1980

The Origins of the
Cold War in the Near East

The Origins of the

Cold War in the Near East

GREAT POWER CONFLICT AND DIPLOMACY

IN IRAN, TURKEY, AND GREECE

Bruce Robellet Kuniholm

PRINCETON UNIVERSITY PRESS
PRINCETON, NEW JERSEY

Copyright © 1980 by Princeton University Press
Published by Princeton University Press, Princeton, New Jersey
In the United Kingdom: Princeton University Press, Guildford,
Surrey.

All Rights Reserved
Library of Congress Cataloging in Publication Data will be
found on the last printed page of this book.

Publication of this book has been aided by a grant from
The Andrew W. Mellon Foundation.

This book has been composed in Linotype Electra.

Clothbound editions of Princeton University Press books
are printed on acid-free paper, and binding materials are
chosen for strength and durability.

Printed in the United States of America by Princeton
University Press, Princeton, New Jersey.

For: My Mother,
Liz, Jonathan, and Erin

Contents

List of Maps

Acknowledgments

I owe a debt of gratitude to the following scholars, statesmen, and friends whose assistance, counsel, criticism, and encouragement contributed to this study: Margaret Ball, William Baxter, Bill and Carol Becker, J. Bowyer Bell, Barton Bernstein, William Chafe, Clark Clifford, Joel Colton, John DeNovo, Arif Dirlik, Elbridge Durbrow, Sydney Fisher, Joel Fleishman, Anthony Furano, John Gaddis, Raymond Hare, W. Averell Harriman, Willis Hawley, Alger Hiss, Ole Holsti, S. Shepard Jones, Alfreda Kaplan, Bruce Lawrence, Cindy Lawson, Walter LeFeber, Warren Lerner, Richard Pfau, Forrest Pogue, Rouhollah Ramazani, Burt and Roberta Rosen, Dick Rumer, William Sands, Moazzam Siddiqi, Gaddis Smith, and Richard Watson.

I owe an especial debt to Loy Henderson, Harry Howard, John Jernegan, George Kennan, Foy Kohler, Gordon Merriam, Harold Minor, Robert Rossow, and Edwin Wright, whose willingness to write letters, subject themselves to interviews, allow me access to some of their private papers, and criticize my manuscript enabled me to piece together certain problems which otherwise I would have been unable to understand. The encouragement and criticism of Calvin D. Davis and William Scott were invaluable in supporting my efforts to grapple with the intricate problems of understanding and writing incisively about the Cold War.

I should like to express my thanks to the Department of History and the Institute of Policy Sciences and Public Affairs at Duke University, the Rockefeller Foundation, the Harry S. Truman Library Institute, and the United States government, whose generous assistance in the form of grants and fellowships made possible the research that was necessary for this work. I also wish to express my appreciation to Judy Hammond, who drew the maps, to Diana L. Witt, who compiled the index, and to the staffs of the National Archives, the Modern Military Records Branch of the National Archives, the Library of Congress, the Franklin D. Roosevelt Library, the Harry S. Truman Library, the State Department, and the manuscript collections of Clemson, Duke, Harvard, Princeton, the University of Virginia, and Yale.

ACKNOWLEDGMENTS

My greatest debt is to my family: my mother, my parents-in-law, my wife Elizabeth, and my children, Jonathan and Erin, without whose combined support this work would never have been started, let alone completed.

I have come across men of letters who have written history without taking part in public affairs, and politicians who have concerned themselves with producing events without thinking about them. I have observed that the first are always inclined to find general causes, whereas the second, living in the midst of disconnected daily facts, are prone to imagine that everything is attributable to particular incidents, and that the wires they pull are the same as those that move the world. It is to be presumed that both are equally deceived.

—Alexis de Tocqueville

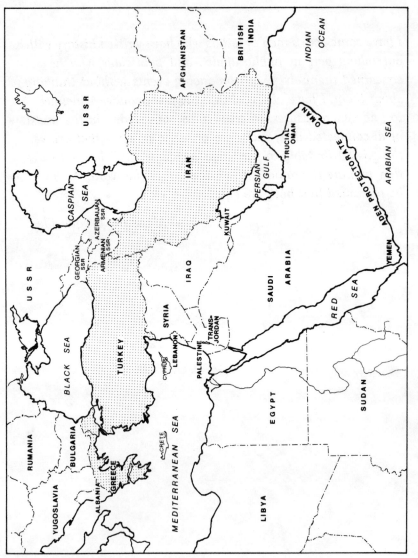

Map 1. The Northern Tier (1946)

Introduction

HISTORIANS writing on the origins of the Cold War have focused on the conflict between the United States and the Soviet Union in Eastern Europe, on the economic underpinnings of America's foreign policies, and on the role of the atomic bomb, but very few have given careful attention to the struggle for power between East and West along the Northern Tier. The term "Northern Tier" describes the northernmost Near and Middle Eastern countries on the border of or near the Soviet Union. It gained currency in the 1950s under John Foster Dulles, when he looked to the countries of the Northern Tier as part of an alliance system whose purpose he saw as containing the expansion of Soviet influence. The concept of a northern tier, however, long predated the policies of the American secretary of state. While historians writing on the subject cannot agree as to which particular countries comprise the Northern Tier, almost all concede that those countries lying within a broad general area in the Near East—especially Turkey and Iran—have been subjected to the same kinds of pressures throughout the last two centuries.[1] Individually, they have been the pawns of Great Powers; collectively, they have constituted a buffer zone between empires. In this sense, they have served both as a northern tier and as a southern tier. Whatever term one chooses invariably depicts a one-sided perspective and implicitly presumes a prior judgment in the struggle that has taken place along an axis formed by the countries. Recognizing the pitfalls accompanying these presumptions, I find, nonetheless, that there is merit in using the term "Northern Tier" to describe the function fulfilled by Greece, Turkey, Iran, and Afghanistan, in attempts by the West to maintain its position in the balance of power in the Near East.[2]

The purpose of this study is to examine the historical struggle for

[1] Rouhollah Ramazani, *The Northern Tier: Afghanistan, Iran, and Turkey* (Princeton, 1966), pp. 3, 9-10; Howard Sachar, *Europe Leaves the Middle East, 1936-1954* (New York, 1972), pp. 336-337; William Polk, *The United States and the Arab World*, 3rd ed. (Cambridge, Mass., 1975), pp. 372-373; Townsend Hoopes, *The Devil and John Foster Dulles* (Boston, 1973), p. 182.

[2] While the terms "Near East" and "Middle East" are often used interchangeably, the former appears to be more appropriate when Greece is included. For a map of the Northern Tier, see Map 1.

power along the Northern Tier as an important factor in the origins and development of what later became known as the Cold War. While the entire Middle East constitutes the larger framework for any history of the international politics of the region, concern here is confined to the Northern Tier because a conception of that region as a whole was crucial historically to the perceptions of most policy-makers responsible for the strategic interests of the Great Powers. By World War II, for example, Saudi Arabia (with its great oil reserves) was essential to Anglo-American strategic conceptions, and its importance is clearly delineated in this work, but of greater immediate concern to American diplomats were policies derived from a conception of the role traditionally played by Iran, Turkey, and Greece in Great Power relations.[3] The categorization of these countries as a geographical and geopolitical unit is arbitrary, of course, but no less arbitrary than other geographical terms whose suitability must be judged by their conceptual usefulness as well as by common usage.

In examining carefully the struggle for power along the Northern Tier, this study is concerned primarily with the postwar formulation of American foreign policy in the region. Of necessity, however, it explores at great length the historical context of British and Russian policies toward the area in order to illuminate the fact that American policies emerge from a framework of traditional European power politics. My intent is to show how traditional interests along the Northern Tier evolve into the postwar conflict between the United States and the Soviet Union, and to follow the process by which American-Soviet rivalry gradually supersedes the earlier Anglo-Russian rivalry in the region.

As a consequence, this book looks carefully at the diplomatic record in Iran, Turkey, and Greece, putting in perspective the efforts of these countries to maintain their independence and territorial integrity in the face of attempts by the Great Powers to exert influence over them.

[3] Although Afghanistan unquestionably forms a part of the buffer zone under examination, it has been consciously excluded. While in the twentieth century Afghanistan has pursued traditional "buffer-state" policies much like those followed by Iran, the pressures to which that mountainous, landlocked, and isolated state has been vulnerable have only recently been as intense as those on the countries west of it. In addition, Afghanistan has been the subject of an incisive analysis that would make its inclusion in this study redundant. See Ludwig Adamec, *Afghanistan's Foreign Affairs to the Mid-Twentieth Century: Relations with the USSR, Germany, and Britain* (Tucson, Ariz., 1974).

It also hazards judgments as to what issues put the Great Powers at odds with one another and what their motives were.

Focus on the entire Northern Tier allows a much broader perspective than would be possible in the study of any single country. At the same time, it has necessitated that, in addition to the wide variety of primary sources on which this work is based, I rely heavily on a small community of scholars whose works are an essential recourse for anyone attempting to appreciate the complexities of Great Power politics in the region. It is important to note that Iran, Turkey, and Greece all came under the jurisdiction of one bureaucratic office in the State Department; since that office, the Office of Near Eastern and African Affairs (NEA), was crucial in the policy-making process (particularly under President Truman), it would have been impossible to examine the policies of the United States in the Near East in the postwar world without first understanding the context of events that took place there. For that understanding, I am beholden to the scholars whose interpretations are incorporated in the text and whose works are cited in the footnotes.

After establishing the historical context of events that took place in the Near East during and immediately after World War II, I attempt to scrutinize the events themselves. Through detailed attention to the manner in which those events were perceived by officials in NEA, I hope to elucidate how events in Greece, Turkey, and Iran, and Soviet actions along the Northern Tier, influenced the policies of the United States and led the Department of State to adopt a regional perspective on the area. In this period, events along the Northern Tier clearly served as a learning experience for those in the State Department who had not yet begun to appreciate the significance of traditional pressures exercised in the area. More particularly, they served as a learning experience for the new president, Harry S. Truman, whose management of foreign policy differed considerably from that of his predecessor.

With Germany defeated in the West, and Japan in the East, Russia looked to its interests in the South, and in the process, together with Britain, inadvertently educated the State Department in traditional power politics. The gradual recognition of American strategic and economic interests in the Near East, accompanied by Harry Truman's decision to rely more heavily than Franklin D. Roosevelt on an informed State Department, led to a revolution in American foreign policy. The United States committed itself to the independence and territorial integrity of countries which had been virtually outside of its prewar cognizance and within Britain's sphere of influence.

The process by which American interests in the region are gradually defined grows out of the traditional rivalry between Britain and Russia; this rivalry, however, takes on a different character as new players—the United States and a powerful Soviet Union—are involved. The ideological baggage which accompanies them tends to confuse the conflict by portraying their rival national interests as a clash between world views, rooted in the different philosophies of Wilson and Lenin. As George Kennan has observed, both Russians and Americans have

> a tendency to attribute to their own political ideology a potential universal validity—to perceive in it virtues that ought, as one thought, to command not only imitation on the part of other peoples everywhere but also the moral authority and ascendancy of the respective national center from which these virtues [are] proceeding.[4]

The tendency that Kennan describes, while it confuses the question of national interests and contributes to the difficulty of examining and understanding the Cold War, makes such an examination all the more necessary—particularly for those interested in contemporary affairs, and for whom an understanding of the Cold War is crucial. Decision-makers, for example, in attempting to formulate the foreign policies of the United States, must constantly ask and attempt to answer the question of where the United States is headed. This question cannot be addressed intelligently, however, without a knowledge of the past. Only with some understanding of how the United States came to be where it is at present does it make any sense to ask where it is headed, and what its policy-makers must do to get it there.

Looking at the recent past, it is clear that American foreign policies in the postwar world were formulated by decision-makers who followed a particular interpretation of the past, a reading of history as it was made. But history, in the process of explaining the past, is largely concerned with creating and destroying myths. "What is commonly called 'a fact,'" Henri Bergson once wrote, "is not reality as it would appear to direct intuition, but an adaptation of reality to practical interests and to the demands of life in society."[5] Appreciation of the historiography

---

[4] George Kennan, "Is Détente Worth Saving?" *Saturday Review*, 6 March 1976, pp. 12-17.

[5] Henri Bergson, *Matière et Mémoire, Essai sur la Relation du Corps a l'Esprit* (Paris, 1911), p. 201.

of the Cold War should give one a feeling for the manner in which facts are subject to interpretation, and for the degree to which history and myth are synonymous. Both are a function of perception and give expression to deep, commonly felt emotions in a changing world. This makes it all the more important that we look closely at the past, and that insofar as our perceptions of the world are predicated upon the past, we have a clear idea of the problems and the biases involved in any one interpretation of it.

One's choice of historical interpretations is a function of many things: of analogies which may or may not be cogent; of developments in the lives of policy-makers which have exposed them to "lessons," and which made a deep impression upon them; of a desire for conscious or even unconscious moral justification for actions, interests, or ideologies. The list is endless.

Whatever the reason for one's interpretation of history, it is clear that policy-makers have used history, and continue to use history. This is particularly true of interpretations of the origins of the Cold War. Ernest May, who has studied the use and misuse of history in American foreign policy, has observed that decision-makers are often influenced by their beliefs about what history teaches. They ordinarily use history badly, he argues, and could, if they wanted, use it more discriminatingly.[6] The first two points are more easily argued than the last, but if we can accept them, and keep them in mind as we look at the policy-making process during the early years of the Cold War, we can see the extent to which beliefs about historical analogies and interpretations were influential in its development. It follows that such beliefs will be extremely influential in the development of future policies, and therefore that it is incumbent upon us to understand how the Cold War developed and what issues it involved.

This, of course, does not deny the centrality of events, and it is upon particular events that this study focuses. But *interpretations* of events are important, too. Ernest May and others have correctly identified the importance of the Munich analogy in the Truman administration's thinking. The appeasement of Hitler and the consequences of appeasement indeed seared themselves on the conscience of a generation. After World War II, a negative model of international behavior—of how *not* to act when confronted by a totalitarian adversary—was reinforced by

[6] Ernest May, *"Lessons" of the Past: The Use and Misuse of History in American Foreign Policy* (New York, 1973).

what happened in Poland and led the administration to adopt policies which later served as the antithesis of the Munich analogy. Positive models—models of how one *should* act when confronted by what the administration regarded as a totalitarian regime—were created by events along the Northern Tier in 1946-47. If Eastern Europe served the Truman administration as an example of how not to deal with the Soviet Union, the countries of the Northern Tier provided a different kind of example, and verified the viability of a firm and determined response to Soviet pressures. In short, the traditional buffer zone between the Russian and British empires came to play the same role between the Soviet Union and the United States, and served as a forge for the latter's policy of containment of the Soviet Union.

The policy of containment in the Near East was a realistic and pragmatic policy. The trouble with it was not its conception. If one were to find fault, it would have to be in its rationalization, in the legacy of that rationalization, and in analogies engendered by the policy's success in the Near East. Subsequent to the Truman Doctrine, the apparent success of American policies in Iran, Turkey, and Greece led the Truman and later administrations to look to those policies as models of how to deal with the Soviet Union and its apparent satellites, not just in Korea, but in Vietnam as well. The public rationalization of American policies in the Near East also created serious impediments to the perceptions of postwar administrations.

While this study addresses these and other consequences of the Truman Doctrine, its main focus is on events that took place in Iran, Turkey, and Greece before 1947. This emphasis attempts to meet an important need. Existing studies of each of the three countries and of particular problems during this period are useful, and there are a few more general works by John Campbell, George Lenczowski, and Rouhollah Ramazani which address the struggle for power in the region, but there are many aspects of American involvement there which have yet to be illuminated. Richard Kirkendall and others have pointed to the need for monographs to explain the reasons for Russian withdrawal from Iran in 1946, for example, and have raised the problem of understanding the role of the United States in the episode.[7] The crux of the matter is not only that Iran has been insufficiently studied, but that its regional context has been ignored, and hence the Northern Tier's role in American

---

[7] Richard S. Kirkendall, ed., *The Truman Period as a Research Field: A Reappraisal, 1972* (Columbia, Mo., 1974), pp. 8, 11-75, 161-191.

foreign policy has been little understood.[8] This study attempts to address that problem by subjecting the Northern Tier to scholarly scrutiny and demonstrating how it provided the historical context for the development of American policy in the Near East. It argues that Great Power relations in the Near East cast significant light on the origins of the Cold War and that the historical struggle for power along the Northern Tier was an important factor in the development of the postwar conflict between the United States and the Soviet Union.

[8] An important recent book which helps to address this imbalance is Rouhollah Ramazani, *Iran's Foreign Policy 1941-1973: A Study of Foreign Policy in Modernizing Nations* (Charlottesville, Va., 1975). See also George Lenczowski, *Soviet Advances in the Middle East* (Washington, D.C., 1971), and his more recent article, "The Arc of Crisis: Its Central Sector," *Foreign Affairs* 57 (Spring 1979): 796-820.

Abbreviations

AF	Division of African Affairs, Department of State
AIOC	Anglo-Iranian Oil Company
AMFOGE	Allied Mission for Observing Greek Elections
APOC	Anglo-Persian Oil Company (later AIOC)
CCS	Combined Chiefs of Staff
CENTO	Central Treaty Organization
EAM	Ethnikon Apelevtherotikon Metopon (National Liberation Front)
EDES	Ellinikos Dimokratikos Ethnikos Syndesmos (Greek Democratic National League)
EKKA	Ethniki kai Koinoniki Apelevtherosis (National and Social Liberation)
ELAS	Ethnikos Laikos Apelevtherotikos Stratos (National People's Liberation Army)
GTI	Division of Greek, Turkish, and Iranian Affairs, Department of State
ICAO	International Civil Aviation Organization
IPC	Iraq Petroleum Company
JCS	Joint Chiefs of Staff
KKE	Kommounistikon Komma Ellados (Communist Party of Greece)
MEI	Division of Middle Eastern and Indian Affairs, Department of State
NATO	North Atlantic Treaty Organization
NE	Division of Near Eastern Affairs, Department of State
NEA	Office of Near Eastern and African Affairs, Department of State
NOF	Narodnoosloboditelniot Front (National Liberation Front)
NKVD	Narodnyi Kommissariat Vnutrennykh Del (People's Commissariat of Internal Affairs)
NSC	National Security Council
OSS	Office of Strategic Services
PEEA	Politiki Epitropi Ethnikis Apelevtherosis (Political Committee of National Liberation)
PGC	Persian Gulf Command
PGSC	Persian Gulf Service Command (redesignated PGC in December 1943)

PRC   Petroleum Reserves Corporation
RAF   Royal Air Force
SOE   Special Operations Executive
UKCC   United Kingdom Control Corporation
SNOF   Slavomakedonski Narodnoosloboditelniot Front (Slavo-
            Macedonian National Liberation Front), reorganized as
            NOF in 1946
UNRRA   United Nations Relief and Rehabilitation Administration
X   Chi, a letter in the Greek alphabet appropriated as a
            designation by a pro-royalist, anti-Communist secret
            society

Part I

═════════════

SOURCES OF GREAT POWER RIVALRY

ALONG THE NORTHERN TIER

Introduction

GREAT power rivalry in the Near East during the Cold War can be traced back to traditional concerns over the balance of power between Britain and Russia along the Northern Tier. These concerns, at once aggressive and defensive, were important factors in the history of the buffer states subject to imperial influence.

The buffer states which were the object of such concerns, the Ottoman Empire (including the Balkans) and Persia, served for centuries as focal points for Great Power rivalry. Together, at least since the nineteenth century, their positions in international affairs were determined by the conflict between Britain and Russia in the Near East. Russia's expansionist policies and her need for warm-water ports clashed with Britain's need to maintain her line of communication through the Eastern Mediterranean to India and her desire to protect a vast area which stretched eastward from the Persian Gulf. As a result, both Russia and Britain became heavily involved in Near Eastern affairs.

Resenting Great Power influence over them and spurred by the forces of nationalism, the Northern Tier countries attempted to maintain their territorial integrity by playing one power off against the other, or by looking to third powers for succor. Their strategies, while partially successful, nonetheless perpetuated Anglo-Russian rivalry, which remained both a guarantee of, and a threat to, their security.

To understand the effect of World War II upon the Northern Tier countries, it is not enough to chronicle the continued incidence of Great Power intrusion and influence. One must also look at the countries themselves, at the difficulties they confronted before the war, and at a problem recognized by all their leaders: that it was necessary to create a national identity in order to ensure national survival. The differential success of Kemal Atatürk, Ioannis Metaxas, and Reza Shah in forging a common identity among Turks, Greeks, and Iranians respectively, helps to explain some of the difficulties their countries encountered during World War II.

The main source of difficulty for the Northern Tier countries, however, was the region's historical instability and the Great Powers' continuing struggle for influence in the Near East—in spite of the fact that the Great Powers occasionally were allied with each other. The

"Eastern Question," the "Balkan Problem," and the "Persian Problem," all of which dated at least from the nineteenth century, were still prominent during World War II in the thinking of Winston Churchill and Joseph Stalin, both of whose policies illustrated the relevance of historical problems. If, after 1943, the Soviets carved out a sphere of influence in the Balkans, supported Bulgarian irredentism in Macedonia and Thrace, asked for a port on the Aegean, and sought to control the Straits; if they attempted to acquire Turkey's eastern provinces, attempted to carve out a sphere of influence in Iran, or contemplated a port on the Persian Gulf, every action had a precedent in tsarist policies. That the Soviets were interested in the entire region, from the Balkans to Iran, is evidenced not only by these actions, but also by the failure of Nazi-Soviet discussions in 1940, when Stalin refused to limit himself to a sphere of interest in Iran and eastern Turkey. Soviet Foreign Minister Vyacheslav Molotov's interest in the Straits and the Balkans made a strong impression on Adolf Hitler and was a crucial element in the worsening of German-Soviet relations at the time.

Russia's historical aspirations toward the countries of the Northern Tier resulted in Britain's attempts to limit them. The diplomacy of 1878 in the Balkans and eastern Turkey is exemplary of British policies, which depended on a strong military and well-chosen allies. Another British policy was to seek a definition of Russia's aspirations through a common understanding over the buffer states. Thus, the two countries divided Persia into spheres of influence in 1907, and partitioned the Ottoman Empire in 1915. They again divided Iran into spheres of influence in 1941, and did the same with the Balkans in 1944. World War II, however, posed serious problems for the declining British Empire; in the face of Russia's growing might, Britain was forced to turn to the United States to protect her line of communications in the Eastern Mediterranean and her oil interests in the Persian Gulf.

Britain's major problem toward the end of the war was to get the United States to join her in maintaining the balance of power against Russia. Winston Churchill, of course, was an old hand at the game. He had engineered the British Admiralty's acquisition of a majority interest in the Anglo-Persian Oil Company in 1914, and had long been sensitive to the strategic value of the region. Joseph Stalin, too, was familiar with such matters. In 1921, for example, he personally negotiated the Soviet Union's borders with Turkey and, against Lenin's wishes, gave armed support to the Soviet Republic of Gilan in northern Iran. But Franklin

D. Roosevelt had little knowledge of, or interest in, the Near East, and in spite of emerging American oil interests—particularly in Saudi Arabia —opposed traditional means of resolving differences there.

The Department of State's Office of Near Eastern and African Affairs (NEA) was more appreciative than the president of the imperatives of European diplomatic history. Close observation of conditions in the Balkans, and Allied policies toward Turkey and the Straits, awakened officials to the role of both Turkey and Greece in the power alignments that were taking shape toward the end of World War II. Roosevelt deferred to Churchill when it came to actual policies in those countries, and the State Department continued to be guided by the principles of the Atlantic Charter, but farsighted diplomats like Lincoln MacVeagh were already trying to create a more realistic attitude toward the region. MacVeagh's influence on thinking was widespread because his best reports were circulated throughout the department, where they were more widely read than those of any other minister or ambassador in the field.[1] Farther east in Iran, the important part played by the United States in the Persian Corridor was providing others with profound insight into both the realities and relative merits of British and Soviet influence in the Near East. The American experience in Iran, combined with a growing recognition of American interests in the Near and Middle East, led officials in NEA increasingly to accept and reiterate British arguments about the identity of British and American interests in the region. Such arguments, which began to emerge with greater clarity as the war progressed, suggested that it was in the American interest to maintain a balance of power along the Northern Tier, and in the process helped to formulate the intellectual framework for subsequent American policies in the Near East.

[1] Foy Kohler, letter to the author.

I
52525252

The Turkish Context

The Historical Background

THE historical conflict between Russia and Turkey dates back three centuries, to the first of their thirteen wars. The source of conflict was in essence a question of power which manifested itself in tsarist Russia's territorial expansion at the expense of the Ottoman Empire. Since this exchange was not in Britain's interests, Russia's conflict with the Ottoman Empire was never entirely separable from its rivalry with Great Britain. Thus, by the time of the Treaty of Küçük Kaynarca between Russia and the Ottoman Empire in 1774, tsarist Russia's expansion was underway, the Ottoman Empire's deterioration had begun, and the Eastern Question—the question of what should take the Ottoman Empire's place—was a matter of international concern.[1]

The Treaty of Küçük Kaynarca, which conveniently dates the Eastern Question, recognized the Russian Empire as a riparian power and guaranteed her merchant ships free passage in the Turkish Straits. By conferring an international status on the Straits it created the problem of their jurisdiction.

A factor further complicating the Eastern Question was the awakening of the declining Ottoman Empire's subject nationalities. Ethnic and religious dimensions compounded what was already an economic, legal, political, and strategic problem. As the nineteenth century drew to a close, the Eastern Question became increasingly central to the rivalry of the Great Powers, whose interests clashed in the Balkans and the Eastern Mediterranean. Thus, out of necessity, the Sublime Porte[2]

[1] Ferenc Váli, *Bridge Across the Bosporus: The Foreign Policy of Turkey* (Baltimore, 1971), p. 167; Edward Weisband, *Turkish Foreign Policy, 1943-1945: Small State Diplomacy and Great Power Politics* (Princeton, 1973), pp. 22-29; Bernard Lewis, *The Emergence of Modern Turkey* (London, 1961), pp. 21-39; L. S. Stavrianos, *The Balkans Since 1453* (New York, 1958), p. 81; M. S. Anderson, *The Eastern Question, 1774-1923* (New York, 1966), pp. xi-xxi; Arnold Toynbee, *A Study of History*, vol. 6 (Oxford, 1939), p. 299; Harry Howard, *The Partition of Turkey: A Diplomatic History, 1913-1923* (Norman, Okla., 1931), pp. 19, 313-314; Harry Howard, *Turkey, the Straits and U.S. Policy* (Baltimore, 1974), p. 1.

[2] The palace inhabited by the chief minister of the sultan, used as a synonym for the Turkish central government. Anderson, p. xii.

developed a broad view of diplomacy and foreign policy which neither the Ottoman Empire nor its successor, the Turkish Republic, has ever relinquished. Throughout the nineteenth and twentieth centuries, Turkey has been forced to maintain tenuous diplomatic positions which, as one historian describes them, "built upon a central strategy of inhibiting the most dangerous and threatening power by invoking the assistance of the others."[3]

Concomitant with this strategy of survival, Turkey has followed a more constructive course, which Bernard Lewis refers to as "the Turkish Revolution." This line of development began not with the establishment of a new political order under the Young Turks in 1908, but in the eighteenth century, when a series of defeats forced the Turks, for the sake of survival, to accept and utilize new ideas and institutions that have served as foundations for the modern state and army. Thus, according to Lewis,

> the basic change in Turkey—from an Islamic Empire to a national Turkish state, from a medieval theocracy to a constitutional republic, from a bureaucratic feudalism to a modern capitalist economy—was accomplished over a long period, by successive waves of reformers and radicals.[4]

While the processes described above were at work, Great Britain and Russia—especially from the 1830s onward—were the powers chiefly concerned with the crumbling Ottoman Empire. Because Britain feared Russian expansion into the Balkans, the Straits Convention of 1841 has been interpreted as representing "the early application of a policy of containment," a policy not unlike that of the Truman Doctrine a century later. With the completion of the Suez Canal in 1869, Britain also feared Russia's potential threat to her newly created lifeline through the Eastern Mediterranean to India. The question of whether or not Russia required containment depends on one's frame of reference. She had strategic as well as economic interests in the Straits. She also had a strong interest in the Slavic peoples of the Balkans and in the many Orthodox Christians who lived in the sultan's dominions. But in the latter half of the nineteenth century, while on the offensive against the

---

[3] Feridun Cemal Erkin, *Les Relations Turco-Soviétiques et la Question de Détroits* (Ankara, 1968), p. 24; James Shotwell and Francis Deak, *Turkey and the Straits: A Short History* (New York, 1940), pp. 1-20; Stavrianos, *The Balkans*, p. 215; Nuri Eren, *Turkey Today—And Tomorrow* (New York, 1963), pp. 227, 234; Váli, pp. 8-9.

[4] Bernard Lewis, pp. 473-474.

Ottoman Empire, Russia may have been more defensive in her position than Britain realized. At least one scholar believes tsarist policy was dominated more by desire to exclude the fleets of the Great Powers from the Black Sea than to project Russian power into the Eastern Mediterranean.[5]

Whatever the motivations behind her foreign policy, tsarist Russia expanded southward, forcing the Ottoman Empire to resort to geopolitics in an effort to contain her. But as the twentieth century began, the Sublime Porte's tactics became increasingly precarious. The settlement of differences between Russia and Britain in the Anglo-Russian Entente of 1907, and the subsequent strengthening of that entente by the inclusion of France, sharply narrowed the options of an emerging nationalist movement in Turkey. After the Young Turk Revolution of 1908, German influence was ascendant. But so was Russian traffic through the Straits. By 1914 approximately 40 percent of all Russian exports and 54 percent of her maritime exports passed through the Straits. The Turks, who continued to harbor a traditional hatred and well-founded fear of Russia, were certain that the Triple Entente would partition the Ottoman Empire whether it won or lost. They were also discouraged by their failure to exact any tangible benefits from Britain and France. Because of these factors and the personal role of Enver Pasha (Turkey's Germanophile minister of war), the Sublime Porte cast its lot with Germany. As A.J.P. Taylor observes:

> This was a supreme blunder, which brought down the Ottoman Empire. The Turks had made up for their internal weakness by a subtle diplomacy playing off one Great Power against another; now they gratuitously involved themselves in the European conflict. Perhaps they had no choice.[6]

At war's end, the sick man of Europe was in his death throes,[7] his

[5] Anderson, pp. 106, 176-177, 389-392; Howard Sachar, *The Emergence of the Middle East, 1914-1924* (New York, 1969), pp. 7-9; Halford Hoskins, *The Middle East: Problem Area in World Politics* (New York, 1964), p. 23; Váli, pp. 165-166.

[6] Váli, pp. 14-15; Harry Howard, "The Turkish Straits After World War II: Problems and Prospects," *Balkan Studies* 11 (No. 1, 1970): 38; Sachar, *Emergence of the Middle East*, pp. 10, 14, 24-31; Stavrianos, *The Balkans*, pp. 55-57; Geoffrey Lewis, *Turkey*, 3rd ed. (London, 1965), pp. 48-50; A.J.P. Taylor, *The Struggle for Mastery in Europe, 1848-1918* (London, 1954), pp. 442-446, 533-534.

[7] Turkey's dead and wounded exceeded 1,400,000; total casualties—if those missing and seriously ill are excluded—number close to 2,500,000 out of an Anatolian population of 12,000,000. Sachar, *Emergence of the Middle East*, pp. 247-248; Stanford Shaw and Ezel Shaw, *Reform, Revolution, and Republic: The Rise of Modern Turkey* (Cambridge, 1977), pp. 238-241, 316.

dismemberment prefigured by four secret treaties which pointed to a resolution of the Eastern Question through the Ottoman Empire's partition. Although the new Russian government renounced Russia's part in the treaties, it was alone. An armistice signed at Mudros on the island of Lemnos in October 1918 provided for the loss of 50 percent of the Ottoman Empire's territory and population. The Straits were opened to the Allies who now had the right to occupy forts on the Dardanelles and the Bosporus, as well as "the right to occupy any strategic points in the event of a situation arising which threatens the security of the Allies" (Article 7).[8]

The ensuing occupation of Turkish territories by the British, French, and Italians aroused the Turkish nationalist spirit, but was of little consequence compared to occupation by the Greeks. The Greek landing at Smyrna (İzmir) in May 1919 had been encouraged by President Wilson, Prime Minister Clemenceau, and Prime Minister Lloyd George —the latter of whom was anxious to safeguard British communications with India. The British prime minister found legitimization of the act in the vaguely phrased Article 7 of the Mudros Armistice.[9]

As a result of the Greek occupation, a nationalist movement gathered momentum in Anatolia. Under the aegis of Mustafa Kemal, whose exploits at Gallipoli in 1915 had frustrated the British and forced their withdrawal, national congresses drafted and endorsed what became known as the National Pact. The National Pact was a declaration that emphasized Turkey's territorial integrity as well as her political, judicial, and financial independence. It expressed the terms on which Mustafa Kemal was prepared to make peace.

Hoping to suppress Kemal, the British occupied Constantinople and deported a number of nationalist deputies. This action, in turn, led to the convocation in Ankara of a Grand National Assembly which established a provisional government. When the sultan's government signed the Treaty of Sèvres in August 1920, the nationalist government promptly rejected its terms and rallied a number of regular forces to the nationalist cause. The Treaty of Sèvres, together with a Tripartite Agreement on Anatolia, would have been far more severe on Turkey

---

[8] Geoffrey Lewis, pp. 52-53; J. C. Hurewitz, *Diplomacy in the Near and Middle East: A Documentary Record, 1914-1956* (Princeton, 1956), pp. 7-12, 18-25; Sachar, *Emergence of the Middle East*, pp. 247-248.

[9] Sachar, *Emergence of the Middle East*, pp. 311-315; Geoffrey Lewis, pp. 52-54; Stavrianos, *The Balkans*, p. 582; Roderic Davison, "Turkish Diplomacy from Mudros to Lausanne," in *The Diplomats, 1919-1939*, eds. Gordon Craig and Felix Gilbert (Princeton, 1953), pp. 174-175; Howard, *Partition of Turkey*, p. 257.

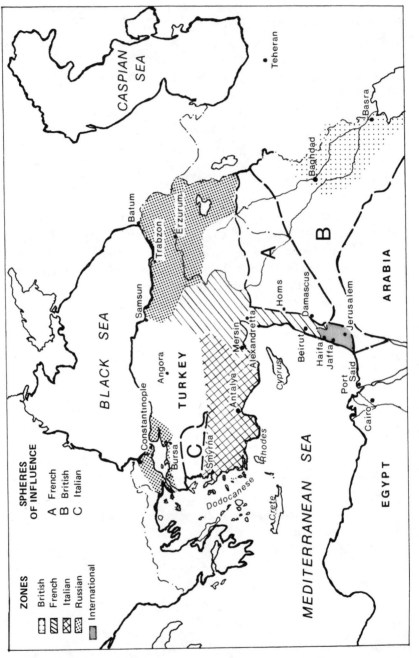

Map 2. The Partition of the Ottoman Empire (1915-1916)
Based on A.J.P. Taylor, *The Struggle for Mastery in Europe, 1848-1918* (London, 1954), p. 562.

ZONES
British
French
Italian
Russian
International

SPHERES OF INFLUENCE
A French
B British
C Italian

CASPIAN SEA

Teheran

Basra

Baghdad

BLACK SEA

Batum

Trabzon

Erzurum

Samsun

Angora

Constantinople

Bursa

TURKEY

Smyrna

Antalya

Mersin

Alexandretta

Homs

Damascus

Beirut

Haifa

Jaffa

Jerusalem

Port Said

Cairo

Rhodes

Cyprus

Crete

Dodocanese

MEDITERRANEAN SEA

EGYPT

ARABIA

A

B

C

than the Treaty of Versailles was on Germany—the two documents would, in effect, have extinguished Turkey's independence. But the nationalists never allowed them to be implemented.[10]

Intent on effecting by force the goals put forward in the National Pact, the Turkish nationalists secured their eastern front and composed their differences with the Soviet regime, which was consolidating its position in the Russian Caucasus.[11] Success against the Armenians in the east was followed by a momentous stand against the Greeks, who in July had come within fifty miles of Ankara. "There is no defense-line," Mustafa Kemal's Order of the Day had proclaimed in response to the Greek attack. "There is a defense-area, which is the whole country. Not one inch of it is to be given up until it is wet with Turkish blood." The new nation heard his call. At the Sakarya River it girded its loins. Women, with babies lashed to their backs, arrived from distant provinces with ox carts laden with food and ammunition. Bound by a sense of solidarity, new recruits held each other's hands as they took

[10] Davison, "Turkish Diplomacy," pp. 175-181; William Helseth, "The United States and Turkey: A Study of their Relations from 1784 to 1962" (Ph.D. dissertation, Fletcher School of Law and Diplomacy, Tufts University, April 1962), p. 94; Sachar, *Emergence of the Middle East*, pp. 318-331, 414 ff.; Lord Kinross, *Atatürk: A Biography of Mustafa Kemal, Father of Modern Turkey* (New York, 1965), pp. 87-113, 189-426, 571; Geoffrey Lewis, pp. 64-65; Hurewitz, pp. 81-89; Stavrianos, *The Balkans*, pp. 582-583.

[11] The Transcaucasian provinces of Georgia, Erivan, and Azerbaijan had been separated from Russia at the outset of the revolution. They had formed a Transcaucasian Federal Republic for a year, and had been established as three independent nations in 1918. They were then subject to German and Turkish occupation, as well as a partial British occupation. Eventually, after being fought over by Russians and Turks, the provinces were absorbed into the Soviet fold, with the exception of certain parts of Erivan that went to Turkey. Acquired by Russia from the Ottoman Empire in 1878, these areas already had been retroceded in the Treaty of Brest-Litovsk (which Russia declared null and void once Germany and Turkey capitulated), and placed within the jurisdiction of the Erivan government by the British army of occupation before it left Transcaucasia. The Soviets formally ceded the areas to Turkey in the 16 March 1921 Treaty of Friendship. Harish Kapur, *Soviet Russia and Asia, 1917-1927: A Study of Soviet Policy towards Turkey, Iran, and Afghanistan* (Geneva, 1965), pp. 93-107; Arnold Toynbee, *Survey of International Relations 1920-1923* (London, 1925), pp. 361-376; Howard, *Partition of Turkey*, pp. 263-264; Adam Ulam, *Expansion and Coexistence: Soviet Foreign Policy, 1917-1973*, 2nd ed. (New York, 1974), pp. 110-111. See also Chapter IV, n. 124. If Turkey was in need of friends owing to the British-supported invasion by Greece, the Soviets were concerned with restiveness in Transcaucasia; in view of the Soviet desire not to diminish Turkish and Persian hostility toward Britain, it was understandable that Russia should court the two Near Eastern countries. See Hurewitz, pp. 90, 95-97; Louis Fischer, *The Soviets in World Affairs* (New York, 1930), pp. 396-400, 428-432.

11

their places in trucks heading for the front. When the Greeks withdrew, scorching the earth as they left, they had lost 18,000 men. The Turks themselves lost nearly as many.

In spite of their losses, the Turks found the drift of events to be in their favor. As a result of the victory at Sakarya, they were able to reach an agreement with France. Three days later, on 13 March 1921, exploiting the problems and jealousies of the Italians, the Turks concluded an accord with them, and three days after that, following detailed negotiations with Joseph Stalin, the Soviet Commissar of Nationalities, they concluded still another treaty with the Soviets. Secure in the northeast, supplied with aid from Russia, and with weapons from France and Italy, the Turks drove the Greeks out of Turkey, and concluded an armistice with the British at Mudanya on the Sea of Marmara in October 1922.[12]

A week later, most of the territory claimed in the National Pact was under Turkish control,[13] and military gains had set the stage for the success of the nationalists' diplomacy. When the Allies invited both the nationalists and the discredited sultan's government to a peace conference at Lausanne, Kemal abolished the sultanate and forced Mehmed VI to leave the country. İsmet Pasha, chief of Kemal's General Staff, hero of two victories over the Greeks at İnönü during the war of liberation, and now foreign minister, was thus able to negotiate freely with Britain's foreign secretary Lord Curzon. The Hapsburg Empire had disappeared; German influence, at least temporarily, was destroyed; and Russia was greatly weakened. As a consequence, the first two countries were not even represented at the conference, while the latter was unable to effect its goal of a Straits regime restricted to the riparian powers of the Black Sea.

In addition to the collapse of the three empires, other factors worked to Turkey's advantage. Following victory over the Central Powers, Allied solidarity collapsed. Russia sought closure of the Straits while Great Britain sought complete freedom of navigation through them. The Turks, whose territorial objectives were severely limited by the

---

[12] Sachar, *Emergence of the Middle East*, pp. 419-433; Hurewitz, pp. 95-100; Geoffrey Lewis, pp. 67-71; Howard, *Partition of Turkey*, pp. 263-264; Stavrianos, *The Balkans*, pp. 583-584; Kinross, pp. 189-426. For Stalin's role in the boundary negotiation with Turkey, see Chapter IV, n. 124.

[13] Prime Minister Lloyd George's resignation at this time resulted from the failure of his policies concerning Turkey. Sachar, *Emergence of the Middle East*, p. 441.

National Pact, were able to manipulate these differences skillfully.[14] The result was a compromise treaty which fulfilled most of the demands of the National Pact and gave Turkey international recognition. If certain questions were unresolved,[15] Turkey's sovereignty was unquestioned over all her territory except the demilitarized Straits; she also held the permanent presidency of a regime with international legitimacy—it was established by an international supervisory commission under the auspices of the League of Nations. The Turks saw the contrast between Sèvres and Lausanne as one between night and day; the nation had been saved from imminent burial at the hands of international diplomacy, and set free to follow its own destiny. The Ottoman Empire was dead, and vast territories had been cut away, but a new Turkish Republic had been born.[16]

The Turkish Republic, in a sense, grew out of the Lausanne settlement. Shortly before the signing of the treaty, elections in Turkey returned a new chamber of deputies which opened its proceedings in August. Its first major political act under Mustafa Kemal's presidency was to ratify the treaty. Then, in October, riding on the prestige which accrued to it from the peace, it made Ankara the new seat of government—a symbolic break with the Ottoman past, and an indication of Kemal's intentions for Turkey's future. Within a month (29 October 1923), Turkey was proclaimed a republic and Mustafa Kemal elected its first president. In March 1924 the caliphate was abolished[17] and

[14] The treaty can be regarded both as Curzon's triumph in splitting Turkey from Russia, and İsmet Pasha's triumph in avoiding dependence on Russia. Davison, "Turkish Diplomacy," p. 203; Sachar, *Emergence of the Middle East*, pp. 442-451; Joseph Grew, *Turbulent Era: A Diplomatic Record of Forty Years, 1904-1945*, 2 vols. (Boston, 1952), 1:569-570.

[15] See Eren, pp. 229-230; Sachar, *Emergence of the Middle East*, p. 451; Váli, pp. 20-21; Davison, "Turkish Diplomacy," p. 207.

[16] Turkey's territory in 1914 consisted of 1,950,000 square miles. By 1923, that area had been cut to 296,107 square miles. J. A. Lukacs, *The Great Powers and Eastern Europe* (New York, 1952), pp. 32-33, quoted in Stavrianos, *The Balkans*, p. 591. Davison, "Turkish Diplomacy," pp. 199-209; Geoffrey Lewis, pp. 72-76, 113; Sachar, *Emergence of the Middle East*, pp. 442-453; Anderson, pp. 388-389; Váli, pp. 20-22, 185-186; Erkin, pp. 61-69; Hurewitz, pp. 119-127; Shotwell and Deak, pp. 111-117; Bernard Lewis, pp. 249-250; Kinross, p. 425; Grew, pp. 569-570; Roderic Davison, "Middle East Nationalism: Lausanne Thirty Years After," *The Middle East Journal* 7 (Summer 1953):324-348; Howard, *Partition of Turkey* pp. 313-314; Kapur, pp. 17-27; D. A. Routh, "The Montreux Convention Regarding the Regime of the Black Sea Straits (20th July, 1936)," in *Survey of International Relations, 1936*, ed. Arnold Toynbee (London, 1937), pp. 595-598.

[17] The caliphate, in the person of the caliph, was responsible for giving effect to

13

Kemal's assault on the entrenched forces of Islamic orthodoxy was underway.[18]

The reforms instituted under Kemal's presidency (which lasted until his death in November 1938) included acts which were both symbolic and substantive: the abolition of the fez and the compulsory wearing of hats;[19] the adoption of an international (Gregorian) calendar and system of time; the adoption of new civil, criminal, and commercial codes; the secularization of the state; the adoption of a latinized alphabet;[20] the political emancipation of women; the compulsory adoption of surnames;[21] and adoption of Sunday as a weekly holiday. While these reforms were revolutionary, one should note that they were conservative in nature. They were carried out from above by an elitist group whose paternalistic guidance, while relatively free of the demagoguery and repression characteristic of later European dictatorships, built on a nationalism that was already mature. Sources of this nationalism were to be found in an elite officer corps and in a bureaucracy which had as its basis two centuries of reform. If Turkey's political system gave voice to democratic ideals, it was democratic only in form; in fact, Turkey under Atatürk could best be described as a paternalistic, single-party state which, while managing to avoid the pitfalls of the European dictatorships, was nonetheless authoritarian.

It is possible that such a rule was necessary to achieve the Kemalist aim: to force the modernization of Turkish society in a manner that would redeem its self-respect. Atatürk recognized the necessity of remodeling not only government and society, but the Turks' sense of

---

the sacred laws of Islam, a system of law and life which had served as a guide to the Ottoman Turks. Geoffrey Lewis, pp. 24-25; Bernard Lewis, pp. 256-262.

[18] See n. 22.

[19] The significance of this and other reforms may not be apparent to the Westerner. To the Muslim, dress, and particularly headgear, expressed and affected his identity. Bernard Lewis, pp. 261-262; Kinross, pp. 467-474.

[20] Arabic letters were not suited to the writing of Turkish and may have been responsible for widespread illiteracy. This particular reform, modeled on that in Soviet Azerbaijan, also served to cut off the younger generation from their Ottoman heritage. Geoffrey Lewis, pp. 97-102; Bernard Lewis, pp. 419-420; Kinross, pp. 501-505.

[21] The Turks, like other Muslims, had not used family names and patronyms, much to everyone's confusion. Kemal dropped the Arabic name of Mustafa and took the patronym Atatürk, or Father Turk. On İsmet Pasha he conferred the name İnönü after the site of his two victories in the war of liberation (Kinross, pp. 537-538). Hassan Arfa notes that this reform was borrowed from the Persians. Hassan Arfa, *Under Five Shahs* (Edinburgh, 1964), p. 249.

identity as well. As a soldier, he had saved the country and won its acceptance by Europe; as a statesman, he renounced foreign ambitions and ideologies which smacked of internationalism (i.e., Pan-Turanism and Pan-Islamic ideologies) and limited his aspirations to the reconstruction of Turkish national territory. By the time of his death, the Turkish people, according to one historian, "were solidly cemented as a national entity around a firm linguistic, cultural and territorial base." Atatürk's biographer, Lord Kinross, has elaborated on his legacy:

> What Atatürk left to the Turkey he had freed was a strong foundation and a clear objective of her future growth. He gave her not merely durable institutions but a national ideal, rooted in patriotism, nourished by a new self-respect, and promising fruitful rewards for new energies. He created, by his deeds and his words, a personal myth, to feed the imagination of a people given to the worship of heroes.[22]

In the period of reconstruction and reform under Atatürk, Turkey renounced expansionist, revisionist ventures and concentrated on internal transformation. International peace and hence the status quo were prerequisites to her development. Development, in turn, was necessary to assure continued independence. As a small power, Turkey followed a realistic policy which, while cognizant of international pressures and the global balance of power, remained rooted in her own, national self-interest.[23]

As a concrete step toward fulfillment of her foreign policy objectives,

[22] Davison, "Turkish Diplomacy," p. 208; Davison, "Middle East Nationalism," p. 347; Kinross, pp. 429-571; Bernard Lewis, pp. 255-287, 297; Geoffrey Lewis, pp. 77-113; Richard Robinson, *The First Turkish Republic: A Case Study in National Development* (Cambridge, 1963), pp. 87-93; Frederick Frey, *The Turkish Political Elite* (Cambridge, 1964), p. 161; Frank Tachau, "Republic of Turkey," in *The Middle East: Its Government and Politics*, ed. Abid Al-Marayati (Belmont, Calif., 1972), p. 379; Váli, p. 22; Eren, p. 19.

[23] For interpretations of the bases of Turkish foreign policy, and the fundamental principles governing Turkey's national interests, see: Váli, pp. 55-56, 68-69; Weisband, *Turkish Foreign Policy*, pp. 3-29; Eren, pp. 226-230; Robinson, pp. 171-177; Geoffrey Lewis, pp. 61-62, 109; Türkkaya Ataöv, *Turkish Foreign Policy, 1939-1945* (Ankara, 1965), p. 1; Dankwart Rustow, "Foreign Policy of the Turkish Republic," in *Foreign Policy in World Politics*, ed. R. C. Macridis (Englewood Cliffs, N.J., 1958), pp. 296, 311, 316, 322; George Harris, *The Troubled Alliance: Turkish-American Problems in Historical Perspective, 1945-1971* (Washington, D.C., 1972), p. 11; Kinross, p. 518; Roger Trask, *The United States Response to Turkish Nationalism and Reform, 1914-1939* (Minneapolis, 1971), pp. 217-218; Helseth, p. 181; Metin Tamkoç, *The Warrior Diplomats: Guardians of the National Security and Modernization of Turkey* (Salt Lake City, 1976), pp. 67-123.

15

Turkey, on 17 December 1925, signed a Treaty of Friendship and Neutrality with the Soviet Union.[24] Each party pledged itself to neutrality in case of military action against the other, undertook to abstain from aggression against the other, and also undertook not to participate in an alliance directed against the other.[25] Other treaties followed: with Yugoslavia (1925), France (1926), Persia and Afghanistan (1926),[26] Britain and Iraq (1926),[27] Hungary (1927), Italy (1928), Bulgaria (1929), and Greece (1930). The treaty with Greece terminated a hundred years of bitter enmity which had often caused tremendous loss of life and had often invited the interference of the Great Powers; it also confirmed Turkey's intention to support the status quo.[28] To this end, she joined Yugoslavia, Greece, and Rumania in the Balkan Pact (1934),[29] a defensive alliance primarily directed against an irredentist

[24] The Turks were reacting to a League decision awarding the *vilayet* of Mosul to Iraq. The Soviets, suspicious of the treaties signed at Locarno, considered friendship with Turkey the key point of their Near Eastern policy and the means by which they hoped to prevent Western (i.e., British) domination of the area. Hurewitz, pp. 142-146; Ulam, *Expansion and Coexistence*, p. 168; Váli, pp. 21, 25; Eren, p. 232; Bernard Lewis, p. 278; Kapur, pp. 133-141.

[25] Ratifications of this treaty were exchanged on 29 June 1926; the treaty was broadened on 17 December 1929 and 7 March 1931, prolonged for five years on 30 October 1931, and further prolonged for ten years on 7 November 1935. On 19 March 1945 the USSR denounced the treaty. Hurewitz, pp. 142-143. See Chapter IV.

[26] The Treaty of Friendship addressed the matter of border disputes and Kurdish uprisings between Turkey and Persia. Desiring independence (promised them in the abortive Treaty of Sèvres), the Kurds had revolted in 1925. As non-Arab Muslims in a former Ottoman territory, they resented Turkish claims on Mosul as well as Turkish rule, and were outraged at the government's abolition of the caliphate. Frontier disputes in 1927 again ruptured relations, and unrest, encouraged by Britain and France, continued for several years until frontier problems were resolved (1932) and the treaty confirmed by Reza Shah's visit to Turkey in 1934. Since the eastern Turkish province of Tunceli remained a seedbed of unrest, the government placed it under martial law in 1936-37, deporting 3,000 Kurdish families to western Turkey. They were permitted to return on 30 December 1946. Kinross, pp. 451-459; Altemur Kılıç, *Turkey and the World* (Washington, D.C., 1959), pp. 69-71; Arfa, pp. 246-252; Geoffrey Lewis, pp. 87-89; Váli, pp. 49-51; Toynbee, *Survey of International Affairs*, 1936, p. 794; Kapur, pp. 134-135.

[27] The treaty defined the border between Iraq and Turkey, resolving the Mosul question and restoring normal relations between the two countries. Kılıç, pp. 60-61; Hurewitz, pp. 143-146.

[28] Hurewitz, pp. 142-143; Kılıç, pp. 69-71; Anderson, p. 389; Routh, pp. 599-600; Eren, pp. 230-231.

[29] From 1930 on the Turks tried unsuccessfully to bring Bulgaria into agreement with her neighbors in order to present a solid front against the designs of the Great Powers in the Balkans. Stavrianos, *The Balkans*, pp. 736-745; Eren, p. 231; Váli, pp. 198-199; Kılıç, pp. 52-54; Ataöv, p. 69.

Bulgaria.[30] The core of the pact was a guarantee of the independence and territorial integrity of each power and an obligation to consult other members of the alliance in the event of threats to peace in the Balkans.

Following the Balkan Pact, however, Turkey's attempts to assure the status quo in the Balkans were gradually undermined. Germany's rapidly increasing economic influence in the Balkans, the Italian conquest of Ethiopia (1935-36), and Hitler's reoccupation of the Rhineland (March 1936) altered the balance of power in Central and Eastern Europe, defeating Turkey's most important foreign policy objectives. Italy's aggression demonstrated the League's impotence, while Hitler's march into the Rhineland did much the same for the Treaty of Versailles and the Locarno treaties of 1925. As a result, Turkey, whose entrance into the League in 1932 had provided her with a forum, now initiated diplomatic discussions to revise the Straits regime. Turkish notes addressed to the signatories of the Lausanne Convention referred to changes in the European situation since 1923. They pointed out the insufficiency of collective guarantees and the necessity of revising the convention in the interests of Turkey's freedom and security. They further requested modification of the convention's demilitarization clauses.

Turkey's initiative was supported by most of the powers—either because of the ends she sought, or because of the peaceful and legal means by which she sought them. The Soviet Union, which since 1923 had desired revision of the convention, supported Turkey because she envisaged at least partial fulfillment of long-standing goals: closure of the Straits to all nonriparian warships; freedom of transit through the Straits for all warships of the Black Sea Powers.[31] France supported the

[30] Bulgaria's grievance was her loss of Dobrudja to Rumania, and her failure to acquire an outlet to the Aegean Sea. Kılıç, p. 81.

[31] Immediately after the October Revolution, the Russians temporarily lost their desire to incorporate the Straits, and to secure the right of passage through the Straits for their warships. As a consequence, they sought permanent closure of the Straits to the warships of all countries except Turkey. (The necessity of this objective had been illustrated during World War I when the British occupied Nikolaev, Kherson, Sebastopol, Batum, and other ports of the Black Sea, thus facilitating Allied support of the armies of General Anton Denikin and Baron Peter Wrangel.) Great Britain, by contrast, seeing no danger from the Russian fleet, sought ingress and egress for warships of all nations. When, at Lausanne, the British point of view largely predominated, the Russians signed (but did not later ratify) the convention (Kapur, pp. 124-128). By the time of the Treaty of Montreux, Russia's desire to secure the exclusive right of free passage through the Straits for Black Sea warships

Soviet Union, believing that increased Soviet influence in the Mediterranean would enhance the value of the recently completed Franco-Soviet Pact (1935). Britain, though opposed to Soviet goals, was seeking allies in the Levant, hoping to wean Turkey from the Soviet Union's influence. As a result of negotiations, Bulgaria, France, Great Britain, Greece, Japan, Rumania, Turkey, the Soviet Union, and Yugoslavia signed the Montreux Convention on 20 July 1936. Turkey's desires were fulfilled: the functions of the International Commission were transferred to Turkey's absolute control; she was allowed to remilitarize the Straits; and although the new convention affirmed "the principle of freedom of transit and navigation by sea in the Straits," that principle was qualified by the regulations of the convention. Turkey had the right to control the passage of belligerent warships in time of war, and to exercise jurisdiction over all warships in time of peace if she were under the threat of war.[32]

The control Turkey now exercised over the Straits was a factor no government could disregard. Until World War II began—and well into the war—England, France, Germany, and the USSR all considered good relations with Turkey an important objective. Meanwhile, Turkey continued to strengthen her diplomatic position, and in 1937 negotiated the Sa'adabad Pact. This agreement with Iran, Iraq, and Afghanistan was directed against interference in their affairs by the Soviet Union and Italy.[33]

Turkey's long-standing apprehensions of Italian designs had been reinforced by Mussolini's speeches advocating Italian occupation of Antalya, by actual Italian occupation of the Dodecanese, and by the Italian conquest of Ethiopia. Apprehensions deepened after the Germans set up protectorates in Czechoslovakia in March, and the Italians invaded Albania in April, leading Turkey and Britain to undertake serious negotiations concerning their common defense. In conjunction with a

---

had revived; her desire to incorporate the Straits was awakened during World War II.

[32] Kılıç, pp. 68-69; Váli, pp. 186-189; Stavrianos, *The Balkans*, pp. 736-745; Trask, pp. 228-233; Routh, pp. 548-651; Eren, p. 235; Robert Wolff, *The Balkans in Our Time* (Cambridge, Mass., 1956), pp. 157-159; Kinross, pp. 544-546; Shotwell and Deak, pp. 124-128; Geoffrey Lewis, p. 117; Hurewitz, pp. 197-203; Ataöv, p. 8; Howard, "The Turkish Straits After World War II," p. 42. For provisions of the convention, see Harry Howard, *The Problem of the Turkish Straits* (Washington, D.C., 1947), pp. 1-35.

[33] Shotwell and Deak, pp. 129-130; Trask, pp. 233-234; Kılıç, p. 72; Hurewitz, pp. 214-216.

British guarantee to Poland in March, and to Rumania and Greece in April, the British joined the Turks in an Anglo-Turkish Declaration of Mutual Assistance on 12 May 1939. The declaration provided for co-operation and assistance in the event of aggression leading to war in the Mediterranean area, and for the conclusion at a future date of a long-term reciprocal agreement.[34] The French (who with the British had offered support to Poland, Rumania, and Greece) followed the British with an identical declaration on 23 June 1939.[35]

Following the two declarations, Germany threatened the Turks with economic retaliation. This was a serious matter since Turkey depended on Germany as a market for her exports. Britain, on the other hand—perhaps because of her own needs, because Turkey was not publicly committed to her side, and because she wanted Turkey to assume additional obligations to Rumania and Greece—failed to meet Turkey's military and economic needs. To complicate Turkey's problems, the Nazi-Soviet Pact of 23 August 1939 meant that her relations with the Western Allies and the Soviets were compromised—especially with the Soviets calling the Allies "warmongers" immediately after the pact.

[34] Germany, in an unsuccessful attempt to frustrate Anglo-Turkish negotiations, sent as the new German ambassador to Ankara a *personalité en vue*, the former chancellor Franz von Papen, who served in Turkey under General Liman von Sanders in 1917-18, and who knew İnönü. The Turks, for their part, expected negotiations between England, France, and the Soviet Union (which had begun in Moscow on 8 April) to benefit from (and be beneficial to) Turkey's association with Britain. Ataöv, pp. 19-29; George Kirk, *The Middle East in the War* (London, 1952), p. 433; Kılıç, pp. 77-81; Franz von Papen, *Memoirs* (London, 1952), pp. 29-52, 443-444; Harry Howard Papers, Harry S. Truman Library, Box 1, "Department of State Special Interrogation Mission in Germany," 15 August-15 November 1945.

[35] Shotwell and Deak, p. 131; Llewellyn Woodward, *British Foreign Policy in the Second World War*, 4 vols. (London, 1970-75), 1:24; Hughe Knatchbull-Hugessen, *Diplomat in Peace and War* (London, 1949), pp. 146-153; Trask, p. 236; Raymond Sontag, *A Broken World, 1919-1939* (New York, 1971), p. 359; George Kirk, "Turkey," in *The War and the Neutrals*, ed. Arnold Toynbee and Veronica Toynbee (London, 1956), p. 346; Kirk, *The Middle East in the War*, p. 443.
The cause for delay in Franco-Turkish negotiations was the questionable status of the *sanjak* of Alexandretta (Hatay), whose annexation by Turkey was recognized by France in June 1939, in return for the strengthening of her defensive alliance system. Trask, pp. 234-236; Ataöv, pp. 29-31; Avedis Sanjian, "The Sanjak of Alexandretta (Hatay): Its Impact on Turkish-Syrian Relations (1939-1956)," *The Middle East Journal* 10 (Autumn 1956):379-394. The peaceful resolution of the *sanjak*'s status was Turkey's second successful effort to revise the post-World War I settlement. Her other success was the Montreux Convention (1936); her one failure was the Mosul question (1925-26). See nn. 15, 24.

19

Earlier assumptions that treaties of mutual assistance with Britain and France would fit into a larger frame of reference in which the Soviets would also have a place were now discarded.[36]

Thus on the eve of World War II Turkey once again was subject to the geopolitical forces which, as in World War I, threatened to bring war into the Eastern Mediterranean. Italian designs, supported by Germany—which had its own economic and strategic interests in Turkey—were made still more ominous by the Nazi-Soviet Non-Aggression Pact. Britain, concerned both with containing Germany and protecting her lifeline in the Eastern Mediterranean, was able to offer little material support in balancing the increasingly lopsided political equation. The Turks, with their long history of restraining the most dangerous powers by invoking the assistance of others, recognized the limited value of agreements such as those at Locarno, or of conventions recognized as international law. Such conventions were a result of the power relationships that existed when they were written. When power was precariously balanced, principle could assert itself; but when that balance was heavily weighted on one side or another, it was realistic to expect changes, and sometimes necessary to adapt to circumstances.

The problem, then, was to understand the complex international situation; to avoid the hasty strategy of World War I; and to do what was possible to safeguard the national interest. Although Atatürk was dead, his successor maintained a firm grip on the reins of the single-party state. Hero of the war against the Greeks, and skillful negotiator of the Lausanne settlement, President İsmet İnönü was keenly aware of international pressures, and no less intent than Atatürk on adhering to the goals set by the National Pact. In pursuit of these goals, he received strong support from a people whose communal sense of identity had been forged in the dying embers of World War I, and wrought in the troubled years that followed.

Turkey in World War II

During World War II, Turkey was again subject to geopolitical pressures. Confronted at first with military threats from both Germany and Russia, she negotiated a qualified alliance with the Western Allies,

[36] Ataöv, pp. 38-53; Howard Sachar, *Europe Leaves the Middle East*, p. 44; Arnold Toynbee and Veronica Toynbee, *The Eve of the War, 1939* (London, 1958), pp. 47, 146-150.

while maintaining a precarious neutrality. The German invasion of the Soviet Union relieved her of some anxiety about possible aggression from the Soviet Union, and focused her attention on Germany. After the Battle of Stalingrad, the situation reversed: the German military threat lessened, while Russia again seemed a menace. Turkey's anxiety over Soviet designs grew throughout the remainder of the conflict. In succeeding conferences between the Allies, and between the Allies and Turkey, two factors stood out as sources of Turkish apprehension: the exigencies of war against the Axis and the historic rivalry between Britain and Russia in the Eastern Mediterranean.

In this rivalry between the two imperialisms, it was the Soviet Union which the Turks most feared. Despite their own imperialist past, the Turks' interpretation of history, like that of many people whose countries had emerged from colonial status, focused on "imperialism" as the great enemy. But there was a difference. As Bernard Lewis points out,

> For the Turks the really important part of the imperialist phenomenon was not the maritime expansion, since the sixteenth century, of Western Europe, which had affected them only indirectly; it was the overland expansion, during the same period, of Eastern Europe, which had brought the old Turkish lands north and east of the Black Sea and the Caspian under Russian rule, and forced the Ottoman Empire to fight a long series of bitter wars, in a rear-guard defence against the Russian advance to the Mediterranean. Thus, while other nationalists looked to Russia for sympathy and support against the West, Turkey looked to the West for help against Russia, and continued, even after many others had turned away, to see in the West and in the Western way of life the best hope for the future. The Turkish nationalist struggle in its final phase—that of 1919-1923—was directed against Western and not Russian encroachments, but it was followed by a more radical and determined effort of Westernization than ever before.[37]

After the winter of 1942-43, the Turks again looked to the West. In several conferences with Allied leaders they revealed their apprehension over Soviet intentions. Analysis of these and other Allied conferences during the war indicates that such concern was not misplaced. The conferences themselves also illustrate how Turkey's geographical position dictated her strategy of restraining the most dangerous and threatening power by invoking the assistance of the others. Accepting George Kennan's dictum that diplomacy must be examined in minute detail if

[37] Bernard Lewis, p. 477.

it is to be fully intelligible,[38] one must trace the evolution of the Turkish Republic's diplomacy during World War II in order to understand her role in the war and to elucidate the reasons why, toward the end of the war, she began to assume an importance comparable to that of the Ottoman Empire when it was the focal point of the Eastern Question.

From the Outbreak of War to the Nazi Invasion of the Soviet Union

Between the outbreak of war and the Nazi invasion of the Soviet Union, the Turkish government had few clear choices. Economically dependent on the Soviets' new ally, Germany, and diplomatically associated with Germany's enemies, Turkey had to consider every move with extreme care.

In August 1939, the Turkish foreign minister, Şükrü Saraçoğlu, was invited to Moscow to discuss a mutual assistance pact. Arriving in Moscow on 25 September (after the invasion of Poland and the outbreak of World War II),[39] he was immediately confronted with harsh demands. They included: (1) modification of the Straits convention so as to give the Soviet Union joint control with Turkey over decisions relating to the Straits;[40] and (2) a reservation (at Germany's insistence) that would exempt the USSR from any obligation to render assistance against Germany should Germany attack Turkey. Saraçoğlu found the Soviet demands completely unacceptable. As a result of his attitude, and because of the fact that the Nazi-Soviet Pact had dictated a reversal in the Soviet attitude toward Turkey's pacts with Britain and France, the talks collapsed.[41] Two days after Saraçoğlu left Moscow, but before he returned to Ankara, his government concluded a Mutual Assistance Treaty with Britain and France (19 October 1939).[42]

[38] George Kennan, *Russia Leaves the War* (New York, 1967), pp. vii-viii.

[39] The similarity in the positions of Turkey and the United States at the outbreak of war is noted in Trask, p. 237.

[40] Altemur Kılıç notes what might have been one of Russia's motives in desiring closure of the Straits: having designs on Bessarabia, she would have had to confront the fact that France and Britain had guaranteed Rumania's independence; according to the Montreux Convention as it then stood, Turkey was obligated to let the British and French navies come through the Straits to Rumania's assistance. Kılıç, pp. 78-79.

[41] Feridun Erkin, who went to Moscow in his capacity as the director general of Turkey's Political Department, suggests that the Soviets invited the German and Turkish foreign ministers to the Soviet Union at the same time in order to play one off against the other. Erkin, pp. 177-178.

[42] For provisions of the treaty, see Hurewitz, pp. 226-228; and Ataöv, pp. 61-62,

The effectiveness of the new treaty depended both on the capacity of the Allies to provide Turkey with the means of resistance, and on Turkey's good faith (especially with regard to its interpretation of Protocol No. 2). As it turned out, circumstances were to qualify both variables. The Allies wanted Turkish aid in containing Hitler, and Britain had a secondary concern in safeguarding Britain's lifeline in the Eastern Mediterranean. But it was necessary that in making such a commitment Turkey receive a quid pro quo, and such was not the case. Because of Turkey's economic dependence on Germany, she attempted to remedy her vulnerability by signing with Britain (January 1940) a two-year agreement by which she would sell Britain the greater part of her chromite production.[43] But the flow of Allied supplies to Turkey remained inadequate, and Turkey found it increasingly difficult to maintain an independent posture. On 10 June 1940 Italy entered the war. Three days later the French and British ambassadors in Ankara, acting on instructions ten days old, asked the Turkish government to declare war. By 13 June, however, the Turks knew that France's fall was imminent. With the collapse of France, the basis of the tripartite alliance was undermined.[44] In addition, Britain had evacuated her army from

for the Special Agreement on Financial and Economic Questions. For the circumstances surrounding these negotiations, see Ataöv, pp. 53-65; Annette Baker Fox, *The Power of Small States: Diplomacy in World War II* (Chicago, 1959), p. 14; Knatchbull-Hugessen, p. 165; Kılıç, pp. 78-79; Necmettin Sadak, "Turkey Faces the Soviets," *Foreign Affairs* 27 (April 1949):452-454; Kirk, *The Middle East in the War*, pp. 443-445; Erkin, pp. 154-184; Raymond Sontag and James Beddie, eds., *Nazi-Soviet Relations, 1939-1941: Documents from the Archives of the German Foreign Office* (Washington, D.C., 1948), pp. 117-118; Toynbee and Toynbee, *The Eve of the War*, pp. 136-150; Woodward, 1:25-27. See also Walter Laqueur, *The Soviet Union and the Middle East* (New York, 1959), p. 129.

[43] In 1939, Turkey produced 16.4 percent of the world's production of chromite (an ore). Both chromium and chrome are derived from chromite, the former being an alloy essential to the manufacture of steel. During the war Turkey was practically Germany's only source of chromite. Weisband, *Turkish Foreign Policy*, pp. 102, 107, 110; Ataöv, pp. 68-69; Fox, p. 18; W. N. Medlicott, *The Economic Blockade*, 2 vols. (London, 1952, 1959), 1:269-276, 601, 605.

[44] A suspensive clause in the treaty absolved Turkey from fulfilling her obligations until the economic and military agreements had been complied with. J.R.M. Butler, gen. ed., *History of the Second World War, United Kingdom Military Series: The Mediterranean and the Middle East*, 6 vols., vol. 1 by I.S.O. Playfair, *The Early Successes against Italy* (London, 1954), p. 52. At the time of the Italian invasion, supplies promised in the 19 October 1939 treaty had not been delivered, and there was little hope that with France out of the war a beleaguered Britain could do any better on her own. Ataöv, p. 74; Knatchbull-Hugessen, p. 166; Andrew Cunningham, *A Sailor's Odyssey* (London, 1951), p. 222; David Gordon and Roydon Danger-

the Continent. If Turkey's entry into the war was desired, it was not clear where she was expected to fight. Finally, Molotov, when asked for the Russian reaction to the possibility of Turkey's belligerence, had given the Turks a menacing response. As a consequence, the Turks invoked Protocol No. 2 of the 19 October 1939 Mutual Assistance Treaty as the reason for not going to war. The British, for their part, fully understood Turkey's position.[45]

Turkey's trade routes were severed in 1940, and German pressures, made more effective by inadequate Allied supplies to Turkey, led the Turks to meet their defensive needs through a commercial agreement with Germany.[46] Her dependency on foreign economies was such that Turkey, seeing tough bargaining as necessary for survival, could not avoid playing the Axis Powers off against the Allies. Commercial agreements, however, did little to relieve political pressures. In October, German troops entered Rumania, while Italy attacked Greece. Turkey, without adequate military equipment, and with no air defense, would have had to denude her defenses to help Greece—a situation which might have brought Bulgaria into the war. Since aid to Greece would have made Turkey vulnerable to attack, even the British saw Turkey's entry into the conflict as a disadvantage. All that Britain asked of her ally was benevolent neutrality, and this Turkey gave; Churchill was grateful, declaring that he fully understood Turkey's "perilous position."[47]

---

field, *The Hidden Weapon: The Story of Economic Warfare* (New York, 1947), p. 120.

[45] Fox, pp. 16-17; William Langer and S. Everett Gleason, *The Challenge to Isolation, 1937-1940* (New York, 1952), pp. 317-318, 647; Gordon Wright, *The Ordeal of Total War, 1939-1945* (New York, 1968), pp. 26-28; Ataöv, pp. 68-75; Kirk, "Turkey," p. 347; Knatchbull-Hugessen, pp. 166-167; Woodward, 1:201, 245-247; Kılıç, pp. 82-83; von Papen, pp. 460-461. The British had little choice but to accept Turkey's position in view of what the Foreign Office on 24 July 1940 saw as the reasons for the vitality of Turkish friendship: Turkey was an ally; a Mediterranean power; politically, the leading state in the Balkans and of the Sa'adabad powers; geographically, on the direct route between Europe and Britain's vital spheres of interest in the Middle East. "It is hardly an exaggeration to say," a Foreign Office memorandum asserted, "that on the friendship of Turkey depends our whole position in the Eastern Mediterranean, Egypt, and the Middle East." Medlicott, 1:601.

[46] The agreement, which was of far greater economic advantage to Turkey than to Germany, did not impinge upon Turkey's determination to remain loyal to the Allies, who were kept informed of the negotiations. Fox, pp. 19-20; Ataöv, p. 71; Medlicott, 1:278-79.

[47] Fox, pp. 18-24; Ataöv, pp. 71-81; Weisband, *Turkish Foreign Policy*, pp. 88-

As if to give substance to Churchill's assessment, Molotov and the German foreign minister, Joachim von Ribbentrop, had been negotiating over Turkey's fate. On 25 November 1940 Molotov handed the German ambassador in Moscow, Count Werner von der Schulenburg, a suggested amendment to a draft protocol of the proposed Four Power Pact outlined by von Ribbentrop earlier in the month. Soviet acceptance of the pact was subject to a number of conditions, which included: "the establishment of a base for land and naval forces of the USSR within the range of the Bosporus and Dardanelles by means of a long-term lease"; and recognition that the Soviet Union's center of aspirations be "the area south of Batum and Baku in the general direction of the Persian Gulf." Turkey's territory and independence would be guaranteed if she joined the pact; if she refused, "the required military and diplomatic measures" would be carried out under a separate agreement.[48]

Fortunately for the Turks, these conditions were unacceptable to the Germans, who were trying to divert the Russians from the Balkans. The Russians, for their part, were becoming concerned about German aims in the area—especially after a Turco-Bulgarian declaration of nonaggression on 17 February 1941 (confirming their 1925 treaty), and the German Army's entry into Bulgaria in early March. Russia's concern was translated into a communiqué, made public on 25 March, which confirmed the antagonisms present since the negotiations in November 1940. Russia now declared her strict neutrality should Turkey be involved in a war (with the Axis). Turkey, for her part, was happy to reciprocate (confirming their 17 December 1925 treaty).[49]

Although the commander in chief of the German Naval Staff desired to concentrate German forces in the Mediterranean, Hitler himself was not interested in the Middle East—at least not until he had smashed

---

115; Gordon Wright, pp. 29-33; Knatchbull-Hugessen, pp. 167-168; Kirk, "Turkey," pp. 348-349; Woodward, 1:548. Bulgaria invaded Greece on 24 April 1941, after the Greeks had been defeated by the Germans.

[48] Ataöv, pp. 82-85; Sontag and Beddie, pp. 257-258; Sadak, pp. 455-457.

[49] Stavrianos, *The Balkans*, pp. 742-756; Paul Schmidt, *Hilter's Interpreter* (New York, 1951), p. 224; Kılıç, pp. 81, 88; Kirk, "Turkey," pp. 349-350; Fox, p. 23; David Dallin, *Soviet Russia's Foreign Policy, 1939-1942* (New Haven, 1942), pp. 310-311; George Gafencu, *Prelude to the Russian Campaign* (London, 1945), pp. 133-134; William Langer and Everett Gleason, *The Undeclared War, 1940-1941* (New York, 1953), p. 404; Sontag and Beddie, pp. 268-269, 277-279; Gerhard Weinberg, *Germany and the Soviet Union, 1939-1941* (London, 1954), p. 154; F. H. Hinsley, *Hitler's Strategy* (Cambridge, England, 1951), p. 134.

the Soviet Union; rather, he regarded the Eastern Mediterranean as falling within Italian Premier Benito Mussolini's sphere. But with the invasion of the Soviet Union pending, he was forced to remove the threat to his flank caused by the Duce's fiasco in the Balkans, and to postpone his plans in order to keep the faltering Italians in the war. In December 1940, as the Greeks were driving the Italians back into Albania, Hitler ordered preparation of an attack across Bulgaria and Yugoslavia into Greece. Although both countries capitulated to German demands for transit of troops, a group of Yugoslav army and air force officers repudiated their government's agreement, causing the Germans on 6 April to launch an attack on both Yugoslavia (where Belgrade suffered a massive air attack) and Greece.[50]

British military leaders had anticipated that Turkey would refuse to enter the war when Germany attacked Greece. They were even somewhat relieved when their anticipations were realized, for they believed that Turkey as a belligerent ally could be more of a liability than an asset. This belief was well-founded. By May, the Greeks were defeated. All Europe was under Nazi control; the Dodecanese islands were in Axis hands; Iraq was under the control of Rashid Ali's pro-Axis government; and General Erwin Rommel had made spectacular gains in North Africa. The Turks considered themselves on the brink of war, and one informed observer believed their army was doomed.

But Hitler, in spite of his Naval Staff's desire for an offensive in the Middle East, was determined to adopt a defensive stance in the Balkans. Plans for operations in the Mediterranean and the Middle East could wait until Russia was defeated. He pressured Turkey to sign an agreement, and suggested that if Germany did not get it, Turkey might be attacked. The Turkish foreign minister, racking his brains to figure out a strategy of survival, kept the British informed throughout negotiations. On 18 June 1941, as a result of German pressures, he had little option but to sign an agreement with the Germans. This agreement was similar to one the Turks had signed with the Soviet Union less than three months before. Each signatory promised to respect the other's territorial inviolability and integrity and to abstain from action aimed at the other. At Turkey's insistence, a reservation respecting existing engagements covered the Anglo-Turkish treaty, which retained precedence.[51]

---

[50] Gordon Wright, p. 36; Sachar, *Europe Leaves the Middle East*, pp. 120, 141-142, 281; Langer and Gleason, *The Undeclared War*, p. 402.

[51] Anthony Eden, *The Reckoning* (Boston, 1965), pp. 226, 237-240, 256-257;

Thus, on the eve of the Nazi invasion of the Soviet Union, Turkey had her bets covered, and awaited with trepidation the next move on the Nazi-Soviet chessboard.

From the Nazi Invasion of the Soviet Union to Stalingrad

Operation BARBAROSSA, Germany's massive invasion of Russia, began on 22 June 1941. Catching the Turks by surprise, it aroused conflicting emotions. On one hand, they were apprehensive that the complete victory of either country would destabilize Central Europe. Short of such a victory, the Turks were anxious that German demands would be made for the passage of troops through Turkish territory, and that political deals (i.e., between the British and the Soviets) might be made at Turkey's expense. At the same time, the Turks were elated by the German invasion. Their traditional suspicions of the Soviet Union had been recently reinforced by Hitler himself, who, on 18 March, had divulged to the Turkish ambassador in Berlin Molotov's demands in 1940 concerning the Straits. The impact of this information on the Turks was enormous, and was one of the principal reasons for their willingness to sign the treaty with Germany four days before.[52]

Woodward, 1:548-549, 571-584; Winston Churchill, *The Grand Alliance* (Boston, 1950), p. 553; Ataöv, pp. 92-94; Hinsley, pp. 154-155; Fox, pp. 26-28; Sachar, *Europe Leaves the Middle East*, pp. 154-155; Bernard E. Fergusson, "Turkey in 1941: Reminiscences," *Journal of the Middle East Society* 1 (Autumn 1947):56, quoted in Sachar, *Europe Leaves the Middle East*, p. 154; Knatchbull-Hugessen, pp. 169-171; Langer and Gleason, *The Undeclared War*, pp. 511-514. Franz von Papen has stated that there was no connection between the pact with Turkey and the attack on Russia—he had been working on the matter since April 1939. "Department of State Special Interrogation Mission in Germany," 15 August-15 November 1945, Box 1, Harry Howard Papers.

[52] Von Papen, p. 479; U.S. Department of State, *Documents on German Foreign Policy, 1918-1945*, Series D, vol. XII, *The War Years, February 1–June 22, 1941* (Washington, D.C., 1962), pp. 308-312, 384, 492; U.S. Department of State, *Foreign Relations of the United States: Diplomatic Papers, 1941*, 7 vols. (Washington, D.C., 1959-1966), III:870-873, 880 (Hereafter, all references to this series will be cited in the following format: FR, year, volume number in Roman numerals, pages. Special conference volumes will be listed in the same way, with the conference title following *FR*.); Sadak, p. 457; Woodward, 2:20; Langer and Gleason, *The Undeclared War*, pp. 789-900. During the German invasion, attempts were made to raise Pan-Turanian sentiment among the Turks; while some Turco-Tatar leaders responded, the Turkish government would not discuss the subject. Ataöv, pp. 96-98; Charles Hostler, *Turkism and the Soviets* (London, 1957), pp. 171-186. For a reliable account of the role of Pan-Turanism in Turkey during the

As the German army moved deeper into Russia, the British and Soviet governments—not yet formally allied—began preparations for occupation of Iran.[53] This action, they knew, would arouse Turkish suspicions. Hoping to quiet Turkish apprehensions, they issued on 10 August a declaration of intent to respect the Montreux Convention and the territorial integrity of Turkey. This declaration, suggested by the British, was purely opportunistic on the part of the Soviets, and did not allay Turkish suspicions when the British and the Soviets invaded Iran on 25 August.

Germany, unsure of Turkey's position, had been putting heavy pressure on the Turks for strategic materials, particularly chromite. When the British and Soviets invaded Iran, the Germans played on Turkish fears of a British-Soviet deal. This strategy, backed by Germany's awesome strength, enabled her to exact from the Turks, in October, a promise to deliver chrome to Germany in January 1943 (after expiration of the January 1940 agreement with Great Britain and France). As in the past, the Turks drove a hard bargain. They gave the Germans much less than they asked for; in return, they were promised essential materials which their allies found difficult or even impossible to supply.

Under the circumstances, the British Foreign Office believed the Turks had given away little and continued to support Turkey. Officials felt they could expect more positive action when the Allied military position in the Eastern Mediterranean was secure. The United States, too, justified continued support of Turkey. On 7 November 1941 President Roosevelt declared Turkey's defense vital to that of the United States. On 3 December, four days before Pearl Harbor, he made public his decision to designate Turkey a recipient—through the medium of the British—of lend-lease aid.

Thus the Turks, whose army had been brought to full strength since Italy's entry into the war, and whose country was surrounded by belligerents, carefully maintained their nonbelligerent status. To avoid using their army, they dealt with both sides impartially, allocating strategically important exports to both sides, creating the impression through their extensive mobilization that German demands could best be secured

---

war, see Weisband, *Turkish Foreign Policy*, pp. 237-256, who finds no government recognition of the Pan-Turanists, and no Pan-Turanian influence in the formation of Turkish foreign policy. See also n. 114.

[53] See Chapter III.

through peaceful commercial interchange. Meanwhile, as one writer has observed, "Turkey's concessions procured arms from the attacking power and thereby contributed to Turkey's own powers of military resistance and to the advantage of its ally at the expense of neither."[54]

Turkey's position, however, became increasingly difficult after the winter of 1942. October and November 1942 saw the turning of what Winston Churchill has called the "Hinge of Fate." General Bernard Montgomery's tank forces broke through the German-Italian front at El-Alamein; the Allies landed in North Africa; and on 19 November the Russians launched their successful counteroffensive at Stalingrad. The Battle of Stalingrad frustrated Hitler's designs in the east, and foreshadowed the collapse of the Third Reich. It also increased Allied pressure on the Turks to abandon their neutral stance.[55]

1943: Conferences over Turkey's Fate

Casablanca (January 1943)
Allied pressure on the Turks to abandon neutrality gained momentum in early 1943, and continued throughout the conferences of that year. Churchill had long sought to open a new route to Russia and to strike at Germany's southern flank. The Turkish Straits and Turkish air bases made Turkey the key to such plans. Before meeting with Roosevelt at Casablanca, Churchill had obtained Stalin's agreement on the desirability of having Turkey in the war. In spite of General George Marshall's opposition to any operation which might delay the invasion of France, the United States accepted "the principle of preparing the way for Turkey's active participation" in the war. President Roosevelt also concurred in Churchill's desire to have Turkey in Britain's theater of

[54] Woodward, 2:20-25; FR, 1941, III:891-892; Kirk, *The Middle East in the War*, pp. 451-452; Kirk, "Turkey," pp. 352, 360; Fox, pp. 29-32; Howard, "The Turkish Straits After World War II," pp. 71-72; FR, 1941, III:828-923 (for a summary of the background to the decision to grant lend-lease to Turkey, see FR, 1941, III:929-934); Langer and Gleason, *The Undeclared War*, pp. 798-799; Helseth, pp. 207-209; Cordell Hull, *The Memoirs of Cordell Hull*, 2 vols. (New York, 1948), 2:1365-1366; Arnold Toynbee and Veronica Toynbee, *The War and the Neutrals* (London, 1958), pp. 82-86; Gordon and Dangerfield, pp. 120-123; Knatchbull-Hugessen, pp. 170-171.
[55] Winston Churchill, *The Hinge of Fate* (Boston, 1950), p. 603; Gordon Wright, pp. 182-183, 188, 194; von Papen, p. 493. Adam Ulam asserts that at this time the Soviets firmly believed Turkey was on the point of joining Hitler against the Soviet Union. Adam Ulam, *Stalin, the Man and His Era* (New York, 1973), p. 567.

responsibility. Earlier policies had deferred to Britain in matters concerning Turkey; and in the event that Turkey participated in the war, a force made up primarily of British troops would have to reinforce her. Thus, if Turkey were to be dealt into the game, the Allies decided that it was Britain who would play the Allied cards—cards which she would hold until the end of the war.[56]

From Adana (January 1943) to Quebec (August 1943)

After the conference at Casablanca, Churchill arranged to meet with President İnönü, Prime Minister Saraçoğlu, and Foreign Minister Menemencioğlu at Adana, there to exchange views and explore the likelihood of Turkey's taking an active part in the war. Churchill—perhaps because of his experience with the Gallipoli campaign in World War I—believed himself an expert on Turkish psychology and policy; presumably, he intended to exercise that expertise at Adana. At Casablanca, he had told Harry Hopkins, Roosevelt's closest advisor, that if the Turks were recalcitrant about entering the war, he would play on their fear of a Russian attempt to seize the Straits—a tactic also suggested by his own Joint Planning Staff. But at Adana the Turks were so worried about Russia's postwar intentions that Churchill found himself reassuring them about Russia, and encouraging their faith in a future international organization which, he assured them, would "secure peace and security."[57]

To the Turks, such faith was misplaced. They were skeptical of international organizations and apprehensive about their own vulnerability to air attack.[58] Above all, they were anxious about their future relations with the Soviets. In October 1939 Prime Minister Saraçoğlu, then foreign minister, had realized the determination with which the Soviets aspired to the historical goals of Tsarist Russia—goals which the Russians had supposedly renounced in 1918. Events since 1939, especially

---

[56] Weisband, *Turkish Foreign Policy*, pp. 119-132; Langer and Gleason, *The Undeclared War*, pp. 800-801; FR, 1941, III:913 ff.; Hull, 2:1366 ff.; Churchill, *The Hinge of Fate*, pp. 696-716; FR, 1943, IV:1067-1070; FR, *Conferences at Washington, 1941-1942, and Casablanca, 1943*, pp. 634, 650, 659-660.

[57] Churchill, *The Hinge of Fate*, pp. 696-716; Gordon and Dangerfield, pp. 123-124; Robert Sherwood, *Roosevelt and Hopkins: An Intimate History*, rev. ed. (New York, 1950), p. 683; FR, *Conferences at Washington and Casablanca*, pp. 764-766; Knatchbull-Hugessen, pp. 188-190; Erkin, pp. 217-225; Weisband, *Turkish Foreign Policy*, pp. 119-139.

[58] For an appreciation of the extent of Turkey's vulnerability, see Ataöv, pp. 107-108; Knatchbull-Hugessen, p. 192; Weisband, *Turkish Foreign Policy*, pp. 136-137.

the Molotov-Ribbentrop negotiations in November 1940, had done little to inspire confidence that these aims had changed.[59]

Churchill did not rely on faith. Instead, he made more likely the possibility that Turkey would enter the war by setting up a Joint Anglo-Turkish Military Commission, arranging for provision of equipment (including fighter aircraft) for the Turkish forces, and planning for their reinforcement in the event Turkey became a belligerent. After the conference, in a letter to Stalin, he expressed the opinion that Turkey would enter the war before the year was out.[60]

He was mistaken—the Turks had no such inclination. Their alliance with the British, after all, was one of expedience; and some Allied causes were downright threatening to Turkey's long-term interests. What, for example, would the total defeat of Germany mean but the ascendancy of the Soviet Union in Eastern Europe? Seeing Churchill's statements and promises as recognition of the services their apparent neutrality had rendered to the common cause, they did not feel they had committed themselves as definitely as Churchill hoped. Rather, they thought they had made clear to him why they had to be prudent. The Russians based their political considerations on cold evaluation of facts. If Turkey remained neutral, the Russians would try to take advantage of that position. If Turkey entered the war, the Russians, as they had with the Poles, would exploit Turkish weaknesses resulting from the fortunes of war.[61] In short, the Turks chose to view Churchill's inducements in a light that reflected their best interests—not Britain's. The result was a legacy of misunderstanding and animosity that contributed to Turkey's problems.

Following the conference at Adana, the British recognized that the Turks would do nothing until they were adequately supplied. Once their conditions were met, Churchill wrongly believed, Turkey's belligerence would be assured. He therefore ordered his Commanders in Chief, Middle East, to work toward fulfillment of Turkey's requirements.[62]

The Turks were not convinced by Churchill's logic, but being the

[59] Weisband, *Turkish Foreign Policy*, pp. 133-139; Erkin, pp. 223-225; Churchill, *The Hinge of Fate*, pp. 706-712; Kirk, "Turkey," p. 356.

[60] Churchill, *The Hinge of Fate*, pp. 712-715; Weisband, *Turkish Foreign Policy*, p. 138; Kılıç, p. 102.

[61] Erkin, pp. 226-277; Weisband, *Turkish Foreign Policy*, pp. 140-142.

[62] Knatchbull-Hugessen, p. 192; Weisband, *Turkish Foreign Policy*, p. 153; Kirk, "Turkey," pp. 355-356.

weaker members of the alliance, they felt unable to resist outright his attempt to force them into belligerency. Tactfully, they turned the discussion from ends to means; or, as Edward Weisband has so aptly put it, "from *what purpose this equipment* to *what amount of equipment* —a much lower-keyed though, to the British, no less frustrating issue." In effect, they turned Operation HARDIHOOD, the British plan for supplying Turkey in preparation for its entry into the war, into a foot-dragging operation. Their purpose was to prevent the British from supplying them to the point where they would be forced into the war.[63]

These tactics require further explanation. The Turks were extremely vulnerable to air attacks. In addition, Hitler had reassured them he had no aggressive intentions against them. As a consequence, President İnönü's primary concern was not Germany, but Russia, whose growing strength and rising hostility toward Turkey again corroborated Turkish beliefs that Soviet diplomatic posture toward Turkey was predicated on the fortunes of war. Thus, the Soviets now chose to disregard their previous criticism that the Turks had entered the path of war by allying themselves with the Allied "warmongers." Easily overlooking their own acknowledgement that Turkey's position had been useful during the German offensive in 1942, they sharply criticized Turkey's supposed pro-Axis orientation (i.e., she was not an anti-Axis belligerent). This line of criticism by the Soviet press, marked after the Battle of Stalingrad, became even more vehement after the Adana Conference.[64]

It is hardly surprising, then, that Soviet Russia should head Turkish worries. To the Turks, for whom the example of Poland was very much in mind, the open break between the Soviet government and the Polish government-in-exile in February 1943 over the question of Poland's eastern frontier was ominous. Severance of diplomatic relations between these two governments in April merely aggravated fears about the Soviets' postwar intentions.[65]

[63] H. Maitland Wilson, *Eight Years Overseas, 1939-1947* (New York, 1951), pp. 155-158; Weisband, *Turkish Foreign Policy*, pp. 153-159.

[64] Von Papen, p. 495; Kirk, "Turkey," p. 356; Weisband, *Turkish Foreign Policy*, pp. 130-146; Ataöv, p. 101; Laqueur, p. 129.

[65] Weisband, *Turkish Foreign Policy*, pp. 134, 150; Kirk, *The Middle East in the War*, p. 457; Erkin, p. 227. For the background to the break in relations between the Polish government-in-exile and the Soviet Union, see FR, III:323-327, 374-393; and Lynn Davis, *The Cold War Begins: Soviet-American Conflict over Eastern Europe* (Princeton, 1974), pp. 44-49. Adam Ulam notes that the spring of 1943 "marked the beginning of a more political phase of the war." *Expansion and Coexistence*, p. 345.

At Adana, and in the months that followed, Turkish statesmen warned the Allies that the position of Soviet forces at war's end would determine the boundaries of Europe, and as a consequence they looked about for a countervailing force to Soviet might. The implications of the Casablanca Agreement between the Americans and the British, reflected in British control of lend-lease goods sent to Turkey, left the Turks with the impression that the United States had withdrawn from the Eastern Mediterranean, and that the British were in control in the Near East. Britain's failure to heed Turkish advice about the Soviet Union's postwar intentions left the Turks with still further distrust of Britain, and a continuing fear of her willingness to work out a deal with the Russians—as she had over Persia in 1907 and 1941, and over Turkey in 1915. The doctrine of unconditional surrender—whose success would leave the Soviet Union dominant in Europe—reinforced Turkish distrust, as did the British attempt to force Turkey into the war. In August 1941 Stalin had promised to help the Turks if they were invaded. But the Turks knew that the Soviets could use their entry into the war as a pretext for entry into Turkey.[66] Entry into the war, then, was to be resisted at all costs. Cooperation with Britain—to the extent that it brought Turkey closer to war—was to be effected at Turkey's peril.[67]

In succeeding months, while insisting that without airfields and air cover they were in no position to enter the war, the Turks obstructed work on British air installations. They were aided by a conference at Quebec in August 1943, where the Combined Chiefs of Staff gave priority to the cross-channel attack and rejected offensive ground operations in the Balkans. From the military point of view, the Combined Chiefs judged that the time was not right for Turkey to enter the war.[68]

[66] The Soviets might have entered Turkey for any of a number of reasons: to fight the Germans on Turkish soil; to defend Turkey from German attack; or to pass through it. In any case, Turkish suspicions were little different from those of the Rumanians and Poles prior to World War II when they refused any agreements sanctioning the crossing of their borders by Soviet troops. This is particularly true since the Turks regarded Soviet actions toward Eastern Europe as indicative of Soviet intentions toward them. Erkin, pp. 226-227; Weisband, *Turkish Foreign Policy*, pp. 132-134, 145; Gordon Wright, pp. 17-20. See also Sontag, pp. 361, 366-367, for a parallel with Estonia.

[67] Weisband, *Turkish Foreign Policy*, pp. 126-145; Erkin, pp. 219-222; Kirk, *The Middle East in the War*, p. 451.

[68] Weisband, *Turkish Foreign Policy*, pp. 160-163; Winston Churchill, *Closing the Ring* (Boston, 1951), p. 58; William Leahy, *I Was There* (New York, 1950), p. 159; FR, *The Conferences at Washington and Quebec, 1943*, p. 1131; Maurice

At this juncture, Churchill, whose plans for the Eastern Mediterranean were predicated on Turkish entry into the war, opted to effect Turkey's belligerency through still another source of pressure—British control of the Aegean. To this end, even without American support, he decided to launch an attack on Rhodes. A day after the Italian armistice (8 September 1943), he accordingly cabled General Wilson, British Commander in Chief, Middle East, whereupon British operations in the Aegean islands began.[69]

Meanwhile, much less concerned with global strategy than Churchill, and increasingly anxious about Soviet intentions in the Near East and the Balkans, the Turks continued to endure hostile accusations in the Soviet press. The Soviets asserted that small states on the border of the Soviet Union (i.e., the Balkan states) were hostile to her, that Turkish neutrality was increasingly favorable toward Germany, and that Turkey's position secured Germany's southern flank.[70] In countering the Soviet attack, the Turkish press expressed cordiality toward the Western Allies, and pointed out that Turkey's nonbelligerence had been determined in part by the Nazi-Soviet pact.[71]

Moscow (October 1943)

Mere expressions of cordiality did not satisfy the British. Unable to acquire desperately needed Turkish bases, they found their position in the Aegean deteriorating as the Moscow Foreign Ministers Conference got underway. At the first formal meeting on 19 October 1943, Molotov momentarily provided the British with a ray of hope which centered on the second of the Soviet foreign minister's three proposals calculated to

---

Matloff, *Strategic Planning for Coalition Warfare, 1943-1944* (Washington, D.C., 1959), p. 229; H. Maitland Wilson, p. 180.

[69] Matloff, pp. 254-259; Weisband, *Turkish Foreign Policy*, pp. 163-166; William McNeill, *America, Britain and Russia: Their Cooperation and Conflict, 1941-1946* (London, 1953), pp. 305, 311-313; Kirk, "Turkey," pp. 356-357; Kirk, *The Middle East in the War*, p. 458; Knatchbull-Hugessen, p. 193; H. Maitland Wilson, pp. 173 ff.; Churchill, *Closing the Ring*, pp. 203-206.

[70] It may be argued that Hitler, fearing losses in the Crimea would encourage Turkish entry into the war against Germany, refused to retreat because of that fear, so inadvertently aiding the Soviet capture of his Sixth Army and, later, of a hundred thousand Rumanians. Weisband, *Turkish Foreign Policy*, p. 164; Hinsley, p. 232; Alan Bullock, *Hitler: A Study in Tyranny* (London, 1954), p. 655; Felix Gilbert, *Hitler Directs His War* (New York, 1950), pp. 91, 95.

[71] Kirk, *The Middle East in the War*, pp. 458-459.

shorten the war: the first asked for a second front; the second asked for a three-power suggestion to Turkey that it enter the war immediately; the third asked that the three powers suggest to Sweden that it provide the Allies with air bases.[72]

Molotov's second proposal pleased the British foreign minister Anthony Eden, who on 20 October agreed that Turkey's entry into the war was desirable; timing was a question, however, especially in light of Turkey's unpreparedness, which made her more of a liability than an asset. In addition, Italian air bases were now available. Nonetheless, Eden expressed willingness to consider the matter if the Soviets desired to press it.[73]

Back in England, Churchill was more enthusiastic. Desirous of lessening German forces in the West, he was quickened by the possibility of resolving the most acute difference he ever had had with General Dwight Eisenhower. Here was the chance to reverse an American decision which, Churchill later acknowledged, caused him one of the sharpest pangs he suffered in the war—the thwarting of his Eastern Mediterranean designs. With Britain losing ground in the Aegean, the prime minister asked Eden to support Molotov and to find out whether the Russians would be attracted to the idea that the British act through the Aegean, involving Turkey in the war. Unable to furnish air support to the Turks because of his limited resources, Churchill hoped to effect Turkey's entry on her own initiative, so avoiding the obligation of providing such support.[74]

Secretary of State Cordell Hull had referred Molotov's initial proposal back to Roosevelt, who in turn referred the matter to the Joint Chiefs of Staff (JCS). Although there were differences within the mili-

[72] Churchill, *Closing the Ring*, pp. 206-221; McNeill, *America, Britain and Russia*, p. 373; Eden, pp. 476 ff.

[73] FR, 1943, I:584-586; Herbert Feis, *Churchill, Roosevelt, Stalin: The War They Waged and the Peace They Sought* (Princeton, 1957), pp. 229-230; Weisband, *Turkish Foreign Policy*, pp. 169-170.

[74] Churchill, *Closing the Ring*, pp. 218, 224, 284-289; Feis, *Churchill, Roosevelt, Stalin*, pp. 230-231. For discussion and explanation of the differences in American and British strategies in the Mediterranean, see J.R.M. Butler, gen. ed., *History of the Second World War, United Kingdom Military Series: Grand Strategy*, 6 vols., vol. 5 by John Erhman, *August 1943-September 1944* (London, 1956), pp. 115-118; see also H. Maitland Wilson, pp. 218-219; and F. W. Deakin, "The Myth of an Allied Landing in the Balkans during the Second World War," in Phyllis Auty and Richard Clogg, eds., *British Policy Towards Wartime Resistance in Yugoslavia and Greece* (London, 1975), pp. 93-116.

tary,[75] the JCS endorsed the Turkish venture with the important qualification that it not jeopardize planned operations in Europe. Roosevelt's reply to Hull, reflecting this note of caution, was negative.[76]

When Molotov, who had earlier suggested coercing Turkey into entering the war, now suggested a three-power request that Turkey could not disregard, Hull held to Roosevelt's view, but agreed the matter might be discussed. With Hull's agreement, Eden later met with Molotov, proposing that Turkish air bases be obtained immediately. The British needed bases from which they could protect Leros (in the Dodecanese) with fighter cover—and they needed them within the next three weeks. If the Turks refused, the British would cease supply shipments to them. Although Molotov had previously insisted, and continued to insist, that Turkey come into the war, he and Eden eventually reached a compromise: Britain would demand immediate use of Turkey's air bases; Britain and Russia would later demand that Turkey enter the war before the end of the year. In effect, Britain had formally accepted Molotov's second proposal,[77] which the Soviets calculated would draw 15 German divisions from the Russian front. When Molotov sought American agreement, Roosevelt also acquiesced (4 November), subject to the proviso that no resources be committed to the Eastern Mediterranean.[78]

---

[75] The Joint Strategic Survey Command, which analyzed many issues for the Joint Chiefs, saw Turkey's belligerency dispersing Germany's forces, while the JCS saw British guarantees to Turkey draining the Allies' forces. Matloff, pp. 296-299; Weisband, *Turkish Foreign Policy*, pp. 170-171.

[76] FR, 1943, I:644; Cordell Hull, 2:1301; Matloff, pp. 296-299; Weisband, *Turkish Foreign Policy*, pp. 170-171.

[77] On the final day of the conference, Andrei Vyshinsky expressed his bitterness over the U.S. attitude on the Turkish question to General John Deane. Vyshinsky said that Turkey's entry into the war would draw 15 divisions from the Russian front, allowing the Russians to be in Prussia in two months. Refusing to accept Deane's explanation that important resources would be drained, Vyshinsky argued that the Turks would have to suffer as the Russians were suffering. John Deane, *The Strange Alliance: The Story of our Efforts at Wartime Cooperation with Russia* (New York, 1947), p. 22; W. Averell Harriman also expressed the opinion that the Russians, who had been bled white, saw no reason why the Turks should not suffer equal treatment. FR, *The Conferences at Cairo and Teheran, 1943*, p. 153.

[78] FR, 1943, I:634, 660-661, 688-695, 698; Eden, pp. 483-484; FR, *Cairo and Teheran*, pp. 144-151; Feis, *Churchill, Roosevelt, Stalin*, pp. 230-231; Weisband, *Turkish Foreign Policy*, pp. 175-176.

Cairo (November 1943)

Following the Moscow Conference of Foreign Ministers, Eden met Turkey's foreign minister Menemencioğlu at Cairo, 4-6 November,[79] to carry out the stipulations of the secret protocol he had signed with Molotov. Menemencioğlu, unaware of the protocol, correctly suspected that a deal had been made. He also saw through the British tactic of trying to get Turkey to enter the war without a guarantee of British support. To Menemencioğlu, permitting the Allies to use Turkish air bases was tantamount to a declaration of war. The Axis might begin hostilities against Turkey in retaliation. The British might consider themselves less responsible for Turkey's protection than if Turkey had declared war as a result of an agreement with the Allies. In view of the Soviet press attack on Turkey, Menemencioğlu expressed concern about the growth of Soviet power. He was fearful that by acquiescing to British demands, the Turks would be setting a precedent for similar demands by the Soviet Union. He repeatedly questioned Soviet intentions, asking Eden specifically about Iran and especially Poland. When asked what business it was of his, Menemencioğlu replied that "for us, Poland is the *pierre de touche*." In the process of what Eden has described as "three days of ding-dong argument," the British foreign minister finally carried out an earlier intention of Churchill's: he warned Menemencioğlu that Turkey's position with regard to Russia would weaken if it did not accede to Britain's wishes. The assertion that Turkish entry into the war would serve only Russian interests had fallen on deaf ears; Menemencioğlu had no choice but to submit the British requests to the Turkish government, and to seek a final answer as to whether in principle Turkey was ready to enter the war.[80]

On 17 November, after almost continuous deliberations, the Turkish cabinet decided to answer Eden's question in the affirmative, while arguing that such steps as would lead her into the war were prevented by military considerations. Turkey had not received the supplies promised at Adana; German strength had not deteriorated to the extent ex-

---

[79] This conference is to be distinguished from the "First" Cairo Conference between Churchill, Roosevelt, and Chiang Kai-shek later in the month (22-26 November 1943). The "Second" Cairo Conference, which is discussed later, was attended by İnönü and Menemencioğlu.

[80] Weisband, *Turkish Foreign Policy*, pp. 176-185; FR, *Cairo and Teheran*, pp. 164-167, 174-175, 180-182, 190-191; Eden, pp. 485-486; Knatchbull-Hugessen, p. 106; Churchill, *Closing the Ring*, pp. 334-335.

pected; Turkey's cities, bases, communications, and industries were vulnerable to air attack; and Eden's proposals had not provided for collaborative action as understood by the Anglo-Turkish Alliance. As a consequence, Turkey required: (1) the equipment necessary for an adequate defense; and (2) specific plans for cooperation between the Allies and Turkey in the Balkans. Until then, Turkey was unwilling to grant air bases to the Allies because she did not share Britain's opinion that war would not result from such action.[81]

Churchill could hardly blame the Turks for their response. The British had failed to attack Rhodes. The Dodecanese islands, Cos and Leros, which the British had held almost from the beginning of the Mediterranean war, had surrendered; and Samos was being evacuated. The British prime minister believed that the Turkish reply was conditioned by these losses only a day or two earlier.[82] It was also affected by the devastating display of Germany's capacity for aerial bombardment on the island of Leros, which was only a few miles from the Turkish mainland. More important than these factors, however, was what Edward Weisband has identified as a tactical shift on Turkey's part. The Turks still were more afraid of Russia's postwar intentions than of a German invasion. Discerning that the Americans had joined the British in giving priority to closer relations with the Soviets, the Turks now shifted from their political arguments. Where before they had concentrated on the Soviets' postwar intentions, arguing that Turkey's entry into the war would work to the detriment of the Western Allies and serve only Soviet interests, they increasingly realized that such arguments were falling on deaf ears. Resistance to Allied demands, while still predicated on fears of the Soviets' postwar intentions, now took the form of logistical and military-tactical arguments. This new tack placed

[81] FR, Cairo and Teheran, pp. 190-192, 261-262, 374-375; Knatchbull-Hugessen, pp. 196-197; Erkin, pp. 247-248.

[82] While the British failure in the Dodecanese may in part have been due to lack of air cover—a function of Turkish refusal to grant them the use of Turkish air bases—the Turks played a far from neutral role in the campaign. Both during the British engagement in the Aegean, and in the subsequent British withdrawal from the Dodecanese, the Turks, at great risk, shipped supplies to the British, facilitated communications, and gave the British enormous help when German aerial bombardment forced them to evacuate. In the process, the British drew upon the military supply dumps they had been building up in Turkey, so depleting Turkey's reserves. Knatchbull-Hugessen, p. 193; Weisband, Turkish Foreign Policy, pp. 165-166; Kirk, "Turkey," pp. 356-357; McNeill, America, Britain and Russia, p. 313; H. Maitland Wilson, p. 181.

more emphasis on equally real if lesser fears of Germany's military power, and on the Allies' weakness—arguments more compatible with the Allied position and calculated to give greater support to Turkish neutrality.[83]

Teheran (November-December 1943)

While the Turks were shifting diplomatic gears, control of their fate continued to be the subject of high-level concern. Throughout the Teheran Conference, which began less than two weeks after the Turkish note of 17 November, Churchill, who had already discussed the matter with Roosevelt at Cairo (24 November), continued to push hard for Turkey's entry into the war. Not wishing to abandon OVERLORD (the code name for the operation which later became the invasion of Normandy), he was still anxious to employ idle British forces in the Mediterranean and to obtain the use of Turkish air bases; he was even willing to entertain the possibility of OVERLORD's delay in light of what he was convinced would be the strategic value not only of Turkey's entry into the war, but of operations in the Aegean and, subsequently, in the Black Sea. An enlarged Mediterranean campaign, he felt, would give a "right hand" to Russia without undermining OVERLORD. Understated was his belief that such a campaign would weaken German ability to resist OVERLORD. One might also speculate that he hoped to bolster Britain's postwar position in the Balkans and the Middle East. As before, Turkey's entry into the war was the key to Churchill's hopes. Perhaps to encourage Soviet support of those hopes, Churchill bluntly noted Britain's intention to point out to the Turks that their failure to respond to an invitation from the Big Three to enter the war would have serious political and territorial consequences in regard to the future of the Straits.[84]

[83] Churchill, *Closing the Ring*, pp. 335, 393; Kirk, "Turkey," p. 357; Weisband, *Turkish Foreign Policy*, pp. 185-191; H. Maitland Wilson, p. 182; Ataöv, p. 111.

[84] FR, *Cairo and Teheran*, pp. 330-333, 516, 523-524, 536, 538-539, 548-549, 586-588; Churchill, *Closing the Ring*, pp. 344-346, 352-353, 355, 357-358, 367-368, 371-373, 389-393; McNeill, *America, Britain and Russia*, pp. 342-343; Ehrman, p. 174; Leahy, pp. 205-207; Eden, pp. 496-497.

Churchill's maneuvering smacks a little of the negotiations between the Russian Foreign Minister Sergei Sazonov and the British Foreign Minister Sir Edward Grey in 1915 (see Chapter III). Churchill was not willing to give up Istanbul, as was Grey, but he was hinting at a greater Russian say in the Straits regime. As in 1915, the British were concerned that the Russians might not remain in the war (see Taylor, *Struggle for Mastery in Europe*, p. 541, and Chapter III). Again, as in

Roosevelt adhered to the position he had taken earlier in October when the question was raised at Moscow. Desiring Turkey in the war and recognizing its importance were one thing. Potential delays to OVERLORD caused by operations in the Eastern Mediterranean were another. Thus, he shared little enthusiasm for Churchill's designs. Though he had no desire to urge Turkey to fight, he eventually agreed to do so, but admitted that if he were the Turkish president he would demand such a heavy price that the cross-channel attack would be indefinitely postponed.[85]

Stalin, who at Moscow only a month earlier had strongly urged Turkey's belligerence, meanwhile revised his former stance. While he, too, was willing to have Turkey enter the war, he saw it as an unimportant question in relation to OVERLORD, and regarded operations in the Mediterranean as merely diversionary. He was willing to promise that if Turkey's entry into the war led to war with Bulgaria, the Soviet Union would declare war on Bulgaria.[86] But he was concerned about the number of Anglo-American troops that would be allotted to the Eastern Mediterranean, and about the dispersal of Allied forces.[87]

Soviet explanations of Stalin's reversal were that he had been convinced—by Menemencioğlu's 17 November reply to Eden—that Turkey would not enter the war. In addition. the Soviets said they wanted no diversion or delays to OVERLORD. To some historians, these reasons suffice: the Russians, observing disagreement among the Western Allies on the implications of operations in the Aegean, and seeing a question of alternatives, felt it important "to throw their weight into the balance." But Stalin's true motivations continue to be the subject of much speculation. Was Turkey's entry, as one writer suggests, really more trouble to Stalin than it was worth? Why, then, did Molotov go to such great efforts at Moscow to secure that entry? If Stalin was concerned that

---

1915, strategic considerations were operative. While Britain's lifeline was important, and had been since the beginning of the war (H. Maitland Wilson, p. 17), British oil fields in Iran were of more value than the Straits. Presumably, if the Russians had to have a warm-water outlet, the Straits would be more acceptable to the British than would the Persian Gulf. This is borne out by British actions in 1947 (see Chapter VI).

[85] FR, *Cairo and Teheran*, pp. 477-482, 496, 520, 537-538, 574, 586-588; Ehrman, p. 176.

[86] As Robert Beitzell points out, this promise was of dubious value. *The Uneasy Alliance: America, Britain, and Russia, 1941-1943* (New York, 1972), p. 333.

[87] FR, *Cairo and Teheran*, pp. 494, 505, 536, 544, 566-567, 571-574, 586-589, 633; Ehrman, pp. 175-179; Churchill, *Closing the Ring*, p. 292.

OVERLORD might be delayed, why, again, did he push so hard to get Turkey in the war only a month before? Eden and Hull had both articulated at that time the possibility of the same diversions and delays.

By the same token, if Stalin was now concerned with postwar spheres of influence, why, another writer asks, did the same concern not dominate his behavior at Moscow? Was he merely throwing the Allies off balance, as still another suggests? One scholar has a plausible explanation: Turkish diplomacy, by insisting on military cooperation in the Balkans, circumvented Soviet machinations; the use of Allied troops would have conflicted with Soviet ambitions in the area. To answer the question as to why this problem did not confront Stalin at Moscow, one can only speculate that he did not then think Anglo-American troops would actually be used. Possibly, as Ambassador W. Averell Harriman suggested in a letter to Roosevelt, the Russians were "entirely indifferent to any moral or actual obligation to assist the Turks in fighting the Germans." The idea that the Americans and British really felt such an obligation was "inexplicable" to them.[88] At the Teheran Conference, on the other hand, it is likely the Soviets took the possibility of Anglo-American assistance more seriously. This is evidenced in the first plenary meeting by Stalin's desire to know whether any Anglo-American forces would be allocated to help the Turks if they entered the war.

Whatever the Soviet motives were, one must agree with Llewellyn Woodward when he observes of the Russians:

> [T]hey could not fail to realize that, if the western Powers were occupied with the Germans in north-west Europe, the Russian armies would be able to advance into all the countries of south-east Europe (except Greece); for this reason also they did not view with favor a proposal made somewhat casually by the President—and supported by the Prime Minister—for an expedition to assist Marshal Tito.

For the Soviets, then, the military situation was now in hand; recent revelations that the British might actually send forces into the Balkans were obviated by apparent disagreement among the Western Allies

[88] In order that the Western Allies be accredited with no undue moral superiority, one may cite Churchill's 23 October 1943 letter to Eden at Moscow, in which he notes: "If we force Turkey to enter the war, she will insist on air support, etc. . . . If, however, Turkey enters the war on her own initiative . . . we should not have the same obligation, and yet greater advantages may be reaped." Churchill, *Closing the Ring*, p. 288.

41

which Stalin could use to his advantage. As the Soviets expanded westward, emphasis on OVERLORD coincided with a desire to avoid any
interference in what they considered as their sphere of influence.[89]

The Teheran Conference seems to have crystallized on a geopolitical
level the Soviet attitude toward Turkey which began to take shape after
Stalingrad. One can also detect an awakening interest in the Straits—
an interest dormant since late 1940 and now activated by Winston
Churchill. Less than twenty-four hours after the British prime minister
had talked of serious political and territorial consequences to Turkey—
particularly with regard to the future of the Straits—he brought up the
question of Russia's access to warm-water ports, observing that the problem would form part of the peace settlement, and that it could be
settled agreeably as between friends. Since Churchill brought the
matter up, Stalin replied, he would like to inquire as to the regime of
the Dardanelles. Because the British no longer objected, he thought it
would be well to relax the regime. Churchill admitted that the British
had had objections in the past, but said that England had none now
with regard to Russia's access to warm-water ports. When Churchill
questioned the advisability of doing anything about the Straits at the
time (since they were all trying to get Turkey into the war), Stalin,
who earlier had noted that at the proper time the question could be discussed, said that there was no hurry about the question. Churchill
reiterated that the question was a legitimate one, and that he hoped to
see Russian naval and merchant fleets on all the seas of the world.[90]

While Churchill and Stalin were having this luncheon conversation,

[89] The discussion of Soviet motives is based on: FR, Cairo and Teheran, pp. 153,
494, 505, 572; Ehrman, p. 177; Feis, Churchill, Roosevelt, Stalin, p. 266; FR, 1943,
I:644, 655, 661, 698; Hull, 2:1301; Deane, pp. 21-23, 44-45; Churchill, Closing
the Ring, p. 294; McNeill, America, Britain and Russia, p. 329-352; Weisband,
Turkish Foreign Policy, pp. 197-200; Helseth, p. 228; Woodward, 2:600; Fox,
p. 34; Louis Fischer, The Road to Yalta: Soviet Foreign Relations, 1941-1945
(New York, 1972), p. 124. If Soviet emphasis on OVERLORD coincided nicely
with other, political interests, the same can be said of Britain's desire for a Balkan
campaign.

[90] Ulam, Expansion and Coexistence, pp. 338, 345, 354-355; FR, Cairo and
Teheran, pp. 536, 566-567. Ulam suggests probable reasons for Churchill's bringing
up the matter of warm-water ports: realization of the losses suffered by Russia;
apprehension over the impending cross-channel attack; and, perhaps, guilt in the
absence of a second front. Another item worth noting is that this discussion over
Turkey is deleted from the official minutes of the conference published by the
Soviet Union. Robert Beitzell, ed., Teheran, Yalta, Potsdam: The Soviet Protocols
(Hattiesburg, Miss., 1970), pp. iv-v.

Molotov was asking Eden to elucidate Churchill's statement of the day before. What would be Turkey's postwar rights at the Straits if she refused the demands Eden was suggesting? While both Stalin and Molotov brought up this matter in a casual manner, their interest appears more than casual, especially in light of Molotov's inquiry into the matter again the next day. When Eden admitted that he did not know what Churchill meant, and talked vaguely about the basis of Britain's relationship with Turkey being changed, Molotov indicated that the Soviets would like further clarification of the matter from Churchill himself. Molotov's and Stalin's expressed desires not to get Turkey into the war if it meant a delay of OVERLORD take on added significance in light of these inquiries. The British had made clear the attitude if not the actions they intended to take toward Turkey in the event the Turks did not enter the war. Anything less than a united front against Turkey would probably not bring her into the war, and would result in a situation which would legitimize Soviet expectations in regard to the Straits. It would be hard to refuse Russian claims against a nonbelligerent power that had traded with the Nazis. If, on the other hand, the Turks suspected the Soviets of maneuvering to put them in a difficult postwar position, and decided to come into the war on their own, they would risk doing so at the expense of Britain's full support. They would also risk the possibility that the Nazis would retaliate against them, and that without British support they would be crippled.[91]

On the last day of the conference, the Big Three agreed to invite İnönü to meet Roosevelt and Churchill at Cairo, where Turkey's entry into the war would be solicited. Assistance to Turkey would be limited to the forces previously discussed: no land forces; 20 squadrons, mostly of fighter aircraft, and three antiaircraft regiments. In the course of the luncheon meeting, Molotov again inquired about Churchill's state-

[91] FR, Cairo and Teheran, pp. 571-574. Turkey's position was made more difficult by the fact that the Germans were fully informed of the conversations taking place. An Albanian agent, alias CICERO, soon passed them photographs of the minutes of the meeting he had obtained from the safe of the British ambassador in Turkey. This information was used by von Papen to make sure the Turks understood the consequences of their succumbing to Allied pressure. Von Papen, pp. 506-519; L. C. Moyzisch, Operation Cicero (London, 1950), pp. 72, 109, 111, 125-126; Louis Hagen, ed., The Schellenberg Memoirs (London, 1956), pp. 388-397; C. L. Sulzberger, A Long Row of Candles: Memoirs and Diaries (1934-1954) (Toronto, 1969), pp. 510-511; and Anthony Cave Brown, Bodyguard of Lies (New York, 1975), pp. 391-405; see also the discussion of Brown's book and of Cicero in The New York Review of Books, 19 February and 1 April 1976.

ment relating to the consequences of Turkey's refusing an invitation to enter the war. Churchill, noting the distance between him and his cabinet (and hence the speculative nature of what he was about to say?), said that he personally favored a change in the regime of the Straits if Turkey proved obdurate. Roosevelt, at this juncture, expressed a desire to see the Straits made free to the commerce and fleets of the world irrespective of Turkey's entry into the war, and the matter was dropped.[92] What changes Churchill had in mind in regard to the Straits are unknown. It was obvious that he was better informed about the matter than Roosevelt, whose emphasis on making the Straits free to the commerce and fleets of the world, if realized, would have been less acceptable to the Russians than the existing regime. Presumably, Churchill's discussion of a change in the regime indicated the possibility of Soviet political control over the Straits, a possibility which now hung fire.

Cairo (December 1943)

Sensing that his country's fate was in balance, Turkey's president, İsmet İnönü, was unwilling to go to Cairo if the object of the conference was to discuss matters already decided. Thus, he demanded assurance that the meeting was for the purpose of discussing freely, equally, and without prejudice the best method by which Turkey would serve the common cause. Given this assurance, he went to Cairo, and as far as the public could tell, the general political situation was reviewed in a spirit of understanding. Traditional friendships were reaffirmed.[93]

The actual talks at the conference, however, were far less assuring than İnönü had been promised. At Teheran, the Allies had reached agreement that he would be asked to bring Turkey into the war by 1 January 1944 (a date which, for military reasons, the British Chiefs of Staff changed to 15 February 1944). Uninformed of these proceedings, the Turks nonetheless were concerned that a deal had been made at their expense, and what ensued at Cairo only confirmed their apprehension.[94]

[92] FR, Cairo and Teheran, pp. 586-590, 633. To compare Roosevelt's suggestion (which is reminiscent of the twelfth of Wilson's fourteen points) with the provisions of the existing convention, see Howard, The Problem of the Turkish Straits, pp. 1-35.

[93] FR, Cairo and Teheran, pp. 663-665, 831-832.

[94] Ibid., pp. 589, 593; Knatchbull-Hugessen, p. 198; Hull, 2:1369; Llewellyn Woodward, British Foreign Policy in the Second World War (London, 1962)

During the course of the Cairo Conference, Churchill, Eden, and General H. Maitland Wilson (Commander in Chief, Middle East, and soon to be appointed Commander in Chief of the Mediterranean Theater), all pressed hard for Turkey to enter the war. Admiral William Leahy, Chairman of the American Joint Chiefs of Staff, in describing one of the dinners that took place during the conference, aptly characterizes the prime minister's conversation on Turkish matters throughout the conference: he pleaded, cajoled, and almost threatened İnönü in an effort to invoke the alliance. He wanted the Turks to come into the war, thereby shortening its length for the Allies. As in the past, his desires to lessen German resistance to OVERLORD and to bolster Britain's postwar position in the Eastern Mediterranean were unspoken. In his discussion with İnönü, Churchill refused to accept the argument that Turkey was in danger of a ground attack—least of all from Bulgaria. Granting Turkey's vulnerability from the air—which he saw as Turkey's only danger—he attempted to press on the Turkish president what he considered an adequate defense plan. He wanted to send support personnel and equipment into the country to prepare for the 20 (later reduced to 17) British squadrons that would arrive in Turkey on 15 February 1944. He stressed, however, not so much the positive value of such actions to Turkey as the harmful effects of failure to take them.[95]

As the conference progressed, Churchill became increasingly impatient with what he called the Turks' circular arguments (i.e., support personnel could not be introduced on the grounds that Germany would be provoked; without the necessary equipment and support personnel, Turkey was not prepared to enter the war). Eden and Wilson, too, took issue with some of the Turkish arguments; while the British had not fulfilled the requirements of the Adana lists, the Turks had received vast quantities of supplies. Arguing that Germany was weaker than ever before, Churchill doubted that Allied squadrons in Turkey would cause Germany to retaliate. While he could not guarantee that

---

(hereafter cited as BFP, to distinguish it from the first four volumes of the more elaborate work with the same title), p. 327; Weisband, *Turkish Foreign Policy*, pp. 201, 206-207.

[95] FR, *Cairo and Teheran*, pp. 691, 695, 698, 726-727, 729-731, 742-743, 745, 747, 752, 754 (for records of the various conversations, see pp. 690-699, 711-718, 726-734, 739, 740-747, 751-756); Leahy, p. 214; Churchill, *Closing the Ring*, pp. 415-418; Eden, p. 497; Knatchbull-Hugessen, pp. 198-201; H. Maitland Wilson, pp. 148, 188.

the Germans would not attack the Turks, he nonetheless wanted the Turks, by 15 February, to decide whether to accept the squadrons. Turkey would not have to enter the war until attacked, but she could, meanwhile, allow the Allies to use her bases.[96] Churchill acknowledged the Turks' preoccupation with Russia. Cooperation with Britain, he asserted, would put their relations with Russia on the best possible footing, since Turkey's only sure course was with the Allies. He even talked of political guarantees in the event that Turkey by her actions were drawn into the conflict, but Roosevelt, noting that such discussion should include Soviet representatives, halted it.[97]

In the course of his conversations with İnönü, Churchill delineated alternatives to cooperation with Britain. After the 15 February deadline, British squadrons would have to be used elsewhere. While remaining Britain's friend, Turkey would count for nothing as an effective ally and, as Eden added, "it was inevitable that the spirit of the alliance would be affected." The implicit threat—which Churchill had made clear at Teheran—was that Britain would not stand in Russia's way at war's end.[98]

In effect the British were attempting to realize the decisions made at Teheran, a decision decidedly in their interest, but questionable in the Turkish view. Without any greater commitment than 17 squadrons, which hardly constituted an adequate defense and certainly was not the collaborative plan the Turks required, the British wanted Turkey to assume an extremely vulnerable posture. İnönü, who felt that Turkey was not in danger so long as she was not in the war, was faced with hard choices.[99]

The Turks' decision was complicated by their erroneous belief that the Russians were trying to push them into the war, and that the British and Americans were the unwitting tools of Moscow. The Turks further believed that the Soviets wanted Turkey to enter the war only if that entry would be followed by a series of defeats which would enable the Soviet government to dominate the situation. But if that analysis had merit at the Moscow Conference, it did not a month later. All evidence indicates that the British were trying to push the Turks into the war— not the Russians. Nonetheless, Russia's absence from the conference,

[96] FR, Cairo and Teheran, pp. 691, 695, 697, 713, 715, 717, 729, 751, 754-755.
[97] Ibid., pp. 741, 751-752, 754.   [98] Ibid., pp. 751-754.
[99] Ibid., pp. 693, 697, 714, 744, 747, 753.

46

while seemingly the result of an accident, tended to confirm certain Turkish suspicions which were not without foundation.[100]

Andrei Vyshinsky, who was supposed to have been the Russian delegate at Cairo, apparently missed the conference because of communications difficulties. Ambassador Vinogradov, the Soviet ambassador in Turkey, persuaded by his British and American counterparts to go to Cairo as İnönü's guest, received no instructions to act as a substitute and refused to attend any meetings. This curious development, concerning as it did a meeting with the heads of state of Russia's two most important allies, was not interpreted by the Turks as an accident.[101]

Vyshinsky's attendance—even Vinogradov's—might have put the Soviets in the position of supporting an Anglo-Turkish expeditionary force in the Balkans, or of supplicating Turkish belligerency. Either alternative would have created difficulties for Soviet postwar designs in that area and would have enhanced Turkey's position vis-à-vis Soviet demands on the Straits. His absence, on the other hand, was interpreted by the Turks as evidence that the Soviets, while trying to push Turkey into the war, did not want to endorse Allied support for that entry. This interpretation was reinforced when Vinogradov informally told Selim Sarper not to pay attention to all the talk of coming into the war. Sarper promptly had gone to İnönü and told him that since their guide to action had always been to do the opposite of what the Soviets wanted them to do, perhaps they should consider coming into the war. As things stood, Turkey could neither characterize her entry into the war as a response to a Soviet request nor ask the Big Three for a declaration similar to that on Iran.[102]

Whatever the Soviet motivations, the Turks regretted Soviet absence from the conference. Sensing the existence of an agreement which, at their expense, worked to the Soviets' advantage, they felt unable to sup-

[100] Erkin, pp. 253-257; Kılıç, pp. 106-107; Eden, p. 497; Knatchbull-Hugessen, p. 198; Weisband, *Turkish Foreign Policy*, pp. 201-203.

[101] FR, *Cairo and Teheran*, pp. 663-667, 858; Beitzell, *The Uneasy Alliance*, pp. 361-362.

[102] Weisband, *Turkish Foreign Policy*, pp. 201-205. Churchill had asked İnönü to take note of the Declaration on Iran, and may have been hinting at something similar when he later talked of political guarantees; discussions of the matter were effectively curtailed, however, after Roosevelt remarked that Soviet representatives should be included (FR, *Cairo and Teheran*, pp. 692, 741). Selim Sarper told Howard of his conversation with Vinogradov some years later. Harry Howard, interview with the author.

port their position by elaborating on their fear of the Soviets' postwar intentions.[103] As a consequence, they reiterated their 17 November response to Eden. They were prepared to enter the war in principle, but were prevented from doing so by two conditions which had to be met: (1) they had to receive the arms and equipment necessary for their defense; (2) they had to have a general plan of collaboration with the Allies in the Balkans.[104]

The Turks believed that British aircraft on their airfields would bring a German attack. They wanted to be prepared. They did not hold the British to the Adana lists, but felt that the supplies the British thought adequate would be insufficient. What the Turks termed reasonable requirements, which the British were reluctant to discuss, were necessary because Bulgaria and Germany had forces on the Turkish frontier. However the British might minimize threats to Turkish security, the Turks saw themselves encircled from the Crimea to Rhodes. They recognized that Germany was losing the war, and that Turkish security ultimately lay in British and American hands, yet they were reluctant to risk everything for a cause that promised so little. As Menemencioğlu put it, the Allies were concerned with time, the Turks with preparation.[105] In short, the determining factor on either side was self-interest.

Hopkins, while impressed with the supplies actually shipped to the Turks, and though he did his best to persuade Roosevelt and Menemencioğlu to bring Turkey into the war, was more understanding of Turkey's position than Eden. Representing a country which had not regarded neutrality as onerous in the first years of the war, Hopkins understood that if a country were to go to war it must do so in its own interests. Roosevelt, although he doubted that Germany could stage a land offensive against the Turks, was even more explicit in his sympathy for İnönü's position, observing that "the Turks did not want to

[103] Weisband, *Turkish Foreign Policy*, pp. 206-207, cites an incident during the conference, recorded by Menemencioğlu, where İnönü seemed to be convincing Roosevelt of the Turkish point of view. Eden, who was in attendance, "leaned forward and whispered in a voice loud enough to be heard by the Turkish translator: 'But Mr. President, you forget we have a commitment vis-à-vis the Russians.'" Such an incident could only contribute to Turkish apprehension that some sort of a deal had been made at Turkey's expense.

[104] FR, *Cairo and Teheran*, pp. 694-696, 712-713, 716, 718, 730, 732-733, 742-744, 747, 752-754.

[105] Ibid., pp. 715-716, 728-731, 741. One source observes that in 1943 the Turkish threat to the Nazi position in the Balkans kept 26 German divisions immobilized on the Bulgarian frontier. Gordon and Dangerfield, p. 123.

get caught with their pants down." Privately, Roosevelt confided in Churchill "that if he, Roosevelt, was a Turk, he would require more assurance of aid than Britain had promised before abandoning neutrality and leading his nation into war."[106]

Like Churchill, Roosevelt understood that the big question for Turkey was Russia; but he was careful to point out to İnönü what Churchill did not: "there was no implication of a threat." Roosevelt, who seemed only moderately informed about Russo-Turkish relations, stressed the desirability of making friends with the Russians. His aims and Churchill's clearly diverged. Near the end of the conference, he managed a private moment with İnönü and expressed hope that Turkey would join the United Nations by 15 February, but he agreed that "everything had to be done to protect Turkey," and told İnönü that he completely understood his reluctance to bring Turkey into the war.[107]

On the morning that Roosevelt left Cairo, Churchill and İnönü had their last meeting. İnönü agreed to return to Ankara to ascertain whether and in what manner the Turks would engage in the preparations envisaged by the British. He promised to give the Allies an answer in three or four days, and to inform them of the conditions under which Turkey would enter the war, or take the risks likely to bring her into the war. Meanwhile, British experts would go to Ankara for talks.[108]

On 11 December, the Turks informed the British that they accepted their plan "in principle," but that the crucial question concerned aid. In effect, their position was unchanged. As one writer has observed, "the Turks were able to insist on objectively reasonable prerequisites which the Allies could not grant, and hence the Turkish Government avoided the onus of saying 'no' outright."[109]

Churchill was inclined to warn the Turks that refusal to honor his request would mean "the virtual end of the alliance," but was dissuaded. The British ambassador was instructed to make an adequate offer of supplies; if the offer were refused, the British would consider cutting off supplies and leaving the Turks isolated at war's end. On 18 December, Knatchbull-Hugessen was further instructed to say that the

[106] FR, Cairo and Teheran, pp. 694, 696, 698, 712-713, 732, 817; Sherwood, p. 800; Leahy, p. 214.
[107] FR, Cairo and Teheran, pp. 694, 712; Weisband, Turkish Foreign Policy, pp. 213-214.
[108] FR, Cairo and Teheran, pp. 753-755; Kılıç, pp. 106-107.
[109] Woodward, BFP, p. 328; Fox, p. 34.

British Commanders in Chief, Middle East, would come to Ankara for discussions.[110]

As the British had expected, discussions proved fruitless. They considered the Turkish request for 180,000 tons of war materiel exclusive of gasoline as too high. The Turks, for their part, were suspicious of Britain's apparent unwillingness to deliver the war materiel requested, and remained concerned that the British and the Soviets had divided Europe into spheres at their expense. The British solicited American assistance in pressing the Turks, but they did not receive full support. The United States made clear its desire that Turkey take an active part in the war, but refused the British request to back any representations they might make.[111]

Turkey's refusal to comply with Churchill's demands brought to a climax the diplomacy of 1943. Examination of that diplomacy reveals that Russia, Britain, and Turkey were all pursuing goals which, however rationalized, always conformed with their national interests. By the end of the year, Russian emphasis on OVERLORD coincided with a desire to avoid British interference in Soviet designs on the Balkans and the Near East. Britain's frustrated hope for a campaign in the Balkans coincided with her desire not only to draw off German opposition to the impending cross-channel invasion, but also to ensure her interests in the Eastern Mediterranean—interests which would increase as the invasion of Normandy succeeded and the war progressed. The United States was not particularly interested in Turkey and could afford to be sympathetic with her position because Roosevelt did not want resources diverted from the cross-channel attack. The Turks, meanwhile, increasingly fearful of Soviet intentions, and suspicious of an Anglo-Soviet deal, kept the Russians at a distance. They dragged their feet in dealing with their British allies, received some moral support from the Americans, and, like both the Russians and the British, acted in accordance with their national interests. A recognition of the interests of Russia, Britain, and Turkey illuminates some of the issues that might otherwise be obscured in their relations; it also illustrates the degree to which arguments based upon historic rivalries were cogent in their strategic thinking.

[110] Woodward, BFP, p. 328.
[111] Ibid., pp. 328-329; FR, 1943, IV:814-817; Weisband, *Turkish Foreign Policy*, pp. 221-223; Ataöv, p. 118.

The Politics of Necessity and the Widening Rift
in Allied Diplomacy over Turkey

As the Allies increased military pressure on Germany in 1944, they forced the Turks to reassess their stalling tactics and to choose a course predicated on the politics of necessity. Desiring to alienate neither the British nor the Russians, the Turks attempted to gauge the differences between them in order to find a course of action most likely to safeguard their position in the postwar world. While they were evaluating their options, they found an unwitting partner in the British Foreign Office. Turkey's refusal to comply with Churchill's demands had inclined the prime minister to send the Turks an ultimatum. He was persuaded otherwise by his Foreign Office, which considered it best not to allow Germany the luxury of discounting a possible declaration of war by Turkey. As a consequence, the British military mission was withdrawn, and its departure in early February was followed by suspension of arms exports to Turkey. But Britain sent no ultimatum.[112]

Increasingly isolated, Turkey now began to modify her position, hoping to placate the Allies by conciliatory policies. If the first phase of her wartime diplomacy had been to meet military threats from Nazis and Soviets alike, she now entered on the second: to limit Russia's influence in Eastern Europe at war's end.[113]

The Turks repealed the Varlık Vergisi (15 March 1944), a tax on wealth that was heavily weighted against minority groups and hence the object of protest on the part of Western democracies. They also suppressed (on 9 May) a small Pan-Turanian movement which had never been backed by the Turkish government, but which, because it had been supported by the Germans and had been popular among a few Turkish youths, was subject to Soviet criticism. These internal shifts in policy, however, were inadequate; the suppression of the Pan-Turanian movement met only sarcasm in the Soviet press.[114]

[112] Woodward, *BFP*, pp. 328-329; Medlicott, 2:542; *FR*, 1943, IV:818.

[113] Weisband, *Turkish Foreign Policy*, pp. 215, 230; Ataöv, p. 119.

[114] Weisband, *Turkish Foreign Policy*, pp. 231-256; Ataöv, pp. 119-120; Kılıç, pp. 107-108; Sachar, *Europe Leaves the Middle East*, p. 364; Hostler, pp. 171-186; Kirk, *The Middle East in the War*, pp. 460-461; Bernard Lewis, pp. 295-296.

Soviet concern about Pan-Turanism probably stemmed from the existence of 21 million Turkish speaking peoples in the Soviet Union, the second largest linguistic or ethnic group after the Slavic groups. A State Department estimate of 1949 gives this regional breakdown: 4,000,000 Turco-Tatars in the European portions of the

As a consequence, Turkey tried another tack. In response to British and American threats of blockade (14 April 1944), and in spite of German pressures, İnönü suspended chromite shipments to Germany (20 April). Since the Germans had paid in advance, with war materiel, for 100,000 tons of chromite, they were alarmed. Their fears of Turkey's active participation on the Allied side revived, and bore out the wisdom of the British Foreign Office's advice to Churchill earlier in the year. Meanwhile, deeply troubled by cessation of Allied arms shipments, and by criticism of Turkish policy in the House of Commons and in the British press, Menemencioğlu in May decided to explore the possibility of bettering Turkey's relations with Russia.[115]

As a means of probing Soviet intentions, Menemencioğlu suggested negotiating a treaty that would guarantee the independence and neutrality of the Balkan states after the war. The Soviets, according to Menemencioğlu, were in agreement with the idea. They even hoped for a general act of mutual assistance, but only if Turkey would enter the war at once. Menemencioğlu concluded that his fears were justified. The Soviets wanted the Turks in the war, but only if they were "mutually assisted" by Russian defense forces which would never leave Turkish

---

Soviet Union; 3,650,000 in the Caucasus; 550,000 in Northeastern and South-central Siberia; and 13,000,000 in Soviet Central Asia. The loyalty of these elements was apparently uncertain due to German success in World War II in recruiting Turco-Tatar prisoners and deserters for the so-called "Turkestani Division." Harry Howard, "The Turkish Speaking Peoples: A Preliminary Estimate of the Problem," 4 March 1949, Box 4, Harry Howard Papers. The above facts and figures contribute to an explanation of Stalin's deportation of eight entire nations from Russia's southern borderlands in 1941 (Volga Germans) and 1943-44 (Kalmyks and the Muslim nations of the Crimea and Caucasus). Of the ten so-called Muslim Republics, four were liquidated, and all of the Muslim Turki reached by the Germans in their attack on Russia were deported. Andrei Sakharov estimates that 46 percent of the Crimean Tatars died, and Robert Conquest that all told 500,000 died during deportation. Roy Medvedev, who is less conservative in his figures, estimates that more than five million people were deported under the pretext of treason, and that hundreds of thousands died of hunger, cold, and disease in the sparsely populated, underdeveloped districts of Kazakhstan, Siberia, and Central Asia. Robert Conquest, *The Nation Killers: The Soviet Deportation of Nationalities* (Glasgow, 1970), pp. 1-12, 64-65; Ivar Spector, *The Soviet Union and the Muslim World, 1917-1958* (Seattle, 1959), p. 189; Medvedev, pp. 491-492; see also Khrushchev's "Secret Speech," in *Khrushchev Remembers*, p. 652.

115 Knatchbull-Hugessen, p. 200; Weisband, *Turkish Foreign Policy*, pp. 224-228, 257-259; FR, 1944, V:827, 832, 853, 863; Medlicott, 2:544-545; Hull, 2:1372; Ataöv, p. 119; Great Britain, Parliament, *Hansard's Parliamentary Debates* (Commons), 5th Series, vol. 400 (1943-1944), cols. 764-766.

soil. In light of Soviet treatment of the Turkish question at Moscow, Teheran, and Cairo, Menemencioğlu's trepidation appears well founded.[116]

June 1944 saw further Turkish concessions to the Allies. As a result of the passage of twelve German vessels from the Black Sea to the Aegean, the Allies again made representations to the Turks. The Soviets and the British had complained before about violation of the Montreux Convention, but these complaints had been of little effect because the matters had been minor, and had concerned conflicting interpretations of the convention. Now, however, the Turks were more inclined to sacrifice interpretation to Allied pressure.[117]

The Montreux Convention was never easy to interpret, and the Turks were always sensitive to the implications of every nuance. Under the convention, for example, in a war in which Turkey was neutral, merchant ships (ordinarily armed during World War II, and so complicating matters of definition) were allowed free passage through the Straits (Art. 4), subject to minor charges (Art. 2) and a cursory sanitary inspection by the Turks (Art. 3). Warships of belligerent powers were prohibited from using the Straits (Art. 19) unless they were acting under the Covenant of the League (Art. 25). Definitions utilized by the convention, however, had been transposed from the Treaty of London (May 1936); they had been conceived in light of the problems of that conference, and were functionally related to the limitation of naval armaments—not to matters which were to confront the Straits regime in World War II. Warships, for example, were narrowly defined (Art. 2; Annex II), while vessels of less than 100 tons displacement were excluded from definition. As a consequence, the convention did not properly account for new types of vessels auxiliary to conventional warships. Nor did it account for those vessels under 100 tons which, while they were not covered by definitions, were in fact capable of being used for warlike purposes.[118] For this reason, Menemencioğlu had followed a strictly legalistic approach to the convention during the war and,

[116] Weisband, *Turkish Foreign Policy*, pp. 228-229; Kirk, *The Middle East in the War*, p. 461; Kirk, "Turkey," p. 361; Erkin, pp. 281-282; FR, 1944, V:864-865.

[117] Kirk, "Turkey," pp. 353, 361-362; Great Britain, *Parliamentary Debates* (Commons), vol. 400, cols. 1986-1988; von Papen, pp. 326-327; Howard, *The Problem of the Turkish Straits*, pp. 48, 50-55; Weisband, *Turkish Foreign Policy*, pp. 261-268; Erkin, pp. 271-281.

[118] Erkin, pp. 271-281; Weisband, *Turkish Foreign Policy*, pp. 261-263; Howard, *The Problem of the Turkish Straits*, pp. 25-28.

under the circumstances, opted to continue such a policy. He felt that sacrificing legal interpretation to political expediency would subject Turkey to a series of demands—especially on the part of the Soviets— which ultimately could only work to Turkey's detriment. According to his interpretation, Turkey had violated the convention neither in letting ships pass on previous occasions, nor in allowing passage of the ships in question—and in a strictly legal sense he probably was correct. Under the convention the Turks had been allowed only a rapid inspection of the ships which, von Papen had assured them, were not auxiliary naval vessels. Their limited inspection had revealed nothing to contradict the German ambassador and the ships were allowed to pass.[119]

When the British protested vehemently, Menemencioğlu offered to submit the dispute to an impartial foreign jurist for arbitration—a solution which was too slow, and hence unsatisfactory to both the Germans and the British. At this juncture, a personal appeal from Churchill persuaded İnönü that Menemencioğlu's resignation was necessary. While generally believed to be pro-Axis, the Turkish foreign minister was less a friend of the Germans than is often imagined. It was he, for example, who helped the British evacuate their troops from the Dodecanese in October and November 1943. Other evidence indicates that if he seemed pro-Axis, it was because of his fear of the Soviets. His essential objective while in office had been to protect Turkey's national interests—a goal which he carried out with full government approval. Now, on 15 June, his resignation indicated a change in the political situation. The Allies had invaded Normandy less than two weeks before, and Allied ascendancy required Turkey to make accommodations to new political realities. But, as one author observes, Menemencioğlu's resignation was "less a factor than a symbol of Turkish realignment."[120]

Prime Minister Şükrü Saraçoğlu, who now became acting foreign minister as well, aptly represented this realignment. While Menemencioğlu was still in office, the Turks had finally insisted on the careful inspection of a German ship they had halted because it refused to be

119 Weisband, *Turkish Foreign Policy*, pp. 263-265; Erkin, pp. 274-279.

120 Erkin, pp. 276-279; Weisband, *Turkish Foreign Policy*, pp. 166, 265-268; *FR*, 1944, V:859. For a wartime evaluation of Menemencioğlu, see the Report of 13 November 1943 in *O.S.S./State Department Intelligence and Research Reports* (Washington, D.C., 1977), Paul Kesaris, ed., 7 vols., vol. VII, *The Middle East*, III:23 (henceforth, these reports on the Middle East will be referred to as *O.S.S./State I&R Reports*, with the Roman numeral referring to the reel, and the Arabic numeral to the report).

inspected. British information concerning its true nature had been correct. As a consequence, on the day Menemencioğlu resigned, Saraçoğlu announced that his government was protesting the matter to Germany. The Turks now prohibited the passage of certain classes of German ships through the Straits, and ordered an intensive inspection of all German vessels applying to pass through the Straits. On 16 June (almost two months after Menemencioğlu had informed the American ambassador of its likelihood), Turkey's realignment was further underscored by a decision to halve exports of commodities other than chromite to the Axis. The remainder would be reduced when the Allies could provide essential imports the Turks could not otherwise obtain.[121]

As Turkish susceptibility to the new influence of the Allies became apparent, the British pressured the Turkish government to sever economic and diplomatic relations with Germany. On 3 July, the Turks were willing to accede to combined British and American representations provided that: (1) Britain treat Turkey as a full ally, and (2) Britain and the United States give Turkey what economic and military assistance they could.[122]

Meanwhile in Moscow on 28 June, at the time that British and American representations to the Turks were being authorized, Molotov called Ambassador Harriman to his office to inform him of developments regarding Turkey. Menemencioğlu a month before had proposed an agreement between Turkey and Russia envisaging political collaboration. The Soviet government had been prepared to effect such an agreement "if Turkey broke with Germany and entered the war on the side of the Allies." Short of that condition, the Soviets were unwilling to negotiate with the Turks. Three days earlier, on 25 June, Molotov had received a British note asking the Soviets to support a demand that Turkey break economic and diplomatic relations with Germany as a first step toward entering the war. Molotov's reaction was that the proposal "was not in accordance with the Moscow decisions." At the Moscow

---

[121] Weisband, *Turkish Foreign Policy*, p. 265-268; Erkin, pp. 276-281; FR, 1944, V:822-823, 825, 827, 839, 840-842, 845-847, 849-852, 855-856. Turkey's position was emphasized by Menemencioğlu's discussion of Atabrine, which helped to prevent malaria. His information was that Britain had failed to deliver promised Atabrine to Egypt, resulting in whole communities being "wiped out" by malaria. When the United States and Britain failed to give effect to their assurances that adequate quantities would be delivered to Turkey, he had been forced to rely on German sources. FR, 1944, V:833.

[122] FR, 1944, V:860-875; Eden, pp. 534-535; Hull, 2:1372-1373; Erkin, p. 282.

Conference the Allies had expected Turkey to enter the war, and Molotov thought it illogical to reduce that demand. Harriman told Molotov that the Allies were not in a position to meet Turkish demands for supplies, but Molotov dismissed these demands as mere excuses.[123]

On the day after his discussion with Harriman, Molotov told the British ambassador that Turkey's breaking of economic and diplomatic relations with Germany was only a half-measure, "and would have no important effect upon hastening the conclusion of the war." The Soviets believed that only entry into the war could demonstrate Turkey's desire to act with the Allies.[124]

In an *aide-mémoire* to the Department of State on 10 July the Soviet embassy reiterated Molotov's views. It mentioned still another Turkish attempt on 27 June to confirm friendly relations between Turkey and Russia, this time through a protocol further prolonging the 17 December 1925 Treaty of Friendship and Neutrality, or through a new treaty. The Russian response had been that such proposals were no substitutes for action against Hitler. The *aide-mémoire* stated that the Soviet position was in accord with the agreement reached at the Moscow Conference in October and confirmed at the Teheran Conference in November and December 1943. The British proposal of 25 June was regarded as a departure from that agreement—which was, according to the Soviet note, to "insist on the immediate entrance of Turkey into the war against Germany." The note went on to point out that the British had made their proposal to the Turks (30 June) in spite of the Soviet note of 29 June.[125]

While Cordell Hull agreed that the Soviet position was in accord with the Moscow agreement, he felt that if the rupture in relations between Turkey and Germany was a first step toward active belligerency, no question should arise concerning the agreement. Hull was more concerned that delay in accepting the Turkish provisions of 3 July (formally made on 4 July) would confirm Turkish suspicions of Allied sincerity in making the request for a break. The British position, which Hull urgently requested, and which he received on 12 July, was that the break was desirable for a number of reasons, one of which was that it would have almost the same moral effect on Germany and the Balkans as a declaration of war—an assessment which the comparative effect of suspending chromite shipments to Germany seemed to support, but which con-

---

[123] FR, 1944, V:863-865; Hull, 2:1373.
[124] FR, 1944, V:865.   [125] Ibid., pp. 875-878; Hull, 2:1373.

flicted sharply with the Soviet position. As a result of this logic, the British were willing to meet Turkey's provisions, and to regard such a break as clarifying Turkey's policy. Apparently British concern over the postwar situation in the Eastern Mediterranean was increasing, for the British believed the break with Germany would place Turkey in a better position at the peace table. Hull was inclined to accept Britain's position if the Joint Chiefs of Staff agreed, and if severance of relations between Turkey and Germany was regarded by both Russia and Turkey as "only the first step toward active belligerency." In addition to political returns, Hull saw immediate military benefits as well: high altitude flights over Turkey; expulsion of Axis agents from Turkish soil; and the possible use of Turkish bases and harbors. On 14 July, he wired Harriman that the British approach to bringing Turkey into the war was more practical and realistic than the simple demand contemplated by the Soviets.[126]

While the British were waiting for American approval of their position, Churchill asked Stalin to regard the break in relations between Germany and Turkey as the first installment of Turkey's entry into the war. Stalin, on 15 July, gave no encouragement, expressing much the same view as Molotov had earlier to the British ambassador. He noted the proposals that had been made to Turkey, and the results of those proposals. He saw no benefit for the Allies in such "half-measures" as a break in relations. Rather, it seems as if he were preparing the ground for postwar Soviet designs:

> In view of the evasive and vague attitude with regard to Germany adopted by the Turkish Government, it is better to leave Turkey in peace and to her own free will and not to exert fresh pressure on Turkey. This of course means that the claims of Turkey, who has evaded war with Germany, to special rights in post-war matters also lapse. . . .

What these special rights might have been, or what their denial portended, was unspecified.[127]

In spite of this Soviet rebuff, the United States on 20 July agreed with the views expressed in Britain's *aide-mémoire*. The American chargé d'affaires in Turkey was authorized to support the British position regarding the severance of economic and diplomatic relations be-

---

[126] FR, 1944, V:878-884; Hull, 2:1373-1375.
[127] FR, 1944, V:881; Winston Churchill, *Triumph and Tragedy* (Boston, 1953), pp. 80-81.

tween Turkey and Germany. While the Americans made clear to the British that they considered this measure as only a first step to active belligerency, they agreed to share with them the burden of any military, financial, and economic assistance they would jointly determine as being necessary for Turkey.[128]

Two days later, on 22 July, an American *aide-mémoire* informed the Soviet government of the coincidence of views between the Soviet *aide-mémoire* of 10 July and those views expressed by the American government at Moscow and Teheran. It further noted that urging Turkey to sever relations with Germany was not a departure from those views since such action was a first step toward active Turkish belligerency—a development which the United States expected to follow the break in relations. In addition, the American *aide-mémoire* noted the "definite practical advantages" of the Turkish action, and promised that a Turkish decision to adhere to the United Nations Declaration would not receive any response until the Soviet Union's views had been sought. Meanwhile, British and American replies to Turkish requests for assurances were given to the Turkish prime minister on 22 July and 24 July respectively. As a consequence, Turkey severed economic and diplomatic relations with Germany at the next session of the Grand National Assembly, 2 August.[129]

Prior to that time, however, the Soviets dissociated themselves from Allied representations. In spite of the advantages of Turkey's breaking relations with Germany, and in spite of assurances that such a break would be only the first step in Turkey's becoming an active belligerent, the Soviets on 27 July informed the United States that Turkey's position with respect to Germany was "unsatisfactory." Turkey, the Soviets declared, was only discussing half-measures which were much too late, and which did "not have any essential significance in the present situation." As a consequence, the Soviet government considered it necessary "to discontinue pressure on the Turkish government and leave it entirely to its own will."[130]

In Moscow, Ambassador Harriman doubted that the Soviets sincerely believed the demands on Turkey contrary to the Moscow agreement; they wanted to avoid recognizing the Turkish action as a concession to

[128] *FR*, 1944, V:844-845.
[129] *FR*, 1944, V:885-890, 896-897; Hull, 2:1375; for the U.N. Declaration, signed at Washington, D.C., 1 January 1942, see *FR*, 1942, I:25.
[130] *FR*, 1944, V:891-894; Hull, 2:1376.

the Soviet Union. On 30 July, when Harriman asked Vyshinsky whether it would be useful to have conversations on how best to implement Turkey's entry into the war, the Soviet First Assistant People's Commissar for Foreign Affairs replied that he did not believe it would, remarking that Turkey should "now be left to its own fate." Whether or not this fate was associated with what Stalin referred to as the lapse of Turkey's claims to special rights in postwar matters required little imagination. As Harriman reported to the secretary of state, "Under this policy, the Soviets get whatever benefits the Turkish actions may bring without paying the price of recognition of any obligation on their part toward Turkey in the peace settlement."[131]

Thus, the widening rift in Allied diplomacy over Turkey reveals that it was a strategic issue over which the Soviet Union and Britain, supported by the United States, came into conflict. While wartime considerations were important in the formulation of their policies, the essential factor in both Russia's and Britain's policies toward Turkey by July 1944 was a desire to ensure their interests in the Eastern Mediterranean in the postwar world.

As we have seen, Soviet desires to bring Turkey into the war lessened when such action was connected to the question of Allied support, and involved the use of British forces in the Balkans. Ostensibly, Soviet attitudes were a result of wartime strategy: Normandy was more important than the Balkans. Later, however, the Soviets were as rigid as ever in their insistence upon Turkish participation in the war. Their position from 1939 to 1941 caused them no embarrassment, and they refused to consider the views of the British and Americans as to which was the common interest of the Allied powers. This insistent, unyielding attitude on the part of the Soviets leads one to the unavoidable conclusion either that they intended to use Turkey's participation in the war to take advantage of her vulnerability, or that they intended to make the price for a voice in postwar matters so high that Turkey could be represented as a moral bankrupt. Either way the Soviet Union would benefit, and she would strengthen her position in regard to the Straits.

Churchill, concerned in 1943-44 with the impending cross-channel attack, initially had intended to use a heavy hand in urging Turkey to enter the war. Out of guilt, perhaps, at the delay of OVERLORD, he had been willing to endorse a degree of Soviet influence at the Straits

---

[131] FR, 1944, V:894-895.

after the war, and had threatened the Turks with that endorsement when they proved recalcitrant. While the cross-channel attack was still pending, he had, in an impulsive mood, thought of handing the Turks an ultimatum, but the Foreign Office stayed his hand. As in the initial stages of the war, so after the successful campaign in North Africa, and the successful invasion of Normandy, the Foreign Office gave greater emphasis to Britain's long-range strategic interests—which included a strong Turkish nation with a seat at the peace table.

The Turks, no doubt, would have agreed with Ambassador Harriman's assessment of the situation. They believed the Soviets were determined to reserve complete freedom of action over Turco-Soviet problems. Soviet actions in Eastern Europe in the latter part of 1944, while in part dictated by wartime strategy, were also a source of anxiety and gave the Turks little hope for anything other than Soviet domination of the Balkans.[132]

Balkan Concerns

Looking to the West, the Turks were particularly concerned about events in Bulgaria. Turkey in 1934 had joined with Greece and Rumania in a defensive alliance whose primary purpose was to contain Bulgarian irredentism. World War II, however, had undermined the Balkan Pact as well as its aims, and had seen the realization of precisely what the pact had sought to prevent.

Bulgaria cooperated with Germany during the war, when she was "neutral for Germany." She joined the Axis under pressure from Hitler and from Bulgarian nationalists whose territorial ambitions Hitler recognized. When Bulgaria's King Boris permitted German forces to cross his country to attack Greece and Yugoslavia in 1941, he accepted portions of those countries as his share of the spoils. Later he declared war against Britain and the United States. Since there was widespread pro-Russian sentiment in Bulgaria, her leaders maintained neutrality vis-à-vis the Russians, and preserved a careful balance between the Russians and the Germans, despite the presence of German troops on Bulgarian soil. Allied bombings in 1943 and 1944 stimulated Bulgaria's deep-seated

[132] Erkin, p. 284; Helseth, p. 243; McNeill, *America, Britain and Russia*, pp. 462-476. See also Wolff, pp. 242, 246-248; Ulam, *Expansion and Coexistence*, pp. 361-364; Thomas Wolfe, *Soviet Power and Europe, 1945-1970* (Baltimore, 1970), p. 21. Hull, 2:1459-1461, discusses American concern over this same issue; in the fall of 1944, the United States was seriously concerned over the hard bargain the Soviets were driving in their armistice terms with Hungary, Bulgaria, and Rumania.

pro-Russian sentiment; but public opinion, while it favored abandoning the Germans and making peace, was fearful of a full-scale German occupation, and was concerned over the possible loss of recently acquired Greek and Yugoslav territory.[133]

As German forces withdrew in 1944, and the Russian army came closer, the Bulgarian government in Sofia underwent several internal changes. In May, Prince Cyril's regency (King Boris died in August 1943 and was succeeded by his six-year-old son Simeon) gave way to a new government. In August, the new government began negotiations with the Western Allies in Cairo.[134] The Russians, ostensibly because they were never at war with the Bulgarians, did not wish to participate in the negotiations, although the Allies kept them fully informed. By September, it appeared that moderates led by the agrarian Kosta Muraviev would assume control of the Bulgarian government, which was following a policy of complete neutrality and resisting Allied demands for a declaration of war against Germany. At this point, *Tass* declared that Bulgaria's actions were not sufficient, and that Bulgaria should join the Allies or suffer the consequences. The Soviet Union, apparently unwilling to allow either control of the government by Muraviev, or a peace negotiated by the Western Allies alone, then declared war on Bulgaria—without consulting her Western Allies. Russian troops marched into the country on 8 September; the next day, a pro-Soviet leader emerged as the head of the Bulgarian government.[135]

The Turks, meanwhile, were concerned with several related issues. Since Stalingrad, they had feared an Anglo-Soviet deal dividing Europe,

[133] Gordon Wright, pp. 136, 196, 220; Wolff, pp. 242-246; Weisband, *Turkish Foreign Policy*, pp. 277-278; Feis, *Churchill, Roosevelt, Stalin*, pp. 417-418; FR, 1944, III:404.

[134] The decision to negotiate with the Allies came at the time of Rumania's surrender—an act which gave the Red Army an open path into the Balkans. The Bulgarian foreign minister's declaration that he would seek peace with the Western Allies, but that Macedonia and Thrace were "Bulgarian by right," indicates both a concern over domestic consequences of the advance and a desire to retain Bulgaria's recent territorial acquisitions. Stavrianos, *The Balkans*, pp. 770, 811.

[135] Edgar Hösch, *The Balkans* (New York, 1968), pp. 164-165; Woodward, 3:139; Stavrianos, *The Balkans*, pp. 769-770, 811; Wolff, pp. 246-247; FR, 1944, III:407. See FR, 144, III:397, 402-403, for Harriman's analyses of: (1) 5 September 1944, where he speculates that the desire to be a party to the Bulgarian armistice and to control the armistice's execution played an important part in the Soviet government's declaration of war; and (2) 7 September 1944, where he notes that the internal political situation in Bulgaria together with the arrival of Soviet forces on the Bulgarian border constitutes the most important factor in Soviet policy.

like Iran, into spheres of influence—at Turkish expense. In the summer of 1944, these fears had been nurtured by reports of such a deal, leaked to C. L. Sulzberger of the *New York Times* by Lincoln MacVeagh, the American ambassador to the emigré Greek and Yugoslav governments in Cairo.[136]

Enis Akaygen, the Turkish ambassador to the Greek government in Cairo, probably was reacting to these reports when he told a high-ranking Greek diplomatic official on 24 July that a cornerstone of Turkey's foreign policy was friendship with Greece. The Turkish diplomat saw friendship between the two countries and, possibly, Yugoslavia, as constituting a barrier to Bulgarian and, more generally, to Soviet aspirations. The British, too, had been thinking along these lines. Anthony Eden in early June had outlined a policy memorandum which advocated abandoning Churchill's tactic of trying to force Turkey into the war under the implicit threat that she would not receive support at the peace settlement; instead, he recommended consolidating Britain's position in Turkey and Greece, arguing that Turco-Greek friendship should be a fundamental factor in Britain's Southeastern European and Eastern Mediterranean policies. The British ambassador to the Greek government, Reginald Leeper, may have been acting on the Foreign Office memorandum when, on 27 July, he suggested to Philip Dragoumis, the Greek undersecretary of state, the desirability of setting up a bloc of countries (Turkey, Greece, Italy) along Britain's imperial lifeline in the Mediterranean. The Greek response came indirectly on 6 August, when Dragoumis hailed Turkey's decision four days earlier to sever relations with Germany. The Greek undersecretary of state stressed the links between Greece and Turkey on geographical, economic, and political grounds, and led the Soviet ambassador in Ankara to wonder if the British were behind this friendly demonstration. The Foreign Office memorandum, British influence over the Greek government-in-exile, and subsequent British policy toward Turkey, are evidence that the British were in fact engaged in much maneuvering behind the scenes.[137]

Another concern of the Turks was the Allies' failure to request them to go to war. After the Turks severed relations with Germany, the

---

[136] FR, 1944, V:899-900; Weisband, *Turkish Foreign Policy*, pp. 288-290; FR, 1944, III:404; Sulzberger, pp. 241-243.

[137] Eden, pp. 533-535; Woodward, 3:119-121, 4:185-186; Stephen Xydis, "New Light on the Big Three Crisis over Turkey in 1945," *The Middle East Journal* 14 (Autumn 1960):416-418.

British ambassador told them that their entry into the war would be too late to be of any value. The Turks, of course, were concerned about the political settlement after the war; they knew that their entry into the war could have some bearing on their future. But the British now appeared reluctant to follow their earlier policies. Presumably, this was due to a change in policy following the June memorandum on Greece and Turkey. The Turks, however, did not appear to be fully informed of the change. As a consequence, they could not understand Britain's attitude. They worried over rumors of an Anglo-Soviet deal, and suspected that Russian occupation of Bulgaria was part of it. Even more worrisome was the possibility that Soviet occupation of Turkey could be as easily sanctioned as that of Bulgaria. Like the Bulgarians, the Turks had been less than fully committed to the Allied war effort. Thus, the Turks were now inclined to comply with any Allied representations, desiring to avoid an ambiguous stance which might subject them, like the Bulgarians, to Soviet occupation.[138] But Turkish anxiety about a possible agreement between the Allies soon gave way to concern over Bulgarian irredentism supported by the Soviet Union.

Bulgaria had long held designs on Thrace and Macedonia, and had sought a port on the Aegean. She had actually incorporated those areas three different times: in 1878, immediately before and during World War I, and then again during World War II. Bulgar irredentism, especially when it was supported by Russia, was nothing new to anyone with even a superficial knowledge of Balkan history. As late as November 1940, Molotov had told Hitler that Russia was prepared to guarantee Bulgaria an outlet on the Aegean. The Turks, of course, had learned of these Nazi-Soviet negotiations,[139] and had been reminded of them periodically during the war. Thus, when Bulgaria capitulated on 9 September, blackout regulations in Turkey were intensified. A joke, then popular in Istanbul, captured the Turkish state of mind at the time:

> The story was that the Russian Ambassador had called on the Turkish Foreign Minister to say: "I am instructed by my government to assure you that there is no need for you to inconvenience your people by this black-out. When we attack, it will be in the day-time."[140]

[138] FR, 1944, V:899-900.

[139] As Barbara Jelavich and Charles Jelavich point out, Bulgaria's desire to acquire further territory led her to support the losing side in three consecutive wars (The Balkans [Englewood Cliffs, N.J., 1965], pp. 66-67). Churchill, too, was very much aware of the history of Bulgarian irredentism. Great Britain, Parliamentary Debates (Commons), vol. 402 (1943-44), cols. 1483-1484.

[140] Weisband, Turkish Foreign Policy, pp. 278-279; Wolff, pp. 247-248; Sontag

What seemed to confirm the Turks' fears of Bulgaria, and to bear out their belief that purely Russian designs were more dangerous than any Anglo-Soviet deal, was an Allied disagreement. In spite of reported agreement among the Western Allies that Bulgarian forces should depart at once, the Bulgarian government refused throughout September and early October to withdraw its forces from Greek and Yugoslav territory. To complicate matters, Bulgarian armies—Bulgaria had declared war on Hitler on 8 September—were now fighting the Germans in Yugoslavia and could not be easily withdrawn. Although the Western Allies had agreed among themselves on the withdrawal of Bulgarian troops, the Soviets disagreed with them over the terms of withdrawal—a problem which the Turks correctly suspected, and which only reinforced their apprehension over Soviet designs. What these designs were can only be guessed, but they may be illuminated by the following facts: the Soviets now wanted armistice negotiations at Ankara or Moscow; they wanted the armistice terms to be assigned to a Soviet general; they wanted Bulgarian troops to stay in certain parts of Greece and Yugoslavia; they wanted Bulgaria to be granted the status of a co-belligerent; and they wanted the Allied Control Commission in Bulgaria to be under the direct control of the Soviet High Command.[141] In short, political control of the Balkans seems to have been one concern that the Soviets were keeping very much in mind.

Such control was obviously of concern to the British, too, who felt that concessions to the Soviet demands would affect British influence

---

and Beddie, pp. 244-246, 252; Kirk, *The Middle East in the War*, p. 462; Geoffrey Lewis, p. 122. For accounts of Bulgarian and Russian concerns in Thrace and Macedonia, see: B. H. Sumner, *Russia and the Balkans, 1870-1880* (Oxford, 1937); Barbara Jelavich, *The Ottoman Empire, the Great Powers, and the Straits Question, 1870-1887* (Bloomington, 1973); Charles Jelavich, *Tsarist Russia and Balkan Nationalism: Russian Influence in the Internal Affairs of Bulgaria and Serbia, 1879-1886* (Berkeley, 1958); Stavrianos, *The Balkans*, esp. pp. 425-447, 513-543, 578-580, 644-660. For the numerous times Germany informed Turkey of the Nazi-Soviet negotiations, see: "Department of State Special Interrogation Mission in Germany," 15 August-15 November 1945, Box 1, Harry Howard Papers. Paul Schmidt, Hitler's interpreter, noted the tremendous impression Soviet demands made on Hitler. Franz von Papen observed that Germany's refusal to meet Soviet demands was the decisive turning point of the war. See also "The Policy of Nationalist Socialist Germany in Southeastern Europe, ca. 1938-1945," Box 3, Harry Howard Papers.

[141] Weisband, *Turkish Foreign Policy*, pp. 278-279; Wolff, pp. 247-248; Feis, *Churchill, Roosevelt, Stalin*, pp. 418-419; Woodward, 3:139; FR, 1944, III:407, 442-443.

in Southeastern Europe, and cause the loss of British authority in Greece and Turkey. British credit and authority in those countries were necessary if Eden's strategy were to be implemented, and if Turco-Greek friendship, supported by Britain, were to be a fundamental factor in Southeastern Europe and the Eastern Mediterranean.

American Attitudes Toward Turkey

Throughout these protracted maneuvers and negotiations in the last months of the war, the United States remained aloof from matters concerning Turkey. In fact, its policies toward the Near and Middle East seemed to follow its traditional isolationist doctrines. Formal relations between the United States and the Ottoman Empire had been established in 1830, but the United States—at least before World War I —had chosen to regard the Middle East as an extension of Europe. The Monroe Doctrine had dictated the rejection of American involvement in Europe. As a consequence, traditional isolationist policies were all that supported American interests in the Near East. And these interests, unlike those of other foreign powers, were neither strategic nor political; rather, they were missionary,[142] philanthropic, cultural, and economic in nature. For the most part, therefore, American policies were relegated to the protection of these nonpolitical interests.[143]

The lack of a more assertive policy in the Middle East did not mean that relations between the two countries were always amicable. In 1917, for example, when the United States declared war on Germany, the Turks severed formal diplomatic relations—a state of affairs which lasted for ten years. The Turks' unfavorable image in the United States (where they were regarded as Central Asian barbarians), American sympathy for Armenians in eastern Turkey,[144] and complications associated with

[142] In 1914, there were 174 missionaries in that part of Turkey which later became the Turkish Republic; they operated or supervised 426 schools in addition to 17 mission stations and 9 hospitals. This number, because of the depression, and perhaps because of the missionaries' focus on the Christian minorities whose number was reduced by the war, dwindled to 54 by 1939. Trask, pp. 9-10; John DeNovo, *American Interests and Policies in the Middle East, 1900-1939* (Minneapolis, 1963), p. 259; Sachar, *The Emergence of the Middle East*, p. 341.

[143] James Field, Jr., *America and the Mediterranean World, 1776-1882* (Princeton, 1969), p. 150; Kirk, *The Middle East in the War*, p. 23; DeNovo, pp. 18-19, 26, 57, 253, 273; Trask, pp. 7, 13-14, 93; Howard Sachar, *The Emergence of the Middle East*, p. 341.

[144] For the background of the Turkish massacres of Armenians during World War I, when at least 200,000 Armenians perished (estimates differ and range up to a million), see: DeNovo, pp. 98-101; Sachar, *The Emergence of the Middle*

65

partisan politics in the United States, all prevented the restoration of formal diplomatic relations until 1927. Following their resumption, however, relations between Turkey and the United States were established on a solid basis: the new nation's reliance on friendship and non-aggression pacts gradually met with American approval.[145]

As diplomatic relations improved, so did commercial relations—a development more important to Turkey than to the United States. The Turks placed great store in their favorable balance of trade with the United States, and sought American assistance in economic development and administration because they appreciated the apparent lack of America's political ambitions in the Middle East in general, and in Turkey in particular. Proof of such an interpretation was the fact that the United States had taken no part in the Montreux Convention. In short, before World War II, the State Department continued to see the protection of its nonpolitical interests as its sole task in Turkey.[146]

Between the wars, of course, the United States had acquired important interests in the Middle East, where strategic resources made the arbitrary distinction between political and nonpolitical interests a tenuous concept. Consequently, Britain's traditional sphere of influence in the region, while it continued to be recognized as such even during World War II for purposes of military strategy, was also the focus of American attempts to oppose both British and French imperialism. These attempts found voice in the principles of the Atlantic Charter

---

East, pp. 87-115; Shaw and Shaw, pp. 200-205, 314-317. For the role of the United States in dealing with the Armenian problem in the period after World War I, see DeNovo, pp. 109-127; and Sachar, *The Emergence of the Middle East*, pp. 336-365. For American policy toward Turkey in general, see Laurence Evans, *United States Policy and the Partition of Turkey, 1914-1924* (Baltimore, 1965). For the stereotyped image of the Turk held by Americans, an image which was not wholly eradicated by World War II, see: Sachar, p. 346; DeNovo, pp. 98-101, 234-236; Trask, pp. 82-83, 92, 244. Particularly illuminating is DeNovo's observation that "the disparaging attitude toward the Turks harbored by most Americans after World War I was the product of a generation of denigration by missionary forces sincerely trying to justify the importance of their efforts to minister to the downtrodden Christian minorities of the Ottoman Empire." DeNovo, p. 234.

[145] Trask, pp. 21, 37, 51. For Turco-American relations during World War I, see Howard, *Turkey, the Straits and U.S. Policy*, pp. 27-50, and Evans, pp. 21-85.

[146] American trade with Turkey was a fraction of one percent of total American trade, and between 10 and 15 percent of total Turkish trade; in addition, the balance of trade was generally in Turkey's favor. Thus, in 1938, U.S. imports from Turkey totaled $18,958,000 (the major import by far being Turkish leaf tobacco), while exports totaled only $13,218,000 (the major export being machinery and vehicles). DeNovo, pp. 232, 241, 264; Trask, pp. 105-107, 145-146.

which, it was assumed, would be sufficient to protect American interests, and which, as one writer notes, were not as altruistic as President Roosevelt imagined them to be.[147]

Turkey, perhaps because she was not subject to the economic rivalry between Britain and the United States so often apparent elsewhere in the Middle East, and because she was the only Middle Eastern country able to maintain more than a nominal independence during the war, was not a bone of contention between Britain and the United States. As one diplomatic historian has observed, she was "the only country in the region in which the United States and Great Britain did not suspect each other's motives."[148] Because of Turkey's adherence to the limited aims of the National Pact, and as a result of her skillful diplomacy, she was never occupied by a foreign army. Thus, she was less susceptible to the kinds of pressures exerted by occupation on the states which bordered her. Her sense of community, of nationhood, provided the moral fiber for her army and kept her from the internal divisions which, aggravated by occupation, were so disruptive in Iran, and even more divisive in Greece. As a consequence, it was possible for the United States to avoid active involvement in Turkish affairs, while continuing to view Turkey in the context of principles on which American policymakers intended to build the postwar world.

President Roosevelt himself knew little about the Near East. He was not especially interested in the area, preferring to concentrate on the cross-channel attack and on the maintenance of Allied unity. As Hitler envisioned the Eastern Mediterranean falling in Mussolini's sphere, so Roosevelt saw it in Churchill's—and continued to regard it as such throughout the war. Reluctant to use Churchill's pressure tactics, he nonetheless allowed the prime minister to control the flow of aid to the Turks and supported many of Britain's policies toward Turkey. If Turkey was vital to the defense of the United States, and lend-lease aid had been granted to the republic, the British dispensed it. Roosevelt endorsed the Moscow agreement between Eden and Molotov, and approved Churchill's desire to regard Turkey's breaking of diplomatic relations with Germany as the first step toward active belligerency. But he was never willing to go as far as Churchill or Stalin in exerting pressure on Turkey. This is not to say that he was more virtuous; rather,

[147] Gaddis Smith, *American Diplomacy During the Second World War, 1941-1945* (New York, 1965), pp. 99, 117; Kirk, *The Middle East in the War*, p. 25; *FR*, 1944, V:27-32.
[148] Smith, *American Diplomacy*, p. 115.

it indicates that Turkey in no way appeared to affect American interests, except in an indirect sense: concentration on Turkey and the Balkans might somehow impede the cross-channel attack; differences over issues in the Eastern Mediterranean might divide the Allies; poor treatment of Turkey would not advance the principles of the Atlantic Charter. In addition, as we shall see, Roosevelt had no intention of getting the United States involved in Eastern Europe let alone the Eastern Mediterranean and the Near East.

Conclusion

Thus, by September 1944, two issues concerning Turkey began to emerge more clearly: the role of the Straits in the postwar world, and the role of the Balkans and the Northern Tier in the power alignments that were taking shape. These issues, while latent in the early stages of the war, were always present. In the course of World War II, they gradually manifested themselves and eventually began to overtake the diminishing exigencies of war.

Throughout World War II, and especially after the Battle of Stalingrad, Turkey was subject to intense pressures. These pressures grew out of the historical rivalry between Britain and Russia in the Near East and the two countries' conflicting interpretations of their immediate and long-range national security interests in the Eastern Mediterranean. Acting on her traditional strategy of inhibiting the most dangerous power by invoking the assistance of the others, and constantly harboring her traditional suspicions of Russia, Turkey necessarily reacted to menacing Soviet pressures by seeking the aid of Britain. Britain's interests in the Near East pitted her against Russia as the historical countervailing force in the region, where her interests were vulnerable, and hence where her assistance could be solicited.

While relying on Britain, the Turks carefully considered every possible means for protecting their vital interests. Turkish neutrality, however, maintained right up to February 1945, is not always understood. It is usual, for example, for some critics to indulge in moral condemnation of some of Turkey's wartime policies. But if one assesses Turkish problems from the point of view of Turkish national interests, one can readily see that such condemnation is unwarranted. Britain and France, after all, handed Czechoslovakia over to Hitler. Russia and Germany contemplated a division of interests in the Near East at Turkey's expense. Both Britain and Russia contemplated pushing Turkey into the war, thereby forcing Germany to redeploy her armies, and so weaken her resistance to attacks directed from East and West. If one remembers these things, it is less easy to take a position on what principles other than self-interest Turkey should have followed.

The difficulty of judging Turkey's role in World War II is particularly true if one recalls that Turkish fear of the Soviet Union, always present, and dominating all other concerns after Stalingrad, was the result of more than traditional suspicions. It was a response to repeated attempts by the Soviet Union to seek advantages at Turkey's expense.[149] It is worth recapitulating, briefly, the evidence of Soviet designs on and ill will toward Turkey:

In September and October 1939 the Soviets attempted to wean the Turks from their alliances with the British and the French, and specifically demanded control over the Straits.

In the summer of 1940 the Soviets' menacing attitude was one of the main reasons the Turks did not honor their alliance with the British.

In November 1940 Molotov, negotiating with the Germans, sought control over the Straits, and was prepared to guarantee Bulgaria an outlet on the Aegean.

After the Battle of Stalingrad in 1943, the Soviets sharply criticized Turkey's supposed pro-Axis orientation. This largely unjustified line of criticism, which ignored previous denunciations of the Anglo-Turco-French Alliance as one between "warmongers," and which contradicted the Soviet government's acknowledgment that Turkey's position during the 1942 German offensive had been useful, grew even more vehement after the Adana Conference in January 1943.

In 1943 Russia sought to coerce Turkey into entering the war, ostensibly to draw 15 German divisions away from the Russian front, and to enable the Red Army to advance with greater rapidity into Germany. Another reason may well have been to create a situation which would have given the Russians an opportunity to occupy Turkey.

Late in 1943 Russia's reversal on the desirability of bringing Turkey into the war against the Axis, her failure to send an official representative to the Cairo Conference, and the advice offered Sarper by Vinogradov at the conference all pointed to two possibilities: (a) the Soviet

[149] For a necessarily selective justification of Soviet actions, see: Ivan Maisky, *Who Helped Hitler?* (London, 1964), pp. 178-202; Ivan Maisky, *Memoirs of a Soviet Ambassador: The War, 1939-1943* (New York, 1967), esp. p. 272.

Union desired to create a situation that would have continued to make the occupation of Turkey possible; or (b) she sought to legitimize Russian interests and claims over those of Turkey at the Straits.

In 1944 Russia, in pursuing the policies outlined above, continued to rebuff attempts by Turkey either to renew existing treaties or to negotiate a new one.

In the summer of 1944 the Soviets refused to accede to a request from their Western Allies that Turkey be asked to do anything less than enter the war (i.e., that she break diplomatic and economic relations with Germany as a first step toward active belligerency). At the expense of her Allies' common interests, the Soviet Union rigidly insisted on Turkish participation in the war, and dissociated itself from British and American representations to Turkey. As in 1943, Russian actions again indicated a desire either to create a situation that would have made the occupation of Turkey possible, or to legitimize Russian claims and interests over those of Turkey at the Straits.

In the fall of 1944 events not only in Bulgaria, but elsewhere in Eastern Europe and the Near East (i.e., Iran), gave the Turks even stronger reasons to doubt the benevolence of Soviet intentions toward Turkey.

In short, the Soviets—for a complex of reasons which were at once defensive and aggressive—appear to have contemplated expanding their sphere of influence in the Near East even before World War II began. After the Battle of Stalingrad, when conditions were more favorable to their interests, evidence seems to confirm that the Soviets hoped to effect such expansion.

The British had misgivings about Soviet intentions in the Near East, and eventually began to contemplate containment of Russia's southern flank. Churchill and his Foreign Office, while focusing on the Balkans primarily as a means of drawing German forces away from the channel prior to the cross-channel attack, also had in mind their own interests in the Near East and the safeguarding of Britain's imperial lifeline in the Eastern Mediterranean. As the war progressed, the latter concerns best explain British policies in Greece and Iran. They also, of course, explain Churchill's policies in Turkey—a country that was both necessary to, and expendable in, Britain's scheme of empire. Turkish territory had always constituted the strategic linchpin in Britain's historic policy of containing Russian influence. But certain Turkish rights, especially at the Straits, had occasionally been negotiable (as in both World Wars) when Britain was confronted with a choice of satisfying Russian needs either at the Straits or in the Persian Gulf. Thus, when developments in Eastern Europe and the Near East led the Foreign Office to consider anew the primacy of Britain's imperial lifeline, British officials looked to Greece (at the cost of cutting off the rest of the Balkans) and Turkey as the best means of containing Russian access to and influence in the Mediterranean. While Churchill was willing to make certain concessions to the Soviets on the Straits, Eden and the Foreign Office caused him to hedge if not suppress his discussions with Stalin over Turkey.

Historical rivalries were clearly in Churchill's and Stalin's thoughts, and operative in their diplomacy. Stalin had personally negotiated the Soviet Union's borders with Turkey in 1921. Perhaps because he came from Georgia, he took great interest in that part of the world[150] and was always well briefed about Turkish matters. Churchill, like Stalin, had a long history of involvement in the area, was aware of Turkish fears, and had no compunction about playing upon the Turks' concerns. In Turkey, both men sought to effect their own interests. Their war aims might have obscured the coincidence between common and self-interest; but eventually, as Hitler was pushed back and common interests required a more precise definition, parochial interests came to the fore.

If the Soviets were drawn to Turkey and the Straits because of what Turkey represented from a strategic point of view, the British were no less susceptible to the same arguments. If the Straits were the key to British penetration of the Black Sea, they were also the key to Soviet penetration of the Mediterranean. And the Mediterranean, as one scholar has pointed out, was the geographic center of British strategy relative to the British Commonwealth and Empire.[151] The Mediterranean's centrality, moreover, was due not only to its strategic value, but to the simple fact that the British were there.[152] The Soviets were not, and the British desired to keep things as they were. This was the essential policy objective behind Eden's Foreign Office memorandum of June 1944.

For the time being, although widening differences between the Allies over Turkey were apparent, the conflict between Russia and Britain

[150] Robert Conquest, *Power and Policy in the U.S.S.R.* (New York, 1967), p. 135; see also Chapter IV, n. 124.

[151] Maxwell Schoenfeld, *The War Ministry of Winston Churchill* (Ames, Iowa, 1972), pp. 129-130. Almost everyone, including the Soviet ambassador, saw Churchill's heart and mind in the Eastern Mediterranean. See Maisky, *Memoirs*, p. 275.

[152] A.J.P. Taylor, *English History, 1914-1945* (Oxford, 1965), p. 522.

over their strategic interests had not yet been joined. As in the past, the source of developing conflict was a question of power. Russia's might was on the rise as she rolled west, a fact of which Stalin was well aware. Britain's was on the wane, and she was struggling to maintain her former position. The United States, not fully awakened either to its interests, or to the role it would play in maintaining the balance of power in the Near East, relied on principle as a means of safeguarding its interests in that area, and watched as the situation developed.

II

The Greek Context

ANALYSIS of Turkey's fortunes in World War II suggests the importance of the rivalry between British seapower and Russian landpower in the Balkans. This rivalry, which can be traced back to the time of Catherine the Great, was quiescent during the German occupation of the Balkans but emerged once Germany's defeat was in the offing, and prefigured the power alignments gradually taking shape in the Balkans.

While British thoughts were directed toward mitigating the consequences of a Second Front, they were also directed toward the protection of Britain's imperial lifeline. This became apparent by 1944 when, on the day after the invasion of Normandy, Eden submitted to the War Cabinet a policy which recommended consolidating Britain's position in Turkey and Greece as a fundamental factor in the Balkans. Russia, of course, wanted bases on the Straits, and had been prepared as late as November 1940 to guarantee Bulgaria an outlet on the Aegean. While Stalin's long-range goals are uncertain, it is clear that by 1944 he desired political control over the Balkans.

Churchill recognized the British Empire's weak position and in 1944 initiated negotiations with Stalin over the Balkans, hoping to salvage Britain's position in the Eastern Mediterranean. Examination of Britain's efforts to secure the establishment of a stable, pro-British government in Athens after the German occupation reveals the undiminished importance to Britain of her imperial lifeline, and emphasizes the role of Greece in British strategic thinking. British perceptions, in turn, provide a convenient baseline for an analysis of developing American attitudes toward Greece—both in the State Department and in the White House. Together, Anglo-American policies help clarify the terms of the October Agreement on the Balkans between Churchill and Stalin, and enable us to assess its significance.

The Historical Background

The modern Greek state was established in the first half of the nineteenth century when, with the help of Great Britain, France, and Rus-

73

sia, the Greeks broke away from four centuries of Ottoman domination. Infused—however inappropriately—with a romantic philhellenism, they struggled to reconstitute themselves as a nation. Once they achieved nationhood, their new identity, together with the idea of an *imperium* (derived from their Byzantine past), enabled them to see themselves not only as a new state, but also as successors to the Byzantine Empire, and crusaders for the redemption of Greeks still living in the Ottoman Empire.[1]

A national obsession with unredeemed Greeks obscured serious domestic shortcomings: a divided administration; a corrupt parliament; a primitive, poorly financed and poorly prepared army. When attention was not focused on the "Great Idea" of an *imperium,* or on the danger of an external threat, these shortcomings surfaced, impinging on the political situation, and revealing the most serious domestic problem of all: the lack in Greece of a range of moral obligations one might expect a citizen to feel toward his state.[2]

An explanation of this phenomenon can be found in the history of Greece's small mountain communities under Ottoman administration —communities where Greek brigands, or *klephts,* hardened by guerilla warfare, were a law unto themselves. Prior to the War of Independence, and long after, moral obligations to a restricted circle limited the extension of loyalties to a larger community (or nation) unless the latter could be represented as an enlargement of the family, or a projection of its values. As a consequence, traditional values made it difficult for either the king, who was not of Greek origin, or the new government to secure the allegiance of the people. Although the government attempted to run the country through corporate parties and centralized bureaucracies, its failure to secure the loyalties of its constituents was a continuing weakness. Incorporating through patronage the narrow interests of divisive particularistic elements, government in general was subject to hostile divisions which were only accentuated by rivalries among the Great Powers. These rivalries, evident throughout the nineteenth century, were reflected in the orientation of Greek political parties toward

---

[1] John Campbell and Philip Sherrard, *Modern Greece* (New York, 1968), pp. 11-49, 102; Frank Smothers, William McNeill, Elizabeth McNeill, *Report on the Greeks* (New York, 1948), pp. 10-11; L. S. Stavrianos, *Greece: American Dilemma and Opportunity* (Chicago, 1952), pp. 21-22; William McNeill, *The Greek Dilemma: War and Aftermath* (Philadelphia, 1947), p. 13.

[2] Stavrianos, *Greece,* p. 23; Campbell and Sherrard, pp. 43-49, 89.

one or another of the Great Powers—a development which continued into the twentieth century.[3]

Eventually, the orientation of Greek political parties along Great Power lines resulted in what became known as the "National Schism." The schism grew out of differing opinions as to which side Greece should join in World War I, and was epitomized by the split between Prime Minister Elevtherios Venizelos and King Constantine I. Venizelos advocated joining the Entente and—upon learning of the Ottoman Empire's projected division—intervening in Asia Minor to prevent Italy from gaining control of unredeemed Greeks. Constantine, who was married to the kaiser's sister, expected his brother-in-law to prevail, and so was receptive to the chief of his General Staff, Colonel Ioannis Metaxas, who advised against joining the Entente and urged him to resist the temptation offered by territory in Asia Minor.[4]

The split between the monarch and his prime minister culminated in a struggle for power whereby Venizelos sanctioned a British and French landing in Salonika, and established a rival "provisional government." The Allies then drove the king into exile in 1917—a fact which was humiliating not only to Constantine's supporters still in the civil and armed services, but to many peasants who saw the king as the hero of the Balkan Wars. It was in the Balkan Wars that Greece, led in battle by the king, and guided by Venizelos, had acquired Crete, southern Epirus, Salonika, and the provinces of Macedonia—at the expense first of the Ottoman Empire, and then of Bulgaria.[5]

Joining the Entente in 1917, Greece sent armies to the Macedonian front in 1918, and gained a prominent seat at the peace table in 1919. As a result, the Treaty of Sèvres in 1920 gave the Greeks eastern Thrace, two Dodecanese islands, and the right to administer the province of Smyrna in Anatolia—which Greek forces began to occupy before the conclusion of the treaty.[6]

The consequences of occupation were noted in Chapter I. Greek in-

[3] Campbell and Sherrard, pp. 57-58, 116-117; C. M. Woodhouse, *Apple of Discord* (London, 1948), pp. 10-12; Smothers et al., p. 13; Theodore Couloumbis, *Greek Political Reaction to American and NATO Influences* (New Haven, 1967), p. 11.

[4] Campbell and Sherrard, pp. 122-123; Stavrianos, *The Balkans*, pp. 566-568, 584, 586; Couloumbis, pp. 11-13.

[5] Bulgaria's consequent irredentism became an important source of friction with Greece. Campbell and Sherrard, pp. 114-122; Stavrianos, *The Balkans*, pp. 567-568.

[6] Campbell and Sherrard, pp. 122-123; Stavrianos, *The Balkans*, pp. 567-568.

vaders pushed the Turks back to the Sakarya River, where the Turks counterattacked, driving them out of Anatolia. Prior to the Turkish victory, however, Venizelos had fallen from power. His countrymen were disappointed over failure to acquire Constantinople and angered by the treatment of Constantine; many were disturbed by his sanction of Allied intervention, or unhappy with the effects of massive mobilization. Middle-class opponents whom Venizelos had ousted from their positions in 1910 added fuel to the fire. When King Alexander (Constantine's son) died of poisoning from the bite of a pet monkey, chance set the stage for an electoral choice between Constantine and Venizelos—and Venizelos lost.[7]

The National Schism

What followed may be briefly told. A plebiscite returned Constantine to the throne; but he, too, was now seduced by the idea of a Greater Greece. Under his command, Greek troops suffered their catastrophic loss to the Turks, and in 1922 the king again went into exile, never to return. The "National Schism" thus developed, and the constitutional question it created came to be the chief political issue between royalists (or Populists) and republicans (or Liberals). According to one author, the issue was so important that it became "almost the sole determining factor in internal affairs." As a consequence, Western political categories were applied to problems that were organic rather than political, and Greek politicians, fixated on the constitutional question, gave little attention to badly needed social problems.[8]

Despite enormous disappointments, Greece did derive certain benefits from the debacle in Turkey. A compulsory exchange of populations after the war removed (except for Turks in western Thrace and Greeks in Constantinople) a source of potential discontent; irredentist activities subsided and the divisive history of Hellenism in Asia Minor ended. In addition, the Greeks benefited from refugee settlements in the disputed area of Macedonia. But the schism was so deeply rooted in Greek political life that it persisted, keeping alive debate over responsibility for defeat and for destruction of the "Great Idea." In the process, the

---

[7] Stavrianos, *The Balkans*, pp. 586-587; Campbell and Sherrard, pp. 116-124; McNeill, *The Greek Dilemma*, p. 18.

[8] Campbell and Sherrard, pp. 120-128; Woodhouse, pp. 12-14; Kenneth Matthews, *Memories of a Mountain War: Greece, 1944-1949* (London, 1972), p. 271.

schism became social as well, preventing friendships and marriages across political lines.[9]

Briefly, there was interest in reform during the early 1920s, and it led to formation of a republic under Venizelos in 1924, but without the unifying element of the Great Idea, and as a consequence of the national schism, the petty nature of Greek politics reasserted itself. Problems associated with the settlement of refugees were compounded by the difficulties of the depression. Recriminations revolved around issues which preceded the losses to Kemal; and chronic instability—not aided by several military coups—eventually precipitated a plebiscite which recalled Constantine's second son, King George II, in 1935. In spite of an obvious manipulation of the results (97 percent of the voters were alleged to have voted for the king), the plebiscite reflected a disillusioned population's hope for political stability.[10]

Sensitive to this hope, the king returned to Greece, granted a general amnesty to those involved in the revolt of 1935, and forced the ultra-royalist premier to resign. He then appointed a nonpolitical prime minister, Alexander Demertzis, who in turn held a general election

[9] Prior to 1912, Greece was homogeneous with the exception of 6,000 Muslims living in Thessaly. The Balkan Wars increased Greek territory by 68 percent and the population by 67 percent. After the Balkan Wars, minorities represented 13 percent of the population (370,000 Turks, 104,000 Bulgars). After World War I, and the exchange of minorities with Bulgaria and Turkey, the Greek element in Macedonia (which prior to the war was only 42 percent of the population) was raised to 88.8 percent of the population. The percentage of Greeks in western Thrace was likewise raised from 17 percent to 62.1 percent. By the mid-twenties, the Slav minority in Greece stood only at 80,000, serving as an effective barrier to serious territorial claims on the part of Yugoslavia and an irredentist Bulgaria. A negative effect of the refugee problem was that it furthered the schism between republican and monarchist. The republic, founded in 1924, had little emotional appeal to those born in Old Greece (Greece before the Balkan Wars); the monarchy, on the other hand, had little appeal for the Greeks occupying the new territories in the north, and even less for the refugees from Anatolia (who believed Constantine to be responsible for their exile). These refugees, who represented a good number of the 1,300,000 Greeks now added to the previous population of 4,500,000, were without traditional attachments, and saw themselves as excluded from the privileged society which supported the monarchy. From this development can be traced some of the social cleavages which gradually came to replace personal rivalries in Greek politics. Campbell and Sherrard, pp. 138-154; Stavrianos, *The Balkans*, pp. 540, 661-670; McNeill, *The Greek Dilemma*, p. 24; Jelavich and Jelavich, *The Balkans*, p. 82; Smothers et al., pp. 16-17.

[10] Ibid. Coups by republican factions took place in 1925, 1926, 1933, and 1935 (in which Venizelos admitted complicity, and for which he was condemned to death *in absentia*).

77

noteworthy for its fairness. The outcome was a more realistic indication of the divisions in Greek politics than the plebiscite, and revealed the split between royalists (with 143 seats in parliament) and republicans (with 141 seats). To make matters even more complicated, the Communist Party (with 15 seats) held the balance of power.[11]

In spite of disagreements on reform, the essential difference between the two main parties in the 1930s was that they represented two exclusive systems of patronage. They both opposed the Communist Party, whose small following could be explained by the nature of Greek loyalties, and by the fact that Comintern resolutions (calling for an independent Macedonian state) continually alienated those groups most likely to support them, whether victims of the depression, refugees dissatisfied with their marginal status, or those opposed to Venizelos's treaty with Turkey in 1930. Comintern policy in the Balkans allowed Bulgarians and Yugoslavs to be both Communists and nationalists, but forced Greeks to choose between the two.[12]

The dichotomy between Communist and nationalist in Greece during the thirties accounts for subsequent events. When the two traditional parties began to negotiate with the Communists, alarm spread among military leaders,[13] who informed the king of their unwillingness to tolerate a coalition with the Communists. As a consequence, the king appointed General Metaxas as his minister of war—an appointment which was warmly approved not only by the military, but by the exiled Venizelos and his Liberal successor, Themistoclis Sofoulis, who believed Metaxas could guarantee control over the military. But political problems continued. Lack of agreement among the factions within parliament led to a compromise "nonparliamentary" government under Demertzis. When Demertzis died within a month, the king appointed Metaxas to succeed him. A parliamentary vote of confidence temporarily legitimized the appointment by a vote of 241-16, and delegated

11 Stavrianos, *The Balkans*, p. 670; Campbell and Sherrard, p. 157; McNeill, *The Greek Dilemma*, p. 30.

12 Woodhouse, *Apple of Discord*, p. 14; Jelavich and Jelavich, *The Balkans*, p. 115; Campbell and Sherrard, pp. 157-159; Stavrianos, *The Balkans*, pp. 670-671; Stavrianos, *Greece*, p. 28; McNeill, *The Greek Dilemma*, p. 33.

13 While republican officers gained power in the armed forces after Greece's defeat by the Turks in 1922 (accounting for subsequent republican coups), royalist control of the government in 1935 led to a purge of the republican officers. As Stavrianos points out, "Thereafter the court and the armed forces were on the same ground and no more was heard of military coups" (Stavrianos, *The Balkans*, p. 662).

to Metaxas the authority to govern by decree. Antagonism between Metaxas and the Communists, however, soon led to a popular, Communist-promoted campaign of industrial unrest, whereupon King George, now deeply worried about the country's international security, granted dictatorial powers to Metaxas. The latter promptly declared a state of emergency, dissolved parliament without provision for a new election, suspended certain provisions of the constitution, and inaugurated what became known as the "Fourth of August Regime."[14]

The Fourth of August Regime

It is difficult to appraise the Metaxas dictatorship, which lasted from 4 August 1936 until his death on 9 January 1941. That he was well intentioned is generally conceded even by his enemies. That his methods were ruthless and repressive is without question. More problematic are the results of his policies.[15]

Recognizing the problem of imposing a modern political system on a society unprepared for it, Metaxas suspended the parliamentary system, hoping to end the political rift of which he had been a part. He also suppressed political parties, believing he could refocus local loyalties and modernize Greek society.[16] Since the king controlled the army, and the army was the source of political power, the monarch's support enabled Metaxas to conduct a repressive campaign against his opponents. His minister of the interior had authority to imprison or exile individuals on the grounds of suspicion, as well as to censor the press and control education, and he used this power freely.[17]

Metaxas' dictatorship should not, however, be equated with the German and Italian dictatorships. Single parties, racial nationalism, personal ambition, and aggressive wars had no place in his regime, which he regarded as an emergency, temporary replacement for constitutional government. His own ambitions, much less grandiose than those of Mussolini and Hitler, were to solve his country's domestic problems. He called for a moratorium on farmers' debts, guaranteed prices for

[14] Campbell and Sherrard, pp. 158-160; Stavrianos, *The Balkans*, pp. 670-672.

[15] Stavrianos, *The Balkans*, pp. 672-676; René Ristelhueber, *A History of the Balkan Peoples* (New York, 1971), p. 298; Woodhouse, *Apple of Discord*, p. 15; Stavrianos, *Greece*, pp. 32-40; Campbell and Sherrard, pp. 161-164; McNeill, *The Greek Dilemma*, pp. 33-35.

[16] Campbell and Sherrard, pp. 161-164.

[17] John Iatrides, *Revolt in Athens: The Greek Communist "Second Round,"* 1944-1945 (Princeton, 1972), p. 13; Stavrianos, *The Balkans*, pp. 672-676.

79

wheat, improved the efficiency of military mobilization, instituted compulsory arbitration in labor disputes, established a minimum wage, legislated public health projects, combated corruption in the public service, organized a National Youth Organization whose loyalties were to the state, and undertook a vast public works program.[18]

Some critics charge that legislation under the regime lacked the necessary funds and was ignored, or that it increased the public debt and caused inflation. Others assert that Metaxas's practical achievements were significant: the public works program, for example, provided much-needed employment, improved communications, and strengthened the country's defenses. In addition, the country's mobilization procedures were made more efficient—a fact of some importance in 1940.[19]

Critics agree that the regime was unpopular, but disagree as to why. Thus, a *New York Times* reporter who lived in Greece under Metaxas asserts that as many as 80 percent of the Greek people were hostile to the regime. Where one historian believes this hostility resulted from the extent and severity of repression under the regime, another argues that any Greek government is alienated from the people it governs until it has provided them with special favors or material benefits, and that it was the philosophy underlying this idea of patronage that Metaxas was trying to eliminate. Both interpretations shed light on the problem. In the final analysis, it is apparent that Metaxas failed to attain his aims.[20] Were one to grant him the purest of motives, one would still confront the fact that during his dictatorship the central issues he attempted to surmount remained unchanged.[21]

It is unfortunate for Metaxas, and for Greece, that during this time international issues changed so rapidly. Greece's problems with Italy over Corfu and Albania had begun almost immediately after her disaster in Anatolia. Other perennial problems were friction with Yugoslavia

[18] Stavrianos, *The Balkans*, p. 675; Woodhouse, *Apple of Discord*, pp. 15-16; McNeill, *The Greek Dilemma*, pp. 33-34; Iatrides, p. 14; Kenneth Young, *The Greek Passion* (London, 1969), p. 218.

[19] Stavrianos, *The Balkans*, p. 675; Campbell and Sherrard, pp. 162-163; Iatrides, pp. 14-15; McNeill, *The Greek Dilemma*, pp. 33-34.

[20] Whether Metaxas could have played in Greece the role that Atatürk played in Turkey, or that Charles de Gaulle later played in France, is a fruitless but interesting line of speculation.

[21] McNeill, *The Greek Dilemma*, p. 35; Stavrianos, *Greece*, p. 39; Campbell and Sherrard, p. 163; Iatrides, pp. 14-15; Woodhouse, *Apple of Discord*, pp. 14-17; Jane Carey and Andrew Carey, *The Web of Greek Politics* (New York, 1968), p. 123.

and Bulgaria over the status of the Slavophone minority in Macedonia. Fortunately for Greece, these problems were not compounded by friction with Turkey. After the exchange of populations, longstanding ambitions subsided, and made possible the negotiation of a treaty between the two countries in 1930. Venizelos was fêted in Ankara, and the first of four Balkan Conferences was convened in an attempt at cooperation among the Balkan states. But if Greece's irredentist ambitions were subsiding, the same could not be said of Bulgaria's. For this reason, the Balkan Conferences may be seen primarily as an effort by the "satisfied" Balkan states (Greece, Yugoslavia, Rumania) and Turkey to oppose irredentist Bulgaria. Italy's efforts to exploit Bulgaria's dissatisfaction— symbolized by the marriage of King Boris of Bulgaria to Princess Giovanna of Italy—added fuel to the fire. Thus the Balkan Entente (1934) between Greece, Rumania, Yugoslavia, and Turkey, officially described as a collective guarantee of existing frontiers, was essentially a defensive alliance against Bulgaria.[22]

The effectiveness of the entente, however, was limited by the desires of Turkey and Greece to avoid entanglement in the ambitions of Russia and Italy. Thus, when Metaxas came to power, he displayed little interest in the pact. But as time passed, he recognized that the Allies' indirect imperialism was preferable to Axis aggrandizement. In addition, Britain controlled the Eastern Mediterranean, and the Greeks recognized the necessity of their sea communications.[23]

When Italy occupied Albania in 1939, Metaxas accepted guarantees of Greek territory by France and Great Britain. After war broke out, he approved of the October 1939 Tripartite Treaty between Turkey, France, and Britain. Greece's neutrality, like that of Turkey, while qualified by commercial dependence on the German market, carefully concealed an ultimate political alignment with the Western Allies. With the fall of France, and as the situation in Greece deteriorated, this alignment became more apparent. Mussolini, meanwhile, humiliated by Hitler's occupation of Rumania, and anxious to acquire more bases in the Mediterranean, looked toward Greece to win the prestige he had failed to find in the closing days of the First Battle of France. As a consequence, he began a calculated policy of antagonism toward

[22] Campbell and Sherrard, pp. 166-167; Kinross, pp. 521-522; Stavrianos, *The Balkans*, pp. 736-740; McNeill, *The Greek Dilemma*, pp. 19-20.

[23] Stavrianos, *The Balkans*, pp. 740-742, 786; Campbell and Sherrard, pp. 167-168.

81

Greece. Disregarding Hitler's wishes, Mussolini on 28 October sent an ultimatum to Metaxas demanding a number of unspecified strategic points in Greek territory.[24]

Without hesitating, Metaxas gave the Italian emissary his response: War. To the Greek people he delivered his summons: "Greeks! Let us clench our fists and elevate our souls." Their sense of national identity temporarily coalesced by the attack, the Greek people determined to resist the Italians with all their strength.[25]

The Italian Attack, the Greek Counterattack, and the German Invasion

When the Italians attacked, full-scale mobilization—delayed by Metaxas in order not to provoke Italy—was effected within two weeks. By 14 November, the Greek Army was able to take the offensive, and by December had driven the Italians back into Albania.[26] The emotional impact of these victories was immense. The Greeks felt they had

[24] Campbell and Sherrard, pp. 169-170; Stavrianos, *The Balkans*, pp. 750-751; Elizabeth Wiskemann, "The Subjugation of South-Eastern Europe, June 1940 to June 1941," in *Initial Triumph of the Axis*, eds. Arnold Toynbee and Veronica Toynbee (London, 1958), pp. 337-340. Stephen Xydis, *Greece and the Great Powers, 1944-1947: Prelude to the Truman Doctrine* (Thessaloniki, 1963), pp. 9-10, notes that a conversation in June between Molotov and the Italians, in which the Soviet foreign minister proposed Italian acceptance of Soviet hegemony in the Black Sea in return for Soviet recognition of Italy's hegemony in the Mediterranean, may have served as a green light for the attack on Greece. See also Sontag and Beddie, p. 161. A key to Russian thinking in 1940 is to be found in a memorandum that Molotov, on instructions from Stalin, gave to the German ambassador Schulenburg. In early July, when the British ambassador suggested to Stalin that both Britain and the Soviet Union ought to agree on a common policy of self-protection against Germany and the reestablishment of the European balance of power, Stalin's answer, according to the memorandum, was that "the so-called European balance of power had hitherto oppressed not only Germany, but also the Soviet Union. Therefore, the Soviet Union would take all measures to prevent the re-establishment of the old balance of power in Europe" (Sontag and Beddie, p. 167). For the British version of this conversation, see Woodward, I:470. Presumably, it was this thinking that was behind the proposal in Italy—a proposal which, in its desire to effect a balance of power in the Eastern Mediterranean and Black Sea, is not unlike that proposed by Britain in 1944.

[25] Wiskemann, pp. 336-340; Ristelhueber, p. 340.

[26] During the Greek Army's thrust into Albania, the party secretary of the Greek Communist Party (KKE) called the action part of an "imperialist war," and requested Soviet mediation (Xydis, *Greece and the Great Powers*, p. 10). His order to desert and to sabotage the war effort was obeyed only by a handful of "professional" Communists, and so did not impinge on the KKE's later, patriotic reputation. McNeill, *The Greek Dilemma*, pp. 67-68.

82

removed the stain of their debacle in Asia Minor—a sentiment which may have made it psychologically easier to establish better relations with Turkey toward the end of the war. Metaxas became a symbol of national honor. With Europe prostrate, and Britain fighting alone against Hitler, opponents of the Axis took heart at the first drubbing of Axis forces. A more tangible consequence was the fact that Greek resistance· upset the timetable for Hitler's attack on Russia.[27]

Anticipating Italy's humiliation, Hitler had foreseen the necessity of intervention in the Balkans. On 12 November, shortly before a conference with Molotov, who was then in Berlin, Hitler signed a directive to that effect. The fact that this directive included plans for an attack on the Soviet Union probably accounts for his and von Ribbentrop's subsequent irritation at Molotov's questions concerning the Balkans, at Soviet proposals regarding guarantees to Bulgaria, and still later at proposals made by the Soviets with regard to the Near East and the Balkans.[28]

If German designs in the Balkans were gradually taking shape, so were the energies of the.Greek government, now aided by Great Britain. By the end of March 1941, more than 30,000 troops (mostly Commonwealth) had arrived in Greece. The British doubted that operations in Greece would be successful. They knew they were running grave risks by sending inadequate forces to face the Axis. But the new Greek prime minister, Alexander Koryzis, successor to Metaxas, who had died during the Italian War,[29] had requested aid, and the British felt that moral and political reasons justified the venture. Germany's attack on Greece on 6 April 1941 confirmed their doubts. By the end of the month, most of the 74,000 Commonwealth troops sent to Greece had had to withdraw, and the Germans had entered Athens. By the end of May, Crete, too, was in Axis hands.[30] The Germans oc-

[27] Stavrianos, *Greece*, pp. 49, 62-63; McNeill, *The Greek Dilemma*, p. 41; Campbell and Sherrard, pp. 170-173; Woodhouse, *Apple of Discord*, p. 9; Iatrides, p. 16; Wiskemann, pp. 340-341; Edgar O'Ballance, *The Greek Civil War, 1944-1949* (New York, 1966), pp. 45-46; Young, pp. 218-219.

[28] Wiskemann, p. 331; Sontag and Beddie, pp. 245-246, 252-253, 257-258; Schmidt, *Hitler's Interpreter*, p. 224. See further discussion of this issue in Chapters I and III.

[29] Metaxas died on 29 January 1941, after a short illness.

[30] The position of Greece's Ionian Islands (which guard the Adriatic), her Aegean Islands (which guard the Turkish Straits), and Crete (which is vital to any Eastern Mediterranean strategy—particularly with regard to the Suez Canal), endowed them with great strategic value (Stavrianos, *Greece*, pp. 92-93). In this

cupied Athens and Piraeus, Salonika, and a few islands, limiting their control to large towns and main lines of communication. Eastern Macedonia and Thrace they left to the Bulgarians (who attacked Greece in late April), and the remainder of the country they left to the Italians.[31]

The Occupation of Greece

The occupation of Greece, from April 1941 until its liberation in October 1944, created intense hardship for its citizens. Enduring famine, deprivation, and terror, they emerged from the experience a divided nation, whose problems were only compounded by ideological categories and international politics. Statistically, the war accounted for nearly 550,000 dead. Seventy thousand Greeks were executed by the Germans; 1,700 villages and one-fourth of all buildings were destroyed; two-thirds of the merchant marine was lost; communications and transportation were broken down. One-third of the forest area was burned; wheat production was half of prewar levels; cultivated acreage was cut by one-fourth. Industry was brought to a standstill and inflation was astronomical: by November 1944, currency circulation since the war had multiplied by a factor of over 800 million.[32]

These objective indices, however, do not fully account for the political consequences of occupation. To grasp what happened in Greece one must examine the effect of occupation on the dynamics of historical forces. In the past, political divisions had generated what

particular case, however, Crete played a different role. Its defense—even if unsuccessful—because it left Germany without any organized paratroop forces, perhaps saved Malta. Malta, in turn, was the key to the Mediterranean, control of which would determine control of North Africa. Schoenfeld, pp. 112-113, 116-117.

[31] O'Ballance, pp. 38-47; Woodward, 3:394; Wiskemann, pp. 361-363; Woodward, BFP, pp. 131-136. After the occupation of Greece, the Soviets on 3 June 1941 requested the accredited Greek diplomatic representative to leave Soviet territory. Diplomatic relations were reestablished shortly after the German attack on the Soviet Union. Xydis, Greece and the Great Powers, p. 10.

[32] Dominique Eudes, The Kapetanios: Partisans and Civil War in Greece, 1943-1949 (New York, 1972); Xydis, Greece and the Great Powers, p. 60; Iatrides, pp. 19, 133. See also FR, The Conferences at Malta and Yalta, p. 249. For some vivid pictures, which capture the consequences of famine and partisanship in Greece, see André Kedros, La Résistance Grecque, 1940-1944 (Paris, 1966). For an analysis of currency circulation in Greece, see Dimitrios Delivanis and William Cleveland, Greek Monetary Developments, 1939-1948: A Case Study of the Consequences of World War II for the Monetary System of a Small Nation (Bloomington, Ind., n.d.).

was known as the constitutional question, which hinged as much on patronage as on principle. Submerged during the Metaxas regime, this question surfaced shortly after his death, and throughout the occupation sharply affected debate over the shape of Greece's postwar government. As the occupation continued, social and ideological influences gradually compounded the question. These influences, in turn, grew stronger as a result of a number of interrelated factors: (1) the increased respect won by the Communist Party for its role in the resistance, (2) the Communist Party's emerging base of support—which included many of the lower strata of Greek society not previously recognized by the more elitist political parties, and (3) reaction to what the Communist Party represented.

The Greek Communist Party (KKE) which, for reasons already discussed, could never have found a broad base of support on the basis of ideology, had organized a much more acceptable popular front whose dominant political sentiment was anti-monarchist. But if opposition to the monarch—who was portrayed as a fascist dictator and a coward—was the dominant sentiment among Greeks in general, and among members of the popular front in particular, the Communist Party which organized that front was also the focus of intense hatred. The consequence of such passions was a curious set of loose political alliances. While the majority of Greeks withheld support both from the popular front and from the monarch, they were unwilling to restrain their hatred either for the KKE or for the monarchy. Thus it was not common purpose, but common hatreds, that allied Greek with Greek. The KKE and the monarchy polarized negative passions— passions which were directed against the two extremes on the political spectrum for fear of what their existence portended.[33]

To say that the process we have just described resulted from the occupation overlooks important developments which contributed to the complexity of the situation in Greece after liberation and which it may be useful briefly to examine: the evolution of the resistance effort during the occupation; the history of the Greek government-in-exile; British efforts to influence both the government-in-exile and the shape of the Greek government which was expected to assume power

[33] Iatrides, pp. 20-22, 288; William H. McNeill, "Greece, 1944-1946," in *The Realignment of Europe*, pp. 389-392, ed. Arnold Toynbee and Veronica Toynbee (London, 1955); McNeill, *The Greek Dilemma*, p. 94; Stavrianos, *The Balkans*, p. 676.

85

in liberated Greece; and finally, American attitudes toward Greece and the Balkans.

The Resistance

During occupation, Greek resistance arose less as a general response to the Axis invasion than as a traditional response to a hostile administration. Already somewhat alienated from their own government, the Greeks were estranged from the forces of occupation, which they detested. In giving vent to hatred, they were also drawn by strong associations between the country's fierce, locally based guerilla bands and the *klephts* who were enshrined in tradition by their feats during the Ottoman occupation and the Greek War of Liberation against the sultan. But if it was still as easy as it was more than a hundred years before to organize guerilla operations in the mountainous countryside, there was a new dimension to guerilla operations in the 1940s. The Communist Party, forced underground during the Metaxas regime, now was the only group capable of organizing guerilla bands into a national resistance movement. For reasons associated with geography, class, and, later, ideology, the KKE's capacity for organization filled a political vacuum caused by the apparent abdication of the old ruling classes.[34]

In September 1941, the KKE, in coalition with other resistance movements, established the National Liberation Front (EAM), an extension of the Popular Front idea of 1936. In the following year, EAM in turn established the National People's Liberation Army (ELAS) whose initials almost reproduced the Greeks' name for their country (Ellas) and thereby emphasized the army's patriotic and national character. While controlled by the KKE[35] (whose influence was deliberately camouflaged), EAM was essentially anti-monarchist in its orientation. Because of the wide spectrum of political opinion in its ranks, EAM/ELAS must be distinguished from the KKE. In spite of assertions that EAM/ELAS was either the tool of a ruthless conspiracy of Slavophile Communists, or the embodiment of every progressive

[34] Campbell and Sherrard, pp. 175-177; McNeill, *The Greek Dilemma*, pp. 61, 80, 91-93; Woodward, 3:386; Stavrianos, *Greece*, p. 87; Woodward, BFP, p. 352.

[35] While it has been estimated that there were not more than 50 Moscow-trained Communists in EAM/ELAS, it is significant that these men filled every position in KKE's political bureau, and most of the positions in its central committee—especially since KKE had ultimate control of EAM/ELAS. Woodward, 3:387; Woodhouse, pp. 60, 115; Stavrianos, *Greece*, pp. 74-75.

force in Greece, it must be regarded as both. While the KKE was ruth-less, many of those associated with EAM/ELAS were primarily mem-bers of islolated, independent resistance bands. Their essential focus had been against the defeated Italians who were now occupying Greece by grace of the Germans. Many guerillas who were members of such bands were gradually incorporated under the aegis of EAM/ELAS, with whose resistance efforts—if not ideals—they were in sympathy. Because such incorporation was of necessity a gradual process, it was not until 1942-43 that EAM/ELAS began to exercise effective control over the guerilla bands. In the process, it assimilated men of all persuasions—including 16 generals, 34 colonels, and 1,450 other com-missioned officers of prewar Greece.[36]

As EAM/ELAS grew in size,[37] KKE ambitions appear to have grown increasingly political, and its methods more ruthless. Its orientation was facilitated by divisions within the population. Most political leaders of the conservative and center parties, as well as the upper and most of the middle class in the towns, avoided association with EAM. In view of this fact and because of KKE's social ideology, EAM grad-ually assimilated many of those who were dispossessed and under-privileged, and became in part a revolutionary class movement. Unlike the upper and middle classes in the towns, the dispossessed and un-derprivileged—most of whom came from the countryside—had little or nothing to lose, and were more willing to risk the dangers of resistance. This was not, of course, the only reason one joined EAM/ELAS. Another reason was coercion: if one failed to join, he was greeted by intolerance, intimidation, and repression. These reasons, nonetheless, are insufficient to explain why EAM/ELAS enjoyed wider support than that of a particular class. The explanation must be found in the fact that in Greece divisions were just not that simple. If they were a function of class, they were just as much a function of fierce individual loyalties.[38]

[36] Elisabeth Barker, "Greece," in *Hitler's Europe*, ed. Arnold Toynbee and Veronica Toynbee (London, 1954), pp. 681-686; Iatrides, p. 27; Stavrianos, *Greece*, p. 68; McNeill, *The Greek Dilemma*, pp. 62, 73-76; Woodhouse, *Apple of Discord*, pp. 71-72; Campbell and Sherrard, p. 174.

[37] According to one of the leaders of ELAS, its ranks included 5,240 officers and 43,700 men on the eve of liberation (Stefanos Sarafis, *Greek Resistance Army: The Story of ELAS* (London, 1951), p. 276). EDES, by contrast, had about 10,000 men. Iatrides, p. 176; O'Ballance, pp. 89-91.

[38] McNeill, *The Greek Dilemma*, pp. 90-93, 109, 133-134, 156-157; Woodhouse, *Apple of Discord*, pp. 75, 96; Stavrianos, *Greece*, pp. 88-89; Iatrides, pp. 17-18,

Personal loyalty and chance as well as class determined the affiliations and confused the allegiance of thousands of Greeks. If army officers could join EAM/ELAS, peasants could join the ranks of those opposed to the resistance army. In the Peloponnese, particularly, the deaths of close relatives at the hands of ELAS caused many peasants and townsmen to join Security Battalions. In the process, ideological factors began to intrude, further confusing the issue of allegiance. Members of Security Battalions, to be sure, were motivated by many personal factors: by loyalties, by hatred, by the necessity of making a living, and even by opportunities for plunder. But the Security Battalions, formed in 1943 by Greeks who got their arms from the Germans and who were ready to use any means available to oppose "Slav-dominated Communism," also counted among their members individuals who were motivated by less personal concerns: by nationalism, and, because of their hatred for EAM/ELAS, by anti-Communism. These individuals could rationalize collaboration as an effort to keep EAM/ELAS from controlling Greece after liberation. Because the anti-Communism which they espoused could easily subsume the more personal motivations of their compatriots, and give them voice, anti-Communism became the common denominator of those who joined the Security Battalions.[39]

Anti-Communism became the rallying cry of other movements as well. One such movement was the National Republican Greek League (EDES), next to ELAS the largest resistance movement. At first opposed to the monarchy, EDES, because of its anti-Communism, gradually became royalist and conservative in its orientation. Some of its elements by 1944 were collaborating with the Germans against ELAS not because they sympathized with the Germans, but because they hated the Communist elements of ELAS. Thus, a brutal vendetta between various resistance bands was generated by issues which were increasingly defined in ideological terms, and which became evident in 1943-44 when each sought the destruction of the other. In 1944, the National Social Liberation (EKKA) was totally destroyed by EAM/ELAS. The fact that many members of EKKA took refuge with the

---

24-25. See also: 15 October 1944 letter from Lincoln MacVeagh to Franklin D. Roosevelt, The Papers of Franklin D. Roosevelt, Roosevelt Library, Hyde Park, Personal Secretary's File (hereafter cited as Roosevelt Papers, PSF), Box 52, File Folder: "Greece: McVeagh, Lincoln."

[39] Ibid.

Germans and the Security Battalions, and that others were in-corporated into ELAS, illustrates the difficulty of categorizing the con-flict as purely political, social, or ideological in character. Even if the vendetta seems in the main to have stemmed from collective fears—fears of the postwar aims held by the KKE on the one hand and the monarchists on the other—this explanation, too, falls short of the mark. C. M. Woodhouse has depicted the nature of the problem:

> A Greek peasant, thinking in terms of his own family and his own patch of stony soil, will vote Communist because he has been told that Russian planes will then come and sow his fields from the air so that he need never work again. He will also vote for the King because he has been told that the British will then divert the stream from the mayor's water mill to irrigate his corn. He will pair off with his brother to vote opposite ways in order to have the best of both worlds. His only objection to Metaxas was based on a law restricting goats in the inter-ests of reafforestation. His wit is quick, but his judgment is weak. These are not imaginary instances: they are records of fact, which may help to explain why ideological conflict so quickly becomes confused in per-sonal vendetta.
>
> This huge majority, having in common only a terrible ignorance of its direction, its dangers, its personal stakes, was divided up and blindly led by the minorities who did not know where they were going. Be-cause all the latter were determined to tolerate no rivals, the ordinary Greek—the man in the street, in the field, on the hillside—was not even free to stay still; for even the decision to stay at home and do nothing was a positive decision involving concrete consequences. He was obliged to choose between the alternative leaderships offered to him; to become either a collaborator or a Communist or a republican or whatever it might be, unaware that these alternatives were not ex-haustive; often only dimly aware that they were mutually exclusive.[40]

The fact that the Germans carried out reprisals—on more than one occasion shooting fifty Greeks for every German killed—and that all sides in the civil war indulged in terror tactics, made it virtually im-possible for anyone in Greece to choose an unambiguous course of action during the occupation. German reprisals, for example, provoked bitter resentment against guerillas among those whose friends suffered unjustly because of guerilla activities. The nagging question always obtruded: How was one to conduct oneself? Personal loyalties, revenge,

[40] Barker, pp. 681-687; Woodhouse, *Apple of Discord*, pp. 57-58, 72-85; McNeill, *The Greek Dilemma*, pp. 56-60; Woodward, *BFP*, p. 352; Iatrides, pp. 26, 41-42.

traditional schisms, politics, chance, and class divisions were only some of the elements providing the framework for what was confusingly presented as an ideological conflict. As one writer has observed: "It was not easy to be a Greek during the years of occupation, nor could any wise man see clearly which way his duty lay." Because of this state of affairs, the resistance effort was as much a response to internal as it was to external matters, and reflected the complex divisions within Greek society.[41]

The Greek Government-in-Exile

The government that assumed power after Greece's liberation in October 1944 reflected many of the divisions within Greek society. This representation resulted from a series of changes in the government-in-exile during the war. After the Germans occupied Greece, the republican prime minister Emmanuel Tsouderos[42] and his cabinet had fled first to Crete, then to Cairo, and then to London (where they arrived in September 1941). At the urging of the British, the government-in-exile returned to Cairo in April 1943 in order to be in closer contact with Greek exiles who swelled the ranks of an already considerable Greek community in Egypt. The Greeks in Egypt had immigrated to the new center of the Hellenistic world in Alexandria after the conquest of Greece by Alexander the Great in the fourth century B.C. They had lived there since, retaining their nationality under the Ottoman Empire's Capitulation laws, and consequently they were able to help the newly arrived exiles form a Greek contingent of 22,000 officers and men. As the war progressed, the government-in-exile, at first largely made up of individuals associated with Metaxas, came to include men with more liberal and republican sympathies, and to reflect concern for the constitutional issue that served as a focus for national passions.[43]

The constitutional question centered around the return of the king who, as noted, was associated both with an oppressive dictatorship and

[41] McNeill, *The Greek Dilemma*, pp. 56-60; Kevin Andrews, *The Flight of Icarus* (Boston, 1959), pp. 194-195, cited by Todd Gitlin, "Counter-Insurgency: Myth and Reality in Greece," in *Containment and Revolution*, ed. David Horowitz (London, 1967), pp. 149-150.

[42] Tsouderos replaced Alexander Koryzis, who had committed suicide prior to Greece's collapse.

[43] McNeill, "Greece," p. 389; Barker, p. 678; Woodward, *BFP*, p. 351; McNeill, *The Greek Dilemma*, pp. 116-117; Iatrides, pp. 31-33; Woodward, 3:384-389.

—however unfairly—with fascism. As opinion gradually polarized on the issue of his return, the king, perhaps unaware of the extent of his unpopularity, continued to assert the legitimacy of his position. He either ignored or actively opposed repeated attempts by various resistance delegations to persuade him not to return until a plebiscite had been held. He responded with *froideur* to similar attempts on the part of the Tsouderos government, which was increasingly sensitive to opinion in Greece. The king's attitude increased the suspicions of anti-monarchists. It prevented clarification of issues among those individuals whose common bond was opposition to him, and served to expand the conflict between the resistance factions.[44]

Eventually, EAM/ELAS attempted to form a rival government in Greece—the Political Committee of National Liberation (PEEA)—with the avowed purpose, announced in March 1944, of seeking a representative national government after liberation. Within two weeks, an anti-royalist mutiny among Greek forces in Cairo demonstrated support for this position. The mutiny was precipitated by several factors: Tsouderos's refusal to recognize PEEA as the legitimate authority in Greece; the king's refusal to appoint a regent; and the king's continued unwillingness to accede to the results of a plebiscite.

As a result, Tsouderos resigned, and the social democrat George Papandreou succeeded him. Under Papandreou, a conference convened in Lebanon in May 1944, where representatives of 17 parties and organizations resolved some of their differences and reached a temporary agreement. The "Lebanon Charter" called for an end to the "reign of terror" in Greece, unification of all resistance forces (including EAM/ELAS, EDES, PEEA, etc.), and formation of a Government of National Unity. Papandreou also took it upon himself to resolve the constitutional question by declaring that the king would not return to Greece pending the results of a plebiscite—a declaration which the king viewed as necessary but to which he was not fully committed.[45]

Britain, the Great Powers, and Greek Politics

British influence, meanwhile, continued to be a factor in Greek politics. More than 70,000 British troops had been sent into Greece to

[44] Stavrianos, *The Balkans*, p. 676; Barker, pp. 682-683; Stavrianos, *Greece*, p. 102; Woodward, 3:385 ff.

[45] Barker, pp. 683-685, 688; McNeill, *The Greek Dilemma*, pp. 25-26; Stavrianos, *Greece*, pp. 83, 106-110; Iatrides, pp. 44, 52-53, 61-65, 68, 100; Campbell and Sherrard, pp. 177-178.

resist the German invasion, and 30,000 had suffered casualties before being withdrawn. Britain also had been actively involved in the resistance movement and in the affairs of the Greek government-in-exile, with which it had signed in March 1942 an agreement for close cooperation in prosecution of the war effort. The liberation of Greece and the reestablishment of her freedom and independence had been accepted as a common objective.[46]

As early as October 1942, the British Special Operations Executive (SOE) had sent a liaison unit into occupied Greece to organize sabotage.[47] While British aid initially went to ELAS, continued rivalry between the resistance forces caused the British to reconsider their policy of allocating assistance. To that end, they attempted to bring the opposing factions into harmony (in the "National Bands" agreement of July 1943 and in the Plaka Agreement of February 1944). They also undertook to build up EDES in an effort to balance the influence of ELAS, which had begun to destroy its rivals with arms captured during the Italian surrender in September 1943.[48]

This rivalry between the resistance forces revealed a conflict in British policies. Military concentration on the war effort had generated a desire on the part of SOE to support the resistance effort. The logic of this view requires little elaboration: the Salonika-Athens railroad link had carried 80 percent of Rommel's supplies prior to El-Alamein—and it was the severance of this link which had led SOE to send a mission to Greece in the first place. In addition, the resistance effort as a whole tied up 300,000 Axis troops (180,000 after the Italian surrender). But Churchill and the Foreign Office, looking to the postwar world, placed less emphasis on support of the resistance effort. They were concerned, rather, with support of the king and of the government-in-exile. A constitutional monarchy in Greece would be more likely to bring about stability than a republic, they believed. A stable government, in turn,

[46] Iatrides, p. 64; O'Ballance, p. 45; Xydis, *Greece and the Great Powers*, pp. 6-7, 683-688.

[47] By agreement between the British SOE and the American OSS, the British Secret Service took the lead in Greece. Roosevelt Papers, PSF, Box 52, "Greece: MacVeagh, Lincoln," 17 February 1944 letter from MacVeagh to Roosevelt.

[48] Woodhouse, *Apple of Discord*, pp. 136 ff.; Barker, pp. 687-688; Campbell and Sherrard, pp. 177-178; Woodward, *BFP*, p. 352; McNeill, *The Greek Dilemma*, pp. 105-107; Iatrides, pp. 39-42; Woodward, 3:398. For an excellent discussion of British aid to ELAS, and the consequences of that policy, see C. M. Woodhouse, *The Struggle for Greece, 1941-1949* (London, 1976), pp. 103-110.

would help ensure the safety of British sea communications in the Eastern Mediterranean.[49]

The difference between Britain's immediate and long-range interests was complicated by the fact that they tended to be mutually exclusive. Aiding the resistance effort, because it meant giving aid to ELAS, also meant less chance of success for the constitutional monarchy. Aware of this conflict, Anthony Eden in late 1943 suggested a change in policy. He recommended withdrawing material support from EAM/ELAS, and undermining the resistance army's popular support by changing Britain's policy on the constitutional question. In view of the king's unpopularity and the undesirable consequences of supporting him, Eden now recommended that the king be advised to name a Regency Council and pledge not to return to Greece until a plebiscite settled the constitutional question. The British government accepted Eden's recommendations.[50]

Shortly after the Teheran Conference, Eden and Churchill met with the king in Cairo.[51] Since the Teheran Conference had ended Churchill's hope for operations in the Balkans, and the Foreign Office had dropped the idea of the king's returning to Greece with a liberating force, the British statesmen advised King George of their new recommendations, only to be thwarted by President Roosevelt.[52] The latter, contrary to advice both from Lincoln MacVeagh, American ambassador to the Greek government-in-exile, and from the State Department, advised the king not to accede to the British suggestion. Erroneously asserting that he had not been consulted previously, Roosevelt acted in a manner which is explicable only in terms of the United States policy of noninterference in Greek affairs, and his suspicions that Britain was trying to "deprive the King of his crown." The president was sentimental about Greece: he liked to recall how his great-grandfather and great-uncle had been responsible for an American frigate's being sent to Greece during the Greek War for Independence; in early 1914, as assistant secretary of the Navy, Roosevelt himself had obtained

[49] Stavrianos, Greece, pp. 103-104; Iatrides, p. 77; McNeill, The Greek Dilemma, p. 123; Eden, pp. 533-534; Woodward, BFP, pp. 352-353; Woodward, 1:525 and 3:121, 151, 383-384, 389-391; Campbell and Sherrard, p. 177; O'Ballance, p. 84.

[50] Eden, pp. 533-534; Woodward, 3:383, 388-393, 398-400.

[51] This was the same conference at which Churchill attempted to get İnönü to agree to enter the war and tried to use Turkey's fear of Russia as leverage.

[52] Roosevelt also helped to thwart British policies with regard to Turkey. See Chapter I.

two battleships "to save Greece from Turkey." In addition, the president liked the king very much, and listened sympathetically when the monarch told him how he was being railroaded.[53]

As a consequence of Roosevelt's attitude, Churchill returned to his earlier position in support of the king. The British fell back on the policy of supporting a united front, which sought to prevent the disintegration of the resistance effort by securing EAM/ELAS participation in the Greek government. This policy was evident in British support for the Plaka Agreement (February 1944)[54] and the Lebanon Agreement (May 1944). But the charge that the British intended to force the king on the country, and that this would mean a dictatorship—a charge which won much popular support for EAM/ELAS—was never refuted either by the king or by the British until after liberation. In the absence of such a refutation, the uneasy alliance between anti-monarchist elements continued to provide EAM/ELAS and the KKE with a powerful base of support, and to worry British Middle East Headquarters. It also worried Churchill who, as a result of the tenuous situation in Greece, in early May initiated a study of the "brute issues" developing between Great Britain and Russia—and took a step toward what became the percentages agreement with Stalin over the Balkans.[55]

[53] See n. 55.

[54] The Plaka Agreement is commonly considered the end of the "First Round" of a struggle for power (which began with the failure of the Cairo talks of August 1943) between the "Left" (EAM/ELAS) and the "Right" (monarchists, etc.).

[55] Barker, p. 682; Woodward, 3:115, 396, 398-403, 410; Roosevelt Papers, PSF, Box 52, "Greece: MacVeagh, Lincoln," 13 December 1943 letter from MacVeagh to Roosevelt, 15 January 1944 letter from Roosevelt to MacVeagh, 1 April 1944 letter from Roosevelt to MacVeagh; Woodward, BFP, pp. 354-355; McNeill, The Greek Dilemma, p. 123; Iatrides, pp. 64, 97-98, 129; Reginald Leeper, When Greek Meets Greek (London, 1950), pp. 34-35. An indication of widespread British concern about the Eastern Mediterranean and the Northern Tier is illustrated by a passage from MacVeagh's 15 May 1944 letter to President Roosevelt: "The chief intelligence officer of our forces here said to me the other day, 'British Middle East Headquarters can't sleep for thinking about Russia,' and he told me of a map which a Britisher had shown him, entitled, 'The next war begins here,' with four places marked on it, namely the Danube, the Dardanelles, the Suez Canal and the Persian Gulf. You may remember the acute British fears of Russia when we were young—Kipling's 'Man who Was' and his 'Bear that walks like a Man.' These fears are all coming back now with a vengeance, and will doubtless be intensified when Russia is no longer one of the great powers but the only great power remaining on the European continent. The British Ambassador to Greece recently said to me, in regard to developments in that country, 'Greece is now at the cross-roads, the question being whether she is to move into the Russian orbit and lose her independence, or remain an European country under British influence." Roosevelt

Meanwhile, the Government of National Unity, conceived at the Lebanon Conference, got off to a shaky start. Its legitimacy was thrown into question as the PEEA (EAM/ELAS's attempt to form a rival government), bargaining for greater influence, initially rejected the work of its delegates. By August, however, the PEEA decided to join the government—perhaps as a result of Soviet influence, but more likely because it recognized its limited bargaining power in a situation it had little hope of changing.[56] Within a week, Papandreou was asking a very concerned British prime minister for help to ensure government control after the liberation.[57] Churchill had already been contemplating this question. In less than a week Roosevelt approved the prime minister's earlier proposal that a British force, not exceeding 10,000 men, be kept in readiness to preserve order in Greece. A month later, Stalin, too, approved plans for landing these forces in Greece. At Churchill's urging, Papandreou meanwhile moved the fragile, newly formed government to Italy, where Harold Macmillan, who had assumed responsibility for British policy in the Balkans, convened a conference of Greek political and guerilla leaders.[58]

Hoping to minimize divisions and strengthen government control over the resistance, Macmillan arranged for the Caserta Agreement, signed on 26 September 1944, in which all Greek guerilla forces recognized the authority of the Government of National Unity. The Government of National Unity in turn placed those forces under the command of a British officer, Lieutenant General Ronald Scobie. Thus, the agreement explicitly acknowledged the Greek government's reliance on Brit-

---

Papers, PSF, Box 52, "Greece: MacVeagh, Lincoln," 15 May 1944 letter from MacVeagh to Roosevelt.

[56] The reason for this shift is still not clearly understood. Some observers see a coincidence between the Soviet ambassador's departure from Cairo (he was gone for 16 months) and the arrival of the Russian (Popov) mission in Greece (see n. 83). Others explain the shift by PEEA's resignation to the fact that it could not oust Papandreou, and its recognition that the Middle East crisis would not discredit king and government to the benefit of PEEA. Xydis, *Greece and the Great Powers*, pp. 38, 49; Barker, pp. 684-685; Woodward, *BFP*, p. 357; McNeill, *The Greek Dilemma*, p. 144; Eudes, pp. 144-150; Sarafis, pp. 224-225; Iatrides, pp. 102-103. See also Woodhouse, *The Struggle for Greece*, p. 92.

[57] See Charles Moran, *Churchill: the Struggle for Survival, 1940-1965, Taken from the Diaries of Lord Moran* (Boston, 1966), p. 173.

[58] Macmillan's position was British Minister Resident at the Allied Force Headquarters, Mediterranean Theater. Woodward, *BFP*, pp. 356-357; Xydis, *Greece and the Great Powers*, pp. 50-53; Woodward, 3:409-410; Iatrides, pp. 110-115; Churchill, *Triumph and Tragedy*, pp. 110-114.

ish forces, which began to land in Greece at the end of September as the Germans withdrew. Within three weeks, the Government of National Unity would be following the British into Athens, and the occupation of Greece would be at an end.[59] Before that time, however, the stage had been set for negotiations between Churchill and Stalin—negotiations which began before the Government of National Unity entered Athens, and which were to have a profound effect on Greek history.

American Attitudes toward Greece and the Balkans

An important element of the negotiations between Churchill and Stalin concerns the role played by Roosevelt in Balkan affairs. The president's failure to take any initiative in the Balkan situation, because by default it gave jurisdiction over that important strategic area to his two allies, deserves attention.

It should be stated at the outset that the president of the United States was well informed about developments in Greece during World War II. The American ambassador to the Greek government-in-exile, Lincoln MacVeagh, was an unusually able man who had excellent contacts in the Greek political world. MacVeagh constantly reported to the State Department and periodically wrote personal letters to the president.[60] The existence of such reports and letters, of course, does not mean that Roosevelt followed their recommendations. When MacVeagh and State Department officials at Cairo in December 1943 advised the president not to support the king, Roosevelt chose to disregard their advice. But MacVeagh's perceptive letters to Roosevelt always illuminated Greece's problems, and were sensitive to the international context of Greek affairs.

MacVeagh kept Roosevelt informed of Greece's internal problems: of the political divisions, of the constitutional question's complexity and its ideological overtones, of important social issues that emerged during the war.[61] But when it came to the external context of Greek affairs, he was more assertive. Appreciating his government's policy of noninterference in Greek affairs, MacVeagh nevertheless attempted to persuade the President to change it. As early as 17 February 1944,[62] he had directed Roosevelt's attention to the traditional rivalry between Russia

[59] Iatrides, pp. 115, 311-313; Woodward, 3:411.

[60] Iatrides, pp. 216, 286. See also the letters cited below.

[61] Roosevelt Papers, PSF, Box 52, "Greece: MacVeagh, Lincoln," 17 March, 15 May, 23 June, and 15 October 1944 letters from MacVeagh to Roosevelt.

[62] Ibid., 17 February 1944 letter from MacVeagh to Roosevelt.

and Britain, and to the fact that their policies had not changed. Pan-Slavism and an outlet to the Mediterranean competed with "the preservation of the Empire connections and the sea route to India." Because of Balkan distrust of England and fear of Russia, and in order to keep Russia and Britain from eventually coming into conflict in the region, MacVeagh believed the United States had a responsibility to undertake the reconstitution of the Balkan states. He understood that British strength was clearly inadequate for this task; if the United States remained aloof, he warned, the area eventually would fall to the Russians.

MacVeagh's letters to Roosevelt told of Britain's preoccupation with the Eastern Mediterranean and expressed concern about Anglo-Soviet rivalry in the region. Shortly after Churchill had begun to consider coming to terms with Stalin over the "brute issues" in the Balkans, MacVeagh on 14 May 1944 wrote Roosevelt:

> I believe that when Athens is restored we may look to see a diplomatic game there (as well as in the rest of the Balkans, Eastern Europe and the Middle East) similar to that which we saw in the past, only this time not between Great Britain and the Axis but between her and the Union of Soviet Socialist Republics.[63]

Recognizing that his earlier recommendation of a United States initiative in the Balkans was out of line with the military policy of the moment, he urged coordination of policies with the British and the Russians.

The British in June told MacVeagh of a tentative agreement between London and Moscow, and the ambassador sensed an improvement in the situation.[64] But on the eve of Greece's liberation in October, he reverted to his earlier premonitions, and stressed once more his view that "what goes on in the Balkans and the Near East generally will have to be recognized as of prime importance to us despite the fact that the countries involved are small and remote." Again he discussed the clashing of Soviet and British interests in the area, placing the rivalry in the context of the historical struggles for hegemony in Europe, and noting the security interests of the United States in its outcome:

> Here both the French Revolution and the Nazi Revolution have made their most dangerous bids to crack England's empire and pick the lock of world dominion. No one can say for certain, of course, that the Empire of the Czars, which has now become the Empire of the Soviets,

[63] Ibid., 15 May 1944 letter from MacVeagh to Roosevelt.
[64] Ibid., 23 June 1944 letter from MacVeagh to Roosevelt.

97

will make a similar attempt in its turn, but the fact remains that—as I have presumed to emphasize in my previous letters—Russian interests are clearly tending to cross with Britain's in this region even now. Nor is this all. Evidence is equally plain right here of Britain's inability to defend alone her Empire against powerful pressure under conditions of modern war. I doubt if in any other part of the world it can appear so clearly as here,—along its principal artery,—that, militarily speaking, the British Empire is anachronistic, perfect for the eighteenth century, impossible for the twentieth. Every day brings its evidence of weakness and dispersion, of consequent opportunism, and dependence on America's nucleated strength. No one, I feel, can keep his eyes and ears open here and fail to believe that the future maintenance of the Empire depends on how far England consents to frame her foreign policy in agreement with Washington, and how far we in our turn realize where that Empire, so important to our own security, is most immediately menaced. British fumbling in the Balkans, fears of what may happen in Palestine, uneasiness as to Syria, doubts regarding Turkey, and alarm over growing Soviet interest in Iran, Saudi Arabia, Egypt and the whole North African Coast, together with the fact that it was only through America's productive strength being thrown into the balance that Rommel's threat to this region was defeated, all seem to me to teach the same lesson in their varying degrees.[65]

In short, MacVeagh believed that the British Empire was crumbling —especially in the Balkans and in the Near East, where Soviet strength was most menacing to British interests. It was up to the United States to recognize that its own security interests were in part dependent on Anglo-American influence along the Northern Tier and in the Balkans. Joint influence depended on the degree to which Britain was willing to follow the American lead on the one hand, and the extent to which the United States was willing to take the initiative on the other. The American lead need not be on Britain's terms—terms with which Mac-Veagh had little sympathy. In fact, MacVeagh recommended an American initiative in part because of American and Balkan suspicions of British intentions in Southeastern Europe. But such an initiative was necessary—especially if Russia's growing influence was to be curbed.[66]

Russia's new influence along her periphery, particularly in Southeastern Europe, resulted partly from Britain's waning strength, as well as from the devastation of war in that region. MacVeagh feared that

[65] Ibid., 15 October 1944 letter from MacVeagh to Roosevelt.
[66] Ibid., 17 February, 17 March, 15 May, 23 June, and 15 October 1944 letters from MacVeagh to Roosevelt.

the Soviet Union would virtually annex much of the area, or, if British strength could be temporarily sustained, that there would be a conflict between Russia and Britain. In either case, the United States inevitably would become involved. MacVeagh argued, therefore, that American intervention was desirable, especially since the United States was the only country sufficiently trusted by all of the countries concerned.[67]

Roosevelt, while appreciative of his ambassador's advice,[68] failed to act upon it. Until October 1944, he neither endorsed a regency nor advocated any sort of American intervention in the Balkans.[69] Instead, he reiterated his country's traditional policy of noninvolvement in the area, consigned the Balkans to Britain's jurisdiction,[70] and focused on the American government's priorities in the war against Germany and Japan.

Any initiative in the Balkans would have been a political gamble, and the president felt that such a gamble should not take precedence over defeat of Germany, the main objective of U.S. military strategy.[71] The defeat of Japan, while taking a back seat to the Atlantic-first policy,[72]

[67] Ibid. Greek trust in the United States may have resulted from the fact that between 1890 and 1931, over 500,000 Greeks immigrated to the United States; of those 500,000, over 40 percent went back as repatriates. Familiarity with the United States, the fact that Greeks had immediate relatives living in America, and the fact that remittances from those relatives (while falling sharply after the depression) had done much to rectify Greece's unfavorable balance of trade, all contributed to a favorable disposition toward the United States. See Couloumbis, p. 25; Stavrianos, *The Balkans*, pp. 480-482, 680-681; Campbell and Sherrard, p. 97. Greek trust was maintained, perhaps even enhanced, during World War II by the Greek-relief program, which by late 1944 had accounted for almost 450,000 tons of foodstuffs, medicines, and related supplies and to which the United States government and public had made payments of more than $20,000,000. Foy Kohler, "The Relief of Occupied Greece," Department of State *Bulletin* 11 (17 September 1944): 300-304.

[68] Roosevelt Papers, PSF, Box 52, "Greece: MacVeagh, Lincoln," 15 January, 1 April, and 1 July 1944 letters from Roosevelt to MacVeagh.

[69] I.e., a political initiative along the lines advocated by MacVeagh—not the military initiative advocated by Churchill in 1943, which was rejected by the United States because of the American desire to concentrate on the Second Front.

[70] As early as 21 February 1944, the president informed the secretary of state that he did not want the United States to bear the postwar burden of reconstituting the Balkans (FR, 1944, I:184; FR, *The Conference at Quebec*, 1944, p. 216). Even before Churchill's May 1944 concern for a division of spheres of action in the Balkans, Roosevelt, on 30 April, had written the secretary of state a letter in which he noted that the "southern zone should be occupied by British forces." FR, *The Conference at Quebec*, 1944, p. 216.

[71] FR, *The Conferences at Washington and Quebec*, 1943, p. 499; *The Conferences at Quebec*, 1944, pp. 155-156, 216.

[72] Gordon Wright, pp. 185, 197.

was also important. As early as August 1943, Roosevelt and Hopkins had been warned of Russia's growing might, and of Britain's concern for building up a position in the Mediterranean that would be useful in balancing the power equation in postwar Europe. Their warning came from a document dated 10 August 1943 and entitled "Russia's Position."[73] The memorandum, which quoted from "a very high level United States military strategic estimate," estimated that British opposition to the Soviet Union in the Mediterranean might be insufficient as a balance unless Britain was otherwise supported. It envisioned such support not in terms of military support for Britain, but in terms of assistance to the Soviet Union. The thrust of such assistance would be to obtain Soviet friendship—an object which was desirable in view of Russia's decisive role in the war, and the fact that *the most important factor the United States has to consider in relation to Russia is the prosecution of the war in Japan*" (italics in original). The train of thought outlined in this estimate, which strongly influenced American decisions at Teheran and Yalta, appears to explain Roosevelt's reluctance to follow MacVeagh's advice on American intervention in the Balkans. Allaying Soviet suspicions and keeping the Soviets informed of Allied actions in the Balkans were uppermost in Washington's thoughts about Southeastern Europe in the fall of 1944.[74]

As a consequence of the thought processes outlined above, Roosevelt was willing to acquiesce to the British lead in the Balkans. He was concerned, he wrote Ambassador Harriman in Moscow two days after Churchill's arrival there, "that such steps as are practicable should be taken to insure against the Balkans getting us into a future war."[75] He was not so concerned, however, that he considered taking any of those steps himself. Instead, he preferred to let Churchill and Stalin work out a solution to their common, historical problems in the Balkans.

The Moscow Conference and the Spheres of Influence Agreement

Prelude

The October Agreement on the Balkans between Churchill and Stalin, while reflecting traditional interests of Britain and Russia, grew out of

[73] Sherwood, pp. 748-749, 977. See also *FR, The Conferences at Washington and Quebec, 1943*, p. 499.

[74] *FR, The Conference at Quebec, 1944*, p. 213.

[75] *FR, 1944*, IV:1009.

the military situation of 1944. Political control of the Balkans had emerged as a clear Soviet objective. The British believed that complete concession to Soviet demands would diminish British influence in Southeastern Europe and cause the loss of British credibility in Turkey and Greece. The Turks and Greeks were also worried about Soviet intentions, and when Soviet forces entered Rumania in April 1944, Americans, too, began to worry.

While the United States appeared willing to accept assurances of Soviet benevolence toward Rumania, Churchill grew anxious as the Red Army advanced. On 4 May he asked Eden for a short paper on the "brute issues" between Britain and the Soviet Union that were developing in Italy, Rumania, Bulgaria, Yugoslavia, and Greece. The next day Eden discussed the matter with Feodor Gusev, the Soviet ambassador to Great Britain, suggesting that the Soviet government take the initiative in trying to get Rumania out of the war. Since Greece was in Britain's theater of command, the Soviets should support British policy in Greece in return for British support in Rumania.[76]

The Soviets agreed with Eden's suggestion, but wanted to know whether the United States had been consulted. Churchill accordingly sent a telegram to Roosevelt in which he dwelt upon a possible divergence of policy between Britain and Russia, and noted Britain's suggestion to the Soviet Union. He made clear that the proposal applied only to "war conditions" and insisted that it not be interpreted as sanctioning a division of the Balkans into spheres of influence, or affecting the rights and responsibilities of the Great Powers at the peace settlement. Rather, he regarded it as a convenient arrangement for preventing a divergence of policy between the Allies in the Balkans.[77]

The State Department was cool to the British proposal. Cordell Hull, especially, saw nothing but "iniquitous consequences" in any system of spheres of influence or in any concept related to the balance of power.

[76] Woodward, 3:115-117, 139; Hull, 2:1451; Churchill, *Triumph and Tragedy*, pp. 72-73; FR, 1944, IV:165-166, 169-174.

[77] Churchill, *Triumph and Tragedy*, pp. 73-74; FR, 1944, V:114-115. A message Churchill sent on 8 June to Edward Halifax, the British ambassador in the United States, deemed it reasonable that the Russians should deal with the Rumanians and the Bulgarians; the British with the Greeks and Yugoslavs. As Stavrianos notes, the casual inclusions meant that the prepared agreement would "cover virtually the entire peninsula" (Churchill, *Triumph and Tragedy*, pp. 74-75; Stavrianos, *The Balkans*, p. 809). Upon being informed of the telegram, Hull's reaction was that it "seemed more urgent even than before to oppose the arrangement which would bring one set of countries under Russia and another set under Britain." Hull, 2:1453-1454.

Influenced by Hull, whose staff helped draft his reply, Roosevelt wrote Churchill of his reluctance to make agreements which had a tendency to broaden and strengthen decisions necessitated by military developments. Despite British intentions, Roosevelt worried that the arrangement could lead to a division of the Balkans into spheres of influence. The president preferred to rely on "consultative machinery" whose purpose would be to dispel misunderstandings.

Churchill immediately took issue with Roosevelt. He proposed a three-month trial of his plan. Without consulting the State Department, Roosevelt acquiesced, counseling Churchill to make it clear that no postwar spheres of influence were being established. On 19 June Eden informed Molotov of Roosevelt's agreement. The proposal was to refer only to military conditions; it was not intended to divide the Balkan states into spheres of influence.[78]

The British believed the Soviets were seeking a predominate position in Southeastern Europe by means of Communist-led movements in Yugoslavia, Albania, and Greece. British support for the Greek EAM and the Yugoslav partisans during the war had worked against their long-range interests, which required a balance between British and Russian influence in the Balkans. To bolster these interests, the British had suggested a confederation of Balkan states after the war, but found their recommendation rejected by the Soviets, who saw it as constituting a "cordon sanitaire" against them. In the nineteenth century Britain had cooperated with Austria-Hungary to counter Russian designs in the Balkans and the Turkish Straits. Now there was no one on whom they could fully rely.[79]

The search for allies presented the British with a dilemma. In Yugoslavia, they had supported Josip Tito, who seemed almost certain to emerge as the ruler of that country. To stop supporting him would be ill advised. In Greece, the Lebanon Agreement for an "all-party" government and a national Greek army embodying all resistance units also precluded a boycott of the Communists. To support Communist ele-

[78] The State Department did not find out about Roosevelt's actions until 26 June, when Lincoln MacVeagh, the American ambassador to the Greek government-in-exile, informed about the proposal by his British colleague in Cairo, cabled Washington what he had learned. Hull, 2:1452-1456; Department of State *Bulletin* 9 (20 November 1943):341-345; Woodward, 3:117-119; FR, 1944, V:112-115, 117-123, 128-129; Churchill, *Triumph and Tragedy*, pp. 74-77; Lynn Davis, pp. 144-151.

[79] Churchill, *Triumph and Tragedy*, pp. 77-78; Woodward, 3:119-121; Hull, 1:128-129.

ments fully in order to wean them from the Russians would be naive and politically distasteful—particularly since the kings of Greece and Yugoslavia had taken refuge in London where they received support from the British government. The only solution appeared to be that suggested by Eden: an understanding with the Soviets in which both powers would promise not to interfere in the politics of their respective areas of operation in the Balkans. This policy would protect Britain's lifeline, and give the British a base for spreading their influence without directly challenging the Soviets. The British had been allowed to "play the hand" in Turkey during the war, and were doing the same in Greece, where the burden for doing so had always rested with them. Consequently, they sought formal sanction to continue their role in Greece.[80]

Cordell Hull's refusal to face this question and his rejection of power politics evidenced a Wilsonian preference for the broad principles of the Atlantic Charter.[81] These principles, if adhered to, perhaps were the only hope for the future independence of small countries such as Turkey and the Balkan states. But principles were useless unless respected, and in the world emerging from the war the dictates of power were the most likely determinants of respect. Considering the British Empire's decline and the Red Army's march through Eastern Europe, Roosevelt's recommendation of consultative machinery appears to have had little merit. Unless there were prior agreement as to spheres of influence, the British believed that de facto spheres would take their place.[82]

A triangular agreement, however, was difficult to attain. Roosevelt grew uneasy over his acquiescence to Churchill's request, and began to doubt the manner in which the request originated. On 22 June he registered his concerns with the prime minister, who immediately reassured the president of his good intentions. A week later a Soviet *aide-mémoire* informed the president of Anglo-Soviet negotiations and requested the American point of view. When Churchill telegraphed Stalin on 11 July

[80] Woodward, 3:120-121; Churchill, *Triumph and Tragedy*, pp. 74-78, 208-209.

[81] See Julius Pratt, *Cordell Hull, 1933-1944*, 2 vols. (New York, 1965), 1:4-6, 29-30; 2:410-411, 524-531, 718-722; Gordon Levin, *Woodrow Wilson and World Politics: America's Response to War and Revolution* (New York, 1968), p. vii. From a more practical point of view, such an arrangement, if it had been made known, would have "aroused fierce antagonisms among the ethnic groups in the United States." Charles Bohlen, *Witness to History, 1929-1969* (New York, 1973), p. 164.

[82] Hull, 2:1452-1453; Wolff, p. 257; Bohlen, p. 164; see also John Lukacs, "The Night Stalin and Churchill Divided Europe," *New York Times Magazine*, 5 October 1969.

about the three-month trial of his plan, stating that the Americans had agreed to it, Stalin wired back that since the United States had doubts about the proposal it was better to hear from Washington first. On the same day, a State Department memorandum to the Soviet embassy noted assent to the arrangement proposed by Churchill. The acceptance was for a trial period of three months, and was agreed to in consideration of the present war strategy. It further expressed hope that the arrangement would not prejudice efforts toward collaboration, observing that a broader system of general security would be jeopardized by any arrangement suggestive of spheres of influence. The British government, which in late July was again informed of the American acceptance, in early August still questioned that there was an agreement. Meanwhile, the Russians (without consulting the British) had sent a mission to ELAS in Greece, and discussion of the agreement ceased. Churchill's concern, however, did not abate, and was exemplified one morning in early August when his private physician heard him shout: "Good God, can't you see that the Russians are spreading across Europe like a tide; they have invaded Poland, and there is nothing to prevent them marching into Turkey and Greece!"[83]

[83] Woodward, 3:121-122; FR, 1944, V:121-131; Hull, 2:1456-1457; Churchill, *Triumph and Tragedy*, pp. 77-81; Stephen Xydis, "The Secret Anglo-Soviet Agreement on the Balkans of October 9, 1944," *Journal of Central European Affairs* 15 (October 1955):256-258; Moran, p. 173. The exact purpose of the Soviet mission under Colonel Gregori Popov has been subject to much speculation. See Stavrianos, *Greece*, pp. 118-119; and *The Balkans Since 1453*, p. 810; Stephen Xydis, "The Secret Anglo-Soviet Agreement," pp. 256-258; Woodhouse, *Apple of Discord*, pp. 198-199; McNeill, *The Greek Dilemma*, pp. 144-146; Eudes, pp. 147-148; Iatrides, pp. 74-76. Iatrides believes that "if there was Soviet influence in the summer of 1944, it most likely took the form of communication to the Greek Communists not as to what to do, but rather as to what Moscow would *not* do for them. From this KKE and EAM were to derive their own conclusions and act accordingly." The question remains as to why the Soviets would not support the Greeks. Was it because of the earlier agreement, or because of what Popov saw? And to what degree did action by default commit them to Greek Communist cooperation as a tactic which would allow the KKE to infiltrate the Papandreou government?

Evidence suggests that the mission went to Greece to seek more information, to check the possibilities, and to find out whether the Soviets could put themselves in a better bargaining position after the three months of the agreement were up. This might explain why the Soviets never gave formal assent to the agreement. The PEEA's decision to join the Papandreou government in August, and Moscow's willingness to make an agreement with Churchill formally in October may also be explained by what Popov saw: a centralized command without much popular support. His observation may have reinforced Soviet adherence to what was initially a temporary tactical maneuver communicated to PEEA through Popov and the

Stalin's reasons for deferring action on Churchill's proposal are subject to speculation. One historian believes he did not want to antagonize the United States. Another has a more plausible explanation. Stalin already had the upper hand in Rumania. The Communists were thought to be strong in Greece, and the opportunity to exploit the situation there was inviting. Since the Allies were not united, it was unnecessary to sacrifice opportunities in Greece for a free hand in Rumania which he already had anyway.[84] It is possible, of course that Stalin was unsure of Communist strength in Greece. If the Communists were weak, striking a bargain was a good idea since it would sanction Soviet moves in the rest of the Balkans. But if they were strong, he could reexamine the matter. Perhaps this explains Stalin's temporizing as well as the Russian mission which went to Greece in late July.

Whatever the explanation, discussions ceased until the Soviets occupied Bulgaria in September. Instead of using all his troops against the retreating German Army, Stalin now diverted some of them to a secondary target, with predictable effects on the Turks, the Greeks, and the British. To make matters worse for the British, Russia was seeking the status of cobelligerent for Bulgaria, now at war with Germany and sending troops into Greece and Yugoslavia. Ever mindful of Bulgarian irredentism, the British felt they should insist that Bulgarian troops withdraw from Greece and Yugoslavia as a preliminary condition to armistice discussions. Agreements could then be reached.

Although the British had been willing to recognize the Soviet position in Bulgaria contingent on acceptance of Britain's position in Greece, they subsequently decided there should be no "bargain" with respect to Bulgaria. They would assert predominance in Greece, and the Soviets could do so in Rumania—but not in Bulgaria, which shared a common border with Greece and Turkey. Their hopes were slightly exaggerated. They continued to insist on evacuation of Greece and Yugoslavia by the Bulgarians in return for a supposedly free hand in Greece, but were forced to make concessions on Bulgaria.[85]

Churchill's and Eden's apparent resolution at this time stemmed

---

Soviet Union's Cairo Legation (see n. 56). Chapter V contains further discussion of this issue.

[84] Walter Roberts, *Tito, Mihailović and the Allies, 1941-1945* (New Brunswick, N.J., 1973), p. 243; Woodward, 3:123; Wolff, pp. 258-259; Woodhouse, *Apple of Discord*, pp. 198-199.

[85] Woodward, 3:139-141; see also Bohlen, p. 161; Xydis, *Greece and the Great Powers*, pp. 50-52.

from a belief that the Soviets were attempting not only to edge them out of the Balkans, but to establish a puppet government in Poland as well.[86] Rumania and Bulgaria were under Russia's influence, but Poland and Greece were not. Britain had declared war to save Poland from Germany, and had made painful efforts for Greece. The fate of the two countries now hung in the balance, and the prime minister was deeply troubled. He had only limited forces to support his position in the Balkans, where British weakness was underscored by the rude intrusion of Soviet power. The Red Army by 1 October had advanced across Poland as far as the Vistula, and into Hungary and Yugoslavia; it occupied Rumania and Bulgaria and had reached the borders of Greece and Turkey.[87]

High-ranking American officials began to realize that the question of control over Southeastern Europe was urgent to the United States as well. On 10 September W. Averell Harriman cabled Harry Hopkins that Soviet-American relations had taken a startling turn during the previous two months. Unless the United States took issue with the Russians, Harriman said, there was every indication the Soviet Union would take a belligerent attitude wherever its interests were involved.[88]

Ten days later, in response to a request by Hull, who was beginning to have doubts about the Soviet Union's long-range policies, Harriman elaborated on his earlier report. Moscow, he observed, was taking the position that it had the right to settle its problems with neighbors unilaterally. For the Soviets the term "friendly governments" meant something quite different from what was understood by the United States. In Poland it translated into Soviet domination—and no understanding on this issue seemed possible in the near future. Harriman also believed the Russians intended to have "a positive sphere of influence over their neighbors in the Balkans." Accepting the Soviet Union's contention that she had the right to penetrate her immediate neighbors for security purposes would logically lead from one country to another. The difficulty of limiting the process frightened Harriman. Molotov, he noted, was unimpressed by the American policy of noninterference in the internal affairs of other countries.[89]

[86] Farther east, the Soviets were pressuring the Iranian government to grant them exclusive rights to oil concessions in northern Iran. See Chapter III.

[87] Woodward, 3:139, 146-150; Churchill, *Triumph and Tragedy*, pp. 159, 208-209, 216; Sherwood, pp. 832-833; Bohlen, p. 161.

[88] Ibid.; FR, 1944, IV:988-990.   [89] Ibid., pp. 991-993.

Harriman recommended that the United States take a definite interest in problems arising over each country. He had in mind not only Poland, but Rumania and Bulgaria, where he suggested the United States strengthen its influence on the Control Commission, and take a firmer attitude toward Soviet transgressions. Such an attitude, he cautioned, required certainty that the American position was right, and prior understanding over how far the United States was willing to go in backing up its position.[90]

In sum, the United States government was unsure how to deal with the Balkan problem. Harriman's recommendations, while reasonable, were neither as realistic nor as practical as Churchill's. In fact, they were hardly more constructive than Roosevelt's earlier recommendation of consultative machinery. Churchill was no doubt correct in believing that such an arrangement, if established, would be "a mere obstruction, always overridden in any case of emergency by direct interchanges" between the Big Three. Without prior understanding, each situation would be subject to de facto control. Since Roosevelt was occupied with the presidential election, and reluctant to commit himself to a policy that would subject him to criticism at this critical time, Churchill took it upon himself to go to Moscow and talk with Stalin. His objectives were settlement on the Polish dispute, and reaffirmation of the earlier arrangement for spheres of action in the Balkans. Since the Soviet Union was responsible for military affairs on the Eastern Front, and since Britain's area of operation included Greece, an arrangement over spheres of action in the Balkans made good sense. Churchill mentioned these aims to Roosevelt in a telegram, although—perhaps to win the president's approval of the journey—he gave as his first object the clinching of Stalin's consent to bring Russia into the war against Japan.[91]

Roosevelt at first was willing to let Churchill speak for the United States, but Hopkins persuaded him otherwise. Charles Bohlen had pointed out to Hopkins that such authority would constitute a confession that European political problems were in Britain's and Russia's domains. At Hopkins' initiative, therefore, Roosevelt wrote Stalin (who had endorsed Churchill's proposed visit) to inform him that there was no question in which the United States was not interested, and that he

[90] Ibid., pp. 994-998.

[91] FR, 1944, V:118; Woodward, 3:146-150; Churchill, Triumph and Tragedy, pp. 208-209; Sherwood, pp. 832-833; Bohlen, pp. 161, 163.

regarded the talks as a preliminary to a meeting of the Big Three. Harriman would attend only as an observer; his presence would not indicate support for any decisions reached. As Roosevelt wrote Churchill, "I could not permit anyone to commit me in advance."[92]

Thus, when Churchill set out for Moscow, he had limited support for a difficult mission: to save what was possible of Eastern Europe. Since there was not much left to save,[93] Turkey and Greece were conspicuous in his thoughts. Churchill had considered asking President İsmet İnönü of Turkey to meet with him while he was en route to Moscow, for he wanted to try again to convince İnönü to bring Turkey into the war. But the Foreign Office dissuaded him, pointing out that Turkey could do nothing to shorten the war. Britain's aim was to keep Turkey within the British orbit and protect her from Russian demands which might endanger her vital interests and hence Britain's position in the Eastern Mediterranean.[94]

Greece was another matter. Churchill met with the Greek prime minister, George Papandreou, in Italy on 8 October—the day before he arrived in Moscow. Papandreou, like the Turks, was concerned about the failure of Bulgarian troops to withdraw from northern Greece. He believed the Russian Army in Bulgaria was encouraging such delays, and that "Balkan Slavism," backed by the Red Army, had become a "mortal threat" to Greece. He asked that the British intervene to effect the withdrawal of Bulgarian troops from Greece, and that they send a substantial number of troops to Greece to reestablish Britain's position in Greece and the Balkans. Churchill assured Papandreou that matters would soon be settled and the Bulgarians would be compelled to withdraw.[95]

Since negotiations between the British and the Russians over Bulgaria were prefaced by British demands, accepted by the Russians, that the Bulgarians withdraw from Yugoslavia and Greece, Papandreou's wishes were partly met. The terms of the Bulgarian armistice were

[92] Bohlen, pp. 162-163; Sherwood, pp. 832-833; FR, *The Conferences at Malta and Yalta*, p. 6; Churchill, *Triumph and Tragedy*, pp. 216-220; Woodward, 3:147-149.

[93] Lukacs, "The Night Stalin and Churchill Divided Europe"; Woodward, 3:119-120 and 4:185-201.

[94] Llewellyn Woodward, BFP, pp. 329-330; Woodward, 3:121 and 4:200; FR, 1944, V:899-900.

[95] Xydis, *Greece and the Great Powers*, pp. 55-56; D. George Kousoulas, *The Price of Freedom: Greece in World Affairs, 1939-1953* (Syracuse, 1953), p. 116.

agreed upon, and Greece could expect the withdrawal to begin soon. Churchill's other assurance, that matters would soon be settled, depended on the negotiations about to take place. When Churchill and Eden landed at Moscow on 9 October, and were received "with full ceremonial," the stage was set for the opening of the Moscow Conference.[96]

The October Agreement

That very evening the British and Russian leaders began discussions. The prime minister at once got down to the problem at hand. After endorsing the frontier line for Poland fixed at Teheran, and exchanging jokes with Stalin over the character of the Poles, Churchill talked about armistice terms for the Eastern European countries, such as Hungary, that had been "coerced by Germany and had not distinguished themselves in the war."[97] The two leaders agreed that Molotov and Eden would discuss these terms.

Churchill made it clear that he was particularly interested in Greece. Britain, he said, must be the leading Mediterranean power. Rumania

[96] FR, 1944, III:449-450; Woodward, 3:151; Feis, *Churchill, Roosevelt, Stalin,* p. 419; Xydis, *Greece and the Great Powers,* p. 58; Churchill, *Triumph and Tragedy,* p. 206.

[97] Except where otherwise noted, the entire discussion of the first meeting between Churchill and Stalin at Moscow in October is based on a British Public Record Office document titled "Record of Meeting at the Kremlin, Moscow, October 9th, 1944 at 10 p.m." (reference: Premier 3/434/7). Since the document consists mainly of indirect quotations from the conversations which took place, I have taken the liberty of using a few of them without quotation marks in order not to confuse what was said with what was recorded. Where quotations are used, as they are here, their intent is not to represent accurately what was said by the principals, but rather to prevent any distortion of the recorder's minutes by further paraphrasing.

Note: It appears from reading the "Record of the Meeting at the Kremlin," that this is the document referred to in the *New York Times,* 5 August 1973, which reports Churchill's agreement in 1944 to concede Soviet hegemony over Poland in exchange for Stalin's support for British efforts to regain Hong Kong and to remain the leading power in the Mediterranean. The article confuses Soviet hegemony over Poland with Churchill's agreement (as fixed at Teheran) on the question of Poland's frontiers, and incorrectly ties this discussion to the spheres of influence agreement as well as to a hypothetical discussion on the Conference at Dumbarton Oaks. See also my letter to the editor in the *International Herald Tribune,* 6 September 1977. For further elaboration on this issue and on the percentages agreement in general, see Albert Resis, "The Churchill-Stalin 'Percentages' Agreement on the Balkans, Moscow, October 1944," *American Historical Review* 83 (April 1978):368-387.

was a Russian affair, but Greece was different. He hoped Britain might have "the first say" in Greece, as Russia did in Rumania. Stalin said he understood the importance of Britain's sea communications and agreed that Britain should have the first say in Greece. Churchill then observed that it was better to express their proposals in diplomatic terms for the phrase "dividing into spheres" might shock the Americans. What he wanted was an understanding with the marshal. If he could achieve this, he could explain matters to President Roosevelt.

At this juncture, Stalin mentioned Roosevelt's message, and noted the president's desire that Anglo-Russian decisions be of a preliminary nature. When Churchill argued that this should not prevent intimate talk, Stalin went on to say that he had noticed some signs of alarm in the president's message, and that on the whole he had not liked it. It demanded too many rights, and left too little for the Soviet Union and Great Britain—who after all had a treaty of common assistance with one another.

Briefly the men discussed the Dumbarton Oaks Conference, then Churchill raised the question of the interests of their governments in the various Balkan countries. Harkening back, perhaps, to Stalin's discussion with Eden in 1941, in which the Soviet leader expressed preference for the practical arithmetic of agreements over the algebra of declarations,[98] Churchill suggested a *modus vivendi*: that the Soviet Union have a 90 percent predominance in Rumania, that Great Britain have a 90 percent predominance in Greece, and that they share Yugoslavia on a 50-50 basis. Churchill wrote these figures on a piece of paper, added "Hungary 50-50," and then "Bulgaria—Russia 75 percent." Using his blue pencil, Stalin made a tick on the paper beside the percentage for Rumania.[99]

As discussion turned to "crimes" committed by Bulgaria, and the relative merit of the parts played by Britain and Russia in Bulgaria and Rumania during the war, Molotov brought up the question of Turkey, and asked whether it was relevant. This question was anticipated by the Foreign Office, which had a surer grasp of Turkey's role in British for-

[98] See FR, 1942, III:502; Woodward, 2:223.

[99] This brief discussion of the initial suggestion regarding the spheres of influence agreement is based on Woodward, 3:150, which in turn is based on Churchill's personal files in the custody of the Cabinet Office. The "Record of the Meeting at the Kremlin" and Woodward together are more reliable, and elaborate in more detail what took place, than Churchill's memoirs (see Churchill, *Triumph and Tragedy*, Book One, Chapter 15, "October in Moscow," pp. 226-243).

eign policy than Churchill. British officials realized that some modification of the Montreux Convention regarding the Straits was necessary;[100] they also thought that Churchill should not go out of his way to agree that Russian demands were justified. This he had done gratuitously at Teheran shortly after Stalin discoursed on the difficulty of preventing bad feeling in the Red Army unless a second front opened in the following spring.[101]

Now when Molotov asked if the question of Turkey were relevant, Churchill evasively replied that he had not touched upon Turkey. He was only saying what was in his mind. He was glad, however, to see how near it was to the Russian mind. When Molotov, ignoring this jibe, countered with the observation that the Montreux Convention was still in effect, Churchill observed that the convention was a Turkish question, not a Bulgarian question. Stalin now entered the fencing match. Turkey was also a Balkan country. As for the convention, it was obsolete. Japan was a signatory, and entitled to the same privileges as Russia. The League of Nations, under whose auspices the convention had been negotiated, was defunct. More specifically, Turkey's control over the Straits was too absolute—if she were threatened, a situation concerning which Turkey was the sole judge, she could close the Straits. Churchill, he continued, had expressed sympathy with Russian views on this question at Teheran. Now they were discussing the Balkans, and Turkey was a Balkan country. Was it not appropriate to discuss Turkey? Churchill agreed.

Stalin compared Britain's interest in the Mediterranean with that of Russia in the Black Sea. Churchill did not comment on this comparison, but expressed the thought that Turkey missed her chance after the Teheran Conference. He said he did not think that the Turks were very clever. But when Stalin remarked that Turkey had 26 divisions in Thrace and asked against whom they were directed, the prime minister was quick to retort that they were directed against the Bulgarians—who were armed, he noted, by French weapons taken from the Germans. It was not Britain's policy, he declared, to begrudge Russia access to warm-water ports or the great oceans of the world. Rather, the British wished to help the Russians. What changes did the marshal desire in the Montreux Convention?

[100] For a discussion of the Montreux Convention, see Chapter I.
[101] Woodward, BFP, p. 330. See also Churchill, *Triumph and Tragedy*, p. 242; FR, 1944, IV:1024; FR, *The Conferences at Malta and Yalta*, p. 328.

Stalin replied that he could not say which specific points required amendment. The convention was unsuitable and should be dropped. Required changes could be discussed if Churchill would agree in principle with his point of view. He compared Turkish control of the Straits to possible Egyptian control of the Suez in the future, or some South American republic's control of the Panama Canal. What would Britain or the United States do if those countries were given the right to close the canals? Russia's situation was worse. While he did not wish to restrict Turkey's sovereignty, he feared Turkey might misuse her powers to restrict Russian trade.

Churchill, agreeing in principle with Stalin's point of view, suggested that the Russians let the British know in due course what they required. He favored free access to the Mediterranean for Russia's merchant ships and warships, but he did not want Turkey to be frightened—a situation which would result, presumably, if such matters were to come out of a conference which Roosevelt had not attended. This, apparently, Stalin understood.

Churchill made it clear that if Stalin were to ask him at the armistice table for free passage through the Straits for merchant ships and warships, he would not object. The Montreux Convention was obsolete. Stalin said he was in no hurry; he merely wanted Churchill to know of the question's existence, and to admit the justice of Russia's claim. Churchill acknowledged that Russia had a moral claim, and suggested that Stalin tell Roosevelt what he had in mind.

Discussion turned to the question of Russian influence in Italy, but not for long. With the Balkans still uppermost in his mind, Stalin suggested that Britain's interest in Bulgaria was not as great as Churchill claimed. Was Britain afraid of Soviet intentions? Was she afraid of a Soviet campaign against Turkey? The Soviet Union, he noted, had no such intentions. After some discussion, Churchill suggested that Molotov and Eden go into the details later. Stalin agreed, and conversation turned to other matters.

Churchill and Stalin discussed Turkey only once again during the entire conference. Stalin raised the question of the Montreux Convention on 17 October, telling Churchill to keep it in mind. The prime minister said the convention ought not remain in force, and asked Stalin to state secretly what improvements he desired. Stalin said he would do so, and that his requirements would not be extravagant.

Churchill, apparently out of pique at İnönü's failure to meet his demands in Cairo a year before, discussed Turkey with more candor than
either Eden or the Foreign Office wished. In principle, the prime minister did not contest Stalin's wish, seeing revision as clearly necessary.
On the other hand, his endorsement was not the general one Stalin
might have obtained. Rather than agree that the Montreux Convention
should be totally scrapped, Churchill suggested that the Soviet Union
make known what changes it required. Those changes the prime minister favored (i.e., free access to the Mediterranean for Russia's merchant
ships and warships) did not depart drastically from the existing
convention.[102]

The real issue over the Straits was not revision of the Montreux Convention. In a war in which Turkey was neutral, merchant ships were
already allowed free passage through the Straits. Warships of belligerent
powers, it is true, were prohibited from the Straits if they were not acting under the Covenant of the League. But this rule had protected
Russia and, very probably, had actually helped her. The closing of the
Straits during the war, moreover, was not a result of Turkey's legal control of the Straits or of Turkey's failure to meet its obligations in
administering the Straits regime, but rather of Germany's control of the
Aegean. Thus, Stalin appeared to be motivated less by an intolerable
situation and more by earlier, traditional interests—he was trying to
secure recognition of Russia's as yet undefined postwar aspirations at
the Straits. By being specific in his endorsement of Russia's aspirations,
and suggesting that the kinds of desires Stalin required at the Straits be
spelled out, Churchill successfully parried Stalin's thrust. But only temporarily. The Turkish question would surface repeatedly in the next
few years.

Balkan questions also were far from settled on 9 October, and were
raised again the next day by Molotov. If Stalin liked arithmetic as a
way of doing business, so did his foreign minister, but with a much more
dogged attention to detail. Molotov opened a meeting with Eden in
characteristic fashion. If agreement had been reached on Greece and
Rumania, he was disposed to haggle over Hungary, Yugoslavia, and
Bulgaria. He asked that Russia's percentage with regard to Hungary be
75 percent. Eden said he wanted to think it over, and turned to the

[102] See Woodward, 4:202-203. For provisions of the Montreux Convention then
in force, see Howard, *The Problem of the Turkish Straits*, pp. 1-35.

armistice with Bulgaria. Molotov promptly asked that Russia's percentage in that country be 90 percent.[103] Eden said he was not concerned with percentages. The British, he complained, were unhappy over the situation in the Balkans, where the Russians always seemed to be presenting them with *faits accomplis*. Essentially, what Britain wanted was a greater share of responsibility in Bulgaria and Hungary than it had in Rumania; in Yugoslavia, it desired a joint policy.[104] As a consequence of these fundamental concerns, Eden refused Molotov's next two suggestions: (1) that Russia should have a 75:25 advantage in the three countries at issue, and (2) that Russia and Britain agree to the 50:50 ratio Britain desired in Yugoslavia, but at the expense of Russia's 90:10 advantage in Bulgaria. Eden could agree to the 75:25 advantage to Russia in Hungary, but the British wanted more of a voice in Bulgaria than in Rumania.[105]

The detailed bargaining that took place between Britain and the Soviet Union at the Moscow Conference may be quickly visualized with the help of the accompanying table.

[103] Woodward, 3:150-151, 349-351; Eden, p. 559. A Soviet historian, writing in 1965, denies that Stalin agreed to Churchill's proposal, or that anything more was said about the matter. He cites a Soviet article, based on unpublished documents, which says that neither Churchill's table nor any agreement on the issue was mentioned in the Soviets' record of the talks (V. Trukhanovsky, *British Foreign Policy During World War II*, trans. David Skvirsky [Moscow, 1965, 1970], pp. 407-409). Ulam, *Stalin*, p. 600, apparently unaware of further discussion over the matter, argues that Churchill's notion of an agreement with Stalin was a delusion: "all that Stalin did was to put his 'tick' on a meaningless piece of paper."

[104] After a luncheon on 10 October, before their formal meeting, Molotov had a vigorous exchange with Eden over Bulgaria. Eden had objected to British officers being placed under house arrest in Grecian Thrace; Molotov, who said the Soviet government had no desire to pursue a separate policy, had begged him to believe that agreement could be reached on the whole Balkan situation. He then let Eden in on a secret: unbeknownst to the British, Tito had recently visited Stalin (23 September-5 October?) to reach an agreement concerning joint military action in Yugoslavia. Since Tito had been living under British protection, and his forces were armed and equipped by the British, Eden took exception to the fact that neither Tito nor the Soviets had told the British of the visit. While Molotov blamed Tito's peasant secretiveness for the secret nature of the visit, Vladimir Dedijer, in his book on Tito, says it was the Soviets who desired secrecy. Whatever the truth of the matter, this episode lends support to the thesis (which Walter Roberts—see n. 84—rejects) that the Soviets were in fact attempting to improve their position in the Balkans prior to the formalization of the spheres of influence agreement. Woodward, pp. 349-350; Eden, pp. 558-559; Churchill, *Triumph and Tragedy*, pp. 230-232; *FR*, 1944, IV:1410; Vladimir Dedijer, *Tito* (New York, 1953), p. 230; Roberts, p. 243; Milovan Djilas, *Wartime* (New York, 1977), pp. 405-407.

[105] Woodward, 3:150-151.

THE SPHERES OF INFLUENCE AGREEMENT

Date:	Original Proposal 9 Oct.	Subsequent Proposals 10 Oct.						Last Proposal 11 Oct.	Implicit Final Agreement	Changes from Original Proposal
Proposer: / Country	Churchill — USSR:GB %	Molotov — USSR:GB %	Molotov — USSR:GB %	Eden — USSR:GB %	Molotov — USSR:GB %	Eden — USSR:GB %	Molotov — USSR:GB (or) USSR:GB %	Molotov — USSR:GB %	USSR:GB %	
Greece:	10 : 90								10 : 90	
Rumania:	90 : 10								90 : 10	
Hungary:	50 : 50	75 : 25	75 : 25	75 : 25				80 : 20	80 : 20	{ +30% for USSR / −30% for GB
Bulgaria:	75 : 25	75 : 25	90 : 10	80 : 20	90 : 10		90 : 10 (or) 75 : 25	80 : 20	80 : 20	{ + 5% for USSR / − 5% for GB
Yugoslavia:	50 : 50	75 : 25	50 : 50	50 : 50	50 : 50		50 : 50 (or) 60 : 40	50 : 50	50 : 50	

When Molotov suggested a 75:25 Russian advantage in Bulgaria, in return for a 60:40 Russian advantage in Yugoslavia, Eden again refused, noting Churchill's concern over Yugoslavia. He countered Molotov's proposal with an offer of Russian advantages of 80:20 in Bulgaria and 75:25 in Hungary for a 50:50 ratio in Yugoslavia. Reverting to his earlier suggestion, which Eden had rejected, Molotov was willing to accept a 50:50 ratio in Yugoslavia only if Russia received a 90:10 advantage in Bulgaria. Eden had his choice of parity in Yugoslavia at the expense of Russia's 90:10 advantage in Bulgaria, or a Russian advantage of 60:40 in Yugoslavia in return for cutting the Russian advantage in Bulgaria to 75:25. The meeting on 10 October ended with Eden again explaining that his concern was not precise percentages so much as it was a greater interest (i.e., influence) in Bulgaria than Britain had in Rumania.[106]

On the next day, Molotov's suggestion of a Soviet advantage of 80:20 in Bulgaria and Hungary in return for a 50:50 ratio in Yugoslavia was agreed to in principle. An understanding of what these percentages meant was also reached. Molotov, for example, understood the 80:20 figure for Bulgaria to mean that the Allied Control Commission would be under Russian control before the German surrender, and subject to joint control thereafter. Churchill, in a memorandum on the agreement, specified his understanding of the percentages: in Greece, for example, Britain would take the lead in a military sense and would try to help the Royal Greek government establish itself on as broad and united a basis as possible. In Yugoslavia, the 50:50 ratio favored the creation of a united Yugoslavia. Its aim was to prevent armed strife between Croats, Slovenes, and Serbs, and to produce "a joint and friendly policy towards Marshal Tito." The system of percentages was "not intended to prescribe the members sitting on Commissions for the different Balkan countries, but rather to express the interest and sentiment with which the British and Soviet Governments approach the problems of these countries." Churchill supposedly regarded the system as only a guide, and recognized that such a guide in no way committed the United States—whose president and secretary of state were informed of the agreement.[107]

[106] Ibid., p. 151.

[107] Ibid., pp. 151-153, 351-352; Churchill, *Triumph and Tragedy*, pp. 231-235; Francis Loewenheim et al., eds., *Roosevelt and Churchill: Their Secret Wartime Correspondence* (New York, 1975), pp. 586-588; FR, 1944, IV:1009-1015, 1018; Hull, 2:1458; Bohlen, pp. 163-164; FR, *The Conferences at Malta and Yalta*,

How, then, should the agreement be regarded, and what was its significance? To begin with, in spite of later criticism that the matter of percentages was unrealistic and puerile if not sinful, the figures arrived at did have some grounding in common sense.[108] As Churchill and Eden attested, they provided a rough guide to Allied influence in the Balkans. Allied influence, however, had long-range political implications. Churchill, certainly, understood this and was less than candid in his repeated stress on the agreement's temporary nature. Confronted with the Red Army's penetration of Eastern Europe, he sought to protect Britain's interests in the Eastern Mediterranean. The political implications of the situation were what led him to seek the agreement in the first place.[109] Stalin, too, recognized what was at stake. Six months later, he would tell Marshal Tito and Milovan Djilas: "This war is not as in the past; whoever occupies a territory also imposes on it his own social system. Everyone imposes his own system as far as his army can reach. It cannot be otherwise." What he described in April 1945 was already true in 1944.[110] Roosevelt was alerted to the agreement's political impli-

p. 104; W. Averell Harriman and Elie Abel, *Special Envoy to Churchill and Stalin, 1941-1946* (New York, 1975), pp. 356-358.

[108] John Lukacs, "The Night Stalin and Churchill Divided Europe"; Wolfe, pp. 15-16; Arthur Schlesinger, Jr., "Origins of the Cold War," *Foreign Affairs* 46 (October 1967): 26 ff.; Ulam, *Expansion and Coexistence*, pp. 364-365; Bohlen, pp. 163-164.

[109] John Wheeler-Bennett and Anthony Nicholls, *The Semblance of Peace: The Political Settlement After the Second World War* (New York, 1972), p. 198; Churchill, *Triumph and Tragedy*, pp. 233-235; FR, 1944, IV:1010-1011.

[110] Milovan Djilas, *Conversations with Stalin* (New York, 1962), p. 114. In his book Djilas observes that the key to Communism in 1944, after the rout of the invasion had passed and the war was being won, was "not *what* is being done but *why*." Much was capable of being rationalized, and only slowly did he come to realize Stalin's desire to subordinate everything to Soviet needs and aims. See, for example, Stalin's treatment of the Bulgarian Communist leader Georgi Dimitrov, pp. 33, 114-117, 176, 195.
The predominance of Soviet influence was recognized in Rumania in September 1944, in Bulgaria in October 1944 (with peace terms requiring Soviet approval), and in Hungary in January 1945. Stavrianos, *The Balkans*, pp. 812-813; C. E. Black, "Soviet Policy in Eastern Europe," *The Annals of the American Academy of Political and Social Science* 263 (May 1949): p. 154; Xydis, *Greece and the Great Powers*, pp. 56-58; Martin Herz, *Beginnings of the Cold War* (Bloomington, Ind., 1966), pp. 114-116, 121-122. Herz points out that the United States and Great Britain, by their actions in Italy, set this precedent for Soviet action in Eastern Europe. Molotov made this analogy plain. But see Ulam, *Expansion and Coexistence*, p. 360.

cations by his secretary of state, who feared an earlier version's long-range consequences. Influenced by Hull's logic, Roosevelt approved of the earlier agreement only after he had made clear that no spheres of influence were to be established.

By October, however, the situation had changed. W. Averell Harriman had warned Washington of Moscow's intentions to settle problems with its neighbors unilaterally and to have a positive sphere of influence over them in the Balkans. The Soviets had demonstrated those intentions in Rumania in September, and would do so in Bulgaria in October. An informal arrangement clearly was better than nothing, and undoubtedly influenced Roosevelt's decision to let Churchill speak for the United States. MacVeagh's warnings that Britain and Russia would clash in the Balkans, Harriman's prophecy that the Russians intended to carve out a sphere of interest there, and Churchill's anxiety over the situation in Greece, all required some kind of response. Churchill's trip to Moscow was just the solution, which explains Roosevelt's initial reaction to it: to wish Churchill "good luck," and to tell him he understood perfectly why the trip had to be made.[111]

The president's decision on 4 October to reserve commitment, due to Hopkins' influence, was unaccompanied by any alternative to Churchill's proposal. Thus, Roosevelt's worries continued. "My active interest at the present time in the Balkan area," he wired Harriman on 11 October, "is that such steps as are practicable should be taken to insure against the Balkans getting us into a future international war."[112]

On the same day, Harriman sent Roosevelt a telegram in which he noted what steps the British and Russians *were* taking:

> Personal for the President. At dinner last night I got for the first time a more definite picture of what the Prime Minister and Eden have in mind working out with the Russians in regard to the Balkan countries and Hungary. In connection with this Churchill has been using the unpopular term "sphere of influence" but as Eden describes his objectives it is to work out a practical agreement on how the problems of each country are going to be dealt with and the relative responsibility of the Russians [and] the British. They stated that they have explained to Stalin and Molotov that they have no authority to commit us and that whatever is worked out will be submitted to us. They consider that on the basis of the armistice terms Russia will have a pretty free hand

[111] Lynn Davis, pp. 160-170; FR, 1944, IV:990-998; Bohlen, p. 162.
[112] Bohlen, pp. 162-164; FR, 1944, IV:1009.

in Rumania since our representatives on the Control Commission have little or no authority. In connection with the Control Commission for Bulgaria and Hungary, Eden is attempting to get Molotov's agreement to greater authority for the British and our representatives. As to Yugoslavia he is attempting to obtain Molotov's agreement that the Russians should not take any independent action but should join with the British and ourselves in bringing the factions together and continue to work with us rather than independently as the Russians have in the past. Eden feels he has made some progress with Molotov.

As to Greece the Prime Minister feels he has already obtained Stalin's approval to keep hands off and to use Soviet influence to prevent the Greek Communists from being a disruptive influence and to induce them to play a constructive part in a national government. Churchill and Eden both hope that you and Mr. Hull will be satisfied with the agreements that are worked out as they feel that unless something along these lines is done there will be political turmoil in these countries if not civil war, and the British will find most difficult situations to deal with. They put Poland in an entirely different category as the Polish question requires specific solution involving all of us. . . ."[113]

Clearly, while Churchill and Eden had no authority to commit Roosevelt to the agreement they were working out, they regarded the problem as one which did not directly concern the American president, and the solution as one which he had little choice but to accept. Time was running out and agreement was essential. Once an agreement was reached, diplomatic language was necessary so that the Americans would not be shocked, and Churchill could explain matters to Roosevelt —which he did on October 18.[114]

Stalin, for his part, resented Roosevelt's reservations concerning the conference. He felt that the president's message of October 4 demanded too many rights and left too little to the Soviet Union and Great Brit-

[113] FR, 1944, IV:1009-1010.

[114] Loewenheim et al., pp. 586-588; FR, 1944, IV:1011; see also n. 107. Churchill's understanding of the percentages is clarified in a memorandum he wrote, but did not send, to Stalin (Churchill, Triumph and Tragedy, pp. 231-233). Harriman was shown the memo on October 12, and was certain that Roosevelt and Hull would repudiate it (Harriman and Abel, p. 358). In a letter to the author, Harriman elaborated: "I can only underline the fact that my relations with Churchill were so intimate through the war years that I could be completely frank with him. It was obviously for that reason that he did not send the letter to Stalin" (W. Averell Harriman, letter to author). Rather than denying Churchill's understanding of what the percentages meant, the incident probably affirmed his belief that diplomatic language would have to be used with the Americans.

ain. His interpretation of the agreement with Churchill must therefore be considered in light of the following facts:

The Balkan problem was one between two realists[115]—Stalin and Churchill—and they were responsible for the negotiations.

The failure of the United States to participate actively in the conference was tantamount to a decision by default, since the Red Army was on the march, and the armistice terms which were to be decided as a result of the agreement would effectively spell out de facto control of Southeastern Europe.

Stalin had no compunction in 1939 and 1940 about negotiating a spheres of influence agreement with the Germans. He did not heed Roosevelt's plea to omit territorial matters from the prospective Anglo-Soviet treaty in 1942 until the very last, and then dropped territorial provisions only in return for the promise of a second front, whose delay had given him cause to act more independently of the president.[116]

At Teheran, agreements in principle were made regarding Poland's frontiers, subject to the qualification that political matters precluded Roosevelt's public participation in any such arrangements. Stalin chose to disregard these qualifications, and to regard the agreements as definite.[117] Since Roosevelt's absence from the Moscow Conference

[115] See Ulam, *Stalin*, pp. 559-560; *Expansion and Coexistence*, p. 357; Djilas, *Conversations with Stalin*, p. 73; A.J.P. Taylor, "The Statesman," in *Churchill Revised: A Critical Assessment*, ed. A.J.P. Taylor et al. (New York, 1969), pp. 15-60 (esp. 56-60).

[116] Hull, 2:1165-1174, 1266; Feis, *Churchill, Roosevelt, Stalin*, pp. 57-67, 174, 261-265; Wheeler-Bennett and Nicholls, pp. 44-50; Eden, pp. 335-352, 376, 382-383; FR, 1941, I:192-195; FR, 1942, III:505-512, 533, 542-543, 558-560, 564-569, 577, 583, 612-614; Woodward, 2:28-54, 220-254, 258-262; Lynn Davis, p. 23; *Correspondence Between the Chairman of the Council of Ministers of the U.S.S.R. and the Presidents of the U.S.A. and the Prime Ministers of Great Britain During the Great Patriotic War of 1941-1945*, 2 vols. (Moscow, 1957), 1:40-41, 44-45, 48-50; 2:22-25; Sherwood, p. 526; George Kennan, *Russia and the West Under Lenin and Stalin* (New York, 1961), pp. 335-336; Bohlen, pp. 123-124; Leahy, p. 185; John Gaddis, *The United States and the Origins of the Cold War, 1941-1947* (New York, 1972), pp. 134-135. For the effects of the second front's delay, see James MacGregor Burns, *Roosevelt: The Soldier of Freedom* (New York, 1970), pp. 374, 422, 593, 609; and Djilas, *Conversations with Stalin*, p. 46. In fairness, it must be argued that Churchill could have used the second front argument, too (Churchill, *The Hinge of Fate*, p. 493). For a criticism of Burns' second front thesis, see Robert Dallek, "Franklin D. Roosevelt as World Leader," *American Historical Review* 76 (December 1971): 1503-1513.

[117] FR, *The Conferences at Cairo and Teheran, 1943*, pp. 594-595; Feis, *Churchill, Roosevelt, Stalin*, pp. 284-287, 455, 459; FR, 1944, III:1323; FR, 1944, IV:922-998; FR, *The Conferences at Malta and Yalta*, p. 204; Hull, 2:1266; Ulam, *Expan-*

also was due to political matters, and since the president had approved the previous spheres of influence arrangement on the Balkans, Stalin may well have seen the Moscow agreement in the same context as those reached in Teheran.

Finally, later events and conversations tend to corroborate the assertion that Stalin (as well as Churchill and Roosevelt) acted within his understanding that the agreement spelled out de facto control of Southeastern Europe.[118]

Thus, when Stalin informed Roosevelt on 19 October of his useful exchange of views with Churchill on policy toward the Balkan states,[119] it seems clear he believed he had made a deal with Churchill, and he saw Roosevelt's reservations of 4 October as equivocations not to be taken seriously.

The State Department, meanwhile, ignored what had taken place. On 8 November 1944, Undersecretary of State Stettinius gave Roosevelt a memorandum on "United States Interests and Policy in Eastern and Southeastern Europe and the Near East." It asserted the independent interest of the United States and advocated maintaining six principles which were in effect an elaboration of the Atlantic Charter. The memorandum showed no understanding that, under present conditions in Eastern Europe, an inability to enforce such principles meant they were worthless. There was no recognition that the Soviets had achieved in fact what the State Department denied them in principle: a sphere of influence in Eastern Europe.[120]

---

sion and Coexistence, pp. 351, 356-357, 367, and The Rivals: America and Russia Since World War II (New York, 1971), p. 51; Kennan, Russia and the West, p. 335; Bohlen, pp. 150-151, 210; Leahy, p. 185; Wheeler-Bennett and Nicholls, pp. 154-157, 163-167; McNeill, America, Britain, and Russia, pp. 364-365, 407; Wolfe, p. 9; Gaddis, The United States and the Origins of the Cold War, pp. 134, 138-139.

[118] FR, The Conferences at Cairo and Teheran, pp. 594-595; Feis, Churchill, Roosevelt, Stalin, pp. 284-285, 450-451, 459; Bohlen, p. 164; FR, 1944, IV:1009, 1011, 1015-1016; for the assertion that the British and the Soviets acted within their understanding of the agreement, see: Churchill, Triumph and Tragedy, p. 293; FR, The Conferences at Malta and Yalta, pp. 103-106, 154, 293, 781, 849; FR, The Conference of Berlin (The Potsdam Conference), 1945, 2 vols., II:150-151, 1044 (hereafter referred to as FR, Potsdam I or II); Herz, pp. 139-140; Loewenheim et al., pp. 661-668.

[119] FR, 1944, IV:1019-1020.

[120] The Department took this position in spite of the fact that both Roosevelt and Hull were informed of the agreement, and that by 25 October the Secretary of State's Policy Committee also knew of the agreement in broad outline. Lynn Davis, pp. 150-156, 158-159, 170-171; FR, 1944, IV:1025-1026.

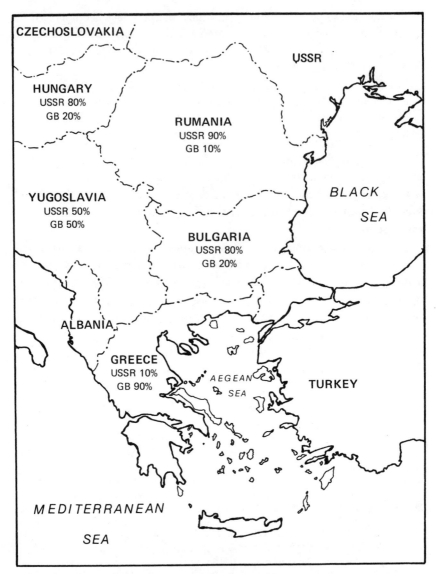

Map 3. The Spheres of Influence Agreement (October 1944)

The State Department's position raises the question of Roosevelt's attitude toward this contradiction in American policies. Where did he stand? The president was informed of the agreement's general outline and had a reasonable idea of its implications. Evidence suggests he agreed with Churchill that an arrangement similar to the one reported was available.[121] At the same time he endorsed the policy put forward by Stettinius, which contradicted the arrangement. How is this possible? One explanation is that Churchill and Stalin, aided by their own diplomatic styles, interpreted Roosevelt's policies in a manner that reflected the more practical aspects of his diplomacy. The State Department, on the other hand, derived its policies from Roosevelt's public pronouncements, and as a consequence reflected the more idealistic aspects of his diplomacy. In short, the contradiction in American policies begins with Roosevelt himself.

One of Roosevelt's biographers has found in the president's character what we have seen reflected in his diplomacy, and has elaborated on Roosevelt's capacity to incorporate within his personality both practical and idealistic qualities. He considers these qualities as characteristic not only of Roosevelt's mind and background, but of the society from which he sprang—a society whose traditions and diplomacy reflected the dualistic qualities of realism and idealism. Roosevelt's problem was that his faith, his moral credo, was a patchwork of attitudes that "crumbled easily under the press of harsh policy alternatives and military decisions." As a consequence, the congruity between his goals and his practical improvisations was less than he led many to expect.[122]

One could argue that Roosevelt proclaimed idealistic goals in order to obtain public support for the war effort. Aside from the fact that he believed in the goals he espoused,[123] he recognized that they fulfilled a public need: a peculiarly American need to justify either force or its potential use in terms of principles with which one could identify. But if such ideals were a necessary response to public opinion, they constrained Roosevelt's behavior in dealing realistically with territorial and political questions in Eastern and Southeastern Europe.[124] Because

[121] In addition to my argument, see Feis, *Churchill, Roosevelt, Stalin*, p. 451.

[122] Burns, pp. vii-viii, 549-551; Daniel Yergin, *Shattered Peace: The Origins of the Cold War and the National Security State* (Boston, 1977), pp. 45-48, 57-58, 72.

[123] Burns, p. 608.

[124] For matters relating to American attitudes and identity concerns, the necessity of characterizing American foreign policy in moralistic terms, and constraints

idealistic rhetoric created expectations which the president was in no position to meet, practical improvisations that fell short left him with two essential options: candor, which risked disillusioning the public, eroding support for his goals, and jeopardizing what Roosevelt saw as necessary mechanisms for the enforcement of peace; or keeping the matter to himself, which risked misunderstandings and recriminations but postponed disagreeable reactions, and which therefore seemed the lesser of two evils.

A more realistic American foreign policy, recognizing the problems of power, and confronting them directly rather than by default, might have been less likely to build false expectations at the end of the war. Both disillusionment and misunderstandings could have been avoided. But Roosevelt apparently did not feel he could educate the public about the realities of power.[125] A more realistic policy would have smacked of cynicism and traditional European politics, which neither he nor the American public believed in. Politically, such a course was worrisome, and its international implications were devastating; revelations of a division of Europe could have damaged the United Nations, as the secret agreements of World War I were damaging to the League of Nations, and the United States might have returned to isolationism.[126] As a result, Roosevelt let things slide. Churchill was given a free hand in Greece, Stalin was given tacit approval of his desires to control the rest of Southeastern Europe, and the State Department was encour-

---

on the conduct of American foreign policy, see: May, *Lessons of the Past*, pp. 9-15; Gaddis, *The United States and the Origins of the Cold War*, pp. 1-31, 149-157; Burns, pp. 359-361, 427-429, 547-548; Arthur Schlesinger, Jr., *The Imperial Presidency* (New York, 1974), pp. 105-130; Feis, *Churchill, Roosevelt, Stalin*, pp. 271-272; Lynn Davis, p. 382, 395; Gordon Levin, *Woodrow Wilson and World Politics*; Elliot West, "The Roots of Conflict: Soviet Images in the American Press, 1941-1947," in *Essays on American Foreign Policy*, ed. Margaret Morris and Sandra Myres (Austin, Texas, 1974), pp. 83-116; Louis Hartz, *The Liberal Tradition in America* (New York, 1955); Albert Hirschman, *Exit, Voice and Loyalty* (Cambridge, Mass., 1970), pp. 106-111; David Calleo, *The Atlantic Fantasy: the U.S., NATO, and Europe* (Baltimore, 1970), pp. 100-122; John Spanier, *American Foreign Policy Since World War II*, 4th ed., rev. (New York, 1971), pp. 3-20; Robert Bellah, "Coming Around to Socialism: Roots of the American Taboo," *Nation* 219 (28 December 1974): 677-685.

[125] It is important to distinguish between Roosevelt's firm grasp of the realities of power and his ignorance of the Soviet Union. See, for example, Bohlen, pp. 140-141, where the American diplomat notes Roosevelt's view of the Bolshevik Revolution as constituting reform from the "bottom." See also pp. 210-211.

[126] Gaddis, *The United States and the Origins of the Cold War*, pp. 134, 139-151.

aged to continue its idealistic pronouncements, while the American people were not prepared to recognize what had happened.

Conclusion

The problem consigned to Churchill and Stalin by Roosevelt in October 1944 can be seen as an extension of Britain's and Russia's historical struggle for power along the Northern Tier. Just as traditional interests explain Soviet demands on Turkey, so they explain Molotov's interest in the Balkans during his negotiations with Ribbentrop in 1940. They also shed light on the Soviet Union's motives in occupying Bulgaria in September 1944.

The designs of any Great Power on the Balkans, because they threatened Britain's strategic interests in the Eastern Mediterranean, made it necessary that she protect them. This logic had been true of the nineteenth century, and was true of more recent history, where it applied to the Germans as well as to the Soviets. Balance of power logic accounts for Britain's support of the Balkan Pact in the 1930s, and for her unconditional guarantee to Greece in April 1939. It renders intelligible her commitment of a large force to the defense of Greece in 1941—in spite of the fact that she herself was beleaguered. It illuminates Churchill's desire to invade the Balkans later in the war, and it explains why the British were so intent on effecting a stable government in Greece after the war.

We have dwelt at some length on the situation in Greece in order that its complexity can be appreciated. We have attempted to show how the chronic lack of stability in Greek politics grew out of Greek history —a history plagued by divided loyalties, by Great Power rivalries, by the Greek political parties' consequent orientation along Great Power lines, by divisive political and increasingly social schisms. While some of these factors contributing to Greece's instability were submerged during the Metaxas regime, they surfaced with a vengeance when World War II swept across the country.

First a battleground, then an occupied country, and then the scene of a bloody civil war, Greece—except for a brief moment in 1940-41—was never able to draw upon the cohesive bonds formed by successful opposition to a common adversary. Turkey, it may be remembered, had done just that during and after World War I, and had forged a common identity under Atatürk, who limited the Turks' aspirations and built upon their successful efforts. During World War II, that identity had served to cement an intangible but unquestionable national will in support of the government's policies, and had made potential aggressors (i.e., Germany and Russia) wary of the costs of interfering in Turkey. Greece, on the other hand, after her victory over Italy, had been subject to the devastating might of the most powerful army in the world, against whom resistance—for a country the size of Greece—was futile, as well as demoralizing. Once Greece was occupied, German brutality, conjoined with the absence of any cohesive bonds that might have united Greeks against the forces of occupation, led to the renaissance of political and social schisms endemic to Greek politics—schisms which the forces of war brutally catalyzed.

As far as the British were concerned, the forces of war reaffirmed the value of securing sea communications in the Eastern Mediterranean. Thus, as the war progressed, as the German Army began to fall back, and as the Red Army pushed inexorably westward, the British transferred their preoccupations from German back to Russian intentions in the area. The safeguarding of Britain's imperial lifeline in the Mediterranean remained an axiom of her strategic thinking.

The only difficulty with an axiom in foreign policy is implementing it. The Foreign Office's 1943 proposal of a regency might have solved Britain's problems in Greece, but the king of Greece, with Roosevelt's support, prevented its implementation. Churchill, temporarily seduced by the plan, then reverted to his earlier solution—reliance on King George as a source of stability in postwar Greece. Measures toward this end included support of the Papandreou Government of National Unity, and an attempt to arrive at some understanding with Stalin.

Anxiety over Russian intentions had surfaced not only in the British Middle East Command, but elsewhere in the British government in May 1944. As a consequence, Churchill began to consider negotiations with Stalin over their spheres of responsibility in Eastern Europe and the Balkans. Concurrently, the British looked to the consolidation of their positions in Greece and Turkey. Increased authority accorded to the Government of National Unity by PEEA in August aided this policy. A request from Papandreou for British military support after the liberation facilitated it. By the end of September, Churchill had received Roosevelt's and Stalin's endorsements for the liberation of Greece by British troops. The spheres of influence agreement merely sanctioned developments in progress.

A day before beginning his conference with Stalin in October, Churchill talked with Papandreou in Italy. Again the latter asked for decisive British military intervention, and expressed fears over the projected aims of "Balkan Slavism." Papandreou, in the course of soliciting the British prime minister's aid, was distressed by the prime minister's failure to understand the political divisions in Greece. Papandreou understood that Greece was divided not between republicans and monarchists, but between those who followed either a revolutionary or an evolutionary approach to government. He saw tragic consequences in Churchill's support for the monarchy: the policy would serve only to divide Greece's moderate forces. But Churchill, confident of a satisfactory solution to the problems in Greece, appeared insensitive to Papandreou's insights. Perhaps this was due to his penchant for royalty; perhaps to his deep concern for the salvation of the British Empire—a concern which, under trying circumstances, may have caused him to look to stereotypic solutions that fit in with the longstanding ideology of the political elite to which he belonged.[127] Whatever the reasons, the prime minister rejected the Greek leader's recommendation of a regency; instead, he subjected him to a "royalist sermon" which expressed his fundamental attachment to the monarchy.[128]

Churchill's increasing reliance on the monarchy reflected Britain's growing concern for her strategic interests in the Eastern Mediterranean. One may grant that Churchill, in his conversations with General George Marshall, chief of staff of the U.S. Army, never expressly advocated joint action in the Balkans as a means of forestalling the Russians,[129] but this does not verify the absence of such thinking on his part. To say, as A.J.P. Taylor does, that "the policy of forestalling Soviet Russia in the Balkans was an invention of the post-war years," and that there is no contemporary evidence for it,[130] belies much of the evidence we have so far examined. That evidence includes not only the presence in the Foreign Office of traditional concern about Britain's role vis-à-vis Russia in the Eastern Mediterranean, but Churchill's continuing interest

[127] Irving Janis, *Victims of Groupthink: A Psychological Study of Foreign-Policy Decisions and Fiascoes* (Boston, 1972).

[128] Xydis, *Greece and the Great Powers*, pp. 53-57; Iatrides, pp. 64, 100, 129-131; Woodward, 3:401, 409-410; Andreas Papandreou, *Democracy at Gunpoint* (New York, 1970), pp. 53-54.

[129] Forrest Pogue, *George C. Marshall: Organizer of Victory* (New York, 1973), pp. 418, 517. Churchill did mention such action tangentially at the Second Quebec Conference in September 1944. Pogue, p. 437.

[130] Taylor, *English History*, pp. 573-576.

in Britain's position in Greece, his conversations with İnönü and Papandreou, his asides to his physician Lord Moran, not to mention his desire to arrive at some agreement with Stalin over the Balkans, and the thrust behind Eden's June 1944 memorandum on Greece and Turkey. If, as one writer asserts, Soviet attitudes toward the Warsaw uprising in the fall of 1944 caused the shadow of Warsaw to lie over British strategic thought,[131] it seems clear that one increasingly important object of that thought was Britain's position in the Eastern Mediterranean, where the sun still set on the Royal Navy. Churchill's desire to effect a solution to Greece's political problems originated from this mode of thinking.[132]

Churchill's solution, tragically, misread the complex situation in Greece. There, the constitutional question had polarized the population around common fears, which the prime minister's support of the monarchy only perpetuated. Had he been willing to force the king to nominate a regency council, and to pledge not to return to Greece until the constitutional question had been settled by a plebiscite, Churchill could have undercut fears in Greece of the return of an unpopular dictatorship, and undermined the anti-monarchist base of support upon which EAM/ELAS and the KKE relied. The British Foreign Office understood this, as did the United States State Department. So did the Greek prime minister, George Papandreou. Churchill did not. And President Roosevelt, if he did, refused to do anything about it.

As a consequence, Churchill's policies continued to hold sway in Greece, where Britain's influence was reinforced by the October agreement. Britain's historical rivalry with Russia in the region, cogent in the strategic thinking of both Churchill and Stalin, had been responsible for Stalin's diverting part of the Red Army to a secondary target in the Balkans, and for Churchill's recognition that an understanding was necessary to safeguard Britain's interests in the Eastern Mediterranean. Their traditional rivalry had helped create a military situation which had then prefigured the postwar alignments taking shape in Southeastern Europe. Complicating the postwar picture, however, was a problem of interpretation. While Churchill and Stalin thought their understanding would receive Roosevelt's sanction, the State Depart-

[131] Ehrman, *Grand Strategy*, 5:367-376, 386; see also Schoenfeld, pp. 226-227.
[132] See the discussion in Elisabeth Barker, *British Policy in South-East Europe in the Second World War* (London, 1976), pp. 111-125, for support of this argument.

ment thought otherwise, and Roosevelt's failure to resolve such differences helped to perpetuate misunderstanding over the matter. What would happen at Yalta, and the recriminations that followed, in part would be a result of the same problem. Because Roosevelt could neither concede portions of Eastern Europe to Stalin, nor deny them to him, he would, in effect, do both—the former through implicit understandings such as the one described; the latter through the promulgation of principles that were interpreted differently by the Soviets and by the American people. Meanwhile, as in Turkey, the State Department relied on principle as a means of safeguarding American interests in the Balkans.

III

~~~~~~~~

The Iranian Context

In Iran, as in Turkey and the Balkans, pursuit of national interests by the Great Powers was the basic issue during World War II.[1] This issue was at the heart of the long-standing rivalry in the region between Britain and Russia, and it accounts for their infringement of Iranian territorial integrity throughout the twentieth century. In 1941 it led to an arrangement somewhat similar to the October agreement on the Balkans—the division of Iran into spheres of influence. The immediate result, simultaneous occupation of Iran by British and Russian forces in August 1941, set the stage for a minor crisis among the Allies in 1944 and was the source of a major crisis among them in 1945-46. To comprehend what the Anglo-Soviet occupation did to Iran, and to understand how subsequent crises grew out of that occupation, it is necessary first to examine the antecedents of Great Power rivalry in Iran, and to place that rivalry in the context of the power struggle along the Northern Tier.

The Historical Background

Persia, like Turkey, has served for centuries as a focal point for Great Power rivalry; and like Turkey, her position in international affairs has been determined at least since the nineteenth century by the conflict between Britain and Russia in the Near East. Russia's expansionist policies and her need for warm-water ports clashed with Britain's need to maintain her line of communication in the Eastern Mediterranean and her desire to protect a vast area which stretched from the

---

[1] Iran, although it was always called "Iran" by the Iranians, was called Persia by westerners after the Greeks, who called Iran by the name of one of its provinces: Fars, or Persia. This tradition continued until 21 March 1935, when Reza Shah made "Iran" the official name of his country and requested that all countries follow his usage. In October 1949, his son, the recently deposed shah, allowed both names to be used. Before this change was made, Winston Churchill, in August 1941, had directed that the British use "Persia" in official correspondence to avoid confusing Iran with Iraq. Consequently, depending on what nationality an author is, and when he is writing, usage varies. Other than attempting most of the time to call Iran "Persia" before 1935, and "Iran" after, I have tried to force no systematic usage.

Persian Gulf to Tibet.[2] The conflict of interests naturally led to pervasive influence by both powers in Iran.

Around the turn of the century Persian nationalists resolved to end their country's subservience to foreign influence. Heartened by Britain's humiliation in the Boer War and Russia's defeat at the hands of the Japanese, they turned against their country's corrupt and autocratic government, convened a National Assembly (Majlis) and in 1906 drafted a constitution. Unfortunately, foreign influence was even stronger than they realized, and foreign interests were soon deeply involved in the internal struggle for power. When the reigning shah, backed by tsarist Russia, attempted to subvert the constitution, he found that his opponents had strong British support. British intervention followed and might have cost him his throne had it not been for the Anglo-Russia Convention of 1907.[3]

As in the past, factors which prompted this agreement were beyond Persia's control: the British for years had wanted a compromise, and feared the Germans, who seemed determined to penetrate the Middle East. The Russians were reeling from their defeat by the Japanese. Turning west, they hoped for a new, friendly British attitude toward their ambitions at the Straits. These considerations led Britain and Russia to bury some of their differences—not only in Persia, but in Afghanistan and Tibet as well. In the resulting division, Persia was partitioned into zones of political and economic influence: a northern zone, which was Russia's sphere; a southeastern zone, which was Britain's sphere; and a central zone, which was neutral.[4] The two

[2] Firuz Kazemzadeh, *Russia and Britain in Persia, 1864-1914* (New Haven, 1968), pp. 5, 13-14, 22-24, 28-31, 219; Peter Avery, *Modern Iran* (New York, 1965), pp. 15-16; Taylor, *Struggle for Mastery in Europe*, pp. 418, 445, 483; Rouhollah Ramazani, *The Foreign Policy of Iran: A Developing Nation in World Affairs, 1500-1941* (Charlottesville, 1966), pp. 36-38; Briton Busch, *Britain and the Persian Gulf, 1894-1914* (Berkeley, 1967), pp. 114-132. Note especially Busch's discussion of the "Persian Problem" as an accepted factor in Near Eastern diplomacy, and the Russian "danger" as viewed from India.

[3] Avery, pp. 126-127, 134; Taylor, *Struggle for Mastery in Europe*, pp. 442-445; Richard Frye, *Iran* (New York, 1953), pp. 65-68; George Lenczowski, *Russia and the West in Iran, 1918-1948* (Ithaca, 1949), pp. 5, 42; John Marlowe, *Iran* (London, 1963), pp. 35-36; Ramazani, pp. 83-86.

[4] Taylor suggests the interesting generalization that "the Anglo-Saxons and perhaps the French believe in buffer states and the Germans and perhaps the Russians believe in partition as the best way to peace between the Great Powers" (Taylor, *Struggle for Mastery in Europe*, p. 239). This generalization may explain some of the problems between the Soviet Union and the West both in Eastern Europe and in the Near East after World War II.

131

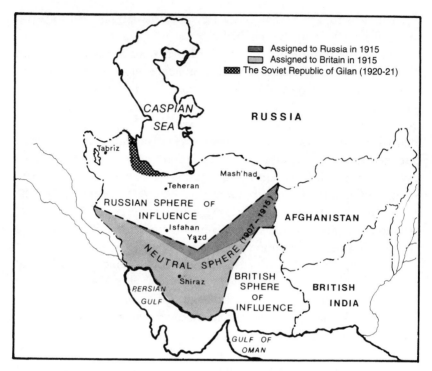

Map 4. The Partition of Persia (1907-1915) and the Soviet Republic of Gilan (1920-1921)

powers sanctimoniously agreed to respect Persia's independence and integrity.[5]

Time, however, revealed that such respect was only nominal, for the two powers continued to view each other's activities in Persia with distrust.[6] The Persians of course trusted neither power. When Bakhtiyari tribesmen in 1909 deposed the tsarist-supported shah, the Majlis (disenchanted with Britain's role in the 1907 partition) sought an ally in Germany, and advice from the United States. But during World War I, in spite of its official neutrality, Persia again was a pawn in Great

[5] Avery, p. 135; Taylor, *Struggle for Mastery in Europe*, pp. 442-445, 462, 475, 482, 507, 512-513; Frye, *Iran*, p. 58; Ramazani, *The Foreign Policy of Iran*, pp. 88-94. Besides a number of other stipulations, the 1907 treaty bound each power not to seek concessions in the zone allocated to the other. George Stocking, *Middle East Oil* (Nashville, Tenn., 1970), p. 6.

[6] This was in part a result of oil having been struck in the neutral zone in 1908. Because of their concern for Russian attitudes toward British interests in this zone, the British acquiesced in Russian interference in the northern zone, and remained concerned about their interests in the central zone. Avery, p. 158.

Power politics. In the Secret Treaty of 1915, Britain gave Russia the right to annex the Turkish Straits and the adjacent Ottoman territories; Russia in return conceded control of most of the neutral zone in Persia to Britain.[7]

Actual military operations in Persia and the Caucasus were of far greater importance to Persia than the abortive treaty of 1915. After the October revolution in Russia, when the Russian front fell,[8] Turkish forces filled the vacuum, and then withdrew from northwest Persia when British forces moved against them. When the British evacuated Transcaucasia in 1920, the Soviet regime quickly took control of the Menshevik republics of Armenia, Georgia, and Azerbaijan. In May of that year, the Red Army, after routing General Anton Denikin, occupied the province of Gilan in Persian Azerbaijan, where it aided the nationalist, anti-British Jangali movement under Kuchik Khan in forming the Soviet Republic of Gilan. Stalin supported the republic, but Lenin overruled him, and eventually ordered that Soviet support cease. The Irano-Soviet Treaty of 26 February 1921 (ratified in December 1921) formally renounced Soviet ambitions in Persia, and Bolshevik Russia returned to more conventional diplomacy in the region.[9]

[7] Taylor, *Struggle for Mastery in Europe*, pp. 512-513, 541-542; Lenczowski, *Russia and the West*, p. 5; Avery, pp. 141, 145; Kazemzadeh, pp. 678-679; Ramazani, *The Foreign Policy of Iran*, pp. 88-89, 96-138. Ludwig Dehio, *The Precarious Balance* (New York, 1926), p. 237, observes that in World War I Britain gave up considerable territory in the Balkans and the Near East in order to assure herself of Russian support against Germany. Obviously, in World War II, the balance of power in Europe again took precedence over Britain's concern for her lines of communication along the Northern Tier—but only to a point. Oil interests in southern Iran were always crucial, and the lifeline again came to the fore in 1944.

[8] At Brest-Litovsk, in December 1917, the German negotiator, Foreign Minister Richard von Kühlmann (who was born in Istanbul of an old German Levantine family, and who was deeply interested in the oriental aspects of the negotiations), adhered to Iranian demands that Russia evacuate Iran and give up tsarist concessions there. In January 1918, Soviet Commissar for Foreign Affairs Leon Trotsky told the Iranian representative at Petrograd that the 1907 agreement was no longer binding; at the same time, Lenin sent the Persian government a note of apology for previous misdeeds. It appears that one purpose of this move by Lenin was to incite Iranian Democrats against the British (Avery, p. 201; Ramazani, *The Foreign Policy of Iran*, p. 148). Needless to say, the Russian revolution brought the 1907 agreement between Britain and Russia to an end.

[9] Marlowe, pp. 39, 41; Frye, pp. 72-73; Lenczowski, *Russia and the West*, pp. 25, 52; Sepehr Zabih, *The Communist Movement in Iran* (Berkeley, 1966), pp. 1-42; Ramazani, *The Foreign Policy of Iran*, pp. 139-167, 186-192; Günther Nollau and Hans Wiehe, *Russia's South Flank: Soviet Operations in Iran, Turkey, and Afghanistan* (New York, 1963), p. 21. See also Chapter I, n.11. In his biography

133

Meanwhile, in February 1921, a nationalist intellectual, Sayid Zia ed-Din Tabatabai, seized power in Teheran with the help of Brigadier Reza Khan, a general in the Persian Cossack Division. Tabatabai, briefly prime minister, denounced an exploitative unratified treaty with Britain, while Reza Khan proceeded to crush the Republic of Gilan (from which, according to prior agreement, Soviet forces had departed in September 1921). Gradually gaining a predominant position in military circles, Reza Khan consolidated his position through the subjugation of local tribes. In 1923 he became prime minister, and by 1925 he had gained control over the army, the police, the Majlis, and the clergy. When the Majlis voted to make him shah, it merely recognized his assumption of sovereignty.[10]

Reza Shah Pahlavi (as he called himself) now turned his attention to the realization of three great objectives: a centralized government; modernization; and freedom from foreign influence. The problems which he confronted, rooted in the historical circumstances we have discussed, seemed almost insurmountable. Foreign rivalries continued throughout his reign, and their divisive effects were profound. Years of foreign encroachments had engendered hatred for, as well as a sensitivity to, the necessities of accommodation. This hatred, together with a suspicion that the throne was especially susceptible to foreign

---

of Lenin, Louis Fischer observes that Lenin favored the withdrawal of Russian troops from Persia in accordance with the February 1921 treaty. Against his wishes, Stalin reinforced Russian troops in Gilan. After Feodor Rothstein, the Russian ambassador in Teheran, protested that Persia was not prepared for a proletarian revolution, and that to expect one would complicate matters not only with the shah, but also with the British, Lenin agreed, whereupon Rothstein urged Reza Shah to suppress the rebellion. Although Stalin was furious, and raised the matter in the Politburo, his protest came to nought. Nonetheless, the episode is revealing insofar as it portrays at such an early date the nationalist-imperialist character of Stalin's attitude toward the countries of the Northern Tier. See Louis Fischer, *The Life of Lenin* (New York, 1964), pp. 420-421. For Article VI of the Irano-Soviet Treaty, see Helen Miller Davis, *Constitutions, Electoral Laws, Treaties of States in the Near and Middle East*, 2nd ed., rev. (Durham, N.C., 1953), p. 133, and Avery, p. 249, for a letter from a Soviet envoy to the Iranian Majlis on 12 December 1921 which clarified the article. See also the extremely useful OIR Report No. 4619, "Iranian and Soviet Interpretations of the Treaty of Friendship of 1921," 28 April 1948, *O.S.S./State I&R Reports*, vol. 7, II:5.

[10] Avery, pp. 203-204, 214-217, 220, 222-227, 235, 267; Zabih, pp. 40-45; Lenczowski, *Russia and the West*, p. 59; Frye, pp. 73-74; Marlowe, pp. 48-49; Kazemzadeh, p. 679; Ramazani, *The Foreign Policy of Iran*, pp. 171-205; Donald Wilber, *Iran, Past and Present* (Princeton, 1976), 8th ed., pp. 125-130; Arfa, pp. 90 ff.

pressures, made it difficult to foster the sense of trust necessary for building national loyalties. Poor communications perpetuated the insularity of local tribes, and their autonomy in turn reinforced the centrifugal forces militating against the shah's efforts at consolidation.[11]

Undaunted, Reza Shah tried to give his country the sense of national unity it lacked. He subdued regional tribes, bringing the tribal Khans to Teheran as hostages. He undertook reforms in industry, agriculture, and education. But his successes were limited: he never established complete authority over the numerous tribes, and most Iranians remained unaffected by his reforms. As a result, the landlord class retained its status, land reform was inconsequential, and basic agricultural problems remained. Nor was there any attempt at constructive political reform. Numerous political factions were permitted to appear, but they were concerned only with short-term political ends; having no common doctrine or platform based on the national interest, they failed to develop into genuine political parties. The reason, of course, was that the shah opposed political challenge; though he acted through the Majlis, he retained control over elections. As a consequence, although his reforms were revolutionary in character, they proved wholly inadequate.[12]

Compounding the difficulty of reform, foreign pressures interfered with the shah's attempts to centralize the government, while foreign interests exercised considerable pressure on the economy. Friction with the Soviet Union, due in part to the shah's policies[13] and to his resent-

[11] Kazemzadeh, p. 679; Avery, pp. 78, 108-109, 141-145, 158-159, 169, 181, 211; Ramazani, *The Foreign Policy of Iran*, pp. 216-257.

[12] The comparisons between Reza Shah and Kemal Atatürk, whom the shah admired greatly, are striking. Their problems, however, were quite different. See Chapter I. Avery, pp. 235-237, 271-272, 282-285, 313, 324; Wilber, pp. 125-130; Irene Meister, "Soviet Policy in Iran, 1917-1950: A Case Study in Techniques" (Ph.D. dissertation, Fletcher School of Law and Diplomacy, 1954), p. 654; Lenczowski, *Russia and the West*, p. 77; Marlowe, pp. 15-63.

[13] During the 1930s there emerged in Persia a group whose members had in common both a sympathy for Marxism and an aversion to dictatorships. Joined in 1936 by supposed Soviet purge victims such as Ja'afar Pishevari, former minister of the interior in the ephemeral Republic of Gilan, the leaders of the group came to be feared by the nationalist shah who eventually arrested and imprisoned 53 of them in 1937. Atatürk, too, faced domestic difficulties of this sort; but Atatürk exercised greater control over the loyalty of his people. In Turkey, the Soviets were careful to overlook Turkish repression of Communists. This was not the case in Iran, where the Soviets had no compunction about denouncing the shah's actions. Lenczowski, *Russia and the West*, p. 224; Zabih, pp. 46-70; E. P. Elwell-Sutton, "Political Parties in Iran," *The Middle East Journal* 3 (January 1949):46-47; Meister, p. 654; Ramazani, *The Foreign Policy of Iran*, pp. 234-240.

ment of Soviet ideology, was largely a consequence of economic rivalry, evident in a series of trade disputes which grew out of Iran's poor internal communications. It was much easier for northern Iran to trade with the Soviet Union than with other provinces—a situation which worked to Iran's detriment.[14]

If Russian influence over Iran was considerable, British influence was even greater as a result of special privileges in the oil industry. Oil was a factor in Anglo-Iranian relations as early as 1901 when Iran granted a concession to the Australian, William D'Arcy, seven years before oil was actually discovered in Iran in 1908.[15] The Anglo-Persian (later Anglo-Iranian) Oil Company was formed in 1909, and the British government acquired a majority interest in the company in 1914.[16] While the British failed to gain a supreme influence in Persian affairs after the war, they nonetheless exercised significant control through the Anglo-Iranian Oil Company (AIOC). The AIOC was an important factor in the shah's economic program, and by the outbreak of World War II it employed 20,000 men.[17]

One writer has described the situation in Iran between 1925 and 1941 as an "armed truce" between the powerful forces of Iranian nationalism, conservative British imperialism, and dynamic Soviet Communism. Better than anyone, the shah understood that he had to balance British and Russian pressures, and that he had to rely on third powers as counterweights against them. For this reason, he first turned to Americans for advice (the Millspaugh Mission, 1922-27), and then sought economic ties with Germany. In addition, he sought friendly relations with his Muslim neighbors.[18] By World War II Iran's trade with Germany

[14] Avery, pp. 239, 310; Ramazani, *The Foreign Policy of Iran*, pp. 216-241.

[15] The D'Arcy concession covered 480,000 of Iran's 628,000 square miles, and was to last for 60 years. The five northern provinces were excluded from the concession in deference to the Russians. Avery, p. 181

[16] It is worth noting that the Admiralty push for government control was engineered by Winston Churchill. Stocking, pp. 17-19.

[17] Avery, pp. 180-182, 203-205, 240, 321-322. A new agreement between Persia and Britain in 1933 gave the former a larger share of the profit and limited the D'Arcy concession to southwest Persia—an area which, by 1938, was restricted to 100,000 square miles. Although by 1930 Persia was the fourth largest producer of oil in the world, the future importance of Middle East oil was still largely unrealized. By 1939, Iran was responsible for 3.4 percent of world oil production (9.5 of 278 million tons). Stocking, p. 21; Stephen Longrigg, *Oil in the Middle East*, 2nd ed. (London, 1961), pp. 48, 59, 123-124; Avery, pp. 321-322; Benjamin Shwadran, *The Middle East, Oil and the Great Powers*, 2nd ed., rev. (New York, 1959), pp. 50-56.

[18] The Sa'adabad Pact of 1937 between Iran, Iraq, Afghanistan and Turkey,

rivaled that with Russia and testified to the shah's gradual success in his efforts to be economically independent of any one power.[19]

Symbolic of the shah's economic policies was the Trans-Iranian Railway. The shah financed it with a tax on tea and sugar, and carefully chose engineers from a selected list of nations in order that none secured undue influence over the project. Completed in 1938, after eleven years' work and a cost of $140 million, the railway was intended to improve Iran's fundamental problem of communications—a problem which the shah correctly saw as the root of most of Iran's internal and international difficulties. Extending 870 miles between the Caspian Sea and the Persian Gulf, it passed through 224 tunnels and over 4,000 bridges. As an official British source noted, it was an engineering accomplishment of awesome proportions:

> Between Andimishk and Do-Rud, a distance of 129 miles, the line climbs 4,000 feet, crosses the River Diz nine times, passes through 125 tunnels totalling over 35 miles in length . . . at one point there is a tunnel 2½ miles long in the form of a double spiral rising 167 feet, and at another point the line goes two miles to cover 328 yards in a straight line.[20]

Ironically, while the railway did little to help Reza Shah attain his objectives, it may have led to Great Power intervention in Iran. On 25 November 1940, one may recall, Soviet Foreign Minister Molotov

---

which was engineered by the shah and signed at his summer palace outside Teheran, was another attempt to escape from the traditional rivalries to which Iran, as well as Turkey and the others, had been subjected (Avery, p. 325; Ramazani, *The Foreign Policy of Iran*, pp. 272-275). The Germans were aware of this situation and attempted to exploit it. In 1937 they were considering an airline service from Berlin to Japan via Iraq, Iran, Afghanistan, and China. A German weekly air service was in operation by 1938. Adamec, p. 225.

[19] Lenczowski, *Russia and the West*, pp. 69-118; Avery, pp. 239, 310; Ramazani, *The Foreign Policy of Iran*, pp. 203, 209-211, 214-215, 228-231, 258-300; Woodward, 2:23. Ramazani points out some revealing statistics:

> In 1940-41 Iran's trade with Germany reached the highest peak in history, with imports up to 47.87 and exports up to 42.09 per cent of the totals. By that time Iran's trade with Russia had been reduced to almost nothing: imports were a mere .04 per cent and exports 1.17 per cent of the totals (pp. 283-284).

[20] Avery, pp. 302-303; Lenczowski, *Russia and the West*, pp. 145-166; T. H. Vail Motter, *The United States Army in World War II: The Middle East Theater: The Persian Corridor and Aid to Russia* (Washington, D.C., 1952), p. 331; Frye, p. 226; Kirk, *The Middle East in the War*, p. 148; DeNovo, pp. 297-302.

submitted to the German ambassador in Moscow a list of conditions for Soviet acceptance of the Four Power Pact outlined by von Ribbentrop earlier in the month. One of these conditions was the establishment of a base for Soviet land and naval forces within range of the Turkish Straits; another was that "the area south of Batum and Baku in the general direction of the Persian Gulf be recognized as the center of the aspirations of the Soviet Union."[21] The existence of the Trans-Iranian Railway may well have been a factor in activating traditional Russian aspirations.[22]

Where the importance of the railway in Soviet ambitions in 1940 is conjectural, there is no doubt of its importance to the Allies when they occupied Iran in August 1941. The Germans had invaded Russia on 22 June. A week later the British began to plan transportation of supplies to Russia through Iran. There was no better way to cross the country than the Trans-Iranian Railway.[23]

It was obvious that the railroad was vulnerable to sabotage, and the British and Russians both regarded the German colony in Iran with concern. There were 1,500 Germans in Teheran in August 1941, and their numbers were steadily increasing. The governments's strong pro-German sentiment heightened Anglo-Soviet concerns, which were aggravated by the shah's reluctance to allow essential supplies to pass through

[21] Sontag and Beddie, pp. 258-259.

[22] In addition to the factors listed above, still another may have been defensively oriented, and related to the publication by the Germans during July 1940 of captured French General Staff documents. Franz von Papen, then German ambassador in Turkey, speculates that Ribbentrop was trying to get the Turkish foreign minister, Şükrü Saraçoğlu, replaced by someone who was more pro-German. Whatever the reason, the Soviet press, with some distortion, depicted the documents as "revealing alleged Anglo-French intentions for an attack upon the Soviet Union, particularly for the bombing of Baku and Batum, implicating Turkey and Iran." At France's suggestion, Britain had in fact entertained the idea of bombing the Baku oil fields in order to prevent Russian oil supplies from being sent to Germany, but had ruled out such a possibility after assessing the risks involved and realizing the plan's doubtful efficacy. FR, 1940, III:209; Ataöv, pp. 76-79; Kirk, The Middle East in the War, pp. 446-448; Avery, p. 327; Woodward, 1:78, 101, 104, 108, 110-113, 454, 523, and 2:25; James McSherry, Stalin, Hitler, and Europe, 2 vols. (Cleveland, 1970), 2:67-70; von Papen, pp. 463-464.

[23] Although Britain's main concern in Iran was to protect its oil interests, the supply line to Russia was an important secondary one—especially since only Murmansk and the Arctic ports (which would freeze in winter) were otherwise practicable as supply routes and involved a dangerous crossing of the North Sea. Winston Churchill, The Grand Alliance (Boston, 1950), pp. 454-455, 463-464, 476-477, 484-485; Philip Swinton, I Remember (London, 1948), p. 175; Ramazani, The Foreign Policy of Iran, p. 290; Woodward, 2:25; H. Maitland Wilson, p. 135.

his country, and his flat refusal to allow the passage of foreign troops.[24] Sir Reader Bullard, British minister in Teheran from 1939 to 1944 and ambassador from 1944 to 1946, in his memoirs tells of Iranian respect for Hitler, and the pro-German sentiment of the press.[25] If the Iranian attitude could be explained by historical mistrust of Britain and Russia, it was nonetheless disconcerting to the two traditional rivals—especially when circumstance made them allies.[26]

Even before the German invasion of Russia compelled drastic revision of Anglo-Russian relations, the British had made unsuccessful representations to Iran about the German colony. On 2 June 1941, three weeks before the German invasion, Eden had invited Ivan Maisky, the Soviet ambassador to Britain, to visit him and discuss the international situation. Eden informed him of German concentrations against Russia, and Britain's determination to maintain its position throughout the Middle East, including Iran. He told the Russian representative that Germany was trying to create conflicts between British and Russian interests in the Middle East, and suggested that a mutual understanding would prevent their occurring.[27]

When the Germans invaded Russia in June 1941, Stalin, too, became concerned about the German presence in Iran. An understanding along the lines Eden had suggested suddenly became possible. After sending a note to Iran on the subject of the German presence, Stalin agreed to a British suggestion of a joint *démarche* to Iran. Such representations were made on 19 July, but with little effect. The Iranians feared acting contrary to their neutrality by expelling large numbers of Germans.

[24] The shah was unwilling to take any action which could be considered a breach of neutrality. Iran had declared neutrality in the European war on 4 September 1939 and in the Russo-German conflict on 26 June 1941 (Avery, pp. 326-327). See also Kirk, *The Middle East in the War*, p. 132; FR, 1941, III:393-394. Figures on the Germans in Iran present a problem. The Iranian minister in the United States believed that there were not more than 700. The British estimated the number to be about 2,000. The Russians estimated the number to be about 7,000 (FR, 1941, III:394; Woodward, 1:616; 2:11, 23-26). Harold Minor, who helped supervise their internment in the German embassy compound in Shimran, recalls that the number was around 900. Minor, letter to the author.

[25] Reader Bullard, *The Camels Must Go* (London, 1961), p. 72.

[26] German activities in Iran were turning it into a center for espionage. The fact that a number of German spies had recently arrived in the country, and that Iran had become a refuge for German sympathizers such as the Iraqi prime minister, Rashid Ali, contributed to Allied concerns. Ramazani, pp. 290 ff.; Churchill, *The Grand Alliance*, pp. 476-477; see also Bernard Schulze-Holthus, *Daybreak in Iran: A Story of the German Intelligence Service* (London, 1954).

[27] Woodward, 1:616 and 2:24.

Since the British thought that economic sanctions without the threat of force were useless—the Iranians would retaliate by cutting off vital oil supplies—they suggested that if their demands were not met, the two powers should resort to force. The Soviets on 28 July agreed to this suggestion. As in 1907, the course of international events again set the stage for the partition of Iran.[28]

The Occupation of Iran

In parallel notes delivered to the Iranian government on 16 August 1941, Britain and Russia demanded expulsion of four-fifths of the Germans in Iran. The two powers found the Iranian answer unsatisfactory, and at dawn on 25 August 40,000 Soviet troops entered Iran from the north while 19,000 British troops entered from the south to protect the oil fields of Ahwaz and the refinery at Abadan, the largest in the world. Joint notes delivered at 4:15 a.m. on the morning of 25 August by the Russian and British emissaries cited reasons for the occupation, promised respect for Iran's independence and territorial integrity, and announced the intention of establishing a supply route across Iran.[29]

There was little resistance to the occupation. British casualties were only 22 killed and 42 wounded, and a cease-fire was called on the third day. Meanwhile, with the dispersal of the Iranian Army—whose main mission was not combat but civil reform—a heavy traffic in arms began among the various tribes, including the Kurds in the western part of the country. The Iranian government's control collapsed and, as one historian has observed, "the normal exercise of sovereignty was so circumscribed by the demands of war as to be virtually suspended for the duration." As a consequence, the centrifugal forces (political, adminis-

---

[28] Avery, p. 327; Woodward, 2:24-25.

[29] A Soviet note handed to the Iranian ambassador in Moscow justified occupation on the basis of Article VI of the Soviet-Iranian Treaty. See FR, 1941, III:397-399, 403, 408, 424; Churchill, The Grand Alliance, pp. 484-485; E. P. Elwell-Sutton, Persian Oil: A Study in Power Politics (London, 1955), p. 83; Motter, p. 388; Bullard, The Camels Must Go, p. 227; Marlowe, p. 65. The recently deposed Shah of Iran has written that prior to the occupation Churchill dealt only with the problem of Germans in Iran; he did not explain the problem of a supply route to Russia, nor did he mention the German threat to India or to the oil fields in the south—which, by 1944, were producing 13,274,243 tons of crude petroleum a year (Mohammad Reza Shah Pahlavi, Mission for My Country [New York, 1960], p. 72; Elwell-Sutton, Persian Oil, p. 83). For the expulsion of Axis nationals from Afghanistan, see Adamec, pp. 255-260. The role of oil in Allied thinking about Iran and the Middle East will be discussed later.

Map 5. Approximate British and Russian Zones of Occupation (1941-1946)

trative, religious, tribal, economic) which had militated against centralization under the shah again came to the fore.[30]

His power undermined, Reza Shah Pahlavi had no desire to remain
on the throne, and he "abdicated" in favor of his son, Mohammad
Reza Pahlavi.[31] The British, Soviet, and American governments prompt-

[30] Kirk, The Middle East in the War, p. 132; Archie Roosevelt, Jr., "The Kurdish
Republic of Mahabad," The Middle East Journal 1 (July 1947):248; Avery, pp. 271-
272, 282-285, 305; Zabih, p. 71; Shwadran (2nd ed.), p. 62; War History Report,
S.D. 124.66, Records and Correspondence, Box 17, Confidential Correspondence,
Post and Lot Files for Iran, Diplomatic Records Branch, Department of State,
Washington, D.C. (Subsequently, this report will be referred to as War History
Report. Hereafter, all State Department records will be cited by the prefix S.D. [for
State Department], followed by the decimal file number of the document in ques-
tion. Records stored in Suitland, Maryland, and examined at the State Department
in Washington, D.C., will be designated as having come from the Post and Lot
Files. Otherwise, they come from the State Department decimal file in the National
Archives, where their official reference is: United States Department of State, Deci-
mal File, Record Group 59, National Archives, Washington, D.C.) See also "The
Tribal Problem in Iran's Domestic and Foreign Politics," 15 March 1945, R&A
No. 2597, O.S.S./State I&R Reports, vol. 7, II:2, for estimations of tribal popula-
tions and their locations.

[31] According to Sir Reader Bullard, the British ambassador in Iran, the Allies did
not arrange the abdication. The Russians moved on Teheran as a result of an agree-

ly recognized the new monarch but made clear that his continued occupancy of the throne was contingent upon good conduct.[32] Inexperienced and unable to rely upon traditional parties for support, the young shah faced tremendous difficulties, both internal and external.

Iran's ports, transportation, oil, capital installations, and currency were now contributing to the Allied cause, but at the cost of extreme hardship to the Iranians.[33] Famine and inflation, only the most noticeable consequences of occupation, were rife.[34] Disruption of the Iranian administration in turn created both the opportunity and the necessity for control by the occupying powers over many aspects of Iran's internal affairs.

As the war progressed, particularly after the Battle of Stalingrad, the historic conflict between Britain and Russia in Iran again came to the fore. The advent of the United States in Iranian affairs added a new and important dimension to this conflict, while the joint ideals which were supposed to govern Allied relations in Iran served mainly to confuse the issues involved. In the process of disentangling various elements of the power struggle taking place in Iran, it will therefore be useful to examine a number of factors crucial to the Allied occupation: the terms of occupation; the context and formulation of American policy in Iran; the background of American oil interests in the Near East as well as in Iran; and finally, the oil crisis of 1944, which clearly illustrated that nineteenth-century diplomacy was still the rule in Iran.

The Terms of Occupation

Soon after occupation began in August 1941 President Roosevelt took note of British and Russian assurances that Iran's territorial integrity would be respected. Secretary of State Cordell Hull, however, was dissatisfied with the terms of occupation and sought a formal joint British

---

ment with the British to occupy the city and pressure the government into ridding Iran of Axis representatives. Seeing the writing on the wall, the shah left of his own accord (Bullard, *The Camels Must Go*, p. 135). See also Shwadran, p. 60, and the discussion in Rouhollah Ramazani, *Iran's Foreign Policy, 1941-1973: A Study of Foreign Policy in Modernizing Nations* (Charlottesville, Va., 1975), pp. 43-44.

[32] *FR*, 1941, III:461-462.

[33] *War History Report*; Woodward, *BFP*, p. 314.

[34] Between 1936 and 1944 the cost of living went up 1,000 percent (Meister, p. 163).

and Russian statement. Ever mindful of principles, he thought that such a statement would have wholesome effects on the entire Muslim world while offering hope to the peoples of small countries everywhere.[35]

The Iranians, meanwhile, feared Anglo-Soviet intentions and consequently sought guarantees of respect for their territorial integrity. Freedom from foreign pressures, which had been one of the principal objectives of Reza Shah, became even more important to his son.[36] Fortunately for the young shah, his efforts to obtain assurances were supported by the American secretary of state.

The joint statement sought by Hull was secured when the United Kingdom, the Soviet Union, and Iran signed a Tripartite Treaty of Alliance on 29 January 1942 at Teheran.[37] The treaty consisted of nine articles and three annexes, all of which were compatible with the principles of the Atlantic Charter. It acknowledged the presence of foreign troops in Iran, but declared that the signatories would undertake to respect the territorial integrity, sovereignty, and political independence of Iran (Art. 1), and that Allied forces would be withdrawn from Iranian territory not later than six months after an armistice or peace between the Allied Powers and Germany and her associates, whichever was the earlier (Art. 5).[38]

The Iranian government was dissatisfied with the guarantees of this treaty. Similar promises had been made in 1907, and Iranians had good memories. They hoped, of course, for a formal American guarantee, but when the Iranian minister in Washington pressed for an American declaration on Iran, Acting Secretary of State Sumner Welles told him

---

[35] FR, 1941, III:406-407, 431-433, 435, 446.

[36] In addition to the fact that Iran was occupied, initial reports, denied by the Soviets, indicated that the Russians were sympathetic to and even assisting separatist movements in the province of Azerbaijan. For a discussion of Iran's diplomatic strategy of relying on a third power as a cornerstone against British and Russian rivalry, see Ramazani, *Iran's Foreign Policy*, pp. 53, 68, 70-71, 91.

[37] The United States ignored three separate Iranian requests to sign or take cognizance of the treaty. FR, 1941, III:468-477; FR, 1942, IV:263; Woodward, 4:412.

[38] Department of State *Bulletin* 6 (21 March 1942):249-252. For the slight significance the treaty appears to have had for the Soviets, see Bullard's discussion of his negotiations with the Soviet ambassador (Bullard, *The Camels Must Go*, p. 231). Once one acknowledges Soviet qualifications of the Atlantic Charter's principles, and recognizes the Soviet understanding that Britain was prepared to sidestep those principles, the insignificance of the treaty in Soviet eyes becomes more apparent.

an American declaration would be detrimental to Allied relations since the United States had no cause to believe that Britain or Russia had any designs on Iran.[39]

By May, however, the United States had reason to change its policy. A Kurdish rebellion broke out in Azerbaijan, and the American consul at Tabriz reported that conditions could not improve without Iranian troops, who were refused entry into Soviet-occupied Azerbaijan. The Kurds had obtained a considerable number of arms abandoned by Iranian troops when the British and Soviets entered the country. This fact and the absence of government control in northwest Iran provided the impetus to Kurdish rebellion.[40]

Fearing general disorder, the Iranian government as early as 6 January 1942 had requested that an American specialist assume direction of Iran's gendarmerie (rural police). When it became apparent that the government needed even more help, the Iranians, encouraged by the British, asked the United States for still more advisors. The government's motives in asking for American assistance were much the same as those which caused Reza Shah to turn to Germany during the 1930s: it wanted to improve Iran's chances vis-à-vis Britain and Russia. Within the next year, the American government granted Iran's requests. Wallace Murray, advisor on political relations in the Department of State and chief of the Division of Near Eastern and African Affairs (NEA), sent instructions to Louis Dreyfus, the minister in Iran, telling him that the United States looked favorably on Iran's desire for assistance. He further elaborated:

> Those who are from the beginning, or later become [,] officials of the Iranian Government will not, of course, be subject to any supervision by the legation, and it seems to us that their chances of success will be much greater if they are able to convince the Iranians that they are working solely for the benefit of Iran. Consequently, it should appear that they should not seem to have too close a connection with the legation. . . .
> Nevertheless, and I think I may properly underline the word, we are prepared to take a strong stand in support of any adviser who may feel himself faced with a problem which his own efforts have proven insufficient to resolve and which seemingly threatens the success of the mission.[41]

[39] FR, 1942, IV:273, 275; see also FR, 1941, III:393.
[40] FR, 1942, IV:222, 318; Archie Roosevelt, p. 247.
[41] Indications that the Iranians would request advisors came as early as 5 Novem-

The instructions were ambiguous on several points. How far were the advisors to go in assisting the Iranians? How much power were they to exercise? How much support could they expect from the United States in accomplishing their mission? There were no answers to these questions, and their omission would cause complications. For the time being, the Kurdish rebellion forced Iran to seek American assistance, which was granted; it also emboldened the Iranian government to make repeated protests to the Soviet government.

The Soviets at first refused to acknowledge Iranian protests, but they eventually directed their military authorities to work with the Iranian government, and permitted 1,500 Iranian troops to enter the Russian occupied area. In September 1942, the Soviets even requested that Iran send a brigade to the area, and reports from the American consul in Tabriz told of improvement in Irano-Soviet relations.[42] This trend, however, probably resulted from expediency, for the war in Russia was not going well. Germany was still on the offensive, and the Russians needed all their troops.[43] They also desperately needed all the supplies they could secure by way of Iran.

A year before, the United States had granted lend-lease to the Soviet Union.[44] Supplies were beginning to reach Russia via the Persian Corridor, at first under British direction, and later under the United States Persian Gulf Command—a service command which would include 30,-000 men at its peak. An essential part of the Corridor was the Trans-Iranian Railway, for it carried three-fifths of all tonnage that crossed

---

ber 1941 (FR, 1941, III:475). See also FR, 1942, IV:214-215, 222-263 (the telegram from Murray is on pp. 248-249); Woodward, BFP, p. 314. The Mills-paugh Financial Mission, whose purpose was to reorganize Iranian finances, is discussed in more detail later. For a general discussion of Iran's initiatives in re-questing various forms of aid, see Ramazani, Iran's Foreign Policy, pp. 72-90. For discussion of American advisors in Iran, see Richard Pfau, "The United States and Iran, 1941-1947: Origins of Partnership," Ph.D. dissertation, University of Virginia, 1975. Pfau is especially good at delineating the roles of and conflicts between the various American groups in Iran.

[42] FR, 1942, IV:319-324.

[43] It is worth noting that Stalin preferred to have Soviet, and then Iranian, troops rather than British troops in northern Iran, in spite of the fact that British troops would have freed five or six Soviet divisions and offered better security than the Iranians (Churchill, The Grand Alliance, p. 485). A study of the historical back-ground of Anglo-Soviet rivalry in Iran makes Stalin's preference understandable.

[44] On 10 March 1942 it had also been granted to Iran. For a good, brief discussion of lend-lease, see "Lend-Lease," by Sir David Waley in McNeill, American, Britain and Russia, pp. 772-789. See also George C. Herring, Aid to Russia, 1941-1946: Strategy, Diplomacy, the Origins of the Cold War (New York, 1973).

Iran to Russia during the period 1941-45. Cooperation between the Allies, of course, was absolutely necessary for the efficient operation of the railroad and other facilities in the Corridor. A few statistics make clear the importance of the project:

1. Between 1941 and 1945, more than 7,900,000 long tons of imports crossed Iran into Russia.

2. Of these imports, 4,159,117 tons were lend-lease goods, carried to Iran on approximately 700 ships.

3. The lend-lease items included more than 180,000 trucks and 4,874 airplanes.

4. British contributions numbered over 14,000 different items, including:
   (a) 3,000,000 pairs of boots
   (b) 360,000 tons of foodstuffs
   (c) 34 power stations (85,000 tons)
   (d) 37,000 tons of aluminum.[45]

Despite the fact that until August 1942 the Allies lost more ships from submarine attacks than they built, by the end of the year more than 2,000,000 tons of supplies had been delivered to the Soviet Union —350,000 tons through the Persian Corridor. Although less than a quarter of the lend-lease supplies that went to Russia before 1943 went via Iran, it is not presumptuous to believe that a large part of the 750 lend-lease tanks that arrived in time for the Battle of Stalingrad came via the Persian Corridor, and that cooperative efforts by the Allies in Iran were necessary for their delivery. By the end of 1942 more than 20,000 combat vehicles had been shipped to Persian Gulf ports, and the Persian Corridor was the most convenient route to Stalingrad. When one considers that Soviet armored strength around Stalingrad stood at 900 tanks on 6 November 1942, the supply effort gains in significance.[46]

Churchill had visited Moscow in August 1942, and his military advisors had then believed the Germans would cross the Caucasus

---

[45] Motter, pp. 4, 6, 138, 330, 498. The Allies even managed to make the corridor functional in two directions, bringing back on their return trips over 115,000 Polish prisoners, many of whom later formed the Polish Divisions. Swinton, pp. 177-178.

[46] McNeill, *America, Britain and Russia*, p. 220; Motter, pp. 4, 484, 488, 508; Kalinov, *Les Maréchaux Soviétiques vous Parlent*, quoted in McNeill, p. 219; Earl Ziemke, *Stalingrad to Berlin: The German Defeat in the East* (Washington, D.C., 1968), p. 50; Alan Clark, *Barbarossa: The Russian-German Conflict, 1941-1945* (New York, 1965), pp. 222-223.

Mountains and dominate the Caspian. Russia's future was grim, and was reflected in the lot of the common footsoldier. "We have no winter clothes," a soldier at the battle front had written; "there are five pairs of *ersatz valenki* per company—great big straw boots on wooden soles. They do not warm the feet and are almost impossible for walking. We have been swindled, and have been condemned to death; we shall die of the war or of the frost." But the Caspian and the Volga provided ready routes of supply. According to one Soviet general, one of the six reasons the Russians managed to hold Stalingrad was "the admirable organization—despite appalling difficulties—of a constant flow of supplies to Stalingrad."[47]

The Battle of Stalingrad was one of the great psychological if not military turning points of the war. It took a supreme Russian effort to throw the Germans back, and until the battle was won military necessity dominated Allied activities in Iran. As a consequence, traditional concerns were of lesser moment and played only a secondary role in the winter of 1942-43. British and Russian actions sometimes contravened their pronouncements endorsing the Atlantic Charter,[48] but justification could be found in the fact that war was approaching the Caucasus and circumstances dictated accommodation to necessity.

Once the battle was won the situation changed. Cooperation in Iran became less important. As the war moved westward across the steppes

---

[47] Churchill, *The Grand Alliance*, pp. 393-394; an anonymous letter from Stalingrad quoted in Desmond Flowers and James Reeves, eds., *The War, 1939-1945* (London, 1960), p. 489; Alexander Werth, *The Year of Stalingrad* (New York, 1947), p. 200.

[48] As early as October 1941, uncooperative Soviet behavior was reported to the Department of State. Besides demonstrating a general unwillingness to cooperate, the Soviets sealed off their area of occupation and pursued a course that included administrative disruption, sympathy for separatists, political intrigue, and propaganda. In October 1942, the Soviets made grain purchases which worked to the detriment of the local population. While the State Department assumed such purchases were based on dire need, later Soviet actions indicated that their intent was to use the grain as a political tool (FR, 1941, III:463-467; 1942, IV:165-166, 173-174; 1943, IV:357; S.D. 891.5018, Dispatch No. 552, 14 May 1943). British contravention of the Atlantic Charter's principles in Iran is less obvious. While it seems unquestionable that the British were involved in political intrigue, much of what they did, so far as American sources reveal, appears to have been a product of the American ambassador's unfounded suspicions rather than fact (FR, 1942, III:179-181, 188-189, 196, 217; 1943, IV:363-370, 600-602; Woodward, *BFP*, p. 315; Pfau, "The United States and Iran," pp. 98-101). The reason for this seems to be that in Iran, unlike Greece, the principles of the Atlantic Charter suited British (and of course American) purposes.

of Russia it became increasingly apparent that Allied actions in Iran were not in accord with the terms of the Tripartite Treaty.[49] The Soviets in particular, suspicious of British designs, pursued their own interests with little regard for the territorial integrity, sovereignty, and political independence envisioned in the Tripartite Treaty. Britain and the United States behaved differently from Russia, but not for purely altruistic reasons. Rather, the ideals to which they subscribed happened to coincide with their long-range interests in Iran.

Ideals and Self-Interest: the Context and Formulation of American Policy toward Iran

American policies toward Iran during World War II had many of the problems of American policies elsewhere. Reflecting President Roosevelt's attitudes and his manner of conducting affairs, they were often misunderstood, and officials charged with their implementation often disagreed as to what they were. For one thing, it was not always clear where ideals left off and practical interests began. For another, it was equally unclear who was responsible for effecting policy. Since policy was ill defined to begin with, confusion was inevitable. Because Americans had never before conducted diplomacy on a large scale in the Middle East, experience was wanting, and confusion was compounded. Nonetheless, through a careful examination of the circuitous process by which American policy toward Iran was actually formulated during World War II, it is possible to understand how confusion developed.

The problems of American policy toward Iran are epitomized by the sojourn there of General Patrick J. Hurley. As Roosevelt's special emissary to Stalin in the winter of 1942 he was the first Allied representative to go to Stalingrad. During his visit to General Vatutin's headquarters at the front, and much as he was wont to do at Perle Mesta's soirées, he leveled a long, savage Comanche war whoop at an honor guard, repeated the performance in the trenches, and thus, like a voice crying in the wilderness, prepared the way for Patrick J. Hurley in Iranian affairs.[50] Handsome, vain, and reckless, the native of Choctaw

---

[49] From the very beginning of the German invasion of Russia, Churchill and Stalin were more concerned with protecting their own interests and with furthering the general effort against Hitler than with establishing a postwar world order. Their backs were to the wall and they were fighting for the existence of their nations, not for the Atlantic Charter (see Chapter II, n. 116 and Chapter III, n. 83). As the war receded from Iran, they found no compelling reason to reorient their priorities.

[50] Don Lohbeck, *Patrick J. Hurley* (Chicago, 1956), pp. 176-179; Robert S. Allen

Nation, Indian Territory, who had once been secretary of war in the Hoover administration, now was happily beginning a diplomatic career under a Democratic president. The general liked to boast of his lethal speed on the draw in the old days in the West, and as a diplomat he soon gave ample evidence that he believed in equally simplistic answers to complicated international questions.[51]

Returning to Washington, Hurley found that the apparent success of his visit to Stalin had led to his rise in Roosevelt's esteem. Soon the general was on his way to the Middle East as Roosevelt's "fact finder." While in Cairo in the spring of 1943, after a brief tour of Iran, he sent Roosevelt a detailed discussion of Iran's problems.[52] Hurley stressed the conflict between British and Russian aspirations. The British wanted to retain a monopoly over their oil resources, while the Soviets wanted a warm-water port. Viewing this conflict in terms of Britain's declining influence in the Middle East, he suggested that the United States either play a strong independent role in Iran, or that it coordinate its efforts with those of the British—but under American leadership. Until now, Hurley asserted, the weight of American influence had been on the Soviet side. He cited as an example the fact that G-2 (Army intelligence) services in Iran had been dispensed with since they were objectionable to the Russians.[53] Planting a seed that was later to grow in Roosevelt's thoughts, he suggested strong action to encourage development of

and William V. Shannon, *The Truman Merry-Go-Round* (New York, 1950), p. 152; Russell Buhite, *Patrick J. Hurley and American Foreign Policy* (Ithaca, N.Y., 1973), pp. 106-108.

[51] Dean Acheson, *Present at the Creation* (New York, 1969), p. 133; Leahy, p. 227.

[52] Lohbeck, pp. 187-188; Buhite, pp. 107-109; FR, 1943, IV:363-370. According to Buhite, Hurley appears to have been "the first American official to whom Stalin made a promise to enter the Pacific War" (Buhite, p. 314).

[53] Edwin Wright, who was born in Tabriz, Iran, who had been principal of the American High School there for many years, and who consequently had contacts with many students in all walks of life, had been recruited by the O.S.S. and worked for Army intelligence in Iran during the first half of World War II. He recounts how the Soviets persistently objected to his presence in Iran, and how the intelligence unit to which he belonged was disbanded—at Soviet behest—on the grounds that an American intelligence unit was superfluous. This was shortly after the unit had trapped a Soviet Turk bribing railway officials to see copies of United States transport plans. See Edwin Wright, "A Personal Narrative—A Retrospective View," 2 April 1975 (in the author's possession). For information regarding United States acquiescence in withdrawing, at Soviet insistence, its Russian-speaking Consul in Tabriz in early 1943, see FR, 1943, IV:337-338, 345-348, 354-355, 360-362.

enlightened governments in Iran and other Middle Eastern countries, "with Russia sharing in a United States trusteeship for these local governments." He believed it essential that the United States uphold the Atlantic Charter, whose principles were necessary for attainment of the proper results in Iran. Hurley concluded his long discussion with four specific recommendations:

1. that Iran be assured of American insistence that the principles of the Atlantic Charter apply to Iran;

2. that Iran be permitted to join the United Nations in a declaration of war against the Axis;

3. that the American and British legations be raised immediately to the status of embassies; and

4. that American and British ambassadors compatible with each other and able to understand and promote British-American-Russian cooperation be appointed to Iran.

Upon receipt of the telegram, President Roosevelt sent a copy to Hull, asking for a recommendation on Hurley's proposals. The president received somewhat defensive comments which could be explained by the fact that Hurley blamed Louis Dreyfus, the American ambassador in Iran, for many Allied problems. In effect, he took a swipe at the State Department, indirectly blaming Hull for the deterioration of Allied efforts in Iran. Needless to say, the issues were more complicated than Hurley could appreciate.[54]

Allied difficulties in Iran were attributable only in part to a clash of personalities. Efforts to cooperate had been founded on the exigencies of war—exigencies whose priority was a matter of one's nationality. Transportation, for example, otherwise used to carry grain in Iran, was being used to carry goods to Russia. The Russians, meanwhile, refused to permit the province of Azerbaijan to deliver wheat to the south, and were themselves taking Azerbaijan's harvest. Currency (which had to be obtained from the Iranian government) and grain were critically short, and while money could be printed, there was no way to produce the grain—a problem which resulted in hunger and hard feelings. All of the Allies tangled on these complex and interrelated issues, and there

[54] Roosevelt Papers, PSF Box 91, File Folder. PSF, Cordell Hull, State, 1943, 31 May 1943 memo from Hull to Roosevelt; including 22 May 1943 memo commenting on Hurley's 13 May 1943 telegram.

clearly was room for improvement in Allied relations, but this is not to say that personalities were solely at fault.

Relations with the Soviets were becoming increasingly distant, not because of personality clashes, but because, as the German threat was pushed back, Soviet policies in Iran changed. As with Turkey, the Soviets grew more aggressive toward Iran when conditions became more favorable to their interests. Starting in January 1943 the Soviets began to negotiate agreements and contracts which consistently exploited the Iranians. The Soviets imposed arms, financial, manufacturing, and other agreements on the Iranians, and the Iranians, out of fear, had no choice but to accept.[55] At the same time, the Soviets stepped up political activity in Iran.

The focus of Soviet political activities was a group of liberal, left-oriented Iranian leaders, some of whom had been expelled from the Soviet Union in 1936, and all of whom had been imprisoned by Reza Shah in 1937.[56] When the new shah ascended the Peacock throne in the fall of 1941, he granted them amnesty. A few months later, on 30 January 1942, they founded the Tudeh (Masses) Party. Tudeh members included 3,500 additional Azerbaijani Turks expelled from the Soviet Union in 1936,[57] many Caucasians who followed the Russian armies into Iran in 1941, and leaders of minority groups who had crossed the border and organized nationalistic groups friendly to the Soviet Union. They were joined by a few intellectuals, some urban poor, many workers, and liberal groups. The Tudeh Party, they believed, would be a means of voicing what were in fact deep-seated grievances.[58]

Because of Azerbaijan's considerable industrialization, its large wheat production, and its lack of geographic barriers, it made a good base for Soviet economic penetration, especially when such penetration was reinforced by the Red Army. A secret study made for American military intelligence in 1946 explains how:

[55] FR, 1943, IV:628 ff.; 1944, V:311-316. For a discussion of some of the instruments of Soviet foreign policy in Iran, see Ramazani, *Iran's Foreign Policy,* pp. 92-96; Avery, pp. 383-384.

[56] See n. 13.

[57] These individuals had avoided imprisonment and obtained key jobs in northern Iran.

[58] Stanley Alpern, "Iran, 1941-1946: A Case Study in the Soviet Theory of Colonial Revolution" (Certificate essay, Russian Institute, Columbia University, 1953), pp. 27-29; Lenczowski, "The Communist Movement in Iran," *The Middle East Journal* 1 (January 1947): 29-30; Meister, pp. 136-137; Zabih, pp. 68-69, 71 ff.

The whole of Iran produces from 1.6 to 2 million tons [of wheat] per year, depending on the amount and distribution of rainfall. Little wheat is grown on irrigated land. Azerbaijan grows about 400,000-450,000 tons of this total. The average wheat consumption of the urban dweller is under 300 pounds (126 kilograms by official figures) and about 345 pounds (156 kilograms) per village dweller.

In normal good years the province exports 25,000-30,000 tons of wheat to Teheran (population 700,000) which consumes about 250 tons per day. Thus the normal Azerbaijan surplus supplies Teheran with 100 to 120 days of its wheat needs. Inasmuch as all Iranians depend largely upon bread for food, this assumes a disproportionate importance in the vital food needs of the capital. During 1941-1943 when the U.S.S.R. took all of this surplus, the Western Allies had to import from Australia, Canada, and the U.S.A. a total of 90,000 tons of wheat in order to avert famine in parts of southern Iran. *Re-allocation of the normal supply of Azerbaijan wheat to the Soviet markets would make this deficit permanent in the south and also give the Soviet government a lever of no mean value in forcing concessions from an underfed capital.* [Italics in original.]

Since Azerbaijan was populated by approximately one-fourth of Iran's 15,000,000 people, and included several large minorities—3,000,000 Turkic-speaking Azerbaijanis, 300,000 Kurds,[59] and tens of thousands of Armenians and Assyrians—it was ideal for political penetration as well. This was particularly true in view of the short-term Soviet policy of supporting autonomous movements among minorities.[60]

Through stenographic reports of Comintern congresses, official and unofficial Iranian documents, Russian periodicals and newspapers, and

[59] To convey the complexity of discussing tribes in the Near East, one need only cite one estimate that 1,700,000 Kurds live in Turkey, 1,000,000 in Iran, 250,000 in Syria, and 20,000 in Soviet Armenia. They are mostly Sunnis as opposed to the Azerbaijani Iranians who are mostly Shi'ites; they have their own language, and in many cases, closer ties with each other than with the Iranians. (Hugh Seton-Watson, *Neither War nor Peace: The Struggle for Power in the Postwar World* [New York, 1950], p. 70). See Chapter IV, n. 176 for an idea of the difficulty in assessing the number of Kurds in each country.

[60] The Russians dismantled frontier and customs posts between Iran and the Soviet Union, and set up military posts on the southern border of the Soviet-occupied zone. The de facto result was that the Soviet frontier extended deep into Iran. Edwin Wright, *Azerbaijan: A Case History of Soviet Infiltration* (Washington, D.C., 1946). This report was loaned to the author by Edwin Wright. See also Meister, pp. 133-140; George Lenczowski, "The Communist Movement in Iran," p. 41.

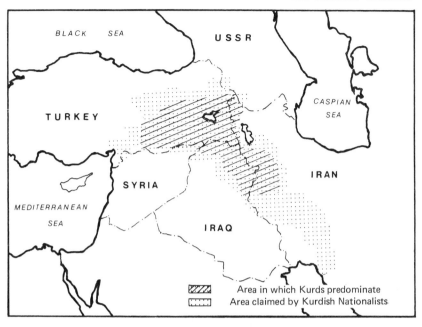

Map 6. Kurdistan
Based on William Eagleton, Jr., *The Kurdish Republic of 1946* (London, 1963), p. 37.

interviews, one scholar has documented the manner in which the penetration of Azerbaijan was carried out: trade unions were infiltrated; women's, workers', and peasants' organizations were formed; Communist propaganda was disseminated. While the Soviets until early 1944 seem to have followed no definite plan to realize their goals, they capitalized upon many movements. Intimidated by the Red Army, the local populace could not refuse cooperation.[61]

Membership in the Tudeh Party initially was ill defined, only its inner core being highly organized. The party ran on a liberal platform which proclaimed concern for the rights of working-class peoples. Apparently it accepted Soviet backing because it could not get such backing from the United States. It was opposed by a disunited hodgepodge of religious

[61] Meister, pp. 147, 645-673; Lenczowski, *Russia and the West*, pp. 197-199. The Soviets exercised control over local populations through their town commandants. These individuals, who were in every town, were responsible to the Soviet consul in Tabriz, who in turn was responsible to the political commissar of Soviet Azerbaijan. Interview with Robert Rossow.

153

elements, governing classes, southern tribesmen, independent trade unions, and merchants.[62] In Azerbaijan, opposition to the Tudeh Party was not allowed. Under the political guidance of the able Soviet consul-general in Tabriz, the capital of Azerbaijan, the Central Council of Trade Unions and the Tudeh Party (which had parallel organizational structures under the same central authority) became increasingly power-ful. Such power was not a consequence of popular support, but derived from the fact that refusal to join either organization brought threats—which the Tudeh Party and Central Council often carried out. People who did not bend to their wishes lost jobs, and some were expelled from Azerbaijan by the Red Army.[63]

Propaganda organizations such as "The Freedom Front" coalition of newspapers, the Irano-Soviet Cultural Societies, and the "Committee of Kurdish Youth" became increasingly pro-Soviet. After the Battle of Stalingrad, when the German menace began to recede and cooperation with the Allies became less important to the Soviets, the Tudeh organ *Rahbar* began to print articles damning reactionary rule, telling its readers they had been saved by Russia's October Revolution, and that the Red Army had delivered their fatherland. Until the oil crisis in 1944 (when the Tudeh Party was recognized as an instrument of Soviet pol-icy), such propaganda was gradually stepped up. One of the costs of this propaganda campaign was Allied unity. Soviet controls on the northern zone prevented anti-Soviet dissension in Azerbaijan,[64] but in Teheran disagreements began to surface between Britain and the United States on the one hand, and the Soviet Union on the other. In short, deteriora-tion of Allied cooperation in Iran did not result from personality clashes, as Hurley had reported to Roosevelt. Rather, it was a consequence of three factors: a relaxation in the critical situation at the front, a growing Soviet influence in the north, and the Allies' mutual suspicions of each other.

It must be observed in passing that Anglo-American relationships in Iran were sometimes strained as a result of the American minister's unfavorable reports about the British minister's pressure tactics. Despite some suspicion of British motives, however, most Americans in Iran

[62] Lenczowski, "The Communist Movement in Iran," pp. 31-41.

[63] Robert Rossow, "The Battle of Azerbaijan, 1946," *The Middle East Journal* 10 (Winter 1956):18; Meister, pp. 147, 165.

[64] Kirk, *The Middle East in the War*, p. 471; Elwell-Sutton, "Political Parties in Iran," p. 54; Lenczowski, *Russia and the West*, pp. 196-198. Assumptions that would have fostered Soviet suspicions of the Allies are discussed elsewhere.

assumed that the two nations were on the same side and were working for the same basic objectives. The common language helped to make relations easy, even warm. One example of Anglo-American cooperation was Sir Reader Bullard's inviting a representative of the American mission to attend his weekly staff meetings, at which very delicate political topics were discussed.[65]

Bullard himself, while not on really friendly terms with Louis Dreyfus, contributed substantially to Anglo-American solidarity. John Jernegan, one of the officers selected by Dreyfus to attend Bullard's staff meetings, has subsequently described Bullard as

> a real old-school British Middle Eastern specialist, with the virtues and the faults that characterized that breed. He looked upon the Iranians as grown-up children, not to be trusted very far but to be protected against themselves and guided in the way they should go. Needless to say, they should also be guided in ways that would protect British interests; that, after all, was what he was paid for. He was not averse to exerting pressure, through the British occupation troops or Britain's control of trade with the outside world, nor was he averse to the traditional methods of oriental intrigue, but he preferred the velvet glove approach when possible, rather than the Russian-style bludgeon. A plus from our point of view was that he considered close cooperation between British and Americans in Iran to be essential, and he practiced what he believed.[66]

American-Russian relations, by contrast, were impeded not only by language, but by Russian standoffishness, and by the emerging American belief that the Soviets were scheming to take over part or even all of Iran. The Russians did not help matters by making it difficult for Americans to get required permits to enter the northern zone—even when Americans were visiting their consulate in Tabriz. The British, on the other hand, did not require permits to travel in their zone.[67]

The American minister in Iran, Louis Dreyfus, was an honest, hardworking, idealistic man who looked on influence in terms of example

[65] FR, 1943, IV:319-329; John Jernegan, letter to the author; Harold Minor, letter to the author.

[66] Jernegan, letter to the author. Harold Minor, who was the first officer selected by Dreyfus to attend Bullard's weekly staff meetings, and who became a personal friend, recalls that when Alan Trott, a capable British diplomat who later became consul-general in Khuzistan and Fars, complained that an Iranian minister was not cooperating, Sir Reader, in his soft voice and unemotional style, replied, "Then, change him." Minor, letter to the author.

[67] Ibid.

155

rather than power. Suspicious of both Britain and the Soviet Union, and sensitive to slights, he often sent critical reports to Washington. While these reports created some discussion between the State Department and the British Foreign Ministry, they caused him no difficulty with Washington until Patrick Hurley's sojourn in Iran. Hurley told the Department that Dreyfus failed to promote good relations, and inadvertently made him a scapegoat for problems which required a more thorough examination.[68]

The need for such an examination had been recognized earlier in the year by John Jernegan, then the Iranian desk officer in the Division of Near Eastern Affairs. Jernegan had little experience in the Middle East. He joined the division in August 1941 when Iran was occupied and was only the eighth man in a regional office whose responsibilities included the Middle East, South Asia as far as Burma, and all Africa except Algeria and the Union of South Africa. The relative importance of these areas to the United States at that time was indicated by the fact that before being assigned to the Iranian desk Jernegan, with one other man, had been assigned responsibility for all Africa. While he had never been in Africa or Iran, Jernegan worked hard to overcome the limitations of a junior foreign service officer. He was aided by Wallace Murray, who had previously served in Iran, and who now headed the Division of Near Eastern Affairs, an office whose somewhat misleading name stemmed from the fact that it originally included all of the old Ottoman territories.[69]

At the beginning of the war, the American mission in Iran was small. Eighteen employees (native and American) served under a chargé d'affaires *ad interim*. They sent or received in that year a total of 214 telegrams and dispatches on such subjects as "Elimination of Latin Characters from Scientific Courses" and "Crown Prince Visits Faculty of Medicine." A year later when Louis Dreyfus went to Iran as minister, the American legation in Teheran was still a small affair; it consisted (aside from servants) of only four persons: Dreyfus, a secretary, a clerk, and an Iranian. There were also two Americans at the consulate in another part of town, but they did no diplomatic work. The contrast between these figures and those at war's end illuminates the increased interest of the United States in Iranian affairs. Instead of a mission, there

[68] Ibid.; FR, 1943, IV:363-370.
[69] Jernegan, letter to the author (Jernegan was posted to the American legation in Teheran in the summer of 1943); Foy Kohler, letter to the author.

was an embassy, and the ambassador headed a staff of ninety-six. The volume of telegram traffic had increased almost tenfold, to 1,965 for the year, and the telegrams concerned far more serious matters. The Near East Division, too, would grow. But in 1942-43 it consisted of only eight men, and John Jernegan was the first desk officer who had been assigned exclusively to Iran.[70]

Jernegan, who had come to share many of the suspicions of Dreyfus and Murray about Russian and British ambitions, had given considerable thought to protecting Iran from the two traditional rivals. American interests in Iran, however, were only vaguely defined until 1943. A memorandum by Cordell Hull in December 1942 noted simply that American policy "is in no way motivated by considerations of self-interest but is directed solely toward the furtherance of the common war effort and the preparation of foundations for satisfactory and lasting peacetime conditions in Iran, as in the rest of the world."[71]

Jernegan, who was aware that the United States had few concrete interests in Iran, nevertheless believed it his duty to save Iran. Young and inexperienced, he idealized the Iranian people and believed the United States could happily influence their destiny. On a more practical level, he hoped to secure a statement of policy which would resolve some of the problems between the State and War departments in Iran —problems which had served as a constant irritant to Dreyfus. The result of Jernegan's efforts was a memorandum Wallace Murray submitted to his superiors in early 1943[72]—a memorandum which was to have great influence in obtaining the agreement on policy that was needed.

While recognizing Iran's value as a supply route, a strategic location, and a source of petroleum, Jernegan pointed out the expediency of American policy regarding these matters. Broader considerations required a more assertive policy in Iran. Specifically, he suggested that Iran constituted "a test case for the good faith of the United Nations and their ability to work out among themselves an adjustment of ambitions, rights and interests which [would] be fair not only to the Great Powers . . . but also to the small nations associated with [them]." The memorandum noted the history of Russia's expansion, countered by

[70] Jernegan, letter to the author; *War History Report.*

[71] Jernegan, letter to the author; *FR,* 1942, IV:214-217. For emphasis on the unselfish character of Murray's interest in reform, see Pfau, "The United States and Iran," pp. 49-52, 94-95, 109, 162-163.

[72] Jernegan, letter to the author; *FR,* 1943, IV:330-336.

Britain's largely defensive reaction, leading to interference by both powers in Iran's internal affairs, and advocated strengthening Iran's political and economic organizations to ensure her survival vis-à-vis the great powers. Survival, Jernegan stressed, had become particularly difficult as a result of pressures from Soviet authorities in the northern provinces. He took due note of Soviet restrictions in Azerbaijan, their encouragement of the Kurds, their refusal to permit grain shipments to leave Azerbaijan, their plans to take over Iranian arms factories, and the fact that "a soviet could be established overnight in Azerbaijan if the Russians gave the word." This fact, coupled with British meddling in Iran's internal affairs, made him wonder about Iran's future.

Jernegan assumed that Iranian leaders based appeals for assistance largely upon such considerations. Since the United States alone was in a position to help Iran free itself from the traditional Anglo-Russian rivalry, he submitted that the United States had a vital interest in ensuring that the United Nations respected the Atlantic Charter. Such respect could be facilitated through an independent, positive program of economic and professional assistance—a program whose cost would be high, but insignificant when compared to that of the war and well worth the risks involved. The program, were it successful, would help prevent postwar friction, and would help make the principles of the Atlantic Charter effective. If, on the other hand, those principles were neglected, the foundations of peace would begin to crumble.

Secretary of State Hull on 17 February approved the memorandum and sent it to Dreyfus for comment. Dreyfus was delighted. He wired back that he was in complete agreement, "being struck, particularly, by the Department's reference to Iran as a proving ground for the Atlantic Charter," but with tongue in cheek he noted four obstacles: "(1) the Soviets (2) the Iranians themselves (3) the British and (4) the Americans." In spite of these obstacles, however, he expressed faith in the resiliency of the Iranians, and concluded that the United States should continue on its way with patience and balance, with its objective ever in view.[73]

Dreyfus meanwhile reported evidence of increased Soviet pressure on Iran, noting that the Russians were using obnoxious means to obtain their ends, and that they both suspected and resented the American advisor program. Considering Dreyfus's report, Hull on 31 March sug-

[73] FR, 1943, IV:343, 356-358.

gested that the minister inform his Soviet counterpart of the similarity between Soviet and American aims in Iran. The United States would be happy to discuss any differences, "whether at Teheran, Moscow, or Washington." While Dreyfus did as he was told, Hull's recommendations had little effect on the Soviet ambassador.[74]

Given the complexity of the Iranian situation and the history of the department's efforts to cope with it, one can understand why Hull was unimpressed with Hurley's telegram to Roosevelt a month later. Asked by the president to make recommendations on Hurley's proposals, Hull first observed that Hurley's statements were in substantial accord with numerous reports already received by the department. He was surprised to note that the United States appeared to be supporting the Soviet Union as opposed to Great Britain, and attributed this impression to the fact that the Soviets held themselves aloof from British and American efforts to resolve common problems. Citing Hurley's suggestion of strong action, Hull referred to the same recommendation in the Jernegan memorandum, the salient parts of which he quoted. He then addressed each of Hurley's four recommendations, declaring his agreement with all but the fourth. He recommended postponing any action on the appointment of an ambassador until he had had a chance to discuss the situation with Dreyfus.[75]

Hurley's recommendations, most of which were certainly not new, were nonetheless influential because they focused the president's attention on issues to which he had theretofore given little thought, and made it necessary for the secretary of state to address these issues with greater resolution. In August the increasingly critical political and economic situation in Iran and the American government's new strategic interest in Middle East oil led Hull to give the president a summary statement of the department's policy toward Iran. Believing that the United States should implement a more active policy, Hull wanted to make sure of the president's support.[76]

Hull's statement, prepared in the Near East Division under Wallace Murray's direction, derived from general ideas articulated earlier by

[74] Ibid., pp. 345-355.

[75] Roosevelt Papers, PSF Box 91, File Folder: PSF, Cordell Hull, State, 1943, 31 May 1943 memo from Hull to Roosevelt; including 22 May 1943 memo commenting on Hurley's 13 May 1943 telegram.

[76] FR, 1943, IV:377-379, 387-388. For the government's recent strategic interest in Middle East oil, see FR, 1943, IV:921 ff., and discussion of the issue later in Chapter III.

Hull, as well as from the Jernegan memorandum. It expressed the belief that the United States "has a vital interest in the fulfillment of the principles of the Atlantic Charter and the establishment of foundations for a lasting peace throughout the world." But it also noted "a more directly selfish point of view." It was in the interest of the United States that "no great power be established on the Persian Gulf opposite the important American petroleum development in Saudi Arabia."[77]

Although the United States government once thought it possessed an unselfish, solely altruistic attitude toward Iran, altruism now coincided nicely with self-interest: an independent Iran would serve as a buffer for American oil interests in Saudi Arabia. The department also had reason to believe that Britain would support its proposed course of action because British interests were served by an American presence between the Russians and themselves. Soviet support, on the other hand, was doubtful because the Russians distrusted American motives, and believed their own interests to be jeopardized.

The coincidence between idealism and self-interest did not appear self-serving either to the president or to lesser officials charged with implementing American policy.[78] The relationship between the two, however, touches on an issue whose roots are profound. Its essence, unappreciated by American policy-makers, is apparent in the very last sentence of the statement on policy toward Iran. "It goes without saying," the statement reads, "that the safeguarding of legitimate British and Soviet economic interests in Iran should be a basic principle of American action." At issue is the meaning of "legitimate," and the extent to which one's interpretation of it is a function of ideology.[79]

However bankrupt the promise of Soviet Russia had become under Stalin, Marxist-Leninist ideas clearly influenced the manner in which Stalin and other members of the Soviet leadership perceived the world. Marxism-Leninism and other variants of the ideology to which they subscribed called into question not only the distinction between ideals and self-interest, but even the very nature of the ideals themselves. Hence, the Soviets could hardly have agreed with American statesmen who characterized United States advocacy of the Atlantic Charter's principles as devoid of self-interest.

What, after all, were the principles of the Atlantic Charter? Were

[77] Hull, 2:1504; FR, 1943, IV:377-379.
[78] FR, 1943, IV:377-379, 386-388; Hull, 2:1504.
[79] FR, 1943, IV:379.

they not but reflections of a ruling class's self-interest? In *The Communist Manifesto* Marx and Engels had written:

> [The bourgeoisie] has resolved personal worth into exchange value, and in place of the numberless indefeasible chartered freedoms has set up that simple, unconscionable freedom—free trade. In one word, for exploitation veiled by religious and political illusions, it has substituted naked, shameless, direct, brutal exploitation.

The principles of the Atlantic Charter among other things called for the access of all states, on equal terms, to the trade and raw materials of the world.[80] Lenin, of course, saw free trade as giving way to monopolies and trusts in a hopeless struggle for spheres of influence in foreign countries, as capitalists strove to arrest the decline of profits at home. He saw the capitalist system falling apart as a consequence of such competition.[81] In short, the concept of free trade was only part of an ideological view advocated by the United States that the Soviets saw in a different light.

While the Soviets would never have described the Atlantic Charter as devoid of self-interest, they might have characterized it as a product of false consciousness. "Ideology," Friedrich Engels wrote in 1893, "is a process accomplished by the so-called thinker consciously, it is true, but with a false consciousness. The real motive forces impelling him remain unknown to him." Which is not to say the motives were unknown to Marx and Engels, or so they thought. They saw man's real motive forces as rooted in economic facts. Individuals who created ideologies, on the other hand, lacked insight. Under an illusion as to the real forces at

[80] The Atlantic Charter proclaimed eight principles common to the foreign policies of the United States and Great Britain. The first four (and most important) principles were: (1) that the two countries sought no aggrandizement, territorial or other; (2) that they desired to see no territorial changes not in accordance with the freely expressed wishes of the peoples concerned; (3) that they respected the right of all peoples to choose the form of government under which they would live, and that they wished to see sovereign rights and self-government restored to all those who had been forcibly deprived of them; and (4) that they would further all states access, on equal terms, to the trade and raw materials of the world. Langer and Gleason, *The Undeclared War*, pp. 677-688; Wheeler-Bennett and Anthony Nicholls, pp. 36-43; Lynn Davis, pp. 16-17; Hull, 2:1114-1126; Herz, pp. vii-ix; Feis, *Churchill, Roosevelt, Stalin*, pp. 24, 60; Churchill, *The Hinge of Fate*, pp. 327-328; Loewenheim et al., pp. 186-187, 311; FR, 1941, I:378; see also FR, 1944, IV:840-841.

[81] Karl Marx and Friedrich Engels, *The Communist Manifesto*, ed. Joseph Katz (New York, 1964), p. 62; Adam Ulam, *The Bolsheviks: The Political History of the Triumph of Communism in Russia* (New York, 1965), pp. 310-312.

work, they propounded through philosophical false consciousness an ideology which served the interests of the ruling class. The right of people to choose the form of government under which they live was thus meaningless if the people in question were victims of false consciousness. And the idea of sovereignty was hardly sacred if nation states were mere reflections of the political power of the ruling classes.[82]

Thus, many of the principles of the Atlantic Charter had little relevance or meaning to the Soviets and could be depicted as products of false consciousness. This helps explain why the Soviets accepted the Atlantic Charter on condition that its principles not deny them the frontiers they occupied when Germany attacked in June 1941, and it illuminates Stalin's suspicious attitude toward the Charter. In December 1941, while discussing with Eden the possibility of Britain's recognizing Russia's 1941 frontiers, Stalin had observed that the Atlantic Charter seemed to be directed against the Soviet Union. In fact, the Charter resulted from Roosevelt's desire to cut the ground from under American isolationist leaders as well as from his anxiety to avoid the mistakes of World War I, and appears to have been the product of expediency. Roosevelt probably took the Charter seriously, but the British saw it as a publicity handout and an answer to German propaganda, while the Russians were suspicious of it and gave it only grudging, qualified acceptance. Undoubtedly the relative vulnerability of the three countries, the range of opportunities afforded them by the war, and the different constraints acting on their leaders, dictated the degree of concern and realism each brought to such matters. It is nonetheless clear that the idealistic pronouncements of the Atlantic Charter concealed serious differences over common goals, and that their relevance to the Soviets was marginal at best.[83]

[82] Letter from Friedrich Engels to F. Mehring (14 July 1893), in *Socialist Thought: A Documentary History*, ed. Albert Fried and Ronald Sanders (Garden City, N.Y., 1964), pp. 324-327; Robert Tucker, *Philosophy and Myth in Karl Marx* (Cambridge, England, 1964), pp. 103-104, 137, 180-181, 192-194; Henri Lefebvre, *The Sociology of Marx* (New York, 1968), pp. 44, 59-88, 117-120, 144.

[83] See Chapter II, n. 116. See also: Loewenheim et al., pp. 57-58, 84; FR, 1941, I:360-369; Woodward, 2:198-206; Wheeler-Bennett and Nicholls, pp. 537-538; Sherwood, pp. 359-363; Sumner Welles, *Where Are We Heading?* (New York, 1946), pp. 1-20; Feis, *Churchill, Roosevelt, Stalin*, pp. 271-272. For discussion of Stalin's domestic political aims, and the role of those aims in reinforcing Soviet suspicions, see: Ulam, *Expansion and Coexistence*, pp. 314-378, 399-404, 418-419, and *Stalin*, pp. 645-650; Kennan, *Russia and the West*, pp. 239, 244; Nikita Khrushchev, *Khrushchev Remembers* (Boston, 1970), pp. 181, 212 ff., 246, 249,

From another point of view, the Soviets could have argued that efforts directed toward maintenance of world order, embodied in the principles of the Atlantic Charter, merely advanced American prosperity and power. Thus, the "Open Door" policy, which the United States claimed to follow in the Middle East, was really a form of imperialism, for the United States was competitively superior to other countries. Those countries accepting the principle of equal trading or exploitation opportunities for all could find themselves within what was tantamount to an American sphere of influence. In early 1945, Francis Lacoste, counselor of the French embassy in Washington, in discussing France's desire for a privileged position in Lebanon and Syria, made precisely this point. A memorandum of his conversation with the assistant chief of the Division of Near Eastern Affairs notes that:

> During this discussion, M. Lacoste made some "personal" observations on the American "open-door" policy. He said that at the turn of the century, when this policy was defined, the United States was only one of a number of powers in the world of relatively equal size and strength. However, we had now become so colossal that if the open-door policy were followed, the others would have been unable to compete with us. Consequently, M. Lacoste implied, other Governments would have to seek exclusive areas and advantages.[84]

The Soviets might have regarded this observation as an indication of weakness, but it applied to them as well. While the United States could happily uphold the principles of the Atlantic Charter, the Soviet Union was more chary of these principles for they could have applied in such a way as to discriminate against Russian interests. Lacking the resources, the technical "know-how," to compete with American interests, it was not illogical for the Soviet Union to resort to force to secure spheres of influence it regarded as rightfully belonging to it—especially when there was a threat of capitalist inroads into those spheres.[85]

393; Robert Conquest, *The Great Terror* (New York, 1968), p. 81; Roy Medvedev, *Let History Judge* (New York, 1971), pp. 90-91, 324-328, 361-366, 474; Djilas, *Conversations with Stalin*, pp. 105-106, 114-117; Alexander Solzhenitsyn, *One Day in the Life of Ivan Denisovich* (New York, 1963); Nicholas Bethell, *The Last Secret* (New York, 1974); Svetlana Alliluyeva, *Twenty Letters to a Friend* (New York, 1967), pp. 171, 180, 188-191, 195. See also Chapters IV and V for Maxim Litvinov's discussions of Stalin.

[84] FR, 1945, VII:1053-1054.

[85] This exposition is not meant to imply an acceptance of economic determinism; neither does it question the genuineness of American ideals, nor condone Soviet

This speculation about possible Soviet perceptions of the situation in Iran may account for what happened in October 1943, when Cordell Hull went to Moscow for a meeting of the foreign ministers. On 24 October, Hull took advantage of a British proposal for a tripartite declaration regarding Iran to advance the policy he had recommended to Roosevelt in August. The secretary suggested to Eden that a declaration should include support for foreign advisors and economic agencies in Iran; he also thought there should be separate declarations by the three powers regarding their intentions to withdraw their forces from Iran after the war.[86]

The Soviets were opposed to further assurances of Allied cooperation in Iran. Molotov stated that major decisions were impossible since the Iranians were not represented at the conference. Soviet Vice Commissar for Foreign Affairs Sergei Kavtaradze argued that several points about Allied cooperation were repetitions of assurances and understandings already made. Andrei Smirnov, former Soviet ambassador to Iran, was as intransigent as Molotov. The Iranian government, he said, had complete faith that the Allied governments would withdraw their troops. He also asserted that foreign troops were not interfering with the internal life of the country. The most that Hull and Eden could obtain was an agreement that a joint declaration might be considered at the forthcoming Teheran Conference.[87]

At Teheran less than two months later there was a change in the Soviet attitude. But before examining this change, it is worth exploring certain difficulties in the management of American foreign policy in Iran that were also brought to light at the conference. Louis Dreyfus, the American minister in Iran, was at the center of these difficulties. A competent diplomat in matters of representation, Dreyfus since 1940 had been responsible for restoration of full relations between Iran and the United States. His quiet manner, however, was displeasing to the military group which began to burgeon under the Persian Gulf Service Command (PGSC), headed by a hard-hitting officer, Major General Donald Connolly. Because Connolly and Harry Hopkins were friends,

---

heavy-handedness in Azerbaijan, Eastern Europe, or elsewhere. It is merely an attempt to examine what may have been the Soviet perception of the situation.

[86] FR, 1943, IV:400-405; I:730-736.

[87] FR, 1943, I:645-649, 674-676; IV:400-405. George Allen, a member of Hull's staff in Moscow, and later an ambassador to Iran, has written that the Soviets' intransigence made the American representatives seriously wonder about their intentions. "Mission to Iran," George Allen Papers, Duke University.

remarks and insinuations against Dreyfus passed from the general to Hopkins, and then to Roosevelt. Dreyfus's credit with the chief executive, already low because of Hurley's criticism, had bottomed out. Before he was shunted off to Iceland in March 1944, he suffered the indignity of being almost totally ignored at the Teheran Conference. "The man just won't get along with anyone," Harry Hopkins said of him. "We have enough problems on our back as it is at this conference without adding trouble by having Dreyfus around."[88]

A factor contributing to Dreyfus's diminished role was Patrick J. Hurley, who temporarily had been carrying out some of his duties. On his own initiative Hurley had suggested that the State Department ask the White House to assign him to Iran to iron out difficulties between the State and War departments, and between the United States and Great Britain. The War Department was agreeable and Roosevelt appointed Hurley his personal representative, with the rank of ambassador. In November, Hurley went to Teheran to prepare for Roosevelt's arrival. During the conference Roosevelt relied upon him when discussion turned to Iran. Roosevelt's comments to his son Elliot are revealing: "I wish I had more men like Pat [Hurley], on whom I could depend. The men in the State Department, those career diplomats . . . half the time I can't tell whether I believe them or not."[89]

Roosevelt's support was one reason Hurley was able to get results. His telegram of 13 May 1943 contained four recommendations for Roosevelt. All four were effected within a year: the first on 1 December 1943, with the Declaration Regarding Iran; the second on 9 September 1943, when Iran declared war on Germany, and on 10 September, when Iran signed the United Nations Declaration; the third on 10 February 1944, when the American (and British) legations became embassies; and the fourth on 21 March 1944, when Dreyfus was assigned to Iceland. Leland Morris was appointed ambassador to Iran.

Dreyfus and the legation had usually worked through a chain of command far removed from the president.[90] Since the president often ignored the State Department, the minister's influence was almost nil.

[88] Lohbeck, p. 109; Minor, letter to the author. Minor's information comes from first-hand knowledge and a conversation later with Dreyfus in Washington. See also O.S.S./State I&R Reports, vol. 7, I:30, 31.

[89] S.D. 123 Hurley, Patrick J./109½; FR, 1943, IV:392-397, 407, 410-413; Buhite, p. 124; Elliot Roosevelt, As He Saw It (New York, 1946), p. 193.

[90] For a chart which represents the organization of the Department of State as of 1 May 1945, see the Department of State Bulletin 12 (13 May 1945): 898-899.

Hurley, on the other hand, had direct access to the president—an asset which was invaluable, especially during the Teheran Conference. It was because of the relationship between Hurley and Roosevelt that the Declaration Regarding Iran was agreed to. Suggested originally by the Iranians themselves, and drafted by John Jernegan with Hurley's advice, the declaration was based on the abortive discussions at Moscow in October 1943. The British, of course, readily agreed to it. When the Soviets seemed doubtful, Roosevelt, at Hurley's request, made a strong personal plea to Stalin and obtained his consent.[91]

Why did Stalin change his mind? Perhaps because he could no longer use as an excuse Iran's absence and hence failure to participate in discussions. It is also possible that Roosevelt's personal appeal overcame lower level opposition. It is more likely that Roosevelt obtained Stalin's approval as a quid pro quo for a later Allied trusteeship on the Persian Gulf. The exchange was certainly not tantamount to an agreement, but Roosevelt may have hinted at the possibility of a trusteeship as an incentive to obtain Stalin's acquiescence—much in the manner that he used his "military proposal" concerning the question of a second front to encourage Soviet territorial claims in 1942.

Before signing the Declaration Regarding Iran, Stalin had already obtained concessions from Roosevelt regarding Eastern Poland and the Baltic states. He also had expressed interest in the question of warm-water ports. Roosevelt, who understood little of the details of such questions, had been sympathetic. Hurley's 13 May telegram had dwelt upon Russia's long-desired access to a warm-water port. Further, Hurley had noted that "at the peace table I believe Russia will insist on either a corridor to the Persian Gulf or to the Indian Ocean or[,] as an alternative[,] freedom of the straits from the Black Sea to the Aegean Sea." Recommending strong action to develop enlightened governments in Iran and the Middle East, Hurley had conceived of a United States trusteeship for local governments in which Russia would share. Roosevelt in November had talked to Stettinius about the possibility of creating such a trusteeship, but nothing had come of it. Nonetheless, it is possible that these thoughts were in the back of Roosevelt's mind as he worked to obtain Stalin's adherence to the Declaration Regarding

[91] FR, *The Conferences at Cairo and Teheran*, pp. 648-649, 840-843; Hull, 2:1506-1507; Elliot Roosevelt, p. 193; Leahy, p. 211; Lohbeck, p. 215; Jernegan, letter to the author; Minor, letter to the author.

Iran.[92] "The Teheran agreement was pretty definite," he later wrote Hull, "and my contribution was to suggest to Stalin and Churchill that three or four Trustees build a new port in Iran at the head of the Persian Gulf (free port), take on the whole railroad from there into Russia, and run the thing for the good of all. Stalin's comment was merely that it was an interesting idea and he offered no objection." The president did not mention Churchill's reaction. Had he felt free to say what he thought, the prime minister undoubtedly would have been less restrained than he was later when he wrote Roosevelt that rather than take any further initiatives in the matter, they might await Russian reactions.[93]

Whatever the reasons for Stalin's acquiescence, he endorsed the Declaration Regarding Iran, and on the last night of the conference, 1 December 1943, Roosevelt, Stalin, and Churchill signed it. In its final form it: (1) recognized Iran's part in the war effort, (2) recognized and affirmed the continuance of economic assistance to Iran, and (3) guaranteed Iran's sovereignty and territorial integrity according to the principles of the Atlantic Charter.[94]

While there was evidence that the Soviets had no intention of adhering to the declaration, Roosevelt had agreed to a statement of principle as a means of resolving Allied problems in Iran and obtaining support for the long-range goals of the United States. He was aware of America's strategic interests in the Middle East, and had been informed of Anglo-Soviet rivalry in Iran, but he had approached the question with little appreciation for the background or the details of the problem. Rather, he was willing to rely on a few principles which, he genuinely believed, would establish a framework for future cooperation. Whether because of his role in the project or his lack of expertise in Iranian affairs, Patrick

[92] They were again on his mind four months later when he spoke to his administrative assistant, Jonathan Daniels, of British and Russian fear of each other in Iran, the Russians' feeling that they had to have a warm water port, and Roosevelt's own suggestion regarding a free port. Jonathan Daniels, White House Witness, 1942-1945 (New York, 1975), p. 221.

[93] FR, 1943, IV:367-368; The Conferences at Cairo and Teheran, pp. 155-156, 162-164; 1944, V:483; Loewenheim et al., p. 500. For an indication that Stalin took the proposal seriously, see FR, 1944, V:455. For departmental reaction to this issue when it surfaced in December 1944, see FR, 1944, V:483-486; 1945, VIII:523-526.

[94] FR, 1943, IV:413-414. The Papers of Harry Hopkins, Franklin D. Roosevelt Library, Hyde Park, New York, File Folder: Book 8: Teheran (B) Meeting w/Stalin, 13 November 1944 memo by Harriman.

J. Hurley shared Roosevelt's views. At the end of the conference he was "pleased as a small boy who had just landed a big fish in a small pond."[95]

Dreyfus's assessment of the declaration's significance was more circumspect: "in many ways it [was] merely a pious wish," whose outcome would depend on concrete steps.[96] As in the case of the State Department's directive concerning advisory missions, its implementation was the crux of the matter.

Implementation of policy in Iran was a continuing problem for the United States. In spite of all the efforts at formulating a policy in 1943, it was not entirely clear what the goals of American foreign policy really were—it was not clear, for example, where ideals left off and practical interests began. As a consequence, many advisors who represented the United States in Iran had never been clearly instructed as to what they were supposed to achieve. Their difficulties were compounded by the fact that no one was certain who in Washington was coordinating American policy in Iran.

Roosevelt thought of Iran as something of a clinic for his postwar policies, one aspect of which was to develop and stabilize backward areas. The president had suggested to Hurley while they were in Teheran that he prepare a plan for United States-Iranian relationships which might be used as a pattern for American relations with all less-favored nations. In response to this suggestion, Hurley sent the president a long memorandum.[97]

Hurley's report envisaged the American purpose in Iran as that of helping the country to become a free, independent nation and of affording it the opportunity to participate in fulfilling the principles of the Atlantic Charter. Regarding those principles as the basis for postwar cooperation, he believed that free enterprise and "world-wide democracy" were approaching an "irrepressible conflict" with the forces of "world-wide imperialism," and that it was absolutely essential for the United States to arrive at an understanding of the kind of freedom it wanted in the postwar world. He submitted that the United States was

[95] Buhite, p. 128; Leahy, p. 227.   [96] FR, 1943, IV:415-416.

[97] S.D. 891.51A/1000 11 January 1944 letter from Arthur Millspaugh to Harry Hopkins; FR, 1943, IV:419-426; Roosevelt Papers, PSF, Box 53, Iran, 21 December 1943 Report from Hurley to Roosevelt. Page 5 of Hurley's report in the Roosevelt Papers contains two paragraphs on the contradictions between imperialism and the Atlantic Charter which were deleted from the version published in the Foreign Relations volume. T. H. Vail Motter notes that Roosevelt requested Hurley's permission to delete these views before circulating the letter (Motter, p. 442).

not fighting to save the imperialisms of others, or to create its own, but rather to bestow upon the world the principles of the Atlantic Charter—principles which apparently neither the Soviets nor the British accepted. As a consequence, he recommended imposing supervision and control over free enterprise in Iran "to protect the unorganized and inarticulate majority from foreign and domestic monopoly and oppression." If the American pattern of self-government and free enterprise could prevail in Iran, he believed the general welfare of the Iranian people would be assured. If this plan worked in Iran, it could serve as a model for the relations of the United States with all nations suffering from monopolies, aggression, and imperialism.

Hurley added a few considerations to these points. He accused the United Kingdom Control Corporation (UKCC) of imperialistic handling of lend-lease,[98] and calumniated the State Department for not negotiating principles to guide relations between American troops and the Iranians.[99] He also assured the president that Iranians praised him for "masterful handling" of the conference at Teheran and his "skill" in procuring the declaration. The praise did Hurley no harm. Roosevelt forwarded this letter to the secretary of state on 12 January 1944, noting that he was "rather thrilled with the idea of using Iran as an example of what we can do by an unselfish American policy." He agreed with Hurley's recommendation concerning lend-lease, and asked for advice on what he should say in reply to Hurley.[100]

[98] For the lack of insight into this charge, and for a discussion of problems relating to it, see: S.D. 891.00/3037; S.D. 891.00/1-2844; S.D. 891.00/3-3044; S.D. 123 Hurley, Patrick J./128½; Swinton, pp. 175-176; Acheson, pp. 133-134, and Hull, 2:1507-1508.

[99] For an insight into this problem, which Hurley did not understand, see Motter, pp. 437-447; FR, 1942, IV:263-276, 336-343; 1943, IV:453-483; War History Report; S.D. 123 Hurley, Patrick J./128½; Pfau, "The United States and Iran," pp. 120-121, 134ff., 157.

[100] FR, 1943, IV:420. Roosevelt also sent the letter to Churchill on 29 February, observing that he liked Hurley's general approach to the care and education of backward countries. He added: "The point of all this is that I do not want the United States to acquire a zone of influence—or any other nation for that matter. Iran certainly needs Trustees. It will take thirty to forty years to eliminate the graft and the feudal system. Until that time comes, Iran may be a headache to you, to Russia and to ourselves" (Loewenheim et al., p. 499; Loewenheim et al. cite the report sent to Churchill as that of 13 May 1943, but it is obviously that of 21 December 1943). Churchill's response on 21 May was that Hurley's ideas of British imperialism made him rub his eyes. Britain had no wish to see foreign "zones of influence" in Iran and was no less interested in encouraging Persia's independence than the United States. He doubted that Persia would welcome an international

Undersecretary of State Edward Stettinius, Jr., on 18 February sent the chief executive a memorandum noting that the president's memorandum to Hull had been helpful for the department. Hurley, he said, could be assured his report was serving as a basis for active measures already underway. Stettinius even wrote Hurley a letter in which he said that "active steps are being taken to implement your excellent and full report of December 21, 1943." But Hurley was soon to be disillusioned. Visiting the State Department in March 1944, he saw a memorandum endorsed by Assistant Secretary of State Dean Acheson which denigrated his Iranian plan.[101]

The memorandum included the observation that Hurley's worldwide plan could "easily turn out to be more than an innocent indulgence in messianic globaloney," whose chief mission would be "to convert the Russians from Communism and the British from what he [called] 'oppressive imperialism.'" Questioning the simplicity of Hurley's formula, Eugene Rostow, one of Acheson's assistants and the author of the statement, noted that advisors were the classic device of imperialistic penetration; he took issue with Hurley over lend-lease distribution, and urged further consideration. The statement was perceptive, if lacking in tact, and it delighted many in NEA. But it had little influence, for it had been rejected by higher authorities. Wallace Murray's office earlier had criticized Hurley's simplistic interpretations and had pointed out that the United States could be accused of imperialism as a result of its activities in Iran. Murray's assistants had cautioned that the United States should bear this latter possibility in mind constantly. But while they had taken issue with some of the items in Hurley's report such as the status of American forces in Iran, they regarded much of it as basically sound, and substantially in agreement with the policies they were already following. As a consequence, Murray had protested Acheson's interference in his office's affairs, and had been supported by Stettinius.[102]

Hurley, of course, did not know of these developments when he lost his temper in Acheson's office, berating Rostow (who had recently been

---

trusteeship, and thought that the advisor program was preferable. He also denied Hurley's accusation regarding the UKCC. Loewenheim et al., pp. 499-501.

[101] Roosevelt Papers, Roosevelt, PSF, Box 53, File Folder: Iran, 18 February 1944 memo from Stettinius to Roosevelt; S.D. 891.00/1-2844; Lohbeck, p. 226; Acheson, pp. 133-134.

[102] S.D. 891.00/3037; 891.00/1-2844; S.D. 123 Hurley, Patrick J./128½; Minor, letter to the author.

discharged from the service), and questioning why he was not in uniform. Acheson, who eventually managed to calm things down, had objected to Hurley's ideas because he believed they would get the United States into commitments beyond the capacity or desire of the government. The president, however, overruled him and supported Hurley's ideas as well as the general's criticism of lend-lease distribution. Even so, whether endorsed by the president or not, Hurley's policy was never fully implemented.[103]

Parts of the program Hurley recommended did take effect. They called for developing Iranian resources to benefit the Iranians and for furnishing advisors to the Iranian government at the latter's expense. Unfortunately for Hurley's place in the history of Iranian-American relations, these policies were being carried out before he thought of them. Beyond these parts of Hurley's program, opposition within the department impeded his recommendation regarding lend-lease.[104] And when it came to the imposition of "supervision and control in either economic or political spheres," it was not so much opposition as diplomatic common sense that obstructed the implementation of his ideas.

Another illustration of State Department "obstruction" may be found in the failure of the Millspaugh Financial Mission. In a letter to the *New York Times* on 30 January 1946, Arthur Millspaugh noted that while his mission to Iran had no official connection with the United States government, it had been established under the auspices and with the assistance of the State Department. His mission collapsed because the department failed to support him, following instead an "appeasement policy" characterized by inconsistency, vacillation, and weakness. That same year he published a book in which he stated: "Probably, our diplomats did not know what they were doing, but in effect they joined the mission's enemies." He blamed the State Department for withdrawing Dreyfus from Iran, for leaving his post vacant for six months, and finally for sending an inexperienced ambassador (Leland Morris) to Iran.[105]

Millspaugh, like Dreyfus, was sensitive to the paradoxes of reform,

[103] Lohbeck, p. 229; Acheson, pp. 133-134; Department of State *Bulletin* 13 (13 December 1945):985-986; S.D. 891.00/3-3044; S.D. 123 Hurley, Patrick J./128½; Roosevelt Papers, Roosevelt PSF, Box 53, File Folder: Iran, 18 February 1944 memo from Stettinius to Roosevelt; March 25, 1944 memo from Hull to Roosevelt; March 25, 1944 letter from Roosevelt to Hurley.

[104] FR, 1943, IV:363-370; S.D. 123 Hurley, Patrick J./128½.

[105] New York Times, 30 January 1946; Arthur Millspaugh, *American in Persia* (Washington, D.C., 1946), p. 233.

but was more assertive about what needed to be done.[106] Just as in 1927, when Reza Shah objected to Millspaugh's first financial mission because he did not want two shahs running the country, so in 1944-45 the Majlis increasingly resented Millspaugh's claim to power. The Majlis had been empowered by the constitution to control the country's financial matters. With the ouster of Reza Shah, it had finally been able to exercise its prerogatives, and it was jealous of them. While many of its members were nationalists who opposed foreign control of Iran, many were also wealthy landowners and entrepreneurs who took advantage of the occupation to look out for their own interests. These men bitterly resented Millspaugh's efforts against the black market, his progressive income tax policies, and his opposition to Majlis control of the vast public works program which, because of the Persian Corridor, employed 67,000 laborers on the building of roads alone. Groups on the right attacked him because they could be hurt by his financial reforms. Others attacked him because he was an agent of the United States.[107]

The American diplomatic mission, meanwhile, confronted the problem of how far it could properly go in supporting the financial mission in its encounters with the Iranian government. While it saved the mission several times—in an income tax dispute in 1943 and in a struggle regarding Millspaugh's powers in 1944—it could not go as far as he wished. The Iranians interpreted any embassy intervention as interference in Iranian affairs; and as Wallace Murray noted, stronger sup-

[106] For Dreyfus's recognition that the American advisor program was endangered by the very people it was intended to help, see FR, 1943, IV:356-358. While well-intentioned and not without insight, Millspaugh was something of a martinet whose lack of tact and difficulty in working with subordinates caused the mission grave problems. War History Report; Jernegan, letter to the author; Paul Atkins, Papers and Correspondence, Yale University, New Haven, Conn., Folder 10, 9 July 1943 letter (29G) to Mrs. Atkins; S.D. 891.51A/1160B/1171, and 22 December 1944 letter from George Hudson to George Allen; S.D. Post and Lot files, Lot No. 54f55, 801.6 Millspaugh, "Comments on Dr. Millspaugh's Book," by John Jernegan.

[107] The shah opposed Millspaugh's attempt to cut the army because he depended on it as his source of strength. Since cabinet responsibility to the Majlis was obscure, the shah's potential role in government was always a factor after 1943, even if the Majlis was dominant. Motter, pp. 467-468; Avery, pp. 359-361, 366-369, 374-375; S.D. Hurley, Patrick J./128½; Millspaugh, p. 26; FR, 1944, V:390-444; 1945, VIII:538-563; Hull, 2:1507-1508; S.D. 891.51A7-844/10-1044/10-1344/10-1444, and 22 December 1944 letter from George Hudson to George Allen; War History Report. According to Ramazani, the landed aristocracy made up 57 percent, and merchants 13 percent, of the deputies in the Majlis. Iran's Foreign Policy, pp. 83-85.

port than that already given would have constituted outright interference in Iran's internal affairs.[108]

Many elements in Iran backed Millspaugh's mission only when they thought American economic support such as lend-lease was contingent on it. When they discovered it was not, Millspaugh's mission did not have long to live.[109] Millspaugh, in turn, was angered by what he believed were the inconsistencies in American policies. He had government support and then lost it on the grounds that it constituted interference.

An explanation of the inconsistencies perceived by Millspaugh requires an understanding of Roosevelt's diplomacy. Where men like Arthur Millspaugh and Patrick Hurley—all euphemisms aside—would have suggested that the United States exert counterpressure to the various pressures existent in Iran, Roosevelt and hence the State Department were both inclined to affirm abstract principles as a means of dealing with those pressures. These policies were predicated on Roosevelt's deep-seated belief that the principles of the Atlantic Charter had wide acceptance. He did not fully understand the degree to which the Soviets did not share his ideals, nor did he appreciate conclusions they might have drawn from the incongruency between his words and deeds. The result was that he occasionally compromised his stated principles and was insensitive to the element of self-interest inherent in them.[110] The problem for the Soviet Union was how to interpret the dualism inherent in Roosevelt's ideals, and apparent in the discrepancies between thought and action. The problem for State Department officials was how to carry out policies which the president endorsed, particularly when the only means by which they could be effectively implemented contradicted his ideals and constituted something closely akin to imperialism. There was never an easy answer.

[108] War History Report; S.D. 891.51A/1106B.

[109] FR, 1945, VIII:545-548; Sydney Morrell, Spheres of Influence (New York, 1946), p. 49. Harold Minor, who was in Teheran when Millspaugh's second mission was conceived and installed, and who, when he returned to Washington, was responsible for recruiting, later observed: "The mission was doomed from the beginning because the Iranians wanted not true reform but the protection, prestige and implied promises inherent in having this body of Americans in Teheran. When the pressure for true reform . . . became too great the mission lost its effectiveness and had to be withdrawn." Minor, letter to the author.

[110] In many cases, of course, as in the pressures which caused the Senate to reject the Anglo-American oil agreement of August 1944, or in the failure to coordinate oil negotiations in Iran (both discussed later), the ideals of free enterprise were not compatible with national self-interest.

In a sense, the conduct of American policy in Iran reflected these confusions—confusions which were compounded by special emissaries such as Hurley.[111] Roosevelt distrusted the State Department in part because of its difficulties in implementing his ideals. As a consequence, he turned to individuals outside the department whom he could trust. Unfortunately, they were often as removed as he from the contextual understanding that effective implementation required.

The State Department's difficulties really began when the Soviets resorted to pressure tactics in Iran. Roosevelt and Hull refused to exert counterpressure to assert the position of the United States. Principle, they hoped, would be respected, and would lead to Soviet restraint. This attitude stemmed from the belief that principles were a necessary element of international politics, that everyone could agree on such principles, and that American policy toward Iran was unselfish. Few recognized or articulated that American self-interest was inherent in the principles of the Atlantic Charter. Some recognized that American interests were served by high-minded principles, and there were disagreements over implementation that amounted to a questioning of sorts, but no one in the Department of State directly questioned the assumption of an unselfish American policy.

Roosevelt, like Hurley, saw no contradiction in using America's power and influence to promote short-run goals—particularly if such expedients advanced the greater ideals in whose name they were pursued. Thus, he could suggest to Stalin that the Big Three impose a trusteeship on Iran, and could endorse Hurley's plan for Iran which clearly intended to impose supervision and control of Iran's economy. The State Department on occasion would take exception to such contradictions. One of the reasons it opposed the trusteeship idea was that it contradicted Roosevelt's ideals. NEA opposed the plan Arthur Millspaugh sent to Harry Hopkins in 1944 for the same reason. Harold Minor, chief of the Division of Near Eastern Affairs, was sensitive to the fine line between support and imperialism, and warned at the time that Millspaugh's idea of imposing reform and reorganization on Iran would eventually lead to some form of imperialism. "If we are going to be Don Quixote going after the windmill," he wrote in a memorandum, "we should not force the poor windmill to be party to the deed."[112]

State Department officials, however, were themselves inconsistent.

---

[111] See the discussion in Buhite, pp. 312-313.
[112] S.D. 891.51A/1000.

On occasion they could support a plan like Hurley's which clearly intended to impose supervision and control on Iran's economy. Perhaps this was because of Hurley's close relationship with the president, or perhaps it was because department officials wished to acquire support where they could for certain aspects of their policies. Harold Minor, for example, in commenting on Hurley's report, was careful to avoid discussing Hurley's personal social philosophy. He cautiously noted that the United States could be accused of imperialism as a result of its activities in Iran, and that it was a danger which the United States should constantly bear in mind. "Imperialism," he wrote, "can be, especially in the beginning, benevolent and well-intentioned." But in spite of these qualifications, both Minor and Wallace Murray endorsed Hurley's plan.[113]

Endorsement, of course, did not mean implementation. In Hurley's case, opposition within the department, a residual idealism, and common sense all obstructed implementation of his ideas.[114] Such obstruction was illustrative, perhaps, of the process which engendered Roosevelt's and others' distrust of the State Department. Following Roosevelt's endorsement of a policy, the State Department's partial implementation of it confused individuals such as Millspaugh and Hurley, both of whom roundly condemned the conduct of American foreign policy in Iran because it was not forceful enough. The root of the problem was that Millspaugh never understood either the president's or his own inconsistencies. Neither did Hurley. En route to China in 1944 as Roosevelt's personal representative to Generalissimo Chiang Kai-shek, Hurley stopped off in Teheran. Soon after arrival in China, he wrote a long letter to Roosevelt. "There are men in the State Department who are upholding imperialism, monopoly and exploitation as opposed to the principles stated in the Atlantic Charter," he said. "That is the one reason for the failure of the Iranian plan." He criticized Ambassador Leland Morris and claimed Millspaugh had not had proper support. His evaluation of the advisory program was grim: "Most of the other so-called American experts in Iran are washouts. Some of them have taken no action whatever."[115]

[113] S.D. 123 Hurley, Patrick J./128½; 891.00/1-2844.

[114] In addition to Minor's, another example of the State Department's idealism would be Hull's refusal to allow arbitration between American companies competing for oil concessions in southern Iran (see n. 150). Hurley, by contrast, and in spite of his contradictions, was really a practitioner of *Realpolitik* in U.N. clothing.

[115] Lohbeck, pp. 233-239.

American advisors could never have taken the action Hurley had in mind without proper support. Such support, however, would clearly have gone against the principles of the Atlantic Charter. Hurley's earlier recommendations of imposing supervision and control over free enterprise in Iran could hardly be construed as anything less than the exercise of imperialistic pressures. But Hurley, unaware of his own contradictions, blamed "imperialists" and "monopolists" in Washington for failure of American policies. Presumably, he was referring to Americans who recognized the acceptable limits of intervention, and so permitted Britain and the Soviet Union to exert influence at the expense of American interests. Hurley closed his letter to the president with a recommendation that there be a restatement or reaffirmation of American policy in Iran. What he really wanted was a more forceful approach to the abstract principles apparently governing American policy.

A forceful approach, however, was no more characteristic of American policy toward Iran in early 1944 than it was of American policies toward Turkey or Greece. Officials in the Department of State recognized this fact and tried to change what they considered an increasing disadvantage in the face of more exacting Soviet policies. On 14 February 1944, for example, Harold Minor, chief of the Division of Middle Eastern and Indian Affairs, wrote a memorandum on Soviet exploitation in Iran. He cited two new Irano-Soviet agreements, representative of numerous others, which were indicative of the Soviet attitude toward the Iranians. The details of one such agreement will suffice to show the nature of agreements the Soviets were imposing on the country it occupied:

> The first of these consists of two contracts, on a cash basis, under which the Iranians will furnish the Russians 36,000 tons of rice at half the price the Iranian Government must pay to acquire the same rice, in exchange for cotton piece goods, newsprint and miscellaneous goods. The cotton piece goods, which comprise two-thirds of the value of the Russian items, are to be furnished at almost 50 percent more than the same goods would cost the Iranians in India.

The memorandum included a list of such agreements. The Russians were exporting shoes to the Soviet Union from Azerbaijani factories while the Iranians had to import shoes. The Iranians had to build and maintain roads which the Soviets used for military purposes. There were other examples of similar arrangements. As a consequence, the memorandum suggested that the Teheran Declaration be taken as "a point of departure to mark the inauguration of a new era of better Allied cooperation in Iran and of more considerate treatment of the Iranians."[116]

The department's apprehension increased steadily through April, although for the next few months it tried to cooperate with the Russians in a common Iranian policy. But such a course failed, and in July the chargé in Iran, Richard Ford, requested clarification of United States policy. Ford recommended a much broader and more forceful policy than had been attempted in the past. He justified his recommendation by reminding the department of its hopes to acquire oil concessions in Iran and its interests in securing long-range protection of American oil concessions in the Persian Gulf.[117]

Acting Secretary of State Edward Stettinius in response told the chargé that the Department of State recognized United States-Iranian relations had become increasingly important. He also noted that now it was "prepared to assume a more active and positive role in Iranian affairs than was possible or necessary in the prewar period." Reasons for this heightened interest included the president's concern for Iran as a "testing ground for the Atlantic Charter," practical international considerations relating to the role of a strong Iran in achieving a lasting peace, and protection and furtherance of American national interests, which included sharing in the development of Iranian and Arabian oil as well as in other Iranian resources. While Stettinius made clear that the United States did not intend to impose its advisors on Iran or to imply that the United States would use armed forces to maintain Iranian independence, he affirmed the department's desire to strengthen Iran and to protect American interests. From now on, he said, "America's position in Iran is not intended to lapse again in any way to that of relative unimportance."[118]

Numerous factors obviously contributed to the acting secretary of state's determination to assert the position of the United States in Iranian affairs, but one of the most important was the pursuit of American national interests. The Standard-Vacuum and Sinclair Oil companies already had entered into arrangements with the Iranian government to secure oil concessions in the south of Iran. These arrangements had been approved by the War and Navy departments, whose senior officials

[116] FR, 1944, V:311-316. See also O.S.S./State I&R Reports, vol. 7, I:33.
[117] FR, 1944, pp. 322-324, 330-335, 340-342.
[118] Ibid., pp. 343-346.

believed Iranian oil could prove of vital importance in the war against Japan.[119] To understand the context of these oil arrangements, however, it is necessary first to discuss the nature of American oil interests in the Near and Middle East.

American Oil Interests in the Near East

Until World War II, the religious, cultural, educational, and economic interests of the United States in the Near East evolved independently of political interests. Americans regarded the Near East as an appendage of Europe, where political noninvolvement was a tradition, and did not consider the competing imperialisms of Russia and Britain as relevant to American policy, which recognized Britain's primacy in the Near East.[120]

This does not mean that American interests were neglected. It is true that before World War II there had been a partial break in diplomatic relations between Iran and the United States and that at the outbreak of the war there were only eighteen employees (native and American) in the United States Mission in Iran. But these facts do justice neither to the role of Iran nor to that of the Near East in general as a focus for American commercial interests between the world wars.[121]

One of the lessons of World War I had been that an adequate supply of oil was essential for national security, and the experience of that war was why Britain and the United States began a rivalry over oil immediately after the war. Standard Oil of New York, spurred on by a fear that American oil reserves were exhausted, contended with the British government for oil rights in Palestine and Mesopotamia. The United States delegation at Paris in 1919 did little to promote American oil interests, and the British government, attempting to capitalize on that fact, sought to exclude all foreign oil companies from the area. As a result, the United States insisted on the Open Door policy in attempts to prevent grants of exclusive concessions. Lord Curzon, the British foreign minister, had little sympathy for the Open Door. He noted that the British share of world oil production (4½ percent) compared unfavorably with that of the United States (70 percent) and that Ameri-

[119] Hull, 2:1508-1509; FR, 1943, IV:625-628; 1944, V:455 ff.

[120] DeNovo, pp. 383-384, 392-393.

[121] In spite of the fact that King Abd al-Aziz Al Sa'ud had requested recognition of his country by the United States, the State Department still had no permanent representative in Saudi Arabia. DeNovo, pp. 275-318, 360-365; *War History Report.*

cans secured an additional 12 percent of world production from Mexico. Curzon also liked to point out that in spite of the Open Door policy, the United States had restricted alien exploitation of oil in the United States and had interfered with British oil prospecting in the Caribbean. As a consequence, the two countries engaged in a bitter dispute over oil rights in the Middle East mandates until, finally, British need for American capital and engineering expertise led in 1928 to a cooperative agreement: the British sold a group of American oil companies a 23.75 percent share of the Turkish Petroleum Company (renamed the Iraq Petroleum Company [IPC] in 1929).[122]

As American oil corporations made inroads into the British sphere of influence, the State Department played an important role. Since British oil companies were partly owned by the British government, American companies were at a disadvantage: they were more vulnerable to the whims of governments which granted concessions. But the Open Door, while it offered little protection to American companies, was an instrument for opening the oil fields to them. This does not mean that it had much value as an idealistic principle: IPC, for example, had a virtual monopoly on the production of oil in Iraq, and the United States acquiesced in restrictive measures which repudiated the basic principles of the Open Door. But regardless of the principle sacrificed, the State Department made good use of it as a rhetorical device for helping American companies get concessions.[123] If the door was not wide open, at least it was not locked.

American oil interests, having gained entrée into the Middle East in the 1920s, proceeded in the 1930s to wedge the door open even further. Standard Oil of California organized the Bahrein Petroleum Company in 1930. The discovery of oil in Bahrein in 1932 stimulated a search for claims on the Arabian peninsula. King Abd al-Aziz (Ibn Sa'ud), concerned about British domination of Saudi Arabia and favoring the superior financial terms offered by Standard Oil of California,[124] in 1933

[122] Gerald Nash, *United States Oil Policy, 1890-1964* (Pittsburgh, 1968), pp. 50-51; Herbert Feis, *Seen From E.A.* (New York, 1947); DeNovo, pp. 167-209; Shwadran (2nd ed.), pp. 242-243. It might be pointed out that the influence of American capital and technical expertise was precisely what made the United States a threat to the interests of its rivals—particularly those who were less competitive and who saw such influence through ideological lenses.

[123] Shwadran (2nd ed.), pp. 242-243, 315; DeNovo, pp. 197-208.

[124] Again, the influence of American capital seems apparent, and is exactly the kind of problem envisaged by the counselor of the French embassy in 1945 (see n. 84 and n. 122).

179

granted the American firm a 360,000 square mile concession. After four years of discouraging results, the company discovered a field of great commercial promise. Standard Oil meanwhile joined with the Texas Oil Company to form a new combine, Cal-Tex. A supplemental agreement between King Abd al-Aziz and Cal-Tex added 80,000 square miles in Saudi Arabia to the earlier concession, and by 1939, following the opening of a new terminal at Ras Tanura on the Persian Gulf, American oil interests in the Middle East had become one of the most important of American foreign investments. In addition to exclusive ownership of the Bahrein, Ethiopia, and Saudi Arabia grants, American holdings included half of a Kuwait concession and approximately a quarter of the extensive IPC holdings in Iraq, Syria, Trans-Jordan, the Trucial Coast, Qatar, Oman, and Dhofar, not to mention other oil exploration rights in Cyprus, Lebanon, Palestine, and Aden. The increasing number of American workers and the large capital outlays in the oil regions of the Middle East indicated even before World War II that the Middle East would play a vital role in the security interests of the United States.[125]

[125] DeNovo, pp. 201-209; Shwadran (2nd ed.), pp. 296-297; FR, *The Conferences at Cairo and Teheran*, pp. 162-164; Sachar, *Europe Leaves the Middle East*, p. 297; U.S. Congress, Senate, Special Committee Investigating the National Defense Program, *Hearings, Part 41, Petroleum Arrangements with Saudi Arabia* (Washington, D.C., 1948), Exhibit No. 2560, after page 25388.

In order to keep the question of national security interests in perspective, the following table indicates the growing production figures for Saudi Arabian and Iranian oil relative to those of the United States and the world. Since some references refer to volume (barrels), others to weight (tons), and since Britain uses short tons while the United States uses long tons, the figures are necessarily approximate. This is especially true because the number of barrels in a ton depends on temperature as well as on the specific gravity of the oil in question. Because the United States Petroleum Council uses a standard measure of 6.349 barrels per short ton, the corresponding figure per long ton should be 7.11 barrels.

Oil Production (long tons per year)

Year	Saudi Arabia	Iran	United States	World
1938	65,618	10,195,371	170,795,350	270,000,000
1939	52,214	9,583,286	177,913,080	278,000,000
1940	672,154	8,626,639	190,325,450	289,000,000
1941	570,046	6,605,320	197,219,120	300,000,000
1942	600,351	9,399,231	195,027,420	282,000,000
1943	645,860	9,705,769	211,759,910	313,000,000
1944	1,034,603	13,274,243	235,992,120	348,000,000
1945	2,825,990	16,839,490	241,020,390	356,000,000
1946	7,889,675	19,189,551	243,796,610	371,000,000
1947	11,813,668	20,194,836	261,179,600	415,000,000

After war broke out in 1939, activities in Saudi Arabian oil fields were curtailed and the pilgrimages to Mecca (which had been an important source of income) ceased. Financially embarrassed, King Abd al-Aziz demanded advances from the American oil firms and the British government. The American oil companies believed that if they did not come through with such advances the king would give concessions to the British; they feared that if they gave the king what he demanded they would not be repaid. The upshot was that the California and Texas companies sought government assistance. President Roosevelt decided that the United States could not assist Saudi Arabia directly, but he arranged for American assistance through the British, within whose political sphere it was felt that Saudi Arabia fell. This decision caused even more concern about British influence among the oil companies. Seeking to gain political credit for American assistance that was being channeled through British sources, the top executives of Cal-Tex in 1943 again sought government assistance. Arguing that British encroachments, the insecurity of their concessions, and the importance of oil all meant that lend-lease aid should be granted to Saudi Arabia, they found an unlikely ally in Secretary of the Interior Harold Ickes.[126]

Roosevelt had appointed Ickes Petroleum Coordinator for National Defense in 1941. In that capacity, he was responsible for promoting government cooperation with the oil industry. Most oil executives distrusted Ickes because he had tried (and failed) to nationalize the oil industry—in 1935, and again in 1940. The federal government, moreover, had tried to restrict the production of oil in order to stabilize the industry, and the oil companies were still suspicious of the Roosevelt administration. But the wartime situation changed the problem from one of stabilization to one of production. Between December 1941 and August 1945, the Allies would require seven billion barrels of crude

---

These figures are based on: Shwadran (2nd ed.), pp. 162, 343; Nash, p. 260; Longrigg, pp. 368, 374; Sachar, *Europe Leaves the Middle East*, p. 636.

An O.S.S. study of oil and power resources in Caucasia, prepared 27 July 1942, estimated Russian oil production in 1938 in and around Baku as 23,935,000 metric tons. This was from the Azneft Trust, consisting of 17 fields and 20,000 wells. The Gruzneft Trust near Tbilisi consisted of 2 fields and produced 45,000 metric tons, while the Grozneft Trust near Groznyi consisted of 7 fields and produced 2,763,600 metric tons. O.S.S./State I&R Reports, vol. 7, I:22.

126 *Hearings, Part 41, Petroleum Arrangements with Saudi Arabia*, 24728-24729, 24745, 24805, 24829-24830, 25090-25095, 25232-25233, 25392; Shwadran (2nd ed.), pp. 301-317; Hull, 2:1511-1512, 1517; Feis, *Seen From E.A.*, p. 95; U.S. Congress, Senate, *Congressional Record* 94 (Part 4):4948.

petroleum, and the United States would have to supply 80 percent of that total. As a consequence, Ickes now supported production through a variety of means: extension of tax benefits, suspension of antitrust laws, and raising ceilings on crude oil. Ickes was given more authority when he was made Petroleum Administrator for War in December 1942. In this new capacity, he did everything possible to increase oil production both at home and abroad. It was as a result of Ickes' influence that the president on 18 February 1943 granted lend-lease to Saudi Arabia.[127]

Ickes in June 1943 went a step further. Prodded by Secretary of the Navy Frank Knox and Secretary of War Henry Stimson, and fully accepting the arguments used by the oil companies to obtain lend-lease for Saudi Arabia, he proposed government purchase of Middle East oil concessions. History compelled the conclusion, he wrote Roosevelt on 10 June, that "American participation must be of a sovereign character compatible with the strength of the competitive forces encountered in such undertakings." Two days earlier, the Joint Chiefs of Staff, because of "an insufficient supply of crude oil from indigenous production," and "in the interest of national security," had urged President Roosevelt that "steps be taken immediately to assure control of sufficient oil reserves to meet our country's needs." The president on 11 June concurred. The next day, James F. Byrnes, director of the Office of War Mobilization, presided over a White House meeting which agreed that the federal government should search out new reserves. Within a week, a State/War/Navy/Interior interdepartmental committee agreed on the organization of the Petroleum Reserves Corporation (PRC), with powers to acquire ownership of petroleum reserves outside the United States—specifically in Saudi Arabia. The secretaries of State, War, and Interior, and Acting Secretary of the Navy James Forrestal then submitted a report to President Roosevelt endorsing the committee decision. The PRC was organized on 30 June, and Harold Ickes was designated president of the Board of Directors.[128]

The PRC, however, never became operational in any real sense. This failure was due in part to differences within the government over the desirability of government ownership, but mainly to the fact that the oil companies which owned the concessions were outraged at the

[127] Nash, pp. 157-172.

[128] Henry Stimson, Diaries, Yale University, New Haven, Conn., 43:94-95 (6/4/43), 99 (6/8/43); Shwadran (2nd ed.), pp. 310-314; Hull, 2:1518-1520; Hearings, Part IV, Petroleum Arrangements with Saudi Arabia, 25237-25238; FR, 1943, IV:921-930; Nash, p. 172.

PRC's proposals. At first they were willing to accept partial government ownership, but they rejected this idea after Rommel had been driven from North Africa and the oil situation had become less critical. Ickes tried a different tack in 1944. When a PRC exploratory mission came back from the Middle East in January 1944 with optimistic estimates of oil reserves in the region,[129] he considered building a government pipeline from the Saudi Arabian oil fields to the Eastern Mediterranean. The pipeline would have been another means of effecting direct government interest in the concession. But this proposal, too, was opposed —not by the big oil companies which were associated with the concession, but by smaller companies which feared the advantages that might accrue to those already ensconced in the Persian Gulf.[130]

Meanwhile, as a result of the increasingly aggressive American attitude concerning oil resources in the Middle East, and following State Department invitations to the British to exchange views on the

[129] In addition to stating that the center of gravity of world oil production was shifting from the Gulf-Caribbean area, the PRC mission report estimated oil reserves in the Middle East to be: nine billion barrels in Kuwait; six to seven billion barrels in Iran; four to five billion barrels in Saudi Arabia, and one billion barrels in Qatar.

According to George Kirk, by 1944 U.S. interests "controlled 42 percent of the proved oil reserves of the Middle East, which themselves had increased 5.8 times by new discoveries since 1936, against only 13 percent of the smaller quantity at the earlier date. Absolutely, their share of Middle East oil had thus increased nineteenfold."

To put Middle East oil in its proper perspective, one needs only to note the following estimate regarding past production and future resources, given by Charles Hamilton of the Gulf Oil Company in June 1945 before the Special Committee of the Senate Committee Investigating Petroleum Resources:

Petroleum Resources:	From U.S.	From Near and Middle East
Percent of World's Estimated Cumulative Production through 1944 (46.6 billion barrels)	63.8	3.8
Percent of Estimated World Resources as of Beginning of 1945 (63.8 billion barrels)	32.0	42.1

Feis, *Seen from E.A.*, pp. 102-103; Shwadran (2nd ed.), p. 319; Kirk, *The Middle East in the War*, p. 25; United States, Congress, Senate, *Hearings Before a Special Committee Investigating Petroleum Resources, American Petroleum Interests in Foreign Countries* (Washington, D.C., 1946), pp. 52-54.

[130] Shwadran (2nd ed.), pp. 314-340; Hull, 2:1513-1514, 1520-1525; *Hearings, Part 41, Petroleum Arrangements with Saudi Arabia*, 25240-25245; John Frey and Chandler Ide, eds., *A History of the Petroleum Administration for War, 1941-1945* (Washington, D.C., 1946), pp. 276-287; Nash, pp. 173-175.

subject, Prime Minister Churchill worried about American intentions in the area. "There is apprehension in some quarters here," he wrote Roosevelt, "that the United States has a desire to deprive us of our oil assets in the Middle East on which, among other things, the whole supply of our Navy depends."[131]

Roosevelt's reply was quick in coming: "You point to the apprehension on your side that the United States desires to deprive you of oil assets in the Middle East. On the other hand, I am disturbed about the rumor that the British wish to horn in on Saudi Arabian oil reserves." Roosevelt felt that mutual apprehensions, and the long-range importance of oil to postwar international security and economic arrangements, necessitated technical discussions at a high level. After Churchill explained his concerns in more detail, and expressed his intention to inquire into the oil situation throughout the world, Roosevelt on 3 March 1944 wrote back: "I am having the oil question studied by the Department of State and my oil experts, but please do accept my assurances that we are not making sheep's eyes at your oil fields in Iraq or Iran." On 4 March, Churchill shot back: "Thank you very much for your assurances about no sheep's eyes at our oil fields in Iran and Iraq. Let me reciprocate by giving you the fullest assurance that we have no thought of trying to horn in upon your interests or property in Saudi Arabia."[132]

As a result of the exchange the two leaders agreed to technical and high-level discussions of mutual problems.[133] These discussions began

[131] Woodward, BFP, pp. 396-398; Nash, p. 176; Loewenheim et al., pp. 440-441; Daniels, White House Witness, p. 222; FR, 1944, III:100-101.

[132] FR, 1944, III:100-103; Loewenheim et al., p. 459.

[133] Herbert Feis's account of why the Soviets were not included is as follows:

The certain interests of the USSR in any agreement that affected the affairs of the region were not forgotten. It was clearly understood that no step should be taken in concert with Britain that might injure the USSR or place it at a disadvantage. But it did not seem feasible immediately to include that country in the preparatory discussions. The American and British governments had virtually pooled their oil supplies for the conduct of the war; the USSR was managing independently and not even exchanging information. Discussions with Moscow, even on matters essential for the conduct of the war, usually took a difficult course. In this matter the first formulations were certain to be groping even between participants who approached it with the same economic conceptions. It was impossible to guess what types of proposals the USSR might make; they might bring the whole pattern of ownership in the region into question. It seemed foolish to take the risk before our own policies were defined. Lastly there was the fact that the USSR possessed no oil rights in the

in April, and arrived at a preliminary agreement in August. Since the basic purpose of the agreement was to place international petroleum trade on an orderly basis, its principles followed logically: respect for valid concessions contracts and lawfully acquired rights in the Near East; orderly development of oil reserves; equal opportunity for exploration or developmental rights in areas not under concession; and freedom from restrictions inconsistent with these principles. There was also provision for an International Petroleum Commission to analyze short-term problems and make long-term estimates of demand and distribution. Despite the evidence of government concern, these principles were essentially academic. Many American oil executives feared the agreement would create a cartel, or lead to nationalization of the industry in the United States, or cause a depression of the domestic oil industry as a result of large-scale imports. So strong were their objections that the agreement was never ratified.[134] Failure of the agreement, however, in no way diminished the importance of Middle East oil to the United States. It only illustrated the obvious fact that economic interests in the United States were not monolithic, and that they often worked at crosspurposes with each other and with policies the administration considered to be in the country's strategic interests.

Thus, burgeoning American business interests throughout the Near East help to explain Stettinius's recognition of the increasing importance of United States-Iranian relations. The Department of State and President Roosevelt as early as 1943 had clearly recognized Iran's strategic importance as a buffer between the Soviet Union and American interests in the Middle East. It was in the interests of the United States, a policy statement then said, that "no great power be established in the Persian Gulf opposite the important American petroleum development in Saudi Arabia." In his instructions to Richard Ford, the chargé in Iran in July 1944, Stettinius said the same thing in a more general way. He stressed the desire to assist Iran in creating a strong

---

region and had shown no recent evident wish to acquire any. *Seen from E.A.*, p. 136.

[134] Hull, 2:1523-1526; Woodward, *BFP*, p. 398; Nash, pp. 176-177. As an increasingly scarce resource, oil was of great value to American business interests and hence to the economy of the United States. Conversely, the success of other countries in obtaining oil concessions would diminish proportionately those resources available for exploitation by American interests. In spite of this fact, the American business community was unable to act in its general interest.

national entity free from foreign domination. He also cautioned against giving the impression that the United States intended to stand at the side of Iran as a "political buffer" to restrain its Allies.[135] Presumably, as in the Balkans, the United States was neither willing nor ready to commit troops to such an enterprise. Hopefully, acceptance of the Atlantic Charter had been sincere and would have a restraining effect upon Britain and Russia. Iran would be the testing ground. But there was no question that if the Charter were observed, a strong Iran would serve the purpose of a strategic buffer. While Department of State memoranda never forgot American interests in Iran itself, they consistently conceived of Iran's importance in the context of its strategic links to American interests in the Arabian peninsula. This relationship was a constant concern of which the department, if not the president, was clearly conscious.

Despite the strident notes which sometimes appeared in American communications to the British about Iran and the Middle East, State Department officials were also conscious of the fact that America and Britain had many interests in that area which did not conflict and which in fact required close cooperation. As a result of the understanding between Churchill and Roosevelt, Anglo-American discussions during the so-called Stettinius Mission to London in April 1944 had touched on such topics as Russian exploitation of Iran, support for the American advisor program, and the maintenance of order throughout the Middle East.[136] Foy Kohler, who as an aide participated in the discussions on the Near and Middle East between Wallace Murray, now director of the Office of Near Eastern and African Affairs, and British Foreign Office Undersecretary Sir Maurice Peterson, asserts that the change toward a more harmonious relationship between the British and the Americans in NEA dates from the Stettinius Misson. It was no secret, Kohler recalls, that until that time,

> Wallace [Murray] tended to be strongly anti-British, perhaps as a result of the long struggle he had participated in to promote American interests in oil and trade in [the] Near Eastern area. He was even more anti-

[135] FR, 1943, IV:377-379; 1944, V:343-346.

[136] In addition, a committee made up of the British, Soviet, and American chiefs of mission was set up in Iran for the purpose of examining problems of an economic nature and more generally of implementing the Teheran Declaration. In spite of repeated Anglo-American attempts to enlist Russian cooperation, the meetings failed to solve common problems and were broken off in July 1944. S.D. Post and Lot files, Lot No. 54f55, 801.6 Millspaugh.

Russian, probably as a result of his earlier experiences in Iran. In fact, some of us used to say that the only way to get a paper through our beloved chief was to persuade him it was more anti-Russian than pro-British.

But wide-ranging discussions with the British appear to have crystallized Murray's thoughts on the relative dangers of British and Russian influence in the area, and as Kohler recalls,

> Wallace was almost completely won over. Both sides agreed that there was entirely too much bickering between British and American representatives in the field who were constantly sending their complaints against their counterparts to their respective foreign offices. Consequently, we agreed with Sir Maurice to send parallel instructions to all our missions to the effect that in the future they were not to complain about the attitudes and actions of their respective colleagues without reporting in the same dispatch what efforts had been made locally to discuss and iron out differences.

Thus, agreed minutes of the discussions "established that there was a general community of aims and outlook between the Foreign Office and the State Department in Middle Eastern questions. It was cordially agreed that in principle there would be great advantage in bringing about in the future an even closer co-operation between British and American policy in the territories concerned."[137]

The beneficial effects of the Stettinius Mission were immediately apparent in terms of improved relations between American and British representatives throughout the Middle East. One of many steps toward Anglo-American cooperation was the assignment of Raymond Hare, second secretary at the legation in Cairo and a Near Eastern specialist, to the American embassy in London in July 1944. Hare's task was to keep in continuous and intimate touch with the appropriate people in the British Foreign Office. Further steps led to the preliminary Anglo-American agreement regarding petroleum in August 1944. Thus, by the time that Roosevelt's year-old proposal to Stalin (made at Teheran) of an international trusteeship in Iran finally surfaced at the department in December, a memo to the secretary of state by Wallace Murray made clear what his office had been thinking all along:

[137] S.D. Stettinius Mission/3-1944/136/144/107/151/124/112½; FR, 1944, V:322-343; Woodward, 4:387, 442-443; Foy Kohler, letter to the author; Papers of Edward R. Stettinius, Jr., University of Virginia, Acession No. 2723, Box No. 251, Folder: London Mission, Conversations—Murray, "Agreed Minute," April 1944.

Our experts on Soviet Russia are most dubious that Russia would be interested, at least for the present, in an international trusteeship or would participate in it in the genuine manner intended by the President.

The British, moreover, would doubtless raise strenuous objections. Britain's policy for a hundred years has been to prevent Russia or any other great power from establishing itself on the Persian Gulf, and there is no indication that British policy has changed in this respect. If we proceed on the assumption that the continuance of the British Empire in some reasonable strength is in the strategic interests of the United States (and I understand the strategists of the War Department proceed on this assumption), it is necessary to protect the vital communications of the Empire between Europe and the Far East. Britain has always tried desperately to keep Russians, whether of the Czarist or Soviet variety, away from the Persian Gulf, and will doubtless continue to do so.

The foregoing considerations might possibly be brushed aside if there were any reason for confidence that the Soviets would participate in an international trusteeship of the high principles the President has in mind. We would be deluding ourselves, however, if we built our plans on such hopes.[138]

Paradoxically, although the United States was Britain's greatest rival for oil in the Middle East, American strategic conceptions of the Northern Tier countries mirrored those of the British. What explains this paradox? Anglo-American mistrust of the Soviet Union in the Near East —a mistrust resulting from tradition, from Soviet actions in Iran following the Battle of Stalingrad, and from the fact that both countries now had important oil interests to protect. Mutual mistrust of the Soviet Union, accompanied by the decline of Britain's military strength, made possible the Anglo-American agreement of August 1944. The agreement reflects the secondary nature of Anglo-American rivalry over oil in the Middle East, and indicates that by late 1944 mistrust of the Soviet Union was a basic notion in British strategic thinking. Already the British were thinking of spheres of influence in the Balkans, and of their

---

[138] Kohler, letter to the author; Raymond Hare, conversation with the author; Jernegan, letter to the author; FR, 1944, V:485-486. The idea that British and American interests were similar in the Near East had been expressed earlier by individuals as different as Patrick Hurley and Lincoln MacVeagh. It was also endorsed in 1945 by Joseph Grew when he was acting secretary of state. See FR, 1945, VIII:523-526.

position in the Eastern Mediterranean. Before Britain and the Soviet Union became allies, Anthony Eden had made clear to Ivan Maisky, the Soviet ambassador, that Britain was determined to maintain its position throughout the Middle East, including Iran. This thought was reiterated at the Dumbarton Oaks Conference in 1944 by Sir Alexander Cadogan, the British undersecretary of state for foreign affairs, who stated that while Great Britain to a very considerable extent was prepared to give in to Russian demands in Eastern Europe and the Balkans, his government could not and would not yield in Iran.[139] The State Department, aware of Cadogan's statement, with the War Department proceeded on the assumption that along the Northern Tier the interests of the British Empire were similar to those of the United States.

Thus, American oil interests in the Near East as a whole constituted an important context within which to view more specific American interests in Iran. Because American interest in Iranian oil and American oil negotiations in Iran during World War II were both part of a long history of American-Iranian relations on the question of oil, we must turn briefly to the background of these relations in order to understand the oil crisis which occurred in 1944.

American Oil Interests in Iran

American interests in Iran before World War II, as in the rest of the Middle East, were primarily concerned with religious, cultural, educational, and economic enterprises. The Presbyterian Church founded a mission in western Persia in 1835, nearly fifty years before the United States established its first diplomatic mission in 1883. The American government had no intention of challenging Britain's primacy in the Near East and the American mission in Persia assumed only a passive role. When Persia appealed to Woodrow Wilson for assistance in maintaining neutrality during World War I, the American president offered only what Roosevelt would offer in 1941: sympathy. British influence, on the other hand, was evident on every occasion when Persia was involved in international affairs: for example, when it opposed the seating of the Persian delegation to Paris in 1919.[140]

We have seen how, as a consequence of British and Russian en-

[139] S.D. 891.6363/12-844.
[140] DeNovo, pp. 278-279, 321-394; Avery, p. 145.

croachments on their territory, the Persians turned in the 1920s to the United States and Germany in an attempt to use them as countervailing powers to the traditional imperial rivals. Thus, the first Millspaugh Mission in Iran (1922-27), which was organized to undertake fiscal and administrative reform, was also looked on as a means of curbing Soviet and British ambitions in Persia.[141]

Even before the arrival of this mission, Persians were attracting American interest in Persia by drawing attention to its oil resources. Persians were anxious to have Americans develop unassigned oil rights in the five northern provinces excluded from the Anglo-Persian concession, and because of the post-World War I oil scare in the United States, American oil interests were receptive.[142]

As early as 1920, the Standard Oil Company of New Jersey was considering a move to secure a concession in Persia, and a year later it let the Persian government know it was ready to accept one. An Anglo-Soviet dispute over the northern provinces, however, complicated matters. A tsarist Russian, Akaki Khoshtaria, had been granted a concession in that area in 1916. While the new Soviet regime and the Persian government both considered it invalid, the Anglo-Persian Oil Company (APOC) was unaware of Soviet and Persian interpretations of that concession and bought it in 1920 for £100,000. A complicating factor was the treaty of alliance between Russia and Persia in 1921, which renounced all previous concessions granted to tsarist Russia, but stipulated that such concessions were not to be ceded to a third power. While the Iranians interpreted the treaty differently, the Soviets insisted that the granting of concessions in the old Russian sphere of influence required Soviet consent. As a consequence, both the British and the Russians opposed the concession which Standard prepared to accept in 1921. At this juncture, the Persians argued that the concession was not valid because the Majlis had not ratified it. Consequently, the Russians had no argument, the British no rights in the north, and the proposed concession to the Americans was valid. Standard Oil, since it needed APOC's permission to transport oil in the south of Persia, and since it now came under British pressure, made a deal with APOC. It admitted

[141] There was an earlier, somewhat similar mission in Iran under W. Morgan Shuster in 1911-12, which was terminated as a result of Russian influence. DeNovo, pp. 53-56, 281-283; FR, 1927, III:527-528.
[142] DeNovo, pp. 283-284. The five northern provinces were: Azerbaijan, Gilan, Mazanderan, Khorasan, and Astrabad.

the legality of the Khoshtaria concession, and agreed to joint participation in the northern provinces in return for transportation rights in the south, as well as in Palestine and Mesopotamia.[143]

Because the concession was nontransferable, the Persian government rejected this arrangement, and in 1922 offered new concessions to Standard Oil and to the Sinclair Consolidated Oil Corporation as well. Sinclair finally signed a concession in 1923, but its concession was undermined by domestic politics. Harry Sinclair, who was on good terms with Soviet authorities, was in a good position to secure transportation rights through Russia to the Black Sea. Apparently he was offering in return his influence to secure recognition of the Soviet Union by the United States and was discussing this possibility with his friends Secretary of the Interior Albert Fall and Attorney General Harry Dougherty. When the Teapot Dome scandal blew up in 1924, implicating Sinclair and his friends, the possibility of such a deal fell through. A glut on the American oil market by the mid-twenties added to his problems, and Sinclair, who now had little reason to pursue oil interests in Persia, was unable to raise the loan necessary to obtain the concession.[144]

From 1925 to 1936 American oil firms showed no interest in Iran, but in the latter year the Amiranian Oil Company (a subsidiary of the Seaboard Oil Company of Delaware) sought concessions in the northern provinces. Warned about transportation problems, Amiranian began discussions with the Soviet Union. The Soviets, despite concern over possible British participation in the concession, allowed the American oil company to ship supplies and materials through their territory. The Anglo-Iranian Oil Company objected on the basis of its claim to the Khoshtaria concession. But the objection was unnecessary. After two years of extensive surveys, Amiranian gave up its concession. While development of oil resources elsewhere may have contributed to the decision, the decisive facts seem to have been the concession's unfavorable inland situation and the unstable situation in the Soviet Union.[145]

[143] Ibid., pp. 284-287; Avery, pp. 256-258; Shwadran (2nd ed.), pp. 89-90; Longrigg, pp. 38-39; S.D. 891.6363 Standard Oil/430. For a useful background survey of the history of Iranian oil concessions, complete with maps, see O.S.S./State I&R Reports, vol. 7, I:32. For the Khoshtaria Concession, see Map No. 5.

[144] Shwadran (2nd ed.), pp. 86-94; DeNovo, pp. 285-286; Avery, pp. 257-258; Nash, pp. 73-81; S.D. 891.6363 Standard Oil/430.

[145] In May 1939, a Dutch company was given an exploration license covering Iran's five northern provinces, but war prevented field operations, and the license was terminated in 1944. Shwadran (2nd ed.), pp. 95-99; Longrigg, pp. 61-62;

Although there were subsequent inquiries by a Standard Oil representative—first in December 1939 about the Iranian government's disposition to grant oil concessions, and then in December 1940 about the possibility of engaging in geological exploration—the Iranian government, which had encouraged exploration in the south, eventually refused. By December 1940, Reza Shah was desirous neither of creating apprehension in Soviet and Axis circles nor of drawing attention to the oil question. Such attention, however, was unavoidable. On 30 August 1941, after the Soviets had occupied northern Iran, they revived an earlier claim to a concession at Kavir Khorian, basing the right to oil exploitation in the area on the old Khoshtaria concession. The Iranians held that the concession was no longer valid, but nonetheless expressed a willingness to discuss a new one.[146] There matters rested until the Battle of Stalingrad, after which the tide of battle turned back toward Europe, and the Soviets began to put pressure on Iran.

The Oil Crisis of 1944 and Its Aftermath

It is against this background of Allied occupation, Great Power politics, the incipient American interest in Iran, and the long history of oil negotiations, that one must view subsequent events. Thus, it seems likely that the Iranian government was seeking support against increased Soviet pressures when its commercial attaché in Washington approached Standard Vacuum in February 1943 on the subject of oil concessions. As was the case in the 1920s, when the first Millspaugh Mission and oil concessions to the United States were a means by which Iran could counter Soviet ambitions, so during World War II the same process was unfolding. At the time, Standard Vacuum was not especially interested and suggested delay because of the political situation in Iran. But by September, probably because of news that representatives of British oil companies had arrived in Teheran to negotiate

DeNovo, pp. 314-315; Feis, *Seen from E.A.*, pp. 174-175; S.D. 891.6363 Standard Oil/430. See also Adamec, pp. 236-237, for activities in Afghanistan.

[146] The Soviet government, apparently without the permission of the Iranian government, began experimental drilling near Gorgan and Shahi in northern Iran shortly thereafter. S.D. Standard Oil/424/430/431/432/433/826; Elwell-Sutton, *Persian Oil*, pp. 41, 107-108. The Soviets on 6 September 1941 took note of Iran's "preparedness to conclude a new agreement for the exploration of Kavir Khorian oil the progress on which has been suspended by Iran over a number of years" (Ramazani, *Iran's Foreign Policy*, pp. 38-39; O.S.S./State I&R Reports, vol. 7, I:32). For the Kavir Khorian concession, see Map No. 5.

concessions in the south,[147] Standard Vacuum became interested. Encouraged by the Iranian government and the State Department,[148] the oil company sent a representative to Iran in December 1943. In March 1944, perhaps as a result of Patrick Hurley's influence, Sinclair Oil also expressed an interest in concessions in the south of Iran.[149]

The oil negotiations that ensued, while initially promising for the American oil companies, dragged on through the summer of 1944. In the process, the State Department followed a contradictory course. It aided the oil companies by facilitating their communications. It sent a petroleum attaché to Iran to assist them in securing concessions, and assisted the Iranian government in procuring the services of two petroleum engineers, Herbert Hoover, Jr., a son of the former president, and A. A. Curtice. These two men had recently reorganized oil concessions in Venezuela, and while carrying out the same task in Iran they, too, assisted the oil companies. But it should be noted that the State Department did not expedite negotiations, nor did it put national interests above those of the two companies. As early as May, when oil negotiations were first widely discussed in the Iranian press, the petroleum attaché predicted that the search for concessions would end in failure because of the way they were being handled. In spite of his efforts, the State Department refused to put pressure on either American company, or to assist in consolidating their bids. As Cordell Hull informed the chargé Richard Ford, such an action would be contrary to policy. What policy? The principle of equal opportunity with respect to new concessions. The State Department was more concerned with the ideals of free enterprise than with seeking a concession that would

[147] Iranian Baluchistan, the southern part of Iran originally covered by the APOC concession which had been reduced in 1938.

[148] For reasons already discussed, American interest in Middle East oil had grown immensely in 1943. As a result, on 17 November 1943 the State Department advised Standard Vacuum "that because of the importance of petroleum, both for the long-range viewpoint and for war purposes, the Department of State looks with favor upon the development of all possible sources of petroleum." Hull, 2:1508-1509, FR, 1943, IV:626.

[149] FR, 1943, IV:625-628; 1944, V:391-392, 446-447; S.D. 891.51A/1000; 891.6363/12-1144; Hull, 2:1508-1509; Shwadran (2nd ed.), p. 65; Elwell-Sutton, Persian Oil, p. 108. The evidence regarding Hurley's influence is only circumstantial: he was traveling in and out of Iran at the time, he was paid considerable sums of money by the Sinclair Oil Company during World War II ($108,000 in 1942, $75,000 in 1945), and conferred with Harry Sinclair 43 times in 1943-44—often, his biographer tells us, for a full day at a time. S.D. 123 Hurley, Patrick J./13 June letter from S. W. Langer to Joseph Grew; Buhite, p. 132.

have redounded to the national interest regardless of the manner of its negotiation. On one occasion Petroleum Attaché John Leavell even complained about it:

> It is quite impossible [he wrote] to utilize the favorable position in which the Department is situated where it can take no action to help either American party where such action might be to the conceivable detriment of the other American bidder, even though such action might result in the award of the concession to an American company. . . .[150]

The United States and Britain were meanwhile seeking an agreement on oil exploitation which, in conjunction with the oil negotiations in Iran, aroused deep suspicions in Iran—suspicions which were quite probably shared by the Soviet government. Soviet apprehension about American claims in the north was apparent in Teheran as early as February 1944 when a Soviet embassy spokesman informed an American correspondent that the Soviet Union possessed prior rights to oil exploitation in northern Iran. In August, when Ford assured the Soviet ambassador that Britain and the United States were interested solely in concessions in the south, Ambassador Maximov remarked that he was "neutral" with respect to the south, but not in regard to the north. Indiscreet (if often justified) criticism of Soviet actions by American advisors in Iran contributed to Soviet suspicions of the West, which were undoubtedly fueled by Anglo-American petroleum negotiations in Washington and Teheran.[151]

In spite of Soviet suspicions, however, it should be noted that the United States never opposed Soviet desires for concessions in the north. The American chargé Richard Ford reassured the Soviets that the American oil companies' interests lay in the south, and the Iranians, too, made this clear. But these assurances were inconsequential when pitted against Soviet suspicions and fears of Allied intentions. Trust, of course, was not the antidote. If there were a remedy, it probably would have been based on the Allies' joint recognition that they held

[150] FR, 1943, V:445-453; S.D. 891.6363/449/451/845/850/853/7-1044 (July 7)/7-1044 (July 10)/7-2544/8-2644/12-1144.

[151] Millspaugh and other members of his staff were vocal in their opposition to various economic agreements imposed on Iran by the Soviets. In the past, others had opposed Soviet handling of grain shipments; and in July, Millspaugh was quoted as saying that if it had not been for the American economic mission in 1943, troubles might have occurred which would have resulted in the occupation (i.e., a much harsher occupation) of Iran by Britain and the Soviet Union. Whatever the merits of the case, this kind of statement was highly annoying to the Soviet ambassador. S.D. 801.6363/8-344/12-1144; FR, 1944, V:311-316.

different conceptions of world order. The Atlantic Charter, which reflected Roosevelt's conception, itself gave rise to suspicions. Was it not Stalin who observed that the Atlantic Charter seemed to be directed against the Soviet Union? The Soviet dictator preferred agreements over declarations, and in Iran there had been no real agreement. Not between heads of state, anyway. And if there had been a declaration, that could be passed off as so much "algebra." Stalin was as aware of Russia's traditional interests in Iran as at the Straits, or in the Balkans. That was what counted in the conduct of Soviet foreign policy in Iran.

As a result, the Soviets decided to act.[152] In September, the Iranians were advised that Russian Vice Commissar of Foreign Affairs Sergei Ivanovich Kavtaradze, who a year before had represented the USSR at the conference in Moscow, would come to Iran to discuss the Kavir Khorian oil concession in northern Iran. After several petroleum geologists accompanying the vice commissar left his party to explore the Kavir Khorian fields, Kavtaradze opened discussions with the shah and Prime Minister Sa'id. As a consequence, the prime minister asked Herbert Hoover, Jr., to draw up a model petroleum contract for a possible Soviet concession in northern Iran. Hoover saw no objection to such a concession. It was his belief that, due to geography, oil from the north could find an outlet only in the Soviet Union.[153]

Two weeks later Kavtaradze's interests shifted. He asked the shah for exclusive exploration rights for five years in an area of northern Iran stretching from Azerbaijan to Khorasan. When the shah told him that the cabinet would consider the matter in conjunction with American and British requests for rights, Kavtaradze indicated that he was not interested in a commercial agreement such as the one at Kavir Khorian. Rather, he was interested in a political agreement between governments. He refused to define its terms, but made it clear that he wanted the concession before his departure.[154]

Fearful of Soviet pressures which would inevitably follow such an agreement, the Iranian cabinet on 8 October postponed all oil concessions until after the war. Kavtaradze, when told of the decision, remarked that it would have unhappy consequences.[155] What he meant

[152] Soviet action in Iran may also have been a consequence of Russia's growing strength in Eastern Europe.

[153] S.D. 891.6363/10-1144/12-1144; FR, 1944, V:452-454.

[154] FR, 1944, V:453-454; S.D. 891.6363/12-1144; Woodward, BFP, p. 317.

[155] The Iranian prime minister told the American ambassador that he believed the Russians were after more than oil in northern Iran; thus, his principal reason

became apparent as soon as the Moscow Conference between Churchill and Stalin ended.[156] The Moscow press began a sustained attack against the Iranian government. Soviet authorities in Iran held up grain shipments and interfered in elections; through the Tudeh and its affiliated newspapers they organized demonstrations, parades, and attacks on the government. The Soviet ambassador even went out of his way to snub the shah. Kavtaradze on 24 October held a press conference. Relations between the Soviet government and the Iranian people were friendly, he declared, but cooperation between Soviet representatives and the Sa'id regime was impossible. The Iranian prime minister, he said, was disloyal and unfriendly. He also expressed the hope that Iranian public opinion would force resolution of Irano-Soviet differences.[157]

---

for refusing the concession was fear that the Soviets would use it as a cover for infiltrating the area (S.D. 891.6363/11-1244). The Soviets, of course, gave the Iranians no reason to trust their motives. As a consequence, while the Iranians took the initiative in encouraging American interest in new oil concessions, their attitude toward the Soviet Union was more defensive. In February 1944, for example, when Millspaugh suspended funds to the Iranian government arsenals because the Soviets were not paying for arms being manufactured and delivered to them, Foreign Minister Mohammed Sa'id pointed out to the American chargé that while Iran lost heavily on all contracts with the Soviets, good relations were worth many times the sum that such relations had already cost (S.D. 891.6363/12-1144). According to Ramazani, the role of the Majlis in opposing Soviet pressure was crucial. *Iran's Foreign Policy*, pp. 102 ff.

[156] Sir Reader Bullard, the British ambassador in Iran, pointed out to Leland Morris, the recently arrived American ambassador, that the Russian embassy's actions in Iran began with Churchill's departure from Moscow (FR, 1944, V:459). It is interesting to speculate as to whether the agreement over spheres of influence between Britain and the Soviet Union in Eastern Europe helped to determine Soviet attitudes regarding the creation of a similar de facto agreement in Iran. Obviously, the Soviets wanted a sphere of influence in northern Iran; but they did not use much pressure until after the agreement between Churchill and Stalin.

[157] FR, 1944, V:455-459; S.D. 891.6363/12-1144. When Kavtaradze visited the Iranian prime minister on 9 October 1944 and talked of the "unhappy consequences" of refusal to grant oil concessions—consequences which he was now in the process of effecting—he was using tactics similar to those advocated by Millspaugh in a draft the American advisor prepared for Roosevelt's signature on 19 May 1944. At a time when Millspaugh had executive authority to effect legislation in Iran, the draft took a strong stand in his favor, ending with the statement "that any reduction in his authority prior to [the termination of the war] would imperil success of his work and the relations between our countries might therefore be prejudiced." The difference here is that the draft Millspaugh wrote was never endorsed. That the Kavtaradze mission was endorsed is evidenced not only by support for his position in the Moscow press, but also by a conversation Stalin had with Anthony Eden at Yalta several months later where Stalin noted Molotov's "resounding diplomatic

Charles Bohlen, chief of the Division of Eastern European Affairs in the State Department, on the same day noted an attack on Iran in *Trud*. Bohlen observed that *Trud*, like all Soviet publications, expressed official Soviet policy, and that it ascribed anti-Soviet action in Iran to "pro-fascist elements" in the Iranian government. Bohlen believed that this was the customary "build-up in order to justify extreme Soviet pressure." He urged the formulation of policy to meet the impending crisis.[158]

The Tudeh Party now came into the open as an "arm of the Soviet Union." It held large demonstrations.[159] The papers of the Freedom Front branded everything that was anti-Soviet or anti-worker as fascist, parroting Moscow's vilification of the government. In turn, *Trud* and *Izvestia* were sharply critical of the Iranian government's attitude, quoting the Freedom Front as representative of Iranian opposition, and criticizing the unlawful presence of American troops in Iran. The Soviets began to use the press censorship provisions of the Tripartite Treaty to censor outgoing news. This meant that news on Iran which appeared in the *New York Times* consisted largely of stories released by the Soviet government, and printed in *Tass*. The privately owned British news agency, Reuters, was subjected to the same censorship.[160]

Thus, the *New York Times* on 30 October cited and quoted from a five-day-old *Tass* dispatch which told of Kavtaradze's news conference. It noted the vice commissar's observation that most newspapers (i.e., the Freedom Front) supported his point of view, and his hope that the public "would make its contribution to the success of the matter." The *Times* did not mention that Kavtaradze's observation was untrue. Again on 31 October, quoting a *Tass* report of the previous day, the

defeat" in Iran and the fact that his foreign commissar was "very sore with Iran." *FR*, 1944, V:404-405, 456; Eden, p. 596.

[158] *FR*, 1944, V:351-352.

[159] The character of these demonstrations is indicated by Sir Clarmont Skrine, a British diplomat at Mash'had in October 1944, who noted a crowd marching by with banners while Red Army soldiers marched alongside, single file, carrying Tommy guns. Clarmont Skrine, *World War in Iran* (London, 1962), p. 208.

[160] Meister, pp. 157-160; Zabih, pp. 89 ff.; Lenczowski, *Russia and the West*, pp. 206-209; FR, *The Conferences at Malta and Yalta*, pp. 331-332; S.D. 891.6363/ 11-1144. When the Iranian prime minister attempted to send his side of the controversy with Kavtaradze to Iranian embassies abroad, his messages were blocked by the Soviet censor. S.D. 891.6363/12-1144; *FR*, 1944, V:472. For the attitude of Soviet press and radio toward Iran after the oil crisis, see *O.S.S./State I&R Reports*, vol. 7, II:3.

Times told of demonstrations of 20,000 in Teheran and 25,000 in Tabriz. The figures were probably closer to 5,000, and most of the demonstrators had been brought in by Soviet trucks and accompanied by Soviet Army detachments, but the *Times* never told this part of the story.[161]

Soviet methods continued to be alarming. The embassy encouraged demonstrations by Russian-employed Iranians. Russian troops interfered when the Iranian police attempted to restore order, and disarmed them. Some of these attacks were directed against the American government. On 1 November 1944, George Kennan, the American chargé in Moscow, gave Molotov a note which stressed that in view of the Teheran Declaration, the American government was unable "to concur in any action which would constitute undue interference in the internal affairs of Iran."[162]

The American note may have had results, for the Soviets soon relaxed their pressure. Kennan surmised that the Soviet government was attempting to undermine influential individuals (i.e., the prime minister) unfavorable to Moscow, and thus keep hanging the problem of oil concessions. He also conjectured that Soviet action was motivated not so much by the need for oil as it was by apprehension of potential foreign penetration and concern for prestige.[163]

Meanwhile, Ambassador Leland Morris in Teheran, aware of a possible divergence between the United States and the Soviet Union, hesitated to encourage Iran to resist Soviet aggression unless the United States was prepared "to back up to the ultimate limit the Iranian Government in its opposition."[164] This was to be a problem throughout the next two years. From this time on, the State Department's belief that United States-Iranian relations were of major importance, and its intention to assume a more active and positive policy in Iran, would be put to a serious test. It was no longer a question of means and ends, of whether or not the United States should back its advisors when that backing meant a contradiction of principles. The question had become essentially one of power. Protecting America's interests in Iran meant strengthen-

161 Lenczowski, *Russia and the West*, p. 220; *New York Times*, 30 and 31 October 1944.

162 FR, 1944, V:462-464. The British delivered a similar note on 2 November. FR, 1944, V:474; Woodward, *BFP*, p. 317, and 4:451.

163 FR, 1944, V:466-471; Woodward, 4:452.

164 FR, 1944, V:465.

ing Iran, and supporting the principles of the Atlantic Charter in that country. Both aims were antithetical to the interests of the Soviet Union in northern Iran. Since Stettinius's earlier policy statement made clear that the United States had no intention of using force to maintain Iranian independence, and since the efficacy of principle was in doubt, the real question was whether the United States intended to back the Atlantic Charter in more than theory, and if so to what extent.

Subsequent diplomatic discussion avoided the question, and followed the pattern set by the Office of Near Eastern and African Affairs (NEA) in a meeting on 3 November with the Iranian chargé, Dr. A. A. Daftary. Wallace Murray, director of NEA and later to replace Morris as ambassador in Teheran, told of United States support for the Declaration Regarding Iran. The United States was at war and Russia was an ally, he reminded Daftary, and he recommended that direct negotiations between Iran and the Soviet Union might be preferable to note writing and protests.[165] This could easily have been construed as an unwillingness to live up to the principles the United States professed—principles which Stettinius was in the process of endorsing as the basis of an 8 November 1944 memorandum he presented to Roosevelt on "United States Interests and Policy in Eastern and Southeastern Europe and the Near East."[166] We have seen that in Southeastern Europe principles meant nothing unless one had the capacity and the will to enforce them. As in Southeastern Europe, it seemed that in Iran the State Department was on the verge of granting the Soviets in fact what it was denying them in principle: a sphere of influence.

George Lenczowski has noted that in Iran "too much restraint and silence was bound to be interpreted . . . as a sign of weakness or as a tendency to compromise principles," and he has pointed out that the failure of the United States to establish a public relations bureau in Iran during the war was evidence of such restraint. He is probably right; American restraint was interpreted as weakness. Although a majority of deputies in the Majlis opposed the actions of the Tudeh Party, lack of visible American support diminished their influence. The Tudeh Party, on the other hand, which in 1943 had garnered only 8 of the Soviet zone's 53 seats in the Majlis, was strongly supported by the Soviets and so exercised influence far out of proportion to its numbers. Because

[165] Ibid., pp. 467-469.
[166] See the discussion of this memorandum in Chapter II.

of these and other factors, the Soviet Union and the Tudeh Party on 8 November effected the ouster of Primer Minister Sa'id.[167]

As Anglo-American concern mounted, Anthony Eden told the British ambassador in Moscow to ask Molotov for a clarification of Russian intentions. George Kennan, when consulted by Sir Archibald Clark-Kerr, declared that such a request would serve no useful purpose.[168] The only way to deter Soviet policies in Iran, Kennan believed, would be to intimate that an explanation of Soviet actions in light of the Teheran Declaration would be required at the next meeting of the Big Three. Eventually this advice was followed. For the time being, however, Sir Archibald Clark-Kerr asked Molotov to clarify Russian intentions. The British government viewed the situation as a test case for future Soviet relations with Iran, and with other countries adjacent to the Soviet Union.[169]

Meanwhile, the Majlis chose a new prime minister, Morteza Bayat, and members of the Majlis began to gather around Sayid Zia ed-Din Tabatabai, the former prime minister (in 1921), who now returned after 23 years in exile in Palestine. The Sayid began forming a new

[167] The organization of a bloc opposed to the Tudeh Party was complicated by the absence of political parties in Iran. Lenczowski, *Russia and the West*, pp. 276-278; Elwell-Sutton, "Political Parties in Iran," pp. 51-53; Frye, p. 117; FR, 1944, V:482-483; Woodward, 4:453. On 13 November 1944, *Pravda* restated the Russian case against the ousted Prime Minister Sa'id by charging that he had armed the Iranian tribes and incited them against the central authorities, and that he had done this in order to interfere with Allied shipments of war materials to the Soviet Union. S.D. 891.6363/12-1144. In view of Sa'id's statement to the American chargé Ford in February 1944 (see n. 155), this charge is patently absurd. See also Pfau, "The United States and Iran," pp. 196-197.

[168] He was right. The formal Soviet reply, delivered by Andrei Gromyko on 28 December 1944, was a blatant distortion of the facts and, as Kennan had predicted, was a recitation of the Soviet position in the press. It asserted that while Prime Minister Mohammed Sa'id had been favorable at first to the Soviet proposals, his attitude had suddenly changed "under hidden influences." Avoiding discussion of the real cause of Sa'id's change in attitude, the Soviet reply further argued that Sa'id was "obviously disloyal" and "hostile" and that his attitude met with the disapproval of wide circles of Iranian public opinion. Since any statements about Soviet interference in Iran's internal affairs were without foundation, the note observed, the Soviet Union could not overlook the unsympathetic attitude of the United States with regard to the negotiations. For the full note, see FR, *The Conferences at Malta and Yalta*, pp. 334-336. For the Soviet position as stated in the press, see I. Svetlov, "Negotiations on Iranian Oil and Soviet-Iranian Relations," *War and the Working Class* (Moscow, 15 December 1944), translation in S.D. 891.6363/12-2944. See also the American embassy's critical comments on the article: S.D. 891.6363/2-645/2-2145.

[169] FR, 1944, V:352, 474-475; Woodward, 4:453-455.

party, the Iradeh-yi-Milli (National Will), which pitted itself against the Tudeh. Led by the nationalist Mohammed Mossadegh, and supported by the Iradeh-yi-Milli as well as the British, the Majlis on 2 December 1944 passed a law forbidding oil negotiations between cabinets and foreigners; thereafter, concessions were to be dependent on the Majlis. This law, which surprised everyone, angered the Soviets. On 7 December, the Soviet vice commissar for foreign affairs called on Bayat to tell him that the 2 December law was objectionable and obstructive. Two days later he returned to the Soviet Union. The crisis, it seemed, was over.[170]

The Soviet attitude, however, was best expressed by Ambassador Maximov, who made it plain to W. Averell Harriman, then passing through Iran en route to his post as ambassador to Russia. According to Harriman, Maximov "had no intention of letting matters drop but intended to take aggressive measures to attain Soviet objectives." These objectives appeared to be much larger than oil concessions, and Maximov justified them by saying that "since the Iranian Government did not truly represent the Iranian people and since the Soviets knew what the Iranian people wanted, it was proper for the Soviet Government to see that this opinion found political expression."[171]

Less than two months earlier, Harriman had informed both the White House and the State Department of Moscow's bullying tactics. He had reported Moscow's belief that it had the right to settle problems with its neighbors unilaterally, and its position that "friendly governments" were those it could dominate. He had then recommended taking "a definite interest in the solution of the problems of each individual country as they arise." Now, after listening to the shah's fears that the Soviets would continue to stimulate agitation in the north, Harriman felt that those fears had basis, and that the situation in Iran should be watched carefully.[172]

In the United States, Secretary of State Edward Stettinius[173] was struggling to formulate a coherent policy toward Iran and asked the president for guidance. Roosevelt suggested that Harriman take up the

---

[170] Elwell-Sutton, "Political Parties in Iran," p. 55; FR, 1944, V:477-484; Woodward, BFP, pp. 317-318 and 4:456-458; Zabih, pp. 78 ff.; S.D. 891.6363/12-1144; Pfau, "The United States and Iran," pp. 208-209.

[171] Maximov's thesis is consistent with the ideological view characterized earlier in Chapter III. FR, 1944, V:345-355.

[172] See discussion of these issues in Chapter II. FR, 1944, V:354-355.

[173] Stettinius became secretary of state on 1 December 1944.

matter of Soviet-Iranian relations with Stalin in person. He observed that "the Teheran agreement was pretty definite," and mentioned his trusteeship idea.[174]

Roosevelt's idea of a trusteeship was previously unknown to the Department of State.[175] The department's policies in Iran and elsewhere along the Northern Tier were diametrically opposed to such a notion; Wallace Murray thought it a great mistake. Undersecretary of State Joseph Grew later agreed and Roosevelt's suggestion was quietly shelved. The State Department meanwhile preferred to follow developments carefully and let Harriman stand by.[176]

Shortly thereafter, a long dispatch from Ambassador Morris reached the Department of State. Morris summarized significant events and incidents which had a bearing on the recent crisis.[177] His analysis confirmed the thinking of individuals in the department who had been dealing with Iran. Morris noted that the British wanted to form a "closely united front with the United States with respect to all questions involving Russia." Bullard had taken great pains to keep him informed of his views and those of his government, and had clearly based his attitude on the assumption that "American and British interests here are identical vis-à-vis the Soviets and that the two governments should and would act as one."

Morris understood Soviet policy although he had not the slightest sympathy with it. A number of factors, he acknowledged, might have given the Soviets the idea that the United States intended to secure a permanent position in Iran. These factors included the extensive opera-

[174] FR, 1944, V:483-484; The Conferences at Malta and Yalta, p. 332.

[175] See discussion of this issue earlier in Chapter III. See also William McNeill's discussion of one of the persistent threads governing Roosevelt's approach to Stalin: "Roosevelt's belief that if he could see Stalin and talk to him as man to man he would be able to break down some of the barriers between Russia and the Western Allies" (America, Britain and Russia, p. 326).

[176] FR, 1944, V:484-486; 1945, VIII:523-526. See also The Conferences at Malta and Yalta, p. 345. As Richard Pfau observes ("The United States and Iran," pp. 162-163, 213, 234), U.S. policy underwent a shift in the Fall of 1944 from more principled ends to the less lofty, more pragmatic goals of strengthening Iran and maintaining stability there. One must be particularly sensitive, however, to the conflicting pressures which influenced many of the policy-makers, the confusions and even contradictions which were implicit in some of their policies, and the constraints which operated on American policy toward Iran.

[177] S.D. 891.6363/12-1144. The dispatch was received at the Department of State on 2 January 1945.

tions of American advisors,[178] negotiations carried on by American oil companies, and the American government's interest in Iran. Whatever the explanation for Soviet policies, Morris saw them as true to the tradition of Great Power diplomacy in Iran. They attested to a determination abundantly demonstrated by history, let alone by events of the last three years. The apparent objectives of Soviet diplomacy were to prevent any foreign power from establishing a foothold in northern Iran, and to continue Soviet dominance in the area. Dominance, in turn, would build up an outer defense zone for Russia's southern frontier and at the same time counterbalance other foreign penetration.

In short, as it appeared to Morris, the greatest significance of the whole affair was that

> it brought out unmistakably the fact that Nineteenth Century diplomacy is still the rule in Iran. It has demonstrated with frightening clarity the tenuous nature of the links binding the Soviet Union to the United States and Great Britain in so far as their relations in this area are concerned.

Conclusion

Morris's assessment captures what was at issue in Iran during World War II: the balance of power along the Northern Tier. The Anglo-Soviet occupation of Iran, because it undermined Reza Shah's earlier efforts to consolidate the centrifugal forces in his country and left Iran even more vulnerable than before, inevitably aggravated mutual suspicions, and revived traditional interests. When the United States entered the picture it, too, looked to its own interests, and sought to capitalize on the fact that Iran had turned to it for succor.

The methods of the Allies in exercising influence over the Iranians were strikingly different. While the Americans appealed to principle, the British used the velvet glove, and the Soviets the bludgeon. But if their methods were different, their ends were all based on conceptions of national interest. Different methods of pursuing these interests derived not so much from varying degrees of benevolence as from the

[178] While Arthur Millspaugh was authorized to engage up to 60 economic experts, technical difficulties prevented that number from being employed. Thirty-five experts were actually recruited, although a number of them left before the mission folded. The total number of American advisors in Iran at any one time thus appears to be well under 100. Lenczowski, *Russia and the West*, pp. 263 ff.

Allies' diverse strengths and weaknesses, and illustrated the bankruptcy of the joint ideals to which they publicly—if not privately—subscribed.

The United States with its vast resources and productive strength could afford to advocate principles which, if no less self-serving than those which guided the Soviet Union, nonetheless were more benevolent toward the Iranian government. Relatively untouched by the scourge of war, the United States was never forced to struggle for economic and political survival to the same degree as its Allies. Therefore, Roosevelt was given the luxury of approaching problems in Iran with a condescending internationalism.[179]

Great Britain was not so fortunate. Because of the empire's increasing weakness relative to Russia, it chose to bury differences with the United States over vital oil interests in the Near East in order to protect them. In contrast to the spheres of influence Churchill and Eden prescribed for the Balkans, the principles of the Atlantic Charter better served the British conception of Iran as a strategic buffer between the Soviet Union and Anglo-American interests to the south; as a result, the Foreign Office chose not to divide Iran into spheres of influence[180] and to emphasize the applicability of the Charter's principles there. That these principles were only tools of British policy, and not its guiding light, was amply evidenced by Churchill's and Eden's negotiations with Stalin over the Balkans, and Britain's subsequent actions in Greece.

The Soviet Union undoubtedly would have accepted a division of Iran into spheres of influence. It had accepted a de facto division in 1941, and was interested in consolidating the zone which it occupied. Wartime circumstances had made such a move possible; the Soviet view of the Atlantic Charter may have made it appear necessary. Unquestionably, application of the Charter's principles to Iran threatened to discriminate against Russia's interests. Her less developed and less sophisticated oil technology, for example, could not compete with that of the United States. Elements potentially hostile to Soviet security

[179] On 29 February 1944, when Roosevelt sent Churchill Hurley's report of 21 December 1943, "for your eyes only," he commented: "I rather like this approach to the care and education of what used to be called backward countries. From your and my personal observation I think we could add something about personal cleanliness as well." Loewenheim et al., p. 499.

[180] At the end of 1944, Anthony Eden opposed the alternative of dividing Iran into spheres of influence as in 1907 because it would involve "an indefinite military commitment, constant friction with the Iranians and Russians, and American criticism." Such a course, he felt, would put Britain at a disadvantage since Russia would be in a better position to exert strong pressure on Iran. Woodward, 4:466.

could refer to the Charter's principles to sanction exploitation of northern Iran.

The Iranians, of course, trusted neither Britain nor Russia, regarded American interest and presence in Iran as crucial to the country's salvation, and were pleased when the terms of the Anglo-Soviet occupation reflected ideals which Roosevelt espoused. Iranian supplication for an American presence in Iran, and the role played by the United States in the Persian Corridor during the war, meant that Roosevelt and the State Department had a much greater interest in Iran than they did in either Turkey or the Balkans. The unique situation which found all three Allies occupying a single, nonhostile country also meant that, unlike the situations in either Turkey or Greece, in Iran the United States could not avoid involvement in Great Power politics.

The conflict between Britain and Russia in Iran did not surface immediately. While the Soviets' good intentions were always subject to question, this was least true before the Battle of Stalingrad, when cooperation between the Allies was essential. It is true that in 1921 Stalin, in opposition to Lenin, had supported the Soviet Republic of Gilan in northern Iran, and that in 1941, in negotiations with the Germans, the Soviets had indicated a desire for a sphere of influence which included Iran. It is also true that Soviet actions in northern Iran had been heavy-handed throughout the occupation. But it was only after the Battle of Stalingrad that Soviet pressures became really serious.

Soviet pressures eventually produced in both the State Department and the Foreign Office a willingness to settle their differences in the Near East. Anglo-American rapprochement in the region became even more desirable in view of Soviet actions in Eastern Europe and the Balkans later in 1944, and in Iran during the oil crisis of late 1944. By this time many officials in NEA, initially wary of both British and Russian intentions in Iran, focused their suspicions on the Soviet Union; and the State Department, if not the president, had begun to act on the assumption of its common interests with Britain along the Northern Tier.

A certain difficulty presents itself to anyone who attempts to appraise the merits and demerits of Allied actions in Iran during the occupation. Some frame of reference is required for such an assessment, and the one that is commonly used—the Atlantic Charter—tends to confuse the issues. An assessment made with reference to the Charter, with its implication that one can come to some judgment about a country's moral worth, fails to question the assumptions one accepts in using such an approach. It fails to recognize immeasurable differences in the degree of suffering and hardship experienced by the Allies, and it does not take into account the psychological consequences of these different experiences.

The traumatic experience of Great Britain and the United States during World War II, for example, can hardly be compared to those of the Soviet Union. While the United States suffered 291,557 battle deaths and the British 373,372, the Soviets suffered something in the neighborhood of 11,000,000, in addition to approximately 7,000,000 civilian deaths.[181] Statistics cited by a Soviet historian give some idea of other damages suffered by the Soviet Union: 1,710 towns and 70,000 villages reduced to rubble; 98,000 collective farms, 1,876 state farms, and 2,890 machine and tractor stations sacked and pillaged; 7,000,000 horses and 17,000,000 cattle lost. Material losses and expenditures ran to 2,600,000,-000,000 rubles in terms of 1941 official prices.[182] However one might question the primacy of security as a motive for Soviet actions, these statistics are a convincing argument for the saliency of that motive.

In addition to the experiential difference between the Allies, there was the difference in ideological perspective. If the source of conflict be-

[181] While there are no generally accepted casualty figures for the Soviet Union, and there is no means of distinguishing those who died as a result of Soviet policies from those who died in battle, or from the 3.3 million who were liquidated in German prisoner of war camps, or from the tremendous number of civilian casualties, there are rough calculations that can be made. Warren Eason, for one, has estimated that the Soviet Union's population declined by 24.1 million from 1941 to 1945. More telling, perhaps, is the fact that whereas in 1941 women outnumbered men by 6.4 million, the 1959 census indicated a difference of 20.7 million—this in spite of the fact that in age groups under 30, men outnumbered women. Of the 373,372 deaths suffered in battle by the British, 264,443 were citizens of the United Kingdom, which also suffered 60,595 civilian deaths. See United States Bureau of the Census, *Historical Statistics of the United States, Colonial Times to 1957* (Washington, D.C., 1960), p. 735; W. Franklin Mellor, ed., *Casualties and Medical Statistics* (London, 1972), pp. 836-838; Warren Eason, "Demography," in *Handbook of Social Science Data*, ed. Ellen Mickiewicz (New York, 1973), p. 53; "Population Changes," in *Prospects for Soviet Society*, ed. Allen Kassof (New York, 1968), p. 220. See also *The Encyclopædia Britannica* (1971), 802J, and the deposition on the *Komissarbefehl* by Hans-Adolf Jacobsen in *Anatomy of the SS State*, ed. Helmut Krausnick et al. (London, 1968). To cite but two different estimates from well-known works, Gordon Wright places the Soviet dead at 16,000,000, while Ulam figures the number to be about 20,000,000. Gordon Wright, p. 263; Ulam, *The Rivals*, p. 6.

[182] Albert Nenarokov, *Russia in the Twentieth Century* (New York, 1968), p. 258.

tween Russia and the West along the Northern Tier was the balance of power, and if the Great Powers generally acted according to the necessities of state, they also rationalized their actions according to different philosophical assumptions. Roosevelt, however, appeared naive about conceptual differences between the Allies,[183] and unaware of the issues at stake. If Hurley, MacVeagh, Murray, and others told him of Russia's aims, and informed him of America's strategic interests, he failed to appreciate the identity of American and British interests in the Eastern Mediterranean and along the Northern Tier. This is evidenced by his trusteeship proposal in 1943, and by his retention of the idea as late as December 1944. As in Greece in 1943, or in the Balkans in 1944, in Iran, too, he ignored the State Department's advice. It is true he eventually heeded the State Department's opposition to his plans in Iran. But it is apparent that before 1945 he did not recognize Russia's historical pressure on Iran or understand the balance of power as an operative mechanism in Iran, any more than he understood these factors in the Balkans or at the Straits, where the United States had no deep-rooted traditional interests.

In the State Department, on the other hand, there gradually emerged a perception of America's interest in maintaining the balance of power in the area. This perception derived from close observation of Allied policies, and from increasingly convincing arguments for sustaining the British lifeline. With this understanding of the problem there also emerged a concern for a more realistic assertion of American influence in Iran. The department sometimes was more idealistic than the president when it came to the implementation of certain policies, but it was more realistic about American interests. Richard Ford's request for a strengthening of American policy resulted in the State Department's more active and positive policy in 1944. This policy, however, still was insufficient for the needs of its representatives. Thus, the subsequent crisis over oil found the newly arrived ambassador Leland Morris hesitant to offer Iran any type of encouragement to resist Soviet aggression on the matters at issue unless the United States was prepared to give the Iranians full support.

Roosevelt's assertion of principle, in the face of Stalin's constant disrespect for it in northern Iran, made it difficult to deal realistically with Iranian problems. When the question was one of power, and of the willingness to use it, diplomatic protests which did not take these fac-

[183] See Chapter II, n. 125.

tors into account were of limited value. Thus, Charles Bohlen advised formulating in advance of any crisis in Soviet-Iranian relations the policy and attitude of the United States government. And George Kennan, in talking to the British ambassador in Moscow, suggested intimating to the Soviets that the subject of Soviet actions in Iran might come up for discussion at the next meeting of the Big Three. Having the Soviets explain their actions at a conference of the Big Three might have had greater merit than mere protests, but only if the Soviets were willing and able to be forthright about their motives, and only if the United States were willing and able to be realistic about the issues involved. In view of the difficulty in meeting all of these conditions, we can see how, in John Jernegan's prophetic words, Iran had indeed become "a test case for the good faith of the United Nations and their ability to work out among themselves an adjustment of ambitions, rights and interests which [would] be fair not only to the Great Powers . . . but also to the small nations associated with [them]." As Leland Morris observed, however, Iran was also a country where nineteenth-century diplomacy was still the rule, and where the links binding the Soviet Union to the United States and Great Britain were tenuous at best. Since Morris's assessment sums up the situation not only in Iran, but in Turkey and the Balkans as well, it fittingly sets the stage for the crises which were soon to follow along the Northern Tier.

Part II

THE NORTHERN TIER AND THE
EVOLUTION OF THE COLD WAR

Introduction

As 1944 drew to a close and the Big Three prepared for the Yalta Conference, the State Department and the Foreign Office became increasingly uneasy about Soviet ambitions in Iran and Turkey. Common concern among their foreign policy bureaucracies, however, in no way suggested that Roosevelt and Churchill were always of the same mind. The president's disregard of America's and Britain's common interests in the Near East, and his desire not to involve the United States in the area, prevented an incipient Anglo-American rapprochement in the region from developing more quickly. Another factor impeding this development was that the ambiguity of Roosevelt's policies in Eastern Europe during the war involved the United States in contradictions which Harry S. Truman was forced to confront at war's end—and that took time. President Truman, of course, was committed to the policies of his predecessor. But before he could effect their continuity, he first had to understand what the late president had done, and then what he had intended to do. This task was especially difficult because the State Department was often uninformed about the subtleties of Roosevelt's personal diplomacy.

Once Truman assumed the burdens of his new office, communications between the White House and the State Department improved, and the chief executive set about fulfilling his responsibilities with a forthrightness that was in marked contrast to the style of Franklin D. Roosevelt. The military situation made it easier for Truman to be more assertive in his dealings with the Russians, but one must keep in mind that the Soviets, too, were acting with greater boldness toward the end of the war, forcing Truman to devote much of his time to the complex problems of Central and Eastern Europe. As de facto boundaries between East and West were established in Eastern Europe and the Far East, Truman gradually became familiar with Soviet diplomatic methods, and like Churchill before him, became more attentive to what was happening in the Eastern Mediterranean. Informed by events in Eastern Europe, instructed by Soviet policies toward Iran and Turkey, and sensitive to Britain's diminished ability to deal with the economic problems of Greece, the Truman administration became increasingly responsive to questions raised by NEA in the State Department, and under Truman's direction began to pursue a more active and forceful policy along the Northern Tier.

In 1945, Allied negotiations demonstrated that high-minded principles and diplomatic conferences were ineffective in deterring the Soviets' ambitions to secure their southern flank and acquire a springboard to the Eastern Mediterranean and the Middle East. Just as Russia's historical aspirations there had resulted in Britain's many attempts to limit them, so contemporary evidence that Russia was pursuing its traditional goals had the same effect upon the United States. Earlier arguments about the coincidence of Anglo-American interests in the Near East and the necessity of confronting Soviet pressures along the Northern Tier gathered force.

As late as 21 February 1946 the Joint Chiefs of Staff argued that the United States should avoid a military commitment to American interests in the Near East, other than through the United Nations, because of geographic distances and the impracticability of assured lines of communication. In March 1946, however, a major crisis in Iran forced the Truman administration to recognize that the United Nations had serious limitations, and taught the State Department that bilateral negotiations between the Soviet Union and the Northern Tier countries were not a practicable means of preventing the Soviets from encroaching upon their Near Eastern neighbors. The administration, in light of its interests in the Middle East, recognized the necessity of dealing firmly with the Soviets, and responded to Soviet maneuvering over Turkey in the fall of 1946 by reformulating American policies toward the Northern Tier and the Eastern Mediterranean. Greece, Turkey, and Iran were seen in their historical geographical role of dividing East and West, and the territorial integrity of the region was defined in terms of the strategic security interests of the United States.

Policy, however, required implementation. After the Iranian crisis in early 1946, Britain's political, economic, and military responsibilities for the defense of the Northern Tier already had begun to devolve more heavily upon the United States, and after the crisis over Turkey in the fall of 1946 the Truman administration was increasingly willing to accept them. But political difficulties in embracing these responsibilities, and a desire not to provoke the Soviet Union, led administration officials to prefer that the British continue their support of the Northern Tier countries. If this was not feasible, the State Department hoped that the British would serve as a front for American support.

The resolution of the Iranian crisis in December, however, demonstrated both the necessity and the efficacy of direct American support and aid as an adjunct to firm policies in dealing with Soviet pressures on the Northern Tier. The United States already was working on the question of aid for the critical situation in Greece when the deterioration of Britain's postwar economy rendered Britain unable to continue its traditional role in the Near Eastern balance of power. This fact, in conjunction with the entire context of recent events along the Northern Tier, galvanized the administration's growing resolve into a public commitment to maintain the balance of power in the region. Recent events had schooled the administration in balance of power politics and the fundamentals of containment inherent in it—even before the containment thesis was consciously propounded. The fundamentals, moreover, seemed to work, and the administration's understanding of them led logically to America's assumption of Britain's role in the Near East. Thus, with the enunciation of the Truman Doctrine and the implementation of Public Law 75, which authorized aid to Turkey and Greece, the United States joined the power struggle which had been taking place in the Near East throughout World War II and the early postwar years, and indeed for centuries.

IV

ᘒᘒᘒᘒᘒ

The Northern Tier in 1945

The Road to Yalta

Iran

In the months before the Yalta Conference,[1] and throughout 1945, the main concern of the United States in Iran was to secure fulfillment of assurances contained in the Tripartite Treaty and in the Declaration Regarding Iran. The United States looked on Iran as a testing ground for Allied cooperation as well as for the principles of Dumbarton Oaks, and sought to strengthen the country internally in order to minimize outside interference.[2]

Britain's concerns were similar, the prime minister himself regarding the Iranian question as "something of a test case." While a telegram he sent Roosevelt on 15 January reflected American sentiments, however, it also noted indications that the Russians did not intend to change their attitude toward Iran, and expressed a desire to discuss Iran at the upcoming conference. The Iranian government on 18 January also requested that high level attention be given to "the desperate

---

[1] The Yalta Conference took place in early February 1945.

[2] FR, *The Conferences at Malta and Yalta*, pp. 340-345. While in Chapter III we pointed out the manner in which self-interest combined with ideals espoused by the United States in Iran, it is necessary here to take issue with Diane Clemens' version of the background to the discussions on Iran which took place at Yalta. The Iranian government was not subservient to American economic interests. American policy in Iran did not exclude the Soviet Union. The United States had not established a virtual protectorate in Iran, and the American government did not advise the Iranian government to postpone concessions in Iran after the Soviet Union followed the Allies in seeking concessions there. In fact, the United States and its independent advisors such as Herbert Hoover, Jr., encouraged granting such concessions until the extent of the Soviets' demands (to be distinguished from the Allies' proposals regarding concessions—which the Iranians had invited) changed the nature of the problem. Allied problems, while they were in great part predicated on questions of relative economic strength, were fundamentally derived from perceptual differences. These differences, and the Allies' inability to discuss them frankly, were the source of most of the problems in Iran—not, as Clemens asserts, Washington's "double standard." Diane Clemens, *Yalta* (New York, 1970), pp. 245-246.

214

situation" which resulted from the Russian occupation of northern Iran.[3]

Thus, at Malta, Anthony Eden proposed to Edward Stettinius that Allied troops begin withdrawal from Iran *pari passu* (at an equal rate) before hostilities ended. The supply route through Iran would not be needed after June, and Eden felt that the Allies should remove all their troops at that time. In addition, he assured Stettinius that Britain opposed any spheres of influence in Iran. After discussing Russia's traditional interest in warm-water ports, the two men agreed on the far-reaching consequences of appearing to default on the Teheran Declaration. Therefore, they decided to seek Soviet agreement on the principle of gradual *pari passu* withdrawal, and acknowledgement that the Iranian government had a right not to negotiate oil concessions while their territory was still occupied.[4]

The Russians, however, refused to discuss these questions at Yalta. There was insufficient time for discussion of troop withdrawals, Molotov told Eden on 8 February. As for oil concessions, tension had lessened and the matter was no longer acute.[5] Stating that it might be advisable to limit the matter to an exchange of views, the foreign commissar offered to have Kavtaradze himself make a report to the conference on the Iranian situation. Eden said he would think over what Molotov had said, adding that he might make new suggestions at a later meeting.[6]

Eden on 9 February submitted a paper to Molotov and Stettinius incorporating the British proposals of the day before. Stettinius was in entire agreement with the British position, but Molotov said he had not had time to study the paper, and the subject was dropped. The exchange which took place on 10 February was of a kind which was becoming familiar and is worth quoting as an illustration.

> *Mr. Eden* inquired whether Mr. Molotov had considered the British document on Iran.

[3] FR, *The Conferences at Malta and Yalta*, pp. 336-337, 339; FR, 1945, VIII: 360-363. See also Woodward, 4:467 ff.

[4] FR, *The Conferences at Malta and Yalta*, pp. 500-501, 748; Edward Stettinius, Jr., *Roosevelt and the Russians: The Yalta Conference* (Garden City, N.Y., 1949), pp. 65-66. See Chapter III, n. 157.

[5] If the Soviets had pressed their desires on the Iranians in late 1944, it would have made suspect their intentions in Eastern Europe in 1945. This may explain why the situation in Iran was no longer acute.

[6] FR, 1945, VIII:362-363; *The Conferences at Malta and Yalta*, pp. 738-740.

Mr. *Molotov* stated that he had nothing to add to what he had said several days ago on the subject.

Mr. *Eden* inquired whether it would not be advisable to issue a communiqué on Iran.

Mr. *Molotov* stated that this would be inadvisable.

Mr. *Stettinius* urged that some reference be made that Iranian problems had been discussed and clarified during the Crimean Conference.

Mr. *Molotov* stated that he opposed the idea.

Mr. *Eden* suggested that it be stated that the declaration on Iran had been reaffirmed and reexamined during the present meeting.

Mr. *Molotov* opposed this suggestion.[7]

So concerned was Eden over Soviet intransigence on Iran that he ignored Stettinius's suggestion to drop the matter. With Churchill's encouragement, he approached Stalin after the afternoon meeting between the heads of government. Stalin laughed when the foreign secretary brought up the subject of Iran: "You should never talk to Molotov about Iran," he told Eden. "Didn't you realize that he had a resounding diplomatic defeat there? He is very sore with Iran. If you want to talk about it, talk with me. What is it?" When Eden mentioned that the time had come to make a joint plan for the withdrawal of Allied troops from Iran effective when hostilities should cease, Stalin said he would think about it, and discussion ended.[8]

Since Eden's talk with Stalin closed the discussion on Iran, and since nothing was resolved by what had taken place, the protocol of the proceedings noted simply that "Mr. Eden, Mr. Stettinius and M. Molotov exchanged views on the situation in Iran. It was agreed that this matter should be pursued through the diplomatic channel." Later, the Shah of Iran wondered why the American secretary of state had not pressed for a reiteration of the Teheran Declaration. If he had read the minutes of the 10 February discussion he could have found his answer.[9] Stalin's advice to Eden never to talk to Molotov about Iran had been unnecessary. At Yalta, both Eden and Stettinius found it impossible.

[7] FR, *The Conferences at Malta and Yalta*, pp. 810, 819-820, 877.

[8] Eden, pp. 595-596.

[9] The Soviet protocol of the proceedings does not mention any discussions on Iran. See Beitzell, *Teheran, Yalta, Potsdam: The Soviet Protocols*, pp. 134-140; FR, *The Conferences at Malta and Yalta*, p. 982; *New York Times*, 20 May 1945.

216

Turkey

During the oil crisis in Iran in late 1944, the Turks anxiously watched the Russians occupy Bulgaria, and wondered why the Allies did not ask them to declare war on Germany. Anxiety turned to elation on 14 October 1944, when the liberation of Athens indicated that Britain had not forgotten its vital interests in the Eastern Mediterranean. Prospects for the future seemed even brighter when, as a result of the agreement between Churchill and Stalin in Moscow, Bulgarian forces withdrew from Greece and Yugoslavia.[10]

But the outbreak of civil war in Athens and subsequent Pan-Slavic irredentist speeches by the Bulgarian prime minister, Kimon Georgiev, and his foreign minister, Petko Stainov, caused new anxieties in Ankara. Fears of a Soviet-supported confederation of Slavic states, and a Slavic descent on the Aegean, were reinforced by the knowledge that in 1940 Russia had been prepared to guarantee Bulgaria an outlet to the Aegean, and were aggravated by Marshal Josip Tito's Pan-Slavic rhetoric in Yugoslavia in January 1945.[11]

The Turks' growing fears explain why they began to identify their in-

[10] Kirk, *The Middle East in the War*, p. 463; Weisband, *Turkish Foreign Policy*, pp. 282-285.

[11] Tito wanted to put an end to conflict among the Balkan states, and in late 1944 took the initiative in attempting to form a federation between Yugoslavia and Bulgaria. The British and the Americans were concerned about these initiatives. They welcomed the idea of a federation if it applied to all of the Balkan states and possibly Turkey, but opposed any federation involving only Yugoslavia and Bulgaria (backed by the Soviet Union) since it would isolate Greece and endanger her position. That their fears were justified is indicated by Milovan Djilas's discussion of the nature of such a federation. There was a general understanding among the Yugoslavs that the Pan-Slavic Committee, created during the course of the war, was meant to rally support around Russia. It was also a fact that the committee was "a naked instrument of the Soviet Government." Thus, in April 1945, Stalin pointed out the meaning of his Pan-Slavic policy to Tito and Djilas: "If the Slavs keep united and maintain solidarity, no one in the future will be able to move a finger. Not even a finger." At the time, Stalin himself was settling affairs in Bulgaria, and would not permit Georgi Dimitrov, one of the organizers of the Bulgarian Communist Party in 1909, and later (in 1946) Premier of Bulgaria, to return to his country. Stalin's excuse was that it was not yet the right time. The Western states would take the return of Dimitrov—who had been general secretary of the Communist International for nine years and who was now a Soviet citizen—as an open sign of the establishment of Communism in Bulgaria. Dedijer, pp. 250, 299-300; *FR*, 1945, VIII:300-303; *The Conferences at Malta and Yalta*, pp. 237-238; Djilas, *Conversations with Stalin*, pp. 25-26, 114, 116-117, 195; Kirk, *The Middle East in the War*, p. 463; Kirk, "Turkey," p. 363; Weisband, *Turkish Foreign Policy*, pp. 282-285; Xydis, *Greece and the Great Powers*, pp. 63-64. See also Chapter I, n. 141, and Chapter VI, n. 59.

terests with those of Greece and the Western Allies. They looked with favor on British efforts to establish a stable government in Greece, and in November renounced claims to the islands of the Dodecanese. When Britain and the United States saw a break in relations between Turkey and Japan as advantageous to their cause—it would deprive Japan of an important point of observation of Allied operations—the Turks decided in December 1944 to sever diplomatic relations with the Japanese. They also accepted almost verbatim a communiqué suggested by the Western Allies which welcomed passage of lend-lease supplies to Russia through the Straits and related the shipments to the reopening of the Aegean.[12]

Meanwhile, as the Yalta Conference approached, the State Department assessed its position on the convention concerning the Turkish Straits and expressed hope the subject would not be raised. The convention had worked well, as the British and Russians stated in August 1941. Failure to use the Straits as a supply route to Russia was not a result of Turkish obstruction, but of Axis control of the Balkans and the Aegean. A major change in the Straits regime would probably violate Turkish sovereignty, and adversely affect the strategic and political balance in the Balkans and the Near East. Internationalization was not a practical solution either since it would set a precedent for similar actions at the Suez and Panama canals, and Turkey would resist it. The Montreux Convention, on the other hand, could be adapted to the collective security system of Dumbarton Oaks. For these reasons the department preferred to defer any changes in the regime until 1946 when, under its terms, the convention could be reconsidered.[13]

While officials in NEA were sensitive to the political balance of the Balkans and the Near East, Roosevelt was not. At Casablanca, when he gave Britain authority to command all Eastern Europe and Eastern Mediterranean operations, he had shown no interest in the area. During the summer and fall of 1944 (when the Balkans had been of such concern to Churchill), he gave no indication of changing his mind. At

[12] The break in relations between Turkey and Japan became effective on 6 January 1945. See Weisband, *Turkish Foreign Policy*, pp. 284-290; FR, 1944, V:900-904; Erkin, p. 284; Anthony De Luca, "The Montreux Conference of 1936: A Diplomatic Study of Anglo-Soviet Rivalry at the Turkish Straits" (Ph.D. dissertation, Stanford University, 1973), pp. 268-269. To appreciate how control of the Aegean can determine access to the Straits, see Map No. 3.

[13] FR, *The Conferences at Malta and Yalta*, pp. 328-329.

Yalta he never seemed especially informed about either the Balkans or Turkey.[14]

The British, on the other hand, had a more important stake in the Eastern Mediterranean, and were better informed. Hence, they had no doubt the Soviets would demand revision of the Montreux Convention. Again, as at Moscow in October 1944, the Foreign Office counseled restraint. Eden warned the prime minister not to be too forthcoming. It would be better, he suggested, merely to note what the Russians said—without entering into discussion, and without giving too much encouragement of British support. At Yalta, Churchill was to be more receptive to this advice than he had been four months before.[15]

At Malta, prior to the meeting of the Big Three at Yalta, Eden acknowledged to Stettinius that he was not sure what the Russians wanted at the Straits. He envisioned something similar to the Suez regime, which enabled warships to pass from one sea to another in time of war. Eden's uncertainty was not dispelled at Yalta where, on 10 February, Stalin brought up the Montreux Convention.[16]

The treaty was outmoded, Stalin said. Japan had played a part in it, and it was linked with the League of Nations, which no longer existed. Since, under the convention, the Turks had the right to close the Straits either in time of war or if they felt under the threat of war, he did not think now that Great Britain would wish to strangle Russia with the help of the Japanese. After this bit of sophistry, perhaps designed for Roosevelt's benefit, he went on to observe that revision was required—what manner he did not know, but Russia's interests had to be considered. It was impossible, he said, to accept a situation in which Turkey had a hand on Russia's throat. He acknowledged that Turkey's legitimate interests should not be harmed, and suggested that the matter was one which the foreign ministers—who were to meet every two or three months—might consider.[17]

Roosevelt, showing both his idealism and his ignorance of Turco-Soviet relations, expressed hope that the Turco-Soviet frontier might

[14] James Byrnes, *Speaking Frankly* (New York, 1947), p. 23; Bohlen, p. 178; Sulzberger, p. 255.

[15] Leahy, p. 295; Eden, p. 587.

[16] FR, *The Conferences at Malta and Yalta*, p. 501.

[17] Ibid., pp. 903-904. Roosevelt believed that the Soviet Union should have unhampered access to warm-water ports and expressed his sympathy for this problem on several occasions. Stettinius, *Roosevelt and the Russians*, p. 268; see also Chapter III, nn. 92, 93.

follow the example of the one between Canada and the United States. After this irrelevant observation from the president, Churchill got down to business and recalled Stalin's discussion of the Straits in Moscow in October 1944. The British had been sympathetic to the question of revision, and had suggested that a note on the subject be sent. None had been received. Churchill endorsed Stalin's method of dealing with the problem, and expressed hope that the Russians would make their proposals known at the meeting of the foreign ministers. Perhaps recalling Allied assurances given Turkey in 1941, or Iran in 1943, Churchill thought it advisable that the Turks be given some guarantee of their independence and integrity. Stalin, noting the impossibility of keeping anything from the Turks, agreed; so did Roosevelt. Churchill thought the proper place for such a discussion should be London, since the matter affected the position of Great Britain in the Mediterranean more than it affected the United States, and the others agreed.[18]

Although the idea of giving Turkey a guarantee was later dropped —it is not clear why or by whom (it may have been Eden)—the working draft of the protocol of the conference proceedings and the minutes of the foreign ministers' meeting which considered the draft contain possible indications of what the Soviets had in mind when it came to the Straits. By seeking to include in the protocol the opinion that the Montreux Convention ceased to correspond to the contemporary situation, Molotov sought to legitimate its revision. It was a hint, he said, that a change was pending. Wary of giving Molotov carte blanche, Stettinius and Eden thought that specific proposals should be considered first. Molotov continued to insist on his general proposal, but Stettinius and Eden refused to go along with him. When one considers what happened in succeeding months, it seems likely that Molotov wanted formal sanction of the Soviet right unilaterally to change the Straits regime. He had to settle for less. The final protocol noted agreement that at the next foreign ministers meeting in London, the Soviets would put forward proposals concerning the Montreux Convention, and that the Turkish government should be informed at the appropriate time.[19]

[18] FR, *The Conferences at Malta and Yalta*, pp. 904, 910-911, 916-917, 948; Clemens, p. 259.

[19] FR, *The Conferences at Malta and Yalta*, pp. 933, 940, 982; Clemens, p. 260. The Soviet minutes of the meeting and the Soviet version of the protocol, published in 1965-66, omit entirely the discussion of Turkey. Beitzell, *Teheran, Yalta, Potsdam*, pp. vii, 122.

One other decision made at the conference which affected Turkey deserves brief attention. During a discussion of criteria for membership in the United Nations, Stalin brought up the question of Turkey's membership, distinguishing between nations which had really waged war and had suffered, as opposed to those which had speculated on the winning side. Roosevelt gave his opinion that only those nations which had declared war should be invited, and suggested that the time limit for such a declaration should be 1 March. Stalin agreed. In the ensuing discussion, Churchill responded to an aspersion Stalin cast at Turkey by confronting the question of Turkey's membership. Turkey, he admitted, would not be greeted with universal approbation, but she had made an alliance with Britain at a very difficult time. Although unequipped for war, she had been friendly and helpful. Stalin, who had little choice but to accept Churchill's point, reluctantly agreed to Turkey's being invited if she declared war before the end of February.[20]

As Admiral Leahy's notes of the discussion on Turkey at Yalta make clear, the real crux of the problem of the Straits did not come into the open at Yalta. "Everyone knew that the Russians desired to get control of this waterway," he tells us. He knew that Churchill, too, was apprehensive. This explains, perhaps, why the United States and Great Britain worked against Molotov's wording of the protocol, and why difficulties over Iran and the Dardanelles were postponed.[21]

Greece

In regard to Greece, conflict between the Soviet Union and the Western Allies had been effectively prevented by Churchill's agreement with Stalin in October 1944. The liberation of Athens, however, led to serious problems for the Greeks and British, and to subsequent difficulties between the British and Americans.

To understand the situation in Greece, it is necessary first to remember that the economic crisis resulting from occupation was acute. Because of the economy's effect on the political divisions within Greece, and because of public disorder resulting from these divisions, it was almost impossible for the Papandreou government to bring order to Greece and deal effectively with the economy. The effects of war

[20] Stalin also may have thought that Turkey would not declare war within the next three weeks. FR, *The Conferences at Malta and Yalta*, pp. 773-774, 783-784, 944; Byrnes, *Speaking Frankly*, p. 39.

[21] Leahy, pp. 317, 321.

221

intensified the dynamics of this vicious circle, whose widening rings sent tremors through the entire nation. Outside Athens, the administration of the country was still under control of resistance groups. Within the capital, there were frequent shootings. Violence had become a patriotic duty, a fixed habit of mind during four years of occupation. So long as economic conditions failed to improve there was little hope of establishing order.[22]

In an effort to restore internal security, the Papandreou government relied on the British and on forces which were either ideologically opposed to the Left (i.e., the Mountain Brigade[23]) or tainted with the stain of collaboration (i.e., the Athens police and the gendarmerie). At the same time, it attempted to demobilize the resistance forces of ELAS and inadvertently divided the polarized country even further. Initially willing to disarm ELAS, EAM's leaders grew increasingly uncertain over government policies and concerned about their disproportionately small representation in the Papandreou cabinet. EAM also sensed that conditions were favorable for a political program of action which could best be supported by the continuation of ELAS. Hence, it was anxious about the Mountain Brigade's intention to bring the king back by force. The Right, on the other hand, claimed that EAM's power was a product of terroristic methods—a claim which was partially true, though not subject to verification because ELAS would not allow government officials to travel outside Athens. Thus, however unfounded and exaggerated, the mutual suspicions of both Right and Left were raised, and compromise became impossible—especially when each side believed it enjoyed public support.[24]

Greece, of course, was central to Britain's strategic interests. Within a month of the liberation of Athens, Churchill made clear to Eden that Britain, having paid the price for freedom of action in Greece, should not hesitate to support the Royal Hellenic government under

[22] McNeill, The Greek Dilemma, p. 135; McNeill, "Greece," pp. 390-391; Iatrides, pp. 129, 133, 148, 151.

[23] After the mutiny in Cairo (which resulted in the internment of over 10,000 Greeks), the British formed a brigade of those who had not participated in the uprising and who were inspired by a hatred of Communism. This unit (of 4,000) participated in the Italian campaign, where it captured the town of Rimini, so acquiring the name of "Rimini," or Mountain Brigade. Iatrides, pp. 54, 152; McNeill, The Greek Dilemma, p. 155.

[24] McNeill, The Greek Dilemma, pp. 152-153, 155-157; Woodhouse, Apple of Discord, p. 215; Iatrides, pp. 156, 164, 168-169, 189; Woodward, 3:411; Stavrianos, Greece, pp. 127-129; Eudes, pp. 186-188.

Papandreou. He fully expected a clash with EAM, and intended not to shrink from it. When confrontation occurred, Churchill opposed any political solution to the problem, and instead prepared to impose his own. Having chosen his course of action, he underestimated his problem. As a result, British forces which he sent into Athens were inadequate to force demobilization of ELAS.[25]

On 3 December 1944, an incident sparked an outbreak of violence which soon developed into a full-scale civil war, commonly referred to as the "Second Round" (i.e., between Left and Right).[26] Neither side planned or prepared for the bitter and bloody conflict that followed. Given the situation in Athens, and the attitude of Churchill toward the Greek government, confrontation was almost inevitable. As the historian of the Second Round, John Iatrides, makes clear, "The real causes must be sought in the economic, social, political and psychological exhaustion inherited from the past and aggravated by the war, foreign occupation, and external manipulation."[27]

The end of the Second Round coincided almost to the day with the termination of the Yalta Conference. And in the final analysis it was Britain's interventionist policies that carried the day. Once violence had occurred, Churchill took more direct control of Greek affairs. In a telegram to General Ronald Scobie, he directed the commander of the Greek resistance forces to maintain order, to neutralize or destroy

---

[25] Churchill, *Triumph and Tragedy*, pp. 286-287; Iatrides, pp. 176, 178, 196, 241-242, 284-285. By the end of October, Britain had 26,500 troops—only half of which were land forces—in Greece. This restricted their use to Athens, Piraeus, and communications centers where they could "show the flag." Their number contrasts with EDES's 10,000 troops and ELAS's 5,240 officers and 43,700 men, Iatrides, p. 176; O'Ballance, pp. 89-91. See Chapter II, n. 37.

[26] The struggle between "Left" and "Right" which began after the Cairo talks of August 1943, and lasted until the Plaka Agreement in February 1944, is commonly referred to as the "First Round."

[27] Iatrides, pp. xi-xii, 161, 169, 178-189, 191-194, 276-277; S.D. 868.00/12-2044; Roosevelt Papers, PSF, Box 52, "Greece: MacVeagh, Lincoln," 8 December 1944 and 15 January 1945 letters from MacVeagh to Roosevelt. MacVeagh's letters, which contain the seed of much of Iatrides' careful study of the Second Round, emphasize the fact that mutual suspicions and fears were rife and that neither pure royalism nor pure Communism had many followers; rather, each enjoyed accretions of strength as a result of suspicions of the other. For a few of the multitude of works which justify or condemn either Papandreou, the Right, and Churchill, or the KKE and Stalin, see: Stavrianos, *Greece*, p. 136; Sarafis, p. 321; Kédros, pp. 510-513; Woodhouse, *Apple of Discord*, pp. 107-116, 181-183; Young, *The Greek Passion*, p. 235; O'Ballance, pp. 95, 110; Kousoulas, *The Price of Freedom*, pp. 118-119; Harold Macmillan, *The Blast of War*, 1939-1945 (New York, 1967), pp. 499-500.

all EAM/ELAS bands approaching the city, and to hold and dominate Athens—"without bloodshed if possible, but also with bloodshed if necessary." In short, Churchill committed Britain's prestige and power to a government which was suspected, however unfairly, of designing to effect the king's return.[28]

Because of suspicions regarding Churchill and the Papandreou government, the lines were drawn. To those on the Left, opposition to the British was equated with a fight for freedom; the Papandreou government, relying on British support, appeared to be opposed to the popular will, and to be supported by reactionary elements from abroad which, the Left believed, intended to bring back a Fascist dictatorship. For those on the Right, the Left appeared bent on establishing a Communist dictatorship.[29] As in the past, Left and Right were bound less by a common cause than by common fears: of KKE ambitions on the one hand, and monarchist ambitions on the other. What fed these fears were Greece's recent political history and social conditions resulting from the occupation.[30]

Churchill's desire to prevent EAM from taking over the Greek government, and his desire to preserve the monarchy, perpetuated and reinforced the polarization of Left and Right. Since earlier he had lost

[28] Churchill, *Triumph and Tragedy*, pp. 288-289; Iatrides, pp. 200-202; Macmillan, p. 500. Secretary of State Stettinius, only a month earlier in his capacity as undersecretary of state, had written a memorandum cautioning the United States not to side with either Britain or Russia in Eastern and Southeastern Europe and the Near East. On 5 December, he unmistakably criticized British interference in Greek affairs. If this made Churchill angry, he was made even more so by the refusal of an American admiral to allow American ships to land British troops in Greece. While these difficulties were eventually ironed out between governments, press reaction, which had been extremely unfavorable, became especially intense after the *Washington Post*, on 12 December 1944, published a summary (leaked by someone in the State Department) of Churchill's message to Scobie. In January 1945, Churchill observed before Commons that he could think of no time in his experience when a British government had been so maligned by its own press and among its own people. See *FR*, 1944, IV:1025; *The Conferences at Malta and Yalta*, pp. 430-433; Churchill, *Truimph and Tragedy*, pp. 283-325; Sherwood, pp. 893-984; Jim Bishop, *FDR's Last Year: April 1944-April 1945* (New York, 1974), pp. 215-218; Stavrianos, *Greece*, p. 121; Great Britain, *Parliamentary Debates* (Commons), 407 (1944-1945): col. 400 (June 16-February 9); Iatrides, p. 211. For Roosevelt's reaction, see Elliot Roosevelt, pp. 222-224. It is worth noting that the Soviet Press, by Churchill's acknowledgment, was careful not to castigate British intervention in Greece. Churchill, *Triumph and Tragedy*, p. 293.

[29] To help give substance to these rumors, KKE circulated reports that they had received Moscow's endorsement to seize power by force. Iatrides, p. 221.

[30] Iatrides, pp. 195-197, 215, 278-279.

the chance to isolate the KKE from EAM/ELAS, his options were limited.[31] It took bloodshed and a trip to Athens on Christmas Day before he finally endorsed the regency solution,[32] urged by almost all responsible statesmen since 1943. Accordingly, on 31 December 1944 Archbishop Damaskinos, who was above the civil strife and enjoyed a good reputation on both sides, was established as regent. He accepted Papandreou's resignation, and on 3 January appointed a new government under General Nikolaos Plastiras, a liberal leader who had forced the abdication of King Constantine back in 1922.[33]

To complement Churchill's political efforts in effecting a regency, British troops began a major offensive. By 4 January 1945 ELAS had decided to withdraw from Athens. An armistice was arranged in mid-January, and peace negotiations concluded with signature of the Varkiza Agreement between the Plastiras government and EAM on 12 February 1945. With this agreement, the Second Round was over, and for the time being British policy was dominant in Greece. But it had required a force of 75,000 to decide the matter, and no one believed a permanent solution had been found.[34]

Nevertheless, relative to November 1944, EAM/ELAS had suffered a great reversal.[35] By the terms of the Varkiza Agreement, they were to

[31] See the articles by C. M. Woodhouse and Richard Clogg in Auty and Clogg, pp. 117-146, 167-205 (esp. 144 and 200-201). Lincoln MacVeagh, in a personal letter to Wallace Murray dated 7 December 1944, blamed Greece's problems not only on Churchill, but also on the United States for its failure to play an active role in the Balkans. S.D. 868.00/12-2944. For a point of view which places blame on the king, and argues that Churchill had little control over British policy due to the king's intransigence, see Ann Karalekas, "Britain, the United States, and Greece, 1942-1945" (Ph.D. dissertation, Harvard Univeristy, 1974), pp. 162-163. See also Woodhouse, The Struggle for Greece, pp. 109-110, who notes the fact that Hitler, Stalin, Churchill and King George all bore some of the blame for the tragic climax of December 1944, but that divisions among the Greeks meant that any scenario one can imagine would have involved bitterness and probably bloodshed.

[32] This meant persuading a reluctant king by threatening to act without him if necessary. McNeill, "Greece," p. 397; Woodward, 3:431-435; Churchill, Triumph and Tragedy, pp. 299-301; FR, 1944, V:150-151, 177-178.

[33] The new government was to include all shades of opinion except that of the official KKE. Woodward, 3:427; Iatrides, pp. 281-285; McNeill, The Greek Dilemma, p. 123; McNeill, "Greece," p. 397; Woodward, BFP, p. 362; Churchill, Triumph and Tragedy, pp. 283-325; S.D. 868.00/1-445.

[34] McNeill, "Greece," pp. 397-398; O'Ballance, p. 108. The regency, even if too late to prevent the conflict that was in progress, had the predictable effect of undermining EAM's base of support.

[35] Many historians—even if they think a different British policy could have been pursued earlier—believe that once the conflict was joined, and if the KKE had

disarm and disband, while elements of the pro-government Greek Army remained as a cadre for the National Army. The KKE was allowed to function openly as a political party, although it was excluded from the new government. In return, the government agreed to guarantee civil rights, to proclaim a partial amnesty, and to purge the state bureaucracy of collaborators. At the earliest possible date, and within a year, a plebiscite would decide the constitutional question, and would be followed by elections to a constituent assembly for the drafting of a new constitution. All sides agreed that the "great Allied Powers" would be requested to send observers.[36]

More damaging to EAM than the agreement was the alienation of many Greeks from their cause by revelations that they had taken as many as 30,000 hostages[37] from Athens during their withdrawal—4,000 of whom died by execution, from torture, or from cruel treatment. As a consequence, the KKE looked on the agreement as a crucial retreat—desirable until their return to popular favor, and necessary to the reemployment of their forces.[38]

With regard to Greece as a whole, the civil war's Second Round merely compounded the already heavy damages of occupation. Only five locomotives and forty cars were left in the entire country, which the Germans had also stripped of livestock and argricultural machinery. In addition to $250 million in property damage, the cost in lives weighed heavily on the nation and reflected the war's bitter fratricidal nature. The Greek dead alone numbered 11,000. Less subject to quantitative estimate were the continually divisive effects of a civil conflict whose

---

seized power, Greece would have been incorporated into the Soviet sphere of influence. Campbell and Sherrard, pp. 181-182; Woodward, 3:439; Iatrides, pp. 279-280. Iatrides attributes this logic to the Communist movement's antinationalist character in Greece, and to its mediocre leadership. See also Chapter IV, n. 27.

[36] Bickham Sweet-Escott, *Greece: A Political and Economic Survey, 1939-1953* (London, 1954), p. 42; McNeill, *The Greek Dilemma*, p. 195; Iatrides, pp. 251, 320-324; McNeill, "Greece," pp. 397-399; O'Ballance, p. 112.

[37] D. F. Fleming asserts that ELAS took hostages after it heard reports that the British had arrested large numbers of people on suspicion of sniping, and transported them to North Africa. Quoted by Todd Gitlin, "Counter-Insurgency: Myth and Reality in Greece," in *Containment and Revolution*, ed. David Horowitz (London, 1967), p. 157. See also McNeill, *The Greek Dilemma*, p. 187, and McNeill, "Greece," p. 399. Woodward notes that after the revelations of atrocities committed during the Second Round, British and American opinion was much more critical of EAM/ELAS than it had been in the past. Woodward, 3:437.

[38] McNeill, "Greece," p. 399; Iatrides, p. 250; McNeill, *The Greek Dilemma*, p. 187; Xydis, *Greece and the Great Powers*, p. 66.

ramifications would subvert recovery and keep the country "in the perpetual turmoil of a mass vendetta."[39]

For the moment, the Plastiras government was given an opportunity to implement the program it had set forth in the previous month. Most Greeks, feeling as if a nightmare had ended, looked for succor to the British, who continued to keep troops in Greece during preparations for the plebiscite on the regime, and for elections to a constituent assembly. The Soviets remained aloof. And the United States continued its policy of noninvolvement—consigning Greece (as it had Turkey) to the British zone of operational responsibility.[40]

Roosevelt's reluctance to involve the United States in the Balkans explains why, at the Yalta Conference, Greece was of limited concern to the United States. State Department planning papers, true to the president's wishes, noted disapproval of and dissociation from any sphere of influence arrangements extending beyond the military field. State Department personnel were aware that dissociation from the policies of others did not constitute an American policy in the area, but executive constraints prevented them from confronting the realities of the situation. All they could do was to urge the need for restraint on Britain and the Soviet Union.[41]

The British, of course, were able to be more realistic. Churchill's conduct of foreign affairs had been schooled by long exposure to traditional diplomacy and the balance of power. Thus, at Malta, the prime minister was still incensed over Stettinius's earlier criticism of British interference in Greek affairs. Stalin, more sensitive to Churchill's operational code, at Yalta referred to Greece only when the Allies appeared

[39] The British suffered 2,100 casualties, of whom 237 were killed in action. Campbell and Sherrard, p. 182; O'Ballance, p. 108; Stavrianos, *Greece*, p. 147; Iatrides, p. 288.

[40] The program of the Plastiras government is set forth in W. Byford-Jones, *The Greek Trilogy: Resistance—Liberation—Revolution* (London, 1945), pp. 265-266. Woodhouse, *Apple of Discord*, p. 225; Campbell and Sherrard, pp. 181-182; Xydis, *Greece and the Great Powers*, p. 66; Stavrianos, *Greece*, pp. 147-148; Woodward, 3:419, 438-439; Iatrides, pp. 221-224, 287; Churchill, *Triumph and Tragedy*, pp. 293, 400, 420, 713; Moran, p. 250; FR, *The Conferences at Malta and Yalta*, p. 249.

[41] FR, *The Conferences at Malta and Yalta*, pp. 103-108, 235, 237, 249-250; *The Conferences at Cairo and Teheran*, p. 259; Leahy, pp. 284-285; Henry L. Stimson and McGeorge Bundy, *On Active Service in Peace and War* (New York, 1948), p. 609; Henry L. Stimson, Diaries, Yale University, New Haven, Conn., 42:83 (2/26/43); Hull, 2:1612; Foy Kohler, letter to the author; Gordon Merriam, letter to the author.

to be selective in their attention to Soviet actions in Poland. Clearly, he intended to draw a parallel between the Allies' actions in their respective military spheres.[42]

At the fifth plenary meeting on 8 February, replying to complaints from Churchill that he could not get information about the situation in Poland, Stalin assured the conference that such information was obtainable, and that the people running the Provisional Government in Poland were popular. After a long monologue on Poland and brief discussion of a few related issues, Stalin brought up the question of Yugoslavia and Greece. There were all sorts of rumors about Greece, he said. While he had no intention of criticizing British policy, he would like to know what was going on.[43]

Acknowledging that he could talk about Greece for hours, Churchill explained briefly his hope that peace would come. He doubted, however, that a government of all the parties would be established, owing to their mutual hatred. After Stalin's comment that the Greeks had not yet become used to discussion and therefore were cutting each other's throats, Churchill went on to say that he would be glad to provide information on Greece. Responding to the thrust of Stalin's remarks, he admitted that the British had experienced a rough time in Greece, and acknowledged his obligation to Stalin for not having taken too great an interest in Greek affairs. Stalin, apparently satisfied with having drawn the parallel between British actions in Greece and Soviet actions in Eastern Europe, repeated that he had no intention of criticizing British actions or of interfering in Greece. He merely had been interested in what was going on.

The next day, after discussing problems associated with Poland's liberation by the Red Army, Stalin again referred to Greece. In proposing an amendment to the Declaration on Liberated Europe,[44] Stalin

[42] Stettinius, *Roosevelt and the Russians*, pp. 60-61.

[43] FR, *The Conferences at Malta and Yalta*, pp. 779-782; Clemens, pp. 198-199; Wheeler-Bennett and Nicholls, pp. 239-240; Beitzell, *Teheran, Yalta, Potsdam*, p. vii.

[44] The Declaration on Liberated Europe was designed by Edward Stettinius, Jr., to reassure the American public, many of whom were sensitive to events in Greece and Poland, and whose support Roosevelt felt was crucial to the United States membership in the United Nations. Stettinius, who knew of the October agreement, saw it as evidence that territorial matters could not wait until the end of the war; agreement would have to be worked out. Because the United States could not commit troops to Eastern Europe, Stettinius's solution was an Emergency High Commission and a Declaration on Liberated Europe—a restatement of the Atlantic Charter's

obviously intended to remind Churchill of the October agreement in Moscow. By making even more apparent the parallel between the Allies' pursuit of self-interest in their respective spheres, he attempted to expand the agreement. The Soviet amendment suggested that support be given political leaders of those countries which had taken an active part in the struggle against Germany. Stalin remarked that Churchill need not be anxious that the amendment was designed to apply to Greece. More than likely, Stalin intended that it embarrass Churchill, who retorted that he was not anxious about Greece—he merely desired that everybody have a fair chance. Continuing to press his point, Stalin said it would have been very dangerous if Churchill had allowed forces other than his own (i.e., Bulgarian and Russian forces) to go into Greece. Thus, he reminded Churchill that he had kept his part of the bargain. The Soviet leader also touched on a sensitive point: Churchill, to protect his own interests, had supported reactionary elements in their battle with forces which had borne the brunt of the resistance. Churchill, of course, had already indicated continued adherence to the Moscow agreement. That agreement, however, had not included Poland. And if the prime minister had agreed at Teheran and Moscow to certain boundary changes, he had not agreed to Soviet control over Poland's internal affairs. Now, apparently with Poland in mind, Churchill made clear that he would welcome Soviet observers in Greece. Stalin, emphasizing his complete confidence in Britain's Greek policy, undoubtedly wanted acceptance of his Polish policy in return. But Churchill did not go that far. He merely expressed gratification that Britain had the dictator's confidence.[45] Agreement on spheres of in-

---

principles. Roosevelt accepted the idea of a declaration, but rejected the Emergency High Commission, thereby rejecting any means of implementing the principles he endorsed. See Stettinius, *Roosevelt and the Russians*, p. 13; FR, *The Conferences at Malta and Yalta*, pp. 97-98, 566, 569-570; Gaddis, *The United States and the Origins of the Cold War*, pp. 157-159; Lynn Davis, pp. 175-176, 197-198; Roosevelt Papers, PFS, Box 89, File Folder: PSF, State Department, 1945, 12 January 1945 and 16 January 1945 memoranda for the president. It is interesting to note that the public in general was not as critical of Russia's relations with Poland as it was of Britain's handling of Greek affairs.

[45] FR, *The Conferences at Malta and Yalta*, pp. 846-849, 854, 857; Stettinius, *Roosevelt and the Russians*, p. 244; Clemens, pp. 263, 329. The parallel between Britain's pursuit of self-interest in Greece, and the Soviet Union's pursuit of self-interest in the Balkans is obvious, and follows from the agreement in October. It was that agreement which got Bulgarian troops out of Greece. Less understood is the parallel Stalin was trying to draw between Greece and Poland, evidenced in the conversation above and more emphatically on 24 April 1945, when he wrote

fluence in the Balkans was clear; acceptance of Soviet aims in Poland was more complicated.

While much too complex to elaborate upon here, the Polish question requires brief attention because of its relevance to subsequent American policies in the Near East. Confusion stems from the fact that for Roosevelt the Polish question was something of a dilemma. If he conceded too much to Stalin he would alienate millions of Polish-American voters. If he did not concede enough to Stalin he would endanger Allied unity. As a consequence, the United States and Britain compromised on the crucial issue of the Polish government's composition, while Stalin, supported in his position by the Red Army, saw his will prevail in Poland. There was little that could be done either by Roosevelt, who did not intend that American troops enter Eastern Europe, or Churchill, who could not have deployed troops there even if he had wanted to. Finally, both Western leaders recognized that the agreement on Poland was the best that could be obtained. It was an extremely ambiguous agreement, and the Declaration on Liberated Europe made it more so. Stalin accepted this declaration of principle with little objection, no doubt because Molotov had secured changes which made its operative clause harmless. All that the declaration provided for was consultation, and unanimity was required before even this would take place. In short, the Soviets conceded nothing, and agreed to a formula which allowed Roosevelt to meet the needs of public opinion.[46]

Truman that the question of Poland had the same meaning for the security of the Soviet Union as the question of Belgium and Greece had for the security of Great Britain (FR, 1945, V:263-264). The Soviet minutes of the Yalta Conference omit both discussions of Greece. Beitzell, *Teheran, Yalta, Potsdam*, pp. vii, 107-108, 116-118.

[46] Clemens, pp. 178, 191-192, 199-215; Leahy, pp. 305-306, 315-316, 323; Burns, p. 580; Churchill, *Triumph and Tragedy*, p. 385; Feis, *Churchill, Roosevelt, Stalin*, p. 550; Ulam, *Expansion and Coexistence*, pp. 374-375; Wheeler-Bennett and Nicholls, p. 217; Herz, pp. 80-84, 86, 100, 104-105; FR, *The Conferences at Malta and Yalta*, pp. 711, 727-728, 776-778, 803-807, 842-843, 862-863, 873; Lynn Davis, pp. 177-187. For an illuminating critique of some of the contradictions in Gaddis's interpretation of the problem of Eastern Europe (Gaddis, *The United States and the Origins of the Cold War*, pp. 133-173), see Barton Bernstein. "Cold War Orthodoxy Restated," *Reviews in American History* 1 (December 1973):453-470. Yergin, pp. 65, 68, 71, 84-85, overstates the clear distinctions in Roosevelt's mind between his *foreign* foreign policy and his *domestic* foreign policy, especially in Poland (see Chapter II, nn. 122-126, and Chapter IV, n. 73). See also Bohlen, pp. 175-177, and Raymond Aron, *The Imperial Republic: The United States and the World, 1945-1973* (Englewood Cliffs, N.J., 1974), pp. 25-27. W. Averell Harriman and

When Roosevelt spoke to Congress on 1 March 1945 about his meeting with Churchill and Stalin, he told them that the Yalta Conference ought to spell the end of "the system of unilateral action, the exclusive alliances, the spheres of influence, the balance of power, and all other expedients that have been tried for centuries—and have always failed."[47] He conveniently forgot that expediency on the Polish question allowed him to make this statement in the first place; that unilateral action had been taken at Yalta, particularly with regard to China;[48] that spheres of influence still existed in the Balkans; and that in the Near East the question of the balance of power had *not* ended—it was *dormant*, and only because discussion of the issues involved had been avoided or obscured.

The Changing of the Guard

Less than two months after his Yalta speech to Congress, Franklin D. Roosevelt was dead, and Harry S. Truman faced the difficult task of carrying out the policies of his administration.[49] The new president at first believed he could identify clearly Roosevelt's policies and intentions. His task was made more difficult by the probability that Roosevelt at the time of his death had not known what he would do about Soviet-

---

Charles Bohlen believe that Stalin might have accepted the Yalta agreement in good faith, operating under the impression that the Poles would receive the Red Army as liberators. Finding this not to be the case, Stalin broke the agreement (Averell Harriman, *America and Russia in a Changing World* [Garden City, N.Y., 1971], p. 36; Bohlen, p. 217). One cannot help but question this interpretation, however, since the consequences of unrealism in Poland had been so clearly demonstrated in 1920. See Warren Lerner, "Attempting a Revolution from Without: Poland in 1920," in *The Anatomy of Communist Takeovers*, ed. Thomas Hammond (New Haven, 1975), pp. 94-106; and Ulam, *Expansion and Coexistence*, pp. 106-109.

[47] Gaddis, *The United States and the Origins of the Cold War*, pp. 164-165; Lynn Davis, pp. 188-191.

[48] The Far East Agreement promised Russia considerable territory and other rights in the Far East as a *quid pro quo* for entering the war against Japan. Roosevelt believed the agreement would save hundreds of thousands of American lives, and he had good reason to justify its expediency, but not if he intended to hold on to principle as the cornerstone of his policies. FR, *The Conferences at Malta and Yalta*, pp. 854, 769-770; Gaddis, *The United States and the Origins of the Cold War*, pp. 161-164; Bohlen, pp. 195-198; Lynn Davis, p. 192. For the background of Roosevelt's proposal regarding a commercial port for the Soviet Union at Darien (a proposal not too different from one he made regarding the Persian Gulf), see: FR, *The Conferences at Cairo and Teheran*, p. 567; Sherwood, p. 792; FR, *The Conferences at Malta and Yalta*, pp. 324, 378, 768-769, 891, 894-897, 984.

[49] Truman became President on 12 April 1945.

American relations.[50] Since the late architect of the New Deal often meant different things at different times, depending on his audience, the question which confronted Truman was not so much what Roosevelt said as it was who Truman would accept as an interpreter of his predecessor's mind.

The new president, as he confronted Soviet actions in Eastern Europe, faced the same dilemmas that had perplexed Roosevelt. The difference in Truman's attitude toward these dilemmas was that the military situation in Europe (if not in the Far East) made it somewhat easier for him to be more assertive in pursuing the letter of the Yalta agreements.[51] Truman was naturally disposed to be more forthright than Roosevelt. Because of his previous military experience, and his inexperience in international affairs, he was also more inclined to believe in clear lines of authority,[52] to rely on bureaucratic channels, and to place more responsibility on the State Department.[53]

[50] Toward the end of his life Roosevelt had serious doubts about Soviet-American relations. While hedging on the question of Rumania, the President was less equivocal about Poland. Transcript, H. Freeman Matthews Oral History Interview, 7 June 1973, Truman Library; Harriman and Abel, p. 444; The Stimson Diaries, 51:61-65 (4/23/45); Bohlen, pp. 213, 239; Arthur Vandenberg, Jr., ed., The Private Papers of Senator Vandenberg (Boston, 1952), p. 155; Grew, 2:1447-1448; Burns, pp. 583-587; Byrnes, Speaking Frankly, pp. 58-59; Walter Millis, ed., The Forrestal Diaries (New York, 1951), pp. 38-41; Stettinius, Roosevelt and the Russians, p. 95; Margaret Truman, Harry S. Truman (New York, 1973), p. 255; Wheeler-Bennett and Nicholls, p. 298; FR, 1945, V:189-190, 194-196, 210, 505-506, 509-510; Loewenheim et al., pp. 668-669, 689-690, 705-706, 709.

[51] FR, 1945, V:252-255. Just before his death, Roosevelt, too, had been thinking along these lines. In answer to a telegram from Churchill which emphasized the importance of a firm and blunt stand by the United States and Britain, Roosevelt expressed his general agreement: "We must not permit anybody to entertain a false impression that we are afraid," he wrote back. "Our armies will in a very few days be in a position that will permit us to become 'tougher' than has heretofore appeared advantageous to the war effort." Loewenheim et al., pp. 704-705.

[52] This made it all the more necessary for Truman to have individuals in his cabinet on whom he could depend. Less than three months after he became president, he would accept the resignations of six cabinet members; by the end of the following year only one, James Forrestal, secretary of the Navy, would be left of the ten in office when Truman became president. See Harry S. Truman, Memoirs, vol. 1, Years of Decisions, vol. 2, Years of Trial and Hope (Garden City, N.Y., 1955, 1956), 1:55-56, 226-227, 324-328, 525, 553-554; Margaret Truman, pp. 65, 274-276; Cabell Phillips, The Truman Presidency: History of a Triumphant Succession (New York, 1966), pp. 13-14. For Leahy's influence, and Truman's reliance on him, see: Harry Truman, 1:18, 70 ff.. Bohlen, p. 213; Leahy, pp. 347-348, 395; Jonathan Daniels, The Man of Independence (New York, 1950), p. 263; Roosevelt Papers, Map Room, Box 9, Folder No. 3.

[53] Contrary to the assertion of one historian, and to occasional derogatory remarks, Truman's actions indicate that he had a high opinion of the State Department as

The State Department, particularly its Russian experts, had been in disrepute during World War II. Roosevelt's and Hopkins' distrust of the men in striped pants,[54] the dictates of military policy, and the president's personal style of diplomacy, all worked to exclude the department from many of the decisions in which it normally would have been involved. State's exclusion from policy may in part explain the idealism (and unrealism) of men like Cordell Hull and Sumner Welles. It also explains the frustration of lower-level diplomats who appeared to have a clearer understanding than the chief executive of what collaboration with the Soviet Union meant. In spite of Roosevelt's and Hopkins' attitudes, however, the two men gradually recognized the need for a closer relationship with the State Department as the war neared its end and foreign policy became more political in nature. One result was that Hopkins appointed Charles Bohlen to coordinate matters between the White House and the State Department, and the State Department was given much greater responsibility in planning for Yalta than it had for any of the other wartime conferences. Roosevelt, unfortunately, did not take advantage of the department's policy papers and briefing books at Yalta, but at Potsdam Truman studied them carefully. Since so many questions at both conferences were handed down to the foreign ministers, these reference materials were important to Secretary of State Edward Stettinius, Jr. and his successor, James F. Byrnes, and were a testimony to State's new role in the decision-making process.[55]

---

well. Shortly after telling Forrestal—in the course of a conversation about reorganizing the government—that "there wasn't much material in the State Department to work with," Truman went to Potsdam, where he stuck closely to the positions which had been worked out by the State Department. Ernest May, "Lessons" of the Past, p. 31; Robert Donovan, Conflict and Crisis: The Presidency of Harry S Truman, 1945-1948 (New York, 1977), pp. 151-152, 154-155, 161, 376; Millis, p. 621; Bohlen, p. 228. Truman's differences with the State Department over the Palestine Problem, of course, involve perceptions that are far more complicated than an off-the-cuff remark might suggest.

[54] See Chapter III, n. 89. The professionalization of the Foreign Service had been gradual, and a relatively recent phenomenon. In 1888, the Pendelton Act of 1883 was applied to the diplomatic service, which was removed from patronage and put under civil service rules. But only in 1924, with the Rogers Act, were Foreign Service officers appointed strictly on a merit basis, and then it still took another bill, which became the Moses-Linthicum Act of 1931, to remedy the maladministration of the Rogers Act. For further details see: Warren Ilchman, Professional Diplomacy in the United States, 1779-1939 (Chicago, 1961); Graham Stuart, The Department of State: A History of its Organization, Procedure, and Personnel (New York, 1949).

[55] Acheson, p. 88; Kennan, Memoirs, pp. 227-228; Wheeler-Bennett and Nicholls,

Facilitating the Department of State's new responsibilities were a number of internal changes. The department, which doubled in size during the war, had badly needed more efficient procedures. Edward Stettinius, Jr., who had acquired a reputation for administrative skills when chairman of the board of U.S. Steel, and who had served effectively as lend-lease administrator during the first half of the war, had been appointed undersecretary of state on 25 September 1943 with the understanding that he would turn his attention to the department's administrative problems. As a result, in less than four months (15 January 1944) he undertook his first major reorganization. Initially disastrous—33 subsequent orders were required to make the changes fully effective and then another order completely reorganized the department—Stettinius's changes included a number of useful innovations. To relieve the undersecretary and the assistant secretaries of many administrative functions, 12 offices were set up under 12 office directors. Four of these were geographical offices, the directors of which, along with the director of the Office of Special Political Affairs, were responsible directly to the undersecretary. The effect of this change was to bring decision-making closer to the country desks where the experts— if they were listened to—could have greater influence in the formulation of policy. In addition, the geographical offices were made responsible for coordinating all aspects of relations with countries under their jurisdiction. Wallace Murray, one of four advisors on political relations, became the first director of the Office of Near Eastern and African Affairs.[56] Stettinius, in spite of his inexperience in foreign affairs, was subsequently appointed secretary of state. Because of Roosevelt's decision to keep control of foreign policy in his own and Hop-

pp. 114, 189, 201-202, 205-208; Feis, *Churchill, Roosevelt. Stalin,* p. 436; Byrnes, *Speaking Frankly,* pp. 23, 60, 67; Bohlen, pp. 165-166, 171, 178, 228; Richard Walker, *E. R. Stettinius, Jr.* (New York, 1965), pp. 24, 36-37, 40; Sherwood, p. 835; George Curry, *James F. Byrnes* (New York, 1965), p. 108; Harry S. Truman, 1:335.

[56] There were other useful innovations, among which was a Joint Secretariat that served as a collection center for the briefing books prepared for the president. Stuart, pp. 383, 389-415, 420; Walker, pp. 8-9, 11, 16-17, 21-22, 36-37; Edward Stettinius, Jr., *Lend-Lease: Weapon for Victory* (New York, 1944); Curry, p. 137; Waldo Heinrichs, Jr., *American Ambassador: Joseph C. Grew and the Development of the United States Diplomatic Tradition* (Boston, 1966). p. 371; Wheeler-Bennett and Nicholls, p. 205; Bohlen, p. 166; Lynn Davis. pp. 259-260. From 1939 to 1945, the number of employees in the State Department increased from 974 to 3,767. The Foreign Service increased from 3,730 to about 7,000 persons. Stuart, p. 414. See also Chapter III, n. 90.

kins' hands after Cordell Hull resigned, the secretary's role in decision-making was nominal, less to make policies than to implement those of the president.[57]

Stettinius recognized that inexperience would force him to rely heavily on department officials, and upon his recommendation Roosevelt appointed a career diplomat, Joseph Grew, as undersecretary of state.[58] Since first Stettinius and then his successor James F. Byrnes often represented the United States at international conferences, Grew served as acting secretary of state for 166 of his 240 days in office (from 21 December 1944 to mid-August 1945). As a consequence, he came to have considerable influence with Truman, whom he saw almost every day. Grew was an exceedingly careful, prudent man. Carefully coordinating State Department policy with the views of the War and Navy departments, Grew was disposed to take advantage of the bureaucratic facilities available to him. He almost never gave Truman a recommendation without consulting experts in his own or other departments, and formulated the daily summary of foreign affairs, which Truman studied carefully each day as his basic source of information, only after careful coordination.[59] In short, both Truman's and Stettinius's inexperience gave special weight to the procedures followed by Grew and to the input of the geographic offices.

While Grew was undersecretary, Stettinius resigned (27 June 1945) and Truman appointed Byrnes secretary of state.[60] Aside from Stettinius's inexperience, the president had been bothered by the fact that his secretary of state had never been a candidate for public office. Because under the law the secretary of state would succeed him were he to die, Truman chose Byrnes as the best qualified candidate

[57] Stettinius was appointed secretary of state on 1 December 1944. An example of the role Roosevelt had in mind for him was the president's directive on 28 February 1945 that Stettinius assume responsibility for putting the Yalta agreements into effect.

[58] Grew, like Roosevelt, Harriman, and Acheson, was a Grotonian, and was close to Roosevelt. His forty-year career included previous service as: undersecretary (1924-27); minister to Switzerland, where he mediated between İsmet İnönü and Elevtherios Venizelos at Lausanne; ambassador to Turkey (1927-32), where he came to know Kemal Atatürk and renewed his acquaintance with İnönü; and ten years as ambassador to Japan. Heinrichs, pp. 5-6, 371; Burns, pp. 21, 136, 552-553; Grew, vols. 1 and 2; Bohlen, p. 106.

[59] Stuart, p. 421; Walker, pp. 25-26; Grew, 2:1449; Heinrichs, pp. 371-373; Harry S. Truman, 1:14-17.

[60] His appointment was announced publicly on 30 June 1945, and his term of office began 3 July.

available—and in part to mitigate the disappointment Byrnes felt over failure to receive the 1944 vice presidential nomination. Byrnes was a competent and highly experienced individual, though unaccustomed to carrying out policies that were not his.[61]

Under Byrnes, Charles Bohlen no longer served as liaison between the White House and State—Byrnes preferred to deal with the White House directly.[62] And Byrnes did not rely on the State Department as much as Stettinius had, but since he was abroad 350 of his 562 days as secretary of state,[63] first Grew and then Dean Acheson served as acting secretary much of the time. Acheson, a brilliant, acid-tongued lawyer with considerable experience in government, like Grew believed in clear lines of authority and functioned accordingly.[64] Thus Byrnes's absence, like the inexperience of Truman and Stettinius, gave the geographical offices greater opportunities to influence policy.

Below the undersecretary, the official with the greatest responsibility for the Northern Tier was the director of the Office of Near Eastern and African Affairs (NEA). As mentioned, Stettinius created that position, and it was he who nominated Wallace Murray as the first director. Shortly after becoming secretary of state in January 1945, Stettinius suggested appointment of Murray as ambassador to Iran,

[61] Byrnes represented South Carolina in both the House and the Senate, served on the Supreme Court in 1941, and after Pearl Harbor resigned his seat on the bench to assume directorship of the Office of War Mobilization, in which capacity he served as Roosevelt's "assistant president." During the 1944 Democratic Convention, Truman was prepared to nominate him as Roosevelt's vice-presidential candidate, and then, of course, was designated in his place. Stuart, p. 425, 493; Harry S. Truman, 1:22-23, 190-193; Margaret Truman, p. 237; Phillips, *The Truman Presidency*, p. 83; James F. Byrnes, *All in One Lifetime* (New York, 1958), pp. 119, 216-230; Samuel Rosenman, *Working with Roosevelt* (New York, 1952), pp. 441-450.

[62] Bohlen stayed on with Byrnes as his special assistant. Bohlen, p. 255.

[63] In the course of Byrnes's frequent comings and goings, a State Department official expressed the sentiments of those who were uncertain of their status under his itinerant tenure of office by quipping, "The State Department fiddles while Byrnes roams." Stuart, p. 425.

[64] Acheson served as undersecretary of the Treasury in 1933, as assistant secretary of state for economic affairs from 1941 to 1944, and as assistant secretary for congressional relations and international conferences from 1944 to 1945. He was designated as undersecretary of state in August 1945, but because the Senate was not in session his appointment was not confirmed until 24 September 1945. Bohlen, pp. 225, 248; Stuart, pp. 426, 436; Heinrichs, p. 380; Acheson, pp. 119-121, 163; Gaddis Smith, *Dean Acheson* (New York, 1972), p. 19; see also Ronald Stupak, *The Shaping of Foreign Policy: The Role of the Secretary of State as Seen by Dean Acheson* (Indianapolis, 1969).

and Roosevelt approved. Murray, a capable diplomat, was an outstanding expert on Near Eastern affairs. The appointment to Iran, a country
which he loved, was regarded by many as an acknowledgement of his
long and dedicated service.[65] It was also a wise move on Stettinius's part,
for the secretary was increasingly concerned about events in Iran.

Since Murray's appointment created a vacancy in NEA, it was up
to Grew, in Stettinius's absence,[66] to name a replacement. Grew, like
most career diplomats who had served in countries on the periphery
of the Soviet Union, had become staunchly anti-Communist. He was
also convinced that most Americans were woefully blind to the fundamental philosophy and doctrine of the Soviets. Even before the summer of 1945 he had begun to doubt that anything could be done to
weaken Russia's stranglehold on Eastern Europe, and to fear that the
Near East and Far East—regions in which he had served—would in
time become virtually subject to the Soviet Union.[67] The appointment of Loy Henderson as director of NEA was probably a result of
Grew's influence, for Henderson agreed with Grew about the Soviets.
Roosevelt's approval of the appointment may also indicate that the
president changed his mind about the Soviets after Yalta.[68]

Few Foreign Service officers have been more highly regarded by
their colleagues than Loy Henderson. His reputation for being tough-
minded about the Soviet Union, however, had made him unwelcome in
Washington from 1943 to 1945. As early as 1919-20, when he worked
with the American Red Cross Commission to Western Russia and the
Baltic States, Henderson had had extended exposure to the conduct of

[65] Roosevelt Papers, PSF, Box 93, File Folder PSF State Department, Edward
R. Stettinius, Jr., 1945, 8, 10, and 20 January 1945 memoranda for the President.
Interviews with William Baxter, William Sands, Robert Rossow; Jernegan, letter
to the author; Merriam, letter to the author; papers in the possession of Loy Henderson, Washington, D.C.; Stettinius Papers, Box No. 224, Calendar Notes, 21 December 1944.

[66] Stettinius left the Department of State on 23 January for the conferences at
Malta and Yalta and did not return to his desk until 13 March 1945. Walker, pp.
37, 53.

[67] In May, Grew, unable to sleep because of his concern about Soviet-American
relations, wrote himself a personal memorandum to this effect, read it aloud to
Harriman and Bohlen the next day, and then locked it away in his private dispatch
box. Grew, 2:1445-1447.

[68] Heinrichs, pp. 49, 159, 186, 217-218, 223, 330, 371-372, 385; interviews with
Loy Henderson and Elbridge Durbrow. For evidence of mutual respect between
Grew and Henderson, see the Joseph C. Grew Papers, Houghton Library, Harvard
University, Cambridge, Mass., AM 1687, v. 121-123: 1945, 1 January 1945 letter
from Henderson to Grew and 18 August 1945 letter from Grew to Henderson.

Soviet affairs. From 1927 to 1930 he was assigned to the Baltic States, which then served as a listening post on the periphery of the Soviet Union. After diplomatic relations were established between the United States and the Soviet Union, he went to Moscow in 1934 with William Bullitt, and remained there for four years as the second-ranking officer in the embassy until he returned to Washington in 1938 to assume the position of assistant chief of the Division of European Affairs.[69]

Even before he went to Moscow, Henderson, like most who served in the State Department's Eastern European Division under Robert Kelley in the 1920s, had pronounced views on the necessity of taking great care in dealing with the Soviets. These views were not the product of shallow or casual thinking. Kelley, a capable, scholarly man who had done exhaustive research on the Soviet Union in the twenties, had insisted that men in his division take special pains to be both objective and careful when trying to verify facts. This Henderson had done, and his experience in the Baltic states led him to believe that there was a limit to the kinds of relations one could have with the Soviet Union. His opinion was reinforced when, in preparing for his assignment in Moscow, he made a study of the agreements previously entered into by the Soviets, and found that nearly all of them had been subsequently broken.[70] Henderson's skepticism about taking the Soviets at face value came to be shared not only by William Bullitt, who valued his work enough to recommend him to Roosevelt, but by virtually all of the Foreign Service officers who served under him in Moscow during the 1930s.[71]

[69] For testimony regarding Henderson, see: Orville Bullitt, ed., *For the President: Personal and Secret* (Boston, 1972), p. 531; Bohlen, pp. 17, 125; Kennan, *Memoirs*, pp. 63-64, 84; Curry, pp. 135-136, 347; Acheson, pp. 170-172, 174; other testimony to the same effect was elicited from an interview with Elbridge Durbrow and correspondence or interviews with many of those who got to know Henderson after he took over the Office of Near Eastern and African Affairs. See also n. 84. For the role of the Baltic as a listening post, see Natalie Grant, "The Russian Section: A Window on the Soviet Union," *Diplomatic History* 2 (Winter 1978): 107-115.

[70] What Henderson did in the thirties was somewhat similar to what Clark Clifford would do in the forties. See Chapter V, n. 185.

[71] George Kennan and Charles Bohlen, who were Russian language officers, and Elbridge Durbrow, who was in charge of the consulate, have all testified to Henderson's profound influence on their thinking and their careers. Since all these men made important contributions in the shaping of American foreign policy at the end of World War II, Henderson's influence cannot be taken lightly (Bohlen, pp. 17-18, 39-41, 125; Kennan, *Memoirs*, pp. 34-35, 63-64, 84; interview with Elbridge Durbrow). Foy Kohler, who served under Henderson in NEA, and later became ambassador to the Soviet Union, has also testified to Henderson's in-

The result of such skepticism was an inner-departmental struggle over the conduct of Soviet-American affairs which was waged from the time of American recognition of the Soviet Union in 1933. Although the influence of the Division of Eastern European Affairs on policy was neutralized when it was merged with the European Division in 1937,[72] the struggle persisted between what some called the government's pro-Soviet and anti-Soviet groups.[73] Henderson, who returned to Washington as assistant chief of the Division of European Affairs in 1938, led the opposition to what the anti-Soviet group felt was Washington's guilt-ridden, syrupy attitude toward the Soviet Union. For the next four years he would stress the necessity of greater realism in America's relations with Russia.[74]

In 1942, however, owing to a four-year rule about the maximum continuous service permitted a Foreign Service officer at the State Department in Washington, Henderson was sent on an inspection trip to Moscow, where he remained for over four months as counselor of embassy.[75] Told by Ambassador Standley in Moscow that Maxim Litvinov, the Soviet ambassador in the United States, had found it im-

---

fluence (Kohler, letter to the author). For a brief analysis of the Moscow embassy in the 1930's, see Thomas Maddux, "American Diplomats and the Soviet Experiment: The View from the Moscow Embassy, 1934-1939," *The South Atlantic Quarterly* 74 (Autumn 1975):468-487, and Yergin, pp. 17-41.

[72] Bohlen, pp. 39-41, 45-55; Kennan, *Memoirs*, pp. 85-90; Fischer, *The Road to Yalta*, p. 211; interviews with Elbridge Durbrow and Loy Henderson; Forrestal Papers, Forrestal Diaries, 4:1301; Yergin, p. 34.

[73] The terms are Henderson's. Daniel Yergin's attempts to codify the axioms of these groups are enlightening, although one must be careful not to overstate the role of Soviet ideology in the "Riga axioms," and underplay the ignorance of Soviet affairs implicit in the "Yalta axioms." See Yergin, pp. 17-68, 415 n. 4. Yergin, for example, gives Davies more credit than he deserves, and attributes more rationality and calculation to Roosevelt's contradictions and ambiguities than they deserve. See Yergin, pp. 32-33, 45-48, 57, 65, 68, 71, 84-85, 417-418; Bohlen, pp. 39-41, 45-55, 140-141; Kennan, *Memoirs*, pp. 85-90; Joseph Davies, *Mission to Moscow* (New York, 1941), pp. 268-272, 357; Fischer, *The Road to Yalta*, p. 211; interviews with Loy Henderson and Elbridge Durbrow.

[74] In 1942, for example, he opposed the wording of the Molotov communiqué regarding the Soviet foreign minister's conversations with Roosevelt on the grounds that it created the impression the United States had committed itself to a second front in 1942, and that the Soviets would take advantage of this fact. He was overruled at the time, although he was later proved right. Interviews with Loy Henderson and Elbridge Durbrow. For the communiqué, see *FR*, 1942, III:593-594, 598, 612-614; Churchill, *The Hinge of Fate*, pp. 341-342; Bohlen, pp. 123-124. See also Chapter II, n. 116.

[75] Henderson, by chance, was the chargé in Moscow when Hurley visited Stalin and made his way to the front at Stalingrad.

possible to work with him, Henderson, on returning to the department in 1943, offered to be relieved of his duties. Cordell Hull at first
refused to bow to such pressures,[76] but later told Henderson that the
White House thought it best that he be transferred. Probably at Hopkins' insistence, Charles Bohlen was appointed to succeed Henderson,
who was sent off as ambassador to Iraq in July 1943. "With the
departure of Henderson," Charles Bohlen notes in his memoirs, "the
Soviet field lost one of its founders, a man who probably did as much
for the Foreign Service as any officer, living or dead."[77]

But the Soviet field's loss was the Near East's gain.[78] After Henderson
officially assumed charge of NEA in 17 April 1945, he was able to use
his understanding of the Soviet Union to particular advantage in assessing the problems that would arise in Iran, Turkey, and Greece—all
of which bordered the Soviet Union or its satellites and which now
came under his jurisdiction. He had a valuable connection, moreover, in
Dean Acheson, who replaced Grew as undersecretary of state in August.
Prior to coming to State, Acheson had asked William Bullitt about
the Soviet Union, and Bullitt's advice had been to see Loy Henderson.
Acheson had done that, and a close, warm relationship based on mutual
respect developed between the two men.[79]

---

[76] Similar tactics were also used to effect the removal of another Soviet expert,
Bertel Kuniholm, who had served with Henderson in Moscow in the thirties and
who had been serving as consul in Azerbaijan, Iran, earlier in the year. See Chapter
III, n. 53.

[77] Interviews with Loy Henderson and Elbridge Durbrow; Bohlen, pp. 121-125.

[78] In addition, Henderson's presence in the Soviet field was no longer essential
to the point of view he represented. The men whom he had helped train, and on
whom he such a profound influence, were well-entrenched. Charles Bohlen, after
interpreting for Ambassador W. Averell Harriman in Moscow, and then Roosevelt
at Teheran and Yalta, was now serving as liaison officer between the White House
and State, as well as advising both Truman and Grew on foreign affairs. Elbridge
Durbrow had replaced Bohlen as chief of the Division of Eastern European Affairs
within the Office of European Affairs, and George Kennan was the second-ranking
Foreign Service Officer in Moscow, where he had the ear of Harriman. Bohlen, pp.
132-133; Harriman, pp. 1-10; Harriman and Abel, pp. ix-x, 229, 547-548; Kennan,
Memoirs, pp. 190, 242-246, 283, 290.

[79] There were naturally differences between them—one in particular which occurred over the organization of intelligence in the government. But this was to be expected between men who acted according to their convictions, and did not lessen
their respect for each other (Acheson, pp. 159-160; interview with Loy Henderson).
It is worth noting here that Acheson had known Harriman both at Groton and at
Yale, where Harriman coached the freshman rowing team, of which Acheson was
a member. Acheson paid close attention to Harriman's views of the Soviets, as well
as to those of Henderson and Durbrow—the latter of whom he frequently called into

While Byrnes would come to have high regard for Henderson, the process took time. It would also take time for the Truman administration to get used to the idea that the Near East merited as much attention as that being accorded Eastern Europe. Meanwhile, Henderson's advocacy of a more significant American role in the Middle East took up where Wallace Murray's left off, and gradually reached attentive ears through Acheson's daily 9:30 meetings, the twice-weekly meetings of the geographic offices, and informal sessions after five in Byrnes's office when he was in Washington.[80]

As Henderson was later to recall, throughout the period 1945-47 he was certain about what the Soviets were after as they continued to exert pressure on Iran, Greece, and Turkey.[81] Many of the European-oriented officers (of whom Acheson was one) were intially uninterested in the area, and in the meetings of the geographic offices Henderson often had to stand alone in his arguments for an increased American role in the Middle East.[82]

Henderson's only experience in the Middle East had been in Iraq, but he was capably supported by an experienced staff which now numbered over fifty. George Allen, his deputy director, had served in Greece.[83] Gordon Merriam, chief of the Division of Near Eastern Af-

---

his office to discuss Soviet affairs. As we shall see, he was also to be influenced by Kennan. Gaddis Smith, *Dean Acheson*, p. 4; Acheson, pp. 85, 151, 159-160; Harriman and Abel, p. 36; interviews with Elbridge Durbrow and Loy Henderson.

[80] Curry, pp. 135-136, 144, 347; Acheson, p. 129; Gaddis Smith, *Dean Acheson*, p. 27. Elbridge Durbrow was in Moscow with Harriman when Roosevelt died, and flew back in April with Harriman to Washington, where he resumed his position as chief of the Division of Eastern European Affairs. His recollection is that he observed an immediate change in America's attitude toward Eastern Europe under Truman. Loy Henderson, whose areas of responsibility were at the time peripheral to the focus of Great Power conflict, recalls that the transition to a firmer attitude toward the Soviet Union in the Near East was much more gradual. Interviews with Elbridge Durbrow and Loy Henderson. This suggests that the situation in the Near East was still waiting to be defined—a process which would take two more years.

[81] In 1947, a separate division under NEA was set up by Loy Henderson to handle Greek, Turkish, and Iranian affairs. GTI, as it was known, was headed by John Jernegan. Jernegan, letter to the author; transcript, Joseph C. Satterthwaite Oral History Interview, 13 November 1973, p. 18, Truman Library. (See Appendix A)

[82] Interview with Loy Henderson. The European-oriented officers looked down on the Near East through their metropolitan glasses, and referred to the Near East desk condescendingly as the "burnoose boys." Interviews with Raymond Hare and William Baxter.

[83] Allen was to impress Henderson, Acheson, and Byrnes so much that when, in 1946, high blood pressure caused Wallace Murray to suffer hemorrhages in his nose

fairs (NE), had long experience in the Near East, having served not only in Iran and Turkey, but also in Lebanon, Iraq, Syria, and Egypt. Harold Minor, chief of the Division of Middle Eastern and Indian Affairs (MEI), was fluent in Turkish, and had spent the first part of the war in Iran. In addition, the Division of Research for Near East and Africa had a number of very capable experts on Middle Eastern affairs, including Kerim Key on Turkey, Harry Howard on the Straits, and Joseph Upton on Iran. Henderson also obtained as his special assistant Edwin Wright, who had been born and reared in Iran, and who knew that country as did few diplomats.[84]

The Office of Near Eastern and African Affairs under Henderson had the same esprit de corps that was evidenced by the men who served under him at Moscow. A modest man, Henderson did not play the role of "expert," and rather let the experts speak for themselves. A hard taskmaster, both on himself and on his staff, he evoked a strong sense of loyalty. His confidence in his staff exacted their best efforts and earned him their mutual respect. As a consequence, Henderson was able to draw upon their expertise, and in conjunction with his understanding of Soviet behavior, to formulate and obtain executive approval for a coherent policy in the Near East which could best represent the national interest.

Throughout 1945-46, Henderson sought support for a more dynamic American policy in the Middle East. The policy which he inherited was essentially a reaffirmation of the principles of the Atlantic Charter—principles which were obviously inadequate by themselves. Gordon

and led doctors to fear the danger of a stroke in Teheran's high altitude, Allen was sent to replace him. Nominated on 16 April and appointed a week later, he arrived in Teheran on 7 May and assumed charge of the embassy on 11 May 1946. Jernegan, letter to the author; papers in the possession of Loy Henderson, Washington, D.C.; S.D. 123 Allen, George/4-1646.

[84] Information about the Office of Near Eastern and African Affairs was obtained from the following sources: "The Division of Near Eastern Affairs," *The American Foreign Service Journal* 10 (Jan. 1933):16-18; U.S. Government, *Register of the Department of State, December 1, 1946* (Washington, D.C., 1947); Evan Wilson, "The Palestine Papers, 1943-1947," *Journal of Palestine Studies* 2 (Summer 1974): 33-54; Loy Henderson, "Foreign Policies: Their Formulation and Enforcement," Department of State *Bulletin* 15 (September 29, 1946):590-596; John Jernegan, letter to the author; Edwin Wright, "A Personal Narrative—A Retrospective View"; Gordon Merriam, letter to the author; interviews with Loy Henderson, Raymond Hare, William Sands, Harry Howard, and William Baxter; Foy Kohler, letter to the author; Harold Minor, letter to the author; and papers in the possession of Loy Henderson, Washington, D.C.

Merriam, chief of the Division of Near Eastern Affairs, recognized that the region was a source of conflict between the economic systems and strategic interests of Britain and Russia. To prevent a situation which either of the traditional rivals might use to their advantage, Merriam recommended that the United States foster the economic advancement of the region. The success of such a course, he reasoned, would promote America's political interests in the region and reduce trade barriers. Although Henderson worked hard to implement such a policy, his efforts were to no avail—at least in 1945. Another memorandum by Merriam, which Henderson and Acheson forwarded to Byrnes in October, noted potential trouble (which we have yet to examine) in Iran and Turkey, American oil interests in Saudi Arabia, a marked Soviet interest in the area, and the fact that Britain was unable to play its traditional role in the Middle East without help. Merriam argued that note writing, propaganda regarding principles, and government loans were inadequate. To effect political and strategic goals one had to have appropriations.[85]

Several factors, however, worked against this recommendation. One was the traditional notion that the area was within Britain's sphere. As with the Balkans, prevailing opinion held that the United States should not become involved in the area. Another factor was the Treasury Department's lack of interest in the Near East. Many of the decision-makers in that department—especially Morgenthau, who resigned in July—had been so opposed to Germany that they did not see the Soviet Union as a threat to the United States or its interests. They kept a sharp eye on Henderson's colleague Elbridge Durbrow in the Eastern European Division, and were not interested in the policies which Henderson advocated, particularly since the thrust of a forward policy in the region was conceived of as a counter to Soviet pressure along the Northern Tier. More significantly, Byrnes felt that such a policy was unfeasible—at least for the time being.[86]

Henderson was persistent. He chose still another course and attempted to elicit from the president himself assurances about overall policy objectives in the Near East. Upon his recommendation, Truman agreed to receive four ministers who were leaving for their posts in the Near East. At a meeting on 10 November Truman agreed that the countries of the Arab world warranted a more important place in

[85] FR, 1945, VIII:34-39, 43-48; interview with Loy Henderson.
[86] Interviews with Elbridge Durbrow and Loy Henderson; FR, 1945, VIII:44.

America's foreign policy, and that requests for technical experts would be sympathetically received. Henderson had specifically asked Truman to assure the ministers that the United States had no intention of withdrawing from the Near East, and the president was as emphatic on this point as Henderson wished.[87] Despite these assurances, however, American policies in the Near East had yet to be realized in anything other than words. It would take another year before events along the Northern Tier would crystallize the Truman administration's conceptions of its national interest in the region. Even then it would take the threat created by Britain's decision to withdraw from the Eastern Mediterranean to galvanize the American government into action.

The Road to Potsdam—and After

In the interim, at least during 1945, the new administration attempted to carry out what it believed to be Roosevelt's foreign policies. The new president immersed himself in international problems and made decisions based on the facts as he saw them. Demonstrating a remarkable sense of responsibility and command, he eschewed the subtle, sometimes ambivalent attitudes characteristic of Roosevelt, impressing everyone with his own decisive attitude, and meeting head-on the central issue, Poland, which had been surmounted at Yalta only through equivocation.[88]

The manner in which the Polish question was resolved was significant in determining the future relations between the United States and the Soviet Union in the Near East. It was Roosevelt's greatest diplomatic problem just before his death, and once it devolved upon Truman, the Polish question remained what the Turkish foreign minister, Numan Menemencioğlu, earlier referred to as the *pierre de touche*.[89]

It is true that Truman never understood the nature of the Yalta compromise on Poland nor the contradiction between a Polish government friendly to the Soviet Union and the holding of free elections

[87] *FR*, 1945, VIII:10-18.

[88] Cabell Phillips, *The Truman Presidency*, pp. 13-14, 79; Margaret Truman, p. 65; Stimson Diaries, 51:50 (4/18/45); Grew, 2:1485; Daniels, *The Man of Independence*, p. 263; Herbert Feis, *Between War and Peace: The Potsdam Conference* (Princeton, 1960), pp. 8-9; Leahy, p. 348; Harriman, *America and Russia*, p. 39; Acheson, pp. 104-101. For details of Truman's earlier career, see: Phillips, pp. 9-47; Margaret Truman, pp. 49-231; Harry S. Truman, 1:1-8, 112-198.

[89] *FR*, 1945, V:212-213, 265-271; Harry S. Truman, 1:76; Gaddis, *The United States and the Origins of the Cold War*, p. 233; Lynn Davis, p. 222.

in Poland.[90] Most of his advisors regarded Soviet actions in Eastern Europe as violations of specific agreements, and Truman acted firmly on the basis of their advice, but he nonetheless sought to be fair and even conciliatory in his relations with the Soviets.[91] Hoping for a clear understanding on the outstanding issues between the Soviet Union and the United States, he sent Harry Hopkins to Moscow to talk with Stalin in late May 1945.[92]

[90] These deficiencies in Truman's understanding appear to have had no appreciable affect on Soviet policies. Maxim Litvinov, former Soviet ambassador to the United States, and then vice commissar of foreign affairs in charge of postwar planning for the European section of Narkomindel, on 6 October 1944 told Edgar Snow, a *Saturday Evening Post* correspondent, that there was no real hope for the London Poles and Lublin Poles getting together and opined that the Soviet Union was "absolutely right about Poland." Litvinov also observed that Stalin attributed hostile press reaction neither to his policies nor to his diplomacy, but to malice and intrigue. Snow later sent a memorandum of this conversation to Roosevelt. Roosevelt Papers, PSF, Box 66, File Folder: Russia—1945.

[91] Truman halted General Omar Bradley's forces (which had reached the Elbe on the day Roosevelt died), allowed the Soviets to capture Prague, and refused to take Churchill's suggestion that he use territory as a bargaining counter for political concessions from the Soviets in Eastern Europe. If he was harsh with Molotov on 23 April 1945, he was not necessarily unfair; his attempt to be forthright in an effort to break the impasse on the Polish question and guarantee a successful meeting at San Francisco, however naive, was not necessarily misplaced. One should not overlook the cogency of Harriman's observations in the briefings prior to that meeting, Stalin's attitude over the Berne episode, the signing of the Polish-Soviet treaty prior to Molotov's visit, and the attitude struck by Molotov in his talks with Stettinius and Eden on 22 April. It is Stalin's attitude, of course, that is at issue. That Molotov was little more than an unyielding defender of Stalin's dictates, totally subordinate to Stalin, is evidenced by his negotiating behavior, and by his inability even to prevent his own wife from being sent into exile by Stalin. In any case, it is doubtful that Stalin, who in 1939 could toast Hitler and call him "molodetz"—a "fine fellow"—would have been bothered by a few blunt words to his foreign minister. For Stalin, actions were more important. Harry S. Truman, 1:9, 23-25, 34, 50, 70-75, 79-80, 97-98, 211-214, 216, 271, 298-303; Leahy, pp. 348-351; Bohlen, pp. 213, 216: Phillips, *The Truman Presidency*, p. 72; Donovan, pp. 37-44; Loewenheim et al., pp. 696-697, 704-705, 707; FR, 1945, V:218-219; Acheson, p. 88; Ulam, *The Rivals*, p. 67; Bohlen, p. 83; Harriman and Abel, pp. 453-454; Wilson D. Miscamble, "Anthony Eden and the Truman-Molotov Conversations, April 1945," *Diplomatic History* 2 (Spring 1978): 167-180.

[92] In this move, as in his decision to be firm with the Soviets, he was following advice of the Russian experts in the State Department—advice whose wisdom and accuracy are often disregarded by those who focus on bureaucratic politics and perceptions. For background see FR, 1945, V:252-255, 299-338; Harry S. Truman, 1:77-82, 110, 257-258; Stettinius Papers, Box 244, Calendar Notes, 21 April 1945; Millis, pp. 48-51; Grew, 2:1446; Vandenberg, pp. 196-197; Byrnes, *Speaking Frankly*, pp. 33-34, 73-75, 98; Bohlen, pp. 192, 215, 217-224; Harriman, pp. 34-35,

Truman soon learned that in Poland Soviet actions tended to dictate events, whether or not an understanding had been reached. In January 1945, against Roosevelt's wishes, the Soviet Union had recognized the Provisional National Government of the Polish Republic. On the day before Molotov met with Truman for the first time in April, the Soviet Union signed a treaty of mutual assistance with the Provisional Government. This move was followed by the arrest of sixteen leaders of the Polish underground. In May, the deadlock over Poland was broken in Moscow only by Harry Hopkins' willingness to overlook the question of the overall interpretation of the Yalta Declaration. After the Hopkins mission to the Soviet Union, lip service only was paid to the Yalta pledges, and Truman learned from experience what Roosevelt had been up against when he dealt with the Soviet dictator.[93]

At Potsdam (17 July-2 August), the president learned that the Soviet Union had incorporated eastern Germany into Poland's western territory. This unilateral action clearly went beyond any previous understanding and was correctly regarded by Truman, Leahy, and Byrnes as still another *fait accompli*. By that time, of course, the Polish issue was dead. The new Warsaw regime already ruled the disputed area, and attempts to reassert the validity of the Declaration on Liberated Europe only led to further attacks on British policy in Greece. As Admiral Leahy observed, "Britain and the United States had to accept at Potsdam many unilateral actions taken by Moscow since Yalta, although this acceptance was concealed in the diplomatic verbiage of the final report. This was especially true of Poland."[94]

40, 70; Stimson Diaries, 51:61-65 (4/23/45); Leahy, pp. 351-352; Arnold Rogow, *James Forrestal: A Study of Personality, Politics, and Policy* (New York, 1963), p. 199; FR, *The Conference of Berlin (The Potsdam Conference), 1945*, vols. I and II (hereafter cited as *Potsdam I* and *Potsdam II*), I:21-62; Herz, pp. 19-37; Kennan, *Memoirs*, pp. 242-246; Yergin, p. 72. A focus on bureaucratic politics sometimes leads one to overlook the *external* problems which bureaucracies face, and the political contexts of those problems. A useful critique of some of the other limitations of this approach can be found in Stephen Krasner, "Are Bureaucracies Important? (Or Allison Wonderland)," *Foreign Policy* 7 (Summer 1972): 159-179, and Robert Art, "Bureaucratic Politics and American Foreign Policy: A Critique," *Policy Sciences* 4 (December 1973):467-490.

[93] Herz, pp. 19-37, 76-111; Lynn Davis, pp. 202-254; Gaddis, *The United States and the Origins of the Cold War*, pp. 234-235; Harry S. Truman, 1:50, 320.

[94] Harry S. Truman, 1:366-373, 404-412, 551; Leahy, p. 406; Byrnes, *Speaking Frankly*, pp. 79-81; Phillips, p. 90; Lisle Rose, *The Coming of the American Age, 1945-1946: Dubious Victory, The United States and the End of World War II* (Kent, Ohio, 1973), p. 288; Bohlen, pp. 234, 240; FR, *Potsdam II*:150-155, 213,

While Truman and Churchill, and Clement Attlee who succeeded him as prime minister during the conference, had no choice but to sanction Soviet domination of Poland, they were more reluctant to acquiesce in Soviet domination of other Eastern European countries. Even so, there was little recourse. When Churchill talked of an iron fence around Allied representatives in Eastern Europe, Stalin dismissed such accusations as fairy tales. The Soviet Union, nonetheless, was tightening control everywhere in the area. It was imposing governments on the Eastern European states and then negotiating with them commercial treaties similar to those negotiated earlier with Iran. As a briefing book paper for the Potsdam Conference put it: Eastern Europe was in fact, if not in name, a Soviet sphere of influence.[95]

What course would the United States pursue? The war in Europe was over (8 May). In a little over a month atomic bombs would drop on Hiroshima (5 August) and Nagasaki (14 August). One event was following hard on another, and the Great Powers were working strenuously to manage the drift of history. After the London Conference of Foreign Ministers in September, differences over increasingly unilateral Soviet policies in Eastern Europe[96] led the United States once

220, 356, 698-699, 1041-1045; Churchill, *Triumph and Tragedy*, p. 636; Lynn Davis, pp. 241-254; Feis, *Between War and Peace*, pp. 198-199, 221-234, 259-271; Leahy, p. 426; Yergin, pp. 114, 118.

[95] Lynn Davis, pp. 255-297; Feis, *Churchill, Roosevelt, Stalin*, pp. 564-570; FR, 1945, V:544-545, 852-853; FR, *Potsdam* I:258-259; *Potsdam* II:362. In June 1945, when Edgar Snow talked with Litvinov in Moscow, he asked the former foreign minister if things were better or worse than when they had spoken in late 1944. "Worse," was Litvinov's reply, and he asked why the United States had waited until then to begin opposing the Soviets in the Balkans and Eastern Europe. He then prescribed what should have been done: "You should have done this three years ago. Now it's too late and your complaints only arouse suspicion here." Vojtech Mastny, in a recent assessment of Litvinov's statements during the war, concludes that his interpretation was independent and fair: "his country's striving for power and influence too far in excess of its reasonable security requirements was the primary cause of the conflict; the West's failure to resist that effort early enough was an important secondary one." If Litvinov's analysis and Mastny's assessment are correct—and I believe they are—the subsequent policies of the Truman administration along the Northern Tier would appear to be in line with what Litvinov believed the United States should have done in Eastern Europe and the Balkans during World War II. Edgar Snow, *Journey to the Beginning* (New York, 1958), p. 357; Vojtech Mastny, "The Cassandra in the Foreign Commissariat: Maxim Litvinov and the Cold War," *Foreign Affairs* 54 (January 1976): 366-376.

[96] This aggressive attitude may well have served to compensate a perceived weakness resulting from America's possession of the atomic bomb. Harriman and Abel, p. 519.

again to affirm the principles of the Declaration on Liberated Europe. Beyond rhetoric, however, little was done to implement those principles, and by October the conflict which had been papered over at Potsdam was becoming more explicit. And more complex. Withholding diplomatic recognition of certain countries in Eastern Europe, or delaying the signing of peace treaties there, had little effect on the Soviets. What was happening in Japan, however, would not be so easily disregarded.[97]

John Gaddis has observed that with the surrender of Japan, Congress gradually reemerged as a major influence in the making of foreign policy and began to push the Truman administration toward a firmer Russian policy. Even before this occurred the administration was slowly changing tactics. This change resulted not only from a new set of circumstances, but from an altered perception of Soviet strategy. Truman's experience at Potsdam made him determined not to allow the Soviets any part in the control of Japan. Stalin was well aware of his weak position in the Far East, a position which the bomb had made even more difficult. According to W. Averell Harriman, who talked to him about this problem, Stalin's failure to receive satisfaction on Japan made it even more certain he would be intransigent over the Balkan countries.[98]

Thus events, as well as the administration's perceptions of those events, had become inextricably interwoven in the warp and woof of policy formulation. In the last half of 1945, Soviet control of Eastern Europe was seen by the United States not only as a warning signal of what could happen in the Far East, but also as a clear indication of Soviet intentions to expand outside Eastern Europe.

In October, Secretary of State Byrnes had sent Mark Ethridge, of the *Louisville Courier-Journal*, as an independent, neutral observer to investigate conditions in Rumania and Bulgaria. His objective was to see if the interim governments in those countries were broadly representative in the sense of the Yalta Declaration. The reports Ethridge sent back stated in no uncertain terms that neither of the interim governments was broadly representative. Rather, they were authoritarian, excluded large democratically inclined segments of the population, and

[97] Lynn Davis, pp. 299-334; Harry S. Truman, 1:412.
[98] Gaddis, *The United States and the Origins of the Cold War*, pp. 263-281; FR, 1945, V:252-255; Loewenheim et al., pp. 704-705; Harry Truman, 1:412; Harriman and Abel, pp. 513-521; Rose, pp. 360-362.

were totally under Soviet control. Further, Ethridge saw the Soviet position in Bulgaria and Rumania as a means of bringing pressure on Greece, Turkey, and the Straits. John Hickerson, deputy director of the Office of European Affairs, endorsed this analysis, envisaging a larger scheme for the establishment of a Soviet security zone throughout the Balkans and the Eastern Mediterranean.[99]

Ethridge's report was to have considerable importance. Byrnes used it when he prepared for his talks with Stalin in Moscow in December 1945. Truman read the report in early January 1946, when it was a factor in convincing him of the need for a much firmer attitude toward the Soviet Union. Confronted in Eastern Europe with an example of how not to deal with the Soviets, Truman then directed his administration's attention to the Eastern Mediterranean. Concurrent Soviet moves in the Near East in the last half of 1945 and in 1946 led him to the belief that a fate similar to that of Poland, or Bulgaria, or Rumania, or Latvia, or Estonia, or Lithuania should not confront the countries of the Northern Tier. Gradually conditioned by Soviet policies in the region, Americans would oppose Russian designs on the countries of the Northern Tier much as the British had before them. While there were many factors in the wide-ranging conflict that was emerging between the United States and the Soviet Union, the balance of power in the Near East was again an important source of Great Power rivalry. We must now analyze its role in the developing Allied conflicts over Greece, Turkey, and Iran.[100]

Greece

In Greece, in spite of the Varkiza Agreement, civil conflict continued to undermine all efforts at creating political stability and revitalizing the badly deteriorating economy. As C. M. Woodhouse has observed, "It was the Government's dilemma that stability could not be assured until an elected Government had the moral power to enforce it, nor could such a Government be elected until stability was assured." Proof of the latter contention could be found in the fact that in 1945 dis-

[99] Transcript, Mark Ethridge Interview, 4 June 1974, Truman Library; Lynn Davis, pp. 288-334; FR, 1945, IV:346-347, 365-366, 407-408; V:622, 633-641; Mark Ethridge and C. E. Black, "Negotiating on the Balkans, 1945-1947," in Negotiating with the Russians, ed. Raymond Dennett and Joseph Johnson (Boston, 1951), pp. 184-203; Yergin, p. 439, n. 13. See also n. 92 above.

[100] FR, 1945, V:643; Byrnes, Speaking Frankly, pp. 107, 115-116; Harry Truman, 1:551-552.

order had delayed four attempts at electoral registration. Despite the presence of 40,000 British troops and substantial aid from the United Nations Relief and Rehabilitation Administration (UNRRA), neither the British nor the Greeks were able to make much progress in re-establishing order of any kind—political or economic. As the country continued to founder, the governments of Britain and the United States became increasingly worried over the complex nature of Greece's recovery problems.[101]

The political situation in Greece seemed to grow more chaotic every day. The Varkiza Agreement in February 1945 had only temporarily halted the civil war. Article IX of that agreement provided that within the current year a plebiscite would decide the constitutional question, and that elections to a constituent assembly for the drafting of a new constitution would follow. The agreement also stipulated that the great Allied powers would be requested to send observers to verify that the popular will had been genuinely expressed. Originally a concession to the Left, Article IX came to favor the interests of the Right. As Leftist excesses were revealed in the aftermath of the Second Round, public opinion swung to the Right. The Left then proceeded to campaign for postponement of the elections until the reaction to the Second Round wore off. The Right—sure that an early plebiscite would bring back the king—now supported early elections. Throughout the year all political parties were preoccupied by the question of whether a plebiscite or an election should come first, whether the two should be nearly simultaneous or widely separate, and whether the elections themselves should be for an ordinary parliament or for a constituent assembly.[102]

In the meantime, while the KKE was allowed to function legally under the Varkiza Agreement, civil liberties were blatantly disregarded by the army and the bureaucracy, both of which came under domination by the Right after the Second Round. As a result, many ELAS weapons were handed over to royalist forces, who used them against

[101] McNeill, *The Greek Dilemma*, pp. 205, 212, 223; Woodhouse, *Apple of Discord*, pp. 248-251; Woodward, *BFP*, p. 558; Woodward, 3:438; S.D. 868.000/5-145, Dispatch No. 965/5-2245, Dispatch No. 1053/6-145, Dispatch No. 114; FR, 1945, VIII:203-205, 207-208, 221-222; Delivanis and Cleveland, pp. 105-128.

[102] FR, 1945, VIII:113, 139-140; Leeper, p. 162; "A Summary of Greek Internal Politics, 1941-1946" (Washington, D.C., January 1946), pp. 40-41. (This pamphlet was obtained from the State Department Post and Lot files and was issued for the use of the United States Mission to Observe the Greek Elections [the American element in AMFOGE]; hereafter, it will be cited as "Summary.")

their previous owners. Although ELAS supposedly demobilized and disarmed, many former ELAS fighters, anticipating their fate, took to the mountains. Others crossed the northern border into Yugoslavia, where Tito not only gave them material support but provided the KKE with a training camp at Bulkes. As a consequence, the constitutional question—marked as it was by Great Power rivalry, confused by ideological categories, and further exacerbated by emerging social issues—again led to the polarization of the population. Both Left and Right expanded at the expense of the Center, and by the fall of 1945, as ELAS bands were forming in the mountains, the royalist "X" organization under Colonel George Grivas boasted 200,000 members.[103]

The regional variation and kaleidoscopic pattern of political sentiment made it extremely difficult to judge support for Left or Right, particularly in Macedonia, where external support for a "Free Macedonia" offered hope to somewhere between 80,000 and 260,000 Slavo-Macedonians. Whatever the number, support for a free Macedonia was convenient for Yugoslav and Bulgarian territorial ambitions, which were gradually defined as diplomatic relations improved in the Balkans.[104]

Also helpful to the territorial ambitions of the Balkan states was the fact that Nikos Zachariadis, general secretary of the KKE, returned to Greece at the end of May after spending nearly three years in the Dachau concentration camp. Arriving in Greece on an RAF aircraft, he began almost immediately to prepare for the next round of the civil war, and by August was declaring to an audience of 150,000 in Salonika that unless the situation took a rapid turn toward normal democratic development, the KKE would retaliate and the ELAS marching song would be heard again in the ravines and on the mountain tops of Greece.[105]

A source of concern not only to the Left but also to the Center was the arrest between February and July 1945 of as many as 20,000 of their

---

[103] McNeill, *The Greek Dilemma*, pp. 196-207; Iatrides, p. 256; Stavrianos, *Greece*, pp. 148-149, 164; Woodhouse, *Apple of Discord*, pp. 234-235; Eudes, pp. 250-251; O'Ballance, pp. 213-214; Campbell, p. 182.

[104] Symbolic of improved relations were: first, the 11 April Treaty of Friendship, Mutual Assistance and Postwar Cooperation between the Soviet Union and Yugoslavia; second, the 28 April resumption of relations between Yugoslavia and Bulgaria; and, third, the recognition of Albania by Yugoslavia in May. McNeill, *The Greek Dilemma*, pp. 199-203; FR, *Potsdam* II:1050-1056; "Summary," p. 38; Woodhouse, *Apple of Discord*, p. 231.

[105] Eudes, pp. 246-250; D. George Kousoulas, *Revolution and Defeat: The Story of the Greek Communist Party* (London, 1965), p. 219.

supporters, many of whom were put to death. According to one source, those already under arrest or about to be charged numbered more than 80,000 by the end of the year. Dissidence was an increasing problem to the government—particularly since KKE support outside Greece was increasing. As early as June, the OSS reported Bulgarian agents in northern Greece stirring up sentiment for "Free Macedonia." In December, KKE made contact with the representatives of Tito and Dimitrov on the Bulgarian frontier. Yugoslavia and Bulgaria promised the party substantial aid in the event of an insurrection in Greece. No Soviet representative was present at this meeting, but Zachariadis was encouraged by Soviet support of the Tudeh Party in Iran.[106]

The Greek government was not prepared to cope with these problems. If anything, it exacerbated them. The Plastiras government, attempting to steer a course between factions on the Left and Right, nonetheless let the royalists gain control over both the army and the bureaucracy. When the royalists managed to oust Plastiras in April, the regent replaced him with the "service" government of Admiral Petros Voulgaris. Because the admiral had been responsible for quelling the mutiny of April 1944, he was regarded by the Left with distaste. His attempts to restore order and security made him even more unpopular. When he announced that elections would take place on 20 January 1946, and both EAM and Liberal Party leaders threatened to boycott the elections if he were not replaced, Voulgaris resigned.[107]

At this juncture, the regent himself assumed the office of prime minister until the appointment of Panayotis Kanellopoulos in early November. Faced with worsening economic chaos and instability, the government of Kanellopoulos gave way to still another under the Liberal Centrist Themistoclis Sofoulis. A former lieutenant of Venizelos, the 85-year-old politician was willing to accede to the regent's desires—which received strong British support—that the plebiscite be postponed for three years and that elections to a revisionary assembly take place not later than March 1946. The regent felt that the plebiscite was best postponed because the country needed time to settle down under a popularly elected government. Such a government could be obtained

---

[106] Iatrides, p. 263; S.D. 868.00/6-145, Dispatch No. 1114; Eudes, p. 258. See the discussion of Iran later in Chapter IV.

[107] One reason for opposition to the elections was that little time had been allowed to compile new electoral lists (which had not been revised since 1936). Iatrides, p. 259; Stavrianos, *Greece*, pp. 150-157; "Summary," pp. 36-37, 41; McNeill, *The Greek Dilemma*, p. 209; FR, 1945, VIII:168-169.

through early elections which, conducted by majority vote, would ensure inclusion of all important figures, and allow modification of minor constitutional provisions.[108]

The election issue had been a bone of contention throughout 1945 in Greece, and those on the Left and Center had favored postponement not only because royalist support was still strong, but also because control of the state machinery was in the hands of the Right. Electoral laws required voters to present identity cards which could be obtained only from the Rightist-controlled bureaucracy. The bureaucracy was willing to issue such cards only to people whose political persuasion it found acceptable. The regent was aware of these problems and was trying to find some means of coming to grips with them.[109]

The election issue and the question of Allied supervision or observation was also causing concern to Britain and the United States. Both countries and France were willing to act as observers of the elections. The Soviets were not. Throughout 1945 both Stalin and Molotov stressed that Poland had the same meaning for the security interests of the Soviet Union that Greece had for the security interests of Great Britain. Stalin's desire not to participate in the supervision or observation of the forthcoming elections in Greece probably stemmed from a desire not to set a precedent for a similar procedure in Eastern Europe. At Potsdam, Phillip Mosely overheard Stalin say that a freely elected government in Eastern Europe would be anti-Soviet. This the Soviet dictator could not permit.[110] The willingness of the United States to become involved in the Greek elections, on the other hand, apparently resulted from a desire to ensure that they were free and fair. This was necessary if the United States were to seek similar assurances about elections in Eastern Europe and thus prevent the Soviets from creating a precedent for recognizing unrepresentative governments elsewhere.[111]

[108] FR, 1945, VIII:150-157, 174-187, 191-193; "Summary," pp. 42-43; Iatrides, pp. 260-266; S.D. 868.00/10-1345, Dispatch No. 1699; FR, Potsdam I:660-661; Stavrianos, Greece, pp. 163-166.

[109] FR, Potsdam I:651-653; Potsdam II:127, 525, 1042, 1077-1078; FR, 1945, VIII:126-139, 144-145.

[110] See the earlier discussion in Chapter IV. See also FR, 1945, V:263-264, 285-287; Churchill, Triumph and Tragedy, p. 636; Feis, Between War and Peace, pp. 198-199; FR, 1945, II:194-201, 243-247; Herz, pp. 140, 152.

[111] FR, Potsdam II:357-362; Lynn Davis, pp. 322-323; Feis, Between War and Peace, pp. 287-288. Foy Kohler, who was handling the Greek election question for NEA at the time and working closely with Elbridge Durbrow, then chief of the Division of Eastern European Affairs, confirms that there was a close tie-up between

So convinced of the correctness of their views were the Russians, British, and Americans that before, during, and after Potsdam, discussions between the Soviets and their Western Allies over Greece and the Balkans were little more than a series of heated monologues by one side or another. Proposals and counterproposals, charges and countercharges, resulted only in a standoff. At Potsdam, it was Stalin's contention that he was not meddling in Greek affairs, and that the proposal for supervising elections in Greece, made in the context of a proposal for implementing the Declaration on Liberated Europe in the Balkans, was unjust.[112] And that was that, except for further wrangling by the foreign ministers. The outcome was the Greek government's announcement in August that Great Britain, the United States, and France would send observers to the elections. In September, after the regent had met with their representatives, they issued a joint statement expressing hope that elections would be held as soon as possible, and that a plebiscite on the future of the Greek regime would be held once stability had been restored.[113]

During the course of these events, the policy of the United States toward Greece had undergone a gradual evolution. In the aftermath of Yalta, the State Department had come to see the Declaration for Liberated Europe as necessitating a reorientation in its earlier policy of nonintervention in Greek affairs. Acutely aware of the relationship between economic and political stability, NEA, under Loy Henderson, took the initiative. As indications of Britain's inability to cope with problems in Greece increased, the State Department decided to recommend economic reforms to the Greek government. Implementation of such reforms would be a prerequisite to further assistance from the United States and Great Britain. While Truman earlier in the year had opposed any United States involvement in the Balkans, he had changed his mind by the end of 1945. As Soviet press campaigns

---

the Eastern European countries and Greece, both in thinking and practice. Kohler, letter to the author.

[112] At this time the British believed some 40,000 to 50,000 people in Bulgaria had been murdered within the past six months—not for collaboration, but for opposition to the present government there. Woodward, BFP, p. 556.

[113] FR, Potsdam II:150-155, 643-644, 698-699, 1041-1045; Byrnes, *Speaking Frankly*, pp. 73-75, 96-99; Feis, *Between War and Peace*, pp. 288-290; Harry Truman, 1:346-397; Churchill, *Triumph and Tragedy*, pp. 634-636; Woodward, BFP, pp. 555-558; Charles Mee, Jr., *Meeting at Potsdam* (New York, 1975), pp. 131-135; FR, 1945, VIII:147, 158.

and radio propaganda attacked the Greek government, the United States was slowly becoming involved in the British effort to stabilize that government. In doing so, it was also indirectly associating itself with the larger British policy of containing Soviet influence in the Balkans.[114]

Turkey

In Turkey, leaders no longer worried that the Balkan states would form a confederation and then descend upon the Aegean through Thrace; they now feared Soviet designs on the Straits and large portions of eastern Turkey. The Turkish government, in order to ensure its participation in the upcoming San Francisco Conference, had declared war on Germany and Japan on 23 February 1945, and had become a member of the United Nations. But such maneuvers did not prevent the Soviet Union from arousing their deepest fears, so bringing a long dormant question back into the public eye. Thus, in May and June, C. L. Sulzberger, of the *New York Times*, noted the role of Iran, Turkey, and Greece in Britain's lifeline, and observed presciently that the future spheres of the three great Allied nations met in the triangle between the Dardanelles, the Suez Canal, and Baluchistan. The Istanbul newspaper *Vatan* on 18 July carried a lead editorial by the distinguished journalist Ahmet Yalman, whose opening statement was more succinct: "The old eastern question has risen from its grave."[115]

The resurrection of the Eastern Question had begun quietly on 19 March, when Molotov handed Selim Sarper, the Turkish ambassador in Moscow, a statement denouncing the Soviet-Turkish Treaty of Friendship and Neutrality of 17 December 1925. The statement said the treaty did not correspond to present circumstances and required important revisions. It had been anticipated by the Turks, who accepted it philosophically. The last of three protocols to the treaty, signed on 7 November 1935, had extended it for ten more years, and had provided for at least six months' notice if either of the parties desired to terminate the treaty. Otherwise, it would be prolonged by tacit consent every two years. Since Sarper was scheduled to leave Moscow within the week, it

[114] FR, *Potsdam* I:651-653, 663-665; FR, 1945, VIII:148-149, 152, 251-255, 263-267, 272, 290-292, 299; S.D. 868.00/6-145, Dispatch No. 1114; Woodward, BFP, p. 558.

[115] Weisband, *Turkish Foreign Policy*, pp. 302-304; *New York Times*, 27 February, 20 and 30 May, 3 June 1945; S.D. 867.00/8-945.

seemed reasonable to the Turks that the Soviets should bring the subject up—particularly if they desired to avoid exaggerating a delicate issue during the conference at San Francisco, scheduled to begin on 25 April.[116]

The American embassy in Moscow, however, was worried over the similarity between Soviet actions in Turkey and those in Bulgaria, and foresaw the possibility of bilateral negotiations leading to strong political pressure on Turkey. In Ankara, the American ambassador, Laurence Steinhardt, believed that the Soviet government regarded Turkey in much the same light as it did Poland, Rumania, and Bulgaria, and that it intended to demonstrate its attitude to Britain by carrying on bilateral discussions with Turkey for a modification of the Montreux Convention. He predicted the pattern of action: criticism of the Turkish government and outbursts in the press and radio (all of which had begun); rumors (already in circulation) of Bulgarian troop movements on the Turkish frontier; and bilateral discussions. Steinhardt did not think the Soviets desired territorial concessions, but if they made excessive demands he had little doubt that the Turks would resist.[117]

When Steinhardt, who had been appointed ambassador to Czechoslovakia, took leave of Hasan Saka, the Turkish foreign minister, at the end of March, the latter was less sanguine than Steinhardt about Soviet intentions. He believed the Soviet government was forcing bilateral discussions on the Turkish government. Their purpose? To present the British with a *fait accompli*. What the *fait accompli* might entail was not outlined, but the implication was clear, as was the government's attitude. Turkey was prepared to modify the Montreux Convention, but would not cede territory or bases to the Soviets. In light of its vulnerability to Soviet pressure, however, the Turkish government on 4 April informed the Soviet Union it was ready to study any proposals the Soviets might make with regard to another pact.[118]

Throughout the next few weeks, during which time Roosevelt died and Truman became president, rumors of aggressive Russian plans in Thrace proliferated. The Soviet press and radio campaign against Tur-

[116] Since there was no meeting of the foreign ministers in London following the Yalta Conference, the Soviets had no formal opportunity to make specific proposals to their Allies about revision of the Montreux Convention.

[117] FR, 1945, VIII:1221-1228.

[118] Ibid., pp. 1229-1231. Steinhardt had served as ambassador to Turkey since 10 March 1942.

key (which had begun during the Battle of Stalingrad) became more vigorous. The new American president met the new Turkish ambassador, Hüseyin Baydur,[119] for the first time on 19 April. Four days later he received one of his first warnings on problems in the Balkans when James Forrestal, secretary of the Navy, observed that the Polish case they were discussing was not an isolated one; it was part of a pattern of unilateral action the Soviets had taken in Rumania, Bulgaria, Turkey, and Greece.[120] If the Russians were to maintain a rigid attitude, Forrestal told Truman, the United States had better have a showdown with them now rather than later. While Forrestal's thinking about Greece was a result of misperceptions, his observations about Rumania, Bulgaria, and Turkey were cogent. That they registered on Truman was obvious two days later when he talked with Edwin Wilson, his newly appointed ambassador to Turkey. Wilson told him about recent developments in that country, and informed him of Turkey's reasonable attitude regarding modification of the convention. The ambassador expressed his opinion that if the Soviet Union should make demands affecting Turkey's independence, Turkey would resist; since Eastern Europe was lost to the Soviet Union, America's interests in the Middle East would lead the United States to support Turkey. The president replied that he agreed, and he asserted that the United States should give Turkey support.[121]

The British, like the Americans, equated Soviet actions in Poland and Turkey. Thus, their anxiety heightened on 7 June (the day after Harry Hopkins' last conversation with Stalin about the Polish question),[122] when Molotov met with Selim Sarper, the Turkish ambassador who had returned to Moscow. Sarper had been encouraged by Sergei Vinogradov, Soviet ambassador to Turkey, to seek an interview with Molotov, and believed that such an interview would lead to a satisfactory basis for discussions. Instead, he received a devastating shock.[123]

[119] Mehmet Ertegün, the former Turkish ambassador to the United States, had died on 11 November 1944. *New York Times*, 12 November 1944.

[120] The discussion took place before Truman's meeting with Molotov on 23 April 1945.

[121] FR, 1945, V:253; Millis, pp. 48-51; FR, *Potsdam* I:1041-1042.

[122] Charles Bohlen, in his memoirs, notes that on his way home from Moscow, Hopkins began to voice for the first time serious doubts about the possibility of genuine collaboration with the Soviet Union. This appears to have been a result of his exposure to the absence of freedom in the Soviet Union, although it may well have resulted from his talks with Stalin. Bohlen, p. 222.

[123] Eden, p. 607; FR, 1945, VIII:1228-1231.

Molotov announced the price for a treaty with Russia: (1) the Kars and Ardahan districts of eastern Turkey, ceded to Turkey in 1921, would have to be retroceded to Russia;[124] (2) the Turks would have to consent to Soviet bases in the Straits; (3) the two countries would have to agree on revision of the Montreux Convention prior to any multilateral agreement. In addition, Molotov coyly mentioned a fourth demand—believed by the Turks to be a rupture with Britain or a re-orientation of Turkish policy—which might make the other demands unnecessary. In reply, Sarper stated that his government was not prepared to reopen the question of the 1921 treaty, nor could he consider granting the Soviet Union bases in the Straits. As for the Montreux Convention, that was a matter for international discussion.[125]

The British found it surprising that Molotov should propose a bilateral understanding while the United States and Britain were still awaiting the Soviet Union's views. They told the Americans that because of their alliance with Turkey, they would support her position, and they expressed hope that the United States would join in a démarche to the Soviet Union. But Undersecretary Joseph Grew declined to make any commitment until the matter could be given careful study; in any case, he preferred to withhold action until conclusion of the San Francisco Conference.[126]

In the meantime, on 18 June Molotov had another discussion with

---

[124] Russia invaded these provinces in 1806, 1828, 1855 and 1877. The first three times, she was forced by the West to restore her conquests to the Ottoman Empire; the last time, she retained possession of them from 1878 to 1921, when Stalin played an important role in settling the frontier line. Except for this forty-three-year period, the districts had been in Turkey's possession for hundreds of years. See O.S.S./ State Department I&R Reports, vol. 7, III:30; Erkin, pp. 300-305; FR, 1945, VIII:1235; George Kirk, The Middle East, 1945-1950 (London, 1954), p. 21. For Stalin's typically Georgian dislike of Kemalist Turkey, see Louis Fischer, The Life of Lenin, p. 542. See also Nikita Khrushchev, Khrushchev Remembers: The Last Testament (Boston, 1974), pp. 295-296, where the former Soviet leader describes how Lavrenti Beria, who was also a Georgian, goaded and teased Stalin about getting back territories which the Turks had seized from Georgia. According to Khrushchev, Beria convinced Stalin that Turkey, weakened by World War II, would not be able to resist Soviet demands.

[125] FR, 1945, VIII:1234-1236; FR, Potsdam I:1017-1022, 1030-1031; Feis, Between War and Peace, p. 292. As Harry Howard has pointed out, these requirements represented "a reversion to and elaboration of the very propositions which Molotov had presented to Hitler and Ribbentrop in November 1940" (Turkey, the Straits and U.S. Policy, p. 219). An indication that these claims originated from Stalin may be found in the fact that they were renounced on 29 May 1953, less than two months after Stalin's death.

[126] FR, Potsdam I:1017-1019.

Sarper, in which he told the Turkish ambassador that Russia and Turkey should conclude a treaty of "collaboration and alliance," but only after the questions referred to earlier had been settled. The Soviet ambassador in Ankara was preparing a more indirect rationale for Soviet goals. He told Turkey's acting foreign minister that Molotov had put aside territorial questions. Denying that the Soviet Union needed additional territory, he said that the Armenian Soviet Socialist Republic did—a statement which Nurullah Sümer would not accept. More annoying to the Turkish government was Molotov's frequent reference to Poland during his second conversation with Sarper in Moscow. The Soviet foreign minister also stated that an earlier Polish treaty with the Soviet Union had been unjust, and that reparation of this injustice had laid the basis for a lasting entente between the two countries. The implication with regard to Turkey was clear, and was not taken lightly by a government that regarded Poland as the touchstone of Soviet intentions.[127]

Despite the hopes of the British and Turkish governments that the United States would take action in Moscow, and a recommendation of such action by the American ambassador in Turkey,[128] the State Department remained silent. Not yet fully informed about the discussion between Molotov and Sarper, the department believed their conversation friendly and exploratory, and thought it premature to protest a preliminary exchange of views. No formal demands had been made, and the department did not want to overemphasize the conversation. To do so could create an unfortunate background for discussion of the Straits. This view contrasted sharply with that of the Turkish ambassador in Moscow, who feared that Russia would close the Straits and expand southward from the Caucasus in two prongs: (1) through eastern Turkey to Alexandretta and the Mediterranean, and (2) through Iran to the Persian Gulf.[129]

As a result of the State Department's unwillingness to join Britain in a *démarche*, Anthony Eden persuaded Churchill to act alone. Accordingly, on 7 July the British ambassador in Moscow was instructed to bring the issues concerning Turkey to the attention of the Soviet

[127] Ibid., pp. 1024-1026, 1031-1032, 1043-1044.

[128] For Secretary of the Navy Forrestal's interest in these telegrams, see Millis, p. 71.

[129] FR, *Potsdam* I:1023, 1026-1030, 1033-1036, 1044-1046. Sarper's opinion of Soviet intentions undoubtedly stemmed from a knowledge and memory of Soviet motives in 1940.

government. It was the British view that the whole question would have to be discussed at Potsdam.[130]

As he prepared for the conference, Eden concluded that the Turks were right in their belief that Soviet demands were the first stage in an attempt to subjugate their country. The British foreign minister was convinced that it was necessary to take a firm line in Turkey to avoid similar demands on Iran, and on other countries of the Middle East. The United States, however, though opposed to any threats against Turkey's independence and integrity, resisted Turkish entreaties and would define no special American objective concerning the Straits question beyond peaceful intercourse. The department speculated that the British were trying to help the Turks resist being drawn into the Soviet orbit, but it recognized that the Turks might assume an attitude which the Soviets could interpret as provocative. Thus, a briefing book paper suggested that the United States maintain a detached, watchful attitude toward British and Soviet policies in Turkey so long as the two countries adhered to the principles of the United Nations.[131]

As for more specific objectives, the briefing book for President Truman outlined the most important American interests in the Straits question as: (1) to prevent the Dardanelles from becoming an area of international dispute and a potential threat to world peace; and (2) to ensure the unrestricted use of the Dardanelles for peaceful commerce. Truman's position paper also asserted that certain changes in the Montreux Convention were advisable. Soviet bases in the Straits, however, would require Turkish consent. If Turkey were at war or threatened with imminent danger of war, it should retain discretion over the passage of warships through the Straits unless interdicted by the United Nations. What was significant was that the United States, while supporting a number of points which favored Soviet interests, wanted preservation of Turkey's independence and sovereignty, and would not support unilateral abrogation of either without Turkey's consent.[132]

At Potsdam, Churchill brought up the matter of the Straits before the Big Three reached that topic on the agenda. When he dined with Stalin on 18 July, the prime minister declared sympathy with Russia, likening her to "a giant with his nostrils pinched by the narrow exits

---

[130] Eden, p. 629; FR, Potsdam I:1046-1048.

[131] FR, Potsdam I:1015-1017, 1034-1036, 1044-1046, 1050-1051, 1053-1054; Eden, pp. 633-634; Feis, Between War and Peace, p. 295.

[132] FR, Potsdam I:1013-1015; Howard, Turkey, pp. 219-225.

from the Baltic and the Black Sea." But the Turks, he noted, were anxious. Stalin explained his version of what had happened: Soviet proposals were made only because the Turks sought a treaty of alliance. Churchill said he would support an amendment to the Montreux Convention which would eliminate Japan and give Russia access to the Mediterranean.[133]

When the subject of the Straits came up in plenary session on 22 July, Churchill again agreed with Stalin on the need for revising the Montreux Convention, but attempted to impress on him the importance of not alarming the Turks. They had been alarmed by troop concentrations in Bulgaria, by press and radio attacks, and by Soviet proposals regarding eastern Turkey and the Straits. In response to Churchill's request for information about the Soviet position, Molotov circulated a letter, the gist of which was that the Montreux Convention was out of date and that it should be abrogated through "proper regular procedure." Molotov's letter also asserted that the Straits regime should fall within the province of the Soviet Union and Turkey, both of whom in effect should become joint custodians of the Straits, with jurisdiction over and bases in the area. Of the proposals mentioned by Churchill, Molotov argued that one resulted from Turkish initiatives regarding an alliance. Before such an alliance could be concluded, a settlement had to be reached over eastern Turkey. As for the Straits, the Soviet government was dissatisfied with present arrangements, and was prepared to make an agreement on that issue with the other Black Sea powers if Turkey refused to settle the question.[134]

As discussion continued, it became clear that Molotov was actually trying to do what the Turks had said the Russians would do—place the Straits question in a regional context so as to justify bilateral talks between Turkey and the Soviet Union. Churchill, standing by his proposal for revision of the Montreux Convention, felt that Molotov's proposal went far beyond the conversations he and Eden had had with Stalin and Molotov on the subject. He was certain the Turks would never agree to such talks and said he felt free of any commitment to the new proposals. Stalin acknowledged that the proposal had gone beyond

[133] Churchill, *Triumph and Tragedy*, pp. 634-635; Feis, *Between War and Peace*, p. 295.

[134] FR, *Potsdam* II:256-258, 1427-1434. For background on Molotov's references to the treaties of 1805 and 1833, and their bearing on the issue of joint defense of the Straits (they had none), see O.S.S./State *I&R Reports*, vol. 7, III:34, "Some 'Precedents' for Joint Turkish-Soviet Control of the Straits," 4 October 1946.

their conversations whereupon Truman suggested that the question be deferred, for he was not ready to express an opinion.[135] On the following day, Truman was prepared, and discussion of the issue began with a squabble between Churchill and Stalin over the number of Soviet troops in Bulgaria and how their strength compared to that of the British troops in Greece. When Churchill said he had 40,000 troops in Greece, Stalin asserted that the Soviets had only 30,000 in Bulgaria. Churchill, who believed the Soviets had 200,000, said he hoped that the meeting would hear Field Marshal Alexander on the subject, but Stalin chose not to pursue the subject. A long discussion then ensued over Soviet proposals, in the course of which Stalin and Molotov repeated many of their previous arguments.[136]

The issue was obfuscated by rhetoric. The Allies all knew that air power had made physical control of the Straits a secondary question in time of war. As for other matters, the existing regime of the Straits, with the exception of the fact that the Japanese were signatories to the Montreux Convention, differed little from proposals advanced by the Western Allies. What was really at issue was whether Russia would control the Straits, and what that meant for Turkey and for Allied interests. Aware of this fact, Truman now advanced a proposal which

[135] FR, Potsdam II:256-259, 266-268, 1427-1428. This entire discussion on Turkey is omitted from the official Soviet Foreign Ministry's published minutes of the plenary sessions at Potsdam. See Beitzell, Teheran, Yalta, Potsdam, pp. vii, 222. Truman's suggestion of deferral was related to the fact that the Joint Chiefs of Staff had recommended limiting discussion of the Dardanelles. The JCS argued that the Soviets had received preferred treatment of their claims, particularly in Eastern Europe, and felt that Russia's reaction had been to demand further special consideration (i.e., at the Straits). So far Russia had been successful because she had been able to seize by force what had not been granted by agreement. The Joint Chiefs doubted that the Soviet Union would break with the United States if some of her demands were denied. They believed that final decisions on the Straits and other territorial issues should wait until a general peace settlement, which alone could establish and stabilize boundaries, delineate the rights and responsibilities of nations in the postwar era, and provide a sound basis for international security. If the United States were compelled to take a position on the Straits, however, the JCS recommended supporting the position of the State Department. Presumably, this was the position that Truman wanted to have time to study. FR, Potsdam II: 1420-1422; Feis, Between War and Peace, p. 296.

[136] Soviet arguments included assertions that Kars and Ardahan had been brought up in response to Turkey's request for an alliance; the Japanese emperor had the same rights as Russia, which Turkey held by the throat; Turkey was too weak to guarantee free passage through the Straits in case complications occurred; the Straits needed to be defended by force—as in the case of the Panama and Suez canals. FR, Potsdam II:301-305; Woodward, BFP, p. 558.

was close to his heart: the free and unrestricted navigation of international inland waterways.[137] Truman told the conference that after a long study of history, he had come to the conclusion that all the wars of the past two hundred years had originated in the area which stretched from the Black Sea to the Baltic, and from the eastern frontiers of France to the western frontiers of Russia. He saw it as the conference's task to make sure that history did not repeat itself, and believed that to a great extent this could be accomplished if all countries had free access to all the seas of the world. He then read a paper on the free and unrestricted navigation of inland waterways.[138] As a first step the president recommended setting up interim navigation agencies for the Danube and the Rhine. Truman recommended that the same procedures should apply in regard to the Kiel Canal and the Dardanelles. In this manner, he linked his proposal to the question of the Straits. Churchill concurred with most of Truman's proposals. Stalin said he wanted to read them closely before he discussed them.[139]

At a banquet given by Churchill that night, Stalin again mentioned the Straits. After drinking a toast with the prime minister, Stalin asked him, "If you find it impossible to give us a fortified position in the Marmora, could we not have a base at Dedeagatch?"[140] Churchill's

[137] The proposal appears to have been engendered by Truman's reading of and belief in the lessons of history. It was catalyzed by the president's discussions with Secretary Byrnes and Admiral Leahy, and supported by the State Department, the JCS, and General Dwight Eisenhower. From a practical point of view, its phrasing in no way jeopardized American interests such as the Panama Canal. General Eisenhower, who looked on the problem of postwar Europe as an administrative problem, urged some variant of the proposal because of the needs of the armies of occupation, as well as the needs of the civilian population under their control. Harry Truman, 1:121, 236, 350; FR, Potsdam II:42, 649-654, 1420-1426; Feis, Between War and Peace, p. 297; Byrnes, Speaking Frankly, pp. 77-78; Leahy, pp. 392, 408-409; Bohlen, p. 235.

[138] One historian believes that this was the boldest paper submitted at Potsdam, and that it could have been the most transforming (Feis, Between War and Peace, p. 298). But this would have been true only if differences between the two state systems which we have described had not existed. A more concrete problem was that international waterways, by definition, excluded the Suez and Panama canals —a fact of which Truman and his advisors were well aware. Harry Howard, for example, recalls that when he wrote a memorandum on this point, he was called into Henderson's office and told, "Damnit! You're not an academician. You're an advocate" (interview with Harry Howard). Although Truman in his memoirs says he included the Suez and Panama canals in the paper he presented at Potsdam, the evidence does not bear him out. Harry Truman, 1:377.

[139] FR, Potsdam II:303-305, 312-313, 654.

[140] Dedeagatch (modern Alexandroupolis) is on the Aegean coast of Grecian Thrace, near the Turkish frontier.

reply was carefully worded: "I will always support Russia in her claim to the freedom of the seas all the year round."[141]

It was apparent by 24 July that no solution compatible with all interests was possible. When the question of the Straits again came up, Stalin pointed out that Truman's proposals did not concern the Straits, but the Danube and the Rhine. He wanted a reply to the Soviet proposal on the Straits. When Truman answered that he wanted the two questions considered together, Stalin said he was afraid they would not be able to reach an agreement on the Straits, and suggested postponement.[142] Churchill hoped to obtain some kind of understanding. When he attempted to clarify what had been agreed to, he was confronted by Molotov's sharp questions concerning the Suez: was the canal under the same international control as proposed for the Straits? Despite arguments by Churchill and Eden, Molotov was unconvinced that there were real distinctions between the Turkish Straits and the Suez or Panama canals. In the end, while Truman and Churchill supported Russia's desire that its ships should move freely in and out of the Black Sea, first the British, and then the Americans hardened their positions on the questions of bases. Following the advice of Admiral Leahy and the JCS, Truman now opposed fortifications of any kind at the Straits. Stalin clearly intended to continue discussing the matter with the Turks, and proposed that each of them work on the matter.[143]

Further attempts to raise the matter at Potsdam were futile. Despite Truman's personal plea, Stalin on 1 August opposed any mention of international inland waterways or the Straits in the final communiqué.[144]

[141] Churchill, *Triumph and Tragedy*, p. 669.

[142] FR, *Potsdam* II:365-366, 372-373. Soviet rejection of Truman's proposal undoubtedly stems from the fact that the proposal excluded some of the principal waterways under British and American control, and that it would have opened up Central Europe to Anglo-American influence.

[143] Ibid., pp. 366-367, 373, 1425; Feis, *Between War and Peace*, pp. 299-301. The Soviet minutes of the meeting drastically cut and grossly distort the conversation on 24 July. The Soviet version makes it appear that the Soviets were not concerned with the Straits, and that they felt Turkey should be consulted over the question of revising the Montreux Convention. See Beitzell, *Teheran, Yalta, Potsdam*, pp. 245-246.

[144] During the discussions on 1 August, Stalin gave five reasons why these questions should not be included in the communiqué: there was enough in the protocol already; the inland waterways question had not been discussed; the question had not been listed as a topic before the conference; the inland waterways question should not have preference over the Straits question; and when Truman said that the Straits question would be mentioned, Stalin said he thought it should not—it would make the communiqué too long (FR, *Potsdam* II: 577-578). Whether

Truman had to be satisfied with the fact that both questions would be mentioned in the protocol (which would remain secret), and that he would be able to mention his proposal before the Senate. On the Straits question, the protocol mentioned simply that the Montreux Convention should be revised since it failed to meet present-day conditions. The Anglo-American version of the protocol further noted that "as the next step the matter should be the subject of direct conversations between each of the three Governments and the Turkish Government." Later, in his memoirs, Truman attempted to explain Stalin's ambitions in the Balkans and the Near East:

> The persistent way in which Stalin blocked one of the war-preventative measures I had proposed showed how his mind worked and what he was after. I had proposed the internationalization of all the principal waterways. Stalin did not want this. What Stalin wanted was control of the Black Sea straits and the Danube. The Russians were planning world conquest.

The president, in his last sentence, overstated the conclusion his administration drew from these events, but his summation otherwise seems accurate.[145]

Similar conclusions about Soviet ambitions were shared by Hüseyin Baydur, the Turkish ambassador in Washington, who conjured up the

---

these reasons were legitimate, or whether Stalin's real motives were more calculating is a moot point. In view of his long hostility toward Turkey (at least since 1921), his interest in Georgia, his attitude toward Turkey during the war, and the fact that postwar Soviet claims on Turkey stopped shortly after Stalin's death, one may reasonably infer that Stalin's reluctance to have the Straits mentioned in the communiqué was related to his desire to have a free hand in pressuring the Turks. This inference is supported by subsequent Soviet interpretation of the protocol on the Straits.

[145] FR, Potsdam I:387, 391, 393, 397-398, 453, 527, 538, 540, 577-578, 584, 606, 655-658, 1434, 1497-1498; Robert Murphy, Diplomat Among Warriors (London, 1964), p. 342; Feis, Between War and Peace, pp. 300-301. The Soviet version of the protocol on the Straits, which was published in its 7 August 1946 note to Turkey (see Chapter V), observed that "as the proper course the said question would be the subject of direct negotiations between each of the three powers and the Turkish Government" (FR, 1946, VII:827-829). As Harry Howard has pointed out, while the United States, Britain and Turkey looked upon "direct conversations" as meaning an exchange of views prior to the conference, the Soviets interpreted "direct negotiations" as meaning something more serious, leading to what they hoped would be a bilateral agreement (Turkey, p. 231). For the Truman quote, see Harry Truman, 1:412. For a different interpretation, see Gardner, Architects of Illusion: Men and Ideas in American Foreign Policy, 1941-1949 (Waltham, Mass., 1970), pp. 81-82.

specter of Hitler and the consequences of appeasement. Responding to Turkish requests for a statement of policy on the Straits, Secretary of State Byrnes was less alarmed. He would not recommend impairment of Turkish control; such a policy would require an American guarantee to the Turks. As a consequence, the State Department never prepared a proposal on internationalization, and while it did consider the possibility of demilitarization, again it did not do so because of the moral obligations involved. Despite bureaucratic delays and the necessity of consultation with the British,[146] the State Department finally suggested a policy acceptable to Byrnes and to Truman—who was deeply concerned, even if somewhat uncertain about the most desirable solution for the Straits problem.[147] The State Department on 2 November 1945 informed the Turkish government that it believed the Montreux Convention should be revised to meet changed world conditions, and that it should be based on the following principles:

1. the Straits to be open to the merchant vessels of all nations at all times;

2. the Straits to be open to the transit of the warships of the Black Sea powers at all times;

3. save for an agreed limited tonnage in time of peace, passage through the Straits to be denied to the warships of non-Black Sea powers at all times, except with the specific consent of the Black Sea powers or except when acting under the authority of the United Nations; and

146 In the course of the State Department's consultation with the British, C. L. Sulzberger, of the *New York Times*, got wind of information to the effect that a joint Anglo-American policy for the Straits was being formulated in order to face Russia with a solid front. It is extremely improbable that this leak originated with Donald Maclean, first secretary of the British embassy and a Russian spy. Whether it can be traced to his compatriot in London, Kim Philby, is a more interesting question. Philby, whose father was a friend of Sulzberger, only a couple of months earlier had flown to Istanbul to oversee the elimination of Konstantin Volkov, a Russian secret intelligence officer and the Soviet vice-consul in Istanbul, who intended to blow the cover of both Maclean and Philby. Had Volkov's defection been successful, the West might have been given a unique insight into Soviet policy in Turkey. FR, 1945, V:1267-1269; *New York Times*, 30 October 1945; Patrick Seale and Maureen McCouville, *Philby: The Long Road to Moscow* (New York, 1973), pp. 179-181, 194-196; Hugh Trevor-Roper, *The Philby Affair* (London, 1968), pp. 48-49; Bruce Page et al., *The Philby Conspiracy* (Garden City, N.Y., 1968), pp. 173-188; Kim Philby, *My Silent War* (New York, 1968), pp. 147-160.
147 See the Department of State *Bulletin* 13 (12 August 1945):212, and 13 (28 October 1945):655-656; FR, 1945, VIII:1255-1256, 1289-1292; S.D. 767.68119/ 12-1345.

4. certain changes to modernize the Montreux Convention, such as the substitution of the United Nations system for that of the League of Nations and the elimination of Japan as a signatory.[148]

The Turks had several reservations about these recommendations, although they accepted them in principle. They did not reply formally, however, since neither the Soviets nor the British had expressed their views. The Turkish foreign minister felt that if Turkey were to accept them formally, the Soviets would consider the Turks committed by that much, declare themselves dissatisfied with the proposals, and then increase their demands.[149]

The British objected to some minor points in the American proposals, but on 21 November agreed with the Americans that revision of the Montreux Convention was necessary; if a conference were called, they would take part. Prime Minister Saraçoğlu, in a press conference on 5 December, then noted that in principle his government also favored the American proposals as a basis for discussion, and that it would make known its opinion after all governments concerned had communicated their points of view to Turkey.[150] Again, the initiative was up to the Soviets.

It would take the Soviets almost a year to send the Turks a formal note on the Straits question, but it took no time at all for them to exercise less formal initiatives. Sergei Vinogradov, the Soviet ambassador in Turkey, attempted to use Nikola Antonov, the Bulgarian minister, and Raphael Raphael, the Greek ambassador, to encourage the Turks to initiate new conversations with the Soviets. But Saraçoğlu was wary, particularly because of his own experiences in Moscow in 1939, and those of his ambassador, Selim Sarper, in Moscow in the summer of 1945.[151]

The Soviets, meanwhile, continued their war of nerves. Rumors of war with Turkey (which the Russians denied), troop concentrations and movements in the Balkans (also denied), government support for irredentist demands by the Armenian and Georgian Soviet Socialist

[148] The American note was also sent to the British and Soviet governments. FR, 1945, VIII:1237-1240, 1242-1245, 1248, 1253-1269, 1289-1292; S.D. 767.
[149] FR, 1945, VIII:1271-1276; Erkin, pp. 314-317.
[150] The immediate reaction of Sergei Vinogradov, the Soviet ambassador in Turkey, was that Russian security was inadequate and required bases in Turkey. FR, 1945, VIII:1271-1283.
[151] Ibid., pp. 1276-1279. For the Soviet note of 7 August 1946, see Chapter V.

Republics, as well as press and radio attacks against the Turks—all contributed to Turkish anxieties. Compounding the Turkish government's difficulties were serious internal problems, whose reform was impeded by the external threat.[152]

Turkey had been struggling with the formidable problem of developing a more democratic system. This meant relaxing press laws and introducing a multiparty system. President İnönü was playing a lead in this reform movement, which was a result of many social, political, and cultural forces, and was in part motivated by desire to assure the world that Turkey would abide by the principles of the Atlantic Charter and that it was worthy of them. The government, even if its citizens were united on issues of foreign policy, also needed a "safety valve" for expression of public discontent with domestic policies.[153] By May 1945, therefore, the nucleus of the future Democratic Party had been formed, and by early January 1946 it would make its debut.[154]

As the Turks waited for a Soviet initiative on the Straits question, Turco-Soviet relations became increasingly strained. Reacting to stepped-up Soviet pressures, particularly to a virulent Soviet broadcast on 29 November, several thousand Turkish students in early December attacked two Communist presses in Istanbul. The Soviets promptly protested and held the Turkish government responsible. The Turks replied that they had greater justification in reading hostile intentions into recent Soviet acts. The Soviets, however, refused to regard the incident as a purely internal matter. As Moscow radio nightly attacked the Turkish government, the United States warned Turkish leaders to avoid any incidents which could be interpreted as provocative. Demonstrations which were being conducted against the Armenians, and

[152] FR, 1945, VIII:1252, 1260, 1263, 1268-1271, 1284-1287; Potsdam I:1031-1032; New York Times, 7 August, 22 and 24 October, 21 December 1945, 1 and 13 January 1946; George Kirk, The Middle East 1945-1950, pp. 25-28; S.D. 867.00/12-445/12-845/12-1945; 867.014/12-2445; 767.68119/12-2445; 860 j.00/11-1945; V. Khvostov, "The Facts of the Case," New Times, 1 February 1946, No. 3. See also nn. 215, 216.

[153] See, for example, a series by Ahmet Yalman in the Istanbul newspaper Vatan in July, where he criticized the one-party system and pointed out the need for an opposition party. S.D. 867.00/8-945.

[154] Bernard Lewis, pp. 299 ff., 308; Kemal Karpat, Turkey's Politics: The Transition to a Multi-Party System (Princeton, 1959), pp. 140-143; Frey, pp. 348-349; Kılıç, pp. 126-127; Geoffrey Lewis, pp. 124-125; Kirk, The Middle East, 1945-1950, p. 29; George Harris, "A Political History of Turkey, 1945-1950" (Ph.D. dissertation, Harvard University, 1956), pp. 184-186, 192, 225, 256-258, 321; S.D. 033.1100/10-1945, Enclosure (c) to Disp. No. 294; 867.00/5-2245/6-2145.

which the Soviets had provoked, were halted as the Turkish government tried to avoid giving the Russians the opportunity of playing up this issue.[155]

The United States and Britain, meanwhile, were both trying to interpret Soviet objectives in the Eastern Mediterranean. At the London Council of Foreign Ministers in September Molotov gave Bevin and Byrnes new reasons for suspicion. He laid claim to a trusteeship over Tripolitania in North Africa, and at the same time obstructed settlement of the Dodecanese question. Hearkening back to the spheres of influence agreement in October 1944, Ernest Bevin noted that the

> British Government had supported the Soviet Government in its claim for adjustments of her western frontier, and in other settlements which had since been made. In view of the vital interest of the British Government in the North Africa area, he was very much surprised that the Soviet Delegation had put forward this claim in respect of Tripolitania. The British claims in that area had been put forward on the same basis as had Russian claims in Eastern Europe, namely security—a perfectly legitimate basis.

But Molotov ignored Stalin's earlier promises, and indirectly attacked British policies in Greece. The Russians wanted Mediterranean bases for their merchant fleets.[156] They would promote a democratic system of government there, though not on the lines recently followed in Greece. Secretary of State Byrnes, faced with these and other Soviet demands, later believed that Molotov's intransigence resulted from a belief that Russia had been inadequately consulted by American officials in Japan. Whatever the reason, Soviet attitudes toward Turkey were gradually seen in the context of larger issues which the United States was slowly coming to appreciate.[157]

By late September, Ambassador Edwin Wilson began to regard the Straits question as a façade behind which the Soviets intended to induce change in Turkey's internal regime, an objective which would mean termination of the Anglo-Turkish Alliance and the end of Western

[155] S.D. 867.00/12-445/12-645/12-845, Dispatch Nos. 1166 and 1153/12-1545/ 12-1745/12-2945/12-3045; Kılıç, pp. 126-127; Karpat, p. 150. For the Soviet role in provoking Turkish antipathy toward the Armenians, see n. 216.

[156] For Russian intentions to construct a greatly expanded fleet, much of which would have to be built in the Black Sea, see O.S.S./State Department I&R Reports, vol. 7, III:28.

[157] FR, 1945, II:164-165, 171-172, 189-192, 200-201, 204-209, 256-257, 297-298; see also p. 566 and pp. 775-776; Byrnes, Speaking Frankly, pp. 95-109.

influence in Turkey, if not in the Middle East. George Kennan, the chargé in Moscow, concurred. He believed that any concessions on the Straits would be exploited by the Soviets with a view to the ends described by Wilson.[158]

Wilson in October again emphasized that the question of the Straits was a pretense for Soviet domination. He doubted that expiration of the 1925 treaty would have much effect upon Turkish-Soviet relations, since the Soviets would prefer to let matters ride. Mobilization of large military forces would strain Turkey's troubled economy and might even lead to a regime more "friendly" to the Soviet Union.[159]

In the Soviet Union, George Kennan, perhaps influenced by the Turkish ambassador in Moscow, wrote an analysis of Soviet policy toward the Near and Middle East which described Turkey as the principal western gap in the Soviet system of defense. Believing security the primary reason for Soviet concern, Kennan noted the Soviet Union's employment of diplomatic negotiations, wars of nerves, and propaganda agencies. He correctly observed the absence of any significant leftist opposition in Turkey. The Soviets, in seeking revision of the Straits regime suitable to their wishes, would have to rely principally on other discontented elements—the Kurds and the Armenians (whose irredentist movement had already begun to gather force).[160]

By December, as events in Iran began to take shape, Wilson predicted a major crisis in the Middle East by spring. Comparing Soviet tactics to those of the Nazis, he observed that the Straits issue was a pretext for Soviet domination of Turkey. NEA accepted this analogy, viewing Soviet support for Armenian and Georgian claims as an extension of earlier demands for Kars and Ardahan and as "a clear piece of press-war effrontery reminiscent of Hitler's press attacks on Czechoslovakia."[161] What caused the State Department's seeming overreaction to events in Turkey was the troubling situation in Iran.

Iran

After the Yalta Conference, Russian interference in internal Iranian affairs continued to be the Iranian government's major concern. Mohammad Reza Shah, however, was reluctant to request permission to move troops into the Soviet-occupied area to quell disturbances. Under

---

[158] FR, 1945, VIII:1248-1251.   [159] Ibid., pp. 1248-1249, 1256-1257.
[160] FR, Potsdam I:1029-1030; FR, 1945, V:901-908.
[161] S.D. 867.00/12-1945; FW 867.014/12-1445.

the Tripartite Treaty, Iran was supposedly responsible for internal security, and the shah did not wish to create a precedent by asking the Soviets for permission to carry out government responsibilities.[162]

The Iranian government's solution to Russian interference was to seek withdrawal of all Allied troops from its territory. On 18 May, shortly after V-E Day (8 May), the shah informed Leland Morris, the departing American ambassador, that Iran intended to send a note to the British and Soviet governments requesting evacuation of troops. This note was sent on the following day, together with a similar note to the United States. The Iranians continued to press these requests for withdrawal throughout the succeeding months.[163]

Meanwhile, with the termination of the Persian Gulf Command (PGC) on 1 June, the Iranian economy faced serious problems. Factions subject to British or Soviet influence were working at cross-purposes in the Majlis, compounding the difficult problem of stabilizing a government whose already poor administration was rapidly worsening. During the summer a new cabinet under Mohsen Sadr ruled without a vote of confidence, but it did not cease to work for the end of foreign intervention. Both the prime minister and the foreign minister told American representatives of their strong hopes that at the next conference the Big Three would work to stop this pernicious foreign influence.[164]

Steps had already been taken in that direction. After the Yalta Conference, the British, to whom the Americans left the initiative, continued to be deeply troubled by the question of troop withdrawals. As the Potsdam Conference approached, they intended to propose that Allied troops withdraw from Iran *pari passu* and in stages before the final treaty date. The State Department endorsed a similar policy, and affirmed opposition to any interference in the affairs of a sovereign nation. But Wallace Murray, who had taken charge of the embassy in Iran on 5 June, recognized political realities. If the Soviets did not leave Iran, the United States would have little with which to influence Soviet

[162] FR, 1945, VIII:361-365, 527-529.

[163] The Iranian note to the United States was apparently sent in order that the government could avoid British and Soviet complaints of discrimination. Ibid., pp. 369-371, 380-381; *Potsdam* I:949, 953-954; *Potsdam* II:1390-1391.

[164] FR, 1945, VIII:375, 380-381, 383, 386, 398; Zabih, pp. 92, 95; Shahram Chubin and Sepehr Zabih, *The Foreign Relations of Iran: A Developing State in a Zone of Great-Power Conflict* (Berkeley, 1974), p. 37. The PGSC was redesignated the PGC in December 1943.

policy. In that event, the most Murray believed the United States could hope for would be *pari passu* withdrawal of all troops to a point where Russian forces in the north would roughly balance Anglo-American forces in the south. This reflected his earlier assumption that the continuance of the British Empire in some reasonable strength was in the strategic interest of the United States and that Americans would be deluding themselves if they built their plans for postwar Iran on the hope that principles could govern relations between the Soviet Union and the West.[165]

At Potsdam, as Tudeh activities increased and the British grew more disturbed at Soviet machinations in Iran,[166] Anthony Eden pressed the question of withdrawal. Noting the Soviet failure to reply to an earlier British suggestion that Allied forces withdraw *pari passu* and in stages before the final treaty date, he now proposed a three-stage withdrawal: (1) from Teheran; (2) from the whole of Iran except Abadan (where the British would remain) and a zone in either northeast or northwest Iran (where the Soviets would remain); and, finally, (3) from all Iran.[167]

Stalin, technically correct in his assumption that the term for the presence of Allied troops in Iran had not expired, and that it would do so only after the end of the war with Japan, accepted the proposal to withdraw from Teheran, but suggested that his compatriots confine themselves to that idea. Since they had until six months after the completion of the war with Japan, the Soviets wanted to think over the other stages. After Truman observed that he expected to have his troops out within sixty days,[168] Stalin gratuitously added: "So as to rid

165 Woodward, *BFP*, p. 319; FR, 1945, VIII:377-378, 546; FR, *Potsdam* I:159, 208, 949-952, 955. Harry Hopkins, in dictating notes for the books he planned to write, observed about this time: "If I were to lay down the most cardinal principle of our foreign policy, it would be that we make absolutely sure that now and forever the United States and Britain are going to see eye to eye on major matters of world policy." Sherwood, p. 922.

166 Soviet actions against Moshen Sadr and his cabinet paralleled those toward Sa'id in the fall of 1944. FR, 1945, VIII:388. See FR, 1946, VII:810-811, for Soviet attempts to change the Turkish government, and FR, 1946, VII:291, for attempts to change the Iranian government.

167 FR, 1945, VIII:386-388; Woodward, *BFP*, p. 320; Eden, p. 633; S.D. 891. 105 A/5-2445; FR, *Potsdam* I:958; *Potsdam* II:195, 237, 1391-1392.

168 Chubin, p. 87, notes that a general belief in America's return to isolationism was reinforced by the withdrawal of American forces before those of Britain and the Soviet Union. In contrast, Iranian ruling groups believed in Britain's ascendancy in the postwar period, particularly because of her intervention in Greece.

the United States of any worries we promise you that no action will be taken by us against Iran."[169]

When it came to the final communiqué, the Soviets—as they had with the problem of the Straits—obtained deletion of the section on Iran. Molotov and Stalin did not want the oil question or other Iranian matters publicized. Thus Iran was mentioned only in the final, secret protocol, which stated that Allied troops would be withdrawn from Teheran, and that further stages of withdrawal should be considered at the London Council of Foreign Ministers in September.[170] As with the Straits, the issue in question was the degree of control Russia intended to exercise over her neighbor to the south, and what that meant for her neighbor and for Allied interests. Again, as with the problem of the Straits, the issue had been postponed.

The Iranian government was disappointed by the results of Potsdam. Their only hope for improvement was the fact that evacuation of foreign troops from Iran was on the agenda of the first meeting of the Council of Foreign Ministers, scheduled to meet in London from 11 September to 2 October 1945. This hope became especially important to the Iranians as the situation in the north continued to deteriorate, and Iranian forces within the Soviet zone were repeatedly unable to exercise their function of maintaining order. Serious rioting inspired by the Soviets appeared imminent.[171]

Expecting conflict over Iran, Loy Henderson, in late August, tried to focus administration attention on Iran in a long memorandum to Secretary Byrnes. Viewing the situation as a threat to Allied solidarity and international security, Henderson questioned present policies. Affirming the department's intention to prevent threats to Iran's sovereignty, he suggested a tripartite advisory commission as an alternative solution to unilateral aid programs.[172] Events of succeeding weeks, however, were to undermine the department's faith in this solution as a viable alternative.

[169] Harry Truman, 1:380; FR, Potsdam II:309-310, 316, 393. As in the case of the discussion of Turkey, the Soviet minutes shorten the discussion of Iran considerably and make the Soviet remarks appear in a much more favorable light. See Beitzell, Teheran, Yalta, Potsdam, pp. 231-232.

[170] FR, Potsdam II:593-594, 1460-1496.

[171] FR, 1945, VIII:389-391, 400 ff. For background on the Iranian government's attempts to control its own military in the north, its efforts to move against the Tudeh, and subsequent interference by the Soviet Union in Iranian affairs, see S.D. 891.00/8-3045/9-2045, and Pfau, "The United States and Iran," pp. 244-245.

[172] Ibid., pp. 393-400.

Meanwhile, armed partisans in Tabriz, protected by Soviet troops, captured government buildings and issued leaflets proclaiming their cultural and administrative autonomy, while the Iranian gendarmerie and army were confined to their barracks. Communications were cut and reinforcements prevented from reaching their destination. Government buildings were soon evacuated and the situation returned to normal, but observers in Teheran agreed that the episode was probably a "rehearsal."[173]

Then, at the end of August, Ja'afar Pishevari founded a new political party which he called the Democratic Party of Azerbaijan. Pishevari had been minister of the interior of the Republic of Gilan in 1921,[174] a prisoner of Reza Shah from 1937 to 1941, and since 1943 an unseated representative to the Majlis from Tabriz. Subsequently described by the American consul in Tabriz as a "small man in his middle fifties, with steely grey hair, and a small brush mustache under a sharp and slightly hooked nose," Pishevari was contemptuous of the traditional Marxist party which until then had been operating under Soviet auspices. The Tudeh Party was the party of Persian intellectuals whose Western European Marxism contrasted with the intellectual heritage of Pishevari's own Azeri patriots. The latter's heritage was rooted in the Leninism of the Bolshevik Party in the Caucasus. This difference, however, was academic in view of the Tudeh Party's vulnerability to Soviet manipulation. Ali Shabustari, who led the Tudeh Party in Tabriz, later said that Pishevari had instructions from the Russians to establish the Democratic Party, and Pishevari's own notebook explains that the Tudeh Party was dissolved and the term "Democratic" used to attract elements not otherwise drawn to Communism.[175]

In western Azerbaijan, the Soviet commander at Miandoab summoned the Kurdish chieftains and transported them to Baku in southern Russia. There, they were harangued by the leader of Soviet Azerbaijan's Communist Party, told that neither their own nationalist party, the Komala,[176] nor the Tudeh Party was looked on favorably, and that

---

[173] Lenczowski, *Russia and the West in Iran*, pp. 286-287.

[174] See Chapter III for a discussion of the Soviet Republic of Gilan.

[175] Zabih, p. 99; Avery, p. 388; Ramazani, *Iran's Foreign Policy*, pp. 112-113; FR, 1945, VIII:417; Rossow, "The Battle of Azerbaijan," p. 18; Nollau and Wiehe, pp. 28-30. See also S.D. 891.00/6-2146.

[176] Komala-i-Zhian-i-Kurd, or Committee of Kurdish Youth. The Kurdish independence movement had been officially inaugurated at the San Francisco Conference in April 1945 in a letter to the delegates written in the name of the Kurdish

they should join the Democratic Party of Azerbaijan. Then they were sent back to Mahabad with a printing press and two tons of paper.[177] Soviet pressure on the Kurds supports the contention that Soviet aims were to make the movement appear more democratic than it was.

The "Democratic" Movement was not created solely by Soviet pressures. In addition to Soviet support, it had as its impetus a reaction to the process of centralization which had been instituted under Reza Shah.[178] The Kurds in particular had reacted strongly to the government's attempts at detribalization; others, like the Azeris, resented the central government's neglect of the province of Azerbaijan. Thus, a concern for identity with their own communal groups seemed logical to both Kurds and Azeris in the aftermath of the Soviet occupation in 1941. Characterizing in terms of class what were communal and regional issues, the Tudeh Party gained their support under the aegis of Soviet occupation and, when Soviet tactics dictated a shift, provided what became the Democratic Party with a ready group of supporters.[179]

Meanwhile, on 6 September, four days after the Japanese surrender, Anushiravan Sipahbodi, Iran's foreign minister, made a formal statement to the effect that Iran was responsible for her internal security and was prevented from accomplishing the task; the end of the war had removed the need for special authorization to assume this responsibility; evacuation was now certain within six months. The foreign minister

---

League. Part of a series of endemic uprisings against controls imposed on the Kurds since 1920, the rebellion found adherents among Iran's and Iraq's Kurds. One contemporary estimate, published in 1946, put the number of Kurds in the Near East as follows:

Turkey	1,000,000
Iran	700,000
Iraq	494,000
Transcaucasian Russia	125,000
Syria	100,000
Total	2,419,000

William Westermann, "Kurdish Independence and Russian Expansion," *Foreign Affairs* 24 (July 1946):675-686. See also Chapter III, n. 59.

[177] Meister, pp. 180-181, 208; Archie Roosevelt, Jr., "The Kurdish Republic of Mahabad," *The Middle East Journal* 1 (July 1947):250, 254. For a map depicting "Kurdistan," see Map No. 6.

[178] See Chapter III for a discussion of this issue.

[179] Rouhollah Ramazani, "The Autonomous Republic of Azerbaijan and the Kurdish People's Republic: Their Rise and Fall," in *The Anatomy of Communist Takeovers*, ed. Thomas Hammond (New Haven, 1975), pp. 456-458.

also asked the American government that Iran be represented at the London Conference of Foreign Ministers. On 9 September a note was sent to the Allies which mentioned that a previous note written in May and requesting evacuation of troops had never received a reply. The new note set the expected evacuation deadline at 2 March 1946.[180]

While the abrupt end of war in the Far East had the effect of speeding up the Soviets' long-range plans in Manchuria, it may have cut short their long-range plans in the Near East where their policy toward Azerbaijan underwent a tactical shift. On 14 September, George Kennan, the chargé in the Soviet Union, noted that the Soviet press devoted three-quarters of a column to an appeal which the Democratic Party issued in Tabriz. The appeal cited Iranian oppression and declared the party's desire to free the Azeris to use their own language and practice their own customs while remaining within the administration of the Iranian government.[181] The publication of this appeal gave Loy Henderson pause. In light of Soviet activities toward the Armenians and Kurds, he believed open Soviet sympathy for the Azerbaijani nationalist movement could be a potential vehicle for securing ascendancy over the central Iranian government. As a consequence, he told his superiors it was absolutely necessary that American military forces withdraw completely from Iran, and that the United States prevail upon the British and Russians to do the same. For their part, the Iranians protested repeated incidents in the northern provinces, while the Soviets ignored their protests and sent them only one reply—a renewed demand for oil concessions.[182]

At the Council of Foreign Ministers in London on 19 September, the British secretary of state for foreign affairs, Ernest Bevin, in a letter asked Molotov to agree to 15 December as the date for withdrawing forces, and 2 March 1946 as the latest date for evacuating troops from

[180] A provision of Article VI and Annex I of the Tripartite Treaty states that "when [a] direct interest of Iran is discussed at an international postwar conference no decision should be taken before consultation with Iran." FR, 1945, VIII:402-403, 408-409.

[181] While the Azeris of Azerbaijan in northwestern Iran share the same culture and religion with the Iranians to the south (they belong to the Shi'a branch of Islam), they speak (but do not write) Turkish, which ties them linguistically to their neighbors in the Soviet Republic of Azerbaijan. It is important to note that neither the Soviet nor the Iranian Azerbaijanis wanted any links with the Turks in Turkey. Seton-Watson, p. 70; Avery, p. 387.

[182] Ulam, Expansion and Coexistence, pp. 395, 477-478; FR, 1945, VIII:407, 410-412.

Azerbaijan and the British oil area. Molotov answered that he saw no need for discussion since the Anglo-Soviet-Iranian Treaty of 1942 had stated the terms for withdrawal. Bevin commented that he was glad the date for mutual withdrawal was set at 2 March 1946, whereupon Molotov again answered that the matter was not a problem since there was a treaty with a provision for it. "I would like you to keep in mind," he continued, "that the Soviet Government attach exceptional importance to the strict fulfillment of obligations undertaken." As a result of these statements, the problem of troop withdrawal from Iran was removed from the agenda.[183] The Iranian note of 9 September, like its predecessor, went unanswered.

Three days later, Wallace Murray, writing the secretary of state, allowed that the Soviets had at least two intentions: the separation and incorporation of Azerbaijan, or (and this was more likely) control of all Iran through the establishment in Teheran of a "popular" government. Going to the Balkans for his analogy, Murray suggested that such a government's form might be similar to that of the Groza regime in Rumania—"led by men under Soviet influence amenable to Soviet demands and hostile to other foreign nations." Murray could see the long-range implications. Such a development, besides being an unjustifiable interference in Iranian affairs, would seriously affect Anglo-Soviet relations, threaten Britain's imperial lifeline, and be harmful to American interests—most important of which were its rich oil holdings in Saudi Arabia, Bahrein, and Kuwait. Deploring conditions in Iran, he argued that control by a minority group under Soviet direction would be worse, and that therefore the time had come for the United States to take a positive stand. The war was over and the Allies had no excuse for keeping troops in Iran.[184]

When the Soviet ambassador returned to Teheran on 27 September from Moscow, a new tactic appeared to be in operation. For the first time in two years the ambassador took the initiative in discussing ques-

---

[183] FR, 1945, VIII:413-415, 428; II:315-316. A careful reading of Article VI of the 1921 Treaty, and the Soviet envoy Rothstein's clarification of it on 12 December 1921, makes clear that it applies only to situations in which preparations for armed attack on the Soviet Union are involved. Molotov's ambiguities in his replies to Bevin suggest that he was already contemplating use of the treaty in September if not before (when the Soviets first occupied Iran), and that the British Foreign Office's concern over his unwillingness to commit himself to a specific date for withdrawal was justified. *O.S.S./State Department I&R Reports*, vol. 7, II:5.

[184] FR, 1945, VIII:417-419.

tions of policy with his American counterpart, emphasizing that reactionary elements in Iran were persecuting "liberal" elements. Murray observed that the ambassador's statements about the reactionary character of the Iranian government followed the line taken by the Soviet government and the Iranian Left ever since the oil crisis in 1944, for they could only be intended to justify Soviet hostility to the regime. Murray further surmised that the Soviet ambassador was trying to get the Allies' passive acquiescence to Soviet policies in Iran.[185]

George Kennan's analysis of the Democratic Party of Azerbaijan, like that of Murray, underlined parallels between events in Iran and Eastern Europe. The party resembled the "nationality" pattern in Bessarabia, Ruthenia, and Eastern Poland, where fissional techniques were based on racial affinity with the Soviet Union. Kennan expressed the opinion that it was impossible to predict what would happen in Iran since the Russians would probably adapt their policies to the whole complex of Middle Eastern developments. He was skeptical, however, of Azerbaijani assurances that government authority would be respected. He agreed with Murray's analysis, but emphasized the regional nature of the movement. Three weeks later, reviewing current trends of Soviet policy with respect to the Near and Middle East,[186] Kennan again addressed the problem. After cataloguing Soviet goals (security, oil, and access to the Persian Gulf) and the instruments for attaining them (the Red Army, the Tudeh Party, the Democratic Party, and the Kurds), he noted that the Democratic Party was attempting, as a preliminary move, to separate northwestern Iran from the rest of the country and so ensure early Soviet predominance in that particular region. The Kurds he likewise saw as a fissional force. In view of his and Murray's analyses, there was little surprise when, on 19 November, press and radio reports carried news of large-scale uprisings in the Azerbaijan province of Iran.[187]

A few days prior to these disturbances the Red Army had distributed arms to the local populace in key areas within the province.[188] When

[185] Ibid., pp. 420-422.

[186] For Kennan's perception of the situation in Turkey, see the previous discussion on Turkey.

[187] FR, 1945, VIII:424, 430; V:901-908.

[188] Meister, p. 186. When Britain and Russia occupied Iran in 1941, the British captured the Iranian Army arsenal in Teheran. When the Soviets expressed a desire for the weapons in it, the British turned them over, but only after recording their serial numbers. Rifles collected from the *fedayin* in Tabriz after the fall of the

the Iranian gendarmerie tried to interfere with the newly armed rebels, the Soviets challenged them and forced them to retire. By 19 November, when the world learned of the disturbances, all major routes entering the province had been seized by the Democratic Party; communications had been cut, and an Iranian force of 1,500 troops (ordered by the shah to Azerbaijan to put down the rebellion) stopped at Qazvin, where the Soviets threatened to open fire if the order to stop were not obeyed. The commander was told that an attempt to advance would be regarded as an attack on the Soviet Union.[189]

In the United States, Loy Henderson noted press and radio reports and elaborated upon their broader implications. The United States had consistently pressed for withdrawal of Allied forces from Iran to avoid a threat to Allied solidarity and international security. Now the situation was fraught with danger. Britain's line of communications was threatened, as was its "empire position" throughout the area. Because of American economic and strategic interests, the United States, too, had a direct interest in the problem.[190]

The Iranian chargé in the United States on 20 November asked the Department of State what the United States intended to do; the confidence of small countries in the promises of the Great Powers had to be maintained if world stability were to exist.[191] As yet, the Department of State took no action, since it possessed no facts from its own sources. In Iran, the British were just as equivocal. Iranian Army Chief of Staff General Hassan Arfa's record of a conversation with Sir Reader Bullard, the British ambassador, captures the Iranians' predicament:

"We are not going to declare war on Russia for that."

"But you have guaranteed our independence and territorial integrity."

"That is up to London," he replied, "here we are just executors."[192]

What London or Washington would do was unknown. Questions in Iranian minds which had surfaced most recently in Arfa's conversa-

---

Democratic Republic in almost every case matched those handed over to the Red Army in 1941. Robert Rossow, "The Flying Wedge of Azerbaijan." This manuscript (in the possession of Robert Rossow, who was consul in Tabriz in the period 1945-46) contains a wealth of information on Soviet activities in Azerbaijan, and served as the basis for chapter 7, "Red Tanks in a Moslem Graveyard," in Peter Lisagor and Marguerite Higgins, *Overtime in Heaven* (Garden City, N.Y., 1964), pp. 131-171. Hereafter it will be cited as: Rossow MS.

[189] Rossow, "The Battle of Azerbaijan," p. 18; FR, 1945, VIII:431-437, 442.
[190] FR, 1945, VIII:430-431.   [191] Ibid., pp. 435-437.
[192] Arfa, p. 349.

tion with Bullard remained: Did either government intend to back the United Nations Charter in more than theory? If so, to what extent? If the United States were not able to effect fulfillment of assurances contained in the Tripartite Treaty and the Declaration Regarding Iran, what course did it propose to follow?

Washington received greater insight into Iranian problems after 21 November, when Murray tentatively confirmed earlier Iranian statements. He told of his inability to get passes into northern Iran for his attachés, speculated that the Soviet ambassador had been withdrawn so that there was no one of any stature to whom he could appeal. The Soviet chargé in Iran insisted that there was complete calm, and blamed the problem of passes on the military, over whom he said he had no control.[193]

The Iranian government sent protests to the Soviet Union on 22 and 23 November.[194] W. Averell Harriman delivered an urgent communication from the American government to Molotov on 24 November.[195] It noted that the Soviets had stopped an Iranian force. Affirming American adherence to the Teheran Declaration, it suggested immediate withdrawal of Allied troops from Iran. Further, it asserted that the United States would be out of Iran by 1 January 1946,[196] and proposed that Britain and Russia do the same. It ended with the observation that nations such as Iran were encouraged at San Francisco to place full trust in the permanent members of the Security Council of the United Nations, and expressed confidence that the Soviet Union and Great Britain were as anxious as the United States to demonstrate that the trust of these nations was not misplaced.[197]

A Soviet reply on 29 November stated that information in the American note did not correspond to reality; reactionary elements had to

---

[193] FR, 1945, VIII:435.

[194] On 23 November, the Central Committee of the Democratic Party, calling itself the "National Congress of Azerbaijan," issued a declaration in which Azerbaijan claimed the right of self-determination under the Atlantic Charter. Denying that the people of Azerbaijan wished to separate from Iran, the declaration stated their desire to form a national government within the framework of the Iranian state. FR, 1945, VIII:455.

[195] The British sent a protest to the Soviets on 23 November. Ibid., p. 457.

[196] By 30 December, the United States had evacuated all of its troops except for those on attaché missions or military missions with the Iranian Army and gendarmerie. Ibid., pp. 453, 522.

[197] United Nations, Yearbook of the United Nations (New York, 1947), p. 328; FR, 1945, VIII:448-450.

be kept outside the province because they were responsible for incidents that had occurred. While affirming Soviet adherence to the Declaration Regarding Iran, the Soviet note observed that the declaration affected neither the number of Soviet armed forces in Iran nor the period of their presence. The length of stay of Soviet troops was determined by the Tripartite Treaty as well as by the Soviet-Iranian Treaty of 1921.[198] Meanwhile, in light of incidents which had occurred, the Soviet government saw no grounds for removing forces from Iran by 1 January.[199] Soviet intransigence again had blocked an attempt to meliorate a situation of explosive character.

That same day, 29 November, Hussein Ala presented his credentials as the new Iranian ambassador to the United States. Sandwiched in between Truman's meeting with a group of senators about Russia and atomic energy, and a discussion with Ham Fisher about Joe Palooka, Ala nonetheless managed in fifteen minutes to describe Soviet machinations in Iran, and to lay before the president the dangers of the political situation. Truman appeared to understand Iran's problems, and was sympathetic.[200]

Perhaps as a result of Ala's interview with Truman, Secretary of State Byrnes a week later reiterated America's pledge to observe the Declaration Regarding Iran. On the day his pledge appeared in the paper, Byrnes also received wide coverage for refuting charges by Patrick J. Hurley, formerly President Roosevelt's trouble-shooter in Iran and later in China. Hurley had publicly asserted that (1) the State Department had been disloyal to American foreign policy, and (2) Presidents Roosevelt and Truman, and Secretaries Hull, Stettinius, and Byrnes all had handicapped his work.[201] In a way, the conflicts which beset American foreign policy in Iran since 1942 were epitomized on 8 December by the vignette portrayed on the front page of the *New York Times*: guarantees of abstract principles were juxtaposed with apparent discord among the statesmen whose job it was to effect them.

[198] For a careful analysis of the 1921 treaty, and for the Soviet distortion of it to suit their ends, see: *O.S.S./State Department I&R Reports*, vol. 7, II:5, "Iranian and Soviet interpretations of the Treaty of Friendship of 1921," 28 April 1948. See also the discussion in Chapter III.

[199] *FR*, 1945, VIII:468-469.

[200] The Harry S. Truman Papers, Harry S. Truman Library, Independence, Mo., PSF, Subject File, Box 180, Folder: Iran, 3 May 1950 memo from Truman to Jim Webb, and letter from Ala to Truman; PSF, Box 82, President's Appointments File, Daily Sheets, President's Appointments Log, 29 November 1945.

[201] *New York Times*, 8 December 1945.

With public disagreement among these statesmen, how could the Iranian government—or, for that matter, the Soviet government—not question the extent to which the United States was willing to support the United Nations Charter?

For this reason, perhaps, the State Department publicly released (on 8 December) the Soviet note of 29 November.[202] The growing dispute between the World War II Allies in Iran was now brought into the open, and with the Moscow Conference[203]—one more test in the efficacy of principle—just a week off, the situation was assuming the proportions of a major crisis.

The Moscow Conference and Its Aftermath

Secretary of State Byrnes departed for Moscow on 12 December 1945. By that date Tabriz was in the hands of Ja'afar Pishevari's Democratic Party. A "National Assembly" had been inaugurated and had proclaimed the autonomous Republic of Azerbaijan, with Pishevari as premier. After the fall of Tabriz (10 December), the head of the Kurdish separatist movement, Qazi Mohammed, had called a meeting of tribal chiefs in Mahabad. There, on 15 December, surrounded by tribal chiefs, leaders of the Kurdish Democratic Party, and three Soviet officers sitting in a jeep and armed with Tommy guns, he inaugurated the Kurdish People's Government. There now existed two virtually independent states in northwestern Iran.[204]

At Potsdam Stalin had confronted Truman with a *fait accompli* on the Polish question. When Byrnes's plane arrived in Moscow, he was faced with the same situation regarding Iran—or so Truman later believed. The Turkish foreign minister, Hasan Saka, earlier in the month had described such a maneuver as a traditional Soviet tactic. Iranian officials in Tabriz, who observed that the moves of the Democrats had been faster than anticipated, were of the same mind: the Democrats wanted to present the foreign ministers at Moscow with a *fait accompli*.[205]

[202] FR, 1945, VIII:473; see also pp. 480-483, 487.

[203] Byrnes had hastily improvised the conference in an attempt to break the impasse reached by the Council of Foreign Ministers in London. Bohlen, pp. 247-248; Byrnes, *Speaking Frankly*, p. 109.

[204] Byrnes, *Speaking Frankly*, p. 110, and *All in One Lifetime*, p. 331; Bohlen, p. 248; Meister, pp. 202-203; Avery, p. 289; Archie Roosevelt, Jr., pp. 256-257.

[205] See n. 94, above; S.D. 867.00/12-845 No. 1553; FR, 1945, VIII:491.

Map 7. Northwest Iran (December 1945-December 1946)
Based in part on William Eagleton, Jr., *The Kurdish Republic of 1946*
(London, 1963), p. 37, and the *Middle East Journal* 1 (July 1947), 249.

The man who confronted this situation had served as Roosevelt's "assistant president," and had long experience in public affairs. Perhaps because of his experience, the secretary tended to function independently of the new president, a fact of which Truman was aware.[206] "More and more during the fall of 1945," Truman writes in his memoirs, "I came to feel that in his role as Secretary of State Byrnes was beginning to think of himself as Assistant President in full charge of foreign policy." Possibly, Byrnes's conception of his role worked to the detriment of Iran's best interests. One of America's stated aims when the secretary of state went to Moscow was "to attempt to get the Soviet troops out of Iran." That he failed possibly resulted from his own actions. Earlier in the year, when Byrnes was appointed secretary of state, Senator Arthur Vandenberg had complained to his wife: "Jimmy is a good guy (for any *other* job down here). But his whole life has been a career of compromise." At Moscow, in regard to Iran, Byrnes's actions justified Vandenberg's concern. "In the present conference his weakness in dealing with the Russians is that his main purpose is to achieve some sort of agreement," George Kennan observed at the time, "he doesn't much care what. The realities behind this agreement, since they concern only such people as Koreans, Rumanians, and Iranians, about whom he knows nothing, do not concern him."[207]

Apparently Byrnes believed that one of his principal tasks at Moscow was to mediate between Bevin and Molotov, and this may be a reason why at the initial session on 16 December he suggested dropping from the agenda the question of evacuating troops from Iran—a topic certain to cause acrimony between the British and Russian foreign ministers and to impede progress on other issues.[208] The Iranian question was at once removed from the agenda, although the foreign ministers agreed to discuss it informally.

As the Moscow Conference opened, Hussein Ala, the Iranian ambas-

[206] For insight into the relations between Truman and Byrnes, see Harry S. Truman, 1:22-23, 190-193, 546; Margaret Truman, p. 237; Phillips, *The Truman Presidency*, p. 83; Byrnes, *All in One Lifetime*, pp. 119, 216-230; Acheson, pp. 136-137; Herbert Druks, *Harry S. Truman and the Russians* (New York, 1966), p. 90; Rosenman, pp. 441-450; William Hillman, *Mr. President* (New York, 1952), pp. 18 ff.; Daniels, *The Man of Independence*, p. 310; Harriman and Abel, pp. 524, 530; Bohlen, p. 250.

[207] Harry S. Truman, 1:546; Byrnes, *All in One Lifetime*, p. 332; Margaret Truman, p. 323; Arthur Vandenberg, Jr., p. 225; Kennan, *Memoirs*, p. 286; Harriman and Abel, p. 525; Bohlen, p. 249.

[208] *Fr*, 1945, II:616

sador to the United States, stated the quintessence of the Iranian question to Acting Secretary of State Dean Acheson. It was not just Iran's sovereignty which was at stake, but the effectiveness and prestige of the United Nations.[209] The potential ramifications of the Iranian question *were*, in fact, incalculable, and the burden on the United States heavy, for almost everyone believed that Iran's only hope now lay with the United States. The implications of failure were ominous. Azerbaijan, Ala told Acheson on 20 December, "[is] only the first move in a series which [will] include Turkey and other countries in the Near East." Without a strong stand, he went on to say, the "history of Manchuria, Abyssinia, and Munich [will] be repeated and Azerbaijan [will] prove to [be] the first shot fired in [the] third world war." That this made an impression on Acheson was apparent in a telegram he sent to Byrnes; it was further indicated by his inclusion of the Manchurian and Ethiopian analogy in another telegram he sent the secretary of state on the implications of Soviet policies in Iran. He hoped that Byrnes would find it possible to impress Stalin with the American government's anxiety. It was important that the Soviet Union recognize the significance of its policies in northern Iran so that if the case came up in the United Nations it could not say the United States had not been frank.[210]

At his first meeting with Stalin on 19 December, Byrnes tried to impress the Soviet leader with his government's concern. With the Democrats firmly entrenched in Tabriz, and the Iranian government powerless to quell the rebellion, Byrnes expressed fear that Iran would raise the question of Soviet interference at the forthcoming United Nations meeting. If the question were raised, he thought it would be difficult to explain why 30,000 Soviet troops in Iran would be endangered by 1,500 additional Iranian troops quelling internal disorders. Stalin told Byrnes what he said he believed were the pertinent facts: Baku was vulnerable to hostile action; the Iranians were hostile to the Soviet Union. The Soviet Union had a right under the 1921 treaty of friendship with Iran to put troops in northern Iran if conditions were disturbed. At present, he pointed out, the Soviet Union was not interfering in Iran's internal, "local" disturbances, and he assured Byrnes that his country had no designs, territorial or otherwise, on Iran. Small na-

[209] Ibid., VIII:435, 461, 500.

[210] Ibid., pp. 501, 508, 512-513. Iranians feared that the British might be willing to settle for another "spheres of influence" arrangement, as in 1907 and 1941. FR, 1945, VIII:497, 500.

tions should be respected, he noted, but were sometimes inclined to promote friction between larger powers. In view of his attitude toward such behavior, he said it was impossible for the Soviet Union to withdraw before the expiration date set by the 1942 treaty. Only when the treaty expired would it be necessary to examine the situation and see whether or not withdrawal were possible. As Byrnes was leaving, Stalin reiterated that his government had no territorial designs on Iran, and cited precautions against hostile action as reason for maintaining troops in Iran.[211]

The British had anticipated Stalin's attitude since the Soviet note of 29 November to the United States. The Foreign Office felt that mention of the 1921 treaty's relevance to the question of withdrawal had "ominous implications" since that treaty could justify retention of Soviet troops in Iran after expiration of the treaty period. Bevin wanted to find out what Soviet intentions were—not only with regard to Iran, but also with regard to Turkey—and that evening, after Byrnes's audience with the generalissimo, the British foreign secretary found his opportunity.[212]

After Stalin told him of his conversation with Byrnes, Bevin put the question directly: was the Soviet government afraid of an attack from Iran? Stalin said he was afraid of sabotage. Bevin ignored this unconvincing explanation and got down to what was troubling him. Explaining that it was not his government's view but one held in the House of Commons and in the country at large, he told Stalin that England feared the Soviet Union's incorporation of Azerbaijan. In response, Stalin told him that "frankly and honestly, he had no claim against Iran."[213]

Although Byrnes had not brought up the question and did not intend to, Bevin was concerned about the situation in Turkey, too. Fully informed about rumors of war, troop concentrations along the Turkish

---

[211] FR, 1945, II:684-687; VIII:510-511. Wallace Murray estimated Soviet strength to be 30,000 in Azerbaijan and 75,000 in northern Iran, compared to 5,000 British troops and 6,000 American troops in the rest of the country. The total number of Soviet combat troops was at least three times that of the Iranian Army. The Kurdish Army had somewhere between 1,000 and 3,000 troops, while the Democratic Republic of Azerbaijan had about 10,000 men under arms at the time of its downfall. It should also be noted that unlike Britain and the United States, the Soviet Union continued to operate that portion of the Trans-Iranian Railway which ran through its zone. FR, 1945, VIII:481-482, 486; Rossow MS; Ramazani, "The Autonomous Republic of Azerbaijan," pp. 460, 462.

[212] FR, 1945, VIII:492-493, 495; II:630-631. See n. 183, above.

[213] Ibid., II:688-690.

border, and Soviet support for irredentist claims on behalf of the Armenian and Georgian Soviet Socialist Republics, Bevin now turned to what he believed was a Soviet war of nerves against Turkey. Pressed by Bevin as to what he wanted, Stalin obliged: the Georgian and Armenian portions of Turkey's eastern provinces and bases at the Straits. Like Churchill before him, Bevin said he would be very interested to see some definite proposals. In the meantime, he expressed hope that Turkey's continued mobilization would not be necessary. Stalin attributed Turkey's actions to its own initiatives. When Bevin remarked that Turkey's initiatives had been due to its fears of the Soviet Union, Stalin disclaimed the need for such fears, and discussion of Turkey ended.[214]

On the next day, however, *Pravda, Izvestia,* and *Red Star* all reprinted an article by S. R. Djanashia and N. Berdzenishvili, both of whom were members of the Science Academy of the Georgian Soviet Socialist Republic. The article, published a week earlier in the Tbilisi newspaper *Kommunisti,* demanded a 180 by 75 mile strip of northeastern Turkey.[215] The Soviet consulate simultaneously, without consulting the Turkish government, began to enlist members of Turkey's Armenian minority for voluntary return to their "homeland."[216] The encourage-

[214] Ibid., pp. 630, 690-691.

[215] According to Turkish sources, of 57,325 Georgian speaking people who had fled from Russia to Turkey, 15,596 lived in the area claimed by the Georgian professors as compared to 1,746,329 autochthonous Turks. S.D. 867.014/1-746.

[216] As early as February 1945, the Soviet Union had started presenting nationalist programs on Erivan radio (in Soviet Armenia). In June, an Ecclesiastical Conclave was called in Soviet Armenia, and a new Catholicos was elected in a ceremony filmed with great pains by the Soviet Union. Subsequently, the Mother Church appealed to all Armenians to return to their homeland. In August, the *New York Times* noted other evidence of Soviet support for Armenian aspirations, including a *Tass* dispatch which reported on a meeting of Armenians in Rumania who approved a resolution "to reunite Soviet Armenian territories unjustly annexed by Turkey." *New York Times,* 7 August 1945; Edward Alexander, "The Armenian Church in Soviet Policy," *The Russian Review* 14 (October 1955):357-362.

At this time, OSS estimates of the distribution of the world's Armenians were as follows:

Palestine	3,000-4,000
Egypt	30,000
Lebanon	60,000-70,000
Iran	60,000-70,000
Turkey	77,433 (by religion)
U.S.A.	95,000
Syria	100,000-120,000
U.S.S.R.	2,150,000

(S.D. 860 j.00/11-1945).

ment of Armenian immigration presumably was meant to reinforce Soviet demands for annexation of Turkey's eastern provinces, and seriously worried the Turks, who anxiously followed developments in Iran.[217]

Byrnes, meanwhile, had no confidence in anything the Soviets were saying about Iran. After assessing his and Bevin's conversations with Stalin, he believed that his worries over Soviet withdrawal had been justified, and determined to make another effort to have Stalin understand the American position.[218] At his second meeting with Stalin, on 23 December, Byrnes said he wanted to talk primarily about Iran, which was the first item on the agenda. Again Byrnes indicated his concern that the Iranian question might be raised at the United Nations. Stalin interrupted, remarking that he would not be frightened if it were. Byrnes continued: *should* the question come up, it would be difficult to take the position that Iran was hostile to the Soviet Union. The United States wished to avoid the embarrassment of having to take sides.

Stalin talked for a while about a proposal by Bevin for a tripartite commission, and about the Declaration Regarding Iran which, he said, still held good. A memorandum of the meeting notes his concluding statement that "no one had any need to blush if this question was raised in the Assembly. All [that] was needed was that the Iranian government should carry out its obligations and cease to be hostile to the Soviet Union." That the Iranian hostility cited by Stalin was either a fantasy or a tactic similar to that used throughout Eastern Europe made little difference. Byrnes was unable to argue with him, and in the car on the way back to the American embassy he told Bohlen that he foresaw real trouble over Iran.[219]

On Christmas Day things looked brighter, for Molotov indicated that the British proposal concerning a tripartite commission would be acceptable. The proposal called for an Anglo-American-Soviet Commission which would assist the Iranian government in reestablishing satisfactory relations with the provinces, and investigate the question of troop withdrawal. That night, Molotov offered several amendments, all but one of which Bevin accepted. It was understood that Molotov would agree to the proposal.[220]

[217] See n. 152, above.
[218] Byrnes, *Speaking Frankly*, p. 119; FR, 1945, II:688.
[219] FR, 1945, II:750-752; Bohlen, p. 250.
[220] FR, 1945, II:771-772, VIII:517-519; Byrnes, *Speaking Frankly*, p. 120.

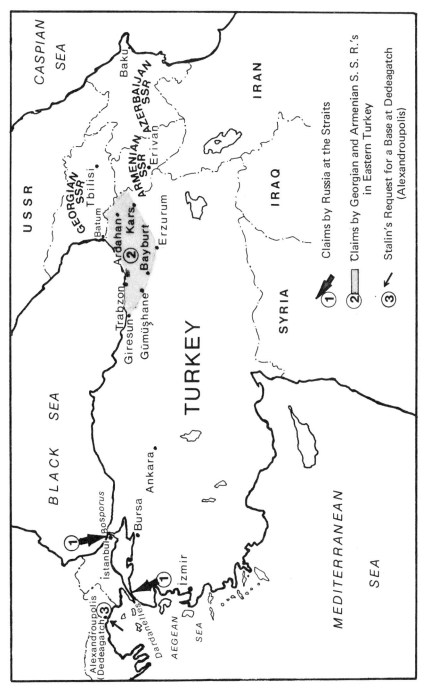

Map 8. Soviet Claims on Eastern Turkey and Demands on the Straits (1945-1946)

The next day, however, Molotov's attitude had changed.[221] His position, similar to that he had taken at Yalta, is best captured in a memorandum of the opening of the discussion on Iran:

> MR. MOLOTOV stated that nothing had come of the Iranian discussions and that they should be dropped.
>
> MR. BEVIN inquired whether that was the Soviet government's decision.
>
> MR. MOLOTOV replied that this was the fact of the matter. He added that Iran was not on the agenda.
>
> MR. BYRNES said that Iran had been on the agenda as enumerated the first day.
>
> MR. MOLOTOV recalled that Iran had been stricken from the agenda by agreement.
>
> MR. BYRNES said this was correct but it had also been agreed to discuss Iran.
>
> MR. MOLOTOV said that Iran had been discussed.[222]

When Bevin again raised the question, Molotov reiterated his opinion that views had been exchanged, that no decisions had been reached, and that since the question was not on the agenda there was no need to mention it in the communiqué. "What is my next step?" Bevin then asked. "You know that well," Molotov replied. Bevin thought he understood, and could only regret the situation.[223]

At the close of the Moscow Conference, the Russians gave the usual banquet and treated their guests to a Soviet film about the Russian victory over the Japanese in 1945. It failed to mention the American

[221] In his autobiography, the British ambassador to Iran, who was in Russia at the time, speculates on "what induced the Russians to make a right-about turn . . . I like to think," he writes, "that they thought at first our scheme would help them, but afterwards realized that it might help Persia, by effecting an improvement in the administration in all the provinces of Persia and reducing to their proper proportions the largely artificial movements in Azerbaijan and Kurdistan."

A better explanation may be found in Adam Ulam's analysis of the 1945-53 period: "Throughout this period . . . Soviet diplomacy often seemed to have operated on the assumption that, confronted with protracted and apparently fruitless negotiations, Americans would simply 'give up' out of sheer exhaustion, out of the inability of a democratic nation to keep attention and energies focused on a subject so peripheral to the interests of a vast majority of its citizens." Bullard, *The Camels Must Go*, p. 267; Ulam, *Expansion and Coexistence*, p. 410.

[222] FR, 1945, II:805. For Molotov's position at Yalta, see the discussion of Iran earlier in Chapter IV.

[223] Bevin expressed regret formally in a note on 27 December. FR, 1945, II:808, 814.

and British roles in the war and ended with an armistice signed by the Russian and Japanese representatives on an undesignated ship.[224] Byrnes passes lightly over the episode in his memoirs, but the incident's significance for Soviet-American relations should not be ignored for what it said about Soviet thinking. As George Kennan suggested in a long essay that winter, when dealing with the Soviets the United States should not assume a community of aims which did not exist. The Soviet Union, certainly, was in no danger of falling victim to this assumption. But the United States, particularly the American public, was often confused. On 28 December, for example, banner headlines in the *New York Times* hailed agreement on the atom, various treaties, Japan, China, and Korea, and characterized the conference in bold letters: "UNITY IN WIDE ACCORD."[225] In an article in the editorial section, however, Arthur Krock noted that no mention of Iran and Turkey "leaves Russian policy in those areas unchallenged for the present." A more analytical appraisal of the situation was made by Herbert Matthews on 30 December. He noted that the Middle East remained the big unsolved problem. Russia had made demands on Turkey for a coastal strip on the Black Sea, sections of Turkish Armenia (including Kars and Ardahan), and rights in the Straits. This fact, Matthews observed, coupled with disturbances in Azerbaijan, made the communiqué's silence on Iran and Turkey ominous. In 1945, Eastern Europe and the Balkans had been settled the way the Soviet Union wanted. In 1946, he predicted, attention would focus on the Middle East.[226]

Matthews' prediction proved correct. American attention already had begun to focus on the Middle East in the waning days of 1945, and much of this new interest was due to the persistence of Loy Henderson. Before Byrnes left for Moscow, Henderson tried to convince him of the importance of the Iranian question and strongly urged that he impress Stalin with the importance the United States ascribed to Soviet

[224] Bullard, *The Camels Must Go*, p. 268; Byrnes, *Speaking Frankly*, p. 213.

[225] Kennan, *Memoirs*, pp. 291, 561; for an indication of the fact that Kennan held this point of view even before the war, see pp. 133-134; for Stalin's attitude toward the Anglo-American "bloc," see FR, 1945, II:756; *New York Times*, 28 December 1945. Yergin, pp. 148-150, 161-162, 183, noting the lack of agreement on Iran, nonetheless overestimates the utility of the "Yalta" strategy at Moscow. Clearly the Northern Tier framework gives one a different perspective for judging such matters.

[226] *New York Times*, 28 and 30 December 1945.

actions in Iran. When Byrnes tried to keep Britain's Ambassador Bullard from attending the Moscow Conference, Henderson suggested that Wallace Murray be present also. The matter was important, Henderson wrote in a memorandum to Byrnes, "not merely because of Iran, but because Soviet interference in the internal affairs of Iran would be certain to undermine the confidence in the good faith of the Soviet Union, necessary for international cooperation in the post war era." Byrnes did not follow Henderson's suggestion on this point, perhaps because of Murray's failing health, but he was mindful of Henderson's advice.[227]

While Byrnes was in Moscow, reports from Iran and Turkey worried Henderson in Washington. There was little opposition to the Soviets in Azerbaijan and Turkey—a problem which no doubt weighed more heavily on Henderson's mind than the principles of the U.N. so often cited in department memoranda. Like others at State, Henderson was skeptical of the "U.N. boys"; he did not have that much faith in the United Nations, even though he supported the organization because the president endorsed it.[228] As a consequence, Henderson on 28 December sent Acheson a long memorandum on the Middle East, which he entitled "A Danger to World Peace." Great Britain, he pointed out, was following its traditional role of holding back Russia's movement south and of maintaining its line of communications to India. The Soviet Union, on the other hand, appeared determined to break down the structure Britain had maintained so that it could sweep into the Mediterranean and the Persian Gulf.

> During the last five years [the memorandum went on], two great barriers to Russian expansion have disappeared, namely, Germany in the West and Japan in the East. Judging from recent events in the Near East, Russia now appears to be concentrating upon the removal of a third barrier in the south.

While Britain's weakened condition made it difficult for her to maintain the ramparts of her empire against Russian encroachments, the United States continued to advocate the policy of the Open Door. No single Great Power, Henderson wrote, had made any effort to restrain the Russians, whose policies in the Near East seriously jeopardized the

[227] S.D. 891.00/12-1045; FR, 1945, VIII:488-490; S.D. 123 Murray, Wallace/ 12-1845/12-2945. See also Chapter IV, n. 83.

[228] Interviews with Loy Henderson, Harry Howard, and William Baxter; FR, 1945, VIII:512-513.

U.N. It was obvious that the United States did not intend to enforce its policies in that area—whether with the use of force, with the threat of force, or with economic power. If steps were to be taken, the United States should do so before the Soviet Union went so far in Iran and Turkey that it could not retreat, and before its activities hopelessly compromised the U.N. Henderson's recommendation as to specific steps was vague; it was embodied in the notion of a comprehensive agreement which would eliminate friction among the Great Powers, which would benefit the peoples of the Near East, and which would in no way contravene the principles of the U.N.[229] Henderson admitted that his recommendation would be difficult, if not impossible, to implement, but made clear the reasons for his anxieties. The United States was not prepared to act. The situation in the Near East was fraught with danger. Something had to be done if conflicts between the Great Powers along the Northern Tier were not to lead to a third world war.

A week later, as Byrnes, who had returned from Moscow, prepared for the first United Nations meeting in London, Henderson sent the secretary a document entitled "Basic Aims of Soviet Policy in Eastern Europe 1939-1941." This document was the work of Harry Howard, of the department's Division of International Organization Affairs. Howard had been in Germany where, as a member of the department's Special Interrogation Mission, he had been reading captured German Foreign Office documents and interrogating German war criminals. Among the latter was Hitler's interpreter, Dr. Paul Schmidt, who had kept full records of talks in which he had participated. A personal memorandum from Henderson suggested that the document was "well-worth reading in its entirety for the light it throws on current Soviet policy in the Near East."[230]

Howard's findings included the Molotov-Ribbentrop conversations of November 1940,[231] and Soviet demands for signing the Axis Tripartite Pact. Among Russian demands specified in the memorandum were:

[229] FR, 1946, VII:1-6.

[230] Interview with Harry Howard. The Papers of James F. Byrnes, Clemson University, Clemson, S.C., 3 January 1946 memorandum (mistakenly dated 3 January 1945) from Loy Henderson to the secretary. Harry N. Howard Papers, Truman Library, Box 1, Folder: "Basic Aims of Soviet Policy in Eastern Europe, 1939-1941"; "Department of State Special Interrogation Mission in Germany," 15 August-15 November 1945; and transcript, Harry N. Howard Oral History Interview, 5 June 1973, Truman Library.

[231] See discussion of this matter in Chapters I and III.

1) Recognition of Soviet security interests in the Black Sea.
2) Establishment of Soviet bases in the Dardanelles.
3) Establishment of Soviet garrisons in certain Turkish districts.

Germany, while it had been willing to see the Soviet Union seek an outlet to the Persian Gulf via Iran in the Near East, was less willing to make concessions in Asia Minor. According to German officials, their refusal of these Soviet claims on Turkey (which were a part of other claims on Finland, Rumania, and Bulgaria) led to the break between the two countries. Howard observed that because the Soviet Union was now seeking in the Near East the identical objectives which it sought from Germany, the Western Allies faced problems in their relations with the Soviet Union similar to those which arose between Germany and the Soviet Union during the years of the Nazi-Soviet Pact.[232]

This characterization of Soviet aims tended to support the interpretation made six months earlier by the Turkish ambassador in Moscow. Selim Sarper based his analysis upon intimate knowledge of many facts Howard had discovered in Germany. These same facts now gave substance to interpretations appearing in the press, to observations of American diplomats in Iran, Turkey, and Greece, and to analyses made in NEA. Inevitably, Secretary Byrnes and other high-level officials of the State Department were influenced by them and by Henderson's arguments that a new policy was necessary.[233]

While attention in the State Department began to focus on the Near East, Congress also began to take strong interest in the region. Arthur Krock, writing in the *New York Times* on 30 December, observed that many influential members of Congress wanted clarification of several questions concerning the Moscow Conference, one of which was: "Why was nothing settled about Russia's activities in Iran and its demands on Turkey?"[234]

There was as much anxiety at the White House as on Capitol Hill. President Truman, who had been kept in the dark about the progress

[232] Byrnes Papers, 3 January 1946 memorandum from Loy Henderson to the secretary.
[233] See n. 129, above. *New York Times*, 28 November and 2, 28, and 30 December; S.D. 891.00/12-1145; and Chapters II-IV for comments by Leland Morris, Wallace Murray, Laurence Steinhardt, Edwin Wilson, and Lincoln MacVeagh. For the effect of the memorandum on Byrnes's thoughts, see Byrnes, *Speaking Frankly*, pp. 255, 284-297.
[234] *New York Times*, 30 December 1945.

of the Moscow Conference,[235] had been further angered by Byrnes's request of 27 December that the White House arrange for him to address the American people on the results of the conference—results Truman did not yet know. When the communiqué came out that night it angered Truman: "I did not like what I read," he later recalled. "There was not a word about Iran or any other place where the Soviets were on the march. We had gained only an empty promise of further talks."[236]

When Byrnes arrived in Washington, Truman summoned him to his yacht, the *Williamsburg*. There Truman took him into his stateroom, closed the door, and belabored the manner in which negotiations had been conducted in Moscow. He did not like being kept in the dark about what was going on, and was shocked that a communiqué should be issued in Washington announcing a foreign policy development of major importance when he had no knowledge of what that development was. He informed Byrnes that he would not tolerate a repetition of such conduct.[237]

Later, studying the documents on the conference, Truman saw that its successes "were unreal":

> There was not a word in the communiqué to suggest that the Russians might be willing to change their ways in Iran—where the situation was rapidly becoming very serious[238]—or anywhere else. Byrnes, I concluded after studying the entire record, had taken it upon himself to

[235] Two reasons for this were: (1) Byrnes had taken only a small staff with him to Moscow, and (2) Byrnes's tendency to function independently. For example, when Averell Harriman and Charles Bohlen suggested that Byrnes notify Truman of the proceedings, Harriman was told that it was not necessary, while Bohlen was rebuffed. Acheson, p. 135; Druks, p. 90; Harriman and Abel, pp. 523-525, 530; Bohlen, pp. 248-251; Vandenberg, pp. 226, 232-233.

[236] Harry S. Truman, 1:550; see also Margaret Truman, p. 323; William D. Leahy Papers, Library of Congress, Washington, D.C., Leahy's Diary entry for 28 December 1945 (p. 199).

[237] Harry S. Truman, 1:550; see also Leahy Papers, Leahy's Diary entry for 29 December 1945 (p. 200).

[238] On 29 December, the vice consul in Tabriz had sent a telegram to the secretary of state which stated: "Unless Soviet position can be altered, Iran Government must accept situation in Azerbaijan as *fait accompli*." By 9 January 1946, he was sending back accounts of heavily armed Soviet troops in that city. Their presence had given rise, Robert Rossow reported, to a "deeply ingrained terrorism" whose reality "pervades even the most casual contact with the natives." His conclusion was startling: "Unless some sort of energetic action is taken, Azerbaijan must be written off." *FR*, 1945, VIII:520-521; 1946, VII:298-299.

move the United States in a direction to which I could not, and would not, agree.[239]

According to Truman, he then wrote a longhand letter which he "read" to Byrnes on 5 January 1946 in the Oval Room of the White House, in order that the two completely understand each other. Besides directing Byrnes's attention toward the proper conduct of foreign policy, the letter addressed the problem of American-Soviet relations. Truman, as he reviewed documents from the conference, for the first time had come across the Ethridge Report. Byrnes had put off publicizing the report and had attempted to use it at Moscow as leverage in settling certain peace treaties with the Soviets. He had been unsuccessful in this endeavor.[240] Truman, on the other hand, appears to have been more receptive to points emphasized by the report: that the Soviet government's position in the Balkans would be used as a means of bringing pressure on Greece, Turkey, and the Straits; and that the United States had to take the necessary steps to ensure application of those principles on which Ethridge thought the present policy of the United States was based.[241]

Although Byrnes had approved a plan for dealing with the Rumanian and Bulgarian situations, which intended to avoid the conflict over the representative nature of their governments, Truman opposed recognition of those governments unless they were radically changed. Turning to the Near East, he was even more adamant, especially because of the analogies he now drew between Eastern Europe and the Near East:

> I think we ought to protest with all the vigor of which we are capable against the Russian program in Iran. There is no justification for it. It is a parallel to the program of Russia in Latvia, Estonia and Lith-

[239] Harry S. Truman, 1:550. William Leahy's Diary entry for 4 January 1946 (p. 2), Leahy Papers, notes Truman's informing Leahy "that his first knowledge of the formal recognition of Yugoslavia was obtained from newspapers and that the matter was not discussed with him." This undoubtedly contributed to Truman's anger.

[240] Molotov's predictable response to the report on Rumania and Bulgaria had been to ask why Ethridge had not been to Greece. Stalin's response had been that if Byrnes published the report, he would ask Ilya Ehrenburg, a Soviet journalist, to publish his views. FR, 1945, II:643-645, 729-731, 752-753.

[241] Harry S. Truman, 1:551-552; FR, 1945, V:633-641. The principles in question were: "that peace will be secure only if based on truly representative governments in all countries with western political traditions, and that to concede a limited Soviet sphere of influence would be to invite its extension in the future." FR, 1945, V:637.

uania. It is also in line with the high-handed and arbitrary manner in which Russia acted in Poland.

At Potsdam we were faced with an accomplished fact and were by circumstances almost forced to agree to Russian occupation of Eastern Poland and the occupation of that part of Germany east of the Oder River by Poland. It was a high-handed outrage.

At the time we were anxious for Russian entry into the Japanese War. Of course we found later that we didn't need Russia there and that the Russians have been a headache to us ever since.

When you went to Moscow you were faced with another accomplished fact in Iran. Another outrage if I ever saw one.

Iran was our ally in the war. Iran was Russia's ally in the war. Iran agreed to the free passage of arms, ammunition and other supplies running into the millions of tons across her territory from the Persian Gulf to the Caspian Sea. Without those supplies furnished by the United States, Russia would have been ignominiously defeated. Yet now Russia stirs up rebellion and keeps troops on the soil of her friend and ally—Iran.

Whether Truman had also seen the memorandum that Henderson sent to Byrnes on 3 January is not clear, but the line of thought about Soviet motives which the memorandum supported was evident in Truman's analysis:

There isn't a doubt in my mind that Russia intends an invasion of Turkey and the seizure of the Black Sea Straits to the Mediterranean. Unless Russia is faced with an iron fist and strong language another war is in the making. Only one language do they understand—"how many divisions have you?"

I do not think we should play compromise any longer. We should refuse to recognize Rumania and Bulgaria until they comply with our requirements; we should let our position on Iran be known in no uncertain terms and we should continue to insist on the internationalization of the Kiel Canal, the Rhine-Danube waterway and the Black Sea Straits and we should maintain complete control of Japan and the Pacific. We should rehabilitate China and create a strong central government there. We should do the same for Korea.

Then we should insist on the return of our ships from Russia and force a settlement of the Lend-Lease debt of Russia.

I'm tired of babying the Soviets.[242]

[242] Gaddis, *The United States and the Origins of the Cold War*, p. 281; Lynn Davis, pp. 328-329; Harry S. Truman, 1:551-552. A transcript of the letter in the

According to Byrnes, Truman never read this letter to him. What really happened? Truman wrote the letter, and probably reiterated its substance to Byrnes. In discussing the conflicting impressions of each over the *Williamsburg* encounter, Dean Acheson has written that Truman was kindly, courteous, and considerate of others' feelings. His bark was worse than his bite. Byrnes, on the other hand, was neither sensitive nor lacking in confidence. A product of South Carolina politics, he was an extrovert who did not take criticism personally. "Both impressions were quite possibly genuine," Acheson observes of the encounter aboard the presidential yacht. The same may be true regarding the incident in the Oval Office. Whatever the circumstances of the exchange, it appears that an understanding *was* reached between the two men. Truman himself asserts that Byrnes accepted his decision, and that it was a point of departure for a new policy.[243] Subsequent evidence bears him out.

Conclusion

At the very end of 1945, elements of a new American foreign policy toward the Soviet Union had begun to coalesce. What the new policy was, and what form it would take, were not at this time specified beyond a determination to compromise no more. Nevertheless, it was clear that the affirmation of abstract principles alone had been insufficient to effect their guarantee. The guarantee of Turkey's and Iran's independence and

---

Truman Library includes one more sentence than the version printed in Truman's memoirs, but the difference is insignificant. For a facsimile of the letter, see Hillman, p. 22.

[243] In support of Truman's account is a note he made on 5 January 1946: "Today I wrote this memo and read it to my Secretary of State. So urgent was its contents that I neither had it typed nor mailed but not only had to read it from manuscript but preferred to do it that way in order to give more emphasis to the points I wish to make" (Truman Papers, PSF, Mr. President Folder, Harry S. Truman's long-hand notes, 5 January 1946). Daily Sheets in the President's Appointments File for January-May 1946 indicate that Truman and Byrnes met at 3:30 p.m. on 5 January 1946. For Byrnes's account, see *All in One Lifetime*, pp. 343-347, 398-403; and his article "Byrnes Answers Truman," *Collier's*, 26 April 1952, where he takes issue with Jonathan Daniels and William Hillman (see n. 206, above); Thomas Campbell and George Herring, eds., *The Diaries of Edward R. Stettinius, Jr., 1943-1946* (New York, 1975), p. 459; Acheson, p. 136; Harry S. Truman, 1:552; Byrnes, *Speaking Frankly*, p. 255; Bohlen, p. 251; Gaddis, *The United States and the Origins of the Cold* War, pp. 282-289; Curry, pp. 185-190; Yergin, p. 160; for different interpretations, see Gardner, *Architects of Illusion*, p. 103, and Donovan, pp. 159-161.

sovereignty had not been furthered appreciably by a resort to conferences either. Conferences had proven increasingly ineffective in the face
of Soviet obstruction and intransigence and had resulted only in what
came to be regarded as compromise. And compromise almost seemed to
be a euphemism, for now, in Iran, events were taking place which
threatened to make a mockery of the principles and guarantees that had
been agreed to during the war.

In Greece, Communist propaganda was attacking a government
whose viability was in serious doubt. The country itself was within
Britain's sphere, and so constituted one of the most important points
of weakness for the Western Allies as they tried to secure an equitable
postwar settlement. But British policy in Greece, while it was vulnerable
to criticism and the subject of considerable embarrassment, was not
really a source of Allied conflict. British dominance in Greece had been
traded off for that of the Soviets in Bulgaria, Hungary, and Rumania,
and the arrangement had clearly recognized the realities of power in
the Balkans.

Turkey and Iran, on the other hand, were entirely different questions.
Roosevelt, it is true, had acquiesced in Soviet and British predominance
in the Balkans and the Near East. He had not been well-informed about
issues within Britain's sphere of operations, and had avoided confronting the realities of power there. Instead, he had attempted to impress on
his Allies the need for restraint. Under his successor, however, things
had begun to change. The United States had slowly become involved in
British efforts to stabilize the Greek government and out of necessity
had also begun to play a political role in Turkey and Iran. Gradually the
United States was assuming Britain's position in the region. Britain's
ability to control events along her line of communications was rapidly
declining, and Whitehall was cognizant of the new realities of power
in the world. Of the thirteen non-Communist states which bordered
Russia before the war, only five were independent when it was over.[244]
Finland was neutralized; Afghanistan, at the extreme eastern end of the
Northern Tier, retained its traditional role of a buffer state. Of the
remaining three, Norway, Turkey, and Iran, the latter two were in serious jeopardy of being drawn into the Soviet fold, and the United
States was the only power capable of seriously confronting this turn of
events.

[244] Chubin, p. 37.

In Turkey, the old Eastern Question had risen from its grave. In the esoteric discussions of the Montreux Convention what was at issue was control of the Straits and respect for the independence and sovereignty of the Turkish government. Churchill at Potsdam had attempted to impress on Stalin the importance of not alarming the Turks, but the generalissimo had not been impressed. The war of nerves waged by the Soviets along Turkey's borders had risen to new heights during the Moscow Conference, and now Stalin's Western Allies were deeply alarmed.

In Iran, the situation in Azerbaijan seemed an extension of the Eastern Question. As in Turkey, the search for security and a desire for access to warm-water ports appeared to be factors in Soviet actions. What was at issue was again the question of Great Power influence in the area, and of Soviet respect for the independence and sovereignty of a border country. Contrary to Allied understandings, and to the question of respect for the principles involved, the Soviets were clearly supporting a separatist rebellion in the zone they occupied. Byrnes's attempt at Moscow to take up where Churchill left off, and to impress on Stalin the importance which the United States ascribed to Soviet actions in Iran, was to no avail.

The Truman administration, faced with what it regarded as a *fait accompli* in Eastern Europe, was gradually coming to the conclusion that a similar fate should not await the Northern Tier. If the administration never fully understood the complex negotiations over Eastern Europe, it did appreciate the fact that the Near East was a totally different problem whose parameters had yet to be defined. If no action were taken by the United States, such parameters would probably be defined by the shifting balance of power in the region.

The United States, however, while willing to endorse the independence and sovereignty of Iran and Turkey, was unwilling to provide either country with a guarantee. In the absence of any apparent American commitments, the Soviets stepped up their pressure along the Northern Tier where their tactics, similar to those which they had used in Eastern Europe, gave the Truman administration pause. Soviet press and radio attacks against "hostile" governments, attempts to effect the ouster of various government leaders, irredentist claims, coupled with troop mobilization, all smacked of Hitler's tactics before the war. If, as one historian has documented, the totalitarian image of the Soviet

Union became popular in American decision-making circles in 1945,[245] close observation of Soviet policies in Iran and Turkey helps to explain *why*. Faced in Eastern Europe with models of how *not* to deal with the Soviets, the Truman administration turned its attention to the Near East, where analogies between Stalin's and Hitler's tactics were too strong to ignore.[246] And if these analogies gave the administration pause, evidence of recent Soviet designs on Iran and Turkey, supplemented by information about Nazi-Soviet negotiations over the Near East in 1940, forced it to recognize the need for a more forceful policy in the region.

Contributing to the administration's resolution was the fact that Truman's close advisors were very much aware of America's recently defined economic and strategic interests in the Near East, and sensitive to Britain's diminished economic and military strength along her line of communications.[247] Because of these factors, the Office of Near Eastern and African Affairs in the State Department by 1944 was already operating on the assumption that British and American interests in the area were synonymous. Under the direction of its new chief, Loy Henderson, NEA and the chiefs of mission assigned to countries in the Near East never challenged this assumption. Accepting the idea that America had vital interests in the Near East, they recognized that an implicit alliance with Britain against Russia was a necessary adjunct to American policy in the Near East. Near the end of his life, Harry Hopkins had come to a somewhat similar conclusion,[248] and so now would the president

[245] Thomas Lifka, chaps. VII-IX.

[246] These analogies seemed cogent not only to Americans, but to Iranians and Turks—the latter of whom had always looked on Poland as a touchstone of Soviet intentions.

[247] Byrnes, Forrestal, and Leahy had all participated in the government's concern for Middle East oil earlier in the war (see Chapter III); in July 1945, Byrnes had been given a recent survey of the vast Near East oil resources. The Near East was then thought to have reserves of 15 billion barrels (compared to United States reserves of 20 billion barrels). Of those 15 billion barrels, 74 percent was controlled by Britain, 24 percent by the United States. Including its own oil reserves, the United States controlled 57 percent of the world's oil resources, Britain 27 percent, and the Soviet Union 11 percent (FR, *Potsdam* I:217-218; see also Millis, p. 81). According to Herbert Matthews, 80 percent of Russia's oil was produced in the Caucasus (*New York Times*, 30 December 1945). For Leahy's opinion about Britain's economic situation, see Francis-Williams, *A Prime Minister Remembers: The War and Post-War Memoirs of the Rt. Hon. Earl Atlee* (London, 1961), pp. 161-162. See also Chapter III, n. 125.

[248] See n. 165.

and his secretary of state. Informed by what they believed had occurred in Eastern Europe, and addressing problems which were now arising in Iran, Turkey, and Greece, both Truman and Byrnes were gradually coming to understand the importance of the power struggle which, for centuries, had been waged along the Northern Tier. From this understanding, a policy would emerge which, as it was enlightened by successive crises in Iran, Turkey, and Greece, would lead the United States to commit itself to maintaining the balance of power in the region.

V

𐂷𐂷𐂷𐂷𐂷

Crisis and Diplomacy—The Reformulation

of American Policy

Toward the Northern Tier in 1946

CRISES in Iran and Turkey led the Truman administration to reformulate American policy toward the countries of the Northern Tier in 1946. The conflicts in question reflected attempts by the Great Powers to define their interests in the region. They grew out of the postwar world's changed power relationships and were activated—at least in this period —by adventurous Soviet policies toward Iran and Turkey. These policies derived from historical goals which were at once defensive and expansionist, and were accentuated by a legacy of contempt for and hostility toward the governments of both countries. Soviet attempts to realize these goals in the postwar world precipitated events that were crucial in advancing the Truman administration's education as to Soviet tactics, and leading the administration to assume Britain's traditional role in the region.

Great Power discussions over Turkey and Iran in 1945 began the administration's education, but it took the Iranian Crisis of 1945-46 to crystallize many of its elements. A conceptual framework for interpreting those elements was articulated most succinctly by George Kennan in a long telegram to the State Department on 22 February 1946. Kennan's telegram, which synthesized and ordered many of the ideas circulating among those concerned with Soviet affairs, significantly shaped the administration's developing views of the Soviet Union. As a result, the Truman administration eventually came to the conclusion that bilateral diplomacy between the Soviet Union and Iran was not a desirable method of solving the Iranian question. Even when sanctioned by the United Nations, bilateral diplomacy created too many opportunities for coercion. Such a course made it difficult to uphold the principles of the United Nations, and threatened the security interests of the United States.

Ultimately what counted—even more than the United Nations—was a desire by the United States to take a firm stand on issues it believed important, and a willingness to support that stand with military power if necessary. If Eastern Europe presented the administration with models of how not to deal with the Soviets, the Iranian crisis served as a model of how it should deal with them. Bolstered by lessons of the Iranian crisis, the administration reacted to the crisis over the Turkish Straits in August 1946 by redefining its military and diplomatic policies in Iran, Turkey, Greece, and the Mediterranean.

The Iranian Crisis

The first major crisis after World War II began in Iran. Occupied by the British, the Russians, and the Americans during the war, Iran— never an actual theater of the war—constituted a unique proving ground for Allied cooperation. In 1946, it was at the center of the first major crisis to come before the United Nations, and proved, in the prophetic terms of a briefing paper for the Malta Conference, a testing ground for the principles of Dumbarton Oaks.[1]

Because the Iranian crisis was so significant, and because it is so little understood, it is necessary to follow in some detail the intricate maneuvers relating to the crisis that were conducted both in and out of the United Nations in 1946. Only then can one truly appreciate the nature of Soviet obstruction and intransigence during the wearying conflict over Iran, and so understand the American response to its involvement in the conflict.

The United Nations: Act 1

On 19 January, Sayid Hassan Taqizadeh, head of the Iranian delegation to the United Nations in London, submitted to the acting secretary general a letter which called for investigation of Russian interference in Iran's internal affairs.[2] The Soviet and Ukrainian delegations countered

[1] FR, *The Conferences at Malta and Yalta*, p. 340.

[2] Neither Great Britain nor the United States encouraged Taqizadeh to file a complaint; Great Britain, in fact, had attempted to discourage such action. S.D. 891.00/1-246/1-346; FR, 1946, VII:293-304; Byrnes, *Speaking Frankly*, p. 123; for a conflicting, unsubstantiated account see Nashrollah Fatemi, *Oil Diplomacy* (New York, 1954), p. 290; Arfa, pp. 352-356, discusses Soviet-supported attempts to stage a coup in December 1945; *United Nations Security Council Journal, 1st Year, Series 1*, Meeting 1-42, 17 January-26 June 1946 (hereafter referred to as *UNJ*), p. 13.

with a demand for investigation into the situations in Greece and Indonesia respectively.[3]

Andrei Vyshinsky, chief of the Soviet delegation, on 24 January attempted to refute the substance of Taqizadeh's complaint. Selectively quoting and distorting previous correspondence with Iran on the question of his government's interference in Iranian affairs, Vyshinsky justified Soviet presence in Iran by the Irano-Soviet Treaty of 1921 and the Tripartite Treaty of 1942. He denied that Soviet troops had any connection with events in Azerbaijan, and asserted that Iran's appeal was unfounded. Negotiations between their governments, he said, had taken place with satisfactory results. In spite of "fascist propaganda" on the part of Iran, he believed that bilateral negotiations could and should settle such differences.[4]

While the Security Council awaited its first meeting in London, the crisis in Iran continued to develop. In Mahabad, Qazi Mohammed, dressed in a traditional turban, but wearing a Soviet uniform, announced establishment of the autonomous Kurdish Republic. In Teheran Soviet pressure caused the Hakimi Cabinet to fall.[5]

The man designated to head the new Iranian government, Ahmad Qavam, was an elderly, heavy-set, enigmatic man who wore dark glasses, had a quick mind, and a habit of giggling quietly to himself. He owned tea-growing estates in the Soviet zone and had supported the Freedom Front—perhaps, it was speculated, as a result of his landholdings. According to State Department sources, Qavam as of 21 January believed that it was better to humor the Russians than to oppose them. By

[3] *UNJ*, pp. 14-15. The Greek question, in no way similar to the Iranian question, came before the U.N. at the beginning of February, and was disposed of after the charge was not substantiated. See also *FR*, 1946, VII:99, 104-115; Xydis, *Greece and the Great Powers*, pp. 163-167. It would appear that the Soviets were attempting to use Greece as a counter to criticism of Soviet policies in Iran, much as they had used it in the Polish question—thus extending their portion of the spheres of influence agreement even more. On 24 January, Ernest Bevin told Stettinius that the reason for the investigation was that Russia was trying to pressure Britain into recognizing Rumania and Bulgaria. Bevin said that Vyshinsky would drop the charges against Greece if Rumania and Bulgaria were recognized. Campbell and Herring, *The Diaries of Edward R. Stettinius, Jr.*, pp. 448-453.

[4] *UNJ*, pp. 17-19. The Irano-Soviet Treaty of 26 February 1921 formalized earlier renunciations of Soviet interests made in 1919. See Chapter III, n. 9. For the Tripartite Treaty of 1942, see Chapter III, n. 38.

[5] The Hakimi Cabinet fell on 20 January 1946. *FR*, 1946, VIII:313; William Eagleton, Jr., *The Kurdish Republic of 1946* (London, 1963), pp. 61-63; Lenczowski, *Russia and the West in Iran, 1918-1948*, p. 295; Meister, pp. 218-219.

making promises to the Russians, he proposed to gain time until their withdrawal, when he felt the government would be able to reassert its authority. Thus, he began his official duties on 27 January by asking the pro-British General Hassan Arfa, the Iranian chief of staff, to step down—a move calculated to calm public opinion on the left and placate the USSR. At the same time, he instructed Taqizadeh not to weaken his efforts to have the Iranian case considered by the U.N.[6]

Taqizadeh needed little encouragement. He had already replied on 26 January to Vyshinsky, quoting relevant passages from previous correspondence to reveal the incredible distortion practiced by the Soviet delegate.[7] Taqizadeh boldly stated that while Iran had discussed with Soviet leaders the withdrawal of their troops, withdrawal was not the question. The real issue was Iran's internal freedom.

Taqizadeh on 28 January gave the Security Council a long memorandum stating the facts of the case. The memorandum ended with the request that Soviet authorities cease interfering in Iran's internal affairs, and withdraw all of their troops and officials from Iran by 2 March 1946. Vyshinsky, however, addressed only the procedural aspects of the question. The Iranian government that made the complaint was not in power. Their claims, moreover, were without foundation. Negotiations between the two countries had taken place, and the results were satis-

---

[6] *New York Times*, 7 March 1946; Skrine, p. 233; Lenczowski, pp. 231, 295; Avery, p. 393; Arfa, p. 364; FR, 1946, VII:315; S.D. 891.00/1-2446; R & A 1090.135-23 Jan. 46. Qavam's experience in government was lengthy; he held his first cabinet post in 1910 and had been prime minister in 1921 and 1922.

[7] One example should suffice to illustrate the differences between the two accounts.

Actual text of 1 December 1945 Iranian Letter, cited by Iranian Letter of 26 January 1946 to Security Council:	Citation of Iranian Letter of 1 December 1945 by Soviet Letter of 24 January 1946 to Security Council:
In answer to the communication in which you reply that the charges made concerning the interference of Soviet officials in our internal affairs, in the northern provinces are unfounded, the Ministry for Foreign Affairs does not wish at this time to throw light on the antecedents of the case. It takes note with satisfaction of the purport of your statements to the effect that henceforth such incidents will not repeat themselves. *UNJ*, pp. 33-34.	It should also be noted that in its reply of 1 December 1945, the Iranian Government not only failed to disprove the facts referred to in the Soviet note of 26 November, but also expressed, as is stated in the abovementioned Iranian note, "its satisfaction that, as was confirmed by the Embassy's reply, the interference of the Soviet officials into the internal affairs of the northern districts of Iran is not in accordance with the facts." *UNJ*, pp. 17-18.

factory. Therefore, the questions raised could not be discussed by the Security Council. As an alternative, he suggested that the Soviet Union and Iran settle the matter between themselves.[8]

When the Security Council reconvened on 30 January, Taqizadeh addressed Vyshinsky's points, and affirmed Iran's willingness to negotiate under the council's aegis, but announced that he was unprepared to let the matter go out of the council's hands.[9] Vyshinsky reiterated the Soviet position: the question was a procedural one; the case should not come before the Security Council. He admitted Russian opposition to the entrance of Iranian troops into the northern provinces, but claimed that forces already there were sufficient to restore order. He denied Soviet interference in the Azerbaijan rebellion, claimed it was an autonomous movement, and ended his remarks with a guarantee of his government's good intentions.[10]

Acrimonious debate followed, the bespectacled, portly British Foreign Minister Bevin countering and being countered by the stocky, hunched Vyshinsky. The "grand inquisitor" of the Moscow purge trials, who at another forum had addressed Nikolai Bukharin as "you son of a bull and a pig," and who in his summation had referred to the old Bolshevik as "that damnable cross of a fox and a swine," now met with witnesses who were better able to defy him openly. Bevin charged the Soviet government with a "war of nerves," while Vyshinsky referred obliquely to the British as "hotheads" and charged them with suspiciousness.[11]

After protracted discussion the matter was referred to bilateral negotiations; the parties would inform the council when agreement was reached. At Vyshinsky's request, it was not formally stated that the question would remain on the agenda; but it was understood, at Bevin's and Stettinius's insistence, that until a settlement was reached, this matter would remain a continuing concern of the council.[12]

Thus ended the first act of the drama unfolding before the U.N. What was its significance? What were its implications? The American delegate, Stettinius, was satisfied. Earlier, Gromyko had assured him that the democratic movement was spontaneous, and that the Soviet armies had nothing to do with the present situation. As a consequence, Stettinius believed that Iran and the Soviet Union would reach a settle-

[8] Ibid., pp. 47-58.   [9] Ibid., pp. 62-65.   [10] Ibid., pp. 65-69.
[11] Ibid., pp. 70-83; *New York Times*, 31 January 1946 and 4 February 1946; Stephen Cohen, *Bukharin and the Bolshevik Revolution: A Political Biography, 1888-1938* (New York, 1973), p. 380.
[12] *UNJ*, pp. 70-83.

ment which conformed with the principles and purposes of the charter. In the Soviet Union, *Pravda* hailed the Iranian question's removal from the agenda as a triumph. The Soviet organ mentioned a possible settlement, but did not speculate on how it might be reached. The Iranian ambassador was disappointed; he had been willing to negotiate providing the item *remained* on the agenda. The question that troubled him was whether the council would take the initiative should the necessity arise. The question was hypothetical, and the United States refused to give definite support on the basis of hypothetical developments.[13]

For Iran, lack of definite support was unsettling—especially since the pointed questions, asked by Bevin in the Security Council debate, remained unanswered: "What is there to negotiate about? . . . And what is to be the result of such negotiations?"[14] According to Article 4 of the 1942 Tripartite Treaty, Iran was responsible for her own internal security. The presence of foreign troops was *not* to constitute a military occupation. The occupying forces were *not* to interfere with Iran's internal functioning any more than necessary. The war was over and the slightest interference was no longer justified. Now Iranian troops had been interfered with by Vyshinsky's admission. What, then, *was* there to negotiate about? What *was* to be the result of such negotiations? These questions must have been in the mind of the wily Qavam as he journeyed to Moscow in February to negotiate with Molotov and Stalin.

Entr'acte

During February Prime Minister Ja'afar Pishevari of Azerbaijan began a vigorous campaign against Qavam's government. Earlier, in order to maintain Moscow's support, he had shown restraint and had merely criticized the Teheran government for its reaction. Now his belligerency seemed dictated by a need to give the Soviet Union an excuse for staying in Azerbaijan.[15] He needed, moreover, a scapegoat for his failures.

Pishevari was a grateful puppet, who never apologized for the Red Army's support of his regime. As a result of this backing, he had been able to institute two badly needed reforms of major consequence: redistribution of land and nationalization of the larger banks. He also began badly needed work on roads, established workers' welfare pensions, and declared Azeri Turqi the official language of Azerbaijan.

---

[13] FR, 1946, VII:326-328; Campbell and Herring, *The Diaries of Edward Stettinius, Jr.,* p. 447; *New York Times,* 4 February 1946.
[14] *UNJ,* p. 70.   [15] FR, 1946, VII:332-333.

These reforms—or at least the intentions which motivated them—were popular, but the economic decline which set in at once was devastating, and the means by which Pishevari coped with economic problems were inane. He abolished unemployment by decree. As economic decline continued, his regime demanded more money from the farmers than the departed landlords had ever asked. With a secret police modeled after the Soviet NKVD, Azerbaijan became a police state, which institutionalized terror under the aegis of a "goon squad" officially titled "The Society of Friends of Soviet Azerbaijan." Even those friendly to Pishevari's rule denounced his abuse of power. When, on 9 February, Pishevari announced creation of an army and the beginning of conscription, and asked the Muslim leaders to declare a Holy War, there was little support from the populace. One reason, certainly, may be attributed to the absurdity of a Communist regime declaring *jihad* on an orthodox Shi'ite Muslim nation. As the police began impressing draft evaders, the American vice consul in Tabriz stated categorically that if the Soviet army left, Pishevari's regime would crumble.[16]

Of more importance than Pishevari's call for a Holy War was a speech on the same day by Joseph Stalin. Three days prior to the speech, Soviet spokesmen had begun a campaign against the "reaction" menacing Russia in Europe and the Middle East. With implicit reference to Iran and Turkey, the Georgian Marshal Lavrenti Beria announced that the collapse of the German offensive shattered the plans of certain countries for a military diversion against the Soviet Caucasus. If that speech (by a man whom Khrushchev later accused of goading Stalin into making demands on Turkey) nurtured anxieties along the Northern Tier, Stalin's speech of 9 February was of equal concern to the United States. Stalin described a capitalist encirclement of the Soviet Union while picturing the capitalist economy as setting the stage for war. In the past, Stalin asserted, crises in the development of the capitalist world economy had produced two world wars. The Soviet Union had survived as a result of its five-year plans. In order to ensure the Soviet Union against any eventuality, industrial production would have to be stepped up. As a consequence, he announced a new five-year plan, a plan with heavy emphasis on rearmament and munitions pro-

16 Lenczowski, *Russia and the West in Iran*, p. 290; "The Communist Movement in Iran," p. 47; Edwin Muller, "Behind the Scenes in Azerbaijan," *The American Mercury*, June 1946, p. 696; Meister, p. 256; Rossow, "The Battle of Azerbaijan," p. 19; Maurice Hindus, *In Search of a Future* (Garden City, N.Y., 1949), p. 52; FR, 1946, VII:333; Rossow MS.

duction. From Moscow George Kennan reported little indication in speeches by any Soviet officials in the "election" campaign that the Soviets placed any reliance on international collaboration.[17]

The ramifications of Stalin's speech were considerable. Justice William O. Douglas told Secretary of the Navy James Forrestal that it was "The Declaration of World War III." Director of the Office of European Affairs H. Freeman Matthews considered the speech "the most important and authoritative guide to post-war Soviet society." Chief of the Division of Eastern European Affairs Elbridge Durbrow urged diligence in counteracting what he predicted would be a Soviet propaganda barrage. Its intent would be to divide Britain and the United States. The purpose of such intent? To give the Soviets a free hand in attaining their ultimate goals. After waiting three days for further comment from Kennan on the speech, Matthews instructed Durbrow to request from Kennan an interpretive analysis of what might be expected in the way of further implementation of the Soviets' announced policies.[18]

Kennan on 22 February responded to Matthews' request with an

[17] *New York Times*, 7 and 10 February 1946; *FR*, 1946, VI:690-691, 694-696; Richard Rosser, *An Introduction to Soviet Foreign Policy* (Englewood Cliffs, N.J., 1969), p. 239; Herbert Feis, *From Trust to Terror: The Onset of the Cold War, 1945-1950* (New York, 1970), p. 75. For discussion of ideological and imperial aspects of Soviet policies from 1944 on, see Donald Treadgold, *Twentieth Century Russia* (Chicago, 1972), p. 422; Aron, p. 37; Schlesinger, "Origins of the Cold War," pp. 43-44; Gaddis, *The United States and the Origins of the Cold War*, pp. 257-258; Franz Borkenau, *European Communism* (London, 1953), pp. 519 ff.; Djilas, *Conversations with Stalin*, pp. 102-103, 114, 129-130, 148 (whose observation of Zhdanov calls Borkenau's Zhdanov thesis into question); Spector, p. 189; Robert Wesson, *The Russian Dilemma: A Political and Geopolitical View* (New Brunswick, N.J., 1964), pp. vii-xi, 104-109. Soviet ideological and political control was necessary because non-Russians, who constituted only 35 percent of the population in the Soviet Union during the interwar years, grew to 44 percent of the population after Stalin's accord with Hitler, to 50 percent of the population by the end of World War II, and to over 60 percent of the population in Russia's de facto "empire." The demographic and ethnic problems of managing large numbers of alien peoples account for Stalin's liquidation of the Volga Germans in 1941, and of the four autonomous Muslim republics of Crimea, Ingush, Chechen, and Balkar in 1943-44. They explain Soviet suspicions of their own soldiers who had been taken prisoner and then repatriated after the war, only to be subject to detention in the Gulag Archipelago. And they help to account for the Soviets' heavy-handed policies that began along the Northern Tier after the Battle of Stalingrad, and in Eastern Europe after its "liberation" by the Red Army. Demographic and ethnic problems of control also make more understandable the increased emphasis on ideology in the Soviet Union—and particularly on its European periphery—at the end of World War II.

[18] Millis, pp. 134-135; *FR*, 1946, VI:695; interview with Elbridge Durbrow.

8,000-word cable. The cable was a perspicacious, reasoned appraisal of Stalinist Russia. It examined Russia's insecurity, and its historical roots. The pressure to extend Russia's border Kennan saw basically as "only the steady advance of uneasy Russian nationalism, a centuries old movement in which conceptions of offense and defense are inextricably confused."[19]

On an official plane, Russia would attempt to advance the official limits of its power; at most, restricted to neighboring points conceived of as being of immediate strategic necessity, such as northern Iran and Turkey. But other points would come into question, such as a request to a "friendly" Iranian government for a port on the Persian Gulf. Aims such as this would be pursued in the U.N., toward which Russia's attitude was pragmatic and tactical.

On an unofficial plane, efforts would be made to weaken the power and influence of the Western Powers, and to keep pressure on governments which opposed Soviet aims. But Soviet power, while neither schematic nor adventuristic, and impervious to the logic of reason, was highly sensitive to the logic of force. Thus, Kennan stressed the necessity of possessing and making clear the readiness to use force in confronting Soviet power.[20] In order to do this, the first step would be to understand the Soviets and educate the American public about the realities of Russia. It also would be necessary to formulate a constructive picture of the sort of world the United States would like to see, and to have the courage and self-confidence to cling to American methods and conceptions of society.

The effects of Stalin's speech and Kennan's cable were profound. Stalin's speech, along with events in Iran, and Truman's desire to take a firmer stance toward the Soviet Union, inspired a speech by Secretary Byrnes at the Overseas Press Club on 28 February—a speech which was correctly interpreted as reflecting a firmer attitude on the part of the United States government toward the Soviet Union.[21] Still other speeches, by Senator Arthur Vandenberg (earlier, on 27 February), John Foster Dulles (1 March), Senator Tom Connally (12 March),

[19] FR, 1946, VI:696-709; Kennan, Memoirs, pp. 308-311.
[20] Yergin, p. 169, overstates Kennan's emphasis on ideology and his ignorance of the role of realpolitik in shaping Soviet policy.
[21] Byrnes, Speaking Frankly, pp. 254-256; Department of State Bulletin 14 (10 March 1946):355-358; Leahy Papers, diary entries for 20 and 21 February 1946; for the effects of the speech on Britain, see New York Times, 2 March 1946; for its effects on Turkey, see S.D. 867.00/3-746.

and again Byrnes (16 March), made this policy shift contemplated by Truman at the turn of the year even more obvious.[22]

The intellectual framework for many of these and other statements was provided by Kennan's analysis, which received wide distribution. His telegram was published as a supplement to the "Office of European Affairs Weekly Review." It was sent to virtually all decision-makers in the State Department. Secretary of the Navy James Forrestal received copies from his own Chief of Naval Operations as well as from his friend W. Averell Harriman, and considered the analysis so important that he distributed copies of it to members of Truman's cabinet who were concerned with foreign and military affairs.[23]

One reason for the popularity of Kennan's analysis stems from the

[22] Arthur Vandenberg, Jr., pp. 250-251; Byrnes, *All in One Lifetime*, pp. 349-350; John C. Campbell, *The United States in World Affairs, 1945-1947* (New York, 1947), p. 103. An interview Maxim Litvinov had with CBS correspondent Richard Hottelet and which was reported to the secretary of state by Ambassador Walter Bedell Smith in June 1946, tended to corroborate the American interpretation of Stalin's speech. Speaking as a private citizen, Litvinov told Hottelet that differences between East and West had gone too far to be reconciled and that the root cause was the prevailing ideological conception in the Soviet Union of the inevitability of conflict between Communist and Capitalist worlds. Asked if Soviet suspicion of the West would be mitigated if all Russian demands were granted, Litvinov said such a course would only result in the West being faced after a period of time with more demands. Litvinov saw little hope and volunteered that there was nothing one could do inside a totalitarian state to change it. See also Litvinov's 24 May conversation with Ambassador Smith, FR, 1946, VI:763-765; Byrnes Papers, Folder 638.

[23] George F. Kennan Papers, Princeton University Library, Princeton, N.J., Box 31 d, 1947 folder; Harriman and Abel, p. 548; James V. Forrestal Papers, Princeton University Library, Princeton, N.J., Forrestal Diaries, vol. 4, p. 906. For the influence of the telegram, see: Acheson, pp. 150-151; Millis, pp. 135-140; Forrestal Papers, esp. Box 24, Folder: Russia; Rogow, pp. 200-203; Joseph Jones, *The Fifteen Weeks* (New York, 1955), p. 133; Curry, pp. 368-369; Gaddis, *The United States and the Origins of the Cold War*, pp. 302-304; George Elsey Papers, Harry S. Truman Library, Box 63; Clark Clifford Papers, Harry S. Truman Library, Box 15; Gardner, *Architects of Illusion*, pp. 270-300, who offers a useful critical comparison of Kennan's arguments and his later article in *Foreign Affairs* (see also Chapter VI, n. 121); John Foster Dulles, "Thoughts on Soviet Foreign Policy and What To Do About It," *Life* 22 (3 June 1946):113-126, and Part II, *Life* 22 (10 June 1946): 119-130, both apparently informed by Kennan's analysis, and subject to problems discussed in Gardner's critique; see also John Foster Dulles Papers, Princeton University Library, Princeton, N.J., Personal Correspondence, 1945-1947, Box 140, File: Communist Party, 1946, 1948, 1949, 9 May 1946 letter from Dulles to Acheson, 28 May letter from Acheson to Dulles, 4 June 1946 letter from Dulles to Walter Lippmann; Folder: 1946 (1), 5 September 1946 letter from Dulles to Lippmann; and Margaret Truman, p. 337, who does not fully appreciate the telegram's impact.

fact that only since 1933 had the United States had official relations with the Soviet Union. Few Americans were trained in Soviet studies, and as wartime policies ended, no conceptual scheme existed for framing American relations with the Soviet Union. Kennan's message articulated such a scheme.[24]

Meanwhile, Qavam, responding to a friendly invitation from Stalin, left Teheran by plane, and on 19 February was received in Moscow by Molotov. The 2 March deadline, set for the withdrawal of all foreign troops from Iran, was approaching, and Qavam was under considerable stress throughout his visit.[25]

On 21 February, in his first meeting with Stalin, Qavam told the Soviet leader that he had come to Moscow to request the immediate evacuation of Soviet forces from Iran in order to prepare the groundwork for friendly relations with the Soviet Union. He discovered, however, that Stalin did not intend to proceed with the evacuation of Azerbaijan. Instead, the Soviet premier asserted that the 1921 treaty gave the Soviet Union the right to maintain forces there. He also brought up the subject of petroleum, which Qavam refused to discuss, and Persian claims to Russian territory made in 1919. Qavam noted that the Persian claim was made prior to the 1921 treaty; he also pointed out that the treaty did not give the Soviets the right to keep troops in Iran unless Soviet frontiers were menaced by a third government through Iran—a threat which did not exist.[26]

Four days later, Molotov sent Qavam a memorandum which suggested that Iran recognize an autonomous government in the northern provinces and that Iran constitute an Irano-Soviet petroleum company. Molotov also told Qavam that Russia would evacuate certain regions of Iran, beginning in March. Complete evacuation would not occur, however, until order and security were established, and the Iranian government had ended its "hostile" and "discriminatory" attitude toward the

[24] Acheson, p. 196; Louis Halle, The Cold War as History (New York, 1967), pp. 104-105.

[25] Qavam was reported to have met three times with Stalin and four times with Molotov (New York Times, 4, 5, 18, and 20 February and 7 March 1946). It is worth mentioning that while Qavam was in Moscow, two consignments of about 5,000 Soviet weapons, including machine guns, arrived in Mahabad. Eagleton, pp. 74, 83.

[26] This account of portions of Qavam's negotiations with the Soviet Union is based on OIR Report No. 4619, O.S.S./State I&R Reports, vol. 7, II:5, pp. 12-16. Since the OIR Report concerns interpretations of the 1921 treaty, it is necessarily selective in its discussion of the negotiations.

Soviet government. For the first time, the Soviets formally declared their intention to disregard the Tripartite Treaty of 1942, and to use the 1921 treaty as a rationale for keeping troops in Iran.

Qavam, on 25 February, protested the Soviet interpretation of the 1921 treaty. Molotov replied at length the next day. He accused the Iranian government of discrimination because of its refusal to constitute an Irano-Soviet petroleum company. Withdrawing his previous suggestion, he now proposed that Iran grant the Soviet Union an outright concession similar to the one sought by Kavtaradze in 1944. Finally, after attacking Iran's governing class and its supposedly discriminatory policies toward the Soviet Union, Molotov asserted the Soviet Union's "obligation" to postpone the evacuation of forces from northern Iran.

Qavam, of course, rejected the Soviet accusations, pointing out that the retention of Soviet forces in Iran after 2 March 1946 would be an infraction of the 1942 treaty, and indirectly denying the applicability of the 1921 treaty. His efforts were to no avail.

By 2 March, the date set for withdrawal of all foreign troops from Iran, British and American troops had departed. The Russians were still there. The Soviet press on 2 March carried a dispatch to the effect that on 25 February, Prime Minister Qavam had been informed of the Soviet government's decision to withdraw a portion of the Soviet troops in northern Iran from the relatively peaceful districts. The terse message concluded with the statement that Soviet troops in other districts would remain in Iran "pending examination of the situation."[27] What the euphemism "pending examination of the situation" entailed was not elaborated, but Kennan was reliably informed that the Soviets had been putting "tremendous pressure" on Qavam, demanding Azerbaijan's autonomy, oil concessions, and the continued presence of Soviet troops in Azerbaijan.[28]

Stalin had indeed been very rough with him, Qavam told Kennan on 4 March. Later, in Teheran, he told Murray how at one point Stalin had said he did not care what the United States or Great Britain thought; he was not afraid of them. Before Qavam left Moscow, the Soviets proposed a communiqué whose phraseology he feared was intended to indicate that agreement had been reached and that negotiations were in progress—indications which could prevent recourse to the U.N. He had changed the wording of the communiqué, and asked to

[27] *New York Times*, 3 March 1946; *FR*, 1946, VII:335.
[28] *FR*, 1946, VII:337; *UNJ*, p. 426.

use the American embassy pouch to send an account of the negotiations to Ambassador Ala in the United States.[29]

In Iran, meanwhile, reaction to the Soviet announcement was immediate. On 3 March, the nationalist leader Mohammed Mossadegh rose in the Majlis. He said that he would protest Russia's violation of the 1942 treaty, and criticized Prince Muzaffar Firuz, Qavam's spokesman, for saying the day before that the maintenance of Russian troops in Iran was a "friendly gesture." All 96 deputies cheered.[30]

An Iranian protest was delivered in Moscow on the following day. So was a note from the British asking for clarification of Soviet intentions. Concern over Iran was growing steadily, as indicated by an editorial in the *New York Times* which compared Soviet action in Iran with previous Soviet moves in Manchuria. If the USSR cited the 1921 treaty (under which occupation was justified *if* a foreign power used Iran as a base for an attack on the Soviet Union) as justification for its remaining in Iran, the editorial asked, who was Russia's enemy? Did Stalin's 9 February speech give any clue?[31]

On 5 March, as news of Soviet espionage activities in Ottawa splashed across the front pages of newspapers throughout the United States,[32] Winston Churchill, speaking as a private person at Fulton, Missouri, delivered a speech whose words rang out to a troubled world. "From Stettin in the Baltic to Trieste in the Adriatic, an iron curtain has descended across the Continent," the former prime minister pro-

---

[29] FR, 1946, VII:337, 350-354.   [30] *New York Times*, 3-5 March 1946.

[31] FR, 1946, VII:377; *New York Times*, 4 and 5 March 1946; Rossow, "The Battle of Azerbaijan," p. 21. The British and Americans were not the only ones disturbed. On 4 March, Rossow notes, the Kurdish People's Republic proclaimed rights of sovereignty over the Kurdish populated areas of southeastern Turkey, creating some consternation in Ankara—where the Soviets continued to press the Turks for their demands of 1945. On 4 February 1946, for example, the Soviet ambassador in Turkey concluded a conversation on the subject with the remark: "We waited [a] long time regarding [the] arrangement we wanted with Poland and finally got it; we can wait regarding Turkey." When Ernest Bevin supported British policy at the Straits in an address to the House of Commons on 21 February 1946, the Soviet ambassador Vinogradov accused the Turks and British of lining up against the Soviet Union. Shortly after that, and in conjunction with the Iranian crisis, the Soviets continued their war of nerves on an even greater scale. FR, 1946, VII:813-819; Great Britain, *Parliamentary Debates* (Commons), vol. 419, cols. 1355-1539.

[32] For the effects of the Canadian spy trial on the perceptions of one State Department official, see: transcript, John D. Hickerson Oral History Interview, 10 November 1972, 26 January and 5 June 1973, pp. 12, 20-30, Harry S. Truman Library.

claimed. Behind this line, only Athens, "with its immortal glories," was free to decide its future. With regard to the Middle East, he noted that "Turkey and Persia are both profoundly alarmed and disturbed at the claims which are being made upon them and at the pressure being exerted by the Moscow Government." The Soviets did not desire war, Churchill asserted, but "the fruits of war and the indefinite expansion of their power and doctrines. . . . I am convinced that there is nothing they admire so much as strength, and there is nothing for which they have less respect than weakness." For that reason, he found the old doctrine of the balance of power unsound. The world could not afford to work on narrow margins, offering temptations to trials of strength. What was required was that the Western democracies stand together in strict adherence to the principles of the United Nations Charter. He ended his oration by endorsing an understanding with Russia under the general authority of the United Nations. He advocated maintaining that understanding by means of the United Nations, supported by Great Britain and the United States.[33]

Churchill's analysis of Soviet pressure in the Near East was in some ways similar to Kennan's. So was his understanding of Soviet admiration for strength and lack of respect for weakness.[34] The former prime minister's call for an alliance of the Western democracies approximated ideas circulating in NEA, and his general interpretation of the contemporary situation was in accord with that of the Truman administration. Although President Truman, who was present at the address, at first refused to comment on it, and Byrnes, responding to Congressional pressure, later asserted that the United States was not interested in an alliance with Britain, their private responses were different. President Truman had read an advance copy and had told Churchill that "it was admirable and would do nothing but good, though it would make a stir." Secretary Byrnes had been excited by it and suggested no alteration. Admiral Leahy was enthusiastic. Loy Henderson saw it as the first forthright speech on the subject, and over in the Eastern European Division, Elbridge Durbrow, his compatriot from Moscow days, was pleased. What Churchill said, and what he repeated in the days that followed, was in many ways descriptive of the international situation and of the drama taking place in the United Nations over Iran.[35]

[33] New York Times, 5 and 6 March 1946.

[34] For a recent exposition of this same thesis, see Hedrick Smith, The Russians (New York, 1976), esp. chap. X, pp. 241-272.

[35] Edward Francis-Williams, A Prime Minister Remembers, pp. 162-164; Yergin,

Only a week before, Byrnes had denied that the United States would divide the world into exclusive blocs and spheres of influence. Churchill on 5 March asserted that the old doctrine of the balance of power was unsound. But these assertions were for public consumption. That there was a de facto alliance between Britain and the United States against the Soviet Union had been an implicit assumption of the administration for some time—at least when it came to the countries of the Northern Tier. Underlying that assumption, as well as Byrnes's and Churchill's speeches, was a growing belief in the Soviets' admiration for strength and their lack of respect for weakness.

Were these interpretations justified? The record shows that in the Balkans heavy Soviet troops had begun moving southward by rail from Bessarabia to Dobrudja and thence into Bulgaria. Among these troops was considerable armor. Hospitals in Bucharest, Rumania, were instructed to be fully equipped by the end of the month, and all convalescents were to be evacuated by that date.[36] This information indicated an impending Soviet move against Turkey. At the same time, events in Iran seemed to confirm the accuracy of the Western leaders' interpretations.

On 5 March, Robert Rossow, the American vice consul in Tabriz, sent the secretary of state an urgent telegram in which he described Soviet troop movements in Azerbaijan. On the night of 3 March, he said, "50 Soviet trucks heavily laden with supplies, mainly ammunition, departed Tabriz toward Iran." On 4 March, 20 tanks and 100 trucks departed in the same direction, while 46 T-34 medium tanks arrived by rail at Tabriz. Night and day reinforcements arrived, and were deployed. On 6 March, Rossow reported, Marshal Ivan Bagramian, a Soviet authority on armor and the commanding general of the Soviet First Baltic Army during World War II, arrived in Tabriz.[37]

Tabriz for a long time had been the center of European trade with Persia. When Marco Polo passed through it in the thirteenth century on his way home from the land of Kublai Khan, it was believed to be the largest city in the world. But the opening of the Suez Canal diverted the

---

pp. 175, 445, n. 39; Leahy Papers, diary entries for 10 February and 3 March 1946; interviews with Loy Henderson and Elbridge Durbrow; Gaddis, *The United States and the Origins of the Cold War*, pp. 307-308; Gardner, *Architects of Illusion*, p. 104-105; *New York Times*, 6, 7, and 9 March 1946.

[36] FR, 1946, VII:818-819.

[37] Ibid., pp. 340 ff.; Rossow, "The Battle of Azerbaijan," p. 20. It is not clear that Bagramian did in fact arrive in Tabriz. See S.D. 861.24591/3-1446 and /3-2146.

flow of trade from Tabriz. While it still had nearly a quarter of a million inhabitants, it had not yet been touched by the twentieth century. The streets were made for donkey traffic, only one road was surfaced, and all but a few sumptuous buildings were built of dried mud. Russian cavalrymen galloped about in groups of four to eight, contributing to what the American vice consul saw as the city's special charm.[38]

Robert Rossow had only recently arrived in Tabriz. The performance of his predecessor, Samuel Ebling, had caused concern in Washington and at the American embassy in Teheran, and Rossow had been sent to replace him. Ebling had been at his post since 1943, when he replaced Bertel Kuniholm, who had reopened the consulate during the war and then had been recalled on Soviet demand.[39] According to Rossow, Kuniholm's keenly perceptive reporting had been so sharp and effective that he had been a thorn in the flesh of the Soviet command. His misfortune had been the fact that in 1942-43 Washington was little disposed to receive reports that might disrupt the wartime alliance. In 1945 the situation changed. With little experience in the political field, Ebling had been trying to get along with the Russians. As a consequence, his perspective had become warped and his analyses inadequate. Replacement had been required.[40]

Rossow, only 27 years old, had been a political officer in Panama earlier in the war, and then had spent a brief period in the army on assignment to the Office of Strategic Services. Earlier, he had attended Georgetown University, and before that had been a cadet in the Black Horse Troop at Culver Military Academy. Rossow's background served him well. To check accounts of troop movements, he followed their route of march, gathering reports from those who had seen the troops, and observing carefully the horses' tracks, droppings, and other signs. Forced to turn back at the first Soviet check point, he sent a contact to check with a civilian broker who supplied forage for the Soviet horses. The supply patterns confirmed his findings and made clear the significance of the movements.

Once Rossow was arrested by the Soviets for driving near the passenger terminal at Tabriz, detained for an hour, and told not to come that way again, but he was not deterred. Taking nightly reconnaissance

---

[38] Rossow MS.   [39] See Chapter III, n. 53.

[40] Interviews with Robert Rossow, 26 June 1975, and Edwin Wright, November 1974; Rossow MS; Edwin Wright, "A Personal Narrative—A Retrospective View." See also Chapter III, n. 53.

runs, he was able to sneak down ravines and clamber up hills from which he could see the Soviet tank park. He counted the medium and heavy tanks, the 122 mm cannons, the 76 mm howitzers, the 3-inch anti-aircraft guns, and the hundreds of trucks, and even photographed them. Using data from the office of the military attaché in Teheran, he was able to check unit and vehicle insignia to avoid double counting. Daily observation enabled him to determine the character and volume of the arrivals and movements of the previous night. All told, between 4 March and 28 March, a heavy Soviet armed force composed of at least 200 tanks was brought into northern Iran.[41] Meanwhile, Moscow Radio had begun a propaganda attack on the Turks. In the Balkans, heavy concentrations of Russian troops and armor were observed moving into Bulgaria.

Concomitant with the beginning of large-scale Soviet troop movements in northern Iran, activity in Teheran began to pick up. On 4 March, several thousand Tudeh members milled about the Majlis, preventing it from meeting. Its term of two years was to expire on 11 March; if no quorum could be achieved, the Majlis's two-year term would end, and Qavam would have the virtual power of a dictator until the Soviets left Iran. On 5 March, delegates trying to run the gauntlet

[41] The above account is based on the sources cited in n. 40, along with *FR*, 1946, VII:340 ff. and Rossow's published article, "The Battle of Azerbaijan." A 1946 document from the American embassy in Teheran updating a department summary of "Issues and Trends in Iran," puts the number of tanks at 200. A 21 March 1946 telegram from Rossow to the secretary of state, repeating a telegram to Washington from Captain Alexis Gagarine, assistant military attaché in Iran, notes that between 4 March and 19 March an absolute minimum of 235 tanks had been processed through Tabriz, along with 3,500 trucks. A 1946 Joint Intelligence Committee memo estimates the number of tanks at 200-300. Rossow, who personally sighted close to 200 tanks, believes that the embassy figure derives from rough summations of specific sightings. Since other British and American officials saw an additional 100 tanks, and since their movements were limited to the vicinity of Tabriz, Rossow figures that 500 is a conservative estimate. All told, Rossow had firm unit identifications of 15 armored brigades which in 1945 consisted of three battalions with 21 tanks each, and which *if* they were fully equipped would have consisted of 945 tanks. I have used the most conservative contemporaneous figure. S.D. Teheran Lot No. 54F55. Enclosure to Dispatch No. 222, 21 November 1946 from the American embassy, Teheran, to the secretary of state, commenting on a *Policy and Information Statement on Iran*, dated 15 July 1946, p. 14; S.D. 861.24591/3-2146; JIC Memo No. 217 (15 May 1946) and enclosure (27 April 1946), ABC 092 USSR (15 November 1944), American-British Command Decimal File, 1942-1948, U.S. Army, Operations Division (hereafter cited as P&O Div.), Records of the Army Staff, RG 319; Rossow, letter to the author; John Milsom, *Russian Tanks*, 1900-1970 (Harrisburg, Pa., 1971), p. 74.

of Tudeh backers, were knocked to their knees, punched, and pummeled. Each day for a week there was a repetition of this scene. On 11 March, shortly after Qavam returned from the Soviet Union, the Majlis ceased to exist.[42]

As events in Iran seemed to be confirming the prevailing interpretations of Soviet logic, George Kennan, on 6 March, delivered a protest to the Soviet government. The protest cited the Tripartite Treaty, and said that the Soviet decision to retain troops in Iran was one to which the United States would not remain indifferent. It expressed hope that the USSR would withdraw its troops from Iran, and acknowledged its appreciation of the Soviet Union's responsibilities under the Charter. It ended by requesting prompt notification of the USSR's decision.[43]

Meanwhile, as Rossow's telegrams continued to arrive in Washington, and the State Department waited in vain for an answer to its protest, Loy Henderson had Edwin Wright prepare a large map of Azerbaijan. Wright did so, placing large red arrows on the roads mentioned in Rossow's dispatches to indicate the direction of Soviet troop movements. Wright was uniquely suited to the task. In addition to the years he had spent in Iran, he had been on a six-week tour of Kurdistan in the spring of 1945 (from both the Iraqi and Iranian sides), after which he had prepared an eighty-page study of the Kurds for the War Department.[44] In the fall of 1945, he had prepared a similar study of Azerbaijan. His experience greatly facilitated his efforts, and at about 3:30 p.m. on 7 March the map was complete.[45]

[42] A quorum, three-quarters of the deputies, was necessary before a continuation of the Majlis's two year term could be put to a vote. It was achieved only once, with no results. Due to a law passed in October 1945, no new elections were to be held as long as foreign troops remained in Iran. This measure was taken for fear of Soviet packing of the parliament under the duress of her military occupation. After 11 March, it meant that until the Soviets left Iran, Qavam was to remain the Iranian premier. S.D. Post Files, 800—Political, 14 March letter from C. Vaughan Ferguson, Jr. to Robert Rossow; New York Times, 6-12 March; Herbert Vreeland, Iran (New Haven, 1957), pp. 56-81; Richard W. Van Wagenen, The Iranian Case, 1946 (New York, 1952), p. 20; Lenczowski, Russia and the West in Iran, p. 297.

[43] FR, 1946, VII:340-343.

[44] For a map of Kurdistan, see Map No. 6.

[45] This account is based on FR, 1946, VII:340-348; Wright, "A Personal Narrative—A Retrospective View," and Alger Hiss, letter to the author. In his memoirs, Truman mentions that he told Byrnes to send a blunt message to Stalin. Later, in a press conference on 24 April 1952, still later at Columbia University in 1959, and in interviews with Nashrollah Fatemi (no date given) and Herbert Druks (21 August 1962), Truman stated that he sent Stalin an "ultimatum." See also Truman's article in the New York Times, 25 August 1957. No record of such an

Henderson called Secretary Byrnes at 4:30 p.m. and said he hoped the secretary would give NEA time to brief him on the events of the day. Harold Minor and Wright took the map and accompanying cables to Byrnes's office. The secretary read the cables for half an hour, and then Wright explained the map. Wright and Minor showed him the size and direction of the Soviet thrusts, aimed at: (1) the Turkish border, (2) the Iraqi border, and (3) the south toward Teheran. Byrnes was convinced the Soviet Union was adding military invasion to subversion in Iran. Beating one fist into his other hand, he dismissed Minor and Wright with the comment: "Now we'll give it to them with both barrels."

By 8 March, as more information came in from Rossow, a committee under Acheson concluded unanimously that the Soviets were using

---

ultimatum exists; Loy Henderson, Edwin Wright, Alger Hiss, George Allen and others have denied that such a message ever was sent. George Kennan, the chargé d'affaires in Moscow in early 1946 and the person who would have delivered such an ultimatum, can recall nothing in the nature of an "ultimatum" given by President Truman to Stalin:

> It is my impression that Mr. Truman (whom in general I much admired) had an unfortunate tendency to exaggerate, in later years, certain aspects of the role that he played when in office in relations with the Soviet Union. His claim that he sent an "ultimatum" to Stalin seems to me to fall in nicely with this pattern.
>
> I strongly doubt, in short, that any communication that would properly answer to this description ever went forward. It was enough for Stalin to learn that a further effort by the Soviet Union to retain its forces in Persia would create serious international complications. He had enough problems, at the moment, without that.

In short, indications point to the message Kennan delivered on 9 March as being the one that Truman had in mind. See FR, 1946, VII:348-349; Harry S. Truman, 2:94-95; Druks, pp. 125-126; Feis, From Trust to Terror, p. 84; New York Times, 25 April 1946; Fatemi, pp. 304-307; Rosser, p. 238; interviews with Loy Henderson and Edwin Wright; Alger Hiss, letter to the author; George Allen Papers, Harry S. Truman Library, Correspondence File, 1945-1969, letter of 4 January 1969 to Alexander George; George Kennan, letter to the author; Ramazani, Iran's Foreign Policy, pp. 138-139; Richard Pfau, "Containment in Iran, 1946: The Shift to an Active Policy," Diplomatic History 1 (Fall 1977):360-361. The fact that Truman, erroneously, remembered that he had issued an ultimatum over the matter merely indicates the importance of the crisis in his thinking of how Russia should be treated. The crisis was also important in illustrating to NEA the desirability of having and using maps in presenting an argument. According to Iselin, NEA had the Office of Intelligence Research prepare two maps—one looking south from Moscow, and one looking north from Ankara. The maps, dated 20 March, were used to present NEA's points in policy debates and illustrated Turkey's pivotal role along the Northern Tier. Xydis, Greece and the Great Powers, pp. 172, 600.

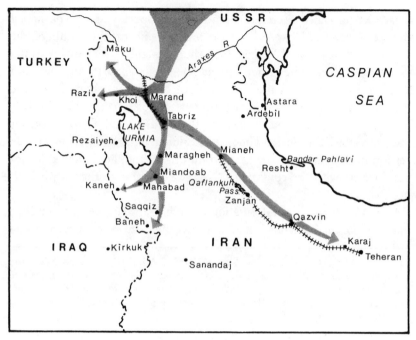

Map 9. Soviet Armored Thrusts into Northern Iran (1946)
Based in part on the *Middle East Journal* 10 (Winter 1956).

military invasion to effect a *fait accompli*. While Wright and Minor
argued that the United States should let the Soviet Union know it considered Soviet actions a clear violation of the 1942 treaty, Charles
Bohlen objected. The United States was not a signatory of that treaty;
the United States had never legalized its position in Iran, and, more important, the United States was in no position to confront the Soviet
Union in Iran. The American Army was largely demobilized. If it were
to be effective, the army would do better confronting the Soviet Union
in Europe. In Iran, Bohlen argued, the Soviet Union would consider
any strong action a bluff, and the United States might wind up in a
worse position than before. Acheson finally ended the meeting by
suggesting that the department let the Soviet Union know the United
States was aware of her move, but "leave a graceful way out" if she
wished to avoid a showdown. Alger Hiss scribbled a draft statement,
and a message was sent to Moscow, which Kennan delivered on 9
March. The note told the Soviet government of the reports that had
been received, expressed a desire to find out whether it was bringing

additional forces into Iran, and, if so, welcomed information regarding the purposes therefore.

Again, the Soviet government did not reply. Instead, the Soviet press on 11 March cited large portions of Churchill's speech of 5 March and excerpts from Truman's press conference on 8 March, in which the president disassociated himself from Churchill's opinions.[46] Stalin, in an interview in *Pravda* on 14 March, castigated Churchill as "a Hitler-like 'warmonger' seeking to set off an armed conflict with the Soviet Union." He spoke of Churchill's 5 March address as a dangerous act. Further, he said Churchill was a racist who called upon the English-speaking people in the same manner as Hitler called upon the Germans. Reaching further back in history to complete the analogy between Britain and Germany, he said Churchill regarded the Anglo-Soviet mutual assistance treaty as "a mere scrap of paper."[47]

Kennan, in a lengthy analysis of Stalin's statement, was inclined to view Soviet reaction to Churchill's speech as closely related to the situation in Iran, where he believed the Soviets' play had been called. Stalin had seized on, distorted, and exploited Churchill's speech, Kennan said, to prepare the Soviet public for coming events.[48]

What those coming events might be was anybody's guess—as for what already had taken place, headlines in the *New York Times* gave a fairly cogent summary of the situation:

March 13: HEAVY RUSSIAN COLUMNS MOVE INTO IRAN:
TURKEY OR IRAQ MAY BE GOAL: U.S. SENDS NOTE:
CONNALLY ASKS BIG 3 MEET AND TALK BLUNTLY

March 14: STALIN SAYS CHURCHILL STIRS WAR
AND FLOUTS ANGLO-RUSSIAN PACT:
SOVIET TANKS APPROACH TEHERAN[49]

In Iran, the tightrope-walking Qavam, when informed of the Soviet movements, said he was officially unaware of them. The Soviet chargé, meanwhile, had heard of Iran's planned complaint and on 14 March advised Qavam not to make it. It would be regarded as a hostile act and would have unfortunate results. On the same day, Murray gave

---

[46] In spite of the stance of the United States toward Soviet actions in Iran and Turkey, Truman wished to avoid the inference that his foreign policy was governed by Churchill's views; apparently, he also wished to divert Soviet reaction from the American government to Churchill. FR, 1946, VI:712-713; Feis, p. 78; *New York Times*, 9 March 1946.

[47] *New York Times*, 14 March 1946.   [48] FR, 1946, VI:716-717.

[49] *New York Times*, 13 and 14 March 1946.

Qavam advance assurance of American support for Iran at the U.N., something Iran had not had at the London meeting, in an attempt to steady Qavam's wavering stance.[50]

As tension increased, speculation became intense. In Iran, rumors of a putsch were rife. In the United States, reporters questioned Truman on Stalin's interview in *Pravda*. Truman said he could not read Russian, did not know if it was the right translation, and so had no comment. When asked about reports that the Russians were moving heavy troops into Iran, the president played down the whole affair. He knew about that, he said, only from what he saw in the papers, and he denied that the situation was fraught with danger. Four hours earlier, however, while trying to persuade W. Averell Harriman to accept appointment as ambassador to Great Britain, the president told Harriman that a dan-

[50] Ibid., 14 March 1946; FR, 1946, VII:355-360. All information utilized by the United States government was initially based on reports from Rossow. Rossow had contacted Pishevari on 29 December. In January, Pishevari's minister of labor, education and propaganda, Mohammed Beriya, had used the media to make the visit appear as American approval of the Azerbaijan regime. It was an attempt to effect Rossow's ouster in a manner more subtle than that used on Kuniholm in 1943 (see Chapter III, n. 53). Rossow was not replaced when Murray insisted that he be kept on, the Department deferring to Murray's judgment. Still further doubts about Rossow were created on 13 March, when the British Foreign Office declared that London had no reports of the troop movements he had described. Within a week, doubts were removed; British information coincided with that of the United States, but its communication channels were slower. Rossow's British counterpart, John Wall, an economy-minded Yorkshireman with few funds at his disposal, had sent only a brief cable. He had held the rest of his reports until the King's Messenger could carry the pouch to Teheran, where further delay caused a lag of nearly ten days. Naturally Qavam's public denial "for diplomatic reasons" confused the issue; so did a report in the *Chicago Sun*, which the Soviet press picked up and used as the basis for an attack on Rossow under the headline, "Imagination Run Wild." FR, 1946, VII:302-303, 359-360; Rossow MS; Rossow, "The Battle of Azerbaijan," pp. 22-23. John Gaddis, *The United States and the Origins of the Cold War*, p. 311, cites an article by James Reston in the *New York Times*, and notes Reston's observation that the seriousness of these troop movements had almost certainly been exaggerated. Presumably, Reston was basing his opinion on earlier reports from the British Foreign Office. Thomas Paterson, *Soviet-American Confrontation: Postwar Reconstruction and the Origins of the Cold War* (Baltimore, 1973), p. 179, makes the same mistake in describing Rossow's "over-excited cables." Gabriel Kolko, *The Limits of Power: The World and United States Foreign Policy, 1943-1945* (New York, 1968), p. 239, simply refers to "rumors of a massive troop build-up." The troop build-up was no rumor, and there was good reason to be excited—particularly in Iran, where, as John Jernegan wrote Rossow, one had gotten so blasé that anything less than U.S. Urgent cables received only a passing glance. S.D. Teheran Post Files, 800—Political, 18 March 1946 letter from John Jernegan to Robert Rossow.

gerous situation was developing in Iran, a situation that might lead to war, and he needed a man in London who knew the British, a man whom he could trust. In the *New York Times*, as headlines continued to keep the Iranian crisis before the public, an editorial focused on the question "What does Russia want?" It examined her argument concerning security, and listed the areas she had annexed during the recent war: Lithuania; Latvia; Estonia; Eastern Poland; Bessarabia; Bukovina; Moldavia; Carpatho-Ukraine; Karelo-Finland; Petsamo, Finland; Tannu Tuva, Central Asia; Southern Sakhalin; the Kurile Islands; naval bases in Porkkala Peninsula, Finland; Port Arthur, China; and the Manchurian trunk railway lines—a total of 273,947 square miles and 24,355,000 people. "Where does the search for security end," the editorial asked, "and where does expansion begin?" It was a rhetorical question, and the answer seemed increasingly obvious.[51]

The Red Army on 15 March moved deeper into Iran. Amid a barrage of Russian radio propaganda and a denial in *Tass* of Soviet movements —the Soviet Union never made an official reply to the U.S. note— Churchill called for a full discussion of the Iranian case in the U.N. Qavam's intention to appeal Iran's case before the U.N. was made official and received wide publicity the next day. So did a speech by Secretary Byrnes on 16 March, in which he refuted Soviet denials of troop movements, urged extension of the Selective Service Act, and pledged that U.S. strength would be used to support the principles of the U.N. Charter should the occasion arise.[52] In Iran, the impending arrival of a Soviet ambassador was expected to confuse the issue, making it possible for Russia to prevent the Security Council from acting, by asserting that bilateral negotiations were taking place.[53]

In the Soviet Union, *Izvestia* said Iran had violated the 1921 treaty, and began printing a series of stories of Iranian plots against the USSR. From Moscow, George Kennan wired his belief that the Soviets, by intimidation, would force the Iranians to bring into power a regime which would accede to their major demands. They were waiting, he

[51] FR, 1946, VII:353, 358; Jones, p. 53; Lenczowski, *Russia and the West in Iran*, p. 298; *Public Papers of the Presidents of the United States, Harry S. Truman, 1946* (Washington, 1962), "The President's News Conference of March 14, 1946," pp. 155-159; Harriman and Abel, p. 550; W. Averell Harriman, letter to the author; Truman Papers, PSF, Appointments Files, Daily Sheets, March 1946; Feis, *From Trust to Terror*, pp. 82-83; *New York Times*, 14 March 1946.

[52] *New York Times*, 15-17 March, 1946; Meister, pp. 260-263.

[53] FR, 1946, VII:361.

felt, for a better justification than the present excuse of security requirements.[54]

The United Nations: Act 2

On 18 March Ambassador Ala brought the dispute between the Soviet Union and Iran to the attention of the United Nations and asked that Iran's appeal for a solution be placed on the agenda for 25 March. The dispute, Ala asserted, resulted from developments which had occurred since 30 January. The Soviet Union had not withdrawn from Iran on 2 March, contrary to the Tripartite Treaty, and, furthermore, continued to interfere in Iran's internal affairs.[55]

Andrei Gromyko, the Soviet representative at the United Nations, on 19 March requested postponement of the date for hearing the Iranian question from 25 March to 10 April. Negotiations were in progress, he said; the complaint was unexpected, and the Soviet Union was unprepared to take part in the discussion.[56]

The United States representative, Edward R. Stettinius, Jr., was unconvinced. He informed the secretary-general of his intention to place Iran's appeal at the head of the agenda, and to request that Iran and the Soviet Union report on their negotiations. Ambassador Ala also requested an immediate hearing of the Iranian question. Negotiations, he said categorically, had failed. The obligation of the Soviet government to withdraw from Iran was not a proper subject for negotiation, and delays had only intensified his country's critical condition.[57]

On the next day, Byrnes informed Bevin of his critical concern. The secretary of state himself intended to attend the council meeting and to insist on final disposition of the question. With Gromyko in Washington seeking support for postponement, President Truman, in a statement to the press, reiterated America's resolve to insist on immediate consideration of the Iranian case.[58]

In Iran, Ivan Sadchikov, the newly appointed Russian ambassador, was putting enormous pressure on Qavam to come to an agreement. Qavam, who had arrested the pro-British statesman Sayid Zia ed-Din Tabatabai as a gesture of appeasement to the Tudeh Party, believed an understanding overdue.[59] Wallace Murray neither encouraged nor dis-

[54] Ibid., pp. 362-364; New York Times, 17-23 March 1946.
[55] FR, 1946, VII:365.   [56] UNJ, p. 353.   [57] Ibid., pp. 353-354.
[58] FR, 1946, VII:369, 372; New York Times, 22-23 March 1946; Campbell and Herring, The Diaries of Edward R. Stettinius, Jr., pp. 457-458.
[59] FR, 1946, VII:369-371; New York Times, 21 March 1946.

couraged the prime minister's line of reasoning. The American ambassador repeated that evacuation should be unconditional, and pointed out that experience with the Soviets in regard to treaties gave little reason to depend on less formal understandings, but he did not know whether the U.S. or the U.N. could save Iran from the consequences Qavam feared if Iran did not negotiate. He realized that Iran, having a long frontier with the Soviet Union, had to get along with its neighbor; besides, it could not appeal to the U.N. for protection all the time.[60]

As the Soviet ambassador and then the American ambassador conferred with Qavam, the prime minister's determination to press his case wavered, first in one direction and then another. Thus, in a press conference on 23 March, Qavam said he felt sure the Soviets were leaving Iran, that Ala had acted without authority in saying negotiations had failed, and that according to his information no additional troops had come into Iran after 2 March. On 24 March Qavam denied ever having made such statements, blamed the remarks on his interpreter, Muzaffar Firuz,[61] and at Wallace Murray's urging called another press conference to correct the impression made by the previous one. The Firuz-Qavam stance was similar to that held by medieval Japanese families which split their loyalty in times of crisis so as to preserve, through one of the factions, the family possessions. It made sense, but it complicated the workings of the Security Council.[62]

Council proceedings were further complicated by Stalin. On 22 March, in a statement that was hailed by Truman, he replied to questions put to him by the Associated Press, saying he attached great importance to the U.N. and that no nation wanted war. On 24 March, after Moscow Radio announced a troop withdrawal from Iran in accordance with what it said was an Irano-Soviet agreement,[63] Stalin made another statement. Asked by the president of the United Press to com-

---

[60] FR, 1946, VII:369-375.

[61] Firuz, who was a member of the Qajar family overthrown in the early 1920s by Reza Shah, was secretary to the Iranian legation in Washington later in the decade. During his tour in the United States he obtained a phony law degree, set up a racket to hand out phony certificates, and finally left in 1930, owing $3,000 in debts. S.D. 891.00/4-846.

[62] FR, 1946, VII:377-378; New York Times, 24 and 27 March and 13 April 1946; see also the statements by Ala and Qavam in the 27 and 28 March issues.

[63] The announcement, printed in Tass on 25 March, stated that withdrawal had begun on 24 March, and should be completed in five or six weeks "if nothing unforeseen should take place." FR, 1946, VII:379; New York Times, 26 March 1946.

327

ment on Churchill's statement that speedy action by the U.N. on Iran was essential, and that delay would be dangerous, Stalin said it was "unconvincing"; withdrawal of Soviet troops from Iran had been decided on 24 March "in a positive way by an understanding" between Iran and the USSR.[64]

The broad outlines of that "understanding" require explanation. Ambassador Sadchikov had called Qavam at 7:00 p.m. on 24 March, and delivered three notes: the first said that the Soviet government would evacuate all Iranian territory within five or six weeks; the second proposed formation of an Irano-Soviet company to develop Iranian oil (51% Russian, 49% Iranian); the third offered to intercede in a settlement of the Azerbaijan situation.[65]

Later that evening, Sadchikov called again to say that the Soviet government was pleased to hear of the arrest of Zia ed-Din Tabatabai, and to announce the withdrawal of troops from Karaj and Qazvin. At that time, the qualifying phrase "if nothing further happened" (otherwise translated as "if no unforeseen circumstances occurred"), was added orally to the first of the three memoranda delivered earlier in the evening. Three days later, Sadchikov told Qavam that agreement on the second and third memoranda (those concerning oil concessions, and an autonomous government for Azerbaijan) would mean that no "unforeseen circumstances" would take place.[66]

In short, the "understanding" mentioned by Stalin was unilateral. Qavam, who privately denied any understanding, meanwhile wired Ala of negotiations in progress, instructing him to say nothing if asked whether or not an agreement had been reached.[67]

Soviet objectives in this period may have been to take control of the Iranian government through support of a Tudeh coup d'état. When Iran complained again to the U.N., the Soviets apparently decided to effect an agreement favorable to their long-range interests before the Security Council could meet. When such an agreement proved slow in the making, Stalin's unilateral announcement was a ploy (whose reality Ambassador Sadchikov had to make good) to keep the matter from coming before the Security Council. Meanwhile, the threat posed by Soviet military forces just outside Teheran forced Qavam to consider the Soviets' terms for an agreement, while the U.N., because it provided

[64] *New York Times*, 27-28 March 1946.
[65] *FR*, 1946, VII:379-380.　　　　[66] Ibid., pp. 380, 402; *UNJ*, p. 452.
[67] *FR*, 1946, VII:385-387, 394, 399.

a forum for discussion, tempered the Soviets' use of force and gave Qavam a bit of leverage against their demands.

When the question of putting the Iranian question on the agenda came up at the Security Council's first meeting in the United States on 25 March, Gromyko cited an "understanding" reached two days before as a basis for stating that negotiations had taken place with positive results; he further argued that placing the item on the agenda contradicted both the facts and the spirit of the 30 January resolution. Byrnes, representing the United States, disagreed; there had been no joint statement of such an agreement, and Iran had not withdrawn its letter. The debate became rancorous, Gromyko refusing categorically to agree that the Soviet statement of 24 March was open to doubt, and accusing Byrnes of being more Iranian than the Iranians.[68]

Having failed to keep the question off the council's agenda, Gromyko then sought to postpone the date of its discussion until 10 April—time enough for Sadchikov to pressure Qavam into an agreement (supposedly already reached). If discussions were not postponed, Gromyko said, the Soviet government would not take part.[69]

On the following day, Gromyko cited a statement by Stalin that a "positive solution" had been reached on the withdrawal of Soviet troops. He also cited a statement by Qavam on 23 March which said, conveniently, postponement was "of negligible importance" to him.[70]

Byrnes countered by stating that his information came not from the press, but from the highest official of the Iranian government to the

[68] *UNJ*, pp. 366-378. Stettinius's diary also records Byrnes's ire over the Iranian crisis, a matter which clearly catalyzed his attitude toward the Soviet Union. On 23 January, he had been convinced that the Iranian problem would not come up and that the Russians would make an arrangement with the Iranians. By 25 March, Soviet methods had sufficiently infuriated Byrnes so that he told Stettinius he had "nursed" the Russians for the last time. Campbell and Herring, *The Diaries of Edward R. Stettinius, Jr.*, pp. 448-449, 461. In his unpublished memoirs, George Allen, too, notes Byrnes's determination to support Iran even if it meant an irreparable break with the Soviet Union ("Mission to Iran," Chapter I); Loy Henderson tells an anecdote, repeated in somewhat different form by Yergin, p. 186, and corroborated by Harold Minor, that supports Allen's account of Byrnes's determination. Interview with Loy Henderson; Minor, letter to the author. The incident they all refer to occurred between 20-24 March 1946.

[69] Gromyko's long statement also included reference to one of Qavam's press conferences. *UNJ*, pp. 385-386, 399-400.

[70] *UNJ*, pp. 407-411. In Iran, meanwhile, in contradiction to a statement by Firuz which *disavowed* that *no* agreement had been reached, Qavam stated that an agreement had *not* been reached. *New York Times*, 27-28 March 1946.

U.S. representative. His information had it that proposals had been made, but not agreed to. Further, he said Gromyko had distorted the sense of Qavam's statement to the press regarding postponement, and cited the statement in full.[71]

Gromyko, in return, berated Byrnes, and reiterated his position. He categorically denied that there had been Russian troop movements in Iran after 2 March. Further, he stated that Ala was acting without instructions in bringing the Iranian case before the U.N.[72] When the council voted down his proposal to postpone the matter, he picked up and left.[73] As members of the council vapidly waited for translations of more repetitive arguments, they watched the grim, stony-faced Gromyko, walking slowly from the room. "In his exit," James Reston noted several days later in the *New York Times*, "Mr. Gromyko stirred the cold winds that swept through the minds of men in the terrible days of doubt and misunderstanding before the war."[74]

After Gromyko's departure the council calmly adopted a procedural vote to hear the Iranian representative, and Ala was given the chance to refute Gromyko's remarks. Adopting Gromyko's tactics, he cited a statement in the morning press in which Qavam denied any agreement between the two governments. Contrary to Qavam's desires, he revealed what had taken place between Qavam and the Soviets in Moscow. The entire matter, he stated, was unjust; demands were being made which

[71] *UNJ*, pp. 411-413.

[72] Trygve Lie, secretary-general of the United Nations during this period, recorded in his memoirs the Council's concern over Ala's representation of his government's point of view. Trygve Lie, *In the Cause of Peace* (New York, 1954), pp. 77-78.

[73] Besides all the damage to the Council's prestige, one significant legal fact of the Soviet walkout, at least insofar as Byrnes *then* interpreted it, was that the Council could not make a substantive decision. Such a decision was not possible, he said, if any one of the permanent members was absent, unless that member had been declared party to a dispute; and the Soviet Union was not officially a party to the dispute. *FR*, 1946, VII:390.

[74] *UNJ*, pp. 415-420; Rossow, "The Battle of Azerbaijan," p. 23; *New York Times*, 28 and 31 March 1946. On 28 March Rossow reported from Tabriz that at the moment he heard Gromyko's voice on the radio denying that Soviet troop movements had occurred in Iran since 2 March, Soviet half-tracks could be seen from the consulate roof, coming from the railroad station to the barracks. S.D. 861.24591/3-2846. Trygve Lie records how, as Gromyko stalked out of the U.N., he paused to confer with Frank Begley, chief of security. Gromyko engaged in brief conversation with him, smiled, then resumed his stern expression and continued on. Reporters never found out why he smiled. The reason, Lie tells us, is that Gromyko was unzipped (Lie, pp. 77-78). If nothing else, this fact may testify to Gromyko's preoccupation with the Iranian question over lesser, mundane matters.

impinged on Iran's sovereignty and threatened world peace. Russia requested delay because it had the most to gain. Iran resisted because it had the most to lose.[75]

On 29 March, after further questioning of Ala by the council, Byrnes proposed that Russia and Iran report to the council by 2 April (later changed to 3 April) on the status of their negotiations, and particularly on whether troop withdrawal was conditional on conclusion of other agreements. The purpose of this questioning, Byrnes had indicated in a confidential meeting of the delegates, was to get Soviet assurance "that withdrawal was not predicated upon Iranian concessions, and that 'unforeseen circumstances' did not refer to further agreements or concessions." Byrnes's proposal was accepted.[76]

On 3 April, as negotiations continued in Iran, members of the Security Council gathered to hear the Russian and Iranian reports. The United States had begun to receive reports of Russian troop movements back toward the Soviet frontier. Were the Russians at last withdrawing? No one could be sure of the answer to this question as the secretary-general read to the council letters from Ambassadors Gromyko and Ala. Gromyko, in his letter, stated that an understanding had been reached on 24 March, and that the withdrawal of troops was not connected with other questions. Ala, who had been firmly endorsed by Qavam on 1 April,[77] had a different story. Negotiations had taken place, but no positive results had been achieved. Not only had the Soviets continued to interfere in Iranian affairs, but Ambassador Sadchikov had told Qavam on 27 March that agreement on oil concessions and an autonomous government for Azerbaijan would mean that no "unforeseen circumstances" would take place—in other words, the withdrawal of troops *was* conditional on conclusion of other agreements.[78]

With one statement directly opposed to the other, Byrnes discussed neither; instead, he asked Ala what the council should do. The Iranian

[75] UNJ, pp. 423-430; for the effect of absence of a permanent member of the Council on voting procedure, see Tae Jin Kahng, Law, Politics, and the Security Council (The Hague, 1964), pp. 132-135.

[76] FR, 1946, VII:391-394, 396-398; UNJ, pp. 433-444; New York Times, 31 March 1946.

[77] On 30 March, Qavam told a reporter from the UP that Ala enjoyed his full confidence, and on 1 April sent an official endorsement of Ala to the secretary-general of the United Nations. New York Times, 31 March 1946; UNJ, p. 450.

[78] FR, 1946, VII:399-400; New York Times, 2 April 1946; UNJ, pp. 450-455. On 4 April, Qavam denied ever giving this information to Ala (though he did not deny its authenticity). He also told Murray that Ala had gone beyond his instructions. FR, 1946, VII:405-407.

331

ambassador had a solution: *if* evacuation were in fact unconditional (if the "unforeseen circumstances" were withdrawn), and *if* the Soviet Union gave to the council an assurance that evacuation would be effected by 6 May, Iran would not press the case further, *provided* the matter remained on the agenda.[79]

On 4 April, Byrnes accepted Ala's solution. Taking note of the Soviet Union's assurances of withdrawal, and of the fact that withdrawal was not connected with negotiations between Iran and the USSR (!), Byrnes recommended that proceedings be deferred until 6 May, when the two countries could report on withdrawal (and the problem could be reexamined). He stressed that developments threatening to impede withdrawal could be brought to the immediate attention of the council. His proposal was adopted, and Byrnes, his work seemingly accomplished, returned to Washington.[80]

In Iran on 4 April, Qavam sent for Ambassador Sadchikov and proposed announcement of a joint communiqué. The Soviet ambassador was agreeable, but Moscow's approval was required.[81]

In Moscow on 4 April, General Walter Bedell Smith,[82] the newly appointed American ambassador, had a long, late-night interview with Stalin. The general had gone over his presentation carefully with Truman, who told him to tell Stalin that he had always considered the generalissimo a man of his word, but that Russian troops in Iran had upset that conviction.[83] Smith bluntly told Stalin that when he left the

[79] *UNJ*, pp. 453-454.

[80] *UNJ*, pp. 458-468; *New York Times*, 5 April 1946. For legal problems involved with resolutions, see Richard Van Wagenen, *The Iranian Case, 1946* (New York, 1952), pp. 63-64; for discussion of whether this resolution (4 April) and the resolution of 8 May were procedural or nonprocedural, see Kahng, pp. 145-146; for consideration of the functional competence of the council, see Kahng, pp. 72-74.

[81] *FR*, 1946, VII:405-407.

[82] Smith replaced Harriman, whose position had been temporarily filled by the chargé d'affaires George Kennan. Information concerning the interview that follows is based on a cable Smith sent to the Department of State—*FR*, 1946, VI:732-736 —and on Smith's memoirs. See Walter Bedell Smith, *My Three Years in Moscow* (New York, 1950), pp. 50-54. Yergin, pp. 163-164, overstates Smith's attitude toward the Russians at this time.

[83] Secretary Byrnes and the State Department's Soviet experts had also told Smith their views. The new ambassador was more optimistic than they, and dubious about some of the views expressed by Churchill. Experience would bring him closer to the points of view of both the State Department and the British prime minister. Walter Bedell Smith, pp. 28-31, 47; Truman Papers, PSF, President's Appointments File, Daily Sheets, January-May 1946, 23 March 1946; interview with Elbridge Durbrow. Interestingly enough, shortly after he had delivered his

United States, the most important question in everyone's mind was, "What does the Soviet Union want, and how far is Russia going to go?" Americans appreciated and understood Russia's desire for security, but Soviet *methods* were causing apprehension. Events in the Near East and in early sessions of the Security Council had created doubts in American minds that the Soviets really intended to support the U.N. These apprehensions, Smith observed, had been somewhat abated by Stalin's statements to the Associated Press, but more was needed. As the dictator listened he doodled in red pencil, drawing what appeared to be lopsided hearts with small question marks in the middle of each. Smith conveyed to him Truman's and Byrnes's belief that he (Stalin) meant to keep his commitments, but the ambassador made clear that holding this belief should not be interpreted as an indication of weakness.

Stalin replied at length and in detail, discussing the long history of the Iranian question. He stated frankly that Qavam's predecessor had been "unfriendly" and that pressures had been exerted to remove him. He was bitter about obstacles to obtain oil concessions, and about American opposition in the U.N. Agreement had been reached, he said, and the commitment would be met. He deplored the American press treatment of Russian objectives in the Balkans, and expressed great resentment over Churchill's speech.

Smith asserted that the United States had no idea of denying the Soviets equal exploitation rights in Iran, but he told Stalin that the Soviet means of obtaining concessions were deplorable. Stalin said that he had not noticed America's support for Russia's just requests, but Smith demurred, and obtained Stalin's admission that the United States had never been in a position to give the Soviet Union moral support. Moving on to Soviet security aspirations, Smith examined what Russia meant by a "friendly government." It seemed to the Americans that the Soviets perceived of such a government as one under Moscow's complete control. This control, Smith implied, was unnecessary. Challenging Smith's assertion that the United States could not take seriously the idea that any combination of powers constituted a threat to the Soviet Union, particularly in the direction of the Baku oil fields, Stalin cited Churchill's activities in 1919, and said he was up to the same old tricks. In response to Smith's question of whether he really believed that the

---

speech at Fulton, Churchill told Smith: "Mark my words—in a year or two years, many of the very people who are now denouncing me will say, 'How right Churchill was.' "

United States and Great Britain were united in an alliance to thwart Russia, Stalin said he believed they were.[84] Smith vigorously denied that this was the case. He held no brief for the Fulton speech, but it did reflect an apprehension common to both the United States and Britain. While the United States had many ties with Britain, their primary concern was world security and justice. Reverting to his initial line of thought, Smith asked again what Stalin's answer was to the question "How far is Russia going to go?"

Looking directly at him, Stalin replied: "We're not going to go much further." "You say 'not much further,'" Smith observed, "but does that 'much' have any reference to Turkey?" Stalin's answer was carefully worded. He admitted that he had assured President Truman the Soviet Union had no intention of attacking Turkey. But Turkey was weak— not strong enough to protect the Straits. The Turkish government was "unfriendly." That was why the Soviet Union had demanded a base on the Dardanelles. When Smith replied that this was a matter that should be handled by the United Nations, Stalin said the Security Council of the United Nations might be able to undertake the responsibility. At the end of the two-hour interview, Stalin affirmed his desire for peace and his adherence to the principles of the United Nations, but expressed hope that in the future differences could be settled outside the U.N. The meeting ended cordially, with Stalin declining an invitation by Truman to come to the United States. His health was a problem, he told Smith, and a man must conserve his strength.

Perhaps this conversation led Moscow that night to approve the communiqué agreed to by Qavam and Sadchikov, and signed by the red-eyed diplomats at 4:00 a.m. on 5 April (though dated 4 April). The communiqué provided for evacuation of the Red Army within six weeks after 24 March, and formation of a joint Irano-Soviet company to exploit oil—provided it was ratified by the Majlis within seven months after 24 March (when, according to Stalin, an understanding had been reached). Azerbaijan, it was agreed, was purely an internal Iranian prob-

---

84 Two weeks earlier, Kennan had written the secretary of state: "If we are to get any long-term clarity of thought and policy on Russian matters we must recognize this very simple and basic fact: official Soviet thesis that outside world is hostile and menacing to Soviet peoples is not a conclusion at which Soviet leaders have reluctantly arrived after honest and objective appraisal of facts available to them but an *a priori* tactical position deliberately taken for impelling selfish reasons of a domestic political nature." *FR*, 1946, VI:721.

lem, and would be settled directly by the Iranian government with the inhabitants of the province.[85]

With an agreement reached, and the United Nations waiting to see if the Soviets would keep their word, the crisis seemed over. The *New York Times* hailed the result as a triumph for the United Nations and a victory for public opinion.[86] Iranians were not so sure. The Soviets would probably get their oil concessions; they would continue to exercise a great deal of influence in the north; and Pishevari controlled Azerbaijan, where Soviet pressure could always be used to support him. Iranians feared that the U.N. had not really saved Iran, but instead had sanctioned its demise—an interpretation which raised the question of what the United Nations represented in practical terms.

One answer to such doubts was suggested by the arrival of the battleship *Missouri* in Istanbul on 6 April.[87] Although the *Missouri's* visit was not entirely a result of American desires to give the Soviets a warning,[88] it was very definitely intended to symbolize American support for Greece and Turkey.[89]

[85] FR, 1946, VII:405-406, 413-415; *New York Times*, 6-7 April, 1946; S.D. Post and Lot Files, 8 April 1946, tel. 1087 from Moscow to Washington. While George Allen could later admit to the Soviet ambassador in Iran that on paper the Soviet oil agreement was much more generous to Iran than existing British concessions, the fact remains that the Iranians were concerned the Soviets would use any oil concession as an instrument of penetration to extend Soviet domination of Iran. Shortly before leaving Iran, Wallace Murray discussed these and other related issues in a cable to State, pointing out that Iran received little benefit from the joint Irano-Soviet Fisheries Company which exploited the caviar fisheries of the Caspian, even though participation in that company was on a 50-50 basis. Payments in rubles would tie the Iranian economy to the Soviet Union, control of the sole outlet would allow the Soviets to fix prices, while control of the company would allow them to manipulate the accounts in such a way that the Iranians would receive little or no profit. Teheran Post Files, Confidential Correspondence 1946, 701-711.9, 710, 21 May 1946; S.D. 891.6363/4-1546. As to what profit the Iranians received for their oil, Elwell-Sutton, *Persian Oil*, p. 83, notes that in 1947, 18,328,692 tons of Iranian oil were sold or exported. AIOC made a profit of £40,561,817 from this oil (before taxes), £7,101,251 of which it paid to the Iranian government.

[86] *New York Times*, 5 April 1946.

[87] Ibid., 7 April 1946. The *Missouri* was the battleship on which the Japanese surrender took place and which played a role (without credit) in the Soviet film shown to Byrnes and Bevin in Moscow in December 1945.

[88] David Alvarez, "The Missouri Visit to Turkey: An Alternative Perspective to Cold War Diplomacy," *Balkan Studies* 15 (2 November 1974):225-236. While useful, this article overstates the methodological implications of its analysis. See Chapter IV, n. 92.

[89] The immediate explanation for the *Missouri's* visit was that Mehmet Ertegün,

Less than two months earlier, on 10 February, a Joint Strategic Survey Report had recommended that the United States avoid military commitment to American interests in the Near East other than through the United Nations because of geographic distances and the impracticability of assured lines of communication. On 21 February, the Joint Chiefs of Staff had approved the memorandum. A week later, however, Secretary of the Navy Forrestal suggested to Secretary of State Byrnes that the United States send a task force to the Mediterranean. The idea was an elaboration of Forrestal's previous conceptions of sea power and global strategy and suited Byrnes's frame of mind, for the secretary was scheduled to speak at the Overseas Press Club that night. Seeing the opportunity to expand on the firm line he intended to take, Byrnes suggested that the task force accompany the *Missouri*. Both men thought the proposal would give encouragement to Greece and Turkey.[90] Because of rapid demobilization and the demand for naval forces in the Far East—and perhaps a change of mind on Byrnes's part as the Iranian crisis developed—the battleship departed without the accompanying task force. But its symbolic character was undiminished.[91]

Ambassador Edwin Wilson wrote Byrnes that the overwhelming re-

---

the Turkish ambassador to the United States and dean of the diplomatic corps, had died in November 1944. At that time the Turkish embassy had suggested the possibility that, as in the past for chiefs of mission who had died in service, arrangements would be made to send the body back to the envoy's country on a battleship. On 25 January 1946, Dean Acheson had suggested that the ambassador's remains be returned aboard a cruiser as a courtesy in keeping with diplomatic practice, and Truman had agreed. Because of a shortage of cruisers in the Atlantic, the *Missouri* was eventually designated to return the body. *New York Times*, 12 November 1944, 7 March 1946; Alvarez, pp. 232-234.

[90] Xydis, *Greece and the Great Powers*, pp. 158-159, 597; United States Army, Operations Division, Modern Military Records Branch, National Archives, Washington, D.C., CCS 092 United States 12-21-45, 10 February 1946 Report by Joint Strategic Survey Committee; Millis, p. 141; Byrnes, *All in One Lifetime*, p. 351; Rogow, p. 179; Robert Albion and Robert Connery, *Forrestal and the Navy* (New York, 1962), pp. 186-187; Alvarez, pp. 234-235.

[91] The State Department announced the voyage on 6 March (as the Iranian crisis was coming to a boil); the *Missouri* sailed on 22 March, and arrived in Istanbul on 5 April. Albion and Connery, pp. 186-187; Xydis, *Greece and the Great Powers*, p. 169. Churchill, informed by Forrestal on 10 March that the task force would not accompany the *Missouri*, was much disappointed. According to Forrestal, Churchill said that "a gesture of power not fully implemented was almost less effective than no gesture at all. He said that to make the gesture effective the entire task force should sail into the Sea of Marmara." Millis, pp. 144-146. See also *New York Times*, 7, 22 and 23 March and 6-7 April 1946.

ception given the *Missouri* in Istanbul could be explained by Turkish hopes that the United States had established an independent policy in the Near and Middle East based on defense of its own interests. Two months later, when Forrestal suggested to Byrnes that the United States send casual cruisers unannounced into the Mediterranean to establish the custom of flying the American flag in those waters, the secretary of state agreed. He had been pleased with reaction to the *Missouri* visit.[92]

If the visit of the *Missouri* to Istanbul did not answer the question of what the United Nations represented in practical terms to the countries of the Northern Tier, that connection was made on 6 April in an Army Day address by President Truman before 70,000 people at Soldiers Field in Chicago. In what was taken as a reply to Churchill's earlier speech at Fulton, Truman called for a unified military service and extension of the Selective Service Act. He was careful not to threaten military action against any nation. Rather, he stated that "the immediate goal of our foreign policy is to support the United Nations to the utmost."[93]

Turning to the grave problems of the Near and Middle East, he noted the area's vast natural resources, and the fact that it lay across important lines of communication. Since the nations of the Near East were not strong enough individually or collectively to withstand powerful aggression, he promised that the United States would do its part to preserve and strengthen peace by helping the people of the area develop their resources, widen their educational opportunities, and raise their standard of living. Pledging that United States military might was behind the U.N., he declared that the United States was dedicated to peace, and expected other powers to pursue the same objectives.[94] In short, the balance of power game as it used to be understood may have been outmoded, but the balance of power between the Soviet Union and the Western Allies (whose forces could acquire legitimacy with United Nations support) was an increasingly apparent fact of life.

The United Nations: Act 3

The United Nations, meanwhile, could serve as a useful forum for addressing problems that arose between the West and the Soviet Union —but only if all parties were willing to cooperate. Doubts about Soviet

[92] FR, 1946, VII:822-823.
[93] Department of State *Bulletin* 14 (14 April 1946):622-624.
[94] Ibid.

intentions were raised when Andrei Gromyko returned to the United Nations and handed to the president of the Security Council a protest over the 4 April resolution. Now that the question of evacuation had been settled, Gromyko asserted that the council's resolution to defer consideration of the Iranian question until 6 May was irrational and illegal. The question, he contended, should be *removed* from the agenda.[95] Although Ala asked that the question *remain* on the Security Council's agenda,[96] the Soviet ambassador in Iran on 11 April pressured Qavam into promising that Iran would request withdrawal of the case from the council.[97]

Ala, however, took matters into his own hands. In a letter to the president of the council on 15 April, he quoted two contradictory statements from his government. The first, received the day before, expressed confidence that the recent agreement between Iran and the Soviet Union would be respected, but noted that Iran had no right to fix the council's course; the second,[98] received that day, noted the Soviet intention to complete evacuation of Iran by 6 May, pointed out the "necessity" of expressing confidence in the Soviet pledge, and instructed him to withdraw Iran's complaint from the U.N.[99] The council required no elaboration. When Gromyko asked that the council meet Iran's request for withdrawal of the question from the agenda, he was firmly opposed. Stettinius declared that the situation had not changed since the decision deferring action until May. *If* on 6 May evacuation was complete, *then* the matter could be removed from the agenda.[100]

On the following day, after listening to Secretary General Trygve Lie's comments on the legal aspects of the Iranian case,[101] the Security Coun-

---

[95] *UNJ*, p. 489. See S.D. 891.6363/4-846 for *Pravda's* discussion of the Iranian negotiations.

[96] *FR*, 1946, VII:415; *UNJ*, pp. 490-491.

[97] *FR*, 1946, VII:415-417, 438; *New York Times*, 8, 10 and 15 April 1946. It is interesting to note that this exchange occurred on the same date that Pishevari, the premier of Azerbaijan, declared on Tabriz radio that the Red Army was responsible for overthrowing the Iranian regime. *Washington Post*, 12 April 1946; *New York Times*, 12 April 1946.

[98] Qavam sent this note at Sadchikov's insistence, and after Moscow had approved it. *FR*, 1946, 426-427.

[99] *UNJ*, pp. 497-498; *FR*, 1946, VII:422.

[100] *UNJ*, pp. 498-515; *FR*, 1946, VII:424-426.

[101] Lie had serious doubts about the Council remaining seized of the Iranian question. For insight into Lie's thinking, see: *UNJ*, pp. 522-524; Trygve Lie, pp. 79 ff.; Andrew Cordier and Wilder Foote, eds., *Public Papers of the Secretaries-General of the United Nations. Vol. I: Trygve Lie, 1946-1953* (New York, 1969), pp. 39-43.

cil focused on two issues: the Iranian government's sudden reversal of its position while Soviet troops were still in Iran; and the question of who—the council or the states who were parties to a dispute—should remain master of the agenda.[102] A week later, after protracted discussion, the council voted against a resolution acknowledging withdrawal of the Iranian complaint. Although Gromyko stated that his government would not take part in further discussion, the Iranian question remained on the agenda.[103]

Meanwhile, Soviet forces began to leave Azerbaijan, where relations with the central government seemed on the mend. Teheran had initiated several reforms and had proposed an accord which, if accepted, would give the recalcitrant province considerable autonomy. On 28 April, Ja'afar Pishevari departed for Teheran to negotiate with Qavam.[104]

On 6 May, the date set by the council for reports concerning the completion of Soviet withdrawal, Ala reported that withdrawal had not been verified and that Soviet influence in the area still made it impossible for his government to exercise effective authority. On the same day, he suggested to Stettinius the desirability of retaining the question on the agenda even after confirmation of Soviet evacuation. To this, Stettinius objected.[105]

Two days later, the Security Council (with the USSR absent) adopted an American resolution which deferred proceedings on the question until Soviet withdrawal could be confirmed, or until 20 May, when Iran could report such information as was available.[106] On 20 May, however, the Iranian government reported that it had insufficient information, that it had no effective authority over Azerbaijan, and that Soviet interference had not ceased. On 21 May, another letter cited new information from Qavam: evacuation of Soviet troops had in fact taken place

[102] *UNJ*, pp. 521-532; *FR*, 1946, VII:426-431.

[103] *UNJ*, pp. 585-598; *United Nations Security Council Official Records, First Year: First Series*, Supplement No. 2, pp. 47-50; *FR*, 1946, VII:432, 435; Lie, pp. 84-85.

[104] Soviet influence in Azerbaijan continued to be apparent. *FR*, 1946, VII:434-440; *New York Times*, 29 April 1946.

[105] *UNJ*, p. 642; *FR*, 1946, VII:452. The State Department on the morning of 6 May had received a cable from Gerald Dooher, the vice consul in Tabriz, stating that Tabriz had been evacuated with great fanfare. S.D. 861.24591/5-546.

[106] *UNJ*, pp. 634-639. On 7 May Dooher reported his belief that Soviet military evacuation of Azerbaijan had been completed the night before. This was a belief, however, not a first-hand observation, and the vice consul had no doubt that the Soviets had the province well in hand. S.D. 861.24591/5-746.

on 6 May.[107] Since a majority of the council's members were dissatisfied with the latest report, the council, after long consideration, adjourned discussion until an unspecified date in the near future, but remained seized of the question.[108]

At the same time, the United States used its influence to prevent Qavam from recalling Ala, who had jeopardized his political life by making his representations before the council. Repudiation of Ala, Byrnes said, would impair the council's ability to aid Iran. Qavam promised not to recall Ala, but was under pressure to take corrective action. On 29 May, the Iranian embassy publicized the fact that Ala had been instructed to make no more statements to the Security Council regarding the Iranian question. George Allen, the new American ambassador to Iran,[109] speculated that this action was as much a result of internal political machinations (a means of placating leftist elements) as Soviet pressure.[110]

Allen's speculation was not ill-founded. With the Security Council temporarily rid of the Iranian question (though remaining seized of it), events in Iran moved out of the limelight of world opinion and onto a stage where motives were not easily perceived by even the most clairvoyant of analysts. Elsewhere along the Northern Tier additional problems were rapidly developing. In Greece, ongoing domestic problems were exacerbated by and tended to mirror the international conflict between the Great Powers, while in Turkey the Soviet war of nerves continued to drain the economic resources of the country and to impede domestic reform. In the United States, the Near Eastern situation was being watched very carefully. Undersecretary Acheson and the members

[107] Verification was carried out by a commission which traveled to Tabriz in a Soviet plane and was taken on a conducted tour of five or six towns in Pishevari's car (FR, 1946, VII:476). Moscow Radio later announced that withdrawal had been completed on 9 May. FR, 1946, VII:479; New York Times, 24 May 1946.

[108] This meant that a meeting on the Iranian question could be called at the request of any member.

[109] Allen replaced Wallace Murray, who had been ill, and officially assumed charge of the embassy on 11 May 1946 (FR, 1946, VII:453). See discussion of this transition in Chapter IV.

[110] UNJ, pp. 699 ff.; FR, 1946, VII:476-489; New York Times, 30 May 1946. Harold Minor, remembering the agony of Ala at the time, and recalling conversations with him later in Teheran, doubts that Qavam secretly instructed Ala to proceed against the Russians while publicly instructing him to do the opposite. Without Ala's courage and persistence, he writes, there would have been no U.N. case. He also notes that Ala had everything to lose since his wife was a member of the Garagozlou family, one of the biggest land owners in Iran. Minor, letter to the author. For evidence of Ala's close ties to the Shah, see S.D. 24591/3-1546.

of NEA had been schooled by the long-drawn-out process of negotiation over the Iranian question at the U.N. Secretary Byrnes, who was attending the Council of Foreign Ministers in Paris, had undergone a similar education. Perhaps this is why on 2 May he told Numan Menemencioğlu, formerly foreign minister of Turkey and now ambassador to France, that if in the past the United States was unaware of Turkey's problems, the government now was "well posted," and took great interest in them.[111]

Four days earlier an incident had corroborated the lessons of the Iranian crisis and encouraged this expression of support for Turkey. At a dinner party which Molotov gave for the secretary, the foreign commissar complained about the American refusal to postpone consideration of the Iranian case until 10 April, and opined that the Soviet government had been the victim of an "anti-Soviet" campaign.[112]

Molotov failed to acknowledge that America's attitude was a result of real fears for which there were legitimate grounds. The question had been postponed once, and the only result of bilateral negotiations had been Soviet pressure to effect a *fait accompli*. Byrnes undoubtedly pointed out such matters to Molotov, and in the course of their discussion both Molotov and Vyshinsky admitted that no agreement had been reached until 5 April.[113] Later, Molotov also stated that the phrase "unforeseen circumstances" was meant to safeguard against the establishment of a new Iranian government hostile to the Soviet Union. Charles Bohlen, concluding a memorandum of the conversation, believed the observations of Molotov and Vyshinsky corroborated the fact that relations between the Great Powers were more important to the Soviets than the principles of the charter.

It is clear from Bohlen's memorandum that toward the end of April Byrnes was already thinking of the United Nations as a forum within which to conduct American foreign policy. By May he was beginning to act upon that line of thought. Earlier, Iran had been characterized as a proving ground for the principles of Dumbarton Oaks. Perhaps it was.

[111] Acheson, pp. 150-151, 195-197; FR, 1946, VII:823; Byrnes, *Speaking Frankly*, pp. 303-304.

[112] FR, 1946, VII:441-442; Byrnes, *Speaking Frankly*, p. 126; *All in One Lifetime*, p. 358; Bohlen, p. 253; Byrnes Papers, Folder 638.

[113] This argument and the complex negotiations over the Iranian crisis are completely misconstrued by Richard Freeland, *The Truman Doctrine and the Origins of McCarthyism* (New York, 1972), p. 53. Gardner, *Architects of Illusion*, pp. 214-215, does better, but he, too, like many others, fails to appreciate what the Iranian episode was all about.

But those principles clearly were not supported by the Soviet Union. As a consequence, principles were of lesser importance than political realities, and the immediate lesson Byrnes drew from the Iranian case was that firmness brought results. A corollary was that firmness ultimately required American strength to back it up, although this aspect of the problem was not really explored until the Turkish crisis in August. The conclusion to this chapter will examine in greater depth the implications of these assessments. For now, suffice it to say that propositions relating to the necessity of firmness in dealing with the Russians were widespread—believed not only by Acheson and Byrnes but by everyone in NEA, and particularly by Loy Henderson.

In June Henderson would elaborate upon some of the themes in Truman's Army Day speech as a means of forcing the administration to go beyond firmness and address impending problems in the Near East. Without a strong army backed by compulsory military training, it was difficult for the United States to conduct a forward-looking policy. What resources it did have included able diplomats, principles, and money. In view of this fact, Henderson believed that defense of American interests required the responsible employment of loans as an instrument of policy in the Near East—an area which now very clearly was a major political battleground.[114]

Respite

As tension over Iran subsided, further complications quietly developed not only in Iran but in Greece and Turkey as well. By August these new developments would cause American statesmen to take a bleak view of the Near Eastern situation and would contribute to a decision whereby the United States would proclaim its policies toward the region more emphatically than at any time during the crisis over Soviet withdrawal from Iran. It is to the events that set the stage for this second crisis that we now turn.

Iran

Historians, in looking at events that took place in Iran after the Security Council discussions in May, cannot agree on answers to two crucial questions: (1) how does one evaluate the key figure, Prime Minister Ahmad Qavam; and (2) how much influence did he exercise relative to

[114] FR, 1946, VII:7-10.

the shah in resolving the situation in Azerbaijan?[115] Before one can address these questions, one must first take note of a new actor who had come on the scene as the drama in Iran continued to unfold.

George V. Allen was now the American ambassador in Iran, where he replaced the ailing Wallace Murray.[116] During the height of the Iranian crisis, Murray had proved a useful balance to the pressures exerted on Qavam by the Soviet ambassador Sadchikov. But Murray's subsequent departure left no one of comparable prestige to counter the continuing influence of Sadchikov.[117]

As a consequence, George Allen was chosen for the job. Allen had concentrated on Iran since the end of World War II, and on Henderson's recommendation had acted as special advisor to both Stettinius and Byrnes at the Security Council. Byrnes had been pleased with his "fellow Carolinian." He suspected that Allen had had a hand in Ambassador Ala's speech to the Security Council in the spring—a notion which Allen never attempted to disabuse—and referred to him ever after as Ala Allen. Allen knew Henderson's attitudes, and agreed with his chief that the Soviets were trying to take advantage of postwar instability to expand their territories along the Northern Tier. The upshot was that Allen was appointed ambassador to Iran. The President met with Allen on 18 April and sent him off with instructions to tell the Iranians to do precisely what their ancestors the Medes and the Persians had done: establish a rule of law. Allen was in Iran within two weeks, and officially assumed his post on 11 May.[118]

[115] Skrine, pp. 235-250; Arfa, pp. 365-381; Mohammad Reza Shah Pahlavi, pp. 116-118; Rossow, "The Battle for Azerbaijan," pp. 25-31; Archie Roosevelt, Jr., pp. 258-268; Kirk, *The Middle East 1945-1950*, pp. 72-83; Avery, pp. 394-401; Eagleton, pp. 87-132; Lenczowski, *Russia and the West in Iran*, pp. 300-315; Elwell-Sutton, "Political Parties in Iran," pp. 58-60; Van Wagenen, pp. 80-88; Sachar, *Europe Leaves the Middle East*, pp. 356 ff.; Ramazani, *Iran's Foreign Policy*, pp. 143 ff. (esp. pp. 148-153); Paterson, p. 181; Gary Hess, "The Iranian Crisis of 1945-46 and the Cold War," *Political Science Quarterly* 89 (March 1974):143 ff.; Eduard Mark, "Allied Relations in Iran, 1941-1947: The Origins of a Cold War Crisis," *Wisconsin Magazine of History* 59 (Autumn 1975): 62-63; Mark Lytle, "American-Iranian Relations, 1941-1947, and the Redefinition of National Security" (Ph.D. dissertation, Yale University, 1973), pp. 298-306; Firuz Kazemzadeh, "Soviet Iranian Relations: A Quarter-Century of Freeze and Thaw," in Ivo Lederer and Wayne Vucinich, eds., *The Soviet Union and the Middle East: The Post World War II Era* (Stanford, 1974), pp. 55-77; Pfau, "Containment in Iran," pp. 359-372; Allen Papers, "Mission to Iran"; Rossow MS.

[116] See Chapter IV, n. 83.

[117] John Jernegan, letter to the author; interviews with Loy Henderson and Robert Rossow.

[118] Interview with Loy Henderson; Henderson Papers; Allen Papers, "Mission to

The situation which Allen confronted required that he understand the Iranian prime minister. This was not an easy task. Murray, of course, had appreciated Qavam's position and was one of the few Americans not discouraged by the prime minister's appointment. In late March, he had cabled Washington that Qavam was operating within the Persian tradition, "which accepts as a matter of course that justice must be cajoled to perform her duties."[119] Murray had long been aware of the necessity of using his personal influence in Iranian politics, a practice which would eventually become clear to Allen, too. Allen, however, at first did not have enough stature to have much influence on Qavam. Like the shah, Allen was much younger than the prime minister, and although highly regarded in Washington, he was unable to impress Qavam with his willingness to "cajole justice"[120] Within six months Allen would take matters into his own hands, but for the time being there was little he could do but watch.

Once, in early June, Allen took the initiative in discussing American reaction to Qavam's apparently pro-Soviet orientation. In late July, he benefited from a decision to continue the Gendarmerie Mission.[121] But if these actions rallied Iranian support for American policies—policies intended to support the Iranians in resisting Soviet pressures—there was a problem convincing Iranians that the Americans were dependable allies. The State Department, for example, felt bound by the Anglo-American oil agreement to respect existing concessions and lawfully acquired rights. This was understandable since British interests in Iran constituted Britain's greatest external asset, and the extent of American interests in the Gulf was enormous. But the department did not want

---

Iran"; Truman Papers, PSF, President's Appointments File, Daily Sheets, January-May 1946, 17-18 April. Byrnes was from South Carolina, Allen from North Carolina.

[119] John Jernegan recalls that during Qavam's visit to Moscow, George Kennan had sent a cable which said in effect that Qavam had sold out during his stay in Moscow. Murray's only comment was: "I think George is playing this over a little too fast on his piano." John Jernegan, letter to the author; FR, 1946, VII:375; interview with Robert Rossow.

[120] Interview with Robert Rossow.

[121] The promotion of Norman Schwarzkopf to brigadier general was interpreted as evidence that the United States strongly supported the mission; consequently, general Iranian support for the mission, which had been lukewarm, changed dramatically. This was important for American interests because the Soviets had been attempting to undermine what constituted the only Iranian security force then capable of maintaining order. S.D. 891.105A/5-46/7-3046; FR, 1946, VII:439, 455, 496-497, 501-502.

its motivation in the Iranian case to appear to be a selfish one; it desired to respect the law forbidding new petroleum concessions, and sought to prevent aggressive American oil representatives from conducting discussions with the Iranians on oil. The result was that the Iranians, who desired concessionary agreements, questioned the American commitment to Iran.[122]

As Allen wrote Henderson in early June, the Iranians demanded that the United States play a more positive role in their country. Allen insisted that his government could not adopt the very tactics to which it had so strenuously objected, but he recognized that Iranians were accustomed to outside interference: "The only way they can think of to counteract one interference is to invite another." Without such interference, many Iranians believed Americans really were not interested in Iran and that the United States was not dependable. As for his relations with Qavam and the shah, Allen told Henderson that the former remained an enigma; the latter, whom he saw frequently, at Allen's advice, was keeping hands off current policy.[123]

The relationships between Qavam and the shah, and between them and the Soviet and American ambassadors, were pivotal to the power struggle in Iran. Qavam, who controlled the gendarmerie but not the army, apparently desired (perhaps because of this fact) to win back control of Azerbaijan through pacific penetration. He therefore made concessions to the Azerbaijan regime in the belief that once he was able to secure election of a Majlis under his control he could steer the government back toward the center.[124]

The shah, on the other hand, both during and after the war, sought successfully to influence the army and prevent others from controlling it until he himself was in a position to exert full control over the nation. Thus, in May and June the shah preferred to rely on the army as a means of resolving the situation in Azerbaijan. Dissatisfied with Qavam's passive policies, the shah opposed any concessions to the dissi-

[122] For discussion of the oil issue, see: S.D. 891/6363/3-2046/5-2046/7-946/7-3146/8-2246/8-2346/8-2946/8-3046/11-1346/11-2146; FR, 1946, VII:18-50 (esp. 34-35, 48-50), 413, 514; S.D. Teheran Lot File No. 54F55: Folder 863.6-1946—Confidential (Ambassador Allen's Correspondence), memo on "Middle East Oil" attached to 1 August 1946 letter from Howard Cowden to George Allen, and 21 August 1946 memo of conversation on the Iranian oil situation.

[123] S.D. Teheran Lot File No. 54F55: Folder 1946-7, 863.6—1946 Confidential (Ambassador Allen's Correspondence), 6 June 1946 letter from George Allen to Loy Henderson. See also S.D. 891.00/5-2246.

[124] FR, 1946, VII:454, 464-465, 491; S.D. 891.00/5-2246.

dent regime, and asked Allen for direct American support.[125] That the shah had fewer options than Qavam followed from his position as monarch and undoubtedly led him to adopt a more forceful attitude toward the rebellion in Azerbaijan.

Meanwhile, until Allen was willing to take the initiative in pursuing a more forceful role in his relations with the two Iranian leaders, the situation in Iran appeared to be deteriorating. In early June Allen became deeply concerned about the government's outright appeasement of leftist and pro-Soviet elements. Qavam's government frequently expressed warm friendship for the Soviet Union without making any reference to other nations. All opposition was being castigated as reactionary and fascist. Newspaper editors published numerous articles against Americans and the United States while those opposed to Qavam and to Soviet policies were arrested without charge or public hearing. Of further concern was the settlement between Qavam's government and the regime in Azerbaijan.[126] An agreement on 13 June granted Azerbaijan a considerable degree of autonomy, and allowed the Democratic Party of Azerbaijan to remain in full control. The Teheran government's only gain was formal acknowledgement of its authority, leading observers to question whether Qavam had gone so far toward the pro-Soviet camp that he could not retreat.[127]

Still more speculation was raised on 29 June, when Qavam formally announced formation of a new political party, the Democratic Party of Iran. Some thought Qavam wanted to use this party as a means of undermining the Democrats of Azerbaijan in the coming elections; others believed it might be another phase in the Soviet Union's political penetration of the country.[128]

These differences of interpretation were still being debated when, in mid-July, a general strike broke out in the British oil fields in southern Iran. The Tudeh-controlled Workers' and Toilers' Union, whose 70,000 workers included almost all the native Iranian laborers of the

[125] S.D. 123/128½ Harold B. Minor; *War History Report*; Arfa, p. 369; FR, 1946, VII: 454, 464-465, 486; S.D. 891.00/9-2146.

[126] Discussion between the two sides had begun in April, possibly as a result of Soviet insistence and due to the Soviet desire to get the case off the Security Council's agenda. FR, 1946, VII:494-495; Rossow, "The Battle of Azerbaijan," p. 25; Eagleton, p. 93.

[127] FR, 1946, VIII:434-435, 491-502; *New York Times*, 12 and 15 June 1946.

[128] Kirk, *The Middle East 1945-1950*, p. 77; FR, 1946, VII:505; see also S.D. 891.00/5-2946.

Anglo-Iranian Oil Company installation in Khuzistan province, were demanding increased wages and improved living conditions. In spite of the appalling situation in the refinery at Abadan, the strike was not of indigenous origin. It was directed from Teheran and appears to have been an attempt by the Tudeh to bring the AIOC to its knees. The strike was politically rather than economically motivated. Sir Clarmont Skrine suggests that it was intended "as an overwhelming demonstration of the power and solidarity of the Tudeh Party and a crushing blow to British prestige and economic interests." In retrospect, Hassan Arfa's assessment is probably correct: it was a Soviet blunder, though at first it might not have appeared to be.[129]

Rioting broke out on the day of the strike and apparently resulted from a clash between the Iranians and a tribal union of marsh Arabs who lived in the region and whose sympathies led them to oppose the Tudeh Party. At least 17 Iranians and Arabs were killed, and 150 seriously injured. The Tudeh suspected that the tribal union was British-sponsored, a suspicion for which there was good argument. To ensure the safety of its workers and its oil interests, Britain dispatched Indian Army troops to Basra (across the border in Iraq) and cruisers to Abadan (an offshore island in the Shatt al-Arab which served as AIOC's pipeline terminus). These precautions Qavam used as a pretext for fulminations against the British, demonstrating to the Tudeh his anti-Western attitude. More important, he sent a government delegation under Muzaffar Firuz to settle the strike. The subsequent agreement which Firuz worked out varied from the workers' demands in only minor details. Robert Rossow, who had flown down to cover the situation, returned to Teheran with the firm conviction that Qavam was conceding to Tudeh pressures to an alarming degree.[130]

Even more disconcerting to many Western observers was Qavam's next move. On 1 August, in an apparent attempt to appease the Tudeh

[129] Arfa, p. 371, makes a good case for Soviet direction of the strike. Rossow MS: S.D. Teheran Lot File No. 54F55, Confidential Dispatch No. 48 from Basra, Iraq, 13 August 1946, "Development of the Labor Union, the Tudeh Party, and the Arab League in the Abadan Area"; "Summary of Issues and Trends in Iran," from Enclosure No. 222, 21 November 1946, from American embassy, Teheran, to the secretary of state; S.D. 891.00/7-1646/8-646; Skrine, pp. 241-250. Sir Clarmont Skrine was then counsellor for Indian affairs at the British embassy in Teheran.

[130] Ibid.; S.D. 891.00/8-3146; S.D. Teheran Lot File No. 54F55, Folder 1946-1947, 800 Political Affairs (July-August) Classified, 1946, tel. No. 1111, 12 August 1946 from Allen to the Department.

Party further, Qavam reformed the government, including three Tudeh members in his new cabinet. As George Lenczowski has pointed out, "this 'popular front' cabinet had many characteristics of classic Communist infiltration into the governing apparatus of a non-Communist country." Qavam's move, about which he had been thinking since early June, was interpreted in a similar light by Robert Rossow, now a political officer at the American embassy in Teheran. Rossow, who had recently been in Tabriz, noted many similarities between the sequence of events that took place there and what was taking place in Teheran. Ambassador George Allen, on the other hand, looked on the change within the government as a means by which Qavam could better handle the Tudeh Party. To support his opinion, the ambassador cited Qavam's backing of the Schwarzkopf mission (the American Military Mission with the Iranian Gendarmerie). That both Allen's and Rossow's interpretations of Qavam's actions were plausible was typical of most interpretations of the prime minister's way of doing things.[131]

What American policy required at this juncture was prescribed in two personal letters from Henderson which Allen received on 29 July. In the first letter, written on 1 July, Henderson was extremely concerned about an impending Irano-Soviet air agreement. Were the agreement to grant the Soviets an exclusive air concession in the northern part of Iran, it would allow the Soviets to consolidate their position there. "We are confident that you will continue to leave Qavam under no illusions as to our attitude in this matter," he wrote Allen. Henderson felt that Qavam could not orient his foreign policy solely toward the Soviet Union and expect to receive the assistance of the United States and the support of the United Nations. Endeavors to impress this fact on Qavam seemed to fail, he said, because Qavam apparently believed in what Edwin Wright termed "devil worship,"

> by which the Iranians traditionally show affection for the strong and ruthless and contempt for those who treat them well. Qavam seems to be so sure of our friendship and our altruism that he counts on our continual assistance despite all developments and despite any words we may utter. We must find some way to shake him out of this com-

[131] Ibid.; Lenczowski, *Russia and the West in Iran*, p. 312; FR, 1946, VII:510-513; New York Times 2 August 1946. Pfau asserts that Qavam agreed to a Tudeh demand for three positions in his cabinet as a price for ending the strike ("The United States and Iran," p. 320).

placency and bring home to him the stark reality of the situation and the nature of the disaster which is about to overtake his country.[132]

Henderson on 3 July had written another letter, this time in response to Allen's letter of early June, which Henderson had shown to Acheson and others in the department. Noting that the department was not sure how to interpret Qavam's new political party (formed on 29 June), Henderson encouraged Allen to indicate to Qavam that his fear of the Soviet Union was exaggerated and that the United Nations could be a determining force. To counter Qavam's playing up to the Soviets, Henderson suggested that "we should perhaps bring home to him the immediate strength of the United States and the United Nations as compared with the basically weak position of the Soviet Union."[133]

This advice, though qualified in its implications, took on added significance in the second week of August, as negotiations between the Iranian government and Azerbaijani authorities broke down and relations between the two "democratic" parties seriously deteriorated. In the south, the Qashqa'i tribes came to the conclusion that Qavam had passed the government irretrievably into the hands of the Tudeh. Aware that a civil war was in the offing, they felt nevertheless that they must act. On 13 August, Qavam—undoubtedly aware of these counterpressures— told Allen he might have to use force to bring Azerbaijan back into the Iranian fold. Concerned that the Soviet Union would support the insurgents, he wanted to know what the United Nations would do to help Iran.[134]

Allen's reply was circuitous, and touched only indirectly on the theme that was elaborated upon in Henderson's letters and suggested by American policies in 1946. The United Nations had no security forces, and the Soviet Union had a veto in the Security Council. But in the event of flagrant support by the Soviet Union for a separatist movement, and in case Iran placed the matter unreservedly before the United Nations, Allen said he did not believe that those nations which were determined

[132] S.D. Teheran Lot File No. 54F55, Folder 800, 1946—Confidential (Ambassador Allen's Correspondence), 1 July 1946 letter from Loy Henderson to George Allen.

[133] Ibid., 3 July letter from Loy Henderson to George Allen.

[134] FR, 1946, VII:511-512; S.D. Teheran Lot File No. 54F55, Folder 1946-1947, 800 Political Affairs (July-August), Classified, 1946, tel. No. 1097 from Allen to the Department. For background on the Qashqa'i, see Kermit Roosevelt, *Arabs, Oil and History, The Story of the Middle East* (New York, 1949), Chapter XVIII.

to make the United Nations a forceful organization (read the United States and Great Britain) would sit idly by. He told Qavam that he thought some means would be found to aid nations who based their policies on the principles of the United Nations.[135]

As in the past, there was a *suggestion* of American support, but this suggestion was *less* than a forthright promise. It was undoubtedly confusing to Qavam, who obviously wanted a concrete indication of American support and apparently understood "devil worship," unadorned by the principled attire of American policies. Contrasted with the stark but serviceable language which cloaked very real Soviet threats, American promises appeared only slightly more substantial than the emperor's new clothes in Hans Christian Andersen's fairy tale. Behind Soviet language, the outlines were clear. American resolve, on the other hand, was as diaphanous as its accoutrement. With the authority of his government in serious jeopardy, Qavam was faced with a difficult choice: give in to Soviet pressures which would ultimately divide, if not subjugate, his country; or rely on the United Nations and the United States —a course which could have the same result while leaving him in a more vulnerable and very embarrassing position. In the meantime, he was attempting to prevent what Henderson had characterized as the disaster which was about to overtake his country.

Greece

In Greece, the situation was equally bleak, although for different reasons. The occupation of Iran had encouraged a centrifugal relationship between the tribes and the central government. The Tudeh Party, with a few important exceptions, had capitalized on this division. In Greece, however, occupation had encouraged a more divisive split which took place not only on ethnic, but on class and ideological lines as well. External interference in Greek affairs exacerbated these divisions, making it impossible for the Greek government to cope with them. If agricultural recovery had begun, industrial recovery was slow,[136] and UNRRA aid was an insufficient antidote. Economic crises, public disorder, and endemic violence continued to polarize the country and to perpetuate the "mass vendetta" which by now had become international in character.

---

[135] FR, 1946, VII:511-512.
[136] McNeill, *The Greek Dilemma*, pp. 205-206; Delivanis and Cleveland, pp. 129-168.

The Soviets, who on 3 March were seeking bases in the Dodecanese,[137] were nonetheless respectful of the spheres of influence agreement made in October 1944. That agreement, it may be recalled, was made over Britain's and Russia's respective interests in the Balkans, and did *not* include Poland, Turkey, or Iran. This is important to remember because so many commentators compare British policies in Greece with Soviet policies in the latter countries.[138] This line of reasoning misconstrues the nature of the problems that had developed since October 1944. Iran and Turkey had never been included in any bargain, and unilateral attempts to acquire influence in those countries were outside the understanding on the Balkans. Soviet antipathy toward Greece should be judged in the context of that understanding, not in the larger context of Turkey and Iran where the Allies' respective interests had yet to be defined. The Soviets, moreover, had been given the opportunity to send a mission to observe the Greek elections, and had declined. Apparently, they desired to establish a precedent for noninterference by the West in elections which they intended to hold in those portions of Eastern Europe and the Balkans which fell in their sphere of influence. For this reason, the Soviets were committed to recognizing the results of the elections in Greece scheduled for 31 March 1946. In February, the KKE emissary Dimitrios Partsalidis had been advised by Molotov and Andrei Zhdanov to form a Democratic Front and to take part in the elections. Western European Communist leaders such as Maurice Thorez of France and Palmiro Togliatti of Italy had given the KKE the same advice. But Nikos Zachariadis, the secretary of KKE, was of a different mind. On the anniversary of the Varkiza Agreement, even before Partsalidis returned from Moscow, the KKE officially decided to abstain from the coming elections and to embark upon what soon would be-

[137] The Soviet ambassador, Admiral Rodionov, hinted to Premier Sofoulis that the Soviets were interested in a base in the Dodecanese islands for the Soviet merchant fleet (FR, 1946, VII:119-120; Xydis, *Greece and the Great Powers*, p. 183). In May, Molotov accused the United States of seeking bases in Iran, Egypt, and Turkey—an accusation whose complete absurdity Byrnes pointed out. A memorandum of the conversation observes that Molotov adopted this absurd propaganda line because he saw that the United States was not prepared to make a deal with regard to the question of Trieste (Byrnes, *Speaking Frankly*, p. 128; Byrnes Papers, Folder 638). In June, Molotov accepted the Dodecanese being given to Greece. Xydis speculates that this change of policy resulted from the belief that Greece would eventually fall into the Soviet orbit. Xydis, *Greece and the Great Powers*, pp. 222, 235, 613; FR, 1946, VII:193-194.

[138] Even the Soviets attempted to do this. See n. 3, above, and n. 168 below.

come the Third Round of the civil war in Greece. Zachariadis had been encouraged by Soviet support for the Tudeh Party in Iran. He also hoped to force Stalin's hand in what members of the KKE saw as a scheme to spread Soviet influence into the Eastern Mediterranean and the Middle East. Tito's help had already been offered and accepted. In March, the Yugoslav leader had further promised all-out help,[139] prompting Zachariadis in a speech at the training camp in Bulkes to predict the coming of the Third Round. Meanwhile, abstention from the election would deny its legitimacy and would give an aura of justice to the armed struggle in preparation. EAM's cause would be supported by the fact that persecution of the Left was real, and that the KKE by claiming all abstentions hopefully could avoid revealing its minority following.[140]

In Britain, policy toward Greece was influenced by the fact that the Iranian crisis profoundly disturbed Clement Attlee. As the crisis broke in early March, the British prime minister began pressing on his Chiefs of Staff the idea of disengagement from areas where there was a risk of clashing with the Russians. It was his belief that the British should pull out from all the Middle East—a view that appealed to Chancellor of the Exchequer Hugh Dalton, who began concentrating his attention on British expenditures in Greece. In July the Greeks were informed of Britain's economic burdens, and of the fact that the Americans had to be brought into their partnership.[141]

[139] Kousoulas, "The Greek Communists Tried Three Times—and Failed," pp. 294, 303-304, surmises that Tito's extensive assistance was probably intended to divert British action against Yugoslavia, so enabling him to consolidate his regime and prevent the reestablishment of a pro-Western regime in Belgrade.

[140] Kousoulas, "The Greek Communists Tried Three Times—and Failed," pp. 294, 302-304, and Revolution and Defeat, pp. 231-232; Eudes, pp. 258-262; O'Ballance, p. 121; FR, 1946, VII:117-118; Xydis, Greece and the Great Powers, pp. 182, 604; McNeill, The Greek Dilemma, p. 229. Xydis, p. 604, notes that the report by Zachariadis—on which much of the above interpretation is based— came only in December 1949. Since the report was made after the Truman Doctrine and after Tito's break with Stalin, the explanation must be taken with a grain of salt. In seeking to blame Tito for the failure of the Third Round, it attempts to absolve the Soviet Union from any responsibility and to conceal whatever role it may have played in the civil war. O'Ballance, p. 122, claims that Stalin approved the formation of the Democratic Army later in 1946, and that he asked the Balkan countries to support the insurgents.

[141] Hugh Dalton, High Tide and After: Memoirs, 1945-1960 (London, 1962), pp. 105, 206; Francis-Williams, A Prime Minister Remembers, p. 165; Xydis, Greece and the Great Powers, pp. 240-243; transcript, Constantine Tsaldaris Oral History Interview, 4 May 1964, Truman Library.

The United States was already in the process of revising its policy of noninterference in Greece and gradually associating itself with the British policy of containing Soviet influence in the Balkans. It had also become involved in efforts to stabilize the Greek government and to address the serious problems of recovery from the war. In January 1946 the United States approved an Export-Import Bank loan to Greece of $25 million. Attention was further directed toward the coming elections, economic assistance, economic stabilization, territorial claims, border violations, and government instability. Symbolic of American attention to Greece's problems was the fact that the *Missouri*, after visiting Istanbul, made its way to Greece, where it was well received. The United States, like Great Britain, recognized that stability required an elected government with the moral power to enforce its will, and that an honest election required stability in the first place. Therefore the State Department continued to support and even encourage the regent's previous decisions to hold elections on 31 March.[142]

On that date, the Populist Party and its allies won 251 of 354 seats by a system of proportional representation. According to the Allied Mission for Observing Greek Elections (AMFOGE) and most Greek observers, the elections for the revisionary parliament (to be convoked on 13 May) had been free and fair. According to the Left, since only 49 percent of those on the electoral lists had voted, 51 percent had abstained, thus giving them a moral victory. This was an unwarranted conclusion. Many of those registered were dead or had moved, and a fair guess suggests that EAM would have seated approximately 25 percent of the representatives in the revisionary parliament.[143]

Meanwhile, on the day before the elections, a guerilla attack on the village of Litokhoron signaled the beginning of the Third Round. In

[142] FR, 1946, VII:91, 98, 125-132, 135-136, 138-144, 154, 156-159, 161, 167; Xydis, *Greece and the Great Powers*, pp. 180, 185-187, 270 ff.

[143] While sampling surveys indicated that only 9.3 percent abstained for political reasons, this statistic, too, was subject to serious question. Sampling was carried out through interviews by AMFOGE representatives whose competence was questionable and whose presence apparently influenced the nature of Greek responses. Estimates of the percentage of votes which would have gone to EAM range from 15 percent (Xydis) and 20 percent (McNeill) to 28 percent (Eudes). McNeill, *The Greek Dilemma*, pp. 231-236; Stavrianos, *Greece*, p. 169; Xydis, *Greece and the Great Powers*, pp. 185, 605-606; Eudes, p. 263. The Statement of the Allied Mission for Observing the Greek Elections, dated 11 April 1946, and a subsequent Report of the Allied Mission to Observe Revisions of the Greek Electoral Lists, dated 19 August 1946, can be found in S.D. Lot M-72 NEA/GTI File: AMFOGE I, Election File II.

succeeding months, the KKE stepped up its guerilla campaign. By the end of July, the problem of restoring public order became more difficult; guerilla bands, aided by Albania, Yugoslavia, and later Bulgaria, forced the government to add detachments of the Greek Army to the gendarmerie units already operating against the guerillas.[144] The serious inflationary implications for the Greek budget were obvious, and in early August a Greek economic mission under former Premier Sophocles Venizelos was telling Acheson of Greece's dire need for economic assistance. Venizelos asserted that if his mission were unsuccessful in obtaining such assistance, the very social order of Greece would be imperiled.[145]

The United States had been extremely critical of the Greek government's inertia in addressing its own problems. The Greek government had not used any of the $25 million credit made available to it eight months before. Apparently, the Greeks felt that British and American strategic and political interests would dictate support of Greece regardless of the government's failure to bring order to its own house—an assumption which was not unwarranted.[146]

The implications of United States involvement in the Balkans had become apparent as early as July, with a Soviet press and radio campaign against Great Britain and the United States. The Western Allies were accused of setting up an Anglo-American bloc, of seeking world hegemony, and of trying to impose their will on other countries. In Yugoslavia, Marshal Tito had declared that he would not abide by the decisions of the Council of Foreign Ministers on Trieste and Venezia Giulia, and on 6 August a Yugoslav fighter plane had forced an unarmed American passenger plane to crash land. Four days before, on 2 August, serious fighting had broken out in northern Greece.

[144] William McNeill notes the Greeks' shock at implied Soviet support for Bulgarian claims to an outlet on the Aegean. He also describes how the Macedonian Communist Party won the support of most Greek Slavs, leading Macedonian Greeks to regard the Communist Party as an anti-nationalist movement. "In reaction, the Right grew stronger than anywhere else in Macedonia. In other words, ideological and national antagonisms aligned themselves; Greek reactionary against Slav revolutionary" (*The Greek Dilemma*, pp. 259, 268-269). The internal struggle between Left and Right had become inextricably confused with the international struggle between Russian Communism and Anglo-American capitalism.

[145] Kousoulas, *Revolution and Defeat*, p. 239; McNeill, *The Greek Dilemma*, pp. 241-245; Xydis, *Greece and the Great Powers*, pp. 254, 261.

[146] FR, 1946, VII:165, 170, 181-182, 187-188, 188-189; Xydis, *Greece and the Great Powers*, pp. 249-251.

While there was no immediate American response to these events, earlier policies—developed during the Iranian crisis and spurred by concern over Trieste—had reached a point where American interest in the region was obvious. On the same day that fighting began in northern Greece, the Navy Department disclosed that it would send the aircraft carrier *Franklin D. Roosevelt* to the Mediterranean for three weeks in late August and early September. Under Forrestal's prodding and with Britain's encouragement, the United States Navy was working to fill the vacuum in the Eastern Mediterranean, where American diplomats had been carrying out government policies without real military support. This development, welcomed by the Greeks, worked to the detriment of internal reform; it reinforced the belief that Greece could rely on the strategic military and political interests of its Western Allies to solve its internal problems.

Thus, while Truman, on 7 August, pointed out to the Venizelos Economic Mission the necessity of internal economic reform, the mission's members were interested in another line of argument. Undersecretary for Coordination Michael Alianos, in his plea for support, stressed the strategic significance of Greece in the Mediterranean and the Balkans, where the respective worth of two ideologies was in the balance.[147] Despite these differences in emphasis, there was no disagreement over the fact that the situation in the Balkans was increasingly grim, and that American interests were involved. As in Iran, however, the United States had not yet indicated the extent of those interests by any concrete commitment.

Turkey

The situation in Turkey at this time was much less complicated than that in Greece or Iran. Because of the communal sense of identity which had been forged among most Turks in the aftermath of World War I, the Turkish Republic was not subject to the divisions which plagued its neighbors. Unlike its neighbors, Turkey had avoided occupation by any country. Thus, Soviet attempts to exercise influence in Turkey, and to undermine the regime, had to come from without. Symbolic of Turkish unity in the face of outside pressure was the fact that, in late summer, when general elections brought in a new government under Prime Minister Recep Peker, the foreign minister Hasan

[147] Xydis, *Greece and the Great Powers*, pp. 262, 267, 269, 624-625; Millis, pp. 183-184; FR, 1946, VII:186-188.

Saka retained his post. Turkey's foreign policy, guided by a general fear of Russia, was unchanged. The Turks' attitude toward the threat from without was uniform.[148]

We have seen that Soviet designs were much in evidence during the crisis over Iran. The events of March bore out the predictions of Ambassador Edwin Wilson in December 1945 that a major crisis would take place in the Middle East by spring, and they impressed Truman with the fact that the security of Turkey was seriously threatened.[149] At least 200 Soviet tanks had crossed the Iranian border, about a third of them mobilizing along the Turkish frontier with Iran. In Bulgaria, large-scale Soviet troop movements and other obvious signs of a potential attack were coupled with a vitriolic press and radio campaign against Turkey.

Edwin Wilson's belief that the Soviets desired to dominate Turkey was not, as one recent interpretation has suggested,[150] an exaggeration. An examination of Soviet attitudes toward Turkey before, during, and immediately after World War II unquestionably supports his analysis, as do the events of 1946. Wilson did not conduct his analysis without consulting Turkish counterparts who were well versed in the intricacies of Turco-Soviet relations. He particularly seems to have benefited from frequent conversations with Feridun Erkin, the very capable secretary general of the Turkish Foreign Ministry. Erkin helped to elucidate many of the obscure problems relating to the Straits, and contributed to Wilson's clear understanding that if the only objective of Soviet foreign policy was a favorable revision of the Straits regime, the American proposals of 2 November 1945 were sufficient. In telegrams to the Department of State, Wilson repeatedly aired these views; and two maps that the Office of Intelligence Research (OIR) prepared for NEA in March—one looking south from Moscow, and one looking north from Ankara—indicated the department's appreciation of Wilson's argument.[151]

Meanwhile, Walter Bedell Smith's conversation with Stalin in April 1946 provided an updated account of Stalin's intentions toward Turkey. Russia still insisted on a base in the Dardanelles. As for assurances that the Soviet Union had no intention of attacking Turkey, these had

[148] Erkin, *Les Relations Turco-Soviétiques et la Question de Détroits* (Ankara, 1968), p. 341; Sir David Kelly, *The Ruling Few: The Human Background to Diplomacy* (London, 1952), pp. 327-328.
[149] See Chapter IV. [150] Paterson, pp. 191, 206.
[151] See Erkin, pp. 298-299, and Chapter IV, nn. 158-161. See also n. 45 above.

to be taken with a grain of salt. Less than four months before, Stalin had assured both Byrnes and Bevin that the Soviet Union had no claims or designs (territorial or otherwise) against Iran, and that he had no intention of infringing upon the sovereignty of Iran. The crisis over Iran had then illustrated the negligible value of Stalin's postwar assurances. As Maxim Litvinov disclosed to Richard Hottelet in June, the Soviet Union had returned to a concept of geographical security. Goodwill, moreover, would be ineffective in meeting the Soviets' security needs since one demand would only follow the satisfaction of another. Within the Soviet Union, attempts to change Soviet policies were equally futile because public opinion had no voice in a totalitarian regime.[152]

In the month prior to this disclosure, President İnönü of Turkey saw the world situation growing darker than he had foreseen a year before. Russian threats had forced the continued mobilization of Turkey's 500,000 man army, a fact which resulted in widespread discontent. In 1946 military needs would require 38 percent of the country's budget. The following year promised no letup; it was expected that national defense expenditures would total 31 percent of a £100.7 million budget. While the British continued to help the Turks, as they had the Greeks, Britain's financial problems were forcing her to reconsider her position in the Eastern Mediterranean. As the British ambassador attempted to inspire confidence in the value of the Anglo-Turkish Alliance, and to uphold what was left of British prestige, NEA was attempting to advance badly needed credits to the Turks.[153]

Secretary of State Byrnes, because of the department's awakened interest in the countries of the Northern Tier, was now well posted on Turkey's situation.[154] In June Ambassador Smith in the Soviet Union alerted Byrnes to the fact that the Soviets had again renewed their war

[152] FR, 1946, VI:736, 763-765; 1945, II:687, 689. For subsequent promises by Stalin that he had no intention of attacking Turkey, see FR, 1946, VII:836. As even the Pope would observe, Stalin, like Hitler, frequently gave assurances of his peace-loving intentions. FR, 1946, VI:795.

[153] Howard, Turkey, the Straits and U.S. Policy, p. 242; FR, 1945, II:691; Kelly, p. 337; E. R. Lingeman, Turkey: Economic and Commercial Conditions in Turkey (London, 1948), pp. 16, 18; FR, 1946, VII:7-10, 809-810, 899-911; S.D. 867.51/11-2346, tel. no. 1208 indicates that national defense expenditures were thought to be as high as 60 percent of the country's budget—if one included the burden of servicing and amortizing debts and credits, along with the drain of mobilization on the labor supply. According to S.D. 867.51/12-1046, total U.S. loans and credits to Turkey totaled about $40 million by December 1946.

[154] See n. 111, above.

357

of nerves on Turkey. Later in the month, when the Soviets tried to lead the Turks into bilateral talks, Feridun Erkin read Wilson a memorandum of the Turkish prime minister's conversation with the Soviet ambassador. Wilson sent the memorandum to Byrnes, including Erkin's surmise that the Russians hoped to create a misunderstanding between Turkey and its Allies, and to exploit the situation that resulted.[155] Turkey's experience in 1945 and Iran's in 1946 clearly had made everyone suspicious of the manner in which the Soviets conducted negotiations.

Then, in early July, the Soviet ambassador was called back to Moscow for consultation. Erkin saw Vinogradov's departure as an indication that a Soviet initiative was in progress. This was a natural conclusion since the Montreux Convention was due automatically to be renewed for a five-year period on 9 November unless one of the signatories to the convention denounced it before 9 August.[156] Attempts to lead the Turks into bilateral discussions had proved fruitless. A denunciation of the convention appeared to be the next alternative, and such a course required preparation.

Events which took place in Moscow are largely unknown, although one abbreviated version has recently surfaced. According to Nikita Khrushchev, Lavrenti Beria played an important part in Russia's demands on Turkey because he was the only person able to advise Stalin on foreign policy. At one of the interminable suppers given by Stalin, Beria had been harping on the fact that the Soviet Union ought to demand the return of territories which once had been part of Georgia and Armenia. Beria, who like Stalin was a Georgian, kept bringing up the subject, teasing Stalin and goading him into doing something about it. Arguing that Turkey was weakened by World War II and would be unable to resist such demands, he convinced Stalin that now was the time to get those countries back. Stalin, of course, was familiar with the territorial question, having himself negotiated the frontier between Turkey and the Soviet Union in 1921. In his capacity as Com-

---

[155] FR, 1946, VII:823, 825-827. When the Soviet Union began playing on the sentiments of Kurdish nationalism, the State Department became concerned not so much about the Kurds of Turkey as about the Kurds of Iraq (S.D. 867.00/4-446/6-1746/6-1946). The Turks were more concerned about the French Communist Party's support for Russian claims to Kars and Ardahan (S.D. 760J.67/7-1146/7-1546). See S.D. 867.00/6-1946 for an analysis of Turkey's Kurdish problem.

[156] Erkin, pp. 338-343; Kirk, *The Middle East 1945-1950*, p. 31.

missar for Nationalities, he had agreed that if Turkey would sacrifice Batum, Russia would sacrifice the area near Kars.[157]

As Khrushchev tells it, Stalin gave in to Beria and sent an official memorandum to the Turkish government pressing Russia's territorial claims. It seems likely that the memorandum Khrushchev had in mind was one dated 7 August and handed to the Turks the following day— the day before the deadline for denouncing the Montreux Convention. Territorial demands in Eastern Turkey were omitted from the memorandum, and it is probable that in searching his memory Khrushchev confused earlier unwritten demands with the later official memorandum. His account, however, rings true insofar as it concerns what may have motivated Stalin's policies. The Straits, as always, were foremost in Russia's thoughts. But territorial questions, while they were omitted, were much in Stalin's mind. In addition, satisfaction of Soviet demands might well have led to a situation where such territorial demands would have been satisfied, for they included a number of propositions which were equally ominous—particularly when accompanied by the familiar propaganda barrage as well as by renewed Soviet troop movements along Turkey's frontiers with Russia and Bulgaria.[158] In conjunction with the uneasy situation in Iran, and the tense atmosphere in the Balkans, the Soviet note set the stage for a drastic revision of American policy toward the Northern Tier.

The Turkish Crisis and Its Ramifications

On 7 August the Soviet Union gave the United States a copy of its note to Turkey. The note asserted that the Montreux Convention did not meet the security interests of the Black Sea Powers, and proposed a new regime at the Straits based on five principles.[159] The first

[157] *Khrushchev Remembers: The Last Testament* (Boston, 1974), pp. 295-296; FR, 1946, VII:816-817. Apparently, Khrushchev's memoirs have been authenticated by voice prints.

[158] Erkin, p. 346; it was estimated in Washington that the Russians had 190,000 troops in Transcaucasia and 90,000 in Bulgaria. Reliable information also indicated that raiding parties had penetrated into Turkish territory to test Turkish reaction, while the Soviet Black Sea Fleet from mid-June to the end of August held maneuvers based on a port 45 miles from the Turkish frontier. This situation led the Turkish General Staff to suspect a real Soviet attack. In September and October, they held a general mobilization disguised as maneuvers, withdrawing their forces from Kars to a position east of Erzurum. Kirk, *The Middle East 1945-1950*, p. 33.

[159] FR, 1946, VII:827-829, 833-834. For a more detailed discussion of this and

three of these principles were in line with those the United States had set forth in its note of 2 November 1945.[160] Principles 4 and 5, however, departed radically from any previous understanding and were in many respects similar to Molotov's demands of November 1940.[161] The fourth principle called for the establishment of a regime on the Straits under the competence of Turkey and other Black Sea Powers. The fifth principle called for a joint Turco-Soviet system of defense for the Straits—a system which implicitly contained the idea of Soviet bases.

Three days later Ambassador Wilson cabled the State Department to tell of Turkish concern. He believed that the timing of the note (delivered just prior to the 9 August deadline for revision of the convention) was an attempt to confuse the issues involved. Wilson again stressed that the Straits question was a pretext for Soviet domination of Turkey. He saw Turkish independence as vital to American interests in blocking Russia's advance to the Persian Gulf and Suez Canal. The Turks, he said, represented a great asset to the stability of the Middle East, and this asset should not be frittered away.[162]

In view of the magnitude of the issues involved, the Departments of State, War, and Navy all studied the situation. Henderson had recommended to Acheson that the Soviets be warned before they took steps from which they could not retreat. Acheson discussed these matters with high administration officials, impressing upon his colleagues that the note he had in mind would not be a bluff, and that it required certainty of American support in the event that Turkey were attacked. On 15 August, they agreed upon and presented to the president a memorandum prepared by NEA on Turkey and the Soviet Union.[163]

The Soviet Union's primary objective, the memorandum said, was to obtain control of Turkey. If such control were obtained through the ostensible purpose of enforcing joint control of the Straits, it would

---

other notes in the exchange over the Straits, see Howard, *Turkey, the Straits and U.S. Policy*, pp. 242-260; Helseth, pp. 348-370.

[160] See Chapter IV, n. 148.

[161] Howard, *Turkey, the Straits and U.S. Policy*, p. 240. See Chapters I-IV for further discussion of these demands.

[162] FR, 1946, VII:836-838. For the Turkish desk officer's analysis, see S.D. 767.68119/8-746.

[163] Ibid., p. 838; S.D. 767.68119/8-746; Acheson, pp. 195-196; United States Army, P & O Div., National Archives, Washington, D.C., File No. 092TS, case No. 76/5; Millis, pp. 191-192; Feis, *From Trust to Terror*, pp. 181-183. For NEA's role in the memorandum, see: transcript, Loy Henderson Oral History Interview, 14 June, 15 July 1973, pp. 233-236, Truman Library.

be difficult for the United States to prevent the Soviet Union from obtaining control of the whole Near and Middle East—the territory lying between the Mediterranean and India. Past experience suggested that when the Soviet Union obtained predominance in an area, all Western influence was gradually eliminated. Since the United States had vital resources and communications interests in the area, the memorandum asserted, it was in the vital interest of the United States that the Soviet Union should not by force or through the threat of force succeed in its unilateral plan with regard to the Straits and Turkey.[164]

The formal proposal for bilateral agreement was unfortunate, the memorandum went on, because the Soviet Union once fully committed on a subject was difficult to persuade otherwise. An appeal to reason was insufficient. The only thing which would deter the Russians would be the conviction that the United States was prepared, if necessary, to meet aggression with force of arms. Belligerency, however, was not the intent of such resolution. Rather, it was that—given a clear understanding of American determination to support Turkey—the Soviet Union would pause and not push the matter further.

The secretaries of war and navy and the acting secretary of state believed that the United States should resist with all the means at its disposal any Soviet aggression against Turkey. They rejected any notion of using threats or provocations in pursuing this course of action, and agreed that the United Nations was the forum within which support for Turkey would be channeled. But they were determined that in the event the United Nations was unsuccessful in stopping Soviet aggression, the United States would join other nations in meeting armed aggression by the force of arms.[165]

Dean Acheson presented the memorandum to the president and discussed the background of the Soviet note. The "trial balloon," he said, should be firmly resisted. At the same time, the president should realize that if the Soviet Union did not back down and if the United States maintained its attitude, the situation might lead to armed conflict. After conducting a thorough discussion of the problem and pondering a map on his desk, the president replied that he was certain the United

---

[164] For an indication of American oil interests, see United States Army, P & O Div., 463.7, JLPC, 33/38, Joint Logistics Plans Committee report on "Oil Resources in the Bahrein-Trucial Oman Area," which estimated oil reserves in the region to be between 25 and 50 billion barrels. For a diagram showing the location of oil fields and refineries in the Middle East, see Annex "A" to Appendix "A" of that report.

[165] FR, 1946, VII:840-842.

States should take a firm position. Americans might as well find out whether the Russians were bent on world conquest now as in five or ten years, and he was prepared to pursue the recommended policy "to the end."

A note explaining the American attitude was prepared for dispatch to Ankara, and when it was ready Truman directed Acheson to have Ambassador Wilson tell the Turkish leaders orally that it had been formulated only after full consideration of the matter at the highest levels. Wilson was also instructed to tell the Turks that their reply to the Soviet government should be reasonable, but firm. The note which Wilson gave to the Turkish government reaffirmed American adherence to its note of 2 November 1945, and rejected the fourth and fifth principles of the Soviet note. It also reaffirmed the belief that the Straits should be administered under the principles of the United Nations, and expressed America's willingness to participate in a conference to revise the Montreux Convention.[166]

After consulting with British and Turkish officials, the State Department on 19 August sent a note to the Soviet Union which basically reiterated its position of 2 November 1945. The note expressed the view that the regime of the Straits was of concern to other powers besides those of the Black Sea, and that it could not agree with the Soviet Union's fourth proposal. As for the fifth proposal, the note emphasized that Turkey should continue to be primarily responsible for defense of the Straits, and warned that an attack on the Straits would clearly be a matter for the Security Council.[167] A British note of 21 August expressed similar views, while a Turkish note of 22 August answered the Soviet charges in detail, refuting allegations that Turkey had not enforced the Convention.[168]

[166] Acheson, pp. 195-196; Harry S. Truman, 2:96-97; Millis, p. 192; FR, 1946, VII:840-844. For the importance that Truman gave to this decision, see Chapter VI, n. 113. For the Turkish foreign minister's appreciation of the note, see FR, 1946, VII:846-847. Peter Lyon, Eisenhower: Portrait of a Hero (Boston, 1974), p. 382, points out that a number of accounts erroneously mention Eisenhower as being present at this meeting. Acheson, while in error on this matter, is nonetheless correct in recalling that Eisenhower was apprehensive lest Soviet occupation of the Dardanelles cause a war. Forrestal Papers, Forrestal Diaries, pp. 1217-1218.

[167] FR, 1946, VII:847-848; Howard, Turkey, the Straits, and U.S. Policy, p. 246.

[168] The Turkish note emphasized the fact that Soviet complaints were not opposed to the legal basis of the convention; rather, they were directed against technical provisions related to the specification of naval auxiliaries and other outdated or inadequate categories which permitted fraud by the Axis Powers. Like the British and

While the Soviet war of nerves with Turkey continued,[169] a second U.S. transport was shot down over Yugoslavia and a brief crisis ensued. Secretary of the Navy Forrestal, apprehensive about the government's capacity to meet sudden emergencies, felt that the tone of American notes to Yugoslavia required that the administraton evaluate what it had to back them up with. Reinforcing this desire for an evaluation of American strength in the Mediterranean was a memorandum from the Joint Chiefs of Staff to the secretaries of war and navy, furnishing their views on the military implications of the Straits question.[170]

The memorandum, dated 23 August, noted that bases on the Straits were ineffective as a defense unless military dominance were extended several hundred miles in all directions. The same logic used to justify the Soviet note of 7 August could be used to justify further Soviet penetration of the Aegean. It was the opinion of the Joint Chiefs of Staff that Turkey was "the most important military factor in the Eastern Mediterranean and the Middle East." The Joint Chiefs saw many indications of "a calculated Soviet policy of expanding Soviet *de facto* geographical political control," with serious impact on the vital interests of the United States. While they believed that British interests were more critical than those of the United States, they suggested that the United States would greatly improve Turkey's military situation if it gave the Turks permission to buy military equipment, and supplied them with technical assistance.

---

the Americans, the Turks accepted the first three proposals as a basis for discussion, but rejected the fourth and fifth as ignoring the interests of other signatories and as being incompatible with Turkey's security and sovereignty. *FR*, 1946, VII:838-840, 842, 850-855; Howard, *The Problem of the Turkish Straits*, pp. 50-55; *Turkey, the Straits and U.S. Policy*, pp. 246-248. On 24 August, probably to confuse the issue in the Balkans and perhaps in reaction to American and British notes on the Straits, the Ukrainian SSR sent a note to the Security Council charging that Greek policies constituted a danger to peace and security in the Balkans, and that the principal factor in Greek policies was the presence of British troops in Greece. The debate that ensued would run on until 20 September, when the Soviet Union vetoed a U.S. proposal to appoint a three-man fact-finding commission, and the case was taken off the agenda. Xydis, *Greece and the Great Powers*, pp. 285-289, 325-355; *FR*, 1946, VII:194-221.

[169] *FR*, 1946, VII:773; *New York Times*, 12 August 1946; Kirk, *The Middle East, 1945-1950*, p. 31; Howard, *Turkey, the Straits and U.S. Policy*, p. 247; see also L. Rovinsky, "Documents on Turkey's Foreign Policy," *New Times* 16 (15 August 1946):26-30, which cites captured German documents allegedly proving a Turkish conspiracy with Germany against the Russians in 1941-43.

[170] Kirk, p. 33; *New York Times*, 18-19 August 1946; Curry, pp. 246-247; Helseth, pp. 358-359; Acheson, p. 196; Millis, pp. 195-197; *FR*, 1946, VII:857-858.

The secretary of war and acting secretary of the navy concurred with the JCS memorandum, and forwarded it to Acheson, who was still acting secretary of state in Byrnes's absence. Acheson, of course, was fully aware of the gravity of the situation. After the decision of 15 August, he had talked off the record to 18 newsmen, emphasizing to them individually that the matter was serious, that it should not be played up sensationally,[171] and that Turkey and not control of the Straits was at issue. Privately, Loy Henderson in talks with the British minister John Balfour in Washington, and H. Freeman Matthews in conversation with the British delegation to the Council of Foreign Ministers in Paris, had been less restrained. They felt the British had been displaying a certain lack of firmness in meeting Soviet challenges at the Straits, just as they had done when facing the Iranian crisis. Hoping to strengthen British resolve, Henderson and Matthews both took pains to stress American resolution and to dwell upon the seriousness with which the United States was viewing the Soviet attitude toward Turkey. Both cited Truman's statement of 15 August that the United States was prepared to pursue its policy "to the end." In Henderson's mind, this helped to convince the British that Americans were not taking lightly Soviet ambitions with regard to the Straits. It also encouraged the British to believe that the United States was prepared to assume a greater responsibility in the Near East and the Balkans.[172]

On 20 August, the British ambassador, Lord Inverchapel, told Dean Acheson that the American view of the Turkish situation had created "quite a bit of excitement" in London, and asked if the United States were prepared to resort to war if necessary to maintain its position. Acheson carefully went over the background of the decision and the problems relating to such a commitment in the conduct of American foreign policy. He did not, however, deny the seriousness with which his government viewed the situation. The British ambassador in Ankara, meanwhile, discovering that his government was unable to modernize

[171] Jonathan Knight, "American Statecraft and the 1946 Black Sea Straits Controversy," *Political Science Quarterly* 90 (Fall 1975):451-475, correctly argues that the adminstration's policy on the Straits crisis was restrained. Force as policy was emerging as a cornerstone of American postwar policy, but in a context which placed persuasion before provocation.

[172] H. Freeman Matthews was director of the Office of European Affairs, serving temporarily as political advisor to the United States delegation at the Council of Foreign Ministers in Paris. *FR*, 1946, VII:849-850, 856-857; Acheson, pp. 195-196; United States Army, P & O Div., 092TS Case No. 67, 20 August; letter from Loy Henderson to the author.

the Turkish Army, suggested that the British explain the situation to the Americans and recommended that the American government undertake the project.[173] Subsequent developments would lead to a private arrangement between the United States and Great Britain. For the time being, events relating to the Near East would receive a more public hearing.

On 6 September as the Soviets gave their support in Paris to earlier Bulgarian requests for restitution of Western Thrace to Bulgaria, and as the public debate raging over the Ukrainian complaint against Greece in the Security Council in New York took a brief respite,[174] Secretary of State Byrnes was in Stuttgart, Germany, delivering an address which essentially recognized the division of Germany and expressed America's intent to maintain its position in Europe.[175]

American resolution, however, was called into question six days later when Secretary of Commerce Henry Wallace gave a speech which was interpreted as an attack on the secretary of state's policies.[176] With implicit reference to Churchill's speech at Fulton, Missouri, Wallace struck out against Britain's "imperialistic policy" in the Near East, a policy which he said would lead the United States straight to war unless it had a clearly defined and realistic policy of its own. He criticized a "get tough with Russia" policy and said he believed cooperation was possible once Russia understood that America's primary objective was "neither saving the British Empire nor purchasing oil in the Near East with the lives of American soldiers." His solution was for the United States to recognize a Soviet sphere of influence in Eastern Europe just as it expected the Soviet Union to recognize that of the United States in Latin America. This he thought the United States should do while insisting on the Open Door for trade throughout the world.[177]

Wallace had cleared this speech with Truman, who scanned parts of

[173] FR, 1946, VII:849-850; Kelly, pp. 328-329.

[174] See n. 168.

[175] FR, 1946, III:203-204, 380; *United Nations Security Council Official Records, 1st Year, Series 2 (Meetings 50-88)* (New York, 1946); Department of State *Bulletin* 15 (15 September 1946):496-501; Harriman and Abel, p. 552; Curry, pp. 299 ff.

[176] As far back as March, at the time of Bedell Smith's appointment as ambassador to Moscow, Wallace had attempted to effect a new approach to the Soviet Union. Truman had ignored him, but had not kept him from speaking out on foreign policy issues. Curry, pp. 249-254; Harry S. Truman, 1:555-560; Byrnes, *All in One Lifetime*, pp. 365-370.

[177] Byrnes Papers, Folder 619; Truman Papers, PSF, Box 84, "Teletype Conference," 19 September 1946.

it, but who undoubtedly had not scrutinized the parts on the Near and Middle East; otherwise, he would have agreed with Loy Henderson and others who gathered in the office of Acting Secretary of State Will Clayton (Acheson was on vacation). They concluded that if the speech had the president's endorsement, the policy which they had been trying to establish for the past year would be repudiated. In Europe, certainly, many thought that the administration was divided and that further concessions might be made to the Soviets, and as a consequence Byrnes was angered by Wallace's inference that American policies were anything but patient and firm. Analysis of the secretary of state's policies in the Near East justifies his indignation on this issue. He was alarmed, moreover, because of the effects of Wallace's speech on the countries of the Northern Tier.[178]

On the same day that Wallace spoke, Will Clayton wrote Byrnes a long letter, enclosing the JCS memorandum of 23 August. In view of the Soviet Union's apparent attempts to undermine stability in and obtain control of Greece, Turkey, and Iran, Clayton wondered whether the United States should revise its general policies toward these countries. They needed military equipment to strengthen their defenses. Refusal to sell them such equipment might undermine their confidence in the United States and weaken their resolve to resist Soviet pressures. A new supply policy was in order. In addition, State, War, and Navy felt that the United States should emphasize its interest in the independence and integrity not only of Turkey (because of the 15 August decision), but also of Greece and Iran.[179]

As the Wallace affair broke, Byrnes had not yet received this letter. But he was sensitive to the same concerns as Clayton. In a teletype conversation with Truman on 19 September, Byrnes referred specifically to disquieting telegrams he had received from American representatives in Greece and Turkey, and told Truman that the bipartisan policy which they had built, and which had appeared permanent and reliable, had been destroyed in a day. As a result of this conversation, the presi-

[178] This analysis of the Wallace affair is based on: Byrnes, *Speaking Frankly*, pp. 239-242; *All in One Lifetime*, pp. 370-376; Margaret Truman, pp. 344-349; Harry S. Truman, 1:555-560; Curry, pp. 252-274; Norman Markowitz, *The Rise and Fall of the People's Century: Henry A. Wallace and American Liberalism, 1941-1948* (New York, 1973), pp. 178-199; Millis, pp. 206-210; Donovan, pp. 222-228. For the affect of Wallace's speech on Iran, see Chapter VI, n. 2.

[179] FR, 1946, VII:209-213.

dent on 20 September asked for and obtained Wallace's resignation. At the same time he gave Byrnes's policies a ringing endorsement.[180]

Bolstered by his success in this bureaucratic battle, and deeply concerned about the situation developing in the Near East, the secretary of state discussed Turkey with Bevin on 21 September. Bevin, needless to say, shared Byrnes's concerns. After the Iranian crisis, Prime Minister Attlee and Chancellor of the Exchequer Dalton had been anxious to withdraw British forces from Greece and bring the United States in as a partner in the Eastern Mediterranean. This explains Britain's great excitement about the 15 August decision. That same month, perhaps after hearing associates say that the United States would resist Soviet pressures at the Straits "to the end," the British ambassador in Turkey, Sir David Kelly, suggested that the United States be brought into partnership with Britain in Turkey as well. A growing belief that the United States and Britain should engage in combined military planning was reinforced after the 1 September plebiscite in Greece indicated overwhelming opposition to the KKE, if not support for the king, and set the stage for British withdrawal. Discussions of combined planning nonetheless proceeded slowly until Field Marshal Bernard Montgomery arrived in the United States on 10 September. On 16 September he talked with the American Chiefs of Staff (Admirals Leahy and Nimitz, Generals Eisenhower and Spaatz) and reached agreement that discussions should begin as soon as possible on Western strategy in the event of a third world war. Of special interest to Montgomery was that when he asked the American Chiefs of Staff what value they attributed to Middle East oil, they replied immediately and unanimously: vital. Four days later, debates over Greece in the Security Council ended, and Wallace resigned. On the following day, Byrnes was discussing Turkey with Bevin.[181]

[180] See n. 178, above. See also *New York Times*, 18-21 September 1946; Leahy Diaries, entry for 18 September 1946; Howard, *Turkey, the Straits and U.S. Policy*, p. 253; for Truman's indignation over Wallace's attitude toward Iran, see Margaret Truman, pp. 346-347. For Stalin's attempt to capitalize on the Wallace affair, see *FR*, 1946, VI:784-787.

[181] See n. 141 and n. 172, above; *FR*, 1946, VII:204-207, 223-224; Kelly, pp. 328-329; Bernard Montgomery, *The Memoirs of Field Marshal the Viscount Montgomery of Alamein* (New York, 1958), pp. 391-396. For further information on the plebiscite, see Kousoulas, "The Greek Communists Tried Three Times —and Failed," pp. 304-307; Stavrianos, *Greece*, p. 175; McNeill, *The Greek Dilemma*, p. 246, who attributes royalist support to the escalation of guerilla warfare,

In the course of their conversation, the foreign ministers agreed that it was Britain's duty to supply military equipment directly not only to Turkey, but to Greece and Iran as well, and that if Britain failed to do so the United States would.[182] On 24 September, Byrnes wired Clayton about his conversation with Bevin, instructing him on the necessity of closely coordinating U.S. policies with the British. He was thinking especially about Turkey and Greece, assistance to whom he felt was of the highest importance. He had just read a revised version of the 23 August JCS memorandum on the military implications of the situation in Turkey, and was aware that the strategic importance of Greece was equally great.[183]

The day after Byrnes sent this telegram to Clayton, the acting secretary read it to a State-War-Navy meeting attended by Secretaries Patterson and Forrestal. They strongly endorsed Byrnes's views, and, on Forrestal's insistence, made less restrictive a State Department draft on military assistance to foreign countries. Under Henderson's prodding, Clayton then decided to draw up new outlines of policy on Turkey, Greece, and Iran, and proposed to Byrnes that they go beyond the military assistance covered by the JCS memo to include political and

---

and S.D. 868.00/9-946/9-1346/10-1046/12-546. Final tabulations showed 1,900,613 Greeks registered to vote, of whom 1,484,748 voted on the basis of their registration and 179,701 on the basis of special identification—or a total of 1,664,449. The king received 1,135,492 votes; 525,005 were opposed; 3,847 were invalid, and 105 were empty. Of those ballots opposed to the king, 343,500 were left blank, 182,-310 were marked "democracy," and 195 bore other political slogans. Since not all persons voting by special identification were required to register, the percentage of eligible voters voting was less than 87.5 percent. Of these, the king received 68.3 percent. During the voting, 94 observer teams visited 625 of 3,523 voting places. Of these, one-third permitted practices in violation of the law, while secret voting was not practiced in 10 percent of the places. As Lincoln MacVeagh wrote the secretary of state in December: "Probably the returns from the plebiscite show that a majority of the voters (all due allowances being made for disturbances at the polls and intimidation both by the right and left) desired, on September 1, the return of King George. But they cannot be made to mean anything more than this."

[182] Byrnes informed Acheson of this agreement on 5 October (FR, 1946, VII:245). The understanding between Bevin and Byrnes was further clarified by a discussion between Byrnes and Britain's minister of defense, Albert Alexander, on 15 October. Byrnes felt it best for the United States not to supply Greece and Turkey with military equipment because of potential charges of aggressive intentions on the part of the United States. Alexander told him of Britain's heavy expenditures in Greece and Turkey and the British desire to reduce expenditures as much as possible. He also promised to communicate further information regarding assistance to Greece and Turkey. FR, 1946, VII:913-915.

[183] FR, 1946, VII:223-224, 245.

economic considerations. Clayton enclosed a draft outline of policy toward Greece in his letter to Byrnes and noted that similar papers on Turkey and Iran were being prepared. Within a month they would be complete and by the first week of November they would all have the secretary's endorsement.[184]

The need for economic and military assistance in all three countries was increasingly apparent, as was American determination to do something about it. Symbolic of this determination was a major report prepared by Clark Clifford and his assistant George Elsey which Clifford gave to the president on 24 September. The report placed great emphasis on Stalin's speech of 9 February 1946 and quoted at length from Kennan's telegram of 22 February 1946. Its assumptions about Soviet policies followed from these documents: the Soviets believed conflict inevitable; their aim was to prepare for this conflict by increasing their power. The memorandum described how the United States had sought throughout World War II to reach understandings with the Soviets, and how the Soviets had violated the spirit of nearly all the agreements which had been reached. Iran was but one clear example. With respect to Soviet foreign policy in the Near East, the memorandum noted Soviet interest in obtaining the withdrawal of British troops and establishing a "friendly" government in Greece; Soviet hopes of making Turkey a puppet state which could serve as a springboard for the domination of the Eastern Mediterranean; and Soviet wishes to continue indirect control of Azerbaijan and northern Iran. It also observed that the Soviet Union's long-range aim was the economic, military, and political domination of the entire Middle East.[185]

[184] Millis, p. 210; Forrestal Diaries, p. 1274; FR, 1946, VII:225-226; for the draft outline of policy toward Greece, see P & O Div., 092TS Case No. 78, 6 September 1946 memo by Colonel James McCormack, Jr.; for the policy statements on Greece, Turkey, and Iran, see FR, 1946, VII:240-245, 894-897, 529-536.

[185] On 10 March, at the height of the Iranian crisis, William Bullitt expressed to Forrestal and Leahy the need to have a small group evaluate U.S. policies vis-à-vis the Soviet Union, with particular reference to American commitments. In early July, not long after the Iranian crisis, and possibly as a result of Bullitt's advice, Truman told his special counsel, Clark Clifford, that he was tired of being pushed around. The Soviets were "chiseling" from the United States, "here a little, there a little," and he felt that the time had come to take a stand. As a consequence, he asked Clifford to conduct a comprehensive study of American-Soviet relations which he could use as a basis for future policy decisions. Clifford, in an interview with the author, opined that the Iranian crisis might well have led Truman to initiate the study. Whatever the reason, Clifford, with his assistant

In an assessment similar to that reached by Loy Henderson in the thirties, Clifford and Elsey believed that there were limits to the relations one could have with the Soviet Union. If it were impossible to enlist Soviet cooperation in world problems, the United States should be prepared to join with Britain and other countries in an attempt to build a world which would pursue its own objectives, recognizing the Soviet orbit as a distinct entity with which conflict was not predestined but with which it could not pursue common aims. Echoing Kennan and others who had dealt with the Soviets, Clifford and Elsey asserted that the language of military power was the only language which the disciples of power politics understood. Compromises and concessions only encouraged the Soviets to make new and greater demands, for they believed that governments willing to compromise and make concessions were merely showing weakness.

This line of reasoning led Clifford and Elsey to the conclusion that the main deterrent to Soviet attacks on areas vital to the security of the United States would be military power. In addition, the United States should support and assist all democratic countries endangered by the Soviet Union. But military support in case of attack was a last resort; economic support was a more effective barrier to Communism. This course required that the American public be fully informed about the difficulties of Soviet-American relations, for only a well-informed public would support the stern policies which Soviet activities made imperative. The memorandum ended with an expression of hope that the Soviet leaders would abandon their belief that the conflict between Capitalism and Communism was irreconcilable, and that the Russians

---

George Elsey, consulted the secretaries of State, War, and the Navy; Admiral Leahy; the JCS; the Director of Central Intelligence; and others, like George Kennan, with special knowledge on the subject. These men prepared careful estimates of Soviet actions, and made recommendations concerning American policy which Elsey, with Clifford's guidance, collated and structured into a coherent report. Clifford on 24 September laid one of twenty bound copies of the 25,000-word report on Truman's desk. Discussion of Clifford's background and his memorandum is based on: an interview with Clark Clifford; Millis, pp. 143-144; Joseph Goulden, *The Superlawyers* (New York, 1972), pp. 72-87; Margaret Truman, pp. 378-380; Arthur Krock, *Memoirs: Sixty Years on the Firing Line* (New York, 1968), pp. 224-231, 417-482 (an appendix which contains the entire memorandum); George Elsey Papers, Truman Library, Box 63; Clark Clifford Papers, Truman Library, Box 15; transcript, George M. Elsey Oral History Interview, Truman Library. Copies of the Clifford study at the Truman Library indicate that 20 copies were made.

would work out a settlement with the United States when they realized the United States was too strong to be beaten and too determined to be frightened.

Truman stayed up late that night reading the memorandum, and on the morning of 25 September called Clifford to his office. The president asked him how many copies of the report existed, and when Clifford told him twenty Truman instructed him to get the rest of them and put them into a safe. As Clifford later recalled, Truman said the report was so hot that if it became known it would blow the roof right off the White House.

Meanwhile, the need for assistance to Iran, Turkey, and Greece grew greater every day. In Iran another crisis seemed to be building. In Greece, Ambassador Lincoln MacVeagh's reports were depicting an increasingly grim picture of the Greek predicament. In Turkey, shortly after midnight on 24 September, the Soviets delivered still another note on the question of the Straits.[186]

The exchange of views on the Straits which now took place was more subdued than that of August. The decision by the United States to stand firm had been implemented; policies for Greece, Turkey, and Iran, which would reflect attitudes expressed in the Clifford memorandum, were being defined. As a consequence, the exchange of views would serve only to reinforce the earlier positions of the Western Allies. The United States and Britain had to be prepared for any occasion which might seem propitious for Soviet initiatives. The process of preparation would give further impetus to collaboration between Britain

---

[186] While MacVeagh acknowledged that there was no conclusive proof of Soviet complicity in Greece's problems, as there was in the problems of Iran and Turkey, he believed that the Soviet government was ultimately responsible for Greece's continued strife. He drew this conclusion from Soviet influence over the KKE and anti-Greek propaganda emanating from Moscow. Without a revision in the policy pursued by Greece's northern neighbors, he did not see how the situation could improve. This analysis was particularly gloomy in light of recent announcements by the British of their gradual military withdrawal from Greece (Acheson, p. 199; FR, 1946, VII:208-209, 226-232, 860-866). Ronald Hingley, *Joseph Stalin: Man and Legend* (New York, 1975), pp. 387-388, deems it likely that Andrei Zhdanov wanted to give all-out support to Communist partisans in Greece. Zhdanov, in his capacity as Stalin's temporary handler-in-chief of the Eastern European satellites, may well have been able to support the Greek Communists for a while, but eventually seems to have clashed with Stalin over this issue. Stalin's admonitions to Edvard Kardelj, vice-premier of Yugoslavia, in February 1948, do not preclude the possibility of a temporary Zhdanov-Tito axis directed against Stalin. See also Djilas, *Conversations with Stalin*, pp. 181-183, and n. 17, above.

and the United States on the matter of assistance to the countries of the Northern Tier.

The Soviet note of 24 September was addressed only to the Turkish government. A reiteration of earlier arguments, it directed the Turks' attention to the fourth and fifth proposals made in the Soviet note of 7 August, and called for direct conversations between Turkey and the Soviet Union prior to convening an international conference for revision of the Montreux Convention.[187]

The Turks considered this note to be much more clever and insidious than the previous one. They had reliable evidence that Litvinov had been brought out of a recent retirement to draft it, and were convinced that its focus on direct conversations could be a trap which would lead only to confusion and misunderstanding.[188] The Turco-Soviet conversations of 1945 and the Iranian crisis of 1946 certainly had made this clear. As a consequence, Turkey sought the views of the United States and Britain which, like Turkey, wanted to maintain a cautious and non-provocative attitude.[189] After consultation, the three countries addressed separate but mutually supporting notes to the Soviet government.[190] The British and American notes, delivered to the Soviet Union on 9 October, reiterated the positions both countries had taken in August. A Turkish note, delivered on 18 October, recapitulated the Turkish government's earlier position, and again gave a detailed reply to Soviet allegations.[191]

[187] The Soviet note also justified excluding (from a future regime) non-Black Sea signatories to the present convention by the argument that the Black Sea was a "closed sea." It cited treaties which had been superseded as precedents for such a course of action. It justified a joint defense of the Straits by citing threats to Soviet security interests. It mentioned the passage through the Straits of the German cruisers *Goeben* and *Breslau* in 1914, and alleged that passage through the Straits contributed to military operations conducted against the Soviet Union in World War II. FR, 1946, VII:866-875; Howard, *Turkey, the Straits and U.S. Policy*, pp. 249-250; S.D. 767.68119/8-1946 (18 October 1946). For a discussion of the "closed sea" question, see Howard, pp. 252-253, and the references cited therein; for the State Department's thinking, see S.D. 767.68119/10-1046 CS/TJ. See also Chapter IV, n. 134.

[188] FR, 1946, VII:868, 878-879. See Chapter IV, n. 145.

[189] Ibid., pp. 870-871, 874-875, 878.

[190] Ibid., pp. 869-970, 893; S.D. 767.68119/10-246/10-346; 740.00119 Council/ 10-746.

[191] For the American note, see: FR, 1946, VII:873-875; Howard, *Turkey, the Straits and U.S. Policy*, pp. 250-251. For the British note, see: FR, 1946, VII: 876; and Howard, p. 251. For the Turkish note, see: FR, 1946, VII:879-893; and Howard, pp. 253-255. The Turkish note observed that the Montreux Conven-

The exchange of notes ended when the Soviet Union on 26 October informed Britain that it did not share the British view that direct conversations contemplated by the Potsdam Conference were complete. At the same time, it viewed as premature the calling of a conference to establish a new regime. The Turks, who expected the Soviets to keep the matter alive, instructed the new Turkish ambassador to the Soviet Union not to engage in any discussions on the question and, if proposals were made, to seek instructions.[192]

By the end of October, the Turkish crisis was over, and Soviet ambitions at the Straits once again were shelved.[193] But Soviet ambitions, even when dormant, were threatening. To confront this problem, the United States continued to develop its policies through bureaucratic channels, and the State Department to be concerned with assistance to the countries of the Northern Tier. The result was that diplomatic and military policies in Iran, Turkey, and Greece, as well as in the Mediterranean, were redefined and brought to bear on the issues at hand.

In the Mediterranean, naval operations were linked with American foreign policy on 1 October by a statement which, for the first time, formally established a Mediterranean force. The purpose of this force, the statement said, was to support the Allies in occupied Europe, to protect American interests and support American policies in the area, and to create good will.[194] By year's end, the Mediterranean command would include one aircraft carrier, three cruisers, and eight

---

tion already gave preferential treatment to the Black Sea Powers and refused to accept the argument regarding a "closed sea." The irrelevance of the German cruisers in World War I was noted, and it was further pointed out that the real threat to Soviet shores in World War II came not from the Black Sea, but from occupation of Russian territory by the German armies, from Rumanian and Bulgarian fleets, and from German and Italian ships sent to the Black Sea by rail or down the Danube.

[192] FR, 1946, VII:897-898; Howard, Turkey, the Straits and U.S. Policy, pp. 258-259. The Soviets never responded to the American note—perhaps because they did not wish to involve the United States in the discussion.

[193] In his memoirs, Feridun Erkin, then secretary general of the Turkish Foreign Ministry and later foreign minister, attributes the end of what he calls "one of the most vigorous diplomatic initiatives in history launched by Russia to obtain control of the Straits," to three factors: the resolution of the Turkish people, well-founded suspicions aroused by the premature divulgence of Soviet designs on the Straits, and the important role played by the United States, which the Soviets at first underestimated. Erkin, p. 369.

[194] Xydis, Greece and the Great Powers, pp. 357-359, 644, described this statement as a Mediterranean counterpart to Byrnes's Stuttgart speech.

destroyers, and the United States would be recognized as the dominant sea power in the Mediterranean, where naval air power combined with the potential of nuclear weapons to create a new strategic environment.[195]

On the heels of the reformulation of American naval policy in the Mediterranean came long, critically important policy statements on Greece, Turkey, and Iran. While these statements were grounded in the special needs of each country, the three statements taken together were closely related. To begin with, they all derived from the 15 August decision on the Straits and from the 23 August JCS memorandum. On a more abstract plane, they all placed symbolic value on the principle of support for the independence and territorial integrity of small countries. Underlying the question of principle was the usual complex of economic and strategic interests. The strategic situation of each country was related to that of the other. Iran, Turkey, and Greece constituted a bulwark which protected American interests in the Near and Middle East as a whole, the focal point of which was Middle East oil.

This marriage between principle and interest provided a convincing rationale for American foreign policy in the region. Under its aegis, a firm policy toward Soviet pressures was seen as a necessary deterrent to recent Soviet designs in the area. To support this policy, economic and military assistance were authorized. At the same time, emphasis was placed on the necessity of maintaining a low profile and not creating the impression that American policy was provocative.[196] For the time being, this emphasis would limit the extent to which the policies could be publicized and the American public informed of Soviet actions and United States interests in the region.

Turning now to the policies themselves, one can sense the gravity with which the administration regarded the recent history of the Northern Tier. The memorandum regarding Greece pictured that country as a focal point in international relations—its fate possibly a deciding factor in the future orientation of the Near and Middle East. It was the only country in the Balkans not yet subject to Soviet hegemony;

---

[195] The policy statement, written at Forrestal's direction, was cleared by the State Department and the White House. Millis, p. 211; Albion and Connery, p. 187; *New York Times*, 1 October 1946; Xydis, *Greece and the Great Powers*, pp. 357-359, 644, 715-716; Rogow, pp. 179-180; Knight, pp. 453-455.

[196] One result of the desire for a low profile was the administration's preference that Britain rather than the United States supply military assistance to Greece, Turkey, and Iran.

374

with Turkey, it formed the only obstacle to Soviet domination of the Eastern Mediterranean. Were Greece to fall victim to Soviet influence or aggression (delegated to Albania, Yugoslavia and Bulgaria), the Soviet Union would be able to exert irresistible pressure on Turkey, and the role of the United States as defender of the principles of the United Nations would be seriously damaged. British withdrawal from Greece would leave a weak government which would face serious problems maintaining internal order and defending its borders against hostile neighbors. In short, the Greek government's stability was questionable without external support. Economic and military assistance were necessary *before* rather than *during* a state of near civil war. In a covering letter, Loy Henderson noted that the critical Greek situation would require very close attention and active interest in the ensuing months.[197]

Another memorandum on Turkey described that country as the most important strategic factor in the Eastern Mediterranean and the Middle East. Recent events clearly indicated Soviet intentions to weaken Turkey, with the object of bringing it under the Soviet Union's direct influence. Were the Soviets to attain their objectives in Turkey even partially, Greece and Iran would be dangerously exposed. Like other nations which faced the spreading power of the Soviet Union, they would be influenced to come to terms with the Soviets and abandon support of the United States in its efforts to uphold the principles of the United Nations—a development which would considerably weaken America's security. Observing Turkey's will to resist Soviet pressures— with a unity nonexistent in Greece or Iran—and recognizing that Turkey possessed a relatively effective military force, the memorandum on Turkey pointed out that the Turks could not stand alone in the face of continued Soviet pressures. The Soviet war of nerves required the Turks to maintain a large military force which was a dangerous drain on their economy. For these reasons, the memorandum recommended that the United States give economic and military support to Turkey.[198]

The memoranda on Greece and Turkey outlined the strategic value

[197] The memorandum was dated 21 October, and was approved by the secretary of state approximately 1 November. *FR*, 1946, VII:240-245.

[198] The memorandum was dated 21 October, and was approved by the secretary of state and the undersecretary, probably in the first week of November. Interestingly enough, it was prepared by John Jernegan, who back in 1943 as a desk officer on Iran had drafted the Jernegan memorandum (see Chapter III), and who subsequently had served in Iran. *FR*, 1946, VII:894-897.

of the two countries and suggested supplying arms and munitions to them if Great Britain were unable to do so. On 30 October, Loy Henderson discussed these matters with British officials in Washington, confirming that inasmuch as Greece and Turkey were of strategic importance to the United States, his government was interested in information on the present state of their armed forces and on British assistance to them. Henderson also noted American concern for what would happen to Greece when UNRRA shipments ended on 1 April 1947. Financial assistance would be required, though it was not clear how this would be done. At the end of the discussion, Henderson observed that his government would be glad to consider the possibility of providing whatever military assistance the British were unable to supply.[199]

Dean Acheson sent the policy memoranda on Turkey and Greece to Ambassadors Wilson and MacVeagh on 8 November and the two diplomats were soon informing foreign officials of their principal ideas. Neither country should obtain the impression that support of its territorial integrity and independence was limited to words and that the United States was unwilling to run the risk of internal or international criticism arising from the supply of military equipment. At the same time, people in the United States and elsewhere should not obtain the impression that the United States was carrying out a provocative policy with regard to the Soviet Union. Acheson made clear that the American government preferred to have the British supply military equipment to both countries, but that it was willing to consider furnishing such supplies directly.[200]

Turning to the policy memorandum on Iran, one can find more clearly delineated some of the issues which dictated the strategic importance of the Northern Tier. On 12 October 1946, a memorandum from the JCS to the Department of State, answering a series of questions prepared by the department on United States strategic interests in Iran, noted that Iran was of major strategic interest to the United States.[201]

---

[199] FR, 1946, VII:913-915. On 28 October the secretary of state had come to the conclusion that Great Britain should furnish arms to Turkey and Greece; in the event that Britain required assistance, the United States would furnish Britain with the necessary arms. Ibid., p. 255.

[200] Ibid., pp. 262-263, 916-917.

[201] It may be remembered that the secretary of state, in his capacity as director of the Office of War Mobilization, in 1943 had been concerned with the government's acquisition of oil reserves in the Middle East. So had a number of other

376

The loss of Middle Eastern oil through Soviet domination of Iran would adversely affect American interests and military capabilities. Iran also was a "cushion" to Soviet advances in the Middle East, and one of the few favorable areas for counteroffensive action against the Soviet Union.[202] Thus, United States strategic interests in Iran were clearly related to its strategic interests in the Near and Middle East as a whole. This meant keeping Soviet influence and forces removed as far as possible from the oil resources of Iran, Iraq, and the Near and Middle East. It also meant opposing the notion of spheres of influence. Spheres of influence would facilitate Soviet operations to the south, nullify Britain's ability to protect its oil fields in the region, and constitute another step in the Soviet attempt to encircle Turkey. Assuming that the immediate security objective of the United States was to prevent civil disturbances which might invite intervention in Iran by the Soviet Union, so endangering American interests in the Persian Gulf, the JCS advocated acceding to the Iranian request for nonaggression items of military equipment.[203]

NEA, after considering the JCS memorandum, on 18 October completed its policy statement on Iran. Like the statements on Greece and Turkey, the memorandum on Iran characterized the problem as one of principle and strategic interests, and placed it in the broader context of American-Soviet relations. American interests, it said, required that the United States give positive encouragement and assistance to Iran if the country were to be saved from falling completely under Soviet domination and rescued from its partial subservience to the Soviet Union.[204]

In a long covering letter, Loy Henderson wrote Acheson that concrete acts were required to keep the Iranians from being discouraged

---

officers. For earlier American interest in the question of oil, see the section on "American Interests in the Near East" in Chapter III; Chapter IV; and Chapter V, n. 122. See also FR, 1946, I:1379-1383; VII:18-50; United States Army, P & O Div., 218 JCS Files, 463.7 JLCP 33/38, 22 October 1946 memorandum, and the appendix (Annex "A" to Appendix "A"), which graphically displays the War Department's knowledge of oil interests in the Middle East.

[202] This line of reasoning could have supported Soviet security concerns as well.

[203] For the JCS memorandum, see FR, 1946, VII:529-532. By "nonaggression" items the JCS meant: small arms and light artillery, ammunition, small tanks, transportation and communication equipment, quartermaster supplies, short-range aircraft, and naval patrol craft.

[204] FR, 1946, VII:535-536.

by Soviet pressures. Recent telegrams from Teheran indicated that the United States was faced with an extremely critical situation that might require quick action. In a few days, it was possible that the shah would remove Qavam and appoint a new prime minister. Moral support, economic assistance, and non-aggression military equipment were required.[205]

In the next chapter we will turn to the context of Iranian affairs which served as a background for the memorandum on Iran, and to another phase of the Iranian crisis which had begun almost a year before. Before doing so, however, it will be useful briefly to reflect on the events which led not only to the creation of an American naval force in the Mediterranean, but to the reformulation of American foreign policy along the entire Northern Tier.

Conclusion

Soviet maneuvering over Iran and Turkey in 1946 significantly influenced the development of American foreign policy during the early years of the cold war. The crisis in Iran crystallized the Truman administration's understanding of Soviet tactics. This understanding, in turn, conditioned the administration's reaction to Soviet notes delivered to Turkey in the fall of 1946. The crisis over Turkey, which set in motion the reformulation of American policies toward the Northern Tier countries, resulted in part from the administration's recognition of the United Nations' limitations, from its experience regarding the hazards of sanctioning bilateral diplomacy between the Soviet Union and its neighbors, and from its growing appreciation of firmness in dealing with the Soviet Union.

Declaring idealistic principles and expressing concern over Soviet intentions had proved ineffectual in moderating Soviet relations with Iran and Turkey in 1945, and direct negotiations between Iran and the Soviet Union had failed to solve the Iranian problem in 1946. The United States, unwilling to provide a guarantee to Iran and Turkey in 1945, was now giving all three Northern Tier countries "positive" encouragement and assistance, and in the event that the United Nations was unsuccessful in stopping Soviet aggression, the United States was prepared to meet armed aggression by the force of arms.

[205] FR, 1946, VII:533-535. The secretary of state also approved Henderson's suggestions that the United States attempt to meet Iran's requirements.

One can infer from Soviet policies toward the Northern Tier that the Soviet Union under Stalin was oriented toward the building and maintenance of its own strength, and that it was interested in expanding its spheres of influence—like any other imperialistic nation. It attempted to do so by deliberately risking diplomatic conflict with Britain and the United States, but stopping short when there was a threat of war. The Soviet regime was very well suited to such a course of action, and it counted on wearing down the resistance of more democratic and less easily managed governments. Soviet attitudes toward these governments were shaped by a tradition of distrust and suspicion. The extent to which this tradition manifested a profound problem inherent in the Soviet system, or reflected a realistic assessment of international politics, is a matter of conjecture; but that suspiciousness, any more than an insatiable desire for security, justified essentially imperialistic tendencies, cannot be accepted.

Accusations by the Soviets that certain elements in other nations were "hostile" and therefore dangerous to the Soviet Union are not convincing. There simply is no evidence that there were elements in Iran which were dangerous to the Soviet Union. Accusations that Turkey was too weak to protect the Straits are also not persuasive. Control of the Aegean was the crucial factor preventing Allied use of the waterway during World War II. New weapons, moreover, had changed the nature of warfare, making strategic control of the Bosporus at the Straits a red herring. What was really at issue was political influence over the Turkish government; control of the Straits, like the acquisition of the provinces of Kars and Ardahan, was a means to that end. In 1921 Stalin had been as much interested in issues relating to those provinces as he had been in supporting the Soviet Republic of Gilan in northern Iran. A quarter of a century later, time and Lavrenti Beria appeared only to have heightened that interest.

What, then, were the Soviets after? It seems certain that they sought to secure their southern flank, to rid that region of Anglo-American influence and at the same time acquire a springboard to the Eastern Mediterranean and the Middle East. In Iran, they exploited several of the opportunities which occupation afforded them with a view to controlling the government in Teheran. The annexation of Azerbaijan and oil concessions in northern Iran were both means to the same end. In Turkey, the Soviets were attempting through a war of nerves and constant pressure to annex Kars and Ardahan, control the Straits, and

379

ultimately control the government in Ankara. In both cases, the Soviets hoped either to incorporate the countries into their sphere of influence, or to establish "friendly governments"—friendly in the sense that they would work toward eliminating American and British influence, while becoming satellites of the Soviet Union.

Why, then, did the Soviets "back down" in Iran? An adequate explanation includes a number of important factors. The U.N. provided a useful forum for debate, and served to focus attention on the issues involved. It also provided a means of mobilizing opinion which the United States needed but which it appeared unable to manage on its own—at least in 1946. Far more important than the U.N., however, was the increasingly firm policy advocated by the United States. This factor is central to an explanation of Soviet withdrawal from Iran, although it must be considered in conjunction with two other explanations.

It is possible that when the Soviets evacuated Iran, they thought that most of their goals would be achieved. They were reasonably assured of being granted their oil concessions, and the puppet regimes in Azerbaijan and Mahabad appeared well established. Through them, perhaps, the long-run goals of making Iran and Turkey satellites of the Soviet Union were real possibilities. After all, the wily prime minister Ahmad Qavam seemed favorably disposed to the Soviets. Once Iran was under Soviet control, the Kurdish question could be used as a means of making inroads into Turkey. So could the claims of the Georgian and Armenian Soviet Socialist Republics. In retrospect, it may be that Qavam, as much as anyone, influenced their decision to withdraw from Iran. He could argue that under the law he was forbidden to negotiate concessions—only the Majlis could carry out such negotiations, and it was prohibited by law from making any concessions until the economic situation of Iran had been clarified. After 11 March, there was no Majlis; the only way for a new Majlis to be elected was for the Soviets to leave Iran. So stated an Iranian law passed in 1945. Why *not* leave, and accede to the pressures of the United States and international public opinion, if they could get almost everything they wanted anyway?

The other explanation of Soviet withdrawal from Iran relates to the Turkish question. If demands were being prepared for Turkey, why should the Soviets use obvious confrontation as the means of effecting their goals? Confrontation served only to mobilize Western opinion. There was also the danger that it would mobilize Western arms. Better to back off from heavy-handed policies and then turn to a calculated war of nerves through bilateral negotiations and other less visible diplomatic pressures. Long-run designs on the Northern Tier dictated getting out of Iran once the Soviet play there had been called. The Soviets apparently regarded the United Nations as a sham, and believed they could confuse both the Iranian and the Turkish questions by bringing up problems in Greece,[206] and by exercising heavy pressures on the governments with which they were "negotiating." In August and October their play had been called in Turkey as well, but not completely. Rather than revise the Montreux Convention they intended to wait for a more auspicious occasion on which to pressure the Turks.

Meanwhile, the United States had become conditioned to Soviet diplomatic maneuvering and had reassessed its policies toward the countries of the Northern Tier. Eight months earlier, on 21 February, the JCS argued that the United States should avoid a military commitment to American interests in the Near East other than through the United Nations because of geographic distances and the impracticability of assured lines of communication. The crisis over the 7 August note from the Soviet Union to Turkey changed this policy. The United Nations, of course, was still recognized as the most appropriate forum for channeling public support for Turkey, but it was the United States and not the United Nations that was prepared to meet aggression with force of arms.

The explanation for this change in American thinking lies in the total context of events which contributed to it: Soviet policies toward Turkey before, during, and after World War II; the Iranian crises of 1944 and 1946; the deteriorating situation in Iran and the Balkans; and the weakened position of the British, who were gradually withdrawing their troops from Greece. Seen in the light of these matters, American interpretation of what clearly was a Soviet threat was not exaggerated, and America's response was not aggressive.[207] Rather, the response was cautious, based on a perception of national and strategic interests, and in keeping with the principles of the United Nations,

[206] See nn. 3, 168.

[207] For a contrary view, see Paterson, pp. 192-193, 206. See also Yergin, pp. 118-191, 234-235, who overlooks evidence that contributed to the perceptual frameworks he discusses. The Russians may never have followed the paths of the arrows in Iran, and they may never have invaded Turkey, but their goals clearly were more aggressive than Yergin allows, and were unrealized only because of America's firmness.

which the people of the Northern Tier countries, in spite of differing degrees of dissatisfaction with their own governments, unquestionably supported.

Soviet designs on the Near East had led the United States and Britain to recognize that their national and strategic interests in the region were synonymous. Support for these interests followed naturally, and in view of the growing discrepancy between the two countries' economic and military capabilities, it was only a matter of time before their policies converged. The British had been forced to contemplate withdrawal of their armed forces from the Eastern Mediterranean after the Iranian crisis in March 1946. Clear indication of American interest in the Near East (in the U.N. over the Iranian crisis, and in private over the Turkish crisis of August 1946) made it easier for the British to pursue this policy. The result was that earlier collaboration with the United States on communications with the Soviet Union now extended to military planning in the Eastern Mediterranean (where the United States had replaced Britain) and to the question of military assistance to Greece, Turkey, and Iran. The British were to continue their aid to those countries as long as possible, and to serve as a kind of front for the United States in order that American policies not appear provocative, but there was little question that they were gradually giving way to the Americans.

The United States already had taken steps to assume the British Empire's role in the Near East. With the help of Britain and the Soviet Union, the Truman administration by the fall of 1946 had arrived at a clear conception of Greece, Turkey, and Iran in their collective historical role of dividing East and West. All three countries were seen as part of a whole, the importance of one inextricably linked to the importance of the others. Their territorial integrity, moreover, was defined in terms of the strategic security interests of the United States. As the viability of all three governments continued to be threatened —by guerillas based in Albania, Yugoslavia, and Bulgaria, by the Soviet Union's relentless war of nerves which forced Turkey to maintain a large and costly military establishment in a state of permanent mobilization, or by Soviet-supported autonomous regimes in northern Iran—the United States found itself increasingly committed to the continuation of earlier British policies and to the defense of the Northern Tier.

VI

꧁꧂꧁꧂꧁꧂

From Policy to Commitment
The United States and the Northern Tier, 1946-47

ONCE the Truman administration's policies toward the Northern Tier had been established, it was up to the Office of Near Eastern and African Affairs (NEA) to translate "positive" encouragement and assistance into something concrete—a task far more difficult than many imagine. Mobilization of the Turkish Army continued to drain the Turkish economy, and the situation in Greece continued to deteriorate. The practical difficulties of advancing American credits remained. In Iran, meanwhile, certain unauthorized representations by Ambassador Allen precipitated events which forced the administration's hand. The effective resolution of the Iranian crisis in December 1946 clearly demonstrated the political utility of American aid and vindicated the notion that firm policies were the correct response to Soviet threats.

With the most recent of a long series of crises finally over, the advent of still another crisis in Greece led the Department of State to determine that economic and military aid must be given directly to Greece. Simultaneous recognition by the British that they had to abandon their support of Greece and Turkey galvanized the administration's growing resolve into action, and with the promulgation of the Truman Doctrine in March 1947, the United States undertook its first public commitment to the balance of power along the Northern Tier.

The Iranian Crisis

Denouement

The apparent resolution of the Iranian question in April 1946 and the withdrawal of Soviet troops from northern Iran in May are often regarded as the virtual end of the Iranian crisis, for the dissolution of the separatist regimes in Azerbaijan quickly followed Soviet withdrawal. The real story, however, is more complicated, and its significance at the time was to add another important element to the Truman administration's understanding of international politics in the Near East.

One may recall that circumstances attending withdrawal of Soviet troops from Iran led the Security Council to remain seized of the question, and that in August, as negotiations with Azerbaijan broke down and a civil war was in the offing, Qavam again needed help. Contemplating military moves against Azerbaijan, he sought United Nations support for Iranian resistance to expected Soviet pressures.[1]

Qavam and the shah asked Allen repeatedly what either United States or United Nations assistance meant in concrete terms. On 13 August, on 24 August, in early September, and on 29 September, Allen received pointed inquiries. But his cautious advice, together with Henry Wallace's speech of 12 September, were taken by the Iranians as evidence that Iran could expect little in the way of concrete assistance from the United States.[2]

Adding to Qavam's worries, Iran's largest tribe, the Qashqa'i, revolted on 20 September, endangering Teheran's control of large areas of southern Iran. The Qashqa'i had long opposed Qavam's flirtations with the Tudeh. The Soviets had opened up two consulates in the south in the first half of 1946, and in June had offered the Qashqa'i tens of thousands of small arms and other weapons as well as full tribal independence if they would ally themselves with Russia. The Qashqa'i had deliberated for two weeks in early July, and then had decided to oppose both Soviet penetration and the Tudeh Party. They also decided to support Qavam, but only if he followed an anti-Tudeh line.[3] Qavam, however, continued to make what the Qashqa'i felt were too many

---

[1] FR, 1946, VII:511-513.

[2] Ibid., pp. 511-513, 518-520; S.D. Teheran Post and Lot Files, Teheran Lot No. 54F55, 1946-1957, 800 Political Affairs, Classified, September-December 1946 (hereafter cited as S.D. Teheran Post Files, 1946, 800), tel. Nos. 1208 (10 September), 1225 (13 September), 1230 (14 September), and 1236 (16 September).

[3] Discussion of the Qashqa'i, the tribal revolt in the south, and the question of British complicity in the revolt, is based on: Rossow MS (pp. 92-97); interview with Robert Rossow; FR, 1946, VII:516-517; S.D. 891.00/2062/11-645; Teheran Post and Lot Files, G-2 Report No. 335 8/28/43; Teheran Post Files, 1946, 800: tel. Nos. 56, 59, 62, 65, 810, 1208, 1219, 1225, 1226, 1231, 1236, 1258, 1275. See also S.D. 891.00/9-2146; Kirk, The Middle East, 1945-1950, pp. 77-78; Skrine, p. 248; Arfa, p. 373; Lenczowski, Russia and the West in Iran, pp. 305-306; Avery, pp. 396-397. It should be noted that documentary evidence does not bear out the thesis that Qavam was behind the revolt, although many still adhere to this interpretation.

concessions to Azerbaijan. On 1 August he appointed three Tudeh Party members to his cabinet, and a week later he appointed Tudeh Party members to local government posts throughout the province of Fars. In September he ordered Firuz to arrest pro-British leaders in Isfahan, including Jahanshah Samson, one of the two paramount Bakhtiyari chiefs. This particularly aggravated the Qashqa'i, who recently had signed an agreement with the Bakhtiyari.[4]

After a tribal conclave, the Qashqa'i sent Qavam a list of demands which included ouster of Tudeh Party members from Qavam's cabinet, expulsion of the Tudeh Party from the local officialdom of Fars, and general autonomy for the Qashqa'i provinces to the south. When their demands were not met they occupied several Gulf ports and besieged Shiraz. The revolt favored British and American policies because it arrested the spread of Tudeh influence in the south. But in spite of allegations of British complicity in the revolt, it was indigenous in origin, and a direct reaction to Qavam's policies. Allen, who was with Qavam when the prime minister received the Qashqa'i demands, doubted that Qavam would be able to withstand the pressures he now faced. But Qavam, as usual, weathered the crisis and on 29 September began to contemplate a sharp change of policy, based on strong insistence upon the central government's authority throughout the country. He had not foreseen the Qashqa'i revolt, but apparently it gave him the excuse he was looking for in dealing with the Tudeh. Before he could act, however, he needed military supplies and financial credits, and Allen again was forced to acknowledge that American aid to Iran was limited.[5]

When Allen wrote the State Department of this conversation with Qavam, he noted the desirability of giving Qavam and the shah a more favorable response on the question of aid. In Washington, Acheson agreed and sent a suggestion to Byrnes in Paris that the department's current policy of economic assistance to Iran be fully implemented to strengthen Qavam's hand. Byrnes, however, had limited knowledge of the situation in Iran and gave Acheson's suggestion only cautious endorsement. Economic help should be extended, not "combat material."[6]

At this juncture, as Qavam entered negotiations with the Qashqa'i,

[4] Ibid.   [5] Ibid.; FR, 1946, VII:518-520.
[6] FR, 1946, VII:518-521. For the State Department's policy at this juncture, see pp. 507-509.

the Soviets began to pressure him to hold elections.[7] In late September, Qavam told the Soviet ambassador that elections were impossible since the Azerbaijan situation was unsettled. That answer was unacceptable in Moscow. The Soviet ambassador therefore insisted that elections take place and that the oil agreement be submitted to the Majlis. Qavam acquiesced, and on 5 October, although no date was specified, the shah signed a decree that elections would be held.[8]

Soviet pressures on Qavam to conduct elections in Iran were of grave concern to Allen, Ala, and NEA. So were reports, denied by Qavam, that Iran was prepared to consider favorably a Soviet request for the creation of an Irano-Soviet aviation company to service northern Iran. Acheson saw the company as a means of facilitating Soviet absorption of northern Iran. Yet, while noting the department's efforts to give Iran support, Acheson, in a telegram to Allen, observed that the responsibility for maintaining Iran's independence and integrity remained primarily with the government of Iran.[9]

As a result of these new Soviet pressures on Iran, Ambassador Ala requested a meeting with Acheson. Preparing for that meeting, Loy Henderson on 8 October sent Acheson a memorandum which expressed the general feeling in his office that the situation was critical and that everything should be done to keep Iran from slipping into the Soviet orbit. Henderson and others had discussed Iran with the JCS, who deemed the oil fields in Iran, Saudi Arabia, and Iraq absolutely essential to American security. In view of American strategic interests in Iran, Henderson believed that Qavam should be encouraged to hope for American assistance, including combat supplies necessary to maintain Iran's internal security. Qavam's concessions to the Soviets were not a result of his inclinations, Henderson argued, but rather of the inability of the United States to take concrete steps to assist Iran. When Ala called on Acheson later that day, however, the acting secretary was unable to support NEA's recommendations. He expressed his close interest in Iran's problems, and his intention to implement the department's declared policy of economic assistance to Iran, but because of Byrnes's cautious support for aid to Iran, there was little that was concrete.[10]

[7] The 5 April agreement between Russia and Iran (dated 4 April) stipulated that elections would take place within seven months of the agreement supposedly reached on 24 March. See Chapter V, n. 85.

[8] FR, 1946, VII:521-522; New York Times, 6 October 1946.

[9] FR, 1946, VII:523-528.

[10] FR, 1946, VII:523-527; letter from Loy Henderson to the author.

In Iran, meanwhile, Qavam's position was becoming increasingly precarious. Azerbaijan, of course, was out of his control. There was open revolt in the south. The Tudeh was demonstrating almost daily in Iran's major cities,[11] and his cabinet was saddled with three Tudeh and two pro-Tudeh members. At this juncture two Iranian businessmen, Reza Afshar and Gholam Hussein Ebtehaj, on 10 October disclosed to the American economic attaché Randall Williams, information whose import was crucial to the situation. Contrary to assurances which Qavam had given Allen only three days before, there were recent developments in the negotiation of an aviation agreement between the Soviet Union and Iran.[12]

According to the information Williams gave Allen, a Soviet proposal was discussed on 30 September by the Iranian cabinet. It was endorsed by Muzaffar Firuz and by the cabinet's Tudeh members, although complications arose. Apparently, the Soviet proposal for monopoly rights violated the International Civil Aviation Agreement which precluded granting cabotage privileges to a foreign airline; further discussion ensued, and it was proposed that the government give notice of withdrawal from the International Civil Aviation Organization (ICAO), thereby enabling Iran after thirty days to grant the Soviet request.[13]

On the following day, one of the Tudeh ministers, Iraj Iskenderi, was approached by the first secretary of the Soviet embassy. The Soviet diplomat asked him why he had proposed a delay, and denounced him unmercifully. Iskenderi, who had been supportive of the proposal but who had suggested the necessary delay as a means of getting around the ICAO regulations, was angered by the rebuke and by the fact that the Soviet embassy was receiving reports of cabinet meetings. With the help of Afshar, Ebtehaj, and Williams, these details eventually reached Allen.[14]

Allen was angered by what he heard. Spurred on, perhaps, by Henderson's advice, by the department's current anxieties, and by his third secretary Robert Rossow, who long had been pushing him to take a firmer attitude toward Qavam, Allen on 11 October called on Qavam

[11] Rossow MS: S.D. 891.00/12-346.

[12] Henderson, in a personal letter to Allen in July, had been concerned about this issue; so had Acheson in a telegram which Allen had just received. S.D. Teheran Post Files, 1946, 800: tel. Nos. 844 (8 October) and 1353 (11 October); Allen Papers, "Mission to Iran"; interview with Robert Rossow; FR, 1946, VII: 528. See also Chapter V, nn. 132, 133.

[13] Allen Papers, "Mission to Iran"; S.D. Teheran Post Files, 1946, 800; tel. No. 1353 (11 October 1946).

[14] Ibid.

and brought the matter to his attention. A member of the Iranian cabinet, he told the prime minister, was a traitor. He described briefly what had happened. The United States, he went on, had always regarded Iran as an independent nation. It had supported Iran in the United Nations. The present government quite obviously had no freedom or independence. He asked Qavam whether he proposed to permit the situation to continue, or not. He wanted to know, he said, so that he could inform his government and enable it to decide what attitude to take toward the Iranian government. The Iranian government could not be regarded as master of its own house when its cabinet members were subject to constant fears that the Soviet ambassador would undermine their positions if they did not carry out his bidding. If Qavam did not denounce the Soviet actions immediately, Allen told him, everyone would consider Qavam to be among the traitors.[15]

Qavam agreed that the matter was serious, and tried to explain it away. He tried to get Allen to name names. Allen refused. Allen said he believed he had done his duty by bringing the situation forcefully to Qavam's attention. Whatever action Qavam took was up to him. The situation was critical and bold action was required. After this interview, Allen told Rossow he would give Qavam a week, and then take matters up with the shah.[16]

For three days Allen mulled the situation over, talking with Rossow for hours. The ambassador was uncertain about the best course. He had no instructions, and was afraid to ask for any since he knew that the decision was one which Washington would not and could not make. He had hesitated a long time already, fully appreciating the seriousness of the move and weighing the consequences carefully. But things were going from bad to worse. Qavam seemed helpless, and Allen did not believe the prime minister would be able to take the bold action required to eliminate increasing Soviet control over Iran. Finally, on 14 October, after spending most of the morning going over and over the situation with Rossow, Allen went to see the shah.[17]

[15] S.D. Teheran Post Files, 1946, 800: tel. No. 1354 (12 October); Allen Papers, "Mission to Iran"; Rossow MS; interview with Robert Rossow. For evidence of Rossow's attempt to encourage the ambassador to take a very firm and forceful attitude, see Teheran Lot File No. 54F55 secret Dispatch No. 148 from George Allen to the secretary of state, 16 September 1946, and the enclosed 11-page memorandum by Rossow. Allen notes that he found the memorandum highly useful.

[16] Ibid.

[17] Interview with Robert Rossow; Rossow MS; S.D. 891.00/12-346.

He told the shah all that had transpired. He had refrained from giving advice until now, but since the Soviet ambassador was involved, he felt it appropriate. He said that in all fairness he did not believe Qavam courageous enough, or strong enough, or decisive enough to take effective action. The government, he said, must be changed if Iran were to preserve its independence. The British ambassador, Sir John Le Rougetel, was in full accord.[18]

When the shah wondered aloud what he could do, Allen said he thought he should demand that Qavam remake his cabinet, dismissing the Tudeh and pro-Tudeh members. When the shah wondered what would happen if Qavam refused, Allen said that if he were the shah he would have Qavam come to the palace in Shimran the next day. He would be waiting for him in full uniform as Commander in Chief of the Iranian Army. He would have Qavam's resignation ready for him

[18] This account of what transpired during the period 14-19 October 1946 is based on the following sources: S.D. Teheran Post Files, 1946, 800: tel. Nos. 1371 (15 October), 1384 (18 October), 1394 (21 October); FR, 1946, VII:533, 536-539; 3 December 1946 letter from George Allen to Harold Minor, S.D. 891.00/ 12-346; Ch. 7 ("Purging the Tudeh") of Allen's "Mission to Iran" in the Allen Papers; Rossow MS; interviews with Robert Rossow and Loy Henderson; letters from Loy Henderson to the author; and a letter from Harold Minor to the author. For the shah's brief account, see Mohammad Reza Shah Pahlavi, pp. 117-118. It should be noted that Allen's memoirs are seriously marred by chronological inaccuracies. They describe the events of October as taking place in 1947 instead of 1946, and they get particular dates confused. These deficiencies can be remedied by the existing documents. His conversation with the shah is more problematic. Although here his memoirs are valuable, and what record there is tends to bear out much of his story, his highly confidential letters to Henderson were destroyed (unlike those Henderson wrote to him). Allen clearly did not tell Washington, or even Henderson, everything about his representations either to Qavam or to the shah. He did, however, inform the department as to the gist of what had happened—enough certainly to disturb some of the officials in the State Department (perhaps members of the Office of European Affairs). Robert Rossow was helpful in providing background to Allen's representations, and corroborated much of what happened independently of Allen's memoirs. While the above interpretation in no way denigrates Qavam's masterful attempt to cope with existing pressures, it does cast considerable light on a situation which is still not very well understood. As Allen wrote Harold Minor on 3 December 1946, his "part in it was primarily to focus a good many forces working to change the Government's direction. Many people wanted the change, not least of whom was Qavam himself, but someone had to take the decision that the time had come to act. Once the Shah made up his mind (and this probably resulted from our conversation), everyone was pleased and relieved." Clearly, Allen's role was crucial. For recent attempts to grapple with the problem of interpreting this episode, see Ramazani, Iran's Foreign Policy, pp. 148-150; and the article by Richard Pfau, "Containment in Iran, 1946," which correctly emphasizes Allen's role.

to sign. If he accepted, he would ask Qavam to form another cabinet. If he refused, he would dismiss him and put him under house arrest. To avoid conflict between the army (loyal to the shah) and the gendarmerie (loyal to Qavam), the whole matter should be of the utmost secrecy. Allen assured the shah that Schwarzkopf,[19] who sympathized with Qavam, would not meddle in the affair. He left the shah with the advice that it would be dangerous to delay, and that any action, to be effective, should be taken within the week.[20]

Allen cabled Washington about what had been said, reporting the gist of his conversation with the Shah. His report aroused great interest in the department, and apparently disturbed some—perhaps members of the Office of European Affairs—who thought that he might have gone too far. But Henderson faced up to their criticism and strongly supported Allen.

Fortunately for both Allen and Henderson the matter was soon resolved. The Qashqa'i tribal leader Nasr Khan on 13 October accepted the central government's terms, and on the following day signed an agreement ending hostilities. It was agreed that local Tudeh officials would be removed, that Fars would have increased local autonomy, and that general amnesty would be declared for all those who had participated in the rebellion. There was no mention of cabinet reform, but an emissary from Qavam had intimated to Allen shortly after receipt of the Qashqa'i ultimatum that while he could hardly be expected to reform the cabinet immediately, he would find reason to do so in 15 or 20 days.[21]

In response to the counterpressures now exerted by Allen and the Qashqa'i, Qavam on 15 October replaced the governor of Teheran (a Tudeh sympathizer) with a member of his own Democratic Party. This would enable him to control the election in Teheran. Meanwhile, following his conversation with Allen, the shah conferred with generals Ahmadi and Yazdanpanah and laid plans to act on Sunday, 20 October. Before then, however, rumors began to circulate that the shah planned to arrest Qavam. Qavam, who was under surveillance, by Wednesday, 16 October, learned that Allen had gone to see the shah and

[19] Brigadier General H. Norman Schwarzkopf, chief of the American Military Mission with the Iranian gendarmerie.

[20] See n. 18 above.

[21] *New York Times*, 14 October 1946; Rossow MS; S.D. Teheran Post Files, 1946, 800; tel. No. 1275 (25 September).

sensed what was in the air. At 11:00 p.m. he called and asked to see the shah, but was told to come to the palace on Thursday at 11:00 a.m.[22]

On Thursday morning, 17 October, when he entered the shah's palace, Qavam appeared to recognize that the locus of power had shifted. He affirmed loyalty to the shah, declared his readiness to resign, and offered to leave the country if the shah wished. But the shah knew of no one else to whom he could entrust the government under the present circumstances. Thus, he told Qavam that he wanted him to dismiss those elements in his cabinet which were hostile to Iranian interests. That meant both Firuzes and the Tudeh Party members. Qavam agreed to all but the dismissal of Muzaffar Firuz, who, rumors had it, had something on Qavam. At this point the shah banged his fist on the table and said he wanted Firuz either in prison or out of the country. Since the Iranian ambassador to Moscow had died a month before, Qavam suggested that Firuz be sent to Moscow, and the shah agreed. He felt that Iranian ambassadors there were always treated like dogs by the Kremlin anyway and he doubted Firuz could do much harm. A new cabinet list was drawn up before Qavam left the palace. Later in the day reports began to circulate that the cabinet had resigned and that because the three Tudeh members of the cabinet had absented themselves from a meeting (in protest over the appointment of a new governor of Teheran), Qavam was trying to take advantage of the situation.[23]

In fact, the shah and Qavam had agreed that to avoid Tudeh demonstrations they should keep the appointment of the new cabinet secret for a day. But Qavam immediately told Muzaffar Firuz what had happened; Firuz in turn told the Soviet ambassador, who demanded to see Qavam that night. Using abusive language, he weakened Qavam's resolve. On Friday, 18 October, Qavam again called on the shah and expressed fear that Soviet troops might enter the country if the cabinet change went through. The shah, however, was determined to exercise his authority and the new cabinet was announced shortly thereafter.[24]

The shah on 20 October made another strong plea for an important American gesture of support for Iran. An extension of credits or at

[22] S.D. Teheran Post Files, 1946, 800: tel. Nos. 1384 (18 October) and 1394 (21 October); FR, 1946, VII:536-539; interview with Robert Rossow; Rossow MS; *New York Times*, 15 September 1946; Allen Papers, "Mission to Iran."

[23] Ibid.; *New York Times*, 18 October 1946.

[24] FR, 1946, VII:537-539.

least some action which would demonstrate publicly U.S. economic interest in Iran would help. The Soviets undoubtedly would protest vehemently, and the Iranians would have to have support in facing Moscow's blasts. The shah reminded Allen of the current support of the United States for Turkey. Again Allen cabled the department that American encouragement for Iran would be appropriate. He reiterated his plea for credits on 22 October. Iranian inquiries were frequent and his inability to give the Iranians satisfactory replies was becoming embarrassing.[25]

In Washington, officials believed that the recent turn of events in Iran was truly critical. The memorandum on policy toward Iran, drafted in the wake of the Turkish crisis, proved convenient to Henderson as he pushed for the kind of support Allen had been requesting. Henderson and others in NEA doubted Qavam's capacity to defend the independence of Iran. Moral, economic, and military support would be required, Henderson had written in his cover letter to the memorandum on Iran, if and when the shah were to appoint a new prime minister.[26]

When Qavam himself was reappointed prime minister the necessity of support became even more urgent. As Allen's requests continued to come in, the secretary of state on 28 October, in a conference on changes in American armaments policy, decided that a limited amount of armaments not to exceed $10 million in value would be sold to Iran. The United States would also give favorable consideration to the credits necessary to furnish such arms. The moral support evidenced by such a decision was perhaps more important than its later realization, and details of the matter were quickly relayed to the Iranians.[27]

In Iran, where Russian propaganda was attacking Qavam, the prime minister asked Allen whether the American policy of firmness toward the Soviet Union was likely to continue. He repeated a question he had asked several times over the last three months: what would the United

[25] S.D. Teheran Post Files, 1946, 800: tel. No. 1394 (21 October); *FR*, 1946, VII:539-540.

[26] *FR*, 1946, VII:533-536.

[27] Ibid., pp. 255, 544. Edwin Wright, who knew well General Abdullah Hidayat, chief of the Iranian military mission to the United States, has written that the Iranians considered this decision to be a crucial indication of U.S. support for their country ("A Personal Narrative—A Retrospective View"). As one scholar has observed, Iran's interest in the United States was political, even if the means were economic. For the problems associated with American aid to Iran, see Ramazani, *Iran's Foreign Policy*, pp. 154-166.

Nations do if he used military force against Azerbaijan, and Russia were to give Azerbaijan substantial help in arms and men? Apparently, he was wondering what to make of recent American support for Turkey, and was curious to know in concrete terms whether that support extended to Iran. In response, Allen again spoke of world opinion, the United Nations, and the principles which guided American foreign policy.[28]

Beyond principle, however, concrete support already had been indicated, and more was in the offing. In Washington, Henderson was pushing hard for an Export-Import Bank loan to Iran. Active measures, he argued, were necessary to encourage Iran to resist external pressures. On 14 November, Acheson was able to wire Allen that helpful information would be forthcoming, and on 22 November it was. After careful consideration of Allen's telegrams, in view of the importance the department attached not only to the Iranian problem, but to the principles involved and to the strategic interests of the United States in the Middle East, the State Department had given its endorsement to the measures recommended in the 18 October memorandum on U.S. policy toward Iran.[29]

The stage was set for the final denouement. Qavam on 28 October already had reiterated the shah's public statement that elections would be held. On 4 November, after learning of Washington's favorable attitude toward a credit of $10 million to purchase military supplies, the prime minister scheduled the elections for 7 December. On 21 November he announced that government troops would be sent into the provinces to maintain peace and order during the elections (which would be held *only* with security forces present). After hearing about the department's decision on more extensive assistance to Iran, Qavam determined to send security forces to Azerbaijan as well. He was prepared to appeal to the Security Council if complications with the Soviet Union ensued, and appeared to feel that he could count on the unqualified support of the United States should he do so—a fact of great importance in view of the Soviet ambassador's increasing pressure on him not to send troops into Azerbaijan. Another equally significant factor was public support of the Iranian decision by George Allen who, when asked by the local paper *Ettela'at* for his opinion on the sending of security forces to Azerbaijan, said it seemed to him "an entirely

[28] S.D. Teheran Post Files, 1946, 800: tel. No. 1434 (3 November).
[29] S.D. 891.51/11-546; FR, 1946, VII:546-547. See also Chapter V, n. 204.

393

normal and proper decision."[30] The statement gave the Iranians a shot in the arm, and focused the brunt of Soviet and Tudeh propaganda on the United States.[31]

Attacks against Allen and Qavam grew sharp in the Tabriz and Soviet presses. The Soviet ambassador, on instructions from Moscow, told Qavam on 28 November that sending troops into Azerbaijan would create difficulties in Azerbaijan and on the Soviet frontier with Iran. Qavam saw these representations as threats, and requested within 24 hours American reaction to the idea that the Security Council be informed of them. Following full and unqualified support from the State Department,[32] Qavam repeated his thanks over and over again. He then instructed Ala to notify the secretary-general of the United Nations of the situation regarding Azerbaijan. Iran made no formal request for action, but Ala made sure everyone knew that a "friendly admonition" of Iran's intended action had been received from the Soviet Union and that Iran desired the Security Council to remain seized of the question.[33]

In spite of further personal threats and strong representations by the Soviet ambassador, Qavam remained steadfastly determined to send security forces into Azerbaijan. Under the shah's leadership, military plans were laid. Opposing patrols established contact on 9 December, and on 10 December the Iranian Army attacked undefended Azerbaijani positions at the Qaflankuh Pass on the road between Zenjan and Mianeh. On 11 December, in spite of a proclamation by Pishevari call-

[30] Allen's reply was approved by the Department of State on 4 December 1946. FR, 1946, VII:549.

[31] New York Times, 29 October, 5 and 22 November 1946; Lenczowski, Russia and the West in Iran, p. 308; FR, 1946, VII:547-549, 552, 556; Rossow MS.

[32] In a personal letter to Harold Minor on 3 December, Allen added a postscript which characterized the State Department telegram as the finest instruction he had seen come out of the department (S.D. 891.00/12-346). Support for Iran by NEA and Acheson was clear throughout this period. One official, in a letter to the author, recalls that at a dinner given by Ala on 1 December 1946, the third anniversary of the Teheran Declaration, Acheson, in responding to a toast, went much further in assuring the ambassador of U.S. support for Iran than had ever been given officially either in writing or orally. It was a very small dinner and the toasts were all "off the record," but they nonetheless delighted Ala who sent a telegram to Qavam that night.

[33] New York Times, 29 November, 4, 5, and 7 December 1946; S.D. Teheran Post Files, 1946, 800: tel. No. 1534 (28 November); FR, 1946, VII:549-556; United States Publication: Security Council Readex Microprint: Documents-s/ 203-s/217; Rossow MS.

ing on the people of Azerbaijan to fight to the death, resistance was negligible.[34] On 12 December, before government troops arrived in Tabriz, bands of armed men roamed the streets, looted the shops of Tudeh sympathizers, and even seized one of the ministers, Mohammed Beriya, dragging his body back and forth around Tabriz in a jeep before depositing it, unrecognizable, in the public square. Pishevari fled to the USSR and the Iranian forces entering Tabriz on 13 December were welcomed by cheering crowds. On 15 December, Qazi Mohammed announced the surrender of Mahabad.[35]

Thus, almost a year to the day after the Soviet-sponsored autonomous republics had been founded, they crumbled. Grim reminders of their existence were embodied for months afterward in rows of bodies swinging from crude gibbets in nearly every public square of Azerbaijan and northern Kurdistan. According to F. Lester Sutton, the American consul in Tabriz, the pall accompanying the Azerbaijan regime had lifted. Never had he seen so many smiling faces. As far as he was aware, the outcome he had witnessed marked the first time in the postwar period that a Russian-sponsored government had fallen anywhere in the world.[36]

In Moscow, Elbridge Durbrow was of the same opinion. Years later he would still remember that he and Ambassador Bedell Smith literally cheered when news arrived of Azerbaijan's demise. Nothing like this had happened in Eastern Europe. Smith's elation was evident in a telegram he sent to the department on 14 December which ended with this

[34] According to Edwin Wright, General Razmara, the Iranian chief of staff, in the summer of 1946 sent a number of Azerbaijanis and Kurds who were in the Iranian Army secretly to Azerbaijan and Kurdistan, where they arranged for the defection of rebel troops. General Razmara did not move his troops into Azerbaijan until the defection of "Democratic" troops was certain. Wright, "A Personal Narrative—A Retrospective View."

[35] Qazi Mohammed was later hanged. Rossow, "The Battle of Azerbaijan," pp. 30-31; New York Times, 14-16 December 1946; Eagleton, pp. 101-132; Archie Roosevelt, p. 266; FR, 1946, VII:556-562; Rossow MS; Allen Papers, "Mission to Iran"; Ramazani, Iran's Foreign Policy, pp. 150-153; Avery, p. 398. Mulla Mustafa Barzani, after further wanderings in and out of Iraq and attempting to sound out Allen on the possibility of the Kurds' migrating to the United States, eventually (June 1947) took his following across the Soviet border, where they would remain for over 11 years. See Map No. 7 for their route.

[36] Ibid.; S.D. Teheran Post Files, 1946, 800: Confidential Dispatch No. 10 from Tabriz, Iran, dated 30 December 1946, and entitled "End of the Democratic Party Control in Azerbaijan." This 17-page document and its two enclosures give a good account of the fall of Azerbaijan.

note: "Incidentally Firuz [the newly appointed Iranian ambassador to the Soviet Union] just called and asked for services of our doctor. He probably had [a] heart attack on recent news from Teheran."[37]

In Teheran, George Allen found that everyone, including the shah, attributed the Soviet Union's failure to assist Azerbaijan to the Soviets' conviction that the United States was not bluffing and that it would support any United Nations member threatened by aggression. The shah, in his tribute to American aid, embarrassed even Allen when he referred to Azerbaijan as the "Stalingrad of the western democracies" and "the turn of the tides against Soviet aggression throughout the world."[38]

In the United States, Loy Henderson transmitted Secretary Byrnes's personal appreciation to Allen for the "admirable manner" in which he had handled an extremely important and delicate situation. Byrnes thought of the achievement of Iranian unity "as proof of the strength and effectiveness of the United Nations in helping those countries which truly desire independence."[39]

Some interpretations of the outcome of the crisis were skeptical. The Turkish foreign minister, as well as certain French officials, believed that Qavam had made still another deal with the Soviets. In their minds, the deal probably centered around ratification of the oil concession. Allen, however, disagreed. So did Henderson and Acheson, and other department officials in Washington. So did Elbridge Durbrow and Bedell Smith in Moscow. While Smith could not exclude such a possibility, he believed that the Soviet Union, caught unprepared, decided not to show its hand by interfering openly. In forwarding the Moscow embassy's assessment of Azerbaijan's collapse, he placed Byrnes's enthusiasm for the United Nations in a more realistic perspective:

> . . . Iran is no stronger than UN and UN, in last analysis, is no stronger than USA. . . .
>
> Collapse of Azerbaijan house of cards was a major victory for UN— and for a firm policy toward USSR.
>
> It must not be thought, however, that Kremlin will resign itself

[37] Interview with Elbridge Durbrow; S.D. Teheran Post Files, 1946, 800: tel. No. 149 (14 December).

[38] FR, 1946, VII:561-563. James Forrestal cites this telegram in his diaries, Forrestal Papers, Forrestal Diaries, p. 1395; Acheson cites it in his memoirs (Acheson, p. 198).

[39] Henderson Papers; FR, 1946, VII:563.

to this humiliating reverse. It will continue to maneuver not only for oil concessions but also for political (and strategic) ascendancy in Iran.[40]

Smith's analysis touched on an important point: the Soviet Union was in a strong position to maneuver for political ascendancy in Iran. Perhaps, as Qavam earlier had suggested they would, the Soviets dropped Azerbaijan in order that the Majlis would later ratify the oil agreement. In any case, Moscow still had the opportunity to conduct bilateral negotiations with and put political pressure on Teheran.[41]

For this reason, when Edwin Wilson sent back to Washington Feridun Erkin's surmise that the favorable turn of events in late 1946 presaged a more favorable Soviet attitude toward the Northern Tier countries, the American embassy in Moscow, better informed about the reasons for the outcome of those events, quickly disabused everyone of the notion.[42]

In Washington, the State Department agreed. Byrnes, of course, would soon depart,[43] and the new secretary of state, George C. Marshall, was unfamiliar with the Near East.[44] But Marshall would leave the formulation of American policies toward the Northern Tier countries to Acheson and Henderson, and to them the issues were clear. Strategic and economic issues were vital,[45] and were best safeguarded

---

[40] FR, 1946, VII:564-567; S.D. Teheran Post Files, 1946, 800: tel. Nos. 16 (23 December), 1068 (28 December), and see also 17 (30 December); interviews with Elbridge Durbrow and Loy Henderson. Acheson, p. 198, cites Smith's telegram in his memoirs, but attributes the analysis to George Allen.

[41] On 7 January 1947, when George Kennan was giving a talk before the Council on Foreign Relations in New York, he addressed precisely this point: Qavam, he noted, "has promised [the Soviets] those concessions and when they get them they will get the province back because the agreement gives them control in the areas where the wells are located" (George F. Kennan Papers). Kennan, when asked, would make no predictions as to whether the Majlis would confirm the oil concessions.

[42] FR, 1946, VII:898-899; 1947, V:2-3, 8-9; S.D. 761.67/1-2947.

[43] After the "minor" peace treaties were completed, Byrnes in December asked Truman to accept his letter of resignation, submitted back in April. His resignation took effect on 20 January 1947. Truman submitted George C. Marshall's name to the Senate for confirmation on 8 January 1947, and it was confirmed the same day. Marshall was sworn in as secretary of state on 21 January. Curry, pp. 253-257; Robert Ferrell, George C. Marshall (New York, 1966), pp. 35-38.

[44] Marshall was also preoccupied with the upcoming Moscow Conference. Acheson, pp. 213, 217-218; Ferrell, pp. 52-53; interview with Forrest Pogue.

[45] Economic interests were most recently emphasized in December 1946 when the Anglo-Iranian Oil Company (in which the British government had a controlling interest) concluded (with the approval of the American government) a major

397

by a firm policy toward the Soviet Union. Henderson had long advocated such a policy and George Kennan in February 1946 had articulated it *before* the arduous trial of pressure and counterpressure with the Soviet Union in Iran and Turkey. The recent success of American actions in Iran confirmed this line of thinking, and completed the education of many in the Truman administration, including Dean Acheson, who learned in 1946 that minds in the Kremlin worked very much as Kennan had predicted they would.[46]

In the meantime, the British Empire was dissolving. Countries that once protected the empire's lifeline to India were becoming more of a burden to Britain than a safeguard, and the imminent withdrawal of British support for Greece and Turkey[47] was threatening to undermine America's recently defined interests in the region.

American policies in Greece and Turkey, moreover, unlike those in Iran, were having no immediate impact. Turkey and Greece—particularly Greece—received larger credits than Iran, but not nearly enough to meet their far greater problems. Greece was further disadvantaged by the fact that it was unable to put what it did get to much use.[48]

Compounding the difficulty of carrying out American policies toward

---

agreement with Standard of New Jersey and Socony Vacuum. The agreement, which included the possibility of constructing a pipeline from the Persian Gulf to the Mediterranean, conceded to the American companies the marketing for 20 years of 134 million tons of oil, or 20% of AIOC's annual production. See FR, 1946, VII:43-50; Kirk, *The Middle East, 1945-50*, p. 9; Woodhouse, *Apple of Discord*, p. 275. See also Chapter III and Chapter IV, n. 247. The chart below, which appears in Kirk, illustrates the rapid expansion of the Arabian-American Oil Company in Saudi Arabia, and that of AIOC in the Persian Gulf:

Production in millions of metric tons

Year	Arabian-American	Anglo-Iranian
1944	1.1	13.5
1945	2.9	17.1
1946	8.2	19.5
1947	12.3	20.5
1948	19.3	25.2

[46] FR, 1947, V:8-9; Loy Henderson, letters to the author; Acheson, p. 196.

[47] Byrnes, *Speaking Frankly*, p. 300, notes that in December Ernest Bevin told him that "the British were anxious to withdraw their troops from Greece and several other places whenever and wherever it could properly be done. However, at no time did he indicate that regardless of conditions in Greece, Britain would withdraw its troops on March 31, 1947, or any specific date."

[48] See Chapter V, nn. 142, 146, 153; Chapter VI, n. 69; FR, 1946, VII:232, 282-283, 285-288, 898-923.

Greece and Turkey was the fact that such policies represented only what the Department of State *wanted* to accomplish. *Practically*, the department encountered serious bureaucratic problems in dealing with independent agencies responsible for granting loans and credits. Concrete and tangible programs of assistance had been handicapped since the termination of lend-lease by the lack of legislation to effect transfers. Existing legislation such as the Surplus Property Act was cumbersome and ineffective. By the end of the year, in spite of the fact that the War Department was also of the opinion that "all practicable measures should be taken to hold the line in the Near East," the problem of implementing such measures remained. Loy Henderson, for one, fully recognized the difficulty of the situation. In spite of his own modest attempts at publicizing American policy in the region, and perhaps because of the cautious manner in which the department was carrying it out, the press was not much interested in the royalist regime in Greece or in the Turkish Republic. The public saw the Turks in stereotyped categories and still associated them with the massacre of Armenians earlier in the century. Nevertheless, Henderson set about reaching a common understanding with the War and Navy Departments so that the State Department would be prepared to move on short notice when conditions were propitious.[49] These preparations had important implications for American policy toward Greece, where still another crisis was coming to the fore.

The Greek Crisis

One may recall that a guerilla attack on Litokhoron on 30 March had signaled the beginning of the Third Round in Greece. As conditions worsened, the Soviets on 20 September vetoed a Security Council resolution to investigate incidents along Greece's frontiers.[50] Then, on

[49] FR, 1946, VII:920-923; S.D. 867.51/12-1846; P & O Div., Case No. 39 400TS, 10 December 1946 memo from Bastion to Henderson, 17 December 1946 memo from Henderson to Bastion, 17 December 1946 memo from Norstad to Chamberlain, 31 December 1946 memo from Chamberlain to Norstad; *The Middle East Journal* 1 (January 1947):85-86; interview with Loy Henderson.

[50] In spite of the Soviet veto, Greece notified the United Nations of further incidents on six subsequent occasions. For an illuminating "case-study" of a Greek Macedonian village (Proastion), see S.D. 868.00/11-646, Dispatch No. 3269, "Life in a Greek Macedonian Village: The Social Background of Political Turmoil," which MacVeagh passed on to the department with the comment that "as a piece of authentic sampling, however restricted, it may shed more light than volumes of statistics or rhetoric on the complex problems of a large area."

399

14 November, a group of about 700 Greek guerillas attacked the village of Skra in northern Greece, killing 19 soldiers and burning 150 of 170 houses before fleeing into Yugoslavia. By the end of the month the Greek civil war was again emerging in full force. Finally, on 3 December, Greece brought the problem before the Security Council, declaring that the guerilla movement was receiving support from Albania, Bulgaria, and Yugoslavia.[51]

In the Department of State, periodic meetings convened to discuss the situation along the northern Greek frontier. By 9 December, a vast body of evidence indicated that the situation there was extremely grave. One report hypothesized that the Soviet Union and its satellites, Albania, Yugoslavia, and Bulgaria, might be seeking to cut Macedonia off from Greece and bring it into the Yugoslav Federation, and to obtain Western Thrace for Bulgaria. Such developments would place the Soviet Union in a much more favorable strategic position relative to Turkey.[52]

Evidence of the three northern countries' interference in Greek affairs was clear. After acrimonious discussions in the Security Council from 10 December to 19 December,[53] the Council unanimously[54] approved

[51] Xydis, *Greece and the Great Powers*, pp. 428, 431; Stavrianos, *Greece*, pp. 179-180; O'Ballance, p. 129; FR, 1946, VII:221, 268, 272-274. See also Chapter V, n. 168.

[52] S.D. Athens Lot Files 54D363, Folder: Border: "Situation Along Northern Greek Frontier," 28 October and 20 November 1946; "Incidents on the Northern Greek Frontiers: A Summary Statement," 9 December 1946; "Incidents on the Northern Greek Frontiers: Some Official Statements from the Governments of Greece, Albania, Yugoslavia, and Bulgaria," DRN Information Note No. 24, 17 December 1946.

[53] *Security Council Official Records, 1st Year, Series 2*, pp. 529-701. Xydis, *Greece and the Great Powers*, pp. 662-663, has made a comparative line count, expressed in percentages, of speeches by Big Three representatives that were devoted to the "Greek Question" in the United Nations in 1946. In the three debates that took place during the year (1-6 February, 30 August-20 September, and 10-19 December), the Soviet Union was responsible for approximately half of the Big Three's contribution to each debate (47%, 58%, and 55%, respectively). While Britain's relative contribution to each debate declined successively (48%, 22%, 20%), that of the United States rose (5%, 20%, 25%), succinctly illustrating the increasing role of the United States in Greek affairs.

[54] Reasons for the Soviet Union's approval of such a commission, particularly after it vetoed an earlier proposal that was similar, are unknown. One factor may have been that the peace treaties with Bulgaria, Hungary, Rumania, Italy, and Finland were finally completed (they were signed on 10 February, and would go into force in September 1947) (Feis, *From Trust to Terror*, pp. 168-170; see also Chapter V, n. 3). But the history of Soviet activity along the Northern Tier argues

an amended American proposal for a commission to investigate on-the-spot alleged violations along the Greek frontier with Albania, Yugoslavia, and Bulgaria. The Commission of Investigation would begin its work on 30 January 1947, and on 23 May 1947 eight of eleven delegations[55] would subscribe to the conclusions set forth in the Report of the Commission of Investigation.[56]

According to the report,[57] Albania, Bulgaria, and Yugoslavia had encouraged, assisted, trained, and supplied guerillas in their actions against the Greek government—actions which had led to over 700 clashes in the provinces of northern Greece alone. The report showed sensitivity to the causes of disturbed conditions in Greece. It recognized that they were a heritage of the war and of the problems faced by the Greek government in its efforts to carry on a program of economic rehabilitation. While the internal situation in Greece could not be ignored, the facts indicated that the majority of clashes occurred in the northern provinces of Epirus, Macedonia, and Thrace. The exist-

---

against this interpretation. Xydis, *Greece and the Great Powers*, pp. 442-443, supposes the Soviets estimated that another veto would have exposed the U.N.'s difficulties in dealing with a situation that was endangering world peace, and so would have catalyzed some new implementation of American interests in the Balkans. Kousoulas, *Revolution and Defeat*, p. 245, believes that to veto such a commission would have constituted a tacit admission that the Greek charges were true.

[55] The eight delegations subscribing to the report were those of the United States (headed by Byrnes's friend Mark Ethridge), Australia, Belgium, Brazil, China, Colombia, Syria, and the United Kingdom. Poland and the Soviet Union did not approve of the report, while France abstained since it had doubts about the advisability of having formal conclusions.

[56] FR, 1946, VII:273, 283-285. For a thoroughly documented analysis and summary of the Report of the Commission of Investigation, see Harry Howard, *The United Nations and the Problem of Greece* (Washington, 1947). The conclusions are set forth in Part II, Chapter I of the report. For background, see also Eudes, pp. 281-288; Matthews, pp. 136-154; and C. M. Woodhouse, *The Struggle for Greece*, pp. 197-198.

[57] The report was based on 33 field investigations (including an investigation of the Skra incident) in various parts of Greece, Albania, Bulgaria, and Yugoslavia, conducted by seven subcommissions or field investigating teams. It included the testimony of 238 witnesses, 32 statements made before the commission by individuals and nongovernmental bodies, as well as over 3,000 communications from various individuals and organizations. Despite delay, obstruction, and an inability to make on-the-spot investigations in Albania, Bulgaria, and Yugoslavia, a Subsidiary Group also worked from May to July and gathered additional evidence. Howard, *The United Nations and the Problem of Greece*, pp. 1-26; Harry Howard, "United States Policy Towards Greece in the United Nations, 1946-1950," *Balkan Studies* 8, No. 2 (1967):263-272; transcript, Harry Howard Oral History Interview, 5 June 1973, Harry S. Truman Library, gives some interesting background details.

ence of disturbed conditions in Greece in no way relieved Greece's three northern neighbors of their duty to prevent and suppress subversive activity within their territory, nor did it relieve them of direct responsibility for their support of the Greek guerillas. Albania, for example, had set up a training camp at Rubik in 1945; Yugoslavia was currently operating a training camp at Bulkes, where, on 25 March 1946, Nikos Zachariadis, leader of the Greek Communist Party, had made a speech urging the refugees to prepare themselves to return to Greece. In addition, it was clear that Yugoslavia and Bulgaria were supporting a separate Macedonian state within a Yugoslav federation through NOF (a Slavic counterpart of EAM), directed from Skopje and Monastir.[58]

It is against the background delineated by the Commission of Investigation's Report that one must view American policies in subsequent months. While the report would not be completed until May, its findings were clear to the Department of State as early as December 1946. Less clear was the role played by the Soviet Union in Albania, Yugoslavia, and Bulgaria.

In the past, the Yugoslavs had often looked in the direction of Salonika—particularly on 25 March 1941, when a former Yugoslav government signed the Axis Pact. Despite official denials, there were indications that Tito dreamed of the acquisition of Salonika as much as did any of his royal predecessors. Whatever Tito's aims, it was certain that their realization would weaken Western positions and serve the general interests of Moscow. Bulgaria, along with Russia, had been interested in Thrace at least since the time of the "Big Bulgaria" policy of 1878. As recently as November 1940, the Soviets had offered Bulgaria both Western and Eastern Thrace in return for Bulgaria's signing a mutual assistance pact with them. By mid-December 1946, Georgi Dimitrov, now installed with Stalin's blessing as prime minister of Bulgaria, was demanding Western Thrace. All this the Department of State knew.[59]

If the Department of State did not know the extent of Soviet complicity in the policies of the three countries bordering northern Greece, it did know that Soviet press and radio propaganda had repeatedly attacked Greece, as well as British and American policies toward Greece. The Soviets also had attacked Greece in the United Nations, where

[58] The report is reproduced as Annex 3 in Howard, *The United Nations and the Problem of Greece*, pp. 52-77.

[59] FR, 1946, VII:226-227, 231-232, 246-247, 265, 268-270, 272, 275-277, 281; David McLellan, *Dean Acheson: The State Department Years* (New York, 1976), p. 101. See also Chapter IV, n. 11.

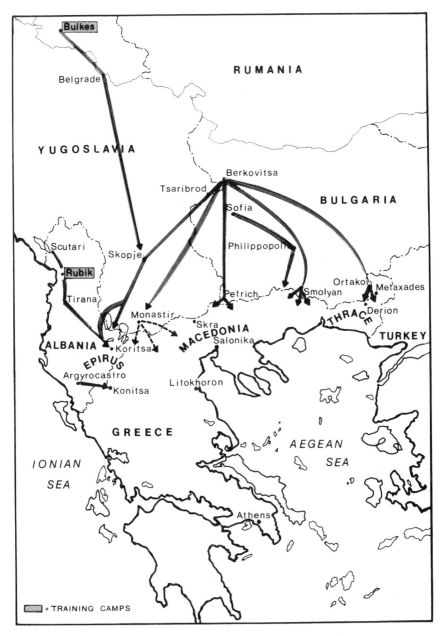

Map 10. Training Camps and Supply Routes of the Greek Guerillas
Based in part on Edgar O'Ballance, *The Greek Civil War, 1944-1949*
(New York, 1966), p. 132.

they supported its Balkan neighbors. Finally, the department was aware of Soviet probing in the Dodecanese, and well knew the recent history of Soviet claims, demands, and activities in Turkey and Iran—a history which could not be taken lightly.[60]

The internal situation in Greece, admittedly, was chaotic. Officials in the Department of State recognized that this situation owed many of its complications not only to the deprivations of war, but also to the inefficiency, pettiness, and irresponsibility of Greece's postwar regimes. The situation could not improve, however, if border activities continued. And this, of course, was precisely the position of Zachariadis, who early in 1946 had been encouraged by Soviet support for the Tudeh Party in Iran. While the British and Americans lacked evidence that the Soviets were directly involved in support for EAM or NOF, the analogy between events in Greece and Iran had occurred to them, too.[61]

In early November, Dean Acheson already was looking to the Iranian case as a model for dealing with any outside attempt to cut off northern Greece and to form a so-called "democratic" unit. Later in the month the British Foreign Office, too, began to link Greece with Iran, fearing that Grecian Macedonia would become another "Azerbaijan area."[62] These analogies had been made before the final resolution of the Iranian crisis in December. Success of the firm stand taken by the administration toward the end of 1946 in Iran strongly reinforced an inclination to take a similar stand in Greece.

Meanwhile, Acheson announced on 11 December that an economic mission under Paul Porter[63] would go to Greece in January to ascertain Greece's reconstruction and development needs. This announcement was followed on 19 December by the visit to the United States of the Greek prime minister Constantine Tsaldaris.[64] In early November Tsaldaris had met with Bevin in Paris, where the British foreign minister

[60] Ibid.; Byrnes, *Speaking Frankly*, p. 300; Harry S. Truman, 2:98.

[61] Gaddis Smith, *Dean Acheson*, p. 45; Acheson, pp. 198-199; FR, 1946, VII: 226-227, 231-232, 259, 282-283; interview with Loy Henderson; see also Chapter V, n. 139.

[62] FR, 1946, VII:259.

[63] Porter had recently been head of the Office of Price Administration. According to Joseph Jones, the administration decided to send Porter to Greece when it became apparent that Greece's economic, financial, and administrative system was totally disrupted, that the Greeks just wanted money, and that if granted it would be wasted. Porter's party arrived in Greece on 18 January. Jones, *The Fifteen Weeks*, pp. 75-76.

[64] Tsaldaris's visit lasted from 19 to 23 December.

encouraged him to go to the United States and ask for aid. He did as Bevin suggested, and was informed that the department intended to request funds for relief to Greece. By the end of the month, Acheson had informed MacVeagh that a relief program was being prepared for Greece's critical economic situation, although Congressional consideration and the necessary appropriations would take at least two or three months.[65]

At the beginning of 1947 the United States was thus concerned with two critical problems along the Northern Tier. First was the continued threat of Soviet pressures on Turkey, which forced the Turks to remain mobilized and caused serious economic problems for the government in Ankara.[66] Second was the more urgent situation in Greece, where Soviet policies were less clear. A full-scale review of American policy toward Greece in January 1947, on the basis of considerable circumstantial evidence inferred that EAM was an instrument of Soviet policy. The broad objective of the Soviets appeared to be to undermine British influence in the Eastern Mediterranean and to establish their own domination of the littoral countries of that region.[67] If, in retrospect, evidence does not bear out the conclusion that EAM was an instrument of Soviet policy, there was and still is little question that the Soviets were indirectly supporting Albania, Yugoslavia, and Bulgaria; there can be no doubt that they would have taken advantage of any situation in the Balkans that proved favorable to their interests.[68]

The American government's commitment to Greece at this time was clear, even though it was inadequate. The Truman administration had given the Greeks $417 million in grants and aid since World War II, and was now contemplating sending a bill to Congress for direct relief to Greece. But urgency on this matter was qualified by the administration's belief that Britain would not withdraw its troops from Greece unless circumstances changed suddenly and drastically.[69]

[65] FR, 1946, VII:278, 286-288; transcript, Constantine Tsaldaris Oral History Interview, 4 May 1964, Harry S. Truman Library.
[66] See, for example, the telegram from Edwin Wilson to the secretary of state, dated 30 December 1946, which Truman cites in his memoirs. FR, 1946, VII:898-899; Harry S. Truman, 2:97-98. See also: FR, 1947, V:2-3; S.D. 767.68119/1-1147/1-1347.
[67] S.D. Lot 55D638, January 1947 memo on "Current U.S. Policy Toward Greece," revising the "Policy and Information Statement on Greece."
[68] Interviews with Loy Henderson, William O. Baxter, and Harry Howard. See also Chapter V, n. 186, and McLellan, pp. 108-109.
[69] S.D. Lot 55D638, January 1947 memo on "Current U.S. Policy Toward

Americans were slow to understand the extent to which the war had devastated Britain's economy, making the situation which confronted the Truman administration in the Near East as much a British crisis as it was either Greek or Turkish. As a result of the war, Britain had lost two-thirds of its exports, one-fourth of its merchant marine, one-half of its overseas investments, and one-fourth of its financial reserves. Before the war, British investments and invisible exports had shored up the difference between imports and exports. Now that difference was gaping wide. To make matters worse, the government had increased its overseas debt by a factor of six. In 1947 these complications were compounded by Britain's severest winter in 66 years. In late January blizzards raged across the country. By the first week in February a severe fuel shortage forced the government to cut off electricity for domestic consumers and for a large part of the country's industry. It was, as Hugh Dalton, chancellor of the exchequer, called it, an "Annus Horrendus."[70]

Dalton had long been asking for a reduction of Britain's financial commitments abroad, and by mid-January had come to the conclusion that Britain's expenditures of manpower and money on defense were making nonsense of its economy and public finance. Against Dalton's arguments Ernest Bevin was unable to rally support, and the result was a pattern which made clear what had long been apparent to the more astute: the British Empire was disintegrating.[71]

A British White Paper on 28 January 1947 announced that Burma would soon have self-government. Ernest Bevin on 14 February declared that Britain had failed to find a solution to the Palestine problem and that it would send the case to the United Nations. Clement Attlee on 20 February read a White Paper announcing the British government's intention to quit India by June 1948. And the British government on 21 February placed before Parliament still another White Paper, "Economic Survey for 1947," which announced a severe economic plan for the coming year. Failure of the plan, said the government, might mean that the foundations of national life would never be restored. As the

Greece"; Lot 54D363, Folder: U.S. Program for Greece, May-July, letter from Robert Patterson to George Marshall. See also FR, 1947, V:491, 497.

[70] Jones, pp. 78-85; Helseth, pp. 387-388; G.D.N. Worswick and P. H. Ady, eds., The British Economy, 1945-1950 (London, 1952), pp. 476-483; Kirk, The Middle East, 1945-1950, p. 36; Dalton, pp. 187, 203.

[71] Francis-Williams, A Prime Minister Remembers, p. 165; Dalton, p. 190; Jones, p. 81; FR, 1947, V:13-14, 27, 37-39, 68.

number of Britain's unemployed reached 2,300,000, or 15½ percent of its labor force, the *London Times* on 22 February characterized the White Paper as "the most disturbing statement ever made by a British Government."[72]

Although two weeks before the British ambassador in Greece had characterized the situation there as desperate, there was little his government could do. Unless some solution to Greece's economic and financial problems could be found, he told his government, Britain's efforts would have been in vain. Economic and political collapse would result, and would be followed by Greece's incorporation into the Soviet system of buffer police states. What the British government could do in response to these warnings from Sir Clifford Norton, and what it did, was its only real option. As Clement Attlee later said: "By giving notice at the right moment that we couldn't afford to stay and intended to pull out we made the Americans face up to the facts in the eastern Mediterranean."[73]

The process of facing up to these facts had begun even before Britain gave the United States notice that it would withdraw from the Eastern Mediterranean. Beginning in February, the American government had been bombarded by a series of anguished reports from Greece. Paul Porter, head of the American Economic Mission to Greece; Mark Ethridge, American representative on the United Nations Commission of Investigation; and Lincoln MacVeagh, American ambassador to Greece, all sent cables expressing concern and alarm at Greece's plight. The internal and economic situations were bad, and guerilla activity was worsening. Secretary of State Marshall on 18 February asked for their concerted views as to the situation's seriousness, and on 20 February they replied. They were unanimous: the situation was critical. To regard the collapse of Greece as anything but imminent would be "highly unsafe." The United States must make it plain to everyone, including the Soviet Union, that it was determined not to permit foreign encroachment, either from within or without, upon the independence and integrity of Greece.[74]

Even before this telegram arrived, Loy Henderson on 20 February had

[72] *New York Times*, 29 January 1947; 15, 21-23 February 1947. Dalton, pp. 191-192, 205.

[73] S.D. Lot 54D363, Folder: U.S. Program for Greece, May-July, "Appendix 'A' to Aide Memoir," extract of a report dated 5 February 1947, from the British representative in Greece; see also *FR*, 1947, V:68.

[74] Harry S. Truman, 2:97-99; *FR*, 1947, V:15-16, 16-17, 17-22, 23-25, 26, 28-29.

written a memorandum to Acheson on the "Critical Situation in Greece." Acheson retitled it, reorganized it slightly, tacked on the most recent telegrams from Porter, Ethridge, and MacVeagh, and sent it on to Marshall on 21 February. Before leaving for Princeton, where he would speak at the university's bicentennial celebration, Marshall instructed Acheson to prepare the steps necessary to carry out NEA's recommendations for economic and military aid to Greece.[75]

It was at this juncture that the private secretary of the British ambassador, Lord Inverchapel, called the department to say that the ambassador wanted to deliver personally an important message to the secretary of state. This was not possible, since Marshall had left for Princeton. Because of the urgency of the situation, the British first secretary, Herbert Sichel, delivered copies of the two documents in question to Loy Henderson late that afternoon.[76]

An *aide-mémoire* on Greece began by noting the strategic problem of preventing Greece and Turkey from falling under Soviet influence. It discussed previous exchanges of views on the subject, including that between Bevin and Byrnes on 15 October 1946. Greece was now on the point of collapse. To support this contention, the 5 February report from Sir Clifford Norton was attached. Noting the urgency of America's decision to help Greece, and what form such help might take, the *aide-mémoire* promised that Britain would maintain Greece's armed forces up to 31 March but indicated that strained resources made further assistance to Greece impossible. In view of the great importance the United States attached to helping Greece, the British trusted that the Americans would find it possible to meet Greece's demands.[77]

An *aide-mémoire* on Turkey also cited the conversations between Bevin and Byrnes and reminded the United States that Byrnes had stressed that his government was as interested in developments in Turkey as in Greece. The British government, it noted, had made a new study of Turkey's problems. The Turks required military and economic assistance that Britain could not provide. The economic situation had been exhaustively discussed, and a full report had been delivered to the American government. Since Britain could not make further credits available to Turkey, the Turks would have to look to the United States.[78]

[75] S.D. 868.00/2-2047; FR, 1947, V:29-31; Acheson, p. 217.
[76] Jones, pp. 3-4; Acheson, p. 217. Lord Inverchapel, formerly Sir Archibald Clark-Kerr, was previously the British ambassador to Moscow.
[77] FR, 1947, VI:32-35.   [78] Ibid., pp. 35-37.

When Henderson learned what was about to happen, he knew what had to be done. So did his colleagues. The administration already was preparing to give aid to Greece, and it was obvious that the Turkish problem had to be faced squarely. Acheson instructed Henderson and John Hickerson, director of the Office of European Affairs, to get their people together that evening and assign tasks for preliminary reports the next day, Saturday. Coordination would be effected with other departments during the weekend, and preparations made for a Monday meeting of key cabinet members. Acheson then called the president and the secretary of state to inform them of the steps he had taken.[79]

On Saturday, reports were received and there was further discussion. There was general agreement that Britain's economic situation was serious and that Britain's motives in presenting the *aide-mémoires* were sincere. The choice was either to accept the general responsibility implied in the British memoranda or face the consequences of widespread collapse of resistance to Soviet pressure throughout the Near and Middle East and large parts of Western Europe not yet under Soviet domination. On Sunday, Henderson took the various reports to Acheson's home in Georgetown. Henderson asked if they were working on a paper bearing on the making of a decision or the execution of a decision, and Acheson said the latter. In the minds of both men, there could be only one decision.[80]

On Monday, 24 February, Secretary Marshall read the department's preliminary recommendations, formally received the British *aide-mémoires* from Lord Inverchapel, and then went to a cabinet luncheon. The British notes, he told Secretary Forrestal before the luncheon, were "tantamount to British abdication from the Middle East with obvious implications as to their successor." Discussion of the matter during lunch left the president and his advisors convinced of what had to be done. In the minds of almost everyone, the latest development was only

[79] Interview with Loy Henderson; Acheson, pp. 217-218; Harry S. Truman, 2:100.

[80] Interview with Loy Henderson; Kennan, *Memoirs, 1925-1950*, p. 331; Acheson, p. 218; FR, 1947, V:41-42, 47-55; Jones, pp. 131-135; John Jay Iselin, "The Truman Doctrine: A Study in the Relationship Between Crises and Foreign Policy-Making" (Ph.D. dissertation, Harvard University, 1964), pp. 83-84, 197-219. Loy Henderson was interested in including Iran in the memoranda that NEA was working on. He gave the matter some thought, discussed it informally with his colleagues, and then abandoned the idea—primarily because Britain had not requested the United States to include Iran in its new responsibilities. Henderson and his colleagues felt that the British government wanted to continue playing a dominant role in Iran in view of its oil concessions there. Loy Henderson, letter to the author.

part of a broader sequence of events which had been in the making for some time. There was no question that security interests were involved, and that only the United States could give Greece and Turkey the support necessary to preserve their independence and territorial integrity.[81]

Later in the afternoon, Loy Henderson chaired the first meeting of the Special Committee to Study Assistance to Greece and Turkey. He summarized the two British notes, observed that they were in line with British withdrawal from Burma, Palestine, and India, and read a memorandum of the 15 August 1946 decision on Turkey. He then read the memorandum which Acheson on Sunday had approved in principle as a basis for discussion; a long discussion followed. Henderson's leadership virtually assured endorsement by the group of his earlier recommendations that the United States should assume responsibility for aid to Greece and Turkey. A drafting committee was appointed to prepare a memorandum for the secretary, setting forth the committee's views.[82]

Meanwhile, President Truman had instructed Admiral Leahy and Clark Clifford to ascertain the views of the military in order to supplement the advice from State. Clifford spent Tuesday, 25 February, at the Pentagon. When he returned, he told the president that there was no alternative but to move into the vacuum created by Britain's withdrawal. Thus, on 26 February, when the Secretaries of State, War, and Navy met to discuss the Report of the Special Committee to Study Assistance to Greece and Turkey, the result surprised no one. The general program of assistance that Acheson and Henderson had put together over the weekend was endorsed and submitted immediately to the president for his approval, which it received before the end of the day.[83]

The Truman Doctrine and its Legacy

The problem which now confronted the Truman administration was to convince Congress and the American people that aid to Greece and Turkey was necessary. The newly elected, Republican-dominated 80th Congress was determined to reduce government spending, and hence

[81] Acheson, pp. 217-219; Kennan, *Memoirs, 1925-1950*, p. 331; Millis, p. 245; see also Millis, p. 251; Harry S. Truman, 2:93-109; *FR*, 1946, V:66-67; Gaddis Smith, *Dean Acheson*, pp. 45, 47; Jones, pp. 130-138.

[82] *FR*, 1947, V:45-47; Iselin, pp. 231-236.

[83] Iselin, p. 250; *FR*, 1947, V:47-55, 56-57, 58, 94.

likely to be antagonistic to foreign aid. As a consequence, the President invited influential Congressional leaders to the White House to hear the administration's case and to give him their reaction to the program.[84]

On 27 February Secretary of State Marshall read to the Congressmen a statement which outlined the current problem. While clearly aware of the Near East's strategic importance, Marshall was insufficiently versed in the recent history of the region to convince the delegation of the problem's urgency.[85] The immediate response of Congressional leaders to his presentation was to question the aid program's cost and the reasons for pulling Britain's chestnuts out of the fire.

Acheson therefore requested and was given the chance to make the case more forcefully. Having been through the ordeals of the past eighteen months, he was better able to describe the Soviet Union's pressures for territorial concessions in eastern Turkey and bases at the Straits, as well as its prolonged and vicious propaganda campaigns. He noted similar pressures against Iran, which for the time being had failed. Now, he said, Communist pressure was concentrated on Greece, where collapse was imminent. Unless Greece received prompt and large-scale aid, Communists would gain the upper hand. In his memoirs, Acheson recalled his impassioned argument: "Like apples in a barrel infected by one rotten one," he said, "the corruption of Greece would infect Iran and all to the east. It would also carry infection to Africa through Asia Minor and Egypt, and to Europe through Italy and France, already threatened by the strongest domestic Communist parties in Western Europe." In short, the Russians were seeking to dominate the Eastern Mediterranean and the Middle East; control of either Greece or Turkey would inevitably lead to control of the region, including Iran, and to the realization of Soviet aims, not only in the Middle East, but in Europe as well.[86]

---

[84] For the 27 February meeting at the White House, see: Jones, pp. 138-143; Acheson, p. 219; Gaddis Smith, *Dean Acheson*, p. 46; Harry S. Truman, 2:103-104; McLellan, pp. 115-118; FR, 1947, V:60-62, 121-123.

[85] For Marshall's speech, see: FR, 1947, V:60-62. The fact that a dry presentation of the problem did not convince the Congressmen undoubtedly influenced Truman and Acheson to believe that the president's speech to Congress required something extra.

[86] Acheson, p. 219. Acheson was well aware that the irredentist and autonomous aspirations of ethnic groups dispersed across the Northern Tier were susceptible to manipulation by the Soviets. Azerbaijanis, Kurds, Qashqa'is, Armenians, Georgians, Grecian Turks (still in Istanbul), Turkish Greeks (still in Thrace), Macedonians and various Slavic minorities all contributed to a situation which made possible the domino pattern he described.

The purpose of the administration's program to strengthen Greece and Turkey, said Acheson, was not to pull British chestnuts out of the fire, but to protect the security of the United States and to safeguard freedom by strengthening free peoples against Communist aggression and subversion.[87] For several moments following his presentation the group was silent. Then Senator Vandenberg, visibly shaken, told Acheson that any request to Congress for funds and authority to aid Greece and Turkey should be accompanied by a message in which the grim facts Acheson had delineated were laid publicly on the line.[88]

One scholar, through a close examination of the drafting process, has carefully traced the manner in which the decision to aid Greece and Turkey was transformed into what later became known as the Truman Doctrine. The contributions of the State Department—in particular those of Dean Acheson—and Clark Clifford were crucial in the nine drafts of the 2,200 word document. Men in the department very early recognized that the situation in Greece was only part of a much larger problem. They saw the importance of what was at stake, and what was required of the United States if it were to meet the larger problem. It fell to Acheson and Clifford to articulate that requirement, and as a consequence the Truman Doctrine bears their stamp.[89]

During recent crises, the United States had put such emphasis on the United Nations that it had created false expectations about that organization's utility. Many officials within the Truman administration, on the other hand, had been disabused of any misconceptions by intimate knowledge of events of the previous year. Acheson and Clifford were among them, and as a result Acheson in particular systematically excised many references to the U.N. from earlier drafts of Truman's

[87] See McLellan, pp. 116-117, for Acheson's convictions about individual freedom.

[88] According to Eric Goldman, Vandenberg, as he left the meeting, remarked to Truman: "Mr. President, if that's what you want, there's only one way to get it. That is to make a personal appearance before Congress and scare hell out of the country." See Eric Goldman, *The Crucial Decade—and After: America, 1945-1960* (New York, 1960), p. 59. Another meeting with Congressional leaders at the White House on 10 March made it clear that the president should put the crisis before the Congress and the United States in its broadest setting. Jones, pp. 143, 168-169; Acheson, pp. 221-222; Harry S. Truman, 2:105.

[89] Iselin, pp. 298 ff., esp. 345; Jones, pp. 148-170; FR, 1947, V:46, 57-58, 73, 94-95; Millis, p. 263; interview with Clark Clifford. The various drafts of the Truman Doctrine and other pertinent documents can be found in the George Elsey Papers, Box 17, and the Joseph M. Jones Papers, Box 1, Harry S. Truman Library. See also FR, 1947, V:41 ff. for departmental concern about publicizing the necessity of giving aid to Greece and Turkey.

speech. The United Nations had no funds and no mechanisms for dealing with the problem at hand. The international organization was slow and subject to delay. The Soviets could always veto its decisions. The United States alone would have to take whatever action was needed, while any action in the U.N. would either lack substance or anticipate the decision of Congress. In short, an appeal to the U.N. was futile, and the "U.N. boys" were not even immediately informed of the situation.[90]

Questions relating to Turkey and the strategic importance of the Middle East, while central in discussions within the executive branch and with Congressional leaders, were consciously played down in the speech. The administration wished to avoid alarming an American public unaccustomed to strategic military thinking in time of peace. It also wished to avoid provoking a Soviet reaction.[91]

Because of Acheson, direct references to Greece's strategic importance and to the vital interests of the United States in the Middle East were also left out of the speech. Why? More fundamental interests were at stake. In retrospect, Clark Clifford, who now admits that the speech overstated the particular crisis, has attempted to outline what those fundamental issues were. The world was prostrate. It needed some kind of hope—a message saying clearly and strongly that the United States was not going to sit back. Truman's speech was intended to give expression to that hope.[92] But whatever hope it was intended to elicit, it also signaled the end of British dominance in the Near East and the beginning of a new role for the United States in the region.

The president's address on 12 March 1947 to a joint session of Congress called for aid to Greece and Turkey. It also expressed the necessity of choosing between alternative ways of life. One alternative, the president said, was based on the will of the majority, and was distinguished by free institutions. The other alternative was based on the will of a minority forcibly imposed on the majority, and relied upon terror and oppression. The president's declared aim was to make possible the messianic hope of everlasting freedom—through support of peoples re-

<hr/>

[90] Iselin, pp. 398-403, 409, 415-416; Acheson, p. 223; interview with Loy Henderson; transcript, George Elsey Oral History Interview, Truman Library. This "oversight" was later corrected by making assistance subject to the United Nations' review.

[91] Jones, p. 162.

[92] Iselin, p. 339; Jones, pp. 154-157; interview with Clark Clifford; transcript, Francis Russell Oral History Interview, 13 July 1973, Truman Library.

sisting subjugation by armed minorities or by outside pressures. His specific aim, however, was to gain Congressional approval for a $400 million appropriation to aid Greece and Turkey. In short, although the problem was partially obscured by rhetoric, the administration was responding to a shift in the balance of power in the Near East, and calling for a public commitment to the defense of the Northern Tier.

The details of Congressional consideration of the bill to aid Greece and Turkey are not relevant to the focus of this study. Suffice it to say that the bill was approved in the Senate on 22 April by a 67-23 vote, and in the House on 8 May by a 287-107 vote. After a Conference Report adjusted differences, a voice vote passed the bill in both houses on 15 May. President Truman on 22 May signed Public Law 75, which gave him the authority he had requested in his address 71 days before.[93]

The effect of the aid program on the Northern Tier countries was to give them moral, political, and—ultimately—economic and military support. While Stalin's attitude toward Turkey never changed as long as he lived, Soviet threats against Turkey were soon subdued. In the Balkans, the American aid program to Greece, coupled with the rift between Tito and Stalin, eventually convinced the Yugoslavs that they should cease aid to the Greek guerillas, and close their borders to them. As a consequence, the civil war ended and the Greek government was stabilized.[94] In Iran, a complicated election process that had begun in January ended in June. The 15th Majlis did not open until July, and did not vote on a controversial oil agreement with the Soviet Union until October. Then, by a vote of 102-2, the agreement was rejected and the issues generated by the Iranian question at the end of the war were finally resolved.

Beyond the question of the aid program's immediate effects is that raised by the Truman administration's rationale for committing the United States to the defense of the Northern Tier. The administration clearly regarded the language employed in the president's speech as nec-

[93] Jones, pp. 197-198; *Legislative Origins of the Truman Doctrine: Hearings held in Executive Session before the Committee on Foreign Relations. United States Senate, Eightieth Congress, First Session on S. 938* (Washington, 1973). For Truman's address, see Appendix B.

[94] Howard, *Turkey, the Straits and U.S. Policy*, pp. 262-264; O'Ballance, pp. 210, 214; Stavrianos, *Greece*, pp. 201-202; D. George Kousoulas, "The Truman Doctrine and the Stalin-Tito Rift: A Reappraisal," *The South Atlantic Quarterly* 72 (Summer 1973):427-439.

essary to obtain public support.[95] This argument may be convincing, although acceptance or rejection of it requires further research into the nature of the political process and the climate of opinion in the United States in 1947. Here, it is sufficient to observe that the Truman administration, in order to rationalize a realistic and sensible policy toward the countries of the Northern Tier,[96] felt the necessity of resorting to imagery and rhetoric which encouraged a misleadingly simplistic view or model of the world.[97]

Whether the language employed by the Truman administration was indeed appropriate historians will long debate, but there is no doubt that the metaphoric representations it used were effective in producing the consensus necessary to respond to Soviet threats along the Northern Tier. The only way that nations can function internationally is to use such representations, with their attending conceptions of morality and power. A corollary, however, is that the moral and power components of such imagery can only be evaluated relative to the particularities of circumstance in which they are applied. This means that they must constantly be evaluated critically, so that the imagery a nation employs can be better reconceived relative to new circumstances. Unfortunately for the United States, this process of evaluation and reconception was overlooked in subsequent years and the view of the world presented by the Truman Doctrine hardened into myth.

[95] For details relating to perceptions of insufficient support, see Iselin, pp. 289, 309; FR, 1947, V:45 ff.; Harry S. Truman, 2:100-109; Acheson, pp. 219-225; Jones, p. 162; McLellan, pp. 115, 119; William Chittick, *State Department, Press, and Pressure Groups: A Role Analysis* (New York, 1970), p. 167. A 21 March 1947 memo from S. Shepard Jones to Dean Acheson, S.D. Lot 54D363, contains results of a telegraphic opinion poll conducted by Denver consultants shortly after Truman delivered his speech. Thirty-nine percent of those polled believed the United States should, and 47% believed that it should not provide military supplies to help the Greek government put down armed attacks led by Greek Communists (14% did not know). Forty-seven percent believed that the United States should, and 41% believed that it should not send some military experts to Greece to improve their armed forces. Forty-three percent believed that the United States should, and 40% believed that it should not provide military supplies and some military experts to Turkey to strengthen her defenses against Russian pressure. See also the undated memo from Elmo Roper, based on interviews in late March, in the Truman Papers, Confidential File, State Department (1946-47) No. 8, Truman Library.

[96] Contrary opinions abound, some of which can be found in Susan Hartmann, *Truman and the 80th Congress* (Columbia, Mo., 1971), pp. 58, 64, 215; Paterson, p. 206.

[97] Gaddis, *The United States and the Origins of the Cold War*, pp. 317-318, 352.

415

How did this happen? For one thing, the Truman Doctrine contributed to a new climate of opinion in which men like Senator Joseph McCarthy could capitalize on the administration's failure to match its rhetoric with concrete policies. McCarthyism would impel the government to pursue a consistently tough policy toward the Soviet Union in order to avoid the charge of being soft on Communism. In the process, decision-makers would adopt a simplistic, inflexible conception of the world, complete (after the "loss" of China in 1949 and the invasion of South Korea in 1950) with monolithic Communism and—in place of rotten apples—falling dominoes. The consequence: a perception of international events which would tend to assume its own reality, and define the world in its own terms.[98]

By following the "lessons of history," the lessons of how to deal with what they believed was a totalitarian adversary, American decision-makers ironically would come to see only the specious abstractions which served as their lenses. They would ignore the historical contexts of situations they faced, and impose on those situations their conceptions of how the world was structured. One could argue that the Truman administration's policies toward the Northern Tier were based on realistic assessments of America's legitimate interests, and that the Truman Doctrine's high-minded definition of the national purpose in 1947 was necessary to acquire support for those policies. But if, in the 1940s, security interests dictated the nation's stated international goals, by the 1950s and 1960s that process would be reversed. Unrealistic rhetoric, once used to mobilize public opinion in support of sensible policies, would itself come to determine what those policies should be, and the State Department's task of continuously redefining the international situation would be discouraged. Instead, abstractions would justify security interests and impose themselves on a world which had changed, a world for which those abstractions were increasingly irrelevant.[99]

[98] Ibid.; Athan Theoharis, *Seeds of Repression: Harry S. Truman and the Origins of McCarthyism* (Chicago, 1971), pp. 28-67; David Caute, *The Great Fear: The Anti-Communist Purge Under Truman and Eisenhower* (New York, 1978), p. 30.

[99] Howard Trivers, "Myths, Slogans and Vietnam: Specious Abstractions and Foreign Policy," in *Three Crises in American Foreign Affairs and a Continuing Revolution* (Carbondale, Ill., 1972), pp. 89-119; Lifka, pp. 530-531; Aron, p. 309. See also McLellan, pp. 426-430, for a discussion of Acheson's views on Vietnam. David Calleo has described how a prudent policy of containment was gradually translated into a new world order. The confrontation between East and West was institutionalized in the North Atlantic Treaty Organization (NATO), so providing

There are still other criticisms of the Truman Doctrine, most of which focus on its overstatement and misleading rhetoric. While some point out that it was meant to have limited application, others recognize that intentions must be distinguished from what in fact happened. While rhetoric, unrealism, and even deceit may be necessary in extreme situations, the consequences of such tactics are dangerous. The manipulation of opinion by the creation of unreal images is not always reversible; sometimes it must be accounted for, and so must be used only when there is no alternative.[100]

---

the groundwork. Where Europeans saw the balance of power as more relevant to diverse peoples, the United States equated such diversity with states' rights. The United States therefore looked to its own federal experience, and transformed it into an ideology of American hegemony in NATO, which saw order and progress tied to the assertion of a central authority. A rule of law supported the status quo which supposedly was based on a tacit social contract, but which served only as a mask for a rule of force over people not content with the status quo. According to Calleo, American nationalism, combined with world federalism, led to a self-righteous imperialism. (Calleo, pp. 42-43, 103-112). For insight into the conflict between pluralistic and synoptic (or "ideal-regarding") notions of justice, neither of which can do without the other, see David Braybrooke and Charles Lindblom, A Strategy of Decision, Policy Evaluation as a Social Process (New York, 1970), and John Rawls, A Theory of Justice (Cambridge, Mass., 1971).

[100] Freeland, pp. 319-360; Iselin, p. 339; Gaddis Smith, Dean Acheson, p. 48; Jones, pp. 154-155; Kennan, Memoirs, 1925-1950, pp. 332-351; George Kennan, "The United States and the Soviet Union, 1917-1976," Foreign Affairs 54 (July 1976): 679; Gaddis, The United States and the Origins of the Cold War, pp. 317-318, 352; Krock, pp. 412-413; Hannah Arendt, "Lying in Politics: Reflections on the Pentagon Papers," in Crises of the Republic (New York, 1972), pp. 3-47. Richard Snyder and others have observed that what they call "motive statements" may sometimes become guides to the conduct of foreign policy: "The notion that a public official can consistently falsify his motives with no consequences for ensuing decision and the surrounding situation is simply misleading. The more important the official the more likely his motive statements will have an effect on the situation." Richard Snyder et al., eds., Foreign Policy Decision-Making: An Approach to the Study of International Politics (New York, 1972), pp. 147-148.

Thomas Lifka takes issue with those who regard the Truman Doctrine's ideological emphasis as an afterthought (Lifka, pp. 505-506). He sees that emphasis as the "central binding quality of both the policy-making and public consensus." His assertion does not deny that events and real interests legitimized in part the images and ideological constructs policy-makers used to cope with complicated phenomena. It points only to the fact that the two were symbiotically related (see pp. 765-768). My argument would be that while there is some truth in Lifka's assertion, policy-makers nonetheless were responding to a reasonably objective interpretation of events and interests, both of which they could judge independently (to a degree) of the ideological framework they used to rationalize their actions to the public. For the difficulty of doing this, see John Steinbruner, The Cybernetic Theory of Decision: New Dimensions of Political Analysis (Princeton, 1974), and

417

What other alternatives did the Truman administration have? The same basic one which had been open to the Roosevelt administration: to lead and to educate. It might have been better for Roosevelt to be more honest with the American people about the differences between America and Russia. But there were good reasons why Roosevelt could not take it upon himself to educate the American public. Such arguments can be made for the Truman administration as well. Acheson, for example, saw first-hand the Congressional reaction to Marshall's presentation on 27 February. Perhaps this influenced his emphasis on rotten apples and, later, his rejection of a more subdued draft of the Truman Doctrine by George Kennan.[101] Acheson's judgment, obviously, was not infallible, but it is seriously questionable whether Kennan's own forthright and realistic speech (which reveals a limited appreciation for the situation in Turkey) would have obtained the necessary aid. When it came to educating the American public, the Truman administration faced an unsympathetic audience as well as a Republican Congress. In addition, the president had to walk in Roosevelt's shadow. These may be the reasons why little was accomplished when the administration first tried to educate the public after its August 1946 decision on Turkey. Could Truman repudiate Roosevelt's characterization of the Soviet Union or his treatment of international affairs? Had the public been informed, things might have been different. They might also have been worse. In any case, the consequences of the Truman Doctrine were profound. As one writer has suggested, the tragedy of American policy in Asia offers abundant proof of what happens if American leaders are less than frank, and if they are unwilling to assume the public's rationality.[102]

On a more concrete level, the program of aid to Greece and Turkey

---

Ole Holsti and James Rosenau, "Vietnam, Consensus, and the Belief Systems of American Leaders," a paper delivered at the 1977 Hendriks Symposium on American Politics and World Order, University of Nebraska, 6-7 October 1977.

[101] Acheson, p. 221; Kennan, *Memoirs, 1925-1950*, pp. 331-332; Jones, pp. 154-155; interview with Loy Henderson. For Kennan's views on one of the drafts of the Truman Doctrine, and for his own draft, see S.D. 868.00/3-647. See also Gaddis, *The United States and the Origins of the Cold War*, pp. 349-350.

[102] Ulam, *The Rivals*, p. 126. For a discussion of the 80th Congress, see Hartmann. See the discussion of domestic constraints on Truman in Gaddis, *The United States and the Origins of the Cold War*, pp. 261-263, 282-284, 312-318, 337-346 (esp.), 350-352, 356-358. Truman's freedom to maneuver was also restricted by troop reductions: from 12,000,000 in June 1945, to 3,000,000 in June 1946, and to 1,500,000 in June 1947. Gaddis, pp. 261-263.

served to reinforce earlier opinions and perceptions associated with the Iranian crisis. It also had a profound influence on the president. If a politician's first political success is important in the formation of his leadership style,[103] the same may be said of a president's first foreign policy success. American policies toward Iran, Turkey, and Greece clearly served this function for Truman. With the Iranian question, the Greek-Turkish question became part of a model of how the United States *should* conduct its relations with the Soviet Union.[104] After the Berlin crisis in 1948, and the "loss" of China in 1949, the administration's growing perception of Communism as an international, monolithic force gave increased relevance to the lessons suggested by events in the Near East. Thus, when North Korea descended on South Korea in 1950, Truman would characterize South Korea as "the Greece of the Far East." "If we are tough enough now," he told an aide in the White House, "there won't be any next step." In his memoirs, the president singled out Iran and Greece, along with Berlin, as cases of successful resistance to aggression. Truman saw Korea as part of a sequence of aggressive moves by the Communist world which tested the United States. Each successful American effort he saw as persuading the Soviets to follow a more cautious policy.[105]

These analogies were not unique to Truman. In early 1950, *before* the Korean War, John Foster Dulles, too, saw Asia in the context of implicit analogies associated with the American experience in the Near East. The fall of Greece in 1947, he wrote, would have led to the encirclement of Turkey, and Soviet Communist domination of the entire

[103] James D. Barber, *The Presidential Character: Predicting Performance in the White House* (Englewood Cliffs, N.J., 1972), p. 6. See also George Ball's comments on experience as a factor in foreign policy decision-making in "A Policy-Maker's View: Experience vs. Character," ed. T. G. Harris, *Psychology Today* 8 (March 1975):39.

[104] Almost immediately, the Truman Doctrine prepared the way for the Marshall Plan. See McLellan, pp. 123-136; Jones, pp. 198-256; Hadley Arkes, *Bureaucracy, the Marshall Plan, and the National Interest* (Princeton, 1972), pp. 3-58. If Soviet actions along the Northern Tier were crucial in the development of American policy toward the Soviet Union, the Marshall Plan had the same effect on Soviet policy. According to Adam Ulam, much of what happened in the next 15 years would be traceable in part to Stalin's reaction to the Marshall Plan (Ulam, *Stalin*, p. 657). As the former Allies' differing notions of how best to meet their security interests became increasingly inflexible, the resulting conflict between self-determination and spheres of influence in Eastern Europe and the Near East gradually assumed global proportions and grew progressively intractable.

[105] Glenn Paige, *The Korean Decision: June 24-30, 1950* (New York, 1968), pp. 54, 148; Harry S. Truman, 2:337-340.

Eastern Mediterranean and Near East. Later in the same book he expressed the desirability of United States help for Vietnam, not only because American prestige was involved, but because Vietnam's defeat, "coming after the reverses suffered by the National Government of China, would have further serious repercussions on the whole situation in Asia and the Pacific." President Eisenhower in 1957 would see the question of Vietnam in light of the lessons of Greece and Turkey. Adlai Stevenson in 1964 would characterize Greece and Korea as models for American action in Vietnam. Lyndon Johnson, too, would see the challenge in Southeast Asia as the same one the United States had already met in Greece, Turkey, Berlin, and Korea.[106] The success of the United States in confronting pressure by the Soviet Union and its satellites along the Northern Tier provided successive postwar administrations with what they believed to be clear and positive models for dealing with the Soviet Union.

In that light, John Gaddis's argument that the Truman Doctrine was not a turning point in American foreign policy bears critical examination. Gaddis argues that the Truman Doctrine, far from being a revolutionary policy,

> was very much in line with previously established precedents for dealing with shifts in the European balance of power; that despite its sweeping language the Truman administration, between 1947 and 1950, had neither the intention nor the capability of policing the rest of the world; and that the real commitment to contain communism everywhere originated in the events surrounding the Korean War, not the crisis in Greece and Turkey.[107]

Turning points in history, however, are rarely abrupt. Gaddis correctly cites a number of specific actions and statements by the admin-

[106] John Foster Dulles, War or Peace (New York, 1950), pp. 44, 231; The Pentagon Papers, The Senator Gravel Edition, vol. 1 (Boston, 1971), p. 615; Ernest May, "Lessons" of the Past, p. 108.

[107] John Gaddis, "Reconsiderations—Was the Truman Doctrine a Real Turning Point?" Foreign Affairs 52 (January 1974):386-402. Gaddis's main point is that the Truman administration did not view monolithic Communism as posing a threat to the world until 1950. In that year there was a change in perception not only of the enemy, but of the means available to contain him. Only then was the problem initially posed by the Soviet Union as a regional threat perceived as being serious enough to require rearmament. John Gaddis, letter to the author. Gaddis, of course, is right in emphasizing some of the critical changes that took place in 1950. My concern is to emphasize some of the factors which contributed to those changes.

istration which rejected the Truman Doctrine's universalizing trend: the rapid acceptance of Tito; the attempt to drive a wedge between Mao and Stalin; the China White Paper; and Acheson's National Press Club speech. He argues persuasively that a commitment to the containment of Communism on a global scale was encouraged by a cumulation of developments—such as Russia's detonation of the atomic bomb in August 1949 and the Communist takeover in China later in the year—and precipitated by events in Korea in 1950. The only concession he makes to the significance of the Truman Doctrine is to acknowledge that the Greek-Turkish crisis was the first situation in which special appropriations were necessary to carry out the administration's program. He recognizes that members of the administration *thought* they were living through a revolution, but he sees their exhilaration stemming "from the way in which policy was formulated—not from the actual decisions that were made." The latter observation, however, points to one of the limitations of his earlier argument. In asserting that a commitment to the containment of Communism on a global scale originated in events surrounding the Korean War, Gaddis gives insufficient attention to the *psychological* impact of events in the Near East on administration officials. The evidence we have examined suggests that the frame of mind which characterized decision-makers during the Korean War, and in the years that followed, was very much affected by the ordeal that led to the enunciation of the Truman Doctrine. In the minds of those officials, it was as difficult to dissociate events in Korea in 1950 from those in China in 1949, or from events in Greece and Turkey in 1947, as it was to dissociate the latter events from those in Iran and Turkey in 1946.[108] In this sense, perhaps, the Truman Doctrine represents an inner turning point.

[108] Nagai Yonosuke, for example, argues that the application of Truman's Cold War doctrine to Asia was due not to the Korean war, but to "the Communist takeover of the China mainland and the loss of America's nuclear monopoly." Walter LaFeber, on the other hand, sees America's involvement in Asia resulting from policies developed through a series of stages in 1945-50, the most significant stage being the application of counterforce in the Eastern Mediterranean and Western Europe in 1947-48. The key to understanding U.S. foreign policy in this period, LaFeber believes, is to be found "in the minds and actions of a small number of executive policy-makers whose view of history, understanding of the Soviet Union, determination of the American system's requirements, and evaluation of U.S. power primarily shaped the nation's foreign policy." While LaFeber's emphasis on the significance of the period 1947-48 coincides with my emphasis on the importance of events in the Near East and the influence of the Truman Doctrine in America's subsequent involvement in Asia, we obviously disagree on

Also important is another matter which cannot be overlooked: the balance of power that was being addressed in the Truman Doctrine was not limited to Europe. Europe's weakness, certainly, was the reason for America's commitment. But what was at issue went beyond Europe to Anatolia and Iran as well. The administration's decisions on policy toward the Northern Tier in the fall of 1946 corroborate the opinion of one official that Iran, too, was "an essential element in the wider situation that the President referred to on March 12." The Shah of Iran, unhappy that the Truman Doctrine conspicuously avoided any reference to Iran, later in the month was consoled by word that Iran, like Greece and Turkey, "would probably be similarly supported if similar need should arise."[109] In short, the American government implicitly had committed itself to maintaining the balance of power in a region which before World War II had been virtually outside its cognizance and within the British Empire's sphere of influence.

Winston Churchill, on 11 and 12 April 1947, in two articles written especially for the *New York Times*, succinctly summarized this fundamental change in international affairs. He observed that his statements at Fulton, Missouri, a year before, which at the time created quite a sensation, were now unchallenged in any part of the non-Communist world. Truman's speech, he further noted, made it plain that vital American interests and duties existed not only in the Eastern Mediterranean, but throughout the Middle East. Dwelling at length on events in Greece, Turkey, and Iran, he again asserted that the Soviet Union did not want war, but only its fruits. Policies directed toward preventing the Soviets from obtaining the fruits of war had been unpopular. Thus, his stand on Greece in 1944-45 had seemed to be out of step. "But today," he wrote, "it seems I was pursuing the exact policy which, little more than two years later, the United States has adopted with strong conviction. This is to me a very intense satisfaction." Churchill acknowledged that the British Empire was declining in the East, and declared that Britain welcomed establishment of American power in her place.[110] In short, he recognized the obvious fact that the United States

---

the administration's wisdom in assessing events in the Near East. Yonosuke Nagai and Akira Iriye, eds., *The Origins of the Cold War in Asia* (New York, 1977), pp. 15-65, 431. See also Lee Ross, "The Intuitive Psychologist and his Shortcomings: Distortions in the Attribution Process," in Leonard Berkowitz, ed., *Advances in Experimental Psychology* (New York, 1977), pp. 173-220.

[109] Jones, p. 58; Allen Papers, "Mission to Iran," chap. 9; FR, 1947, V:901.
[110] *New York Times*, 11-12 April 1947. See also chapter V, n. 83.

had assumed responsibility for maintaining the balance of power along the Northern Tier.

The Truman administration's recognition of this responsibility was symbolized in the Office of Near Eastern and African Affairs (NEA) by Loy Henderson's creation in 1947 of GTI, the Division of Greek, Turkish, and Iranian Affairs, formally established in NEA in 1948.[111] The policy implications that followed were evidenced in the "Pentagon Talks" on the Middle East that began in October 1947 between the United States and Britain. In these talks, the United States explicitly recognized the tremendous value of the Middle East, particularly the value of its oil. The United States also recognized the necessity of containing Soviet expansion in the region, the possibility that the American government might have to make full use of its political, economic, and military power to support such a policy, and the desirability of both immediate planning and parallel policies with the British. Central to this elaborate scheme was the territorial integrity and independence of Iran, Turkey, Greece, and now Italy. All four countries were seen as constituting a political and strategic bastion for vital American and British security interests in the Eastern Mediterranean and the Middle East. The newly formed National Security Council (NSC) approved these views on 21 November 1947, and the president subsequently endorsed them. By 6 January 1948, Admiral Souers, executive secretary of the NSC, would note the council's concurrence in the following report:

> . . . The security of the Eastern Mediterranean and of the Middle East is vital to the security of the United States. . . . The security of the whole Eastern Mediterranean and Middle East would be jeopardized if the Soviet Union should succeed in its efforts to obtain control of any one of the following countries: Italy, Greece, Turkey, or Iran. In view of the foregoing, it should be the policy of the United States, in accordance with the principles, and in the spirit of the Charter of the United Nations, to support the security of the Eastern Mediterranean and the Middle East. As a corollary of this policy the United States should assist in maintaining the territorial integrity and political independence of Italy, Greece, Turkey, and Iran. In carrying out this policy the United States should be prepared to make full use of its political, economic, and, if necessary, military power in such manner as may be found most effective. . . . It would be unrealistic for the United States to undertake to carry out such a policy unless the British maintain their

[111] John Jernegan, letter to the author. See Appendix A.

strong strategic political and economic position in the Middle East and Eastern Mediterranean, and unless they and ourselves follow parallel policies in that area. . . .[112]

In the final months of negotiations which ended in the North Atlantic Treaty in April 1949, when the question arose of American support for Greece, Turkey, and Iran, the United States government considered issuing a formal declaration of support for them, but instead decided to rely on previous and future public statements by the secretary of state and the president. On 23 March 1949, for example, Secretary of State Dean Acheson reiterated in a press conference what he had said earlier in a radio discussion of the North Atlantic Pact:

> In the compact world of today, the security of the United States cannot be defined in terms of boundaries and frontiers. A serious threat to international peace and security anywhere in the world is of direct concern to this country. Therefore, it is our policy to help free peoples to maintain their integrity and independence, not only in Western Europe or the Americas, but wherever the aid we are able to provide can be effective. Our actions in supporting the integrity and independence of Greece, Turkey and Iran are expressions of that determination. Our interest in the security of these countries has been made clear, and we shall continue to pursue that policy.

Twelve days later, in a speech at the ceremony for the signing of the Atlantic Pact, President Truman again made it clear that American adherence to the pact in no way signified a lessening of concern for the security and welfare of the Near East. And on 12 April 1949 Dean Acheson told Turkish Foreign Minister Necmeddin Sadak that after ratification of the pact the United States planned to study what further steps it could take to strengthen international security. Whether such steps included extension of the Atlantic Pact to the Middle East, or support of an Eastern Mediterranean bloc, depended on events that developed.[113]

[112] FR, 1947, V:485-626 (esp. 513-514, 551, 561, 575-580, 592-594, 623-624); 1948, IV:2.
[113] FR, 1949, VI: 8, 44, 500, 1647-1653. In his conversation with Sadak, Acheson underlined America's vital interest in Turkey by citing his government's decision of August 1946 in support of Turkey—a decision which had been taken with full knowledge of the possible consequences. "The President," he told Sadak, "considered this the most important decision he had made subsequent to the bombing of Hiroshima." While American capabilities did not permit negotiations on security pacts with Greece, Turkey, and Iran before the Korean War, policy

In short, the invitations to Greece and Turkey in 1951 to join NATO, and their accession to the North Atlantic Treaty in 1952, the Baghdad Pact of 1955, the Eisenhower Doctrine of 1957, and the Baghdad Pact's heir, CENTO, which included Turkey, Iran, and Pakistan, all were extensions not so much of the Korean War as of problems inherent in the struggle for power in the Near East and the policies outlined in 1946-48. The first serious postwar confrontation between the United States and the Soviet Union, and the Truman administration's subsequent commitment to the countries of the Northern Tier, together thwarted Soviet ventures in the Near East, and invariably extended the perimeters of America's defensive concerns. Both experiences created a model for the nation's subsequent international behavior and began the process, which gradually assumed global proportions, of containing Communism in the postwar world. Commitment to the defense of the countries of the Northern Tier also involved the United States inextricably in the problems of the Middle East—problems which in many respects represent a continuation of the old Eastern Question and which continue to make the countries of the Northern Tier as important to the security interests of the United States as they were when the United States first assumed responsibility for maintaining the balance of power in the region.[114]

Conclusion

Whatever the far-reaching consequences of the Truman Doctrine and Public Law 75, their immediate result was to complete the transformation of the State Department's policies into concrete commitments by the United States to Greece and Turkey, and to conclude the revolution in American foreign policy toward the Near East.

---

planners seriously considered the problem, as did the countries in question. FR, 1948, IV:41, 148; 1949, VI:31-45, 233, 473n, 1662.

[114] For a general discussion of American foreign policy toward the Middle East in the postwar world, see John C. Campbell, *Defense of the Middle East: Problems of American Foreign Policy*, rev. ed. (New York, 1960), and Polk. For Soviet policy, see Lederer and Vucinich; and Lenczowski, *Soviet Advances in the Middle East*. The assertion regarding the present attitudes of the United States toward the countries of the Northern Tier was elicited from a conversation with General George Brown, former chairman of the Joint Chiefs of Staff. His assertion about the importance of the Northern Tier has been underscored by recent events in the broader "Arc of Crisis." See also John C. Campbell, "The Soviet Union in the Middle East," *Middle East Journal* 32 (Winter 1978):1-12, and Lenczowski, "The Arc of Crisis: Its Central Sector."

One of the last contributing factors in this transformation was the crisis in Iran, whose resolution reinforced the administration's inclination to assume a greater responsibility for the emerging crisis in Greece. George Allen and the confidence in American support that he inspired together were decisive in prompting Prime Minister Ahmad Qavam to exercise control over the province of Azerbaijan. The resolution of the crisis in December 1946—however convoluted the process—demonstrated the effectiveness of direct American support and aid to the Northern Tier countries, and strengthened the Truman administration's growing belief that firm policies, formulated in response to Soviet threats, were correct.

The Iranian crisis also completed the administration's education in the regional realities of power. It was now certain that nineteenth-century diplomacy was still the rule, and the balance of power still the governing factor along the Northern Tier. When another crisis in Greece precipitated Britain's recognition in February 1947 that it would have to abandon its traditional role as a balance to Russian aspirations in the Balkans and at the Straits, department officials were conditioned as to their responsibilities.

Lincoln MacVeagh and others in NEA had predicted long before the British crisis in February 1947 that the British Empire was disintegrating, and had counseled that the United States should exercise its influence in the Eastern Mediterranean. Because of Britain's relative weakness, and America's recently-defined economic and strategic interests in the Near East, Soviet hostility toward the countries of the Northern Tier had nurtured the development of Anglo-American cooperation in the region. By 1947, America's role in the Near East had evolved to a point where the United States was playing an important part in the region's geopolitical developments. It was supporting Iran, Turkey, and Greece politically, assisting them economically, and preparing to subsidize Britain's faltering military assistance to them as well. Britain's sudden collapse only hastened the process.

Soviet responsibility for the crisis in Greece was much less clear than it had been for the crises it initiated in Turkey and Iran, but whether or not the Soviets were *directly* involved in this most recent problem, and the available evidence suggests that they were not, there was no question that they associated themselves with the efforts of Albania, Yugoslavia, and Bulgaria to support the Greek Communists. What was known of Russia's pronouncements on the Balkans, and the inferences

426

that could be made on the basis of its performances in Iran and Turkey, moreover, redounded to its complicity in the Greek crisis, and strongly suggested that it would take advantage of any situation that proved favorable to Soviet interests.

President Truman's decision to aid Greece and Turkey, therefore, must be understood in light of these considerations and in the context of events which had taken place along the Northern Tier in recent years. Repeated Soviet maneuvers against Turkey, three crises in Iran, the deteriorating situation in the Balkans, and the weakened capacity of Great Britain to fill its traditional role in the Eastern Mediterranean, all were part of the larger problem addressed by Truman's decision of 26 February to aid Greece and Turkey, and his speech before Congress on 12 March 1947. The problem was one of political, economic, and military power, and of America's willingness to use it. Perhaps, as Clark Clifford has noted, the speech itself overstated the crisis in Greece. But it did not overstate the larger crisis of instability and disequilibrium along the Northern Tier that was bound to follow the collapse of British influence.

The Administration's motives for committing American power to the Near East have often been questioned. Were the ideals espoused by the United States merely a rationalization for economic interests—the pursuit of which dominated American concerns and caused the Soviets to act menacingly and aggressively toward the Northern Tier countries? As we have indicated elsewhere, America's competitive superiority meant that countries accepting the principles of the Atlantic Charter, and the principle of equal trading opportunities for all, and which therefore were subject to the economic influence of the most able, often found themselves within what was tantamount to an American sphere of influence—a liberal capitalist international order dominated by the United States. Thus, while the United States could happily uphold the principles of the Charter and the United Nations, the Soviet Union was more chary of them. Not having the technical "know-how" to compete with American interests and threatened by capitalist inroads in the Near East, Stalin resorted to forceful methods to obtain control over areas he hoped to include within the Soviet Union's sphere of influence. This logic applies especially to a postwar world where changed power relationships created a situation conducive to the redefinition of earlier understandings.

The claim that economic interests *dominated* American foreign pol-

427

icy, however, except in the sense outlined above, imputes too much to a thesis which, while it enlightens, explains everything only at the expense of distortion. As one historian has written, "political behavior consists of an aggregate of individual actions influenced by diverse factors and therefore seldom if ever comprehensive in terms of any pervasive or underlying force."[115] Events in the Near East point less to cynicism and strictly imperialistic economic motives on the part of the United States than they do to an aggressive idealism which, to a considerable degree, derived from a profound belief in the virtues of America's political and economic system. This belief was reinforced by perceived "lessons" of the past,[116] and indirectly although clearly promoted American interests. As a consequence, the United States was willing to play the balance of power game within the context of the principles of the United Nations. The governments supported by the United States agreed with those principles because the United Nations protected their interests as well. Unfortunately for the Soviet Union, the United Nations' principles did not serve Soviet needs.

There is an almost insurmountable difficulty in differentiating between the Soviets' aggressive and defensive actions, just as there is in distinguishing between the nationalistic and ideological elements of their policies. This problem is somewhat analogous to that of distinguishing between ideals and self-interest in American foreign policy. Again, the debate over motivation is of little use and will probably not be of much ultimate significance. As one scholar has observed, American decision-makers did not make any distinction between economic and political goals, ideologies and self-interest. Rather, these factors were inextricably related.[117] Thus, there is little to be gained by quibbling over the most conspicuous motives of either the Russians or the Americans

[115] Ernest May, *American Imperialism: A Speculative Essay* (New York, 1968), p. 15.

[116] Some of these lessons included the notion that support for an international organization such as the League of Nations, and the dissolution of barriers to international trade and investment, would prevent the recurrence of a cycle which began with economic nationalism, led to depression, gave impetus to militarism and fascism, and ultimately resulted in war. Ernest May, *"Lessons" of the Past*, p. 9.

[117] Lifka, p. 353. This point of view is substantiated in a recent work by Edward Weisband, which shows how a paradigm of Lockian liberalism transforms concerns with wealth, power, status, moral virtue, and the freedom of mankind into a single set of mutually reinforcing values. Edward Weisband, *The Ideology of American Foreign Policy: A Paradigm of Lockian Liberalism* (Beverly Hills, Calif., 1973).

428

in the Near East; nor is there much benefit in describing the conflict that occurred there in the normative terms of one or the other country. Such a course leads only to the kind of history that supports a national point of view. The latter frame of reference is occasionally useful, but in international rivalries and disagreements it often obscures the nature of the historical problem which caused nations to come into conflict in the first place. It is preferable to characterize the conflict along the Northern Tier as another episode in the historical struggle for power in the region, a clash between competing national entities whose interests were intimately related to the world views or philosophies they espoused. Underlying their different perceptions of the world was the fundamental belief of each that its interests were compatible with those of other nations, and that its own system could best serve mankind.[118] The question of the relative merits of each system is universally debated today, and is in part a continuation of the debate between Wilsonian-

[118] See Introduction, n. 4. Lloyd Gardner has characterized what he feels was part of America's world view in his treatment of American perceptions of Eastern Europe:

> "America's direct interests in Eastern Europe were far less important than the rebuilding of an effective European and world economic system; but the only way to promote such reconstruction was for America (the only nation powerful enough to do it) to take the lead in keeping the door open in Eastern Europe. This fact and not simple economic motives alone prompted Washington's strong efforts to enforce equal opportunity. Had he lived, Roosevelt would have been faced with the same situation" (Gardner, *Architects of Illusion*, p. 57).

Much controversy has taken place over attempts by "revisionist" historians to deal with the issue of American liberal objectives and the question of their universal applicability. In part, revisionists have attempted to compensate for previous histories of the Cold War that have been written from a nationalistic point of view. They desire to counter the moral righteousness which such a view presumes. In the late sixties and early seventies when many were writing, the war in Vietnam was seen as a particularly vivid example of what happens when a nation imposes its values on another; many were led to question the righteousness of the United States not only in Vietnam, but in the past as well. In doing so, these historians irritated the more traditional of their colleagues for a variety of reasons: the polemical quality of much that they wrote; the systemic frames of reference some of them used, the validity of which many traditional historians questioned; the fact that they threatened the identities of the nationalistic historians, many of whom had been Cold Warriors; and because the parochial nature of much that was written evidenced a failure adequately to understand the nature of the Soviet system under Stalin, or truly to appreciate its repressive character. Because of these factors, the debates that took place between traditionalists and revisionists often degenerated into heated and irrational arguments which obscured the insights that some of the latter had to offer.

ism and Leninism that began during World War I.[119] The task of resolving the debate is left to the moralist. Our interest here is to recognize and delineate the problem, and to point out that during the early years of the Cold War, the vast majority of people in Greece, Turkey, and Iran preferred alignment with the United States.

The Russians, in attempting to redefine the balance of power along the Northern Tier, were doing what they had done for centuries along their southern flank. The United States, on the other hand, had never made clear (nor did the State Department know) the degree to which it was willing or able to back up the principles President Roosevelt had espoused during the war. Perhaps, as Maxim Litvinov told Edgar Snow in 1945, the United States should have begun opposing Soviet interests in the Balkans and Eastern Europe back in 1942. This, of course, would have been difficult to do until the war was over, as Roosevelt well knew, and when the war was over, the postwar boundaries of Europe were virtually established. Whether the United States could have opposed the Soviet Union effectively along the Northern Tier before 1947, and could thereby have prevented the confrontations that occurred, is a moot point. The Soviets had been allies of the Americans, and Stalin had been treated kindly by the American press. Would public opinion have tolerated the use of force against him? On 5 February 1945 Roosevelt had indicated to Churchill and Stalin at Yalta that he did not believe he could obtain support from Congress or the American public for the maintenance of an appreciable American force on the Continent for more than two years. Truman had less prestige than Roosevelt, and the Near East was even more remote than the Continent. In 1946, especially during the crisis in Iran in March, and even during the Turkish crisis in August, the ideological arguments used in the Truman Doctrine in 1947 could not have been used as effectively to sway public opinion. In December 1946, when the Iranian crisis was resolved, it was still not clear that the United States would have seriously contemplated using force. By this time, one should remember, a Republican Congress had been elected, and possession of the atomic bomb notwithstanding, options open to the American government in the Near East were at a premium.

In February 1947, however, the administration was forced to act.

---

[119] See Gordon Levin, *Woodrow Wilson and World Politics*. See also Lloyd Ambrosius, "The Orthodoxy of Revisionism: Woodrow Wilson and the New Left," *Diplomatic History* 1 (Summer 1977):199-214.

Within a month its public policies toward Soviet aspirations in the Eastern Mediterranean were in line with what Litvinov believed they should have been toward Soviet designs on Eastern Europe and the Balkans during World War II. Events along the Northern Tier had educated department officials in balance of power politics and served as a forge for the administration's emerging policy of containment—a policy inherent in the idea of an equilibrium of forces and a cornerstone of British diplomacy in the Near East for over a century.[120] One crisis after another had given American policy-makers a clear conception of Greece, Turkey, and Iran in their collective historical role of dividing East and West, and fostered the increasingly close association between British and American policies in the Near East. By 1947 these policies had become inseparable. In giving expression to the idea of containment implicit in the Truman Doctrine,[121] President Truman was not pulling Britain's chestnuts out of the fire. He was not acting primarily on the basis of economic imperatives (which were important) or cynically in the context of domestic politics; nor was he overreacting to events in Greece, which by themselves, admittedly, were ambiguous. What he was doing, essentially, was responding to his responsibilities for protecting the broad, complex, and inextricably interwoven strategic and security interests of the United States, and to the State Department's well-founded belief that those interests were best served by maintaining the balance of power along the entire Northern Tier.

[120] See Chapter I, no. 5.

[121] The policy of containment, of course, was first articulated publicly by George Kennan in *Foreign Affairs* 25 (July 1947):566-582. For recent assessments of the notion, see John Gaddis, "Containment: A Reassessment," *Foreign Affairs* 55 (July 1977):873-887; Eduard Mark, "The Question of Containment: A Reply to John Lewis Gaddis," *Foreign Affairs* 56 (January 1978):430-440; see also Gaddis's response, pp. 440-441, George Kennan's letter to the editor, *Foreign Affairs* 56 (April 1978):643-645, and Mark's response, pp. 645-647.

The Organization of the Office of Near Eastern and African Affairs (NEA)

The Office of Near Eastern and African Affairs (NEA) was created in 1944 during the administrative reforms of Undersecretary of State Edward Stettinius, Jr. While Greece and Turkey came under the jurisdiction of the Division of Near Eastern Affairs (NE), Iran came under that of the Division of Middle Eastern and Indian Affairs (MEI). There was also a Division of African Affairs (AF). During 1947, conditions in Greece, Turkey, and Iran led Loy Henderson, Director of NEA, to place those countries under the jurisdiction of a separate division, an arrangement that was formalized by the creation of the Division of Greek, Turkish, and Iranian Affairs (GTI) in 1948.

The "Truman Doctrine"

ADDRESS of the President of the United States delivered before a joint session of the Senate and the House of Representatives, recommending assistance to Greece and Turkey, March 12, 1947.

Mr. President, Mr. Speaker, Members of the Congress of the United States:

The gravity of the situation which confronts the world today necessitates my appearance before a joint session of the Congress.

The foreign policy and the national security of this country are involved.

One aspect of the present situation, which I wish to present to you at this time for your consideration and decision, concerns Greece and Turkey.

The United States has received from the Greek Government an urgent appeal for financial and economic assistance. Preliminary reports from the American Economic Mission now in Greece and reports from the American Ambassador in Greece corroborate the statement of the Greek Government that assistance is imperative if Greece is to survive as a free nation.

I do not believe that the American people and the Congress wish to turn a deaf ear to the appeal of the Greek Government.

Greece is not a rich country. Lack of sufficient natural resources has always forced the Greek people to work hard to make both ends meet. Since 1940, this industrious and peace-loving country has suffered invasion, 4 years of cruel enemy occupation, and bitter internal strife.

When forces of liberation entered Greece they found that the retreating Germans had destroyed virtually all the railways, roads, port facilities, communications, and merchant marine. More than a thousand villages had been burned. Eighty-five percent of the children were tubercular. Livestock, poultry, and draft animals had almost disappeared. Inflation had wiped out practically all savings.

As a result of these tragic conditions, a militant minority, exploiting human want and misery, was able to create political chaos which, until now, has made economic recovery impossible.

434

Greece is today without funds to finance the importation of those goods which are essential to bare subsistence. Under these circumstances the people of Greece cannot make progress in solving their problems of reconstruction. Greece is in desperate need of financial and economic assistance to enable it to resume purchases of food, clothing, fuel, and seeds. These are indispensable for the subsistence of its people and are obtainable only from abroad. Greece must have help to import the goods necessary to restore internal order and security so essential for economic and political recovery.

The Greek Government has also asked for the assistance of experienced American administrators, economists, and technicians to insure that the financial and other aid given to Greece shall be used effectively in creating a stable and self-sustaining economy and in improving its public administration.

The very existence of the Greek State is today threatened by the terrorist activities of several thousand armed men, led by Communists, who defy the Government's authority at a number of points, particularly along the northern boundaries. A Commission appointed by the United Nations Security Council is at present investigating disturbed conditions in northern Greece, and alleged border violations along the frontier between Greece on the one hand and Albania, Bulgaria, and Yugoslavia on the other.

Meanwhile, the Greek Government is unable to cope with the situation. The Greek Army is small and poorly equipped. It needs supplies and equipment if it is to restore the authority of the Government throughout Greek territory.

Greece must have assistance if it is to become a self-supporting and self-respecting democracy.

The United States must supply that assistance. We have already extended to Greece certain types of relief and economic aid, but these are inadequate.

There is no other country to which democratic Greece can turn.

No other nation is willing and able to provide the necessary support for a democratic Greek Government.

The British Government, which has been helping Greece, can give no further financial or economic aid after March 31. Great Britain finds itself under the necessity of reducing or liquidating its commitments in several parts of the world, including Greece.

We have considered how the United Nations might assist in this crisis. But the situation is an urgent one requiring immediate action and the United Nations and its related organizations are not in a position to extend help of the kind that is required.

It is important to note that the Greek Government has asked for our aid in utilizing effectively the financial and other assistance we may give to Greece, and in improving its public administration. It is of the utmost importance that we supervise the use of any funds made available to Greece, in such a manner that each dollar spent will count toward making Greece self-supporting, and will help to build an economy in which a healthy democracy can flourish.

No government is perfect. One of the chief virtues of a democracy, however, is that its defects are always visible and under democratic processes can be pointed out and corrected. The government of Greece is not perfect. Nevertheless it represents 85 percent of the members of the Greek Parliament who were chosen in an election last year. Foreign observers, including 692 Americans, considered this election to be a fair expression of the views of the Greek people.

The Greek Government has been operating in an atmosphere of chaos and extremism. It has made mistakes. The extension of aid by this country does not mean that the United States condones everything that the Greek Government has done or will do. We have condemned in the past, and we condemn now, extremist measures of the right or the left. We have in the past advised tolerance, and we advise tolerance now.

Greece's neighbor, Turkey, also deserves our attention.

The future of Turkey as an independent and economically sound state is clearly no less important to the freedom-loving peoples of the world than the future of Greece. The circumstances in which Turkey finds itself today are considerably different from those of Greece. Turkey has been spared the disasters that have beset Greece; and during the war, the United States and Great Britain furnished Turkey with material aid. Nevertheless, Turkey now needs our support.

Since the war Turkey has sought financial assistance from Great Britain and the United States for the purpose of effecting that modernization necessary for the maintenance of its national integrity.

That integrity is essential to the preservation of order in the Middle East.

The British Government has informed us that, owing to its own difficulties, it can no longer extend financial or economic aid to Turkey.

As in the case of Greece, if Turkey is to have the assistance it needs, the United States must supply it. We are the only country able to provide that help.

I am fully aware of the broad implications involved if the United States extends assistance to Greece and Turkey, and I shall discuss these implications with you at this time.

One of the primary objectives of the foreign policy of the United States is the creation of conditions in which we and other nations will be able to work out a way of life free from coercion. This was a fundamental issue in the war with Germany and Japan. Our victory was won over countries which sought to impose their will, and their way of life, upon other nations.

To insure the peaceful development of nations, free from coercion, the United States has taken a leading part in establishing the United Nations. The United Nations is designed to make possible lasting freedom and independence for all its members. We shall not realize our objectives, however, unless we are willing to help free peoples to maintain their free institutions and their national integrity against aggressive movements that seek to impose upon them totalitarian regimes. This is no more than a frank recognition that totalitarian regimes imposed on free peoples, by direct or indirect aggression, undermine the foundations of international peace and hence the security of the United States.

The peoples of a number of countries of the world have recently had totalitarian regimes forced upon them against their will. The Government of the United States has made frequent protests against coercion and intimidation, in violation of the Yalta agreement, in Poland, Rumania, and Bulgaria. I must also state that in a number of other countries there have been similar developments.

At the present moment in world history nearly every nation must choose between alternative ways of life. The choice is too often not a free one.

One way of life is based upon the will of the majority, and is distinguished by free institutions, representative government, free elections, guarantees of individual liberty, freedom of speech and religion, and freedom from political oppression.

The second way of life is based upon the will of a minority forcibly imposed upon the majority. It relies upon terror and oppression, a controlled press and radio, fixed elections, and the suppression of personal freedoms.

I believe that it must be the policy of the United States to support

437

free peoples who are resisting attempted subjugation by armed minorities or by outside pressures.

I believe that we must assist free peoples to work out their own destinies in their own way.

I believe that our help should be primarily through economic and financial aid which is essential to economic stability and orderly political processes.

The world is not static, and the status quo is not sacred. But we cannot allow changes in the status quo in violation of the Charter of the United Nations by such methods as coercion, or by such subterfuges as political infiltration. In helping free and independent nations to maintain their freedom, the United States will be giving effect to the principles of the Charter of the United Nations.

It is necessary only to glance at a map to realize that the survival and integrity of the Greek nation are of grave importance in a much wider situation. If Greece should fall under the control of an armed minority, the effect upon its neighbor Turkey, would be immediate and serious. Confusion and disorder might well spread throughout the entire Middle East.

Moreover, the disappearance of Greece as an independent state would have a profound effect upon those countries in Europe whose peoples are struggling against great difficulties to maintain their freedoms and their independence while they repair the damages of war.

It would be an unspeakable tragedy if these countries, which have struggled so long against overwhelming odds, should lose that victory for which they sacrificed so much. Collapse of free institutions and loss of independence would be disastrous not only for them but for the world. Discouragement and possibly failure would quickly be the lot of neighboring peoples striving to maintain their freedom and independence.

Should we fail to aid Greece and Turkey in this fateful hour, the effect will be far reaching to the West as well as to the East.

We must take immediate and resolute action.

I, therefore, ask the Congress to provide authority for assistance to Greece and Turkey in the amount of $400,000,000 for the period ending June 30, 1948. In requesting these funds, I have taken into consideration the maximum amount of relief assistance which would be furnished to Greece out of the $350,000,000 which I recently requested that the Con-

438

gress authorize for the prevention of starvation and suffering in countries devastated by the war.

In addition to funds, I ask the Congress to authorize the detail of American civilian and military personnel to Greece and Turkey, at the request of these countries, to assist in the tasks of reconstruction, and for the purpose of supervising the use of such financial and material assistance as may be furnished. I recommend that authority also be provided for the instruction and training of selected Greek and Turkish personnel.

Finally, I ask that the Congress provide authority which will permit the speediest and most effective use, in terms of needed commodities, supplies, and equipment, of such funds as may be authorized.

If further funds, or further authority, should be needed for purposes indicated in this message, I shall not hesitate to bring the situation before the Congress. On this subject the executive and legislative branches of the Government must work together.

This is a serious course upon which we embark.

I would not recommend it except that the alternative is much more serious.

The United States contributed $341,000,000,000 toward winning World War II. This is an investment in world freedom and world peace

The assistance that I am recommending for Greece and Turkey amounts to little more than one-tenth of 1 percent of this investment. It is only common sense that we should safeguard this investment and make sure that it was not in vain.

The seeds of totalitarian regimes are nurtured by misery and want. They spread and grow in the evil soil of poverty and strife. They reach their full growth when the hope of a people for a better life has died.

We must keep that hope alive.

The free peoples of the world look to us for support in maintaining their freedoms.

If we falter in our leadership, we may endanger the peace of the world —and we shall surely endanger the welfare of our own Nation.

Great responsibilities have been placed upon us by the swift movement of events.

I am confident that the Congress will face these responsibilities squarely.

439

Selected Bibliography

Archives, Manuscript Collections, and Private Papers

Acheson, Dean. Harry S. Truman Library. Independence, Mo.

Allen, George. Duke University Library. Durham, N.C.

Atkins, Paul. Yale University Library. New Haven, Conn.

Baldwin, Hanson. Yale University Library. New Haven, Conn.

Byrnes, James F. Clemson University Library. Clemson, S.C.

Clayton, William. Harry S. Truman Library. Independence, Mo.

Clifford, Clark. Harry S. Truman Library. Independence, Mo.

Connally, Tom. Manuscript Division, Library of Congress. Washington, D.C.

Daniels, Jonathan. Harry S. Truman Library. Independence, Mo.

Dulles, John Foster. Princeton University Library. Princeton, N.J.

Elsey, George M. Harry S. Truman Library. Independence, Mo.

Feis, Herbert. Manuscript Division, Library of Congress. Washington, D.C.

Forrestal, James V. Princeton University Library, Princeton, N.J.

Grew, Joseph C. Houghton Library, Harvard University. Cambridge, Mass.

Henderson, Loy. Personal papers in the possession of Loy Henderson, Washington, D.C.

Hopkins, Harry. Franklin D. Roosevelt Library. Hyde Park, N.Y.

Howard, Harry N. Harry S. Truman Library. Independence, Mo.

Hull, Cordell. Manuscript Division, Library of Congress. Washington, D.C.

Jones, Joseph M. Harry S. Truman Library. Independence, Mo.

Kennan, George F. Princeton University Library. Princeton, N.J.

Leahy, William D. Manuscript Division, Library of Congress. Washington, D.C.

Modern Military Records Branch. Record Group 218, National Archives. Washington, D.C.

Patterson, Robert P. Manuscript Division, Library of Congress. Washington, D.C.

Roosevelt, Franklin D. Franklin D. Roosevelt Library. Hyde Park, N.Y.

Rosenman, Samuel I. Harry S. Truman Library. Independence, Mo.

Rossow, Robert. Personal papers in the possession of Robert Rossow, Washington, D.C.

Steinhardt, Laurence. Manuscript Division, Library of Congress. Washington, D.C.

Stettinius, Jr., Edward. University of Virginia. Charlottesville, Va.

Stimson, Henry. Yale University Library. New Haven, Conn.

Truman, Harry S. Harry S. Truman Library. Independence, Mo.

U.S. Army, Operations Division. National Archives. Washington, D.C.

U.S. Department of State. Decimal File. Record Group 59, National Archives. Washington, D.C.

————. Diplomatic Records Branch, Post and Lot Files. Suitland, Md.

U.S. Office of Strategic Services. Research and Analysis Branch. Records, National Archives. Washington, D.C.

Vaughan, Harry H. Harry S. Truman Library. Independence, Mo.

Interviews, Letters, and Conversations

Baxter, William. Interview. 23 June 1975.

Brown, George. Conversation. 10 October 1974.

Clifford, Clark. Interview. 6 May 1975.

Durbrow, Elbridge. Interview. 10 April 1974.

Gaddis, John. Letter to the author. 10 September 1978.

Hare, Raymond. Interview. 11 April 1974.

Harriman, W. Averell. Letter to the author. 20 June 1977.

Henderson, Loy. Interviews. 18 April 1974 and 16 May 1974.

————. Letters to the author. 20 and 28 June 1976, 2 January 1977.

Hiss, Alger. Letter to the author. 7 June 1977.

Howard, Harry. Interview. 23 June 1975.

————. Letter to the author. February 1977.

Jernegan, John. Letter to the author. 15 April 1975.

Kennan, George. Conversation. 11 April 1975.

————. Letter to the author. 6 December 1977.

Kohler, Foy. Letter to the author. 22 June 1977.

Merriam, Gordon. Letters to the author. 25 September 1975, 22 and 28 January, and February, 1977.

Minor, Harold. Letter to the author. 14 June 1977.

Pogue, Forrest. Interview. 23 June 1975.

Rossow, Robert. Interview. 26 June 1975.

————. Letter to the author. 6 July 1977.

Sands, William. Interview. 23 June 1975.

Wright, Edwin. Interview. November 1974.

————. "A Personal Narrative—A Retrospective View." 2 April 1975. In the author's possession.

Truman Library Oral History Collections

Daniels, Jonathan

Elsey, George M.

Ethridge, Mark K.

Henderson, Loy W.

Hickerson, John D.
Howard, Harry N.
Matthews, H. Freeman
Russell, Francis H.
Satterthwaite, Joseph C.
Tsaldaris, Constantine
Vaughan, Harry H.

Public Documents and Papers, Documentary and Statistical
Collections, and Official Publications

Beitzell, Robert, ed. *Teheran, Yalta, Potsdam: The Soviet Protocols*. Hattiesburg, Miss., 1970.

Butler, J.R.M., gen. ed. *History of the Second World War, United Kingdom
Military Series: Grand Strategy*. 6 vols. Vol. 5 by John Ehrman, *August
1943-September 1944*. London, 1956.

———. *History of the Second World War, United Kingdom Military Series:
The Mediterranean and the Middle East*. 6 vols. Vol. 1 by I.S.O. Playfair,
The Early Successes against Italy. London, 1954.

Cordier, A. W., and Foote, W., eds. *Public Papers of the Secretaries-General
of the United Nations*. Vol. I: *Trygve Lie, 1946-1953*. New York, 1969.

*Correspondence Between the Chairman of the Council of Ministers of the
U.S.S.R. and the Presidents of the U.S.A. and the Prime Ministers of
Great Britain During the Great Patriotic War of 1941-1945*. Moscow,
1957.

Ehrman, John. See Butler, J.R.M.

Great Britain, Parliament. *Hansard's Parliamentary Debates* (Commons),
5th series, vols. 400, 402, 407, 500.

Great Britain. Public Record Office. Premier 3/434/7. "Record of Meeting
at the Kremlin, Moscow, October 9th, 1944 at 10 p.m."

Howard, Harry. *The United Nations and the Problem of Greece*. Washington, D.C., 1947.

Hurewitz, J. C., ed. *Diplomacy in the Near and Middle East: A Documentary Record, 1914-1956*. Princeton, 1956.

Kesaris, Paul. See *O.S.S./State Department Intelligence and Research Reports*.

Medlicott, W. N. *The Economic Blockade*. 2 vols. London, 1952, 1959.

Mellor, W. Franklin, ed. *Casualties and Medical Statistics*. London, 1972.

Motter, T. H. Vail. *The United States Army in World War II: The Middle
East Theater, The Persian Corridor and Aid to Russia*. Washington, D.C.
1952.

O.S.S./State Department Intelligence and Research Reports. 7 vols. Vol.
VII, *The Middle East*, Paul Kesaris, ed. Washington, D.C. 1977.

443

The Pentagon Papers. The Senator Gravel Edition. Vol. 1. Boston, 1971.

Playfair, I.S.O. See Butler, J.R.M.

Public Papers of the Presidents of the United States: Harry S. Truman, 1946. Washington, D.C., 1962.

Roosevelt, Kermit. *War Report of the O.S.S.* New York, 1976.

Sontag, Raymond, and Beddie, James, eds. *Nazi-Soviet Relations, 1939-1941: Documents from the Archives of the German Foreign Office.* Washington, D.C., 1948.

United Nations. *United Nations Security Council Journal.* 1st year, Series 1, Meetings 1-42 (17 January-26 June 1946). London, New York, 1946.

――――. *United Nations Security Council Official Records.* 1st year, Series 1, Supplements 1-2. New York, 1946. Readex Microprint: Docs s/203-2/217. New York, 1946.

――――. *United Nations Security Council Official Records.* 1st year, Series 2, Meetings 50-88 (10 July-31 December 1946). New York, 1946.

――――. *Yearbook of the United Nations, 1946-1947.* New York, 1947.

U.S. Bureau of the Census. *Historical Statistics of the United States: Colonial Times to 1957.* Washington, D.C., 1960.

U.S. Congress. Senate. *Congressional Record.*

――――. Senate. *American Petroleum Interests in Foreign Countries: Hearings Before a Special Committee Investigating Petroleum Resources.* Washington, D.C., 1946.

U.S. Department of State. The Department of State *Bulletin.*

――――. *Documents on German Foreign Policy, 1918-1945.* Series D, vol. XII, *The War Years. February 1-June 22, 1941.* Washington, D.C., 1962.

――――. *Foreign Relations of the United States, 1927,* III. Washington, D.C., 1942.

――――. *Foreign Relations of the United States, 1940,* III. Washington, D.C., 1958.

――――. *Foreign Relations of the United States, 1941,* I. Washington, D.C., 1958.

――――. *Foreign Relations of the United States, 1941,* III. Washington, D.C., 1959.

――――. *Foreign Relations of the United States, 1942,* I. Washington, D.C., 1960.

――――. *Foreign Relations of the United States, 1942,* III. Washington, D.C., 1961.

――――. *Foreign Relations of the United States, 1942,* IV. Washington, D.C., 1963.

――――. *Foreign Relations of the United States, 1943,* I. Washington, D.C., 1963.

444

————. *Foreign Relations of the United States*, 1943, III. Washington, D.C., 1963.

————. *Foreign Relations of the United States*, 1943, IV. Washington, D.C., 1964.

————. *Foreign Relations of the United States*, 1943, V. Washington, D.C., 1965.

————. *Foreign Relations of the United States*, 1944, I. Washington, D.C., 1966.

————. *Foreign Relations of the United States*, 1944, III. Washington, D.C., 1966.

————. *Foreign Relations of the United States*, 1944, IV. Washington, D.C., 1966.

————. *Foreign Relations of the United States*, 1944, V. Washington, D.C., 1966.

————. *Foreign Relations of the United States*, 1945, II. Washington, D.C., 1967.

————. *Foreign Relations of the United States*, 1945, IV. Washington, D.C., 1968.

————. *Foreign Relations of the United States*, 1945, V. Washington, D.C., 1967.

————. *Foreign Relations of the United States*, 1945, VIII. Washington, D.C., 1969.

————. *Foreign Relations of the United States*, 1946, I. Washington, D.C., 1972.

————. *Foreign Relations of the United States*, 1946, III. Washington, D.C., 1970.

————. *Foreign Relations of the United States*, 1946, VI. Washington, D.C., 1969.

————. *Foreign Relations of the United States*, 1946, VII. Washington, D.C., 1969.

————. *Foreign Relations of the United States*, 1947, I. Washington, D.C., 1973.

————. *Foreign Relations of the United States*, 1947, V. Washington, D.C., 1971.

————. *Foreign Relations of the United States*, 1948, IV. Washington, D.C., 1974.

————. *Foreign Relations of the United States*, 1949, VI. Washington, D.C., 1977.

————. *Foreign Relations of the United States: The Conferences at Cairo and Teheran, 1943*. Washington, D.C., 1961.

————. *Foreign Relations of the United States: The Conferences at Malta and Yalta, 1945*. Washington, D.C., 1955.

445

U.S. Department of State. *Foreign Relations of the United States: The Conference of Berlin (The Potsdam Conference), 1945.* Vols. I and II. Washington, D.C., 1960.

――――. *Foreign Relations of the United States: The Conference at Quebec, 1944.* Washington, D.C., 1972.

――――. *Foreign Relations of the United States: The Conferences at Washington, 1941-1942, and Casablanca, 1943.* Washington, D.C., 1968.

――――. *Foreign Relations of the United States: The Conferences at Washington and Quebec, 1943.* Washington, D.C., 1970.

U.S. Government. *Register of the Department of State: December 1, 1946.* Washington, D.C., 1947.

U.S. House of Representatives. *Assistance to Greece and Turkey: Hearings Before the Committee on Foreign Affairs, House of Representatives, Eightieth Congress, First Session on H.R. 2616.* Washington, D.C., 1947.

U.S. Senate. *Foreign Relief Aid: 1947, Hearings Held in Executive Session Before the Committee on Foreign Relations, United States Senate, Eightieth Congress, First Session on H.J. Res. 153 and S. 1774.* Washington, D.C., 1973.

――――. *Legislative Origins of the Truman Doctrine: Hearings Held in Executive Session Before the Committee on Foreign Relations, United States Senate, Eightieth Congress, First Session on S. 938.* Washington, D.C., 1973.

Wright, Edwin. *Azerbaijan: A Case History of Soviet Infiltration.* Washington, D.C., 1946.

Newspapers

Christian Science Monitor.
Le Monde (Paris).
New York Herald Tribune.
New York Times.
Washington Post.

Books, Articles, and Secondary Sources

Acheson, Dean. *Present at the Creation.* New York, 1969.

Adamec, Ludwig. *Afghanistan's Foreign Affairs to the Mid-Twentieth Century: Relations with the USSR, Germany, and Britain.* Tucson, Arizona, 1974.

Albion, Robert, and Connery, Robert. *Forrestal and the Navy.* New York, 1962.

Alexander, Edward. "The Armenian Church in Soviet Policy." *The Russian Review* 14 (October 1955):357-362.

Allen, George. "Mission to Iran." Manuscript in the George Allen Papers, Duke University, Durham, N.C.

Allen, Robert S., and Shannon, William. *The Truman Merry-Go-Round*. New York, 1950.

Alliluyeva, Svetlana. *Twenty Letters to a Friend*. New York, 1967.

Alpern, Stanley. "Iran 1941-1946: A Case Study in the Soviet Theory of Colonial Revolution." Certificate essay, Russian Institute. Columbia University, 1953.

Alperovitz, Gar. *Atomic Diplomacy: Hiroshima and Potsdam*. New York, 1965.

Alsop, Joseph, and Alsop, Stewart. *The Reporter's Trade*. New York, 1958.

Alvarez, David. "The Missouri Visit to Turkey: An Alternative Perspective on Cold War Diplomacy." *Balkan Studies* 15 (1974):225-236.

Ambrosius, Lloyd E. "The Orthodoxy of Revisionism: Woodrow Wilson and the New Left." *Diplomatic History* (Summer 1977):199-214.

Anderson, M. S. *The Eastern Question, 1774-1923*. New York, 1966.

Arendt, Hannah. *Crises of the Republic*. New York, 1972.

Arfa, Hassan. *Under Five Shahs*. Edinburgh, 1964.

Arkes, Hadley. *Bureaucracy, the Marshall Plan, and the National Interest*. Princeton, 1972.

Arlen, Michael. *Passage to Ararat*. New York, 1975.

Aron, Raymond. *The Imperial Republic: The United States and the World, 1945-1973*. Englewood Cliffs, N.J., 1974.

Art, Robert. "Bureaucratic Politics and American Foreign Policy: A Critique." *Policy Sciences* 4 (December 1973):467-490.

Ataöv, Türkkaya. *Turkish Foreign Policy, 1939-1945*. Ankara, 1965.

Atiyeh, George N. *The Contemporary Middle East, 1948-1973: A Selective and Annotated Bibliography*. Boston, 1975.

Auty, Phyllis, and Clogg, Richard, eds. *British Policy Towards Wartime Resistance in Yugoslavia and Greece*. London, 1975.

Avery, Peter. *Modern Iran*. New York, 1965.

Aydemir, Şevket S. *İkinci Adam*, II Cilt. Istanbul, 1968.

"The Azerbaijan Problem." *The World Today* 2 (February 1946):48-57.

Bagguley, John. "The World War and the Cold War." In *Containment and Revolution*, pp. 76-124. Edited by David Horowitz. Boston, 1967.

Bailey, Thomas. *The Marshall Plan Summer: An Eyewitness Report on Europe and the Russians in 1947*. Stanford, 1977.

Ball, George W. Comments in "A Policy-maker's View: Experience vs. Character." Edited by T. G. Harris, *Psychology Today* 8 (March 1975): 39.

Banani, Amin. *The Modernization of Iran, 1929-1941*. Stanford, 1961.

447

Barber, James D. *The Presidential Character: Predicting Performance in the White House*. Englewood Cliffs, N.J., 1972.

Barghoorn, Frederick. "The Soviet Union Between War and Cold War." *Annals* 263 (May 1949):1-8.

Bargman, Alexander. "The Polish Question." *Survey* 58 (January 1966):159-167.

Barker, Elisabeth. *British Policy in South-East Europe in the Second World War*. New York, 1977.

——. "Greece." In *Hitler's Europe*, pp. 678-690. Edited by Arnold Toynbee and Veronica Toynbee. London, 1954.

——. *Macedonia—Its Place in Balkan Power Politics*. London, 1950.

Beitzell, Robert. *The Uneasy Alliance: America, Britain, and Russia, 1941-1943*. New York, 1972.

Bellah, Robert. "Coming Around to Socialism: Roots of the American Taboo." *Nation* 219 (28 December 1974):677-685.

Berkhofer, Robert, Jr. *A Behavioral Approach to Historical Analysis*. New York, 1969.

Bernstein, Barton J. "Cold War Orthodoxy Restated." *Reviews in American History* 1 (December 1973):453-462.

——. "Roosevelt, Truman and the Atomic Bomb, 1941-1945: A Reinterpretation." *Political Science Quarterly* 90 (Spring 1975):23-69.

Bernstein, Barton J., ed. *Politics and Policies of the Truman Administration*. Chicago, 1970.

Bethell, Nicholas. *The Last Secret*. New York, 1974.

Bishop, Jim. *FDR's Last Year: April 1944-April 1945*. New York, 1974.

Black, C. E. "Soviet Policy in Eastern Europe." *The Annals of the American Academy of Political and Social Science* 263 (May 1949):152-164.

Black, C. E. et al. *Communism and Revolution: The Strategic Uses of Political Violence*. Princeton, 1964.

Blum, John. *V Was for Victory: Politics and American Culture During World War II*. New York, 1976.

Bohlen, Charles. *Witness to History, 1929-1969*. New York, 1973.

Borkenau, Franz. *European Communism*. London, 1953.

Braybrooke, David, and Lindbloom, Charles. *A Strategy of Decision: Policy Evaluation as a Social Process*. New York, 1970.

Brown, Anthony Cave. *Bodyguard of Lies*. New York, 1975.

Bryson, Thomas. *American Diplomatic Relations with the Middle East, 1784-1975: A Survey*. Metuchen, N.J., 1977.

Brzezinski, Zbigniew. *The Soviet Bloc: Unity and Conflict* (Revised and enlarged). Cambridge, Mass., 1967.

Buhite, Russell. *Patrick J. Hurley and American Foreign Policy*. Ithaca, 1973.

Bullard, Sir Reader. *Britain and the Middle East*. London, 1964.

————. *The Camels Must Go*. London, 1961.

Bullitt, Orville, ed. *For the President, Personal and Secret*. Boston, 1972.

Bullock, Alan. *Hitler, A Study in Tyranny*. London, 1954.

Burns, James MacGregor. *Roosevelt, The Soldier of Freedom*. New York, 1970.

Busch, Briton. *Britain and the Persian Gulf, 1894-1914*. Berkeley, 1967.

————. *Mudros to Lausanne: Britain's Frontier in West Asia, 1918-1923*. Albany, 1976.

Byford-Jones, W. *The Greek Trilogy: Resistance—Liberation—Revolution*. London, 1945.

Byrnes, James F. *All in One Lifetime*. New York, 1958.

————. "Byrnes Answers Truman." *Collier's*, 26 April 1952, pp. 15 ff.

————. *Speaking Frankly*. New York, 1947.

Calleo, David. *The Atlantic Fantasy: The U.S., NATO, and Europe*. Baltimore, 1970.

Campbell, John, and Sherrard, Philip. *Modern Greece*. New York, 1968.

Campbell, John C. *Defense of the Middle East: Problems of American Foreign Policy*. New York, 1960.

————. "The Soviet Union in the Middle East," *Middle East Journal*. 32 (Winter 1978):1-12.

————. *The United States in World Affairs 1945-1947*. New York, 1947.

Campbell, Thomas, and Herring, George, eds. *The Diaries of Edward R. Stettinius, Jr*. New York, 1975.

Carey, Jane, and Carey, Andrew. *The Web of Greek Politics*. New York, 1968.

Caute, David. *The Great Fear: The Anti-Communist Purge under Truman and Eisenhower*. New York, 1978.

Chittick, William O. *State Department, Press and Pressure Groups: A Role Analysis*. New York, 1970.

Chubin, Shahram, and Zabih, Sepehr. *The Foreign Relations of Iran: A Developing State in a Zone of Great-Power Conflict*. Berkeley, 1974.

Churchill, Winston. *Closing the Ring*. Boston, 1951.

————. *The Grand Alliance*. Boston, 1950.

————. *The Hinge of Fate*. Boston, 1950.

————. "If I Were an American." *Life*, 14 April 1947, pp. 106 ff.

————. *Triumph and Tragedy*. Boston, 1953.

Clark, Alan. *Barbarossa: The Russian-German Conflict, 1941-1945*. New York, 1965.

Clemens, Diane. *Yalta*. New York, 1970.

Cohen, Stephen. *Bukharin and the Bolshevik Revolution: A Political Biography, 1888-1938*. New York, 1973.

449

Collins, Larry, and Lapierre, Dominique. *Freedom at Midnight*. New York, 1975.

———. *O Jerusalem!* New York, 1972.

Conquest, Robert. *The Great Terror*. New York, 1968.

———. *The Nation Killers: The Soviet Deportation of Nationalities*. Glasgow, 1970.

———. *Power and Policy in the U.S.S.R.* New York, 1967.

Copeland, Miles. *The Game of Nations: The Amorality of Power Politics*. New York, 1969.

Cottam, Richard W. *Nationalism in Iran*. Pittsburgh, 1964.

Couloumbis, Theodore. *Greek Political Reaction to American and NATO Influences*. New Haven, 1967.

Cunningham, Andrew. *A Sailor's Odyssey*. London, 1951.

Curry, George. *James F. Byrnes*. New York, 1965.

Dallek, Robert. "Franklin D. Roosevelt as World Leader." *American Historical Review* 76 (December 1971):1503-1513.

Dallin, David. *Soviet Russia's Foreign Policy, 1939-1942*. New Haven, 1942.

Dalton, Hugh. *High Tide and After: Memoirs, 1945-1960*. London, 1962.

Daniels, Jonathan. *The Man of Independence*. New York, 1950.

———. *White House Witness, 1942-1945*. New York, 1975.

Davies, Joseph. *Mission to Moscow*. New York, 1941.

Davis, Forrest. "Roosevelt's World Blueprint." *Saturday Evening Post* 215 (10 April 1943):20 ff.

Davis, Helen Miller. *Constitutions, Electoral Laws, Treaties of States in the Near and Middle East*. 2nd ed., rev. Durham, N.C., 1953.

Davis, Lynn. *The Cold War Begins: Soviet-American Conflict over Eastern Europe*. Princeton, 1974.

Davison, Roderic. "Middle East Nationalism: Lausanne Thirty Years After." *The Middle East Journal* 7 (Summer 1953):324-348.

———. "Turkish Diplomacy from Mudros to Lausanne." In *The Diplomats, 1919-1939*, pp. 172-209. Edited by Gordon Craig and Felix Gilbert. Princeton, 1953.

Deane, John. *The Strange Alliance: The Story of Our Efforts at Wartime Cooperation with Russia*. New York, 1947.

Dedijer, Vlademir. *Tito*. New York, 1953.

Dehio, Ludwig. *The Precarious Balance*. New York, 1926.

Delivanis, Dimitrios, and Cleveland, William C. *Greek Monetary Developments, 1939-1948: A Case Study of the Consequences of World War II for the Monetary System of a Small Nation*. Bloomington, Ind., no date.

De Luca, Anthony. "The Montreux Conference of 1936: A Diplomatic Study of Anglo-Soviet Rivalry at the Turkish Straits." Ph.D. dissertation, Stanford University, September 1973.

DeNovo, John. *American Interests and Policies in the Middle East, 1900-1939*. Minneapolis, 1963.

"The Division of Near Eastern Affairs." *The American Foreign Service Journal* 10 (January 1933):16 ff.

Djilas, Milovan. *Conversations with Stalin*. New York, 1962.

———. *Wartime*. New York, 1977.

Dobney, Frederick J. *The Selected Papers of Will Clayton*. Baltimore, 1971.

Donovan, Robert J. *Conflict and Crisis: The Presidency of Harry S Truman, 1945-1948*. New York, 1977.

Druks, Herbert. *Harry S. Truman and the Russians*. New York, 1966.

Dulles, John Foster. *War or Peace*. New York, 1950.

Eagleton, William, Jr. *The Kurdish Republic of 1946*. London, 1963.

Eason, Warren. "Demography." In *Handbook of Soviet Social Science Data*, pp. 49-63. Edited by Ellen Mickiewicz. New York, 1973.

———. "Population Changes." In *Prospects for Soviet Society*, pp. 203-240. Edited by Allen Kassof. New York, 1968.

Eden, Anthony. *The Reckoning*. Boston, 1965.

Edson, Charles. "Greece During the Second World War." *Balkan Studies* 8 (1967):225-238.

Eisenberg, Carolyn. "Reflections on a Toothless Revisionism." *Diplomatic History* 2 (Summer 1978):295-305.

Elwell-Sutton, E. P. "Political Parties in Iran." *The Middle East Journal* 3 (January 1949):45-62.

———. *Persian Oil: A Study in Power Politics*. London, 1955.

Eren, Nuri. *Turkey Today—And Tomorrow*. New York, 1963.

Erickson, John. *The Soviet High Command*. London, 1962.

Erkin, Feridun Cemal. *Les Relations Turco-Soviétiques et la Question des Détroits*. Ankara, 1968.

Esmer, Ahmed. "The Straits: Crux of World Politics." *Foreign Affairs* 25 (January 1947):290-302.

Ethridge, Mark, and Black, C. E. "Negotiating in the Balkans, 1945-1947." In *Negotiating with the Russians*, pp. 184-203. Edited by Raymond Dennett and Joseph Johnson. Boston, 1951.

Eudes, Dominique. *The Kapetanios: Partisans and Civil War in Greece, 1943-1949*. New York, 1972.

Evans, Laurence. *United States Policy and the Partition of Turkey, 1914-1924*. Baltimore, 1965.

Fatemi, Nasrollah. *Oil Diplomacy*. New York, 1954.

Feis, Herbert. *Between War and Peace: the Potsdam Conference*. Princeton, 1960.

———. *Churchill, Roosevelt, Stalin: The War They Waged and the Peace They Sought*. Princeton, 1957.

Feis, Herbert. *From Trust to Terror: The Onset of the Cold War, 1945-1950.* New York, 1970.

———. *Seen from E.A.* New York, 1947.

Ferrell, Robert. *George C. Marshall.* New York, 1966.

Field, James A., Jr. *America and the Mediterranean World, 1776-1882.* Princeton, 1969.

Firouz, Prince Mozaffar. *L'Iran Face à L'imposture de L'histoire.* Paris, 1971.

Fischer, Louis. *The Life of Lenin.* New York, 1964.

———. *The Road to Yalta: Soviet Foreign Relations, 1941-1945.* New York, 1972.

———. *The Soviets in World Affairs.* New York, 1930.

Fleming, Denna F. *The Cold War and its Origins, 1917-1960.* 2 vols. Garden City, N.Y., 1961.

———. *The Issues of Survival.* Garden City, N.Y., 1972.

Flowers, Desmond, and Reeves, James, eds. *The War, 1939-1945.* London, 1960.

Fox, Annette Baker. *The Power of Small States: Diplomacy in World War II.* Chicago, 1959.

Francis-Williams, Edward. *Ernest Bevin: Portrait of a Great Englishman.* London, 1952.

———. *A Prime Minister Remembers: The War and Post-War Memoirs of the Rt. Hon. Earl Attlee.* London, 1961.

Freeland, Richard M. *The Truman Doctrine and the Origins of McCarthyism: Foreign Policy, Domestic Politics, and Internal Security, 1946-1948.* New York, 1972.

Frey, Frederick. *The Turkish Political Elite.* Cambridge, Mass., 1964.

Frey, John, and Ide, Chandler, eds. *A History of the Petroleum Administration for War, 1941-1945.* Washington, D.C., 1946.

Fried, Albert, and Sanders, Ronald, eds. *Socialist Thought: A Documentary History.* Garden City, N.Y., 1964.

Frye, Richard. *Iran.* New York, 1953.

Gaddis, John. "Containment: A Reassessment." *Foreign Affairs* 55 (July 1977):873-887.

———. "Reconsiderations: Was the Truman Doctrine a Real Turning Point?" *Foreign Affairs* 52 (January 1947):386-402.

———. *Russia, The Soviet Union, and the United States: An Interpretive History.* New York, 1978.

———. *The United States and the Origins of the Cold War, 1941-1947.* New York, 1972.

Gafencu, George. *Prelude to the Russian Campaign.* London, 1945.

Gardner, Lloyd. *Architects of Illusion: Men and Ideas in American Foreign Policy, 1941-1949.* Rev. ed. Chicago, 1970.

———. *Economic Aspects of the New Deal*. Madison, 1964.

Gardner, Lloyd, with Schlesinger, Arthur, Jr., and Morgenthau, Hans. *Origins of the Cold War*. Waltham, Mass., 1970.

Gati, Charles. "What Containment Meant." *Foreign Policy* 7 (Summer 1972):22-40.

George, Alexander. "The Causal Nexus Between 'Operational Code' Beliefs and Decision-Making Behavior: Problems of Theory and Methodology." A paper presented to the annual meeting of the International Studies Association, 22-25 February 1978.

Gilbert, Felix. *Hitler Directs His War*. New York, 1950.

Gimbel, John. *The American Occupation of Germany: Politics and the Military, 1945-1949*. Stanford, 1968.

Gitlin, Todd. "Counter-Insurgency: Myth and Reality in Greece." In *Containment and Revolution*, pp. 140-181. Edited by David Horowitz. London, 1967.

Goldman, Eric. *The Crucial Decade—and After: America, 1945-1960*. New York, 1960.

Gordon, David, and Dangerfield, Roydon. *The Hidden Weapon: The Story of Economic Warfare*. New York, 1947.

Goulden, Joseph. *The Best Years*. New York, 1976.

———. *The Superlawyers*. New York, 1972.

Graebner, Norman. "Cold War Origins and the Continuing Debate: A Review of Recent Literature." *Journal of Conflict Resolution* 13 (March 1969):123-132.

Grant, Natalie. "The Russian Section: A Window on the Soviet Union," *Diplomatic History* 2 (Winter 1978):107-115.

Gregorian, Vartan. *The Emergence of Modern Afghanistan: Politics of Reform and Modernization, 1880-1946*. Stanford, 1969.

Grew, Joseph. *Turbulent Era: A Diplomatic Record of Forty Years, 1904-1945*. 2 vols. Boston, 1952.

Griffith, Robert. "Truman and the Historians: The Reconstruction of Postwar American History." *Wisconsin Magazine of History* 59 (Autumn 1975):20-50.

Groseclose, Elgin. *Ararat*. New York, 1939.

Gulick, Edward Vose. *Europe's Classical Balance of Power: A Case History of the Theory and Practice of One of the Great Concepts of European Statecraft*. New York, 1955.

Hagen, Louis, ed. *The Schellenberg Memoirs*. London, 1956.

Halle, Louis. *The Cold War as History*. New York, 1967.

Hamby, Alonzo. *Beyond the New Deal: Harry S. Truman and American Liberalism*. New York, 1973.

453

Hammond, Thomas, ed. *The Anatomy of Communist Takeovers*. New Haven, 1975.

Hamzavi, A. H. *Persia and the Powers: An Account of Diplomatic Relations, 1941-1946*. London, 1946.

Harriman, W. Averell. *America and Russia in a Changing World*. Garden City, N.Y., 1971.

Harriman, W. Averell, and Abel, Elie. *Special Envoy to Churchill and Stalin, 1941-1946*. New York, 1975.

Harrington, Daniel. "Kennan, Bohlen, and the Riga Axioms." *Diplomatic History* 2 (Fall 1978):423-437.

Harris, George. "A Political History of Turkey, 1945-1950." Ph.D. dissertation, Harvard University, 1956.

————. *The Troubled Alliance: Turkish-American Problems in Historical Perspective, 1945-1971*. Washington, D.C., 1972.

Hart, B. H. Liddell, ed. *The Red Army*. New York, 1956.

Hartmann, Susan. *Truman and the 80th Congress*. Columbia, Mo., 1971.

Hartz, Louis. *The Liberal Tradition in America*. New York, 1955.

Haynes, Richard. *The Awesome Power: Harry S. Truman as Commander in Chief*. Baton Rouge, 1973.

Heinrichs, Waldo, Jr. *American Ambassador: Joseph C. Grew and the Development of the United States Diplomatic Tradition*. Boston, 1966.

Helseth, William. "The United States and Turkey: A Study of Their Relations from 1784-1962." Ph.D. dissertation, Fletcher School of Law and Diplomacy, Tufts University, April 1962.

Henderson, Loy W. "American Political and Strategic Interests in the Middle East and Southeast Europe." Department of State *Bulletin* 17 (23 November 1947):996-1000.

————. "Foreign Policies: Their Formulation and Enforcement." Department of State *Bulletin* 15 (29 September 1946):590-596.

Herring, George C., Jr. *Aid to Russia, 1941-1946: Strategy, Diplomacy, the Origins of the Cold War*. New York, 1973.

Herz, Martin. *Beginnings of the Cold War*. Bloomington, Ind., 1966.

Hess, Gary. "The Iranian Crisis of 1945-46 and the Cold War." *Political Science Quarterly* 89 (March 1974):117-146.

Hewlett, Richard G., and Anderson, Oscar E., Jr. *A History of the United States Atomic Energy Commission: The New World, 1939-1946*. University Park, Pa., 1962.

Hillman, William. *Mr. President: The First Publication from the Personal Diaries, Private Letters, Papers and Revealing Interviews of Harry S. Truman*. New York, 1952.

Hindus, Maurice. *In Search of a Future*. Garden City, N.Y., 1949.

Hingley, Ronald. *Joseph Stalin: Man and Legend*. New York, 1974.

454

Hinsley, F. H. *Hitler's Strategy*. Cambridge, England, 1951.

Hirschman, Albert. *Exit, Voice, and Loyalty*. Cambridge, Mass., 1970.

Hodgson, Marshall G. S. *The Gunpowder Empires and Modern Times*. Chicago, 1974.

Hodson, Henry V. *The Great Divide: Britain-India-Pakistan*. London, 1969.

Holsti, Ole, and Rosenau, James. "Vietnam, Consensus, and the Belief Systems of American Leaders." A paper delivered at the 1977 Hendriks Symposium on American Politics and World Order, University of Nebraska, 6-7 October 1977.

Horowitz, David. *The Free World Colossus: A Critique of American Foreign Policy in the Cold War*. New York, 1965.

Horowitz, David, ed. *Containment and Revolution*. London, 1967.

Hösch, Edgar. *The Balkans*. New York, 1968.

Hoskins, Halford. *The Middle East: Problem Area in World Politics*. New York, 1964.

Hostler, Charles. *Turkism and the Soviets*. London, 1957.

Hough, Jerry. "Ideology and Ideological Secretaries as a Source of Change in the Soviet Union." Paper prepared for delivery at the Mid-West Association for the Advancement of Slavic Studies, 11 April 1969, Lincoln, Nebraska.

Hovannisian, Richard. *Armenia on the Road to Independence*. Berkeley, 1967.

Howard, Harry. "The Development of United States Policy in the Near East, 1945-1951. An Historical Note: Part I." Department of State *Bulletin* 25 (19 November 1951):809-816.

———. "The Development of United States Policy in the Near East, 1945-1951. An Historical Note: Part II." Department of State *Bulletin* 25 (26 November 1951):839-843.

———. "Germany, the Soviet Union, and Turkey during World War II." Department of State *Bulletin* 19 (18 July 1948):63-73.

———. "Greece and the United Nations, 1946-49." Reprinted from the Department of State *Bulletin* 21 (19 September 1949):407-431. Washington, D.C., 1949.

———. *The Partition of Turkey: A Diplomatic History, 1913-1923*. Norman, Okla., 1931.

———. *The Problem of the Turkish Straits*. Washington, D.C., 1947.

———. "The Soviet Alliance System, 1942-1948." *Documents and State Papers* 1 (July 1948):219-249.

———. *Turkey, the Straits and U.S. Policy*. Baltimore, 1974.

———. "The Turkish Straits After World War II: Problems and Prospects." *Balkan Studies* 11 (1970):35-60.

Howard, Harry. "The United States and the Problem of the Turkish Straits." *Middle East Journal* 1 (January 1947):59-72.

———. "The United States and Turkey: American Policy in the Straits Question (1914-1963)." *Balkan Studies* 4 (1963):225-250.

———. "United States Policy Towards Greece in the United Nations, 1946-1950." *Balkan Studies* 8 (1967):263-296.

Hull, Cordell. *The Memoirs of Cordell Hull.* 2 vols. New York, 1948.

Hurewitz, J. C. *The Struggle for Palestine.* New York, 1950.

Hutson, James H. "Intellectual Foundations of Early American Diplomacy." *Diplomatic History* 1 (Winter 1977):1-19.

Hyman, Herbert. "The Value Systems of Different Classes: A Social Psychological Contribution to the Analysis of Stratification." In *Class, Status and Power,* pp. 426-442. Edited by Reinhard Bendix and Seymour Lipset. Glencoe, Ill., 1953.

Iatrides, John. *Revolt in Athens: The Greek Communist "Second Round," 1944-1945.* Princeton, 1972.

Ilchman, Warren. *Professional Diplomacy in the United States, 1779-1939.* Chicago, 1961.

Iselin, John J. "The Truman Doctrine: A Study in the Relationship Between Crisis and Foreign Policy-Making." Ph.D. dissertation, Harvard University, 1964.

Janis, Irving. *Victims of Groupthink: A Psychological Study of Foreign-Policy Decisions and Fiascoes.* Boston, 1972.

Jelavich, Barbara. *The Ottoman Empire, the Great Powers, and the Straits Question, 1870-1887.* Bloomington, Ind., 1973.

Jelavich, Charles. *Tsarist Russia and Balkan Nationalism: Russian Influence in the Internal Affairs of Bulgaria and Serbia, 1879-1886.* Berkeley, 1958.

Jelavich, Barbara, and Jelavich, Charles. *The Balkans.* Englewood Cliffs, N.J., 1965.

Jones, Joseph. *The Fifteen Weeks.* New York, 1955.

Kahng, Tae Jin. *Law, Politics, and the Security Council: An Inquiry into the Handling of the Legal Questions Involved in International Disputes and Situations.* The Hague, 1964.

Kapur, Harish. *Soviet Russia and Asia, 1917-1927: A Study of Soviet Policy Towards Turkey, Iran and Afghanistan.* Geneva, 1965.

Karalekas, Ann. "Britain, the United States, and Greece, 1942-1945." Ph.D. dissertation, Harvard University, September 1974.

Karpat, Kemal. *Turkey's Politics: The Transition to a Multi-Party System.* Princeton, 1959.

Kaufman, Arnold. "The Cold War in Retrospect." In *A Dissenter's Guide to Foreign Policy,* rev. ed., pp. 65-94. Edited by I. Howe. Garden City, N.Y., 1968.

456

Kazantzakis, Nikos. *The Fratricides.* New York, 1964.

Kazemzadeh, Firuz. *Russia and Britain in Persia, 1864-1914.* New Haven, 1968.

Kedourie, Elie. *In the Anglo-Arab Labyrinth: The McMahon-Husayn Correspondence and its Interpretations.* Cambridge, England, 1976.

————. *The Chatham House Version.* London, 1964.

Kedros, André. *La Résistance Grecque, 1940-1944.* Paris, 1966.

Kelly, David. *The Ruling Few: The Human Background to Diplomacy.* London, 1952.

Kennan, George. *American Diplomacy, 1900-1950.* Chicago, 1951.

————. "Interview with George Kennan." *Foreign Policy* 7 (Summer 1972):5-21.

————. "Is Détente Worth Saving?" *Saturday Review,* 6 March 1976, pp. 12-17.

————. *Memoirs: 1925-1950.* Boston, 1967.

————. *Russia and the West Under Lenin and Stalin.* New York, 1961.

————. *Russia Leaves the War.* New York, 1967.

————. "The United States and the Soviet Union, 1917-1976." *Foreign Affairs* 54 (July 1976):670-690.

Khrushchev, Nikita. *Khrushchev Remembers.* Boston, 1970.

————. *Khrushchev Remembers: The Last Testament.* Boston, 1974.

Khvostov, V. "The Facts of the Case." *New Times* 3 (1 February 1946): 24-25.

Kılıç, Altemur. *Turkey and the World.* Washington, D.C., 1959.

Kinross, Lord. *Atatürk: A Biography of Mustafa Kemal, Father of Modern Turkey.* New York, 1965.

Kirk, George. *The Middle East, 1945-1950.* London, 1954.

————. *The Middle East in the War.* London, 1952.

————. "Turkey." In *The War and the Neutrals,* pp. 345-366. Edited by Arnold Toynbee. London, 1956.

Kirkendall, Richard, ed. *The Truman Period as a Research Field: A Reappraisal, 1972.* Columbia, Mo., 1974.

Knapp, Wilfred. "Cold War Origins." *Survey* 58 (January 1966):153-158.

Knatchbull-Hugessen, Hughe. *Diplomat in Peace and War.* London, 1949.

Knight, Jonathan. "American Statecraft and the 1946 Black Sea Straits Controversy." *Political Science Quarterly* 90 (Fall 1975):451-475.

Kocaeli, Nihat Erim. "The Development of the Anglo-Turkish Alliance." *The Asiatic Review* 42 (October 1946):347-351.

Koestler, Arthur. *The Thirteenth Tribe: The Khazar Empire and its Heritage.* New York, 1976.

Kohler, Foy. "The Relief of Occupied Greece." Department of State *Bulletin* 11 (17 September 1944):300-304.

457

Kolko, Gabriel. *The Limits of Power: The World and United States Foreign Policy, 1945-1954*. New York, 1972.

Kolko, Gabriel, and Kolko, Joyce. *The Politics of War: The World and United States Foreign Policy, 1943-1945*. New York, 1968.

Kousoulas, D. George. "The Greek Communists Tried Three Times—and Failed." In *The Anatomy of Communist Takeovers*, pp. 293-309. Edited by Thomas Hammond. New Haven, 1975.

———. *The Price of Freedom: Greece in World Affairs, 1939-1953*. Syracuse, 1953.

———. *Revolution and Defeat: The Story of the Greek Communist Party*. London, 1965.

———. "The Truman Doctrine and the Stalin-Tito Rift: A Reappraisal." *South Atlantic Quarterly* 72 (Summer 1973):427-439.

Krausnick, Helmut et al., eds. *Anatomy of the S.S. State*. London, 1968.

Krock, Arthur. *Memoirs: Sixty Years on the Firing Line*. New York, 1968.

Kulski, Wladyslaw W. *Germany and Poland: From War to Peaceful Relations*. Syracuse, 1976.

LaFeber, Walter. *America, Russia, and the Cold War, 1945-1975*. 3rd ed. New York, 1976.

Langer, William, and Gleason, S. Everett. *The Challenge to Isolation, 1937-1940*. New York, 1952.

———. *The Undeclared War, 1940-1941*. New York, 1953.

Laqueur, Walter. *The Soviet Union and the Middle East*. New York, 1959.

Lasch, Christopher. "The Cold War, Revisited and Re-Visioned." *The New York Times Magazine*, 14 January 1968.

Leahy, William. *I Was There*. New York, 1950.

Lederer, Ivo, and Vucinich, Wayne, eds. *The Soviet Union and the Middle East: The Post World War II Era*. Stanford, 1974.

Leeper, Reginald. *When Greek Meets Greek*. London, 1950.

Lefebvre, Henri. *The Sociology of Marx*. New York, 1968.

Lenczowski, George. "The Arc of Crisis: Its Central Sector." *Foreign Affairs* 57 (Spring 1979):796-820.

———. "The Communist Movement in Iran." *Middle East Journal* 1 (January 1947):29-45.

———. *Russia and the West in Iran, 1918-1948*. Ithaca, N.Y., 1949.

———. *Soviet Advances in the Middle East*. Washington, D.C., 1971.

Lenczowski, George, ed. *Iran Under the Pahlavis*. Stanford, 1978.

Leopold, Richard. *The Growth of American Foreign Policy*. New York, 1962.

Lerner, Warren. "Attempting a Revolution from Without: Poland in 1920." In *The Anatomy of Communist Takeovers*, pp. 94-106. Edited by Thomas Hammond. New Haven, 1975.

Levin, Gordon. *Woodrow Wilson and World Politics: America's Response to War and Revolution.* New York, 1968.

Lewin, M. "Stalin and the Fall of Bolshevism." *Journal of Interdisciplinary History* 7 (Summer 1976):105-117.

Lewis, Bernard. *The Emergence of Modern Turkey.* London, 1961.

Lewis, Geoffrey. *Turkey.* 3rd ed. London, 1965.

Lewis, Wm. Roger. *Imperialism at Bay: The United States and the Decolonization of the British Empire, 1941-1945.* New York, 1978.

Lie, Trygve. *In the Cause of Peace.* New York, 1954.

Lifka, Thomas E. "The Concept 'Totalitarianism' in American Foreign Policy, 1933-1949." Ph.D. dissertation, Harvard University, September 1973.

Lingemen, E. R. *Turkey: Economic and Commercial Conditions in Turkey.* London, 1948.

Lipset, Seymour, and Bendix, Reinhard. *Social Mobility in Industrial Society.* Berkeley, 1959.

Lisagor, Peter, and Higgins, Marguerite. *Overtime in Heaven.* Garden City, N.Y., 1964.

Loewenheim, Francis et al., eds. *Roosevelt and Churchill: Their Secret Wartime Correspondence.* New York, 1975.

Lohbeck, Don. *Patrick J. Hurley.* Chicago, 1956.

Longrigg, Stephen. *Oil in the Middle East.* 2nd ed. London, 1961.

Lukacs, John. *A New History of the Cold War.* Rev. ed. Garden City, N.Y., 1966.

———. "The Night Stalin and Churchill Divided Europe." *The New York Times Magazine,* 5 October 1969.

Lyon, Peter. *Eisenhower: Portrait of a Hero.* Boston, 1974.

Lytle, Mark H. "American-Iranian Relations, 1941-1947, and the Redefinition of National Security." Ph.D. dissertation, Yale University, 1973.

MacMillan, Harold. *The Blast of War, 1939-1945.* New York, 1967.

McLellan, David S. *Dean Acheson: The State Department Years.* New York, 1976.

———. "Who Fathered Containment?" *International Studies Quarterly* 17 (1973):205-226.

McNeill, William. *America, Britain and Russia: Their Cooperation and Conflict, 1941-1946.* London, 1953.

———. *The Greek Dilemma: War and Aftermath.* Philadelphia, 1947.

———. "Greece, 1944-1946." In *The Realignment of Europe,* pp. 389-408. Edited by Arnold Toynbee and Veronica Toynbee. London, 1955.

McSherry, James. *Stalin, Hitler, and Europe.* 2 vols. Cleveland, 1970.

Maddox, Robert James. *The New Left and the Origins of the Cold War.* Princeton, 1973.

459

Maddux, Thomas. "American Diplomats and the Soviet Experiment: The View from the Moscow Embassy, 1934-1939." *South Atlantic Quarterly* 74 (Autumn 1975):468-487.

Maier, Charles. "Revisionism and the Interpretation of Cold War Origins." *Perspectives in American History* 4 (1970):313-347.

Maisky, Ivan. *Memoirs of a Soviet Ambassador: The War, 1939-1943.* New York, 1967.

————. *Who Helped Hitler?* London, 1964.

Mandelstam, Nadezhda. *Hope Abandoned.* New York, 1974.

————. *Hope Against Hope: A Memoir.* New York, 1970.

Mark, Eduard. "Allied Relations in Iran, 1941-1947: The Origins of a Cold War Crisis." *Wisconsin Magazine of History* 59 (Autumn 1975): 51-63.

————. "The Question of Containment: A Reply to John Lewis Gaddis." *Foreign Affairs* 56 (January 1978):430-440.

Markowitz, Norman D. *The Rise and Fall of the People's Century: Henry A. Wallace and American Liberalism, 1941-1948.* New York, 1973.

Marlowe, John. *Iran.* London, 1963.

Marx, Karl, and Engels, Friedrich. *The Communist Manifesto.* Edited by Joseph Katz. New York, 1964.

Mastny, Vojtech. "The Cassandra of the Foreign Commissariat: Maxim Litvinov and the Cold War." *Foreign Affairs* 54 (January 1976):366-376.

————. *Russia's Road to the Cold War: Diplomacy, Warfare and the Politics of Communism, 1941-1945.* New York, 1979.

Matloff, Maurice. *Strategic Planning for Coalition Warfare, 1943-1944.* Washington, D.C., 1959.

Matthews, Kenneth. *Memories of a Mountain War: Greece, 1944-1949.* London, 1972.

May, Ernest. *American Imperialism: A Speculative Essay.* New York, 1968.

————. *"Lessons" of the Past: The Use and Misuse of History in American Foreign Policy.* New York, 1973.

Mayer, Arno. *Politics and Diplomacy of Peacemaking: Containment and Counterrevolution at Versailles, 1918-1919.* New York, 1967.

Medvedev, Roy. *Let History Judge.* New York, 1971.

Mee, Charles, Jr. *Meeting at Potsdam.* New York, 1975.

Meister, Irene. "Soviet Policy in Iran, 1917-1950: A Case Study in Techniques." Ph.D. dissertation, Fletcher School of Law and Diplomacy, Tufts University, 1954.

Messer, Robert. "Paths Not Taken: The United States Department of State and Alternatives to Containment." *Diplomatic History* 1 (Fall 1977): 297-319.

Miller, R. H. "Roots of the Cold War." *Commonweal*, 21 January 1972, pp. 375-380.

Millis, Walter, ed. *The Forrestal Diaries*. New York, 1951.

Millspaugh, Arthur. *American in Persia*. Washington, D.C., 1946.

Milsom, John. *Russian Tanks, 1900-1970*. Harrisburg, Pa., 1971.

Miscamble, Wilson D. "Anthony Eden and the Truman-Molotov Conversations, April 1945." *Diplomatic History* 2 (Spring 1978):167-180.

Mohammad Reza Shah Pahlavi. *Mission for My Country*. New York, 1960.

Montgomery, Bernard Law. *The Memoirs of Field-Marshal the Viscount Montgomery of Alamain*. New York, 1958.

Moran, Charles, *Churchill: The Struggle for Survival, 1940-1965, Taken from the Diaries of Lord Moran*. Boston, 1966.

Morrell, Sydney. *Spheres of Influence*. New York, 1946.

Moyzisch, L. C. *Operation Cicero*. London, 1950.

Muller, Edwin. "Behind the Scenes in Azerbaijan." *American Mercury*, June 1946, pp. 696-703.

Murphy, Robert. *Diplomat Among Warriors*. London, 1964.

Nagai, Yonusuke, and Iriye, Akira, eds. *The Origins of the Cold War in Asia*. New York, 1977.

Nash, Gerald. *United States Oil Policy, 1890-1964*. Pittsburgh, 1968.

Nenarokov, Albert. *Russia in the Twentieth Century*. New York, 1968.

Nollau, Günther, and Wiehe, Hans. *Russia's South Flank: Soviet Operations in Iran, Turkey, and Afghanistan*. New York, 1963.

O'Ballance, Edgar. *The Greek Civil War, 1944-1949*. New York, 1966.

Osgood, Robert. *Ideals and Self-Interest in America's Foreign Relations*. Chicago, 1953.

Page, Bruce et al. *The Philby Conspiracy*. Garden City, N.Y., 1968.

Paige, Glen. *The Korean Decision: June 24-30, 1950*. New York, 1968.

Pandey, B. N. *The Break-up of British India*. New York, 1969.

Papandreou, Andreas. *Democracy at Gunpoint*. New York, 1970.

Papen, Franz von. *Memoirs*. London, 1952.

Paterson, Thomas. *Soviet American Confrontation: Postwar Reconstruction and the Origins of the Cold War*. Baltimore, 1973.

Pfau, Richard. "Containment in Iran, 1946: The Shift to an Active Policy." *Diplomatic History* 1 (Fall 1977):359-372.

————. "The United States and Iran, 1941-1947: Origins of Partnership." Ph.D. dissertation, University of Virginia, 1975.

Philby, Kim. *My Silent War*. New York, 1968.

Phillips, Cabell. *The 1940s, Decade of Triumph and Trouble*. New York, 1975.

————. *The Truman Presidency: History of a Triumphant Succession*. New York, 1966.

Pickersgill, John, and Forster, D. F. *The Mackenzie King Record.* 4 vols. Toronto, 1960-1970.

Pogue, Forrest. *George C. Marshall: Organizer of Victory.* New York, 1973.

Polk, William. *The United States and the Arab World.* 3rd ed. Cambridge, Mass., 1975.

Powell, Anthony. *The Military Philosophers.* Boston, 1968.

Pratt, Julius. *Cordell Hull, 1933-1944.* 2 vols. New York, 1964.

Pynchon, Thomas. *Gravity's Rainbow.* New York, 1973.

Ramazani, Rouhollah. "The Autonomous Republic of Azerbaijan and the Kurdish People's Republic: Their Rise and Fall." In *The Anatomy of Communist Takeovers,* pp. 448-474. Edited by Thomas Hammond. New Haven, 1975.

————. *The Foreign Policy of Iran: A Developing Nation in World Affairs, 1500-1941.* Charlottesville, Va., 1966.

————. *Iran's Foreign Policy, 1941-1973: A Study of Foreign Policy in Modernizing Nations.* Charlottesville, Va., 1975.

————. *The Northern Tier: Afghanistan, Iran, and Turkey.* Princeton, 1966.

Rapoport, Anatol. *The Big Two: Soviet-American Images of Foreign Policy.* Indianapolis, 1971.

Rawls, John. *A Theory of Justice.* Cambridge, Mass., 1971.

Rees, David. *The Age of Containment: The Cold War, 1945-1965.* New York, 1968.

Resis, Albert. "The Churchill-Stalin 'Percentages' Agreement on the Balkans, Moscow, October 1944." *American Historical Review* 83 (April 1978): 368-387.

Ristelhueber, René. *A History of the Balkan Peoples.* New York, 1971.

Roberts, Chalmers. "How Containment Worked." *Foreign Policy* 7 (Summer 1972):41-53.

Roberts, Walter. *Tito, Mihailović and the Allies, 1941-1945.*

Robinson, Richard. *The First Turkish Republic: A Case Study in National Development.* Cambridge, Mass., 1963.

Rogow, Arnold. *James Forrestal: A Study of Personality, Politics, and Policy.* New York, 1963.

Roosevelt, Archie, Jr. "The Kurdish Republic of Mahabad." *Middle East Journal* 1 (July 1947):247-269.

Roosevelt, Elliot. *As He Saw It.* New York, 1946.

Rose, Lisle. *The Coming of the American Age, 1945-1946: Dubious Victory, The United States and the End of World War II.* Kent, Ohio, 1973.

Rosenman, Samuel. *Working with Roosevelt.* New York, 1952.

Ross, Lee. "The Intuitive Psychologist and his Shortcomings: Distortions in the Attribution Process." In Leonard Berkowitz, ed., *Advances in Experimental Psychology.* New York, 1977.

Rosser, Richard F. *An Introduction to Soviet Foreign Policy*. Englewood Cliffs, N.J., 1969.

Rossow, Robert. "The Battle of Azerbaijan, 1946." *Middle East Journal* 10 (Winter 1956):17-32.

———. "The Flying Wedge of Azerbaijan." Manuscript in the personal files of Robert Rossow, Washington, D.C.

Routh, D. A. "The Montreux Convention Regarding the Regime of the Black Sea Straits (20th July 1936)." In *Survey of International Affairs, 1936*, pp. 584-651. Edited by Arnold Toynbee. London, 1937.

Rovine, Arthur W. *The First Fifty Years*. Leyden, 1970.

Rovinsky, L. "Documents on Turkey's Foreign Policy." *New Times* 16 (15 August 1946):26-30.

Runciman, Walter G. *Relative Deprivation and Social Justice: A Study of Attitudes to Social Inequality in Twentieth-Century England*. Berkeley, 1966.

Rustow, Dankwart. "Foreign Policy of the Turkish Republic." In *Foreign Policy in World Politics*, pp. 295-322. Edited by R. C. Macridis. Englewood Cliffs, N.J., 1958.

Ryan, Henry R. "The American Intellectual Tradition Reflected in the Truman Doctrine." *American Scholar* 42 (Spring 1973):294-307.

Sachar, Howard. *The Emergence of the Middle East, 1914-1924*. New York, 1969.

———. *Europe Leaves the Middle East, 1936-1954*. New York, 1972.

———. *A History of Israel from the Rise of Zionism to Our Time*. New York, 1976.

Sadak, Necmeddin. "Turkey Faces the Soviets." *Foreign Affairs* 27 (April 1949):449-461.

Sanjian, Avedis. "The Sanjak of Alexandretta (Hatay): Its Impact on Turkish-Syrian Relation (1939-1956)." *Middle East Journal* 10 (Autumn 1956):379-394.

Sarafis, Stefanos. *Greek Resistance Army: The Story of ELAS*. London, 1951.

Schlesinger, Arthur M., Jr. *The Imperial Presidency*. New York, 1974.

———. "Origins of the Cold War." *Foreign Affairs* 46 (October 1967): 22-52.

Schmidt, Paul. *Hitler's Interpreter*. New York, 1952.

Schoenfeld, Maxwell. *The War Ministry of Winston Churchill*. Ames, Iowa, 1972.

Schulze-Holthus, Bernard. *Daybreak in Iran: A Story of the German Intelligence Service*. London, 1954.

Schwartz, Morton. "The 'Motive Forces' of Soviet Foreign Policy, A Reappraisal." *Monograph Series in World Affairs* 8 (Monograph No. 2): 1-48. Denver, Colo., 1971.

Seale, Patrick, and McCouville, Maureen. *Philby: The Long Road to Moscow.* New York, 1973.

Seton-Watson, Hugh. *Neither War nor Peace: The Struggle for Power in the Postwar World.* New York, 1950.

Shah, Linda, and Shah, Khalid. *Refugee.* New York, 1974.

Shaw, Stanford, and Shaw, Ezel. *Reform, Revolution, and Republic: The Rise of Modern Turkey, 1808-1975.* Cambridge, 1977.

Sherwin, Martin. *A World Destroyed: The Atomic Bomb and the Grand Alliance.* New York, 1975.

Sherwood, Robert. *Roosevelt and Hopkins: An Intimate History.* Revised ed. New York, 1950.

Shotwell, James, and Deak, Francis. *Turkey and the Straits: A Short History.* New York, 1940.

Shulman, Marshall. *Stalin's Foreign Policy Reappraised.* Cambridge, Mass., 1963.

Shwadran, Benjamin. *The Middle East, Oil and the Great Powers.* 2nd ed., rev. New York, 1959.

———. *The Middle East, Oil and the Great Powers.* 3rd ed., rev. and enlarged. New York, 1973.

Skrine, Clarmont. *World War in Iran.* London, 1962.

Slusser, Robert. "A Soviet Historian Evaluates Stalin's Role in History." *American Historical Review* 77 (December 1972):1389-1398.

Smith, Gaddis. *American Diplomacy During the Second World War, 1914-1945.* New York, 1965.

———. *Dean Acheson.* New York, 1972.

Smith, Geoffrey. " 'Harry, We Hardly Knew You': Revisionism, Politics and Diplomacy, 1945-1954, A Review Essay." *American Political Science Review* 70 (June 1976):560-582.

Smith, Hedrick. *The Russians.* New York, 1976.

Smith, Walter Bedell. *My Three Years in Moscow.* New York, 1950.

Smothers, Frank; McNeill, William; and McNeill, Elizabeth. *Report on the Greeks.* New York, 1948.

Snell, John. *Illusion and necessity: The Diplomacy of Global War, 1939-1945.* Boston, 1963.

Snetsinger, John. *Truman, The Jewish Vote and the Creation of Israel.* Stanford, 1974.

Snow, Edgar. *Journey to the Beginning.* New York, 1958.

Snyder, Richard C. et al., eds. *Foreign Policy Decision-Making: An Approach to the Study of International Politics.* New York, 1962.

Solzhenitsyn, Aleksandr. *The Gulag Archipelago, 1918-1956.* New York, 1973.

———. *One Day in the Life of Ivan Denisovich.* New York, 1963.

Sontag, Raymond. *A Broken World, 1919-1939*. New York, 1971.

Spanier, John. *American Foreign Policy Since World War II*. 4th ed., rev. New York, 1971.

Spector, Ivar. *The Soviet Union and the Muslim World, 1917-1958*. Seattle, 1959.

Stavrianos, L. S. *The Balkans Since 1453*. New York, 1958.

————. *Greece: American Dilemma and Opportunity*. Chicago, 1952.

Steinbruner, John. *The Cybernetic Theory of Decision: New Dimensions of Political Analysis*. Princeton, 1974.

Stettinius, Edward, Jr. *Lend-Lease: Weapon for Victory*. New York, 1944.

————. *Roosevelt and the Russians: The Yalta Conference*. Garden City, N.Y., 1949.

Stimson, Henry L., and Bundy, McGeorge. *On Active Service, in Peace and War*. New York, 1948.

Stocking, George. *Middle East Oil*. Nashville, Tenn., 1970.

Stuart, Graham. *The Department of State: A History of its Organization, Procedure, and Personnel*. New York, 1949.

Stupak, Ronald. *The Shaping of Foreign Policy: The Role of the Secretary of State as Seen by Dean Acheson*. Indianapolis, 1969.

Sulzberger, C. L. *A Long Row of Candles: Memoirs and Diaries (1934-1954)*. Toronto, 1969.

Sumner, B. H. *Russia and the Balkans, 1870-1880*. Oxford, 1937.

Sweet-Escott, Bickham. *Greece: A Political and Economic Survey, 1939-1953*. London, 1954.

Swinton, Philip. *I Remember*. London, 1948.

Sykes, Christopher. *Crossroads to Israel, 1917-1948*. Bloomington, Ind., 1965.

Tachau, Frank. "Republic of Turkey." In *The Middle East: Its Government and Politics*, pp. 377-400. Edited by Abid Al-Marayati. Belmont, Calif., 1972.

Tamkoç, Metin. *A Bibliography on the Foreign Relations of the Republic of Turkey, 1919-1967*. Ankara, 1968.

————. *The Warrior Diplomats: Guardians of the National Security and Modernization of Turkey*. Salt Lake City, 1976.

Taylor, A.J.P. *English History, 1914-1945*. Oxford, 1965.

————. *The Struggle for Mastery in Europe, 1848-1918*. London, 1954.

Taylor, A.J.P. et al., eds. *Churchill Revised: A Critical Assessment*. New York, 1969.

Theoharis, Athan. *Seeds of Repression: Harry S. Truman and the Origins of McCarthyism*. Chicago, 1971.

Thomas, Brian. "Cold War Origins, II." *The Journal of Contemporary History* 3 (January 1968):183-198.

465

Thomas, John R. "The Rise and Fall of the Azerbaijan People's Republic as Reflected in Izvestia, 1945-1947." Certificate essay, Russian Institute, Columbia University, 1953.

Tinker, Hugh. *Experiment with Freedom: India and Pakistan, 1947*. London, 1967.

Toland, John. *The Last 100 Days*. New York, 1966.

Toynbee, Arnold. *A Study of History*. Vol. 6. Oxford, 1939.

————. *Survey of International Relations, 1920-1923*. London, 1925.

Toynbee, Arnold, and Toynbee, Veronica. *The Eve of the War, 1939*. London, 1958.

Toynbee, Arnold, and Toynbee, Veronica, eds. *The War and the Neutrals*. London, 1958.

Trask, Roger. *The United States Response to Turkish Nationalism and Reform, 1914-1939*. Minneapolis, 1971.

Treadgold, Donald. *Twentieth Century Russia*. 3rd ed. Chicago, 1972.

Trevor-Roper, Hugh. *The Philby Affair*. London, 1968.

Trivers, Howard. *Three Crises in American Foreign Affairs and a Continuing Revolution*. Carbondale, Ill., 1972.

Trukhanovsky, V. *British Foreign Policy During World War II*. Translated by David Skvirsky [1970]. Moscow, 1965.

Truman, Harry S. *Memoirs*. Vol. 1: *Year of Decisions*. Vol. 2: *Years of Trial and Hope*. Garden City, N.Y., 1955, 1956.

Truman, Margaret. *Harry S. Truman*. New York, 1973.

Tsirkas, Stratis. *Drifting Cities*. New York, 1974.

Tucker, Robert C. *Philosophy and Myth in Karl Marx*. Cambridge, England, 1964.

Tucker, Robert W. *The Radical Left and American Foreign Policy*. Baltimore, 1971.

Ulam, Adam. *The Bolsheviks: The Political History of the Triumph of Communism in Russia*. New York, 1965.

————. "The Cold War According to Kennan." *Commentary* 55 (January 1973):66-69.

————. *Epansion and Coexistence: Soviet Foreign Policy, 1917-1973*. 2nd ed. New York, 1974.

————. *The Rivals: America and Russia Since World War II*. New York, 1971.

————. *Stalin: The Man and his Era*. New York, 1973.

Váli, Ferenc. *Bridge Across the Bosporus: The Foreign Policy of Turkey*. Baltimore, 1971.

Van Wagenen, Richard. *The Iranian Case, 1946*. New York, 1952.

Vandenberg, Arthur, Jr., ed. *The Private Papers of Senator Vandenberg*. Boston, 1952.

Villiers, Gérard de et al. *The Imperial Shah: An Informal Biography*. Boston, 1976.

Vreeland, Herbert H. *Iran*. New Haven, 1957.

Walker, Richard. *E. R. Stettinius, Jr.* New York, 1965.

Warner, Geoffrey. "The Truman Doctrine and the Marshall Plan." *International Affairs* 50 (January 1974):82-92.

Weinberg, Gerhard. *Germany and the Soviet Union, 1939-1941*. London, 1954.

Weinstein, Allen. *Perjury: The Hiss-Chambers Case*. New York, 1978.

Weisband, Edward. *The Ideology of American Foreign Policy: A Paradigm of Lockian Liberalism*. Beverly Hills, Calif., 1973.

————. *Turkish Foreign Policy, 1943-1945: Small State Diplomacy and Great Power Politics*. Princeton, 1973.

Welch, William. *American Images of Soviet Foreign Policy*. New Haven, 1970.

Welles, Sumner. *Where Are We Heading?* New York, 1946.

Werth, Alexander. *The Year of Stalingrad*. New York, 1947.

Wesson, Robert. *The Russian Dilemma: A Political and Geopolitical View*. New Brunswick, N.J., 1974.

West, Elliott. "The Roots of Conflict: Soviet Images in the American Press, 1941-1947." In *Essays in American Foreign Policy*, pp. 83-116. Edited by Margaret Morris and Sandra Myres. Austin, Texas, 1974.

Westerfield, N. Bradford. *Foreign Policy and Party Politics: Pearl Harbor to Korea*. New Haven, 1955.

Westermann, William. "Kurdish Independence and Russian Expansion." *Foreign Affairs* 24 (July 1946):675-686.

Wheeler-Bennett, John, and Nicholls, Anthony. *The Semblance of Peace: The Political Settlement after the Second World War*. New York, 1972.

Wilber, Donald. *Iran, Past and Present*. 8th ed. Princeton, 1976.

————. *Riza Shah Pahlavi: The Resurrection and Reconstruction of Iran*. Hicksville, N.Y., 1975.

Williams, William A. *The Tragedy of American Diplomacy*. Rev. ed. New York, 1972.

Wilson, Evan. "The Palestine Papers, 1943-1947." *Journal of Palestine Studies* 11 (Summer 1973):33-54.

Wilson, H. Maitland. *Eight Years Overseas, 1939-1947*. New York, 1951.

Winterbotham, F. W. *The Ultra Secret*. New York, 1974.

Wiskemann, Elizabeth. "The Subjugation of South-Eastern Europe, June 1940 to June 1941." In *Initial Triumph of the Axis*, pp. 319-363. Edited by Arnold Toynbee and Veronica Toynbee. London, 1958.

Wolfe, Thomas. *Soviet Power and Europe, 1945-1970*. Baltimore, 1970.

Wolff, Robert. *The Balkans in Our Time*. Cambridge, Mass., 1956.

467

Woodhouse, C. M. *Apple of Discord*. London, 1948.

————. *The Struggle for Greece, 1941-1949*. London, 1976.

Woodward, Llewellyn. *British Foreign Policy in the Second World War*. London, 1962.

————. *British Foreign Policy in the Second World War*. 4 vols. London, 1970-1975.

Worswick, G.D.N., and Ady, P. H., eds. *The British Economy, 1945-1950*. Oxford, 1952.

Wright, Gordon. *The Ordeal of Total War, 1939-1945*. New York, 1968.

Wright, William Livingstone. "Truth About Turkey." *Foreign Affairs* 26 (January 1948):349-359.

Xydis, Stephen. *Greece and the Great Powers, 1944-1947: Prelude to the "Truman Doctrine."* Thessaloniki, 1963.

————. "Greece and the Yalta Decision." *The American Slavic and Eastern European Review* 20 (February 1961):6-21.

————. "New Light on the Big Three Crisis over Turkey in 1945." *Middle East Journal* 14 (Autumn 1960):416-432.

————. "The Secret Anglo-Soviet Agreement on the Balkans of October 9, 1944." *Journal of Central European Affairs* 15 (October 1955):248-271.

————. "The USSR and the Creation of the Commission of Investigators Concerning Greek Frontier Incidents." *Balkan Studies* 4 (1963):1-14.

Yalman, Ahmet. "The Struggle for Multi-Party Government in Turkey." *Middle East Journal* 1 (January 1947):46-58.

Yergin, Daniel. *Shattered Peace: The Origins of the Cold War and the National Security State*. Boston, 1977.

Yeselson, Abraham. *United States-Persian Diplomatic Relations, 1883-1921*. New Brunswick, N.J., 1956.

Young, Kenneth. *The Greek Passion*. London, 1969.

Young, Peter. *Atlas of the Second World War*. New York, 1974.

Zabih, Sepehr. *The Communist Movement in Iran*. Berkeley, 1966.

Ziemke, Earl. *Stalingrad to Berlin: The German Defeat in the East*. Washington, D.C., 1968.

Index

This index identifies persons, organizations, places, and specialized terms. Terms that appear in the footnotes have been included. Entries under countries are subdivided with appropriate subheadings. Names including de and von are alphabetized under the major part of the name. Organizations with acronyms are filed alphabetically under the acronym. The list of abbreviations at the front of the book provides a guide to them.

Library of Congress Cataloging in Publication Data

Kuniholm, Bruce Robellet, 1942-
   The origins of the cold war in the Near East.

   Bibliography: p.
   Includes index.
   1.   Near East—Politics and government—1945-
2.   United States—Foreign relations—Russia.
3.   Russia—Foreign relations—United States.
4.   United States—Foreign relations—1945-1953.
I.   Title.
DS63.K86   327'.09'045   79-83999
ISBN 0-691-04665-4
ISBN 0-691-10083-7 pbk.